A Dictionary of COMPUTER

A Dictionary of COMPUTER

W.R. Spencer

CBS Publishers & Distributors
4596/1-A, 11 Darya Ganj, New Delhi - 110 002 (India)

ISBN : 81-239-1029-0

First Indian Edition : 1994
Reprint : 2000
Reprint : 2003

This edition has been published in India by arrangement with Academic Science, Inc., U.K.

Published by S.K. Jain for CBS Publishers & Distributors,
4596/1-A, 11 Darya Ganj, New Delhi - 110 002 (India)

Printed at :
Asia Printograph, Shahdara, Delhi - 110 032

Preface

This dictionary contains accurate definitions of the working vocabulary of A Dictionary of Computer while compiling the dictionary, the author has concentrated on terms which seem to him to be in the widest use. A very useful system of cross references assists the reader to find his way from one related topic to another. It also allows the greatest account of information to be given in a small space. Thus many of the entries contain words which are themselves defined elsewhere. SI units are used throughout this dictionary.

In compiling a book of this kind it is necessary to draw upon the work of many authorities and seek the advice of colleagues, to all of whom the author is deeply indebted. All comments from users on omissions or shortcomings will be most welcome.

A

abelian group (commutative group) *See* group.

abnormal termination A termination to a process brought about by the operating system when the process reaches a point from which it cannot continue, e.g. when the process attempts to obey an undefined instruction. In contrast, a process that reaches a successful conclusion terminates normally by issuing a suitable supervisor call to the operating system. It is common practice to inform the initiator of the process as to whether the termination was normal or abnormal.

abort (of a process) To undergo or cause *abnormal termination. Abortion may be a voluntary act by the process, which realizes that it cannot reach a successful conclusion, or may be brought about by the operating system, which intervenes because the process has failed to observe system constraints. Thus, computationally, the term has a rather similar meaning to its medical meaning of spontaneous or induced fetal death.

absolute address *Another name for* machine address.

absolute code Program code in a form suitable for direct execution by the central processor, i.e. code containing no symbolic references. *See also* machine code.

absorption laws The two self-dual laws

$$x \vee (x \wedge y) = x$$
$$x \wedge (x \vee y) = x$$

(*see* duality) that are satisfied by all elements x,y in a *Boolean algebra possessing the two operations $\vee$ and $\wedge$.

abstract data type A *data type that is defined solely in terms of the operations that apply to objects of the type without commitment as to how the value of such an object is to be represented (*see* data abstraction).

An abstract date type strictly is a triple (D,F,A) consisting of a set of domains D, a set of functions F each with range and domain in D, and a set of axioms A, which specify the properties of the functions in F. By distinguishing one of the domains d in D, a precise characterization is obtained of the *data structure that the abstract date type imposes on d.

For example, the natural numbers comprise an abstract data type, where the domain d is

$$\{0,1,2,\ldots\}$$

and there is an auxiliary domain

$$\{\text{TRUE},\text{FALSE}\}$$

The functions or operations are ZERO, ISZERO, SUCC, and ADD and the axioms are:

$$\text{ISZERO}(0) = \text{TRUE}$$
$$\text{ISZERO}(\text{SUCC}(x)) = \text{FALSE}$$
$$\text{ADD}(0,y) = y$$
$$\text{ADD}(\text{SUCC}(x),y) = \text{SUCC}(\text{ADD}(x,y))$$

These axioms specify precisely the laws that must hold for any implementation of the natural numbers. (Note that a practical implementation could not fulfill the axioms because of word length and overflow.) Such precise characterization is invaluable both to the user and the implementer.

abstract family of languages (AFL) A class of formal languages that is closed under all the following operations: *union, *concatenation, Kleene-plus (*see* Kleene star), *intersection with *regular set, Λ-free homomorphic image, and inverse homomorphic image (*see* homomorphism). An AFL is *full* if it is also closed under Kleene star and homomorphic image. The motivation for the concept of an AFL is to investigate properties of classes of languages that follow merely from the assumption of certain *closure properties. Each member of the *Chomsky hierarchy is an AFL; all except type 2 are full.

abstraction The principle of ignoring those aspects of a subject that are not relevant to the current purpose in order to concentrate solely on those that are. The application of this principle is essential in the development and understanding of all forms of computer system. *See* data abstraction, procedural abstraction.

abstract machine A machine can be thought of as a collection of resources together with a definition of the ways in which these resources can interact. For a real machine these resources actually exist as tangible objects, each of the type expected; for example, addressable storage on a real machine will actually consist of the appropriate number of words of storage, together with suitable address decoders and access mechanisms. It is possible to define an abstract machine, by listing the resources it contains and the interactions between them, without building the machine. Such abstract machines are often of use in attempting to prove the properties of programs, since a suitably defined abstract machine may allow the suppression of unneeded detail.

acceleration time (start time) The time taken for a device to reach its operating speed from a quiescent state.

accept (recognize) *See* automaton.

acceptance testing *See* testing.

accepting state *See* finite-state automaton.

access The reading or writing of data, with the connotation that the content of the reading or writing is taken into account. The word is also used as a verb: to gain entry to. It is most commonly used in connection with filed information and is often qualified by an indication as to the types of access that are to be permitted. For example, read-only access means that the contents of the file may be read but not altered or erased.

access arm *See* arm.

access control The process by which access to resources of a computer system is limited or controlled. Access control is carried out by appropriately limiting the abilities of using resources (users or computer processes) to act on used resources (files, computer processes, etc.). Access control is commonly carried out according to information provided in an *access matrix*, which describes, in a two-dimensional array, the allowable actions between using and used resources.

access matrix (authorization matrix) *See* access control.

access method The technique used for selecting records in a file, one at a time, for processing, retrieval, or storage. The access method is related to but distinct from the *file organization, which determines how the records are stored. A number of different access methods are available, mainly categorized as *sequential access or *random access. *See also* keyed sequential access method, skip sequential access method, virtual storage access method.

access time The time taken to retrieve an item of information from storage. The access time may be counted in nanoseconds for a semiconductor device or in minutes

6
1 3 7
4 2
5 8 9

row-ragged array

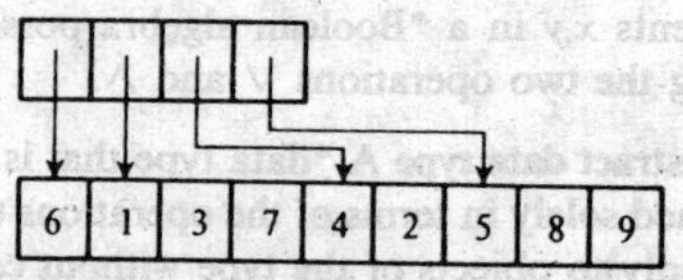

representation using an access vector

Access vector

if the file containing the required data is on magnetic tape.

access vector A vector that is used in the representation of a *ragged array. For example, the elements of a row-ragged array, A, would be stored row by row in a vector B. The ith element of the access vector would then point to the position in B where the first element of the ith row of A was stored (*see* diagram). A column-ragged array would be similarly represented using an access vector referring to the beginning of columns and a listing of the elements column by column.

accountable file A file that will be taken into account when evaluating system usage. An example is a user's permanent file holding the text of a program. Files that have only a transient existence, for example to hold spooled files, will not be accountable.

accounting file A file that contains records of the resources used by individual jobs. These records are required both to regulate the amount of resource used by a job and, in a commercial environment, to manage the charging for use of the system. As each job is started, an entry is opened in the accounting file into which records concerning system utilization are written as the job is processed. *See also* system accounting.

accumulator A *register that is used to contain the results of an operation performed by the *arithmetic and logic unit (ALU). It can normally be one of the inputs to the ALU, thus the results of a number of successive operations may be built up – hence the name. In addition to holding results, the accumulator commonly has the ability to perform the various *shift and *circular shift instructions.

ACE *Acronym for* Automatic Computing Engine. An electronic stored-program computer designed in 1945–46 by Alan Turing while he was at the National Physical Laboratory (NPL), near London. The high-performance prototype version *Pilot ACE* was built at the NPL, ran its first program in 1950, and was in full-time use in 1952. The final version was working by 1957.

ACIA *Abbrev. for* asynchronous communications interface adapter. An integrated circuit that can be used in data communication interfaces. The function of the device can be varied by signals applied to its control inputs.

ACK *See* acknowledgment.

Ackermann's function The *function A defined inductively on pairs of nonnegative integers in the following manner:

$$A(0,n) = n + 1$$
$$A(m+1,0) = A(m,1)$$
$$A(m+1,n+1) = A(m,A(m+1,n))$$

where $m,n \geqslant 0$. Thus

$$A(1,n) = n + 2$$
$$A(2,n) = 2n + 3$$
$$A(3,n) = 2^{n+3} - 3$$

The highly recursive nature of the function makes it a popular choice for testing the ability of *compilers or computers to handle *recursion. Named for W. Ackermann, it provides an example of a function that is general *recursive but not *primitive recursive because of the exceedingly rapid growth in its value as m increases.

Ackermann's function may also be regarded as a function Ack of a single variable:

$$Ack(n) = A(n,n)$$

where A is defined as above.

acknowledgment A message that describes the status of one or more messages sent in the opposite direction. A *positive acknowledgment (ACK)* confirms that the previous messages were received correctly. A *negative acknowledgment (NAK)* indicates that the previous messages were not received correctly and should be retransmitted. In some protocols, acknowledgments are also used as a simple form of *flow control: sending an ACK implies that another message may be sent in the same direction as the message being acknowledged.

Piggyback acknowledgments are acknowledgments that are carried in a special field in regular data messages. Thus, as long as there is data ready for both directions of a circuit, no extra messages are needed to carry acknowledgments.

Different layers of a protocol hierarchy may have their own acknowledgment systems operating simultaneously. For example, an end-to-end transport protocol may be used to send a message reliably from one host to another in a packet switching network. When the message reaches its destination, an acknowledgment will be generated and sent in the opposite direction. Both the original message and its acknowledgment will cause data link layer acknowledgments to be generated as they travel from node to node in the network. *See also* backward error correction.

ACM Association for Computing Machinery, a US organization founded in 1947 with the following purposes.

"To advance the sciences and arts of information processing including, but not restricted to, the study, design, development, construction, and application of modern machinery, computing techniques, and appropriate languages for general information processing, for scientific computation, for the recognition, storage, retrieval, and processing of data of all kinds, and for the automatic control and simulation of processes.

"To promote the free interchange of information about the sciences and arts of information processing both among specialists and among the public in the best scientific and professional tradition.

"To develop and maintain the integrity and competence of individuals engaged in the practices of the sciences and arts of information processing."

In 1982 the ACM had approximately 55 000 members world-wide.

acoustic coupler A type of *modem that converts serial digital data into a *frequency shift keyed sound signal in the audio range for transmission down telephone lines, and decodes similar incoming sound signals. The connection between the acoustic coupler and the telephone system is made by means of a small microphone and loudspeaker held close to the earpiece and mouthpiece of an ordinary telephone handset in a sound-absorbent enclosure.

This system is ideal for connecting portable terminals or data-capture devices to remote computers using any convenient telephone. The lack of any electrical connection between terminal and phone lines is of benefit when obtaining the approval of the PTT for the use of such a device. The quality of ordinary switched voice circuits normally limits the speed of transmission to 300 baud or less.

acoustic delay line *See* delay line.

actigram *See* SADT.

active *Another term for* running.

active star A network topology in which the outer nodes connect to a single central node. The central node processes all messages in the network, including messages that it forwards from one outer node to another. A failure of the central node causes the entire network to fail. *See also* passive star, star network, network architecture.

activity Any read or write operation performed on a file. In some systems a record is kept of file activity and the information is used to optimize the use of available storage resource. For example, a file for which the activity has fallen below a certain level may be moved off line.

actual address *Another name for* machine address.

actuator of a disk drive. The mechanism that causes the head carriage and heads to be moved to the desired track. There are two main types: the *voice coil* and the *stepper motor*. The former gains its name because its operating principle is similar to that of a moving-coil loudspeaker. This type of actuator invariably forms part of a closed loop servosystem. The reference information is often provided by a disk with a dedicated servosurface. The servohead positions itself symmetrically between two servotracks by sensing positioning information from both tracks (di-bits) and moving in such a way that the amplitudes of the two signals are equal. A recently developed alternative method employs bits recorded on all surfaces that fall between sectors containing stored information; this technique is known as *embedded servo*.

The second type of actuator is essentially open loop in that it makes use of a stepper motor – a motor that moves in discrete steps when currents of the correct phase relationship are applied to its windings. This type of actuator is only used in low-cost systems where the track density may be as low as 150 tracks per inch.

ACU *Abbrev. for* automatic calling unit. A device that allows a computer or terminal to originate calls over the public switched telephone network, or in some cases over a private switched network. An ACU is often used in conjunction with a *modem: the ACU is responsible for placing the telephone call, while the modem is responsible for data transfer and call termination. Since the ACU is needed only when the call is being placed, a single ACU can often be shared among multiple modems and phone lines. ACUs are used when the traffic between two nodes (terminals or computers) is too large for manual call origination, but not large enough to justify a dedicated connection. Computer networks that use ACUs usually function as *store-and-forward message switches.

acyclic graph A *graph possessing no *cycles; when the term is applied to directed graphs the direction associated with the edges must be taken into account. *See also* tree.

Ada *Trademark* A programming language developed at the behest of the US Department of Defense for use in embedded systems, i.e. systems in which a computer is used for control purposes. (Aircraft navigation systems are an obvious example.) Such systems require concurrent activity and have severe response-time constraints, thus Ada is a *real-time language.

The design requirements of Ada were elaborated in a sequence of reports, successively more detailed specifications being identified as Strawman, Woodenman, Tinman, Ironman, and Steelman. When the specification was complete, four contractors were invited to implement a language to meet the specification. The language developed by CII-Honeywell-Bull was chosen: originally code-named *Green*, it was renamed Ada in honor of Augusta Ada Lovelace who, as assistant to Charles Babbage, has some claim to be the world's first programmer.

In addition to facilities for real-time concurrent programming, Ada incorporates novel ideas of modular structure and separate compilation to support the development of very large systems. It also introduces the idea of a *programming support environment* (*APSE*) whereby program development tools are specified along with the language as an integrated whole.

adaptive channel allocation A process by which the capacity of a communication channel is multiplexed (shared) among several sources depending upon their relative requirements. The resource distribution varies with time to match changing requirements. *See* multiplexing.

adaptive-control system An automatic (process) control system that uses adaptation as part of its prediction of process behavior in order to optimize the control. *See* adaptive process.

A	B	Σ	C_o
0	0	0	0
0	1	1	0
1	0	1	0
1	1	0	1

Fig. *a* Truth table of binary addition

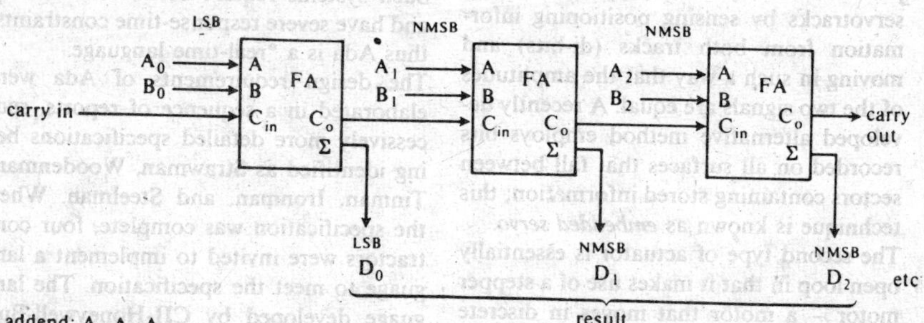

addend: $A_0\ A_1\ A_2$

augend: $B_0\ B_1\ B_2$

result: $D_0\ D_1\ D_2$

LSB : least significant bit

NMSB : next most significant bit

Fig. *b* Parallel 3-bit ripple-carry adder using cascaded full adders

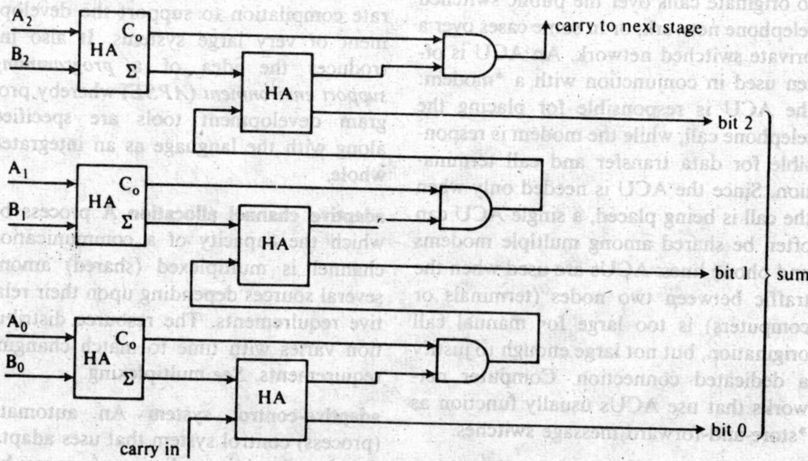

Fig. *c* Parallel 3-bit ripple-carry adder using half adders and additional gating

adaptive process The process of performing computations on a set of measured or presented data (believed to be) from a physical, i.e. natural, source in such a way as to develop a "best" parametric model of that physical source, i.e. one that best fits the observed data according to some error criterion. *See also* adaptive-control system, self-organizing system.

adaptive quadrature *See* numerical integration.

ADC *Abbrev. for* analog-to-digital (A/D) converter.

ADCCP *Abbrev. for* advanced data communication control procedure. A bit-oriented *data link control protocol developed by ANSI and similar to *SDLC and *HDLC.

A/D converter (ADC) *Short for* analog-to-digital converter. A device that can accept an analog, i.e. continuous, signal whose amplitude lies within a given range, and produce an equivalent digital signal, i.e. an *n*-bit parallel binary word that represents this analog signal. The analog signal is "examined" at discrete fixed intervals of time by means of a *sampling process in order to produce the digital signal. Analog signals originating from devices such as analog sensors or tachogenerators may thus be converted into a form that can then be processed by, say, a microprocessor.

The *resolution* of an A/D converter gives the smallest change in analog input that can be discriminated by the device. If the voltage range of an *n*-bit A/D converter is V, then its resolution is

$$V(2^n - 1)$$

Since the resolution is finite, the conversion process introduces quantization noise (*see* discrete and continuous systems). A/D converters are available in integrated circuit form. *See also* D/A converter.

adder In its simplest form, a digital electronic device that performs the operation of modulo-two addition on two binary digits, the *augend* and the number to be added, the *addend*. It is therefore also known as a *binary adder*. This operation is exemplified by the truth table shown in Fig. *a*, where Σ is the sum and C_o is the carry. From this it can be seen that binary addition may generate a carry to subsequent stages.

A *full adder* has provision for inputs of addend, augend, and carry bits and is capable of generating sum and carry outputs. These adders may be cascaded when it is desired to add binary words greater than one bit in length by connecting together the carry inputs and outputs of adjacent stages. The circuit shown in Fig. *b* is a *parallel adder operating on two 3-bit binary words ($A_0A_1A_2$ and $B_0B_1B_2$) to produce a 3-bit result ($D_0D_1D_2$) and a carry. The adder uses a *ripple-carry* technique: the carry at each stage of addition must propagate or ripple through the succeeding stages of addition in order to form the result.

A *half-adder* is an implementation of an adder that has provision only for input of addend and augend bits and is capable of generating sum and carry outputs. These devices cannot directly be cascaded as can full adders but may be made to perform a similar function by including additional logic gating, as shown in Fig. *c*. This type of adder is relatively slow in operation. *See also* BCD adder, serial adder.

address 1. The term most generally used to refer (in some way) to a location within the computer memory; the word *location* is actually used as a synonym. Such reference is usually made for the purpose of retrieving or storing some information at that location. The reference may be explicit (*see* machine address) or it may be made in any of a number of ways for convenience or brevity (*see* addressing

schemes). In some architectures the registers in the CPU and/or the I/O devices are also addressed.
The word address is also used as a verb: to specify a location.
2. In communications, *see* addressing.

addressable location A location whose position in a storage medium is precisely defined and can be accessed. As a safeguard it is usual to arrange that not all memory locations are addressable by all programs.

address bus A *bus that is dedicated to passing address information. It may be a set of conductors that are physically separate from other dedicated buses or it may be a subset of a system bus. The number of conductors is often the same as the maximum allowable number of bits in the address.

address calculation sorting A form of *sorting that uses extra storage space to improve upon a *straight insertion sort. One method employs *n* *list heads, corresponding to *n* different ranges of the sortkey, together with a *link field on each record.

address format *See* instruction format.

addressing The method used to identify the location of a participant in a *network. Ideally, addressing specifies where the participant is located rather than who they are (*see* name) or how to get there (*see* routing). This is true for *flat addressing*, in which addresses are assigned independently of each other and carry no internal structure. More common, however, is *hierarchical addressing*, in which addresses are grouped to reflect relationships among the addressed entities. Often the grouping reflects the physical topology of the network, so addressing and routing are interrelated. Sometimes the grouping reflects administrative or functional relationships (*logical addressing*), so addressing and naming are interrelated.
In a system employing layered protocols (*see* X.25, seven-layer reference model), different forms of addressing may be used at different levels. The data link level may use addresses that identify specific stations on a multidrop line. The network level uses addresses that identify the source and destination hosts associated with a packet. Higher protocol layers may use addresses that distinguish different connections or processes.
Addresses may be fixed-length or extensible. In *fixed-length addressing* all addresses occupy a fixed number of digits. An example is the Ethernet protocol, which uses 48-bit addresses. In *extensible addressing* the length of an address may vary from case to case. For example, in *X.121 "international data numbers" are defined and these may be from 3 to 14 decimal digits in length.

addressing schemes The wide variety of schemes developed in order to provide compact or convenient *address references in cases where the *machine address is too large to be comfortably included in an instruction (*see* instruction format) or where it is not possible or even necessary to assign an explicit address. *Augmented, *indirect, *implied, *immediate, and *relative addressing schemes provide compact references. *Indexed, relative, and *symbolic addressing schemes provide convenient references. In the absence of any of these addressing schemes *direct addressing is used.

address mapping Use of one of the *addressing schemes to convert an address that is specified in an instruction into a *machine address. *Virtual memory and *cache memory use forms of address mapping for additional memory-management functions.

address mark The special code or d.c.-erased area on a magnetic disk track that occurs just prior to the address information of a *sector. In the case of an MFM drive using a special code (*see* disk format), the encoding rules for MFM are broken so that the code is unique. The

purpose of the address mark is to bring the drive control electronics into byte synchronization.
The *data mark* fulfills the same function with respect to data as the address mark to the address.

address register A *register in which an *address is stored. *See also* control unit.

address-relative Having or involving a relative address or relative addresses. *See* relative addressing.

address space The number of distinct locations that may be referred to with the *machine address. For most (i.e. binary) machines it is equal to 2^n, where n is the number of bits in the machine address. In many large machines the address space is larger than the number of physical or real addresses that are present in the system. Additionally, the number of bits available to specify an address is restricted (*see* instruction format), and some form of *address mapping or *addressing scheme is used to obtain the machine address from the specified address.

address table sorting A form of *sorting that is useful when the information records are long. A table of addresses that point to the records is formed and these addresses, rather than the records themselves, are manipulated.

add-subtract time The time required by a computer to find the sum or difference of two numbers; it may or may not include the time required to obtain the numbers from memory. This is often used as one form of (speed) figure of merit for computers. *See also* computer power.

adjacency list *Another name for* adjacency structure.

adjacency matrix (connectivity matrix; reachability matrix) A *matrix used as a means of representing a *graph. If A is the adjacency matrix corresponding to a given graph G, then

$$a_{ij} = 1$$

if there is an edge from vertex i to vertex j in G; otherwise

$$a_{ij} = 0$$

If G is a directed *graph then

$$a_{ij} = 1$$

if there is an edge directed from vertex i to vertex j; otherwise

$$a_{ij} = 0$$

If the vertices of the graph are numbered 1,2, ... m, the adjacency matrix is of a type $m \times m$. If

$$A \times A \times \ \ldots \ \times A$$
$$(p \text{ terms}, p \leqslant m)$$

is evaluated, the nonzero entries indicate those vertices that are joined by a *path of length p; indeed the value of the i,jth entry of A^p gives the number of paths of length p from the vertex i to vertex j. By examining the set of such matrices,

$$p = 1,2, \ldots, m-1$$

it can be determined whether two vertices are connected.
It is also possible for adjacency matrices to be formed from *Boolean matrices.

adjacency structure (adjacency list) A means of representing a *graph. The adjacency structure corresponding to a *path G is the set

$$\{\text{Adj}(v) \mid v \text{ is a vertex in } G\}$$

If G is an undirected graph, then a vertex w is in Adj(v) if and only if there is an edge in G between v and w; if G is a directed graph, then w is in Adj(v) if and only if there is an edge in G directed from v to w.

ADP *Abbrev. for* automatic data processing. *See* data processing.

advance-feed tape *See* paper tape.

AED *Acronym for* Algol extended for design. A programming language based on *Algol 60 with extensions for computer-aided design. The major extension was the ability to manipulate *plex structures built from records and pointers. The language is now obsolete.

AFIPS American Federation of Information Processing Societies, Inc., founded in 1961 to provide a structure for societies and associations interested in information processing to join together in order to advance the state of the art. AFIPS includes: the American Society for Information Science, American Statistical Association, Association for Computing Machinery, Association for Computational Linguistics, Association for Education Data Systems, Data Processing Management Association, IEEE Computer Society, Instrument Society of America, Society for Computer Simulation, Society for Industrial and Applied Mathematics, Society for Information Display. It is the US member of IFIP.

AFL *Abbrev. for* abstract family of languages.

AHPL *Abbrev. for* a hardware programming language. *See* hardware description.

AI *Abbrev. for* artificial intelligence.

aleph null *See* cardinality.

algebra 1. The investigation both of mathematical properties of numbers and of mathematical structure employing the use of symbols.
2. A *set A, say, together with *operations of the form

$$f : A^n \rightarrow A$$

mapping elements of the *Cartesian product

$$A \times A \times \ldots \times A \text{ (} n \text{ terms)}$$

into A itself. Examples of algebras include:
(a) the integers together with, for example, the operations of *monadic and *dyadic addition and subtraction, together with multiplication and finding the remainder;
(b) the set {TRUE, FALSE} together with the operations AND, OR, and NOT (*see* Boolean algebra);
(c) sets together with the operations of *union, *intersection, and *complement (*see* set algebra);
(d) strings together with the operation of *concatenation.
In computing terms an algebra can be identified with the notion of type; thus there typically exist in programming languages the type integer, the type Boolean, etc. The operations that are defined on elements of that type can then be considered. By stating the axioms concerning the operations involved in the algebra, an *abstract data type is obtained. *See also* algebraic structure.

algebraic language *Another name for* context-free language.

algebraic specification *See* module specification.

algebraic structure The notion combining *algebras, *functions, and propositions, giving properties and operations relevant to sets of values in one or more *abstract data types. The simplest case will contain or be only a single algebra.
In general there may be several interrelated algebras, functions, and propositions: each algebra represents a data type together with the operations on the elements of that type (i.e. functions from the type to itself);
other functions have operands and produce results in data types that are not necessarily the same;
propositions may have operands from various data types and produce results that are truth values (either TRUE or FALSE).
The notion of an algebraic structure thus represents the mathematical model that underlies the basic design of programming languages.
It is usually understood that there are algorithms for performing any calculation involving the various operations and functions, and algorithms for deciding the truth or falseness of a proposition in any particular case. Formally it is said that the operations and functions are effectively computable and that the propositions are effectively decidable. A distinction is therefore sometimes made between algebraic structures and effective algebraic structures.

algebraic symbol manipulation language A programming language in which the data are algebraic expressions in symbolic form, and the operations are the operations of algebra. The operations provided usually include multiplying out brackets, simplification, factorization, polynomial division, and differentiation with respect to one or more variables.

Algol *Acronym for* algorithmic language. The generic name for a family of high-level languages of great significance in the development of computing. In 1958 the Association for Computing Machinery (ACM) in the US and the Gessellschaft für Angewante Mathematik und Mechanik (GAMM) in Europe set up a joint committee to define an *international algorithmic language (IAL)*. The language that was designed became known as Algol, and was later called *Algol 58* to distinguish it from later versions. Algol 58 was not intended to be a viable language, and in 1960 an augmented committee was convened to devise the second iteration, which was published as the language *Algol 60*. *See also* JOVIAL.

Algol 60 was much more popular in Europe than in the US, probably due to the dominance of IBM and FORTRAN in the North American market, and to the extent that it was at all widely used, that use was in Europe. It introduced many new concepts, notably block structure (*see* block-structured languages), nested scopes, modes of parameter passing to procedures, and the definition of the language introduced the now classic *BNF notation for describing syntax. The influence of Algol 60 can be seen in all succeeding languages, and it stands as a milestone in the development of programming languages.

In the years following the publication of the Algol 60 Report, a working group of the International Federation for Information Processing (IFIP – WG2.3) was set up to consider the definition of a successor to Algol 60. There were many dissensions within the group, and eventually a minority report was issued proposing the language *Algol 68*. The first implementation of Algol 68, named ALGOL 68R, was produced at the Royal Radar and Signals Establishment in the UK. ALGOL 68R demonstrated that Algol 68 was a viable language (not at the time a self-evident proposition).

Although Algol 68 introduces many novel concepts of great theoretical interest and significance, its practical application has been almost nil. One of the most notable features of Algol 68 is its formal specification using a VW-grammar. Although a very precise definition, it is very difficult to understand, and this difficulty partly accounts for the low acceptance of the language. One of the most significant effects of the split in the Algol 68 working group is that it led indirectly to the development of *Pascal.

algorithm A prescribed set of well-defined rules or instructions for the solution of a problem, e.g. the performance of a calculation, in a finite number of steps. The word is thought to derive from the name of the 9th-century Persian mathematician abu-Ja'far Mohammed ibn Mūsa al-Khuwārizmi. Expressing an algorithm in a formal notation is one of the main parts of a *program; much that is said about programs applies to algorithms, and vice versa. An *effective algorithm* is one that is effectively computable (*see* effective computability). The study of whether effective algorithms exist to compute particular quantities forms the basis of the theory of algorithms.

Save for the simplest of algorithms it is difficult to *prove* that an algorithm is correct (*see* program correctness proof), or even to specify the effect it is intended to achieve. In practice it is usually necessary to be content with *algorithm validation*. This process certifies, or verifies, that an algorithm will perform the calculation required of it. It involves testing the routine against a variety of instances of the problem and ensuring that it performs satisfactorily for these test cases. If the test set is chosen sufficiently well there can then be confidence in the algorithm.

Algorithm analysis is the study of the performance characteristics of a given algorithm. One branch of this study, *average-case analysis*, examines the average behavior of the algorithm. *Worst-case analysis* studies the behavior when all circumstances are as unfavorable as possible.

algorithmic language A language or notation used to express clearly an algorithm. It is usually part of a programming language.

allocation routine A routine that is responsible for the allocation of resources to a process. *See* resource allocation.

alphabet An ordered *character set. *See also* formal language.

alphabetic code A code whose target alphabet contains only letters and/or strings of letters from the Roman alphabet.

alphanumeric character Any of the 26 letters of the Roman alphabet, or any of the decimal digits, 0 through to 9.

alphanumeric code A code whose target alphabet contains both letters and digits and/or strings thereof.

ALU *Abbrev. for* arithmetic and logic unit.

S

if c1 then S

if c2 then s2 else s1

S

if c1 then S else s2

if c2 then s2

Two derivation trees in an ambiguous grammar

ambiguous grammar A *context-free grammar that derives the same word by different *derivation trees, or equivalently by different leftmost *derivation sequences or by different rightmost derivation sequences. A familiar programming language example is:

S → if C then S else S

S → if C then S

where S and C stand for statement and condition. This grammar is ambiguous since the following compound statement

if c1 then if c2 then s2 else s1

has two derivation trees, as shown in the diagram. *See also* inherently ambiguous language.

Amdahl A company that was founded in 1969 by Gene Amdahl, the prime architect of the IBM 360 series, for the purpose of making very high speed computers that could run IBM software. These computers have been successful primarily because they could run the IBM operating systems languages and applications programs. Gene Amdahl left Amdahl Corporation in 1980 to form a new venture known as Trilogy Ltd., which is also aimed at very high speed computers.

amplitude *See* signal.

amplitude modulation (AM) *See* modulation.

amplitude quantization *See* discrete and continuous systems, quantization.

analog computer A computer that performs computations (such as summation, multiplication, integration, and other operations) by manipulating continuous physical variables that are analogs of the quantities being subjected to computation. The most commonly used physical variable is voltage; time may also be used. Some analog computers use mechanical components: the physical variables become, for example, angular rotations and linear displacements. *See also* discrete and continuous systems.

analog signal A smoothly varying value of voltage or current, i.e. a signal that varies continuously in amplitude and time. It often represents a measured physical quantity. *See also* A/D converter, D/A converter, analog computer, discrete and continuous systems.

analog-to-digital converter *See* A/D converter.

analysis of variance A technique, originally developed by R. A. Fisher, whereby the total variation in a vector of numbers $y_1 \ldots y_n$, expressed as the sum of squares about the mean

$$\sum_i (y_i - y_.)^2,$$

is split up into component sum of squares ascribable to the effects of various classifying factors that may index the data. Thus if the data consist of a two-way $m \times n$ array, classified by factors A and B and indexed by

$$i = 1, \ldots, m \qquad j = 1, \ldots, n$$

then the analysis of variance gives the identity

$$\underset{\text{Total}}{\sum_{ij} (y_{ij} - y_{..})^2} = \underset{\text{A main effect}}{\sum_{ij} (y_{i.} - y_{..})^2} +$$

$$\underset{\text{B main effect}}{\sum_{ij} (y_{.j} - y_{..})^2} + \underset{\text{A.B interaction}}{\sum_{ij} (y_{ij} - y_{i.} - y_{.j} + y_{..})^2}$$

where dots denote averaging over the suffixes involved.

Geometrically the analysis of variance becomes the successive projections of the vector $\boldsymbol{y}$, considered as a point in n-dimensional space, onto orthogonal hyperplanes within that space. The dimensions of the hyperplanes give the *degrees of freedom* for each term; in the above example these are

$$mn - 1 \equiv (m-1) + (n-1) + (m-1)(n-1)$$

A statistical model applied to the data allows mean squares, equal to (sum of squares)/(degrees of freedom), to be compared with an error mean square that measures the background "noise". Large mean squares indicate large effects of the factors concerned. The above processes can be much elaborated (*see* experimental design, regression analysis).

Analytical Engine The logic design for a mechanical computer conceived by Charles Babbage around 1833, but never built. The design envisioned a memory of a thousand 50-digit numbers. The machine, which could do addition, subtraction, multiplication, and division, was to have been programmed by punched cards and was to have included a printer to obtain the results. The design was remarkable in anticipating so many elements of modern computers.

analyzer A program, such as a parser, that determines constituents in a string; the word is rarely used except in the combinations syntax analyzer and lexical analyzer.

ancestor of a node in a *tree. Any node on the unique path from the root of the tree to the node in question. A *proper ancestor* of a node, *A*, is a node, *B*, such that *B* is an ancestor of *A* and $A \neq B$. *See also* parent.

AND gate An electronic *logic gate whose output is logic 1 (true) only when all (two or more) inputs are logic 1, otherwise it is logic 0 (false). It therefore implements the logical *AND operation on its inputs and has the same *truth table. The diagram shows the usual circuit symbol and the truth table of a two-input gate.

AND operation The logical *connective combining two statements, truth values, or formulas *P* and *Q* in such a way that the outcome is true only if both *P* and *Q* are true; otherwise the outcome is false (*see* table). The AND operation is usually denoted by $\wedge$, and occasionally by . or by

A1, A2 → B

inputs	A1	0	0	1	1
	A2	0	1	0	1
output	B	0	0	0	1

Two-input AND gate, circuit symbol and truth table

P	F	F	T	T
Q	F	T	F	T
$P \wedge Q$	F	F	F	T

Truth table for AND operation

juxtaposition, as in *PQ*. It is one of the binary operations of *Boolean algebra and is both *commutative and *associative. When implemented as a basic machine operation on computers, the AND operation is usually generalized to operate on complete words. Then the operation described above is applied to the corresponding bits in each word. In this context AND is often used for *masking purposes, i.e. to select parts of words, such as the address field.

annotation Explanation added to a program to assist the reader. This may take the form of manuscript additions to the program listing, but more often takes the form of *comments included in the program text.

ANSI American National Standards Institute, an industry-supported standards organization, founded in 1918, that establishes US industrial standards and their correspondence to those set by the *ISO (International Standards Organization). ANSI determines hardware-related standards for such items as link-level protocols, pin positions and meaning in chips, and recordings on tape and disk, and some software standards, e.g. the FORTRAN and COBOL standards.

ANSI–SPARC schemata A general standard for the description of a *database management system by the use of three separate *schemata: the conceptual schema, which provides the logical description of the data with a semantic meaning, one or more versions of a user schema, which represent the data structure as apparent to the user, and a physical schema, which defines the physical structure of the data stored within the system.

antisymmetric relation A *relation *R* defined on a set *S* and having the property that

$$\text{whenever } x\,R\,y \text{ and } y\,R\,x \text{ then } x = y$$

where *x* and *y* are arbitrary members of *S*. Examples include "is a subset of" defined on sets, and "less than or equal to" defined on the integers. *See also* asymmetric relation, symmetric relation.

APL *Acronym for* a programming language. Originally devised by Iverson as a mathematical notation in the mid-1960s, and only later implemented as a programming language, APL has had a meteoric rise in popularity. The main feature of APL is that it provides a rich set of powerful operators for handling multidimensional arrays, together with the capability for the user to define his own operators. The built-in operators are mainly represented by single characters using a special character set. Thus APL programs are very concise and often impenetrable.

Apple One of a plethora of microcomputer systems. The Apple, manufactured by Apple Computer, Inc., is remarkable because it has been a very big commercial success. Observers credit the development of a spread sheet program (VisiCalc) for the Apple as the principal reason for this success.

application layer of network protocol function. *See* seven-layer reference model.

application package (software package) A suite of programs or modules that is directed at some generic application and can be tailored (perhaps with some additions) to the needs of a specific instance of that application.

applications program Any program that is specific to the particular role that a given computer performs within a given organization and makes a direct contribution to performing that role. For example, where a computer handles a company's finances a payroll program would be an applications program. By contrast, an *operating system or a *software tool may both be essential to the effective use of the computer system, but neither makes a direct contribution to meeting the end-user's eventual needs.

application terminal A combination of input and output devices configured into a unit to meet the requirements of a particular type of business activity and environment. They usually have some built-in processing capability and are connected to a controlling processor via a data communication link. Examples include point-of-sale terminals and bank teller terminals.

applicative language *Another name for* functional language.

applied robotics *See* process control, robotics.

approximation theory A subject that is concerned with the approximation of a class of objects, say F, by a subclass, say $P \subset F$, that is in some sense simpler. For example, let

$$F = C[a,b],$$

the real continuous functions on $[a,b]$, then a subclass of practical use is P_n, i.e. polynomials of degree n. The means of measuring the closeness or accuracy of the approximation is provided by a metric or *norm*. This is a nonnegative function that is defined on F and measures the size of its elements. Norms of particular value in the approximation of mathematical functions (for computer subroutines, say) are the *Chebyshev norm* and the *2-norm* (or *Euclidean norm*). For functions

$$f \in C[a,b]$$

these norms are given respectively as

$$\|f\| = \max_{a \leqslant x \leqslant b} |f(x)|$$

$$\|f\|_2 = \left(\int_a^b f(x)^2 \, dx\right)^{1/2}$$

For approximation of data these norms take the discrete form

$$\|f\| = \max_i |f(x_i)|$$

$$\|f\|_2 = \left(\sum_i f(x_i)^2\right)^{1/2}$$

The 2-norm frequently incorporates a weight function (or weights). From these two norms the problems of *Chebyshev approximation* and *least squares approximation* arise. For example, with polynomial approximation we seek

$$p_n \in P_n$$

for which

$$\|f-p_n\| \text{ or } \|f-p_n\|_2$$

are acceptably small. Best approximation problems arise when, for example, we seek

$$p_n \in P_n$$

for which these measures of errors are as small as possible with respect to P_n.

Other examples of norms that are particularly important are *vector* and *matrix norms*. For n-component vectors

$$\boldsymbol{x} = (x_1, x_2, \ldots, x_n)^T$$

important examples are

$$\|\boldsymbol{x}\| = \max_i |x_i|$$

$$\|\boldsymbol{x}\|_2 = \left(\sum_{i=1}^{n} x_i^2\right)^{1/2}$$

Corresponding to a given vector norm, a subordinate matrix norm can be defined for $n \times n$ matrices A, by

$$\|A\| = \max_{\|x\| \neq 0} \frac{\|A\boldsymbol{x}\|}{\|\boldsymbol{x}\|}$$

For the vector norm

$$\|x\| = \max_i |x_i|,$$

this reduces to the expression

$$\|A\| = \max_i \sum_{j=1}^{n} |a_{ij}|$$

where a_{ij} is the i,jth element of A. Vector and matrix norms are indispensible in most areas of numerical analysis.

APSE *Acronym for* Ada programming support environment. *See* Ada. *See also* software engineering environment.

arc of a graph. *See* graph.

architectural design (high-level design) *See* program decomposition, program design, system design.

architecture The specification of a (digital) computer system at a somewhat general level, including description from the programming (user) viewpoint of the instruction set and user interface, memory organization and addressing, I/O operation and control, etc. The implementation of an architecture in members of a given *computer family may be quite different, yet all the members should be capable of running the same program. Implementation differences may occur in actual hardware components or in subsystem implementation (e.g. *microprogramming as opposed to wired control), generally in both. Different implementations may have substantially different performances and costs. An implementation feature – such as a cache memory – that is *transparent to the user does not affect the architecture. Common architecture provides compatibility from the user's viewpoint.

archived file A file that has been transferred to a lower level in the *memory hierarchy, usually from magnetic disk to magnetic tape. The decision for this transfer to take place may be made as a conscious decision by the owner of the file, or it may arise from the operations of the appropriate resource management.

Arden's rule A rule, used in formal language theory, stating that A^*B is the smallest solution for X in the equation

$$X = AX \cup B$$

where X, A, B are sets of strings. (For notation, *see* concatenation, Kleene star.) A^*B is furthermore the only solution, unless A contains the empty string, in which case any A^*B' is a solution,

$$\text{where } B \subseteq B'$$

Although simple, Arden's rule is significant as one of the earliest fixed-point results in computer science. In conjunction with the normal process of eliminating variables, it can be used to solve any set of simultaneous linear equations over sets of strings. *See also* Kleene's theorem (on regular expressions).

argument A value or address passed to a procedure or function at the time of call. Thus in the BASIC statement

Y = SQR(X)

X is the argument of the SQR (square root) function. Arguments are sometimes referred to as *actual parameters.*

arithmetic and logic unit (ALU; arithmetic unit, AU) A portion of the *central processor that (generally) forms functions of two input variables and produces a single output variable. These functions usually consist of the common *arithmetic operations, the common *logic operations, and *shift operations.

arithmetic instruction An instruction specifying that one of the *arithmetic operations is to be carried out by the computer.

arithmetic operation An operation that forms a function of two variables. This function is usually one of the class of operations: add, subtract, multiply, and divide. These operations may be carried out as operations on integers, fractional numbers, or floating-point numbers. The operation is normally performed in the *arithmetic and logic unit.

arithmetic operator A type of *operator appearing in an expression denoting one of the operations of arithmetic, e.g. +, –, * (multiplication), / (divide).

arithmetic shift *See* shift.

arithmetic unit (AU) *Another name for* arithmetic and logic unit.

arm 1. (access arm) A lever or bar that supports and moves the read/write head to the correct track on a disk.
2. (tension arm) A lever or bar that is fitted with rollers or guides and is automatically moved so that it maintains the right tension in a low-speed tape transport. *See also* buffer.
3. To bring a device to a state of readiness.

ARMA *Abbrev. for* autoregressive moving average. *See* time series.

ARPA *See* DARPA.

ARPANET or **Arpanet** *Acronym for* Advanced Research Projects Agency Network. The collection of *host computers plus *backbone network making up the first major *packet-switching network. Begun through research grants provided by ARPA (now *DARPA) to universities and private organizations for computer science, the ARPANET started as a four-node network in December 1969. It now connects over 100 host computers throughout half the world.
The ARPANET utilizes minicomputers called interface message processors (*IMPs) as a backbone network of message-switching nodes. The IMPs are primarily connected by 56K bps leased lines, although other links are also used (such as the satellite link between the US and Europe). Each IMP takes blocks of data from its hosts, subdivides them into 128 byte packets, and adds a header specifying destination and source addresses. Then, based on a dynamically updated routing table, the packet is routed over whichever line is currently the fastest route to the destination. Upon receiving a packet, the next IMP acknowledges it and repeats the routing process independently.
The ARPANET pioneered many of the network concepts that are in use today. An important contribution is the ARPANET routing algorithm, which is completely distributed, is performed on a packet-by-packet basis, and is based on a continuous evaluation of the network's topology, capacity, and utilization. The practical demonstration of distributed routing was viewed as an important step in demonstrating that packet switching networks would be cost-effective and reliable.
The ARPANET technology has been successfully replicated for several other military and intelligence-gathering networks used by the US. The ARPANET itself was transferred to the Defence Communication Agency in 1975, and is no longer the direct responsibility of DARPA.

array (subscripted variable) An ordered collection of a number of elements of the same type, the number being fixed unless the array is *flexible. The elements of one array may be of type integer, those of another array may be of type real, while the elements of a third array may be of type character string (if the programming language recognizes compound types).
Each element has a unique set of *index values that determine its position in the ordered collection. Each index is of a discrete type. The number of dimensions in the ordering is fixed.
A one-dimensional array, or *vector, consists of a list of elements distinguished by a single index. If v is a one-dimensional array and i is an index value, then v_i refers to the ith element of v. If the index ranges from L through U then the value L is called the *lower bound* of v and U is the *upper bound*. Usually in mathematics and often in mathematical computing the index type is taken as integer and the lower bound is taken as one.
In a two-dimensional array, or *matrix, the elements are ordered in the form of a table comprising a fixed number of rows and a fixed number of columns. Each ele-

ment in such an array is distinguished by a pair of indexes. The first index gives the row and the second gives the column of the array in which the element is located. The element in the *i*th row and *j*th column is called the *i,j*th element of the array. If i ranges from L1 through U1 and j ranges from L2 through U2 then L1 is the *first lower bound* of the array, U1 is the *first upper bound*, L2 is the *second lower bound* and U2 is the *second upper bound*. Again it is common practice to take the indexes as integers and to set both L1 and L2 equal to one. An example of such a two-dimensional array with U1 = m, U2 = n is given in the diagram.

$$\begin{bmatrix} a_{11} & a_{12} & \cdots & a_{1n} \\ a_{21} & a_{22} & \cdots & a_{2n} \\ \vdots & \vdots & & \vdots \\ a_{m1} & a_{m2} & \cdots & a_{mn} \end{bmatrix}$$

Two-dimensional array

In *three-dimensional arrays* the position of each element is distinguished by three indexes. Arrays of higher dimension are similarly defined.

array processor A computer/processor that has an architecture especially designed for processing *arrays (e.g. matrices) of numbers. The architecture includes a number of processors (say 64 by 64) working simultaneously, each handling one element of the array, so that a single operation can apply to all elements of the array in parallel. To obtain the same effect in a conventional processor, the operation must be applied to each element of the array sequentially, and so consequently much more slowly.

An array processor may be built as a self-contained unit attached to a main computer via an I/O port or internal bus; alternatively, it may be a *distributed array processor* where the processing elements are distributed throughout, and closely linked to, a section of the computer's memory.

Array processors are very powerful tools for handling problems with a high degree of parallelism. They do however demand a modified approach to programming, which has not yet reached full maturity (1983). Conversion of conventional (sequential) programs to serve array processors is not a trivial task, and it is sometimes necessary to select a different (parallel) algorithm to suit the parallel approach.

See also vector processing.

articulation point *Another name for* cut vertex.

artificial intelligence (AI) A discipline concerned with the building of computer programs that perform tasks requiring intelligence when done by humans. However, intelligent tasks for which a decision procedure is known (e.g. inverting matrices) are generally excluded, whereas perceptual tasks (e.g. seeing and hearing) are generally included. For this reason, AI is better defined by indicating its range. Examples of tasks tackled within AI are: game playing, inference, learning, natural-language understanding, plan formation, speech understanding, theorem proving, and visual perception.

Perceptual tasks have been found to involve a lot more computation than is apparent from introspection. This computation is unconscious in humans, which has made it hard to simulate. AI has had relatively more success at intellectual tasks (e.g. game playing and theorem proving) than perceptual tasks. Sometimes these computer programs are intended to simulate human behavior (*see* computational psychology). Sometimes they are built for technological application (*see* computer-aided instruction, expert systems, robotics). But in many cases the goal is just to find any technique for doing some task, or to find a technique that does the task better than hitherto.

Computational techniques and concepts that have been invented in AI include *list processing, *interactive (multiaccess) computing, *augmented transition networks, *means/ends analysis, *production-rule systems, *resolution, *semantic networks, and various *line finders.
The term *machine intelligence* is synonymous with artificial intelligence, although it is sometimes used to indicate only the technologically oriented aspects.

ASCC *Abbrev. for* Automatic Sequence Controlled Calculator. *See* Harvard Mark I.

ASCII (American standard code for information interchange) A standard character encoding scheme introduced in 1963 and used widely on many machines. It is a 7-bit code with no parity recommendation, providing 128 different bit patterns. The character set is shown in the table. The control characters of ASCII include
DEL (delete)
STX (start of text)
ETX (end of text)
ACK (acknowledge)
HT (horizontal tab)
LF (line feed)
VT (vertical tab)
CR (carriage return)
NAK (negative acknowledge)
SYN (synchronous idle)
ETB (end of transmission block)
FS (file separator)
GS (group separator)
RS (record separator)
See also character set.

assembler 1. A program that takes as input a program written in *assembly language and translates it into machine code or relocatable code.
2. *Colloquial* An assembly language.

bits b7 b6 b5 →					0 0 0	0 0 1	0 1 0	0 1 1	1 0 0	1 0 1	1 1 0	1 1 1
b4	b3	b2	b1	row ↓ / column →	0	1	2	3	4	5	6	7
0	0	0	0	0	NUL	DLE	SP	0	@	P	`	p
0	0	0	1	1	SOH	DC1	!	1	A	Q	a	q
0	0	1	0	2	STX	DC2	"	2	B	R	b	r
0	0	1	1	3	ETX	DC3	#	3	C	S	c	s
0	1	0	0	4	EOT	DC4	$	4	D	T	d	t
0	1	0	1	5	ENQ	NAK	%	5	E	U	e	u
0	1	1	0	6	ACK	SYN	&	6	F	V	f	v
0	1	1	1	7	BEL	ETB	'	7	G	W	g	w
1	0	0	0	8	BS	CAN	(	8	H	X	h	x
1	0	0	1	9	HT	EM	)	9	I	Y	i	y
1	0	1	0	A	LF	SUB	*	:	J	Z	j	z
1	0	1	1	B	VT	ESC	+	;	K	[	k	|
1	1	0	0	C	FF	FS	,	<	L	\	!	|
1	1	0	1	D	CR	GS	–	=	M	]	m	|
1	1	1	0	E	SO	RS	.	>	N	^	n	~
1	1	1	1	F	SI	US	/	?	O	_	o	DEL

ASCII code chart with binary and hex equivalents

assembly language A notation for the convenient representation of machine-code programs in human-readable terms. An assembly language allows the programmer to use alphabetic operation codes with mnemonic significance, to use symbolic names of his own choice for machine and memory registers, and to specify *addressing schemes (e.g. indexing, indirection) in a convenient way. It also allows the use of various number bases (e.g. decimal, hexadecimal) for numerical constants, and allows the user to attach *labels to lines of the program so that these lines can be referenced in a symbolic manner from other parts of a program (usually as the destination of a control transfer or jump).

assertion A Boolean formula whose value is claimed to be true. The following are all examples:

4 + 5 = 9
4 is even and 5 is odd
x is even or y is odd
$x - y > 15$
for all relevant i, x[i] < x[i+1]

The last assertion states that the array x is sorted into ascending order, with no repeated values.
Assertions are employed extensively in proofs of *program correctness, where they are used to characterize program states.

assertion checker An automated system for checking whether *assertions attached to the text of some program are consistent with the *semantics of that program as given by some formal semantic definition of the programming language. *See also* mechanical verifier.

assignment-free language A programming language that does not include the concept of assigning values to variables. It is usually a *functional language.

assignment statement A fundamental statement of all programming languages (except *declarative languages) that assigns a new value to a variable. The typical form in Algol-like languages is

variable := expression

where := is read as "becomes"; it is sometimes written as a left-pointing arrow to signify the conveyance of a value to the variable on the left. Older languages (notably BASIC, FORTRAN) use = as the assignment operator, e.g.

A = B + C

This leads to consequent problems in expressing the concept of equality of two values in a comparison, leading to such statements as FORTRAN's

IF (A.EQ.B) . . .

associative addressing A method of addressing a location by what is in the memory rather than where it is. This is achieved by specifying something about the contents of the desired location rather than by a normal address. An *associative memory (or content-addressable memory) is used to provide a search mechanism to match on partial memory contents for a word that satisfies the match. In some applications it may be permissible for more than one word to be found. The desired data will be in close association or proximity, most often as an additional field of the retrieved word.

associative computer A computer containing an *associative memory.

associative law *See* associative operation.

associative memory (content-addressable memory, CAM) A memory that is capable of determining whether a given datum – the *search word* – is contained in one of its addresses or locations. This may be accomplished by a number of mechanisms. In some cases parallel combinational logic is applied at each word in the memory and a test is made simultaneously for coincidence with the search word. In other cases the search word and all of the words in the memory are shifted serially in synchronism; a single bit of the search word is then compared to the same bit of all of the memory words using as many single-bit coincidence circuits as there are words in the memory. Amplifications of the associative memory technique allow for *masking the search word or requiring only a "close" match as opposed to an exact match. Small parallel associative memories are used in *cache memory and *virtual memory mapping applications.

Since parallel operations on many words are expensive (in hardware), a variety of stratagems are used to approximate associative memory operation without actually carrying out the full test described here. One of these uses *hashing to generate a "best guess" for a conventional address followed by a test of the contents of that address.

Some associative memories have been built to be accessed conventionally (by words in parallel) and as serial comparison associative memories; these have been called *orthogonal memories*. *See also* associative addressing.

associative operation Any *binary operation $\circ$ that satisfies the law

$$x \circ (y \circ z) = (x \circ y) \circ z$$

for all x, y, and z in the domain of $\circ$. The law is known as the *associative law*. An expression involving several adjacent instances of an associative operation can be interpreted unambiguously; the order in which the operations are performed is irrelevant since the effects of different evaluations are identical, though the work involved may differ. Consequently parentheses are unnecessary, even in more complex expressions.

The arithmetic operations of addition and multiplication are associative, though subtraction is not. On a computer the associative law of addition of real numbers fails to hold because of the inherent inaccuracy in the way real numbers are usually represented (*see* floating-point notation), and the addition of integers fails to hold because of the possibility of *overflow.

astable An electronic circuit that has no stable output state and whose output therefore oscillates between two voltage levels. As a result it functions as a square-wave oscillator or a pulse generator. *See also* multivibrator.

asymmetric relation A *relation R defined on a set S and having the property that

$$\text{whenever } x\ R\ y$$

then it is never the case that

$$y\ R\ x$$

where x and y are arbitrary elements of S. The usual "is less than" ordering defined on the integers is an asymmetric relation. *See also* antisymmetric relation, symmetric relation.

asynchronous Involving or requiring a form of computer control timing in which a specific operation is begun upon receipt of an indication (signal) that the preceding operation has been completed. *See also* interrupt. *Compare* synchronous.

asynchronous circuit An electronic logic circuit in which logical operations are not performed under the control of a clock signal with the result that logic transitions do not occur simultaneously. Significant delays may thus occur between signals.

asynchronous TDM *See* time division multiplexing.

Atanasoff–Berry computer (ABC) The first known attempt at an electronic digital computer, designed in 1936–38 by John Atanasoff, a mathematics professor at Iowa State College, primarily for the solution of linear algebraic equations. It was built by Atanasoff and his assistant Clifford Berry, using vacuum tubes (valves) as the logic elements, but was never fully operational and was abandoned in 1942.

ATL *Abbrev. for* automated (or automatic) tape library.

Atlas The first computer to incorporate many features now considered standard, including: a virtual (logical) address space larger than the actual (physical) address space; a *one-level memory using core backed by drum; an architecture based on the assumption of a software operating system, with hardware features to assist the software (e.g. extracodes). The design commenced in 1956 under Tom Kilburn at the University of Manchester, UK, and the project was supported from 1958 by Ferranti Ltd. The prototype was operating in 1961 and production models appeared in 1963.

atom A value that cannot be decomposed further. In *LISP an atom is a representation of an arbitrary string of characters or the special atom NIL, i.e. nothing. The word is also used as a predicate in LISP-like languages to determine whether an arbitrary value is or is not an atom:

(Atom (CONS(h,t)))

always yields FALSE but

(Atom NIL)

and

(Atom "word")

evaluate to TRUE.

atomic formula *See* propositional calculus.

atomicity A term used in connection with the extent to which a resource can be subdivided. For some resources the amount allocated to a process can be completely arbitrary; an example is processor time (outside *critical sections). For other resources allocations must be in terms of a smallest allowable amount; an example might be memory, which may only be allocated in multiples of, say, 1024 bytes.

attach To make a device available for use by a system. On simple systems this may be achieved by simply engaging the appropriate plug and socket of the interface and putting the device into a state of readiness. In more complex systems it is often necessary to make the operating system aware of the type of device and the address of the connector to which it is attached. It is also necessary to ensure that the operating system has available the appropriate utility program for that device. In some designs the operating system can itself determine the type and address of all the peripherals that are electrically connected.

attenuation The reduction in amplitude of a *signal when it passes through a medium that dissipates its energy. It is usually measured in decibels (attenuation then being negative while *gain* is positive).

attribute grammar A *context-free grammar that has been augmented with attribute evaluation rules or conditions enabling non-context-free aspects of a language to be specified. Associated with each symbol of the grammar is a finite set of attributes or conditions. Rules for evaluating the attributes are associated with the productions of the grammar. Using these rules the attributes of each node in a *parse tree may be evaluated. The attributes may either be *inherited*, meaning that their values are a function of the attribute of their parent node in the parse tree, or *synthesized*, meaning that their values are a function of the attributes of their children in the parse tree.

The concept of an attribute grammar was introduced by D. E. Knuth who suggested that the semantics of a program could be specified by the attributes of the root node in its parse tree.

AU *Abbrev. for* arithmetic unit. *See* arithmetic and logic unit.

audio response unit An output device that can give a spoken response. The message may be prerecorded phrases, a collation of prerecorded words, or synthesized from digital data. The range of applications includes prompts to operators of application terminals and acknowledgment of input via a telephone keypad.

audit trail (audit log) A permanent record of every transaction taken by a computer system, indicating, for example, when users log in and out, what transactions they perform, when files are accessed and the type of access. Examination of this record provides a way of observing patterns of security violation and/or serves as a deterrent to violations.

augmented addressing (augmenting) A method of expanding a short specified address by concatenating the specified address (as low-order address bits) with the contents of the *augmented address register* (as high-order bits) to produce a *machine address. *See also* addressing schemes.

augmented transition network A generalization of *finite-state automata that is used to represent natural-language grammars and hence to parse and generate natural-language text (*see* parsing). The grammar is represented as a set of labeled directed *graphs whose labels are word categories, or recursive calls to itself or other graphs, or calls to update or access a set of registers. Procedures can be associated with the arcs to build a *parse tree, to build a semantic representation, to generate text, etc.

authentication The act of verifying the identity of a potential user (or using process). In systems that hold sensitive data or for which charges are levied for use of system resources, users are given a password that they are required to enter at the time of attempting to log into the system. This password is checked against the stored version, providing a simple check that the user is indeed who he claims to be. Where greater levels of security are needed, users may be issued with a "badge" containing a mechanically readable version of a password.
The term also applies to techniques that guarantee that information has not been altered since its construction by an authorized person.

authentication code (message authenticator) A cryptographically derived check that is appended to a plain text message or is part of a cipher text message. The check is made in such a way that tampering with the message will be exposed. *See* cryptography.

authorization The granting of access. *See* access control.

authorization matrix *Another name for* access matrix.

autocode The generic name given to the precursors of modern high-level programming languages. The term is now obsolete.

autodump *See* autoload.

autoload 1. A facility provided on some tape transports whereby a tape reel is automatically located and clamped on the hub and the tape is then automatically threaded. However the term is widely used as if synonymous with *autothread, even when the reel has to be manually placed on the hub. It is also used as a verb: to load a tape reel on a tape transport automatically by the use of the autoload.
2. A facility in a magnetic tape subsystem whereby a single unqualified command from the host causes a quantity of data from the tape mounted on a transport, selected according to predetermined rules, to be read and transferred to the host. The function is provided to assist in initial program loading. The corresponding process in which data is written to tape is known as *autodump*.

autoload cartridge *See* magnetic tape cartridge.

autoload success rate The proportion of tape volumes presented to a magnetic tape transport that are successfully autoloaded (or autothreaded) after a defined number of attempts. For ½″ tape about three attempts are usually made and the success rate is typically about 97%; failures are mainly due to the end of the tape being damaged, often as a result of manual threading on another tape transport. The operator should then trim the end of the tape, or load it manually.

automated tape library (ATL) A peripheral device in which a large number of cartridges or reels of magnetic tape are stored in *cells* in a *storage matrix*. Any chosen cartridge can be transferred mechanically to a tape transport (directly or by way of a further mechanism called a *shuttle*) where it can be accessed by the host system, and then returned to the same or another cell. The device also contains one or more *drawers* that can also be reached by the transfer mechanism: these are accessible to an operator so that cartridges can be introduced to or removed from the library. An ATL is functionally equivalent to a conventional *tape library but without the need for a human operator except to add or remove cartridges. In one brand of ATL, standard reels of ½″ tape are used, but more often the cartridge is specially designed for the purpose and generally contains a single reel with a relatively short length of tape several inches wide. The virtues of the ATL are the rapidity with which any cartridge can be selected and mounted on the transport, typically a few seconds, and the elimination of human operators. Its disadvantages are cost and mechanical and functional complexity. At the time of writing (1983) ATLs are not widely used.

An equivalent arrangement for storing and accessing *optical disks is likely to come into use in the 1980s; prototypes already exist.

automatic calling unit *See* ACU.

automatic check Any automatic (as opposed to programmed) computed check on the validity of a segment of data. *See also* error detection and correction.

automatic coding A term used in the early stages of development of computers to signify the use of a primitive high-level language or *autocode, as contrasted with the more usual "hand coding".

automatic data conversion The conversion of data from one form to another without any direct action by the programmer, e.g. decimal integers on input to stored form of integer. Such facilities are commonly available for individual items of data in modern programming languages. Many database input systems carry out more complex transformations of the data, and at the extreme may translate data from the format of one database system to another.

automatic data processing (ADP) *See* data processing.

automatic programming 1. The use of a high-level programming language. The term in this sense is now obsolete.

2. Generation of programs automatically from a nonprocedural description of their desired effect. Thus in artificial intelligence we describe the required actions of a robot, and the system generates a program that will cause the required movements to take place. In commercial data processing we describe the various documents – orders, invoices, delivery notes, etc. – and the relationship between the quantities involved, and the system generates a suite of programs to do the required processing. Automatic programming in this sense is at an early stage of development.

automatic tape library (ATL) *See* automated tape library.

automaton A general term for a device that mechanically processes an input string with the aim either of deciding whether it belongs to some set of strings, i.e. a *formal language, or of producing an output string.

There are two senses in which an automaton A is said to *recognize* (or *accept*) a language L:

(a) for any input string w, A halts and indicates that it *accepts* or *rejects* w, according to whether or not $w \in L$;

(b) A halts if $w \in L$ and fails to halt otherwise.

In the case of *Turing machines, the languages recognizable in sense (a) and the weaker sense (b) are the *recursive sets and the *recursively enumerable sets respectively. Hence, if a language is recognizable (in either sense) by any kind of automaton, it is so recognizable by a Turing machine.

Turing machines are a particular kind of automaton. Other kinds include the *finite-state automaton, *pushdown automaton, and *linear-bounded automaton. *Sequential machines are automata that produce an output string.

automorphism An *isomorphism from one *algebraic structure into another, the two algebraic structures sharing a common set of elements.

autoregression *See* time series.

autothread A facility provided on some tape transports whereby magnetic tape is automatically threaded from the file reel through the tape path and secured to the hub of the take-up reel (*see also* autoload). The first autothreading transports, introduced by IBM in the 1960s, required the tape reels to be placed within an Easyload *magnetic tape cartridge and manually mounted on the transport hub; later designs dispensed with the cartridge but still required the reel to be manually mounted. The most recent types only require the tape reel to be "posted" through a slot in the transport housing; this has the advantage that transports can be mounted horizontally and stacked, giving a very compact layout. The arrangement was pioneered by Cipher in 1980.

auxiliary memory *Another name for* backing store.

available list (free list) A list of the unallocated parts of a sharable resource. Some resources, such as processors, are shared by being allocated in their entirety to a process for a period of time. Other resources consist of a number of functionally similar units, e.g. pages within memory, and the resource is shared by units of the total resource being allocated to a process. This allocated share remains with the process until the process releases it. The available list provides the resource controller with a convenient record of which parts of the resource are not allocated to a process. *See also* free-space list.

available time The amount of time in a given period that a computing system can be used by its normal users. During available time the system must be functioning correctly, have power supplied to it, and not be undergoing repair or maintenance. Available time is comprised of *productive time* and *idle time*. Productive time is the amount of time in a given period that a system is performing useful work for the users. Idle time is the amount of time in a given period that a system is performing no useful function. It usually occurs when waiting for completion of some I/O function or backing-store transfer.

average-case analysis *See* algorithm.

AVL tree (height-balanced tree) A *binary search tree such that for each node the *heights of the left and right subtrees differ by at most one. Thus the *balance of each node is −1, 0, or +1. During insertion or deletion, a node in an AVL tree may become *critical* or unbalanced and then the tree has to be reorganized to maintain its balanced property. The tree is named for its originators, Adel'son-Vel'skii and Landis.

axiomatic semantics An approach to the *semantics of programming languages in which the meaning of a construct or program in a language is given by an "axiom". For a particular statement the axiom specifies what should be true after the execution of the statement in terms of what was true before the execution. This approach grew out of the work of Floyd who attached assertions to the links of flowcharts. It was developed and applied to high-level languages by Tony Hoare. It is an important technique for proving the correctness of programs.

B

Babbage A machine-oriented high-level language (*MOHLL) for the GEC 4080 series machines and their derivatives. Particularly noteworthy is the fact that it is supplied by the manufacturer and entirely replaces the assembler for these machines.

backbone network The underlying nodes of a multilevel distributed network, providing communication services for the rest of the network (the hosts). The backbone network usually consists of dedicated packet, message, or circuit switches connected by high-capacity trunk circuits, along with some special diagnostic and control equipment. An example is the *ARPANET's *IMP subnet.
An important requirement for backbone networks is that they must be extremely reliable. For this reason they are usually built out of homogeneous (essentially similar) processors and run by a centralized administration, although the rest of the network may be highly heterogeneous and under distributed authority. Distributed procedures are often used to control the operation of the backbone network in order to reduce the possibility that a single failure might disrupt the entire network. When a central control system is used, there is usually a standby system ready to take over when the active system fails.
Backbone networks are often characterized by distributed traffic patterns. *Packet switching may be used internally by backbone networks to take advantage of these traffic patterns, even though the backbone network may present a *circuit-switching appearance to external hosts (*see* virtual connection). Traffic-pattern analysis may be used to construct backbone networks that minimize certain network parameters, such as average delay, circuit costs, etc. Backbone networks may themselves be multilevel, incorporating low-capacity terrestrial links, high-capacity terrestrial links, and satellite links.

back-end processor A processor that is used for some specialized function such as database management, or a special-purpose arithmetic and logic unit.

background processing Processing without the opportunity for interaction with the user, within a system that provides for interaction by *foreground processing. The jobs are submitted by users from terminals but are not processed immediately. They are placed into a *background queue* and run off as resources become available.

backing store (auxiliary memory; bulk memory; secondary memory) The memory on which information is held for reference but not for direct execution. Backing store is the lower part of the *memory hierarchy, in which the speed of access to the information stored is matched to the requirements of the system so as to achieve the greatest economy. The term may be used either in an absolute sense, in which case it usually refers to a disk, or it may be used in a relative sense to refer to the device next down in the memory hierarchy.

backplane A device that may be considered as the physical "plane" by means of which a computer or similar device communicates with its various peripherals. Normally a backplane consists of a series of multiway sockets that are wired in parallel and are connected to the internal wiring, or *buses, of the computer. Peripherals may then be attached to the computer simply by inserting compatible interface cards into any one of these sockets.

backtracking A property of an algorithm that implies some kind of tentative search for a goal, and the possibility that any search path may turn out to be a deadend; the algorithm then retreats back down the search path to try another path. The technique is generally suitable for solving problems where a potentially large but finite number of solutions have to be inspected. It amounts to a systematic tree search, bottom-up.

backup A resource that is, or can be used as, a substitute when a primary resource fails or when a file has been corrupted. The word is also used as a verb, to back up, i.e. to make a copy in anticipation of future failure or corruption. Thus a *dump forms a backup to be used in cases where a user's file has become unusable; the taking of the dump can be regarded as backing up the version on disk.

Backus normal form, Backus–Naur form *See* BNF.

backward error analysis *See* error analysis.

backward error correction (backward correction) Error correction that occurs in a channel through the detection of errors by the reciever: the receiver responds to any errors in a *block by requesting the transmitter to retransmit the affected block. Backward correction requires a *return channel, by contrast with *forward error correction.

There are two ways in which the return channel can be used to indicate errors: *positive acknowledgment* and *negative acknowledgment*. With positive acknowledgment, the receiver returns confirmation of each block received correctly, and the transmitter is prepared to retransmit a block that is not acknowledged within an appropriate time. With negative acknowledgment, the receiver returns a request to retransmit any block received erroneously, and the transmitter is prepared to retransmit such a block (implying that the transmitter retains a copy of every block sent, indefinitely).

Since the return channel itself may be prone to errors, and to limit the amount of storage necessary at the transmitter, the positive acknowledgment and retransmission (PAR) technique is generally preferred.

badge reader A device designed to read information encoded into a small plastic card. It is often part of a data collection system in which each operator can be identified by the badge they present to the machine. It can also be used to control access to areas associated with electrically operated door locks, and when built into keyboards and other parts of information systems it can control access to information.

The badge is usually of plastic, or paper laminated between plastic, and may contain a photograph and other information in addition to what is encoded. The encoding takes many forms, some of which are proprietary and complex to achieve greater security. The most common form for data collection systems in an industrial environment was originally the punched badge: there were five standardized formats using the rectangular punched holes common to the 80-column punched card. The punched badge reader is being superseded by devices that sense information encoded by printed marks or characters, by capacitive or magnetic elements embedded within the card, or by magnetic recording on a strip of material on the surface.

bag (multiset) 1. An unordered collection of items where more than one instance of the same item is allowed.

2. Any data structure representing a bag. Representations are similar to those used for *sets. In a set, however, it is only necessary to represent the presence (or absence) of an element whereas in a bag it is also necessary to represent the number of times it occurs.

balance of a node in a *binary tree. A measure of the relative size of the left and right subtrees of the node. Usually, the balance is defined to be the height of the left subtree minus the height of the right subtree (or the absolute value thereof). However, formulas are also used that measure balance in terms of the total number of nodes in the left and right subtrees.

balanced (height-balanced; depth-balanced) Denoting a tree that has *height (and thus *depth) approximately equal to the logarithm of the number of nodes in the tree. This property is usually achieved in a binary tree by ensuring every node is balanced according to some measure. *See also* AVL tree, B-tree.

band 1. A set of adjacent tracks on a magnetic disk.
2. A loop of flexible material, in particular the loop of steel tape that acts as the font carrier in a *band printer.
3. A section of the frequency spectrum lying between limits that are defined according to some requirement or to some functional aspect of a given signal or transmission channel. When used as a suffix the word is a contraction of *bandwidth, as in narrowband, wideband.

band-limited channel A transmission channel with finite *bandwidth. All physically realizable channels are band-limited. *See also* channel coding theorem, discrete and continuous systems.

band matrix A sparse matrix in which the nonzero elements are located in a band about the main diagonal. If A is a band matrix such that

$$a_{ij} = 0 \text{ if } j - i > p \text{ or } i - j > q$$

where p and q are the distances above and below the main diagonal, then the *bandwidth* w is given by

$$w = p + q + 1$$

band-pass filter A *filtering device that permits only those components in the *Fourier transform domain whose frequencies lie between two critical values to pass through with little attenuation, all other components being highly attenuated.

band printer (belt printer) A type of *impact *line printer in which the font – characters and timing marks – is etched on a steel band. The operating principle is similar to that of the *chain printer and train printer. Although demonstrated in the mid-1960s it was 1972 before machines with satisfactory print quality and band life were available. Band printers have price/performance advantage over *drum (or barrel) printers and satisfy the preference for printers in which the font moves horizontally: any mis-timing of the impact on a horizontal-font machine results in a change in the space between characters, which is less noticeable than the vertical displacement that occurs with mis-timing in a drum printer.
The majority of new impact line printers in the late 1970s were band printers. Machines were available at speeds from 300 lpm to 2500 lpm when using a 64 character repertoire. Designs for the lower-speed machines often time-share a print hammer between adjacent print positions. In one implementation this is achieved by having a wide hammer head that spans two columns and in another a bank of single-width hammers is moved – or shuttled – laterally by one or more column pitches. An advantage of some shuttle printers is the ability to print at "compressed pitch", i.e. 15 characters per inch as well as the standard 10 characters per inch.

band-reject filter *Another name for* band-stop filter.

band-stop filter (band-reject filter) A *filtering device that permits only those components in the *Fourier transform domain whose frequencies lie below one critical value or above another (higher) critical value to pass through with little attenuation; all components whose frequencies lie between the critical values are highly attenuated.
If the two critical values are very close together, the device is called a *notch filter.* Notch filters are used, for example, in *modems in order to prevent certain components of the data signal from interfering with equipment in the telephone system.

bandwidth 1. of a transmission *channel. Usually, the range of *frequencies passed by the channel. This will often consist of a single *passband, but may instead consist of several distinct (nonoverlapping) passbands. Each passband contributes to the bandwidth of the channel a quantity equal to the difference between its upper and lower frequency limits; the sum of all such differences gives the total bandwidth.

In these cases bandwidth is measured in frequency units: hertz (Hz) or, colloquially, cycles per second (cps). If the bandwidth is considered in a transform domain other than frequency (such as *sequency) then it is measured in the appropriate units.

There are several loose classifications of frequency bandwidths employed for convenience of description in various areas of technology; one classification is as follows:

narrowband (up to 300 Hz)
voiceband (300–3000 Hz)
wideband (over 3000 Hz)

See also band-limited channel, channel coding theorem (for Shannon–Hartley law), Nyquist's criterion.

2. *See* band matrix.

bank switching A technique for *memory management commonly used in microcomputer systems that require more memory than the microprocessor can directly address. A typical 8-bit microprocessor can directly reference a 16-bit address space (64K bytes). In systems requiring more than 64K bytes of memory, such as multiuser systems, bank switching can be used to overcome the addressing limitations of the microprocessor.

In a bank-switched system, different *banks* of memory are selected by writing different bit patterns to a specified output port. Each bank may contain as much memory as the processor can address, and the number of banks supported can be very large. In practice one bank is often dedicated to each user of the system with an additional bank reserved for the operating system.

Bank switching is similar in concept to memory segmentation (*see* segment) but does not require the use of a processor that knows about a segmented address space. Note also that an entire bank of memory may be allocated to a single task, whether it needs all of it or not, whereas more sophisticated memory-management schemes can make more efficient use of physical memory.

bar code A printed machine-readable code that consists of parallel bars of varied width and spacing. The application most commonly observed is the coding on food and other goods that is read at the checkout and translated into a line of print on the bill showing product and cost. The information is also used to update stock records and provide sales statistics.

In the US the code used for this purpose is the Universal Product Code (UPC) and in Europe it is the European Article Numbering (EAN) code. The UPC decodes initially into two five-digit numbers. The first five identify the supplier and the next five are the item number within that supplier's range of goods. From this information the checkout terminal can access the details to be printed on the bill. The EAN code has a two-digit number to indicate country of origin, then the two five-digit numbers, followed by a check digit. The EAN arrangement simplifies the allocation of codes to suppliers. Only the two-digit code and the format need to be agreed internationally.

Other codes are used for shop-floor data collection, library systems, and monitoring the circulation of confidential documents. The advantage of bar codes is that they can be produced and read by relatively simple equipment. Codes used for these purposes are Code 39, Codabar, and "2 of 5".

Barker sequence In data communications, a sequence of symbols (binary or *q-ary) that, when embedded in a string of randomly chosen symbols (from the same alphabet), has zero autocorrelation except in the coincidence position. Barker sequences are used to check, and if necessary to correct, the synchronization and framing of received data.

barrel printer *UK name for* drum printer.

base *Another name for* the radix of a positional number system. Hence decimal numbers are base 10 numbers and binary numbers are base 2 numbers. *See* number system.

base addressing *See* relative addressing.

baseband networking Communication in which a digital signal is placed directly on the transmission medium without requiring a carrier, i.e. without modulation. Only one signal may be present on the baseband channel at a time. This type of signaling, *baseband signaling*, is also called *d.c. signaling* because in some baseband networks a continuous d.c. voltage is present when the data does not change. Baseband networks may use twisted pair or coaxial cables for data transmission. The *Ethernet is a prototype *local area network using baseband signaling on a coaxial cable. *Compare* broadband networking.

base-bound register (datum-limit register) Hardware used for *virtual-memory allocation. A base-bound register is associated with each *segment of data or code and defines the position in physical memory of word zero for that segment, the so-called *base* or *datum*, and the number of words available to that segment, the so-called *bound* or *limit* (or alternatively the physical memory address of the next word after the end of the segment, in which case it is a *bounds register). Whenever a process attempts to access the memory segment, the hardware of the system checks that the address of the word lies within the range

$$0 \leqslant \text{word address} < \text{bound}$$

and then adds the address to the value contained in the base register to give the physical address. A restriction on this system is that the storage for the segment must be allocated in a contiguous area of memory (*see* best fit, first fit).

The *base register*, used in the construction of relative addresses, should not be confused with the base of a base-bound system; the result of modifying an address by a base register's contents is still an address within virtual memory space of the process, and is not necessarily a physical address.

base field *See* polynomial.

base-limit register *See* base-bound register.

base register *See* relative addressing.

BASIC or **Basic** *Acronym for* beginner's all-purpose symbolic instruction code. A simple programming language, developed in the mid-1960s to exploit the then novel capability of interactive use of a computer from a remote terminal. BASIC as originally conceived was a very simple language that could be learned very quickly. The BASIC system included crude editing facilities as part of the language so that the user was insulated from the complexities of any underlying operating system. At first BASIC only handled numeric values, but it was later extended to allow string variables and was provided with a set of procedures for simple string manipulation that have become a de facto standard.

The simplicity of BASIC made it a natural choice as a programming language for the early microcomputers, and it became established as a common language for programming personal computers. Unfortunately, almost every machine has its own dialect of BASIC so that programs are not readily portable. The establishment of an ANSI Standard for BASIC has not made any appreciable improvements in this situation.

batch control Correctness checks built into *data-processing systems and applied to batches of input data, particularly in the data-preparation stage. There are two main forms of batch control: *sequence control* involves numbering the records in a batch consecutively so that the presence of each record can be confirmed during the data-vet run; *control totals* involve establishing record counts, or totals of the values in selected fields within each record, and checking these totals during the data-vet run. Control totals may be "meaningful", in the sense that they may have a use (for instance to an auditor) that is additional to their function within the system. Most commonly they are meaningless totals (e.g. of employee numbers), often referred to as *hash totals.

The scope of batch control may extend beyond the data-vet program, for as far into the system as batches retain their separate identities. In particular, they may be used to check that incorrect records, rejected during the data vet, are resubmitted before a batch is released for further processing.

Batcher's parallel method (merge exchange sort) A form of *sorting by selection that chooses nonadjacent parts of sortkeys for comparisons. The sequence of comparisons was discovered by K. E. Batcher in 1964. It is particularly appropriate for *parallel processing.

batch processing Originally, a method of organizing work for a computer system, designed to reduce overheads by grouping together similar jobs. One form avoided reloading *systems software. The jobs were collected into batches, each batch requiring a particular compiler, the compiler was loaded once, and then the jobs submitted in sequence to the compiler. If a job failed to compile it took no further part in the processing, but those jobs that did compile led to the production on magnetic tape or other backing store of an executable binary. At the end of the batch of compilations those jobs that had produced an executable binary form were loaded in sequence and their data presented to the jobs. Another form avoided the time taken to read cards and print on paper by off-line processing, having a batch of jobs on magnetic tape.

The term has also come to be applied to the *background processing of jobs not requiring intervention by the user, which takes place on many multiaccess systems.

baud rate The number of times per second that a system, especially a data transmission *channel, changes state. In the particular case of a binary channel, the baud rate is equal to the bit rate, i.e.

1 baud = 1 bit per second

For a general channel,

1 baud = 1 digit per second

1 baud = 1 symbol per second

or whatever the states of the system represent. The rate was named for J. M. E. Baudot.

BCD *Abbrev. for* binary-coded decimal.

BCD adder A 4-bit binary *adder that is capable of adding two 4-bit words having a BCD (*binary-coded decimal) format. The result of the addition is a BCD-format 4-bit output word, representing the decimal sum of the addend and augend, and a carry that is generated if this sum exceeds a decimal value of 10. Decimal addition is thus possible using these devices.

BCH code *Short for* Bose-Chandhuri-Hocquenghem code.

BCPL A systems programming language that incorporates the control structures needed for *structured programming. Its main distinguishing feature is that it is type-free, i.e. the only type of data object that can be used is a word made up of bits (hence the suitability for systems programming). BCPL has been implemented on many machines, and programs written in the language are readily portable. *See also* CPL, C.

BCS British Computer Society, formed in 1957 to further development and use of computer machinery and related techniques and to facilitate exchange of information and views by means of conferences, meetings, and publications. It is the UK member of IFIP.

bead A *data structure consisting of several fields, some or all of which are instances of the same data structure. It is now obsolete, having been replaced by the more general concept of a *record.

Bell Telephone Laboratories The research and development laboratories for American Telephone & Telegraph (AT&T), jointly owned by AT&T and Western Electric Corporation (the manufacturing arm of AT&T). The products of Bell Labs include Shannon's seminal work on information theory, the transistor, and, more recently, the UNIX operating system.

belt printer *Another name for* band printer, used to describe the early versions of those machines, but also used to describe printers in which the font is carried on plates or fingers attached to a flexible belt. The operating principle is similar to that of the *chain printer but the font carrier is lower in cost. In some designs it was possible to change individual type carriers.

benchmark (benchmark problem) A problem that has been designed to evaluate the performance of a system (hardware and software). In a *benchmark test* a system is subjected to a known workload and the performance of the system against this workload is measured. Typically the purpose is to compare the measured performance with that of other systems that have been subject to the same benchmark test.

best fit A method of selecting a contiguous area of memory that is to be allocated for a segment. The available areas are examined in order of increasing size; the area that exceeds the request by the smallest amount is taken and the request met by allocating the amount requested from this area.

beta reduction *See* lambda calculus.

bias 1. The d.c. component of an a.c. signal.

2. The d.c. voltage used to switch on or off a *bipolar transistor or *diode (*see* forward bias, reverse bias), or the d.c. gate-source voltage used to control the d.c. drain-source current in a *field-effect transistor. The word is also used as a verb: to switch.

3. In statistical usage, a source of error that cannot be reduced by increasing sample size. It is systematic as opposed to random error.

Sources of bias include (a) bias in *sampling, when members of the sample are not fully representative of the population being studied; (b) *nonresponse bias* in sample surveys, when an appreciable proportion of those questioned fail to reply; (c) *question bias*, a tendency for the wording of the question to invite an incorrect reply; (d) *interviewer bias*, a problem of personal interviewing when respondents try to reply in the way the interviewer is thought to expect.

A narrower definition of bias in statistical analysis (*see* statistical methods) is the difference between the mean of an estimating formula and the true value of the quantity being estimated. The estimate

$$\sum_i (x_i - \bar{x})^2 / n$$

for the variance of a population is biased, but is *unbiased* when n is replaced by $(n-1)$.

4. (excess factor) *See* floating-point notation.

biased exponent *Another name for* characteristic. *See* floating-point notation.

P	F	F	T	T
Q	F	T	F	T
$P \equiv Q$	T	F	F	T

Truth table for biconditional

biconditional A logical statement combining two statements, truth values, or formulas P and Q in such a way that the outcome is true only if P and Q are both true or both false, as indicated in the table.
The biconditional *connective can be represented by

$$\equiv \quad \leftrightarrow \quad <-> \quad \text{or} \quad <=>$$

and is read as "if and only if" or "iff" or "is equivalent to". Note that $P \equiv Q$ has the same truth table as the conjunction

$$(P \rightarrow Q) \wedge (Q \rightarrow P)$$

where $\rightarrow$ denotes a simple *conditional. The biconditional connective itself is also known as the biconditional.

biconnected graph A *graph G, either directed or undirected, with the property that for every three distinct vertices u, v, and w there is a path from u to w not containing v. For an undirected graph, this is equivalent to the graph having no *cut vertex.
Two edges of an undirected graph are said to be related either if they are identical or if there is a *cycle containing both of them. This is an *equivalence relation and partitions the edges into a set of *equivalence classes, $E_1, E_2, \ldots E_n$, say. Let V_i be the set of vertices of the edges of E_i for $i = 1, 2, \ldots n$. Then each graph G_i formed from the vertices V_i and the edges E_i is a *biconnected component* of G.

bifurcation A splitting in two. The term can be applied in computing in various ways.
1. Bifurcation is the generic name for a collection of algorithms that initially convert a *decision table into a *tree structure, which can then be systematically encoded to produce a program.
The *bifurcation method* involves choosing some condition C and eliminating it from the decision table to produce two subtables, one corresponding to the case when C is true and the other to when C is false. The method is then applied recursively to the two subtables. From this approach a *decision tree can be built, each node of the tree representing a condition and subtrees representing subtables; leaf nodes identify rules.
2. *Bifurcation theory* is the theory of equilibrium solutions of nonlinear differential equations; an equilibrium solution is a steady solution, a time periodic, or quasi-periodic solution. Generally *bifurcation points* are points at which branches and therefore multiple solutions appear.

bijection (one-to-one onto function) A *function that is both an *injection and a *surjection. If

$$f : X \rightarrow Y$$

is a surjection, then for each y in Y there is a unique x in X with the property that

$$y = f(x)$$

i.e. there is a one-to-one correspondence between the elements in X and the elements in Y. Such functions always have *inverses. The sets X and Y will have the same number of elements, i.e. the same *cardinality.

binary adder *See* adder.

binary chop *Informal name for* binary search algorithm.

binary code A *code whose alphabet is restricted to $\{0, 1\}$. In general, any *q-ary code has the important special case $q = 2$.

binary-coded decimal (BCD) A code in which a string of binary digits represents a decimal digit. In the *natural binary-coded decimal (NBCD)* system, each decimal digit 0 through 9 is represented by the string of four bits whose value is equivalent to the decimal digit. For example, 3 is represented by 0011 and 9 is represented by 1001. The NBCD code is the *8421-code such that the weighted sum of the bits in a codeword is equal to the coded decimal digit.

binary-coded octal The representation of any octal digit by its three-bit binary equivalent.

binary counter *See* counter.

```
IF      t is empty THEN v not present
ELSE    case 1:  t = root  → v present
        case 2:  t < root  → search left subtree
        case 3:  t > root  → search right subtree
```

Binary search tree, search algorithm

binary digit (bit) *See* binary system.

binary encoding 1. The representation of symbols in a source alphabet by strings of binary digits, i.e. a *binary code. The most commonly occurring source alphabet consists of the set of *alphanumeric characters. *See* code.
2. of a set *A*. Any assignment of distinctive bit strings to the elements of *A*. *See also* character encoding; Huffman encoding.

binary notation *See* binary system.

binary operation 1. (dyadic operation) defined on a set *S*. A *function from the domain $S \times S$ into *S* itself. Many of the everyday arithmetic and algebraic operations are binary, e.g. the addition of two integers, the union of two sets, and the conjunction of two Boolean expressions. Although basically functions, binary operations are usually represented using an infix notation, as in

$$3 + 4, \quad U \cup V, \quad P \wedge Q$$

The operation symbol then appears between the left and right operand. A symbol, such as $\circ$, can be used to represent a generalized binary operation.
When the set *S* is finite, *Cayley tables and sometimes *truth tables are used to define the meaning of the operation.
2. An operation on binary operands.

binary relation A *relation defined between two sets.

binary search algorithm (logarithmic search algorithm; bisection algorithm) A searching algorithm that uses a file in which the sortkeys are in ascending order. The middle key in the file is examined and, depending upon whether this is less than or greater than the desired key, the top or bottom part of the file is again examined. Continuing in this way the algorithm either finds the desired record or discovers its absence from the file. Thus the algorithm treats the file as though it were a *binary search tree.

binary search tree A *binary tree in which the data values stored at the nodes of the tree belong to a *well-ordered set, and the value stored at any nonterminal node, A, is greater than the values stored in the left subtree of A and less than the values stored in the right subtree of A. To search a binary search tree, t, to see if the value, *v*, is present, the recursive search algorithm shown in the figure is used.
In data-processing applications, the data values stored at the nodes of a binary search tree will be key values with an associated link to the record to be retrieved. The same principle is used in the *binary search algorithm. The concept can be generalized to a *multiway search tree. *See also* AVL tree, optimal binary search tree.

binary sequence A sequence of binary digits. Such a sequence, produced randomly or pseudorandomly (*see* random numbers) and generally of known statistical properties, may be employed either as a model of noise affecting a binary channel or as a means of controlling synchronization between transmitter and receiver.

binary signal *See* digital signal.

binary symmetric channel (BSC) A binary communication channel on which errors (substitution of a 1 for a 0, or vice versa) occur randomly: substitution of a 0 for a 1 occurs with the same probability as substitution of a 1 for a 0. Much of the theory of *error-correcting and *error-detecting codes assumes a BSC.

binary synchronous communications *See* BISYNC.

binary system Usually, the binary number system, i.e. the positional number system with base 2. This is the number system most commonly used in computers. A *binary digit* (or *bit*) is either 0 or 1. The representation of numbers by binary digits is called *binary notation*.
The term binary system is also used to describe any system in which there are just two possible states. For example, each of the elements comprising the memory of any computer is a binary system, one of whose states is used to denote the binary digit 0 and the other to denote the binary digit 1. It is customary to refer to such a storage element, or to the unit of information in any binary system, as a *bit*.

binary tree 1. A finite set of nodes that is either empty or is such that firstly there is a single designated node called the *root* and secondly the remaining nodes are partitioned into *disjoint sets, T_l and T_r, where each of these sets is itself a binary tree. T_l is called the *left subtree* and T_r the *right subtree* of the root.
At *level h of a binary tree there is a maximum of 2^h nodes. A binary tree of *depth d thus has at most $(2^{d+1} - 1)$ nodes and one with n nodes has a minimum depth of $\log_2 n$.
The term binary tree is also used to describe any (ordered) tree of *degree two. *See also* tree.
2. Any data structure used to represent a binary tree. Each node would be represented by pointers to the left and right subtrees as well as to the data value associated with the node. The binary tree could then be represented as a pointer to its root node.

binary-tree representation 1. A binary tree constructed to represent a tree of arbitrary *degree. For any node, the root of the left subtree in the binary-tree representation is the eldest child of the node in the original tree and the root of the right subtree is the next eldest sibling (*see* diagram).

2. *See* binary tree (def. 2).

bind To resolve the interpretation of some name used in a system for the remaining lifetime of that instance of the system. For example, upon invocation of a procedure the formal parameters are bound to the actual parameters that are supplied for that invocation, and this binding remains in force throughout the lifetime of that invocation. Similarly, at some time the variables in a program must be bound to particular storage addresses in the computer, and this binding typically remains in force for as long as the variable continues to exist. In a *virtual memory system, there is further binding between the virtual ad-

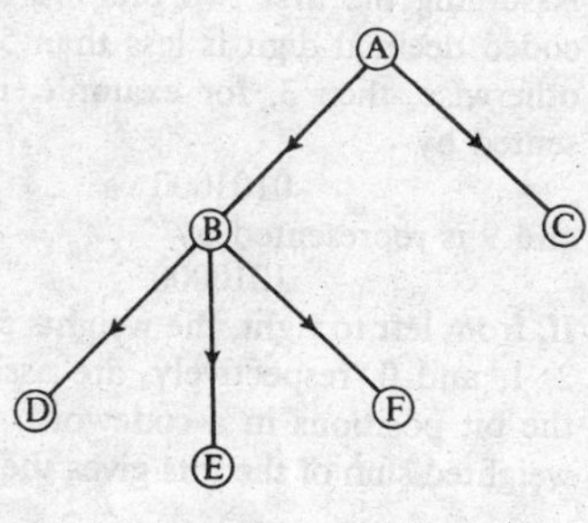

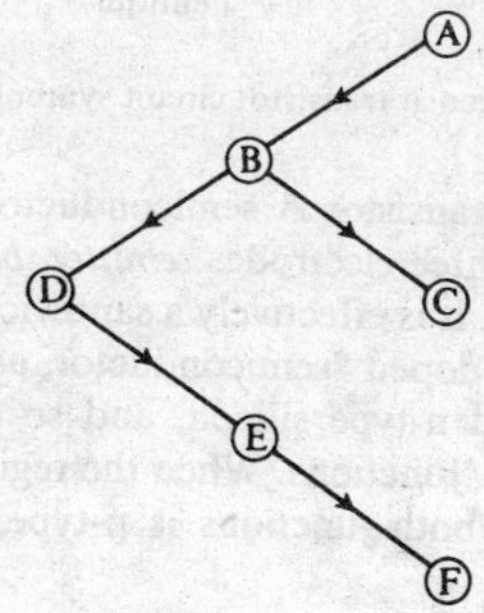

A tree and its binary representation

dresses used in the program and the physical addresses of the hardware.

binomial distribution The basic discrete *probability distribution for data in the form of proportions. An event, E, can occur with *probability p. In a sample of n independent trials the probability that E occurs exactly r times is

$$^{n}C_{r}\, p^{r}(1 - p)^{n-r}$$

(*see* combination). The distribution is discrete, taking only the values 0, 1, 2, . . . , n. The mean of the binomial distrubution is np and the variance is

$$np/(1 - p)$$

bipartite graph A *graph G whose vertices can be split into two *disjoint sets, U and V, in such a way that the only edges of G join a vertex in U and a vertex in V. Bipartite graphs tend to provide a convenient graphical representation of *relations and therefore *functions.

bipolar integrated circuit *See* integrated circuit.

bipolar signal A signal whose signaling elements consist of both positive and negative voltages. Bipolar signals are used in data-communication systems. *Compare* unipolar signal.

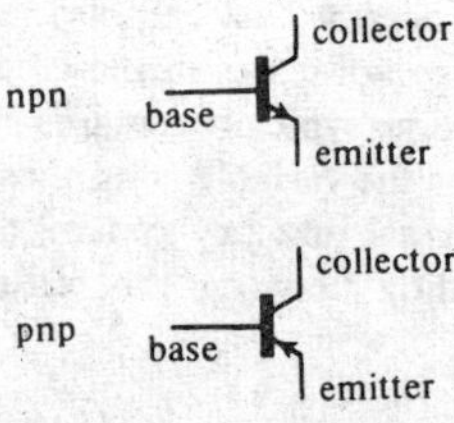

Bipolar transistor circuit symbols

bipolar transistor A semiconductor device having three electrodes: *emitter*, *base*, and *collector*. It is effectively a sandwich of two types of doped *semiconductor, usually p-type and n-type silicon, and so contains two p-n *junctions. When the region common to both junctions is p-type, an *npn transistor* is formed; when it is n-type a *pnp transistor* is formed. This central region forms the base electrode.

Current flow between collector and emitter is established by applying a *forward bias between base and emitter. In linear (i.e. *nonsaturated*) operation, the magnitude of this current is proportional to the input current drawn at the base. The directions of current flow are indicated on the circuit symbol by an arrow on the emitter connection (*see* diagram).

If the base current is increased but the collector current is restrained, so that the transistor effectively receives more base current than it would seem to require, the transistor is driven into a state of *saturation*. It then behaves as a very efficient switch since the base-collector junction becomes *reverse-biased and, in saturation, the collector-emitter voltage can fall as low as 20 millivolts. The device thus seems virtually a short circuit. Bipolar transistor switches, working into saturation, are the basis of *TTL circuits. Saturated transistors do however have a fairly low switching speed. The much higher switching speeds of *Schottky TTL and *ECL circuits are achieved by using a nonsaturated mode of operation.

biquinary code (quibinary code) A seven-bit *weighted code, two bits of which are used simply to indicate whether or not the coded decimal digit is less than 5. Four of the remaining five bits are zero, the position of the nonzero bit indicating which of the five possible decimal digits is required. Assuming the first two bits are 01 if the coded decimal digit is less than 5 and 10 otherwise, then 3, for example, is represented by

0101000

and 9 is represented by

1010000

If, from left to right, the weights 5, 0, 4, 3, 2, 1, and 0, respectively, are assigned to the bit positions in a codeword, then the weighted sum of the bits gives the value of the decimal digit represented by that codeword.

bisection algorithm *Another name for* binary search algorithm.

bistable An electronic circuit, usually an integrated circuit, whose output has two stable states to which it is directed by the input signal or signals. It is more usually known as a *flip-flop. *See also* multivibrator.

BISYNC (BSC) *Abbrev. for* binary synchronous communications (protocol). A *line protocol created by IBM for synchronized communication between mainframe computers and remote job-entry terminals. BISYNC is a character-oriented protocol: it uses special control characters to mark the beginning and end of a message, to acknowledge previous messages, to request retransmission of missing or damaged messages, etc. The BISYNC protocol may be used with the 6-bit Transcode, 7-bit ASCII, or 8-bit EBCDIC character codes, and multidrop or point-to-point communication lines.

A BISYNC block (message) generally starts with two or more synchronization characters. Thc next field is an optional start-of-header code and header. The presence and contents of the header depends on the devices that are communicating. The header is followed by the start-of-text code and text (the data of the message). Finally an end-of-text code is followed by the block check characters, which terminate the message.

Several variations of the general format may be employed. Special codes are inserted to acknowledge previous messages, or to request retransmission. The particular character(s) used to represent the BISYNC functions depend upon the character set being used. The protocol has a *transparent mode*, which allows the presence of arbitrary data in the text field. Special provision is made for the automatic insertion and deletion of *idling* characters, which are used in synchronous communications when a sender has more data to send but is temporarily unable to send it on time. There are various other options.

The protocol is inherently half duplex: a message is sent, a reply is sent, the next message is sent, etc. Thus BISYNC communication usually uses half duplex communication lines and modems. Full duplex communication lines and modems may be used but most of the additional capacity is wasted.

BISYNC is being replaced in computer communications by newer data link control protocols, such as *SDLC and *HDLC. BISYNC's retransmission and acknowledgment scheme does not work efficiently over connections with long delay times. This is particularly important in the US and other areas where the telephone system is converting to satellite transmission systems for voice and data traffic.

bit *Acronym for* binary digit. *See also* binary system.

bit density The number of bits stored per unit length or area of a magnetic recording medium. The figure is usually calculated as the maximum density achieved, i.e. it does not take account of the unrecorded areas between blocks, tracks, sectors, etc.

bit handling The faculty provided in some programming languages to manipulate the individual bits of a byte or word. Operators provided usually include bitwise "and" and "or" between two bytes (or words), bitwise "not" (inversion) of a single byte (or word), and circular shifts. Many of the programming operations traditionally regarded as bit handling can be achieved in Pascal by use of sets.

bit mapping A graphics display technique wherein each pixel (picture element) of the displayed image corresponds to one or more bits in the processor's memory. In a monochromatic display the number of bits corresponding to each pixel determines the number of *gray-scale levels supported. If there is one bit per pixel the image will be strictly black-and-white with no shades of gray. In a color display the number of bits per pixel determines how many colors can be displayed.

bit matrix A two-dimensional *array in which each element is equal to 0 or to 1. *Compare* Boolean matrix.

bit rate The number of bits transmitted or transferred per unit of time. The unit of time is usually one second, thus giving rise to bits per second, bps.

bit-slice architecture A computer architecture or design, used especially for microprocessors, in which the CPU is constructed by concatenating a number of high-performance processing units. Each of these "slice" elements represents a limited width (commonly 2, 4, or 8 bits) of an ALU and CU section; a parallel computer of any desired word size can therefore be constructed. Specific system customization is accomplished by *microprogramming. This form of architecture permits the use of standard (thus low-cost) VLSI elements to produce different computer systems.

bit string A *string of bits.

bit stuffing 1. A means of providing synchronization in a *data link control protocol such as HDLC where, for example, a 0 is automatically inserted whenever a determined number of 1s is present in a data stream at the sending end of the link. The receiving equipment automatically deletes the extra 0s before delivering the received message to the receiving terminal.
2. A means of inserting and deleting bits on multiply connected high-speed digital transmission links that are not synchronously clocked.

blank Empty, i.e. not containing meaningful data. In a memory, blank cells may contain a particular bit pattern that has no assigned value.

blank character A character that creates a blank space when displayed or printed.

blast *Another term for* blow.

blink An attribute that causes a character to be intermittently displayed on a screen at a regular rate, usually in the range 1–10 Hz. The technique used for presenting data on a cathode-ray tube inherently causes it to blink at a rate usually in excess of 50 Hz; this is not usually apparent to the eye but when it is it is referred to as *flicker*.

block 1. A collection of data units such as words, characters, or records (generally more than a single word) that are stored in adjacent physical positions in memory or on a peripheral storage device. A block can therefore be treated as a single unit whereby data can be (and usually is) transferred between storage device and memory, using one instruction. Blocks may be fixed or variable in size.
A stream of data to be recorded on magnetic tape is divided into blocks for convenience of handling and particularly of error recovery. (The equivalent on disks is *sectors.) Successive blocks are separated by *interblock gaps* and often also by control signals introduced by the magnetic tape subsystem and invisible to the host (*see* tape format). It is usual but not essential for the block length to be the same for all blocks of data within a volume or at least within a file, though this may not apply to *labels; where the end of a file occurs partway through a block, the remainder of the block may be filled with *padding characters*.
The choice of block length is largely dependent on *error management considerations. The minimum length of the interblock gap is defined by the standard for the tape format in use; the maximum length is usually undefined, except that a very long stretch (typically 25 feet) of blank tape is taken to mean that there is no more data on the volume. To avoid wastage of tape the gap written is usually

fairly close to the minimum but it may be elongated in some circumstances, e.g. by error recovery actions or to leave space for the *editing* of a file (which in this context means its replacement by a new version of the same length).
In conventional magnetic tape subsystems the division of data into blocks is carried out by the host. However some buffered tape subsystems, particularly streaming cartridge tape, accept a continuous data stream from the host, and the subsystem itself divides the data into blocks (in this case often called *blockettes*) in a manner that is not visible to the host.
2. In coding theory, an ordered set of symbols, usually of a fixed length. The term is generally synonymous with word or string.
3. *See* block-structured languages.
4. In parallel programming, to prevent further execution of one sequence of instructions until another sequence has done whatever is necessary to unblock it. *See also* blocked process.

block code A type of *error-correcting or *error-detecting code in which a number (conventionally k) of digits are taken into the encoder at a time and then output as a *codeword* consisting of a greater number (conventionally n) of digits. It is often specified as an (n, k) *code*, with block length k and codeword length n. The corresponding decoder takes in n digits, and outputs k digits, at a time. Although the codewords are longer than the input words, they are no more numerous. They are only a selection of all possible words of their length: the selection method gives any code its particular properties. *See also* code.

block compaction *Another name for* memory compaction.

block diagram A diagram that represents graphically the interconnection relationships between elements of a computer system. These elements may range from circuits to major *functional units; they are described as labeled geometric figures. The whole block diagram may represent any level of computer description from a compound circuit to an overall computer complex.

blocked process A *process for which a process description exists but which is unable to proceed because it lacks some necessary resource. For example, a process may become blocked if it has inadequate memory available to it to allow the loading of the next part of the process.

blockette *See* block.

blocking factor *See* record.

block length 1. *See* block (def. 1).
2. The input word length, k, of an (n, k) *block code. The term is also applied to the codeword length, n, of an (n, k) block code.
3. The input word length (i.e. the *extension of the source) used in a *variable-length code.

block retrieval Fetching a block from backing store as part of a *memory-management process.

block-structured languages A class of high-level languages in which a program is made up of *blocks* – which may include *nested blocks* as components, such nesting being repeated to any depth. A block consists of a sequence of statements and/or blocks, preceded by declarations of variables. Variables declared at the head of a block are visible throughout the block and any nested blocks, unless a variable of the same name is declared at the head of an inner block. In this case the new declaration is effective throughout the inner block, and the outer declaration becomes effective again at the end of the inner block. Variables are said to have *nested scopes*.
The concept of block structure was introduced in the *Algol family of languages, and block-structured languages are sometimes described as *Algol-like*. The concept of nested scopes implicit in block struc-

ture contrasts with FORTRAN, where variables are either local to a program unit (subroutine) or global to several program units if declared to be COMMON. Both of these contrast with COBOL, where all data items are visible throughout the entire program.

blow (blast; burn) *Jargon* To program a *PROM, i.e. to record information in a programmable read-only memory using a *PROM programmer.

Blum's axioms Two axioms in complexity theory, discovered by M. Blum. Let

$$M_1, M_2, \ldots, M_n, \ldots$$

be an effective *enumeration of the Turing machines and let f_i be the *partial recursive function of a single variable that is computed by M_i. (For technical reasons it is simpler to think in terms of partial recursive functions than set (or language) recognizers.) If

$$F_1, F_2, \ldots, F_n, \ldots$$

is a sequence of partial recursive functions satisfying
axiom 1:
$f_i(n)$ is defined if and only if $F_i(n)$ is defined,
and axiom 2:
$F_i(x) \leqslant y$ is a recursive predicate of i, x, and y,
then $F_i(n)$ can be thought of as the amount of some "resource" consumed by M_i in computing $f_i(n)$. This notion represents a useful abstraction of the more usual resources – time and space – and helps to understand their relationship.

BNF *Abbrev. for* Backus normal form, Backus–Naur form. The first widely used formal notation for describing the *syntax of a programming language; it was invented by John Backus. BNF was introduced as a defining mechanism in the Algol 60 Report (editor Peter Naur) to describe the syntax of Algol 60. BNF is capable of describing any *context-free language, and variants of it are still in use today.
A BNF grammar consists of a number of *production rules,* which define syntactic categories in terms of other syntactic categories, and of the *terminal symbols* of the language. Examples are shown in the diagram. The name of the syntactic category that is being defined is placed on the left, its definition on the right; the two are separated by the symbol ::=, read as "is defined to be". The names of syntactic categories are enclosed by angle brackets. The symbol | is read as "or".
See also extended BNF.

board 1. The thin rigid board of insulating material on which a circuit is constructed, often a *printed circuit. *See* circuit board. **2.** *Short for* circuit board.

book A term used in connection with the organization of files in Algol 68. A file is regarded as one or more books, each book being composed of numbered pages; within a page data is organized into lines made of individual characters. It is important to distinguish "page" in this context from a *page in memory management systems.

Boolean algebra An *algebra that is particularly important in computing. Formal-

⟨digit⟩ ::= 0|1|2|3|4|5|6|7|8|9
⟨integer⟩ ::= ⟨digit⟩|⟨digit⟩⟨integer⟩
⟨fractional number⟩ ::= ⟨integer⟩|⟨integer⟩.⟨integer⟩
⟨number⟩ ::= ⟨integer⟩|⟨fractional number⟩
⟨signed number⟩ ::= ⟨number⟩|+⟨number⟩|–⟨number⟩

Production rules of a BNF grammar

ly it is a *complemented *distributive lattice. In a Boolean algebra there is a *set of elements B that consists of only 0 and 1. Further there will be two *binary operations, usually denoted by $\wedge$ and $\vee$ (or by . and +) and called *and* and *or* respectively. There is also a *unary operation, denoted here by ′, and known as the *complement operation*. These operations satisfy a series of laws, given in the table, where x, y, and z denote arbitrary elements of B.

There are two very common examples of Boolean algebras. The first consists of the set

$$B = \{\text{FALSE, TRUE}\}$$

with the binary *AND and *OR operations replacing $\wedge$ and $\vee$ respectively, and the *NOT operation producing complements. Thus 1 and 0 are just TRUE and FALSE respectively. This idea can be readily extended to the set of all n-tuples

$$(x_1, x_2, \ldots, x_n)$$

where each x_i is in B. The AND and OR operations are then extended to operate between corresponding pairs of elements in each n-tuple to produce another n-tuple; the NOT operation negates each item of an n-tuple.

The second common example of a Boolean algebra is the set of subsets of a given set S, with the operations of *intersection and *union replacing $\wedge$ and $\vee$ respectively; set *complement fills the role of Boolean algebra complement.

Boolean algebras, named for George Boole, the 19th-century English mathematician, are fundamental to many aspects of computing – switching theory, logic design, logic itself, and aspects of algorithm design.

Boolean function (logic function) A *function in *Boolean algebra. The function is written as an expression formed with binary variables (taking the value 0 or 1) combined by the binary and unary operations of Boolean algebra, e.g.

$$f = (x \wedge y) \vee (x' \wedge z)$$

For any particular values of its constituent variables, the value of the function is either 0 or 1, depending on the combinations of values assigned to the variables. A Boolean function can be represented in a *truth table. It can also be transformed into a *logic diagram of logic gates.

Boolean matrix A two-dimensional *array in which each element is either TRUE or FALSE. *Compare* bit matrix.

idempotent laws:
$x \vee x = x$
$x \wedge x = x$

associative laws:
$x \vee (y \vee z) = (x \vee y) \vee z$
$x \wedge (y \wedge z) = (x \wedge y) \wedge z$

commutative laws:
$x \vee y = y \vee x$
$x \wedge y = y \wedge x$

absorption laws:
$x \vee (x \wedge y) = x$
$x \wedge (x \vee y) = x$

distributive laws:
$x \wedge (y \vee z) = (x \wedge y) \vee (x \wedge z)$
$x \vee (y \wedge z) = (x \vee y) \wedge (x \vee z)$

identity laws:
$x \vee 0 = x$
$x \wedge 1 = x$

null laws:
$x \vee 1 = 1$
$x \wedge 0 = 0$

complement laws:
$x \vee x' = 1$
$x \wedge x' = 0$

Laws of Boolean algebra

Boolean value (logical value) Either of the two values TRUE and FALSE that indicate a truth value.

bootstrap In general, a means or technique for causing a system to build up from some simple preliminary instruction(s) or information. The preliminary instruction may be hardwired and called by the operation of a switch. The word is used in a number of contexts.

For example, a bootstrap can be a short program, usually held in nonvolatile memory, whose function is to load another longer program. When a computing system is first powered-on, the contents of its memory are in general undefined except for those parts that are fabricated from read-only memory or for the contents of nonvolatile memory. The bootstrap routine is stored in ROM and is capable of reading from backing store the complete operating system, which is loaded into the empty machine.

A bootstrap is also a method by which a compiler is transferred from one machine to another, and which depends on the compiler being written in the language it compiles. To transfer from machine A to machine B, given a compiler that runs on machine A, it is first necessary to make the compiler generate B's machine code. The source code of the compiler is then compiled by this modified compiler, so generating a version of the compiler for machine B. In practice it is usually necessary to recode some machine-dependent portions of the compiler by hand to complete the transfer.

The term originates from a story told by Baron Munchausen who boasted that finding himself trapped and sinking in a swamp, he lifted himself by the bootstraps and carried himself to safety on firm ground.

Bose–Chandhuri–Hocquenghem codes (BCH codes) An important family of *binary *linear *error-correcting *block codes. They are reasonably efficient and have reasonably good error-correcting abilities, but their importance lies in their ease of encoding (by means of *shift registers) and of decoding. They can be regarded as a generalization of *Hamming codes, and as a special case of *Reed–Solomon codes. BCH codes can be arranged to be *cyclic.

BOT marker *Short for* beginning of tape marker. A physical feature of a magnetic tape by which the tape transport senses on the tape the start of the volume into which data can be recorded, or has been recorded. When the transport senses the marker it commences the logical sequence of recording or reading data. The marker may be, for example, a rectangular strip of reflective material adhering to the tape, a transparent part of the tape, or a hole in the tape, according to the type of tape and transport. The distance of the marker from the physical beginning of the tape allows the tape to be loaded, threaded through the transport, and wound on to a point at which data will be reliably recorded. This distance, and the form of the marker, are defined by the standard pertaining to the type of tape. *See also* EOT marker. *Compare* tape mark.

bottom-up development An approach to program development in which progress is made by composition of available elements, beginning with the primitive elements provided by the implementation language and ending when the desired program is reached. At each stage the available elements are employed in the construction of new elements that are more powerful in the context of the required program. These new elements will in turn be employed at the next stage in the construction of still more powerful elements, and so on until the available elements can be employed directly in the construction of the desired program.

In practice, "pure" bottom-up development is not possible; the construction of new elements must always be guided by a look-ahead to the requirements of the eventual program, and even then it will often be discovered at a later stage that some earlier construction sequence was inappropriate, leading to a need for iteration. *Compare* top-down development.

bottom-up parsing (shift-reduce parsing) A strategy for *parsing sentences of a *context-free grammar that attempts to construct a *parse tree beginning at the leaf nodes and working "bottom-up" toward the root.
Bottom-up (or shift-reduce) parsers work by "shifting" symbols onto a stack until the top of the stack contains a right-hand side of a production. The stack is then "reduced" by replacing the production's right-hand side by its left-hand side. This process continues until the string has been "reduced" to the start symbol of the *grammar.
The string of symbols to be replaced at each stage is called a *handle*. Bottom-up parsers that proceed from left to right in the input must always replace the leftmost handle and, in so doing, they effectively construct a rightmost *derivation sequence in reverse order. For example, a rightmost derivation of the string *abcde* might be

$$S \Rightarrow ACD \Rightarrow ACde \Rightarrow Acde \Rightarrow abcde$$

A bottom-up parser would construct this derivation in reverse, first reducing *abcde* to *Acde*, then to *ACde*, then to *ACD*, and finally to the start symbol *S*. The handle at each stage is respectively *ab*, *c*, *de*, and *ACD*.
See also LR parsing, precedence parsing.

boundary protection *See* bounds registers.

boundary-value problem *See* ordinary differential equations, partial differential equations.

bounds registers Two registers whose contents are used to denote an area of memory for which there is *access control. The area may be defined by beginning and ending addresses, or by the beginning address and the area length – in which case it is a *base-bound register. The use of bounds registers is a form of hardware security, and is sometimes known as *boundary protection*. *See also* memory protection.

Box–Jenkins forecasting techniques *See* time series.

bps *Abbrev. for* bits per second. *See also* bit rate.

branch instruction (jump instruction, transfer instruction) An instruction in a program that breaks the normal sequential program flow.

breadboard An easily adapted *circuit board on which experimental arrangements of electronic components may be realized. Access to the individual components is simple and hence the overall arrangement may be readily modified. Breadboards are used mainly for the development of prototype circuit designs.

breadth-first search A technique of searching through a tree whereby all nodes in a tree at level *k* are searched before searching nodes at level *k* + 1. *Compare* depth-first search.

breakpoint *See* debugging.

bridge *See* gateway.

bridgeware Any software or hardware that eases the transition from use of one computer system to use of another not entirely compatible one. Bridgeware is normally supplied by a computer manufacturer when a new range of machines does not offer complete upward *compatibility from some previous range. Typically the bridgeware will permit programs developed for the previous range to be executed (perhaps after minor modifications) on the new range of machines.

broadband coaxial systems Communication systems that use *broadband networking techniques on coaxial cable. The 300 megahertz (MHz) bandwidth of a coaxial cable is divided into multiple channels through *frequency division multiplexing. The channels can transmit signals at different data rates, allowing diverse applications to share the cable by means of dedicated channels. Channel bandwidth may range from a few kilohertz to several megahertz. A single cable may carry both digital data and analog data (voice, television) simultaneously. Access to the cable is provided through radio-frequency *transceivers (modems) assigned to a particular channel. *Frequency-agile modems* may be used to communicate on different bands at different times.

There are two classifications of broadband coaxial systems. In a one-way system signals travel in only one direction in the cable. This kind of system is common in cable TV (CATV) systems. In a two-way system signals can travel in both directions on the cable. All traffic that originates from network nodes travels on the inbound channels to the *headend*. The headend is the origin of all traffic on the outbound channels, routing all messages on inbound channels to the proper outbound channel to reach their destination. Network nodes transmit messages on inbound channels and receive messages on outbound channels.

Two-way systems fall into *midsplit* or *subsplit* categories. Midsplit systems divide the cable bandwidth equally between inbound and outbound channels. Subsplit systems put inbound traffic in the 5 – 30 MHz bands and outbound traffic in the 54 – 100 kHz bands. This format is the easiest way to retrofit onto a one-way CATV system, and leaves the VHF TV channels on their normal "off-the-air" frequency assignments.

broadband networking **1.** Communication using a modulated carrier (*see* modulation) to apply a data signal to a transmission medium in analog form. Multiple signals can be present simultaneously using *frequency division multiplexing. Different bandwidths may be allocated to different signals, and different kinds of traffic (digital data, analog voice, television) may be carried at the same time. *See also* broadband coaxial systems. *Compare* baseband networking.

2. A term sometimes used for wideband networking, i.e. networking with wideband channels (*see* bandwidth).

broadcasting A message-routing algorithm in which a message is transmitted to all nodes in a network. Some data-communication media, such as the *Ethernet, are inherently broadcast in nature. Address filtering is used to restrict the set of messages that any one host actually reads. The network service that delivers the message is known as *broadcast service* and is implemented using a special address, which all stations are prepared to accept. Other communication systems, such as the *ARPANET, may require that a copy of the message be separately addressed to each possible recipient in order to implement broadcasting.

Broadcasting may be used for a variety of purposes. For instance, to find the shortest path to a destination, a message can be broadcast to all intermediate nodes repeatedly until the destination node is reached. If path information is recorded as the message traverses the network, the same path can be used for future messages to the same destination node. As a second example, in local area networks with a tree-like topology, or in satellite communication links with multiple ground stations within a beam radius, broadcasting can be used to simplify addressing. This allows certain messages, such as request for a bootstrap, to be sent to all hosts with the expectation that at least one host will be able to satisfy the request. Thirdly, a broadcast message may be one that carries general information of potential interest to all nodes on the net.

A generalization of broadcasting is *multicasting*, in which special address flags are used to indicate that particular messages are of interest to particular classes of nodes, but not necessarily to all nodes on the net.

brother *Another name for* sibling.

browsing Searching of files by an unauthorized user for information that is not specifically known to exist. This is one of the *threats to a computer system.

BSC 1. *Abbrev. for* binary symmetric channel.
2. *Another abbrev. for* binary synchronous communications. *See* BISYNC.

B-tree or **b-tree 1. (balanced multiway search tree)** of *degree n ($\geqslant 2$). A *multiway search tree of degree n in which the root node has degree $\geqslant 2$, every nonterminal node other than the root has degree k,

$$\text{where } n/2 \leqslant k \leqslant n$$

and every leaf node occurs at the same level. Originally defined by R. Beyer and E. McCreight, the data structure provides an efficient dynamic retrieval device.
2. A binary tree with no nodes of degree one.

bubble memory *See* magnetic bubble memory.

bubble sort (exchange selection) A form of *sorting by exchanging that simply interchanges pairs of elements that are out of order in a sequence of passes through the file, until no such pairs exist. The method is not competitive with *straight insertion.

bucket 1. A sector on a disk file.
2. A capacitor whose electric charge is used as a form of *dynamic random-access memory (RAM). A fully charged bucket, or *full* bucket, is equivalent to a logic 1; an uncharged or *empty* bucket is equivalent to a logic 0. The charge may be passed through an array of capacitors and associated electronics, which together form a *bucket brigade.*

bucket sort An external sort in which the records to be sorted are grouped in some way, and each group stored in a distinct *bucket. Different buckets will probably be stored on different storage devices. If searching is to be performed on the data, then each bucket should contain records with the same hash value (*see* hashing). In this way all the records that might contain the required key may be fetched from the external memory at once.

buddy system A method of implementing a *memory management system. The available memory is partitioned into blocks whose sizes are always exact powers of two. A request for m bytes of memory is satisfied by allocating a block of size 2^{p+1} where

$$2^p < m \leqslant 2^{p+1}$$

If no block of this size is available then a larger block is subdivided, more than once if necessary, until a block of the required system is generated. When memory is freed it is combined with a free adjacent block (if one exists) to produce a larger block, always preserving the condition that block sizes are exact powers of two.

buffer 1. A temporary memory for data, normally used to accommodate the difference in the rate at which two devices can handle data during a transfer. The buffer may be built into a peripheral device, such as a printer or disk drive, or may be part of the system's main memory. *See* buffering.
2. A means of maintaining a short but varying length of magnetic tape between the reels and the *capstan and head area of a tape transport, in order that the acceleration of the tape at the reels need not be as great as that of the tape at the capstan. There are two principal types of buffer: *tension arm* and *vacuum column*. In the first, the tape passes over a series of rollers, alternate rollers being fixed in position and the rest being attached to a sprung pivoted arm, so that a variable length of tape is taken up in the resulting loops; in the second, the tape is drawn by a difference of pressure into a chamber

whose width is just that of the tape. Vacuum column transports are more expensive and noisier but can handle higher tape speeds.
Streaming tape transports and many types of cartridge drives do not use buffers and are therefore limited to lower accelerations of the tape in the area of the head and (if there is one) capstan.
3. Any circuit or device that is put between two others to smooth changes in rate or level or allow asynchronous operation. For example, line *drivers can be used to isolate (or buffer) two sets of data lines.

buffering A programming technique used to compensate for the slow and possibly erratic rate at which a peripheral device produces or consumes data. If the device communicates directly with the program, the program is constrained to run in synchronism with the device; buffering allows program and device to operate independently. Consider a program sending output to a slow device. A memory area (the *buffer) is set aside for communication: the program places data in the buffer at its own rate, while the device takes data from the buffer at its own rate. Although the device may be slow, the program does not have to stop unless the buffer fills up; at the same time the device runs at full speed unless the buffer empties. A similar technique is used for input. *See also* double buffering.

buffer register A storage location or device for the temporary storage of information during the process of writing to or reading from main memory. It generally has a capacity equivalent to one byte or one word.

bug An error in a program or system. The word is usually used to mean a localized implementation error rather than, say, an error introduced at the requirements or system-design stage. *See also* debugging.

bulk memory *Another name for* backing store.

burn *Another term for* blow.

Burroughs A company that was incorporated in 1886 and assumed its present name in 1953. The products of Burroughs Corporation include everything from mechanical bookkeeping machines through a family of large-scale processors starting with the B5000 and including the B7700 of today. The distinguishing feature of the large-scale machine family is an operating system that provides the run-time environment for programs written in high-level languages. The initial machine of the family, the B5000, was designed around the capabilities of Algol 60. Later, FORTRAN and COBOL were added to the languages supported on that system. Architecturally, Burroughs machines feature a built-in automatic stack, and had a *virtual-memory capability as early as 1962.

burster A mechanism for separating continuous fan-folded paper used in line printers and some page printers into separate sheets. Frequently it also performs the function of separating out interleaved carbon and sorting the multicopy output into sets. It may also trim the edges to remove the sprocket holes and the ragged edge left by the perforations between sheets. Generally this is done off-line but some versions can be linked directly to the output printer.

burst error (error burst) An error pattern, generally in a binary signal, that consists of known positions where the digit is in error ("first" and "last"), with the intervening positions possibly in error and possibly not. By implication, digits before the first error in the block and after the last error in the block are correct.

burst mode Usually, dedicated use of a multiplexer *channel for a single I/O device, thus permitting that device to operate at high (burst) speed.

bus A signal route to which several items of a computer system may be connected in parallel so that signals can be passed between them. A bus is also called a *trunk* in the US, and a *highway* in the UK. The signals on a bus may be only of a particular kind, as in an *address bus or *data bus, or they may be intermixed. To maximize throughput, the number of lines in the bus should equal the sum of the number of bits in a data word, the maximum address, and the number of control lines. As this is expensive to implement, a *multiplexed bus may be used.

There are a number of widely used proprietory bus systems, such as DEC's *Unibus and Intel's *Multibus. There is also a widely used communications bus standard, referred to as *IEEE 488* or as *GPIB, general-purpose interface bus*; it is defined by ANSI/IEEE 488–1978. It was initially promoted by the Hewlett Packard company as *HP–IB* and they have patent rights on the three-wire *handshake system that it incorporates. For microprocessors there are a number of standardized bus systems, one of the most widely used being the *S-100 bus.

busbar 1. A physical signal carrier that connects several parts of a computer system. The term is frequently contracted to *bus.

2. An electrical conductor that is usually substantial compared to its associated conductors and is common to several electrical loads and/or sources.

bused interface *Another name for* daisychain.

bus terminator An electrical circuit connected at the end of a bus to hold it at a predetermined signal level when it is not active, and also to ensure impedance matching and thus avoid unwanted reflections of signals. It is often available as a single package for mounting onto a printed circuit board.

It is important to ensure that the electrical impedance of a bus carrying high-frequency signals does not have any abrupt changes. If the ends of the conductors are not terminated, the signals see an almost infinite impedance and are reflected back along the conductor. A fast switching circuit connected close to the end of an unterminated bus could detect both the signal and the reflection and so give rise to errors.

bus topology *See* network architecture.

byte A subdivision of a *word in a machine, usually comprising eight bits. *Compare* character.

byte machine *See* variable word length computer.

C

C A systems programming language developed for implementation of the *UNIX operating system, and widely used for software development in the UNIX environment. C combines the control and data structures of a modern high-level language with the ability to address the machine hardware at a level more usually associated with assembly language. The terse syntax is attractive to professional systems programmers, and the compilers generate very efficient object code. C is derived from *BCPL, via a short-lived predecessor B.

cache memory (cache) A type of memory that is used in high-performance systems, inserted between the processor and memory proper. The *memory hierarchy on a system contains registers in the processor, which are the highest-speed storage, and, at a slightly lower level of accessibility, the contents of the main memory. The cache is intended to reduce the discrepancy in accessibility between these two types of unit, and functions by holding small regions that map the contents of main memory. The formal behavior of the cache corresponds closely to that of the *working set in a *paging system.

CAD *Abbrev. for* computer-aided design.

CAI *Abbrev. for* computer-aided (or -assisted) instruction.

calculator A device, now usually electronic, by means of which arithmetic operations can be performed on numbers entered from a keyboard. Final solutions and intermediate numbers are generally presented on *LCD or *LED displays. Present-day calculators range from very cheap simple devices capable of performing the basic arithmetic operations to those whose capabilities extend to sophisticated mathematical and statistical manipulation and that may be programmed with large numbers of steps. Add-on memory modules containing sets of specialist programs for particular fields – engineering, navigation, or business for example – may be purchased as accessories to the more expensive calculators, as can small printers.

call To transfer control to a *subroutine or *procedure, with provision for return to the instruction following the call at the end of execution of the subroutine/procedure.

calling sequence The code sequence required to effect transfer of control to a subroutine or procedure, including passing of parameters and the recording of the return address. Uniformity of calling sequences is vital if it is required to call procedures written in a different language from the calling program.

call instruction An instruction that saves the contents of the *program counter before branching to a *subroutine or *procedure. *Compare* return instruction.

CAM *Abbrev. for* **1.** computer-aided manufacturing, **2.** content-addressable memory.

CAMAC A standardized multiplexing intermediate interface. It does not usually connect directly to a processor or a peripheral, but provides a standardized interface to which a number of *peripheral interface adapters and a single computer interface controller can be connected.

The peripheral adapters may each have different functions, e.g. digital to analog converter, level changers, parallel to serial converter, and thus have different interfaces facing outward from the CAMAC. Similarly the controller module connects to the CAMAC interface but the outward-facing interface can be chosen to suit the available computer. The name CAMAC was chosen to symbolize this characteristic of looking the same from either direction. The adapters are typically a single printed circuit card that plugs into the internal 86-way connector. The outward-facing connections are usually mounted on a panel attached to the circuit card or may be made via a second connector mounted above the 86-way CAMAC connection. The interface is widely used for connecting instruments and transducers to computers.

CAMAC was proposed as a standard by the UK Atomic Energy Authority and further development and documentation was done by the European Standards of Nuclear Electronics and the Nuclear Instrument Module Committee of USA. It has also been adopted and documented as a standard by IEEE. The internal electrical interface, the size of the cards, and the physical parameters of the casework and connectors are defined by the standard.

Cambridge ring A high-speed *local area network developed as a *ring network at Cambridge University, UK. It has pioneered many aspects of local and ring network design.

cancellation The loss of significant digits in subtracting two approximately equal numbers. This is a frequent cause of poor accuracy in numerical results but it can usually be avoided by some reorganization of the calculation. Consider, for example, the quadratic equation

$$ax^2 + bx + c = 0$$

The formula for the roots of a quadratic is

$$(-b \pm \sqrt{(b^2 - 4ac)})/2a$$

If b^2 is large compared with $4|ac|$ severe cancellation occurs in one of the roots. This root can be computed from the fact that the product of the roots is c/a.

capability architecture (capability-based addressing) An architecture that extends across both the hardware and the (operating system) software of a computer system. It is intended to provide better protection features to facilitate both multiprocessing and computer security. In this form of architecture or addressing there are two types of words in memory: data (including programs) and *capabilities*. Capabilities can only be manipulated by privileged portions of the system. The capability descriptor tells where data is and what sorts of access to that data are permitted.
Examples of systems with capability architecture are the Plessy 250 and the Cambridge CAP. *Object architecture is an extension of this concept.

capability-based addressing *Another name for* capability architecture.

capability list The list of permitted operations that a user can perform upon an object. *See* object architecture, capability architecture.

capacity **1.** The amount of information that can be held in a storage device. The amount may be measured in words, bytes, bits, or characters.
2. The maximum range of values that can be held in a register.
3. of a transmission channel. *See* channel coding theorem.

capstan The component of a tape transport that transmits motion (sometimes indirectly) to the magnetic tape and controls the speed of its motion past the head; the motion of the tape reels is usually separately controlled. *Streaming tape transports often have no capstan.

CAR The *LISP function that when applied to a list yields the *head of the list. The word was originally an acronym for contents of address register. *Compare* CDR.

card *See* punched card, magnetic card, chip card, circuit card.

card cage A framework in which *circuit boards can be mounted. It comprises channels into which the boards can be slid and sockets and wiring by means of which they are interconnected.

cardinality A measure of the size of a *set. Two sets S and T are said to be of the same cardinality or to be *equipotent*, often written as $S \sim T$, if there is a *bijection between the elements of S and the elements of T. If the set S is finite, then the cardinality of S is the number of elements in the set.
If S is equipotent to the set of natural numbers

$$\{1,2,3, \dots\}$$

then S is an infinite set and it is said to have cardinality $\aleph_0$ (a symbol called *aleph null*). A number representing the cardinality of an infinite set is said to be *transfinite*.
If S is equipotent to the set of real numbers then S is infinite; it has cardinality **C** and this is called the *power of the continuum*. It can be shown that in some sense

$$\mathbf{C} = 2^{\aleph_0},$$

the number of subsets of natural numbers.

card punch A machine that is used to punch a pattern of holes in a punch card. The pattern has a coded relationship to the data that has been passed to the machine from another data-processing machine or an operator at a keyboard.

card reader A machine that senses the data encoded on a card and translates it into binary code that can be transmitted for further processing (*see also* magnetic card, chip card, punched card).
The *magnetic card reader* can have a power-driven transport that will draw the card

into the machine and move it past the read head. In some designs there are cleaning brushes before the read head. The direction of travel is reversed after the card has been read and thus the card is returned to the operator. In designs used with automatic cash dispensers, the direction of travel may not reverse if the card and/or the associated identification number are not valid.

A *slot reader* is a relatively simple device for reading badges or plastic cards. The badge or card is manually moved along a slot that guides it past a sensing station. The data to be read may be encoded magnetically or printed in *bar code or a machine-readable font. Since the rate of movement past the read head is not controlled by the device, the sensing head and electronics are generally designed to work over a range of speeds. Compared to a reader with a powered transport the device is much cheaper and quicker. Some designs for use with bank teller terminals can read the printed encoding on checks and the magnetic encoding on plastic cards.

The *chip card reader* has a guide and a connector that engages contacts on the card. When the machine senses that the card is in place and the related code has been keyed in, the memory device embedded in the card can be read.

See also punched card reader.

card verifying The process of checking that the data encoded on a punched card or magnetic card has the intended relationship to the original data. It is being made obsolete by systems in which the data is stored and verified before being encoded onto a card. *See also* verification.

carriage-control tape *See* vertical format unit.

carriage return (CR) A control code that is used to affect the format of printed or displayed output. It indicates that the next data character is to appear in the leftmost position on a line. In some serial printers, the CR code may cause a physical movement of the printing carriage to the leftmost print position. In line printers and serial printers designed for high productivity, the characters will be correctly positioned although the printing of a line may commence at either the left or the right end.

carrier *See* modulation.

carrier sense multiple access (CSMA), CSMA with collision detection *See* CSMA/CD.

carry lookahead A method that is used in multibit *parallel adders whereby an individual element in the adder can detect when the immediately preceding stage of the adder is about to generate a carry as the result of the addition of the next least significant bits in the addend and augend. The logic required to generate the carry lookahead signal is available in integrated-circuit form.

Carry lookahead affords a considerable improvement in performance over, say, ripple-carry *adders since the carry is generated in parallel at all stages of addition rather than sequentially, as in the ripple adder. Adders using the lookahead technique are thus often called high-speed adders.

Cartesian product of two *sets S and T. The set of all *ordered pairs of the form (s,t) with the property that s is a member of S and t is a member of T; this is usually written as $S \times T$. Formally,

$$S \times T = \{(s,t) | (s \in S) \text{ and } (t \in T)\}$$

If R denotes the set of real numbers, then $R \times R$ is just the set of points in the (Cartesian) plane or it can be regarded as the set of complex numbers, hence the name. The concept can be extended to deal with the Cartesian product of n sets,

$$S_1, S_2, \ldots, S_n$$

This is the set of ordered n-tuples

$$(s_1, s_2, \ldots, s_n)$$

with the property that each s_i is in S_i. In the case where each S_i is the same set S, it is customary to write S^n for

$$S \times S \times \ldots S \text{ (}n\text{ terms)}$$

Cartesian structure Any data structure where the number of elements is fixed and linearly ordered. The term is sometimes used as a synonym for *record.

cartridge A container used to protect and facilitate the use of various computer-related media such as *magnetic tape, *magnetic disk, or printer ink ribbon. It is usually designed so that the medium remains permanently within the cartridge or at least attached to it, and the medium itself is not touched by an operator. *See* magnetic tape cartridge, disk cartridge.

cartridge drive Either a tape transport for handling cartridge tape, or a disk drive for handling disk cartridges.

cartridge tape Tape carried in a *magnetic tape cartridge. The term is generally used in reference to the 3M-type cartridge.

cascadable counter An individual counter element, usually a *flip-flop, in a chain of such elements. Each element has facilities for a count input and is capable of generating an overflow (or carry) output. The counter elements may typically have count lengths of integer powers of 2 (binary counters) or integer powers of 10 (decimal counters). Cascading a counter that has a count length of 4 with one having a count length of 10 will give a counter that has a count length of 40.
Since cascadable counters are available as integrated-circuit blocks or modules, cascadable counters are also called *modular counters*. *See also* counter.

cassette A container that is similar to a *cartridge, but conventionally the two terms are applied to different types of device. A cassette is usually interchangeable with an ordinary domestic audio cassette. *See* magnetic tape cartridge.

cassette drive A tape transport for handling magnetic tape contained in cassettes. *See* magnetic tape cartridge.

CAT *Abbrev. for* computer-aided testing.

catastrophic code A *convolutional code that is prone to *catastrophic error propagation*, i.e. a situation in which a finite number of *channel errors causes an infinite number of decoder errors. Any given convolutional code is or is not a catastrophic code.

catastrophic error propagation *See* catastrophic code.

category A collection of *objects* $\boldsymbol{A}$, together with a related set of *morphisms* $\boldsymbol{M}$. An object is a generalization of a *set and a morphism is a generalization of a *function that maps between sets.
The set $\boldsymbol{M}$ is the *disjoint *union of sets of the form $[A,B]$, where A and B are elements of $\boldsymbol{A}$; if α is a member of $[A,B]$, A is the *domain* of α, B is the *codomain* of α, and α is said to be a morphism from A to B. For each triple (A,B,C) of elements of $\boldsymbol{A}$ there is a *binary operation $\circ$ from the *Cartesian product

$$[B,C] \times [A,B]$$

to $[A,C]$. The image $\beta\circ\alpha$ of the ordered pair (β,α) is the *composition* of β with α; the composition operation is *associative. In addition, when the composition is defined there is an *identity* morphism for each A in $\boldsymbol{A}$.
Examples of categories include the set of *groups and *homomorphisms on groups, and the set of *rings and homomorphisms on rings. *See* functor.

cathode-ray tube (CRT) An electronic display device in which an electrical signal is used to modulate one or more well-defined and controllable beams of electrons; in a color CRT three electron beams are used. The electron beam or beams are directed onto a target surface, usually a phosphorescent screen, the controlled movement and intensity of the beam(s) producing a visible display, or sometimes a display that must be detected other than by eye. *See also* oscilloscope, storage oscilloscope.

Cayley table (composition table; operation table) A tabular means of describing a finite *group, first used by the 19th-century mathematician Arthur Cayley. To illustrate, the set

$$\{1,-1,i,-i\}$$

forms a group under the *binary operation ∘ as described by the Cayley table given below. The value of $-1 \circ i$, for example, is $-i$. The name composition table is usually used when the group operation is *composition of functions.

	∘	1	−1	i	$-i$
		right operand			
	1	1	−1	i	$-i$
left operand	−1	−1	1	$-i$	i
	i	i	$-i$	−1	1
	$-i$	$-i$	i	1	−1

Cayley table

CBL *Abbrev. for* computer-based learning.

CCD, CCD memory *See* charge-coupled device.

CCITT Comité Consultatif Internationale de Télégraphique et Téléphonique (International Telegraph and Telephone Consultative Committee), an agency of the International Telecommunication Union (ITU), itself an agency of the UN. The CCITT provides worldwide coordination for telephone and data communication systems. Its technical recommendations often become internationally recognized standards.

The CCITT has the following five classes of members. Class A: national telecommunication administrations such as the *FCC in the US and *PTTs in Europe; class B: recognized private administrations such as AT&T; class C: scientific and industrial organizations; class D: international organizations such as the *ISO; class E: organizations whose primary purpose is in another field, but with some interest in CCITT work. Only the first two classes vote.

CDC Control Data Corporation, a spin-off from *Sperry Univac that included a number of key people from the pre-UNIVAC organization known as Engineering Research Associates (ERA). CDC is one of the major suppliers of large-scale high-speed scientific computers throughout the world. CDC machines of the 6600 family include the architectural approach of providing a number of I/O computers called *peripheral processors to manage the movement of data into and out of a very high-speed arithmetic engine.

CDL *Abbrev. for* computer description language. *See* hardware description.

CDR The *LISP function that when applied to a list yields the *tail of the list. The word was originally an acronym for contents of decrement register. *Compare* CAR.

Ceefax One of the UK's two *teletext systems.

cell An address, a location in memory, or a register, usually one capable of holding a binary number. It is sometimes a location capable of holding one bit.

cellar *Another name for* stack, rarely used.

center-feed tape *See* paper tape.

central processor (CPU; central processing unit) The principal operating part of a computer. It is usually defined as the *arithmetic and logic unit (ALU) and the *control unit (CU) and sometimes (but not always) the *primary memory. As the functions in a computing system have become more distributed and autonomous, the specification of the CPU has become less significant.

chad The piece of material that is removed when a hole is punched in a data medium. The preparation of punched cards and tape produces large volumes of chad. The punching of the tractor holes in continuous form paper also produces chad. If the pieces are not cleanly removed they can cause errors. Line printers are often fitted with chad traps to prevent chad from falling between the ribbon and the paper and causing loss of data on the top copy.

chain 1. A *singly linked linear *list.
2. *See* complete lattice.

chain code 1. A method of describing contours by a succession (chain) of symbols representing a discrete set of directional vectors. It is used in computer graphics and pattern recognition for description of line drawings (including characters).
2. *Another name (chiefly UK) for* simplex code.

chained file A file constructed such that each entry contains the address of the next entry in a sequence. The entries may be randomly distributed within a storage device. *See also* data chaining.

chained list *Another name for* linked list.

chaining search A search in which each item contains the means for locating the next.

chain printer A type of *solid-font *line printer in which the font is etched or engraved on small plates that are linked together to form a chain. The chain is connected around two sprocket wheels so that the straight part of the chain between the wheels runs parallel to the paper and spans the line to be printed. This was one of the first types of computer printer to use the *hit-on-the-fly* principle, developed in the mid-1950s: the chain carrying the type font moves continuously at high speed relative to the paper, and the characters are printed by impacting the paper and an inked ribbon against the moving type font with an electrically operated hammer. The duration of the impact is measured in microseconds and the smear due to the movement of the font is very slight in a well-adjusted machine. The timing of the impact is achieved via detectors that sense index marks on the rotating chain.
Early machines had speeds of 150 lpm, adequate for the input/output rates of the time. IBM was the major promoter of chain printers. By the early 1960s speeds of 600 lpm were achieved when printing alphanumerics, and a speed of over 1200 lpm could be achieved if the repertoire was limited to a numeric and symbols set of 16 characters.
The problems associated with guiding the chain in a horizontal plane, maintaining precise position relative to the timing marks, and achieving very short impact times led to the development of the *train printer, which superseded the chain printer. *See also* band printer.

change dump An output, usually printed, that lists the content of all memory locations that have changed subsequent to a defined event. This is usually the result of a routine that is written and used as an aid to debugging a program.

change file A file of change records.

change record A record containing information that is to change data values in, or insert or delete records on, a *master file.

channel 1. A specialized processor that comprises an information route and associated circuitry to control input and/or output operations. It normally provides for formatting and buffering and has the necessary control to meet the timing requirements of an I/O device. In an interface that has a number of parallel channels, each is usually separately dedicated to the passing of a single type of information such as data.
Several different I/O devices may be connected to one channel and the control circuitry within the channel directs the data

streams to or from the appropriate device. If the I/O devices have a relatively slow data rate, e.g. line printers, displays, document readers, then a *multiplexer channel* is used to connect them to the processor. The transfers to or from the separate devices are multiplexed, i.e. interleaved, character by character, such that several devices can work simultaneously.
When a number of devices with high data rates, e.g. magnetic disk and tape, are to be connected, a *selector channel* is used. This will transfer a complete record to or from a device before reselecting. Usually the selection of a device remains stable for the passage of more than one record. While the selector channel is dealing with one device, the other devices connected to it cannot transfer information but they may still be active, e.g. in a search or rewind mode.
A channel is often a *wired-program processor. As channels have become more elaborate they have tended to become programmed computers (*I/O processors*) in themselves. *See also* peripheral processor.
2. (transmission channel; communication channel) A unidirectional information route in data transmission. *See also* Shannon's model.
3. A link (physical or virtual) to a *host computer in a communication network.
4. One of the longitudinal rows in which holes may be punched in paper tape. In addition to its use as a data input/output medium, punched tape was widely used in *vertical format units for controlling the format of printer output. Although the paper loop has been replaced by binary information in a memory, the term channel is sometimes still used to refer to the equivalent electronic signal.

channel capacity *See* channel coding theorem.

channel coding The use of *error-detecting or *error-correcting codes in order to achieve reliable communication through a transmission *channel. In channel coding, the particular *code to be used is chosen to match the channel (and especially its *noise characteristics), rather than the source of the information. *See* channel coding theorem, Shannon's model. *Compare* source coding.

channel coding theorem In *communication theory, the statement that any channel, however affected by *noise, possesses a specific *channel capacity* – a rate of conveying *information that can never be exceeded without error, but that can, in principle, always be attained with an arbitrarily small probability of error. The theorem was first expounded and proved by Claude Elwood Shannon in 1948.
Shannon showed that an *error-correcting code always exists that will reduce the probability of error below any predetermined level. He did not, however, show how to construct such a code (this remains the central problem of *coding theory), although he did show that randomly chosen codes are as good as any others, provided they are extremely long.
Among Shannon's results for specific channels, the most celebrated is that for a *power-limited continuous-amplitude channel subject to *white *Gaussian noise. If the signal power is limited to P_S and the noise power is P_N, the capacity of such a channel is

$$C = \tfrac{1}{2}\nu \log_2(1 + P_S/P_N) \text{ bit/s}$$

If it is a discrete-time channel, ν is the number of *epochs per second; if it is a continuous-time channel, ν is the minimum number of samples per second necessary to acquire all the information from the channel. In the latter case, if ν is to be finite, the channel must be *band-limited; if W is its *bandwidth (in Hz), then, by *Nyquist's criterion,

$$C = W \log_2(1 + P_S/P_N) \text{ bit/s}$$

This is sometimes called the *Shannon–Hartley law*, and is often applied, erroneously, in circumstances less restricted than those described. This and other expressions for the capacity of specific chan-

nels should not be confused with the channel coding theorem, which states only that there is a finite capacity and that it can be attained without error.
See also Shannon's model, source coding theorem.

channel controller The control unit for an I/O *channel. *See also* I/O processor.

channel error An error, in a signal arriving at the *decoder in a communication system, whose occurrence is due to *noise in the channel. By contrast, a *decoder error* is an unsuccessful attempt by the decoder (of an *error-correcting code) to correct a channel error.

channel switching 1. A means of communicating on or switching between several different communication channels.
2. *Another name for* circuit switching.

channel time response *See* convolution.

character 1. An element of a given *character set.
2. A subdivision of a *word in a machine, usually comprising six, seven, or eight bits. This is sometimes called a *byte*.
3. The smallest unit of information in a *record.

character encoding A *binary encoding of a given *character set. Examples include ASCII and EBCDIC.

characteristic (biased exponent) *See* floating-point notation.

characteristic function of a *subset S of a *universal set U. A *function that indicates whether or not an element is a member of the subset S. It is the function

$$f : U \to \{0,1\}$$

defined as follows:

$$f(x) = 1 \quad \text{if } x \in S$$
$$f(x) = 0 \quad \text{if } x \notin S$$

The codomain might also be given as {true,false} or {1,2}.

characteristic vector 1. A *vector of bits representing a set in a finite universe. If the universe has n elements $a_1, a_2, \ldots, a_n$ then any set, A, can be represented by a vector of n bits where the ith bit is 1 if and only if $a_i \in A$.
2. *English form of* eigenvector. *See* eigenvalue.

character machine *See* variable word length computer.

character recognition A process in which a machine senses and encodes printed characters that are also readable by a person. The characters may be printed using a special magnetic ink and/or a special style of character, but modern machines can read good-quality typewritten or equivalent standard of print, in a variety of type fonts. *See* MICR, OCR.

character representation A representation of a character as a distinctive bit string that is defined by some *character encoding.

special characters	operation characters
space	+ −
, ; : . ? !	* /
( ) [ ] { }	> = <
$ % # & @ ~	
| \ " ' ' →	

Character set

character set 1. The set of characters that is handled by a specified machine. The set usually includes the English *alphanumeric characters, *special characters*, and *operation characters* (*see* table), all of which are *graphics characters*, and various *control characters*. Graphics characters thus denote a printed mark or a space while control characters produce some particular effect.
Two of the widest used character sets are *ASCII (American standard code for information interchange) and EBCDIC (ex-

tended binary coded decimal interchange code). EBCDIC is used primarily on the IBM 360–370 series while ASCII, introduced in 1963, is in more general use.
2. The set of characters that is valid within a given programming language.

character string A string of elements from a given *character set.

charge-coupled device (CCD) A semiconductor device that has the structure of a *MOSFET with an extremely long channel and many gates, perhaps 1000, closely spaced between the source and drain electrodes. A MOS capacitor is formed between each gate and the substrate; since this capacitor is capable of storing a charge, CCDs can be used as memory devices. The CCD essentially acts as a long (high-density) *shift register since, by manipulating the voltages applied to the gates, charge can be transferred from one MOS capacitor to its neighbor, and so on along the channel.
The physical structure of the device and the way in which the gate voltages are manipulated determines the number of gates needed to store one bit of information, typically two or three gates being required. Since the stored charge leaks away, CCDs must be continuously clocked, typically at a frequency of one megahertz.
Charge-coupled memories are particularly suited to applications where memory contents are accessed in a serial manner, as in *refresh memories for CRT terminals. They are slower than comparable RAMs but faster than magnetic bulk storage devices.

chassis In general, a mechanical system that is designed to provide a supporting and/or enclosing medium for an item of electronic equipment. The system may be equipped with supporting structures to carry standard-sized *circuit boards in addition to a *mother board or *backplane into which the boards are inserted and connected via sockets. Alternatively the individual components may be hardwired onto tag strips attached to the chassis.
For safety reasons the metal parts of a chassis should be permanently connected to a local zero-voltage reference or ground. In some equipment, however, it is more convenient to connect the chassis to one side of the a.c. or d.c. line (mains) supply; the equipment is then said to have a *hot chassis*. The chassis may also be left unconnected or floating.

CHDL *Abbrev. for* computer hardware description language. *See* hardware description.

Chebyshev approximation, norm *See* approximation theory.

check Some means or process of validating the accuracy of a segment of data, the result of a computation, or completion of a successful message transmission (across a network or to an I/O device). *See also* error detection and correction.

check character A character, or more generally some element of specified size ranging from a single bit to a few bytes, that contains the result of a check computation performed on a segment of data. *See also* error detection and correction.

checking program A program that examines other programs or data for certain classes of error, usually relatively straightforward ones such as syntax errors in the source text of a program.

checkout All activities concerned with bringing a program to the state where it produces some results (as distinct from, say, failing to compile or terminating abnormally) so that *testing can begin. Such activities might include *desk checking*, i.e. checking by human inspection, and use of a special "checkout" mode of compilation and execution that provides extensive information on erroneous use of the programming language or abnormal program termination.

checkpoint A point in a process or job at which a *dump check is taken (and hence also referred to as a *dump point*), and the point from which a subsequent *restart will be effective.

checksum (molulo-n check, residue check) A simple error detection method that operates on some set of information (usually data or program). If this information is in units that are m bits wide, a sum is taken molulo n, where $n = 2^m$, and appended to the information. At a later time or different location the check may be recomputed and most simple (all single) bit errors will be detected. A *parity check is the simplest version of this check with $m = 1$ and $n = 2$.

chief programmer team A programming team in which responsibility for program design and implementation rests entirely with one highly skilled member, the *chief programmer*. The other team members provide various forms of support. A typical team could consist of the chief programmer, a backup programmer, librarian, administrator, and secretary: the backup programmer assists the chief programmer and is able to take over that role if necessary; the librarian maintains all technical documents on the project, such as design documents, source modules (in all versions), and test histories; the administrator relieves the chief programmer of all administrative duties on the project. Various other services might be obtained from outside the team as needed.

This team organization has been advocated for the production of large programs: a single highly skilled programmer, when properly supported, can produce programs more quickly and more reliably than a team of less talented programmers working as equals. In particular, the problem of communication within the team is minimized.

The approach was pioneered in the early 1970s by the Federal Systems Division of IBM, particularly by Harlan D. Mills. Successful results have been reported from various projects, including some that produced more than 100 000 lines of source code.

child (son; offspring; daughter) Any node in a *tree, except the root. Every child thus has a *parent.

CHILL A programming language developed by CCITT and adopted as the standard language for the programming of computer-based telecommunication systems and computer-controlled telephone exchanges. CHILL is a *real-time language, bearing a substantial resemblance to *Ada.

Chinese remainder theorem Let $m_1, m_2, \ldots, m_r$ be positive integers that are relatively prime to one another, and let their product be m:

$$m = m_1 m_2 \ldots m_r$$

Let $n, u_1, u_2, \ldots, u_r$ be integers; then there is exactly one integer, u, that satisfies

$$n \leqslant u < (m + n)$$

and

$$u \equiv u_j \text{ (modulo } m_j) \text{ for } 1 \leqslant j \leqslant r$$

chip A small section of a single crystal of *semiconductor, usually silicon, that forms the substrate upon which is fabricated a single semiconductor device or all the individual devices comprising an *integrated circuit.

chip card A plastic card similar to a credit card but having some memory and a microprocessor (or specialized logic) embedded within it. It is thought to require a very much higher level of technical competance before fraud or forgery can be achieved. In addition to its use in funds transfer it is also proposed for use in connection with medical treatment. The first cards and associated equipment to be produced commercially were made in Europe by Siemens, Philips, and CII Honeywell Bull; trials were carried out in 1982. The CII Honeywell Bull card contains a variant of the Motorola 6805 microcomputer and up to 8K of *EPROM. *See also* card reader.

chip set A set of integrated circuits that when connected together form a single functional block within a computer system.

Cholesky decomposition *See* LU decomposition.

Type	Grammar	Automaton
0	arbitrary	Turing machine
1	context-sensitive	linear-bounded
2	context-free	pushdown
3	regular	finite-state

Chomsky hierarchy

Chomsky hierarchy A series of four classes of *formal languages whose definition in 1959 by Noam Chomsky marked the beginning of formal language theory, and that have ever since remained central to the subject. The are called *type 3*, *type 2*, *type 1*, and *type 0*, each one a subclass of the next. Each type can be defined either by a class of *grammars or by a class of *automata, as indicated in the table. Type 0 consists of all *recursively enumerable languages. Type 1 is a subclass of the languages definable by *primitive recursive functions. Types 2 and 3 are significant in providing abstractions of the computational ideas of iteration and recursion respectively.

Chomsky normal form A restricted type of *context-free grammar, namely one in which each production has the form

$$A \rightarrow BC \text{ or } A \rightarrow d,$$

i.e. each right-hand side consists of either two nonterminals or one terminal. Any context-free language is generated by such a grammar, except that derivation of the empty string, Λ, requires the additional production

$$S \rightarrow \Lambda$$

Church–Rosser theorem A theorem, proved jointly by A. Church and J. B. Rosser, concerning Church's *lambda calculus. It states that if a lambda-expression x can be reduced in two ways leading respectively to expressions y_1 and y_2 then there must be an expression z to which both y_1 and y_2 can be reduced. The choice of ways to reduce an expression arises from the possibility of separately reducing different "parts" of the expression. The Church–Rosser theorem shows that either part can be worked on first, without the loss of any possibilities obtainable from working on the other part first. A corresponding theorem has been proved for combinatory logic. More generally, any language for which there is a notion of reduction is said to have the *Church–Rosser property*, or to be *confluent*, if it admits the Church–Rosser theorem.

Church's thesis A proposition, put forward by A. Church in 1936, claiming that the concept of Turing computability (*see* Turing machine) is the correct formalization of our intuitive concept of *effective computability. The evidence in favor of Church's thesis is (as it must be) empirical in nature. The several attempts that were made to formalize the concept of computability have all yielded concepts (formally) equivalent to Turing computability. Among these are the notions of *lambda-definability*, developed by Church, and *general recursiveness*, introduced by Gödel.

CIM *Abbrev. for* computer input microfilm, i.e. the process, or the input itself: it is not widely used. Input devices that have been produced have relied on optical character recognition (*OCR) to recode alphanumeric data on microfilm or have read special microfilm on which the data was recorded as binary code. *See also* COM.

cipher *See* cryptography.

CIR *Abbrev. for* current instruction register.

circuit 1. The combination of a number of electrical devices and conductors that, when interconnected to form a conducting

path, fulfill some desired function. *See also* logic circuit, integrated circuit, printed circuit.
2. A physical (electrical) connection used for communication. *See also* circuit switching.
3. of a graph. *Another name for* cycle.

circuit board A single rigid board of insulating material on which an electrical circuit has been built. It often has an *edge connector at one end for making all the connections to other circuits so that the board may be plugged into a piece of equipment. Circuit boards come in a variety of sizes, some of which are standardized. The term *circuit card* is often used synonymously but is sometimes considered smaller than a circuit board. *See also* printed circuit, backplane.

circuit card *See* circuit board.

circuit design *See* digital design.

circuit switching A method of communications that is used in telephone systems and requires a physical transmission path – a *circuit* – to exist between the two devices wishing to communicate. The end-to-end path must exist before data can be sent. The only delay to which the data is subject is the propagation delay along the transmission medium (6 microseconds per 100 km for copper telephone lines). Since the path is reserved during the entire connection, any unused bandwidth is wasted. *Compare* message switching, packet switching.

circular list A *linked list in which the last item contains a link to the first. This allows access to all of the list from any given point. Circular lists are most useful if the pointer to the list links to the last node, allowing easy access to both ends of the list. *See also* ring.

circular shift (end-around shift) A *shift operation, specified by a *circular shift instruction*, that causes the contents of some register (usually the accumulator) to be shifted circularly to the left or right a prescribed number of positions.

circulating register A *shift register in which quantities (data) shifted out at one end are entered into the other end. This accomplishes a *circular shift and may be performed in either direction.

CIS–COBOL *Acronym for* compact interactive standard COBOL. A version of the programming language *COBOL that runs on many of the popular *personal computers above the hobby level. CIS–COBOL has been implemented for the 6809, 8080, 8086, and similar microprocessor chips, making it widely available. A particularly important point is that CIS–COBOL programs are portable between different micros, thus making it a very useful language for the development of program packages on the commercial market.

clamp An electronic circuit that is designed to return the d.c. voltage level at a given point in the circuit to a fixed reference value at fixed points in time, often in response to an externally generated clamp pulse.

clear An *instruction or *microinstruction that causes a designated register or counter to be set to the all-zero state (i.e. cleared).

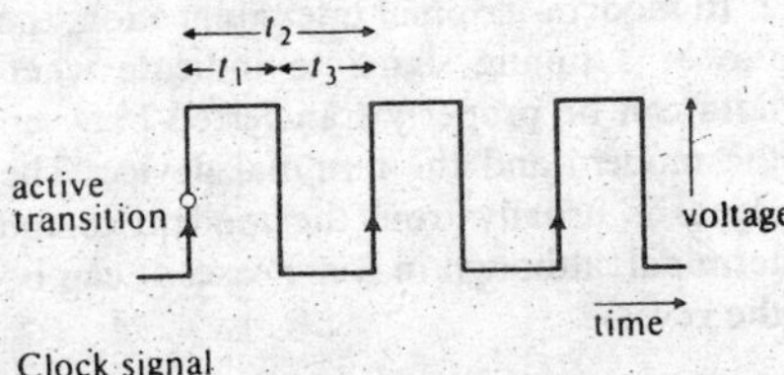

Clock signal

clock An electronic device, generally a stable oscillator, that generates a repetitive series of pulses, known as *clock pulses*, whose repetition rate, or frequency, is accurately controlled.
The *clock rate* is the frequency, expressed in *hertz, at which active transitions of a

given clock signal occur. The active transition may be from a low to a high voltage level, or vice versa, but will always be followed after a fixed time by an opposite inactive transition. The clock signal is thus formed as a series of fixed-width pulses having a fixed rep :tion rate (*see* diagram). The pulse width, t_1, is often 50% of the pulse repetition period, t_2, i.e. $t_1 = t_3$. The clock rate is $1/t_2$ hertz. A *clock cycle* is considered to be one complete cycle of the clock signal and will always contain one active transition of the clock. For the clock signal illustrated, a clock cycle occurs in t_2 seconds.
Clock pulses are used to initiate actions within a *sequential logic circuit and to synchronize the activities of a number of such circuits. These circuits are said to be *clocked*.

clock cycle *See* clock.

clocked flip-flop *See* flip-flop.

clocking 1. In synchronous communication networks, the use of a single time standard to control all bit transmissions and switching throughout the network. The clocking signal is sent as part of the data or as non-data-carrying clock-transmission signals, depending upon the exact link protocols involved.
2. In modem-terminal interconnection, the use of a timing signal to indicate when data can be properly transferred between the modem and the terminal device. The signal is usually from the modem to the terminal, although in some cases it can be the reverse.

clock pulses *See* clock.

clock rate *See* clock.

clock skew *See* skew.

closed A term applied to a *set S on whose elements a *binary operation $\circ$ is defined and that possesses the property that, for every (s,t) in S, the quantity $s \circ t$ is also in S; S is then said to be closed under $\circ$. A similar definition holds for *unary operations such as $\sim$. A set S is closed under $\sim$ provided that, when s is in S, the quantity $\sim s$ is also in S.
The set of integers is closed under the usual arithmetic operations of addition, subtraction, and multiplication, but is not closed under division.

closed loop A term used in the early development of programming to describe the repetition construct now known just as a *loop. (Since a loop is necessarily closed, the short term suffices.)

closed semiring A *semiring S with two additional properties:
(a) if $a_1, a_2, \ldots, a_n, \ldots$ is a *countable sequence of elements of S then

$$a_1 + a_2 + \ldots + a_n + \ldots,$$

exists and is unique; the order in which the various elements are added is irrelevant;
(b) the operation $\cdot$ (*see* semiring) distributes over countably infinite sums as well as finite sums.
A special unary operation called *closure* can be defined on closed semirings. Given an element a in S, powers can be defined in the expected manner:

$$a^0 = 1$$
$$a^n = a \cdot a^{n-1} \quad \text{for all } n > 0$$

Then the closure a^* can be defined as follows:

$$a^* = 1 + a + a^2 + \ldots + a^n + \ldots$$

The properties of a semiring imply that

$$a^* = 1 + a \cdot a^*$$

Closed semirings have applications in various branches of computing such as automata theory, the theory of grammars, the theory of recursion and fixed points, sequential machines, aspects of matrix manipulation, and various problems involving graphs, e.g. finding shortest-path algorithms within graphs.

closed shop A method of running a computing facility such that the design, development, writing, testing, and running of programs is carried out by specialist computing staff and not by the originators of the problem. *Closed shop operation* is the operation of a computing system, excluding terminals, by specialist computer operators and not by other computing staff or computer users. *Compare* open shop.

closed subroutine *See* subroutine.

closure *See* closed semiring. *See also* Kleene star.

	closed under complement	closed under intersection
3	yes	yes
2	no	no
1	unknown	yes
0	no	yes

Closure properties for Chomsky hierarchy

closure properties A class of *formal languages L is *closed* under an operation f if the application of f to languages in L always yields a language in L. For example, if, for any L_1 and L_2 in L,

$$L_1 \cup L_2$$

is also in L, then L is closed under union. Typical operations considered are:
*union, *intersection, *complement, intersection with *regular set;
*concatenation, *Kleene star;
image under *homomorphism, inverse homomorphism, *substitution;
*gsm-mapping, etc.
Most familiar classes of languages are closed under these operations. The detailed picture for the *Chomsky hierarchy is given in the table. Certain classes of languages, e.g. *regular languages, are definable by their closure properties.

cluster A group of magnetic tapes, videos, or terminals usually under the control of one master. As an illustration, a cluster of magnetic tape is a *magnetic tape subsystem consisting of two or more magnetic tape units (MTUs) sharing a single physical interface to the host (processor or network) so that only one MTU can perform a data transfer at a time, although other MTUs may be completing off-line operations such as rewind or tape mark search. The software is not necessarily aware that the MTUs share an interface.
In some cases, particularly on large systems, a tape cluster may be provided with two interfaces, which gives *dual access* to the cluster and hence resilience in the event of a failure of one interface or the host equipment supporting it.

cluster analysis Any statistical technique for grouping a set of units into clusters of similar units on the basis of observed qualitative and/or quantitative measurements, usually on several variables. Cluster analysis aims to fulfill simultaneously the conditions that units in the same cluster should be similar, and that units in different clusters should be dissimilar. It is not usually possible to satisfy both conditions fully, and no single method can be recommended as best for all sets of data. Among other desirable properties of clusters are that some variables should be constant for all units within a cluster, which makes it possible to provide a simple scheme for identification of units in terms of clusters.
Most cluster analysis methods require a *similarity* or *distance* measure to be defined between each pair of units, so that the units similar to a given unit may be identified. Similarity measures have been proposed for both quantitative (continuous) variables and qualitative (discrete) variables, using a weighted mean of similarity scores over all variables considered. The term distance comes from a geometric representation of data as points in multidimensional space: small distances correspond to large similarities.
Hierarchical cluster analysis methods form clusters in sequence, either by amalgamation of units into clusters and clusters into larger clusters, or by subdivision of clusters into smaller clusters and single units. Whichever direction is chosen, the results

can be represented by a *dendrogram* or family tree in which the units at one level are nested within units at all higher levels. *Nonhierarchical cluster analysis* methods allocate units to a fixed number of clusters so as to optimize some criterion representing a desired property of clusters. Such methods may be iterative, involving transfer of units between clusters until no further improvement can be achieved. The solution for a given number of clusters need bear little relation to the solution for a larger or smaller number.
Cluster analysis is often used in conjunction with other methods of *multivariate analysis to describe the structure of a complex set of data.

CMI *Abbrev. for* computer-managed instruction.

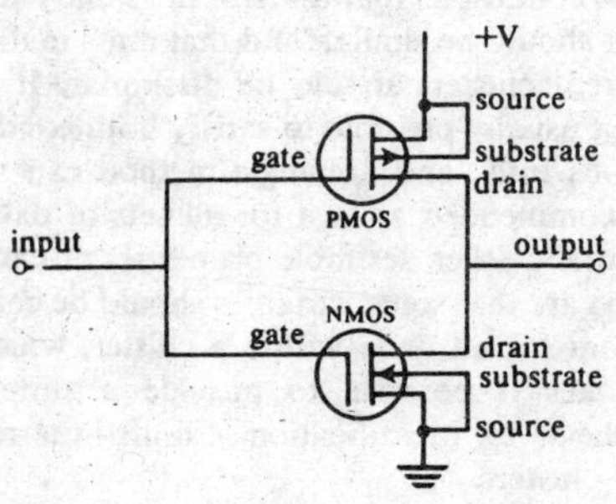

CMOS inverter

CMOS (COSMOS) *Acronym for* complementary metal oxide semiconductor (field-effect transistors). A family of logic circuits that uses pairs of complementary *MOSFETs, i.e. PMOS plus NMOS, to implement the basic logic functions. The complementary transistors are arranged so that there is no direct current flow through each pair of PMOS and NMOS. In the circuit of the CMOS inverter (*see* diagram), the PMOS conducts when the input is logic 0 and the NMOS conducts (to ground) when the input is logic 1.
By scaling down the dimensions of the MOS devices, higher switching speeds and larger packing densities are possible; these devices are often termed *HMOS.

CMS *See* VM/CMS.

CNF *Abbrev. for* conjunctive normal form. *See* conjunction.

CNF satisfiability *See* P = NP question.

COBOL or **Cobol** *Acronym for* common business-oriented language. A programming language that was developed by *CODASYL and is a de facto standard for commercial data processing. COBOL first came into use in 1960; the version in general use at present is COBOL 66, though discussions about COBOL 80 are at an advanced stage.
A COBOL program is divided into four divisions, of which the most important are the DATA division and the PROCEDURE division. In the DATA division the programmer defines the files to be used by specifying their record structure. The PROCEDURE division is made up of statements, grouped into sentences, paragraphs, and sections. These statements define manipulation of data from the current record(s) of one or more files. The notation is English-like, e.g.

```
IF X = Y MOVE A TO B;
IF GREATER ADD A TO Z;
OTHERWISE MOVE C TO D.
```

Input-output is defined in terms of complete records, so the typical program reads a record from its input file, processes it, and writes a record to its output file, repeating this sequence until the whole file is processed. A powerful feature allows the data definition to specify editing that will take place as a side-effect of output, e.g. suppressing nonsignificant zeros.

cocktail shaker sort A refinement of the *bubble sort in which alternate passes go in opposite directions.

CODASYL 1. *Acronym for* Conference on Data Systems Languages. An organization of computing personnel from the computer industry, user organizations, software

houses, and other related groups that was founded at a meeting convened at the Pentagon in 1959. Its aims were primarily to develop a standard data-processing programming language. After a number of years it produced the COBOL standard, which was adopted by the US Department of Defense for all its data-processing installations. CODASYL then extended its activities to all developments that could be useful to COBOL, one of which was the specification of a database system (*see* def. 2).
2. A particular formally defined *database management system controlled by standards committees. It is a *network database system and has been widely implemented both by software corporations and by computer manufacturers.

code 1. A rule for transforming a message from one symbolic form (the *source alphabet*) into another (the *target alphabet*), usually without loss of information. The process of transformation is called *encoding* and its converse is called *decoding*. These processes are carried out by an *encoder* and a *decoder* respectively; the encoder and decoder may be implemented in hardware or software, the encoding and decoding processes being algorithmic in nature. The term "an encoding" is sometimes used synonymously with "a code". From a more formal viewpoint, a code is a one-to-one *homomorphism h from the set of Σ-words, Σ_1*, to the set Σ_2*, where Σ_1 and Σ_2 are alphabets (*see* word, formal language). Since h is one to one, $h(w)$ may be "decoded" to obtain w for any w in Σ_1*.
See also fixed-length code, variable-length code, error-correcting code, error-detecting code, channel coding theorem, source coding theorem, encryption.
2. Any piece of program text written in a programming language (as opposed to a data structure or algorithm illustrated by a diagram or flowchart, or a program specified or sketched out in natural language prose). The term sometimes implies executable code as opposed to declarations or tables, but this is by no means always the case. *See also* coding.
3. The particular language in which some code is written, e.g. *machine code, *source code.

8421 code A *weighted code in which each decimal digit 0 through 9 is represented by a four-bit codeword. The bit positions in each codeword are assigned weights, from left to right, of 8, 4, 2, and 1. *See also* binary-coded decimal, excess-3 code.

codebook *See* cryptography.

codec *Short for* coder-decoder. A device that converts a continuous analog signal into an encoded representation in a digital bit stream, and decodes incoming digital signals back into analog form. Codecs are used in telephone systems to convert analog voice signals into digital signals, which can be transmitted at higher data rates and with lower error rates. Digital signals can be multiplexed to make more efficient use of the transmission medium. Telephone system codecs operate at 8000 samples per second (125 μs/sample), sufficient for the 4 kilohertz bandwidth analog signal. A codec is the inverse of a *modem. A codec may also be used to convert a digital signal between its original form and one with additional bits containing redundant information. The original digital signal may be recovered with low probability of error, even when it has passed through a noisy communication path such as some satellite transmission systems.

code length In an encoder, the number of symbols output when an encoded operation takes place. Usually the number of symbols input to the encoder is fixed; the number output may or may not vary, depending on whether the encoder is designed to give a *variable-length code or a *fixed-length code.

coder-decoder *See* codec.

codeword, codeword length *See* block code.

coding The transformation of a detailed design into an actual program, normally done automatically. Use of the term coding generally implies a straightforward activity – simply expressing an existing design in some formal programming language – and that any decisions made during the activity (such as the choice among arbitrary locations for particular variables) would not be classed as design decisions since they are of a relatively trivial nature. *See also* software life-cycle.

coding bounds A variety of inequalities that apply, generally or specifically, to *error-detecting and *error-correcting codes, setting bounds to their performance as expressed by parameters such as the number of codewords (*see* block code), minimum *Hamming distance, codeword length, and efficiency. Of the many bounds that are known, the most important are the *Hamming bound and the *Gilbert–Varshamov bound.

coding standards *See* programming standards.

coding theorems *See* source coding theorem, channel coding theorem.

coding theory The branch of *communication theory that deals with the mathematical study of *codes with a view to their employment in *communication systems, usually for the purpose of increasing their efficiency and reliability. *See* source coding, channel coding.

codomain *See* function, relation, category.

collating sequence An ordering of the internal character set, used in alphabetic and alphanumeric sorting.

collator A machine associated with card-based data processing that could merge two packs of punched cards: header cards, containing the address and other account information, could automatically be placed in the card file ahead of the related new cards that carried data on current transactions. Some collators could also perform the decollate function.

collector *Another name for* link editor, but rarely used.

collision, collision detection *See* CSMA/CD.

color display A VDU capable of displaying data in full color.

Colossus An electronic special-purpose digital "computer" that was built in great secrecy by the Post Office Research Station in London and began useful work at the government establishment at Bletchley Park, Buckinghamshire, in late 1943. It contained 1500 vacuum tubes (valves) and could operate at high speed. The strategy or "program" was controlled from patchboards and switches. The faster Mark II machines, operating by mid-1944, contained 2500 tubes. Both versions were used for code-breaking purposes during the war.

column-major order One way of mapping the elements of a two-dimensional *array onto a vector, e.g. for representation in memory. If a two-dimensional array, *A*, with *m* rows and *n* columns is mapped in column-major order onto a vector ***b*** with $m \times n$ elements then

$$a_{ij} = b_k$$
$$\text{where } k = m(j - 1) + i$$

See also row-major order.

column-ragged *See* ragged array.

column vector *See* matrix.

COM *Abbrev. for* computer output microfilm. Either the process by which data is recorded on microfilm – in a roll or on aperture cards – or on microfiche, or the resulting output itself. The facility has been available since the early 1960s and currently most COM devices are run off-line. *See also* CIM.

COMAL *Acronym for* common algorithmic language. A programming language developed initially for use in schools in Denmark, now used in the UK as well. It is defined as a set of extensions to *BASIC, combining "modern" control constructs with the well-known simplicity and familiarity of BASIC. It therefore facilitates the teaching of *structured programming to beginners. COMAL is at present (1983) available on only a few machines.

combination 1. A *subset of a finite set of elements. The number of combinations of n distinct objects taken k at a time is

$$^{n}C_k = n!/[k!(n-k)!]$$

2. A method of combining *functions in a parallel manner, (*compare* composition). For functions f and g,

$$f : S \rightarrow T \quad \text{and} \quad g : U \rightarrow V$$

the combination $f \times g$ is such that

$$f \times g : S \times U \rightarrow T \times V$$

where $S \times U$ and $T \times V$ are *Cartesian products, and

$$(f \times g)(s,u) = (f(s),g(u))$$

(*see* ordered pair).

combinational circuit (combinatorial circuit) A *logic circuit whose outputs at a specified time are a function only of the inputs at that time. In practice, any physically realizable combinational circuit will have a finite transit time, or delay, between the inputs changing and the outputs changing; the intention of the term combinational is to include algebraic elements (*AND gates, *OR gates, etc.) and preclude memory elements (*flip-flops, etc.). Analysis and synthesis of combinational circuits is facilitated by *Boolean algebra and *Karnaugh maps. *Compare* sequential circuit.

combinatorial circuit *Another (UK) name for* combinational circuit.

combinatorics The branch of mathematics concerned with the counting problems and enumeration problems associated with such topics as *combinations, *permutations, number theory, arithmetic, and the theory of *graphs, *groups, and other *discrete structures. *Induction, *recursion, and *recurrence relations tend to play a significant role in much of this work. In computational combinatorics the underlying theory is applied to algorithms of any kind.

combinatory logic *See* lambda calculus.

command 1. *See* job-control language.
2. *Obsolete name for* instruction or statement, i.e. the elementary unit from which a program is built up.

command control program A program that controls some piece of equipment, especially in the military context. (*JOVIAL is described as a command-and-control language.) Such programs are now more usually called *embedded systems.

command language *Another name for* job-control language.

comment Part of a program text included for the benefit of the reader and ignored by the compiler. Each language has its own syntax for comments, usually a form of bracketing, e.g.

{.....} in Pascal,
/*.....*/ in PL/I

Some languages, including Ada, prefer "end-of-line" comments, which are introduced by a characteristic symbol and are automatically terminated at the end of a line. Older languages such as BASIC and FORTRAN restrict comments to be whole lines and do not allow them to be appended to a line of code.

COMMON area In FORTRAN, an area of storage accessible from more than one program unit (subroutine). Data is local to the subroutine in which it is defined unless it is declared to be in a COMMON area. There is one anonymous COMMON area, called "blank COMMON", and any number of other areas, which are named ("labeled COMMON").

common carrier In the US, a private business or corporation that offers to the public general communication services such as telephone, teletype, or intercomputer communications. Common carriers are regulated by the Federal Communications Commission (FCC), and all services offered must charge according to tariff schedules filed with and approved by the FCC.

communication channel *See* Shannon's model.

communication network *See* communication system, network.

communication processor A specialized *I/O processor that is used to control a number of communication lines and/or communication devices. These lines/devices operate slowly in comparison to computing speeds so that one communication processor is usually multiplexed across a large number of lines/devices. Communication processors are used for the handling of data (in *blocks, *packets, *messages, *datagrams, etc.) for purposes of protocol, error checking and correction, acknowledgment, and buffering. They are now (mostly) programmed computers; earlier generations tended to be less general wired-program systems.
Communication processors are sometimes called concentrators, transmission control units, or front-end processors.

communication server *Another name for* gateway. *See also* server.

communication subnetwork (subnet) The dedicated processors and *trunk circuits that are responsible for communication functions in a distributed network. *See* backbone network.
The term is sometimes used to refer to the communication circuits in a computer network, exclusive of any switching equipment.

communication system Any system whereby a source of information is enabled to convey that information, with due regard for efficiency and reliability, to a destination. Such a system may contain more than one source and/or more than one destination, in which case it is called a *communication network*. Communication systems are usually studied with *Shannon's model in mind.

communication theory The study of *communication systems through mathematical models of their operation. It is broadly divided into *information theory (the entropy formulation of sources and channels) and *coding theory (source coding and channel coding).

commutative group (abelian group) *See* group.

commutative law *See* commutative operation.

commutative operation Any *binary operation ∘ that satisfies the law

$$x \circ y = y \circ x$$

for all x and y in the domain of ∘. The law is known as the *commutative law*. The usual addition of integers is commutative but subtraction is not.

commutative ring *See* ring.

commutative semiring *See* semiring.

compaction 1. Any of a number of methods to reduce unused or unusable space in primary, secondary, or other memory. *See* memory compaction.
2. Removal of redundant data from a record. Many systems work with fixed-length records as a convenient method of handling files. This has the disadvantage that all records must be capable of holding the longest record, giving uneconomic use of storage. The fixed-length records can be processed (compacted) into a variable-length form. One method involves the removal of trailing spaces; another involves the replacement of long strings of identical characters by a *flag that indicates the occurrence of such a string, together with a count of the number of characters and a

single instance of the character. Compaction will require CPU time when the record is stored and again when it is unpacked to fixed-length form, but the consequent saving in storage may justify this.

comparator An electronic circuit that is capable of examining the magnitude of two input signals and producing outputs indicating whether one of these inputs is greater than, equal to, or less than the other. There are both analog and digital comparators.

comparison counting sort A sorting algorithm that stores, for each sortkey, the number of keys less than the given key. If N_j denotes the number of keys less than the *j*th key then (assuming that keys are unique) the *j*th record should be in position $N_j + 1$ in a file sorted into ascending order of the keys. This is a simple but inefficient algorithm.

compartmentalization (compartmentation) The process of keeping resources with differing access attributes in separate groupings.

compatibility 1. of hardware. The ability of a subsystem (e.g. memory) or an external device (e.g. terminal) to be substituted for the originally designated equipment. To designate that one manufacturer's hardware can be connected to another manufacturer's hardware, the terms *plug-to-plug compatible*, or *plug-compatible*, are used.
2. of software. The ability of a computer to directly execute program code that was compiled, assembled, or written in machine language for another computer. Generally this occurs for successive computers in a given manufacturer's line. Since later computers are usually more capable (i.e. have a larger instruction set and/or more memory), the ability to run the program of a less capable machine is usually called *upward compatibility*. *See also* portable, emulation.
3. of a new piece of software. The ability to reproduce the behavior of its predecessor, in particular to accept the same input formats.

compilation time The time at which a high-level language program is translated into some other representation, such as machine code, so that the program can subsequently be executed by some computer system. *Compare* run time.

compiler A program that translates high-level language into *absolute code, or sometimes into *assembly language. The input to the compiler (the source code) is a description of an algorithm or program in a problem-oriented language; its output (the object code) is an equivalent description of the algorithm in a machine-oriented language.

compiler-compiler A program that accepts the syntactic and semantic description of a programming language and generates a *compiler for that language. The syntax is expressed in *BNF or a derivative thereof, and must conform to the rules dictated by the parsing technique to be used in the generated compiler. The semantics of the language are usually described by associating a code-generation procedure with each syntactic construct, and arranging to call the procedure whenever the associated construct is recognized by the parser. Thus the user still has to design the run-time structures to be used, and decide how each syntactic construct is to be mapped into machine operations. Then he has to write the code-generating procedures. A compiler-compiler is therefore a useful tool to aid the compiler writer, but nothing more.

complement 1. of a *set, S, with respect to some universal set U. The set consisting of elements that are in U but not in S; it is usually denoted by S', $\sim S$, or $\bar{S}$. Formally,

$$S' = \{x \mid (x \in U) \text{ and } (x \notin S)\}$$

The process of taking complements is one of the basic operations that can be performed on sets.
The *set difference (or *relative complement*) of two sets S and T is the set of elements that are in S but not in T; it is usually written as $S - T$. Thus

$$S' = U - S$$

See also operations on sets.
2. *See* Boolean algebra.
3. of a *subgraph G', with vertices V' and edges E', of a *graph G, with vertices V and edges E. The subgraph consisting of the vertices V and the edges in E but not in E'.
4. *See* radix-minus-one complement. *See also* radix complement, complement number system.

complemented lattice A *lattice in which there are identity elements 0 and 1 and in which each element a has at least one complement b, i.e.

$$a \wedge b = 0 \quad \text{and} \quad a \vee b = 1$$

It will also be the case that b is a complement of a and that 0 and 1 are the complements of each other.

complement number system An alternative representation of numbers in a fixed-radix *number system. In a complement system each positive integer is represented in its usual form in the given radix system except that it is prefixed by at least one leading zero. Each negative number is then represented by the complement of the corresponding number. For example, in both the ten's complement system and the nine's complement system any number with leading digit 9 represents a negative number. *See also* radix complement, radix-minus-one complement.

complete graph A *graph G in which there is an edge joining every pair of distinct vertices; every vertex is adjacent to every other vertex. If G contains n vertices then the number of edges is

$$n(n - 1)/2$$

complete lattice (domain) A *set D on which there is a *partial ordering and in which every subset of D has both a least *upper bound and a greatest *lower bound in D. A *chain* is a *countable set

$$X = \{x_i | i = 0,1,2 \ldots\}$$

of elements of D with the property that

$$x_0 \sqsubseteq x_1 \sqsubseteq x_2 \sqsubseteq \ldots$$

where $\sqsubseteq$ is the partial ordering, sometimes called the *approximation relation*, underlying D.

complete tree Any tree constructed from a *full tree of depth k by deleting some of the leaf nodes and the arcs leading to them. In a complete binary tree, the deleted nodes are often constrained to be the rightmost terminal nodes.
The term is also sometimes used as a synonym for full tree.

complexity The "difficulty" of solving computational problems, measured in terms of some resource consumed during computation. The resource can be an abstract measure or something specific like space or time. The analysis of the complexity of computational problems is a very active area of research at present and has important practical applications. *See also* complexity classes, complexity measure.

complexity classes A way of grouping algorithms or computable functions according to their *complexity. Computable functions with the same *complexity measure are placed in the same complexity class; functions in the same class are equally difficult to compute (with respect to the measure).
The classification is characteristically done for *formal languages that can be recognized by *Turing machine programs. If L is a formal language that can be recognized by a deterministic Turing machine program M, and the time complexity (*see* complexity measure) for M is $T_M(n)$, then L is classified according to the nature of $T_M(n)$. If $T_M(n)$ is bounded

(polynomially or exponentially) then there exists a bounding function $S(n)$ such that

$$T_M(n) \leqslant S(n)$$

For a particular function $S(n)$ there is consequently a class of languages for which the above bound holds. This class is denoted by

$$\text{DTIME}(S(n))$$

Thus DTIME($S(n)$) is the class of languages recognizable within time $S(n)$.
There is a similar definition of a class of languages

$$\text{DSPACE}(S(n))$$

in terms of the space complexity (*see* complexity measure).
There are various known relations between complexity classes. For example, if for two bounding functions S_1 and S_2

$$\lim_{n \to \infty} S_1(n)/S_2(n) = 0$$

then there is a language in DSPACE($S_2(n)$) that is not in DSPACE($S_1(n)$). Note that this applies if S_1 is polynomial and S_2 is exponential. There are similar results for time complexity classes.
It can be shown that the class of languages with exponential bounding functions is the union of an infinite set of languages with polynomial bounding functions. If p is any polynomial then *exponential time* and *exponential space* are the union of the complexity classes

$$\text{DTIME}(2^{p(n)})$$
$$\text{DSPACE}(2^{p(n)})$$

respectively, for all nonnegative integers n.
Complexity classes can also be defined for nondeterministic *Turing machine programs. Thus a language L is in

$$\text{NSPACE}(S(n))$$

if there is some nondeterministic Turing machine program that recognizes L and such that on an input string of length n none of the possible computations uses more than $S(n)$ tape squares. Time complexity classes,

NTIME,

can be similarly defined. It is known for example that

$$\text{NSPACE}(S(n) \subseteq \text{DSPACE}(S(n)^2)$$

complexity function (work function) If A is an algorithm for solving a particular class of problems and n is a measure of the size of a particular problem in this class, then $f_A(n)$, the complexity function, is that function of n giving an upper bound on the maximum number of basic operations that algorithm A has to perform to solve any problem of size n. For example, n might be the number of records in a file and $f_A(n)$ the maximum number of comparisons required to sort the file. *See also* complexity measure.

complexity measure A means of measuring the resources used during a computation. During any Turing machine computation various resources will be used, e.g. space and time. These can be defined formally as follows.
Given a Turing machine program M and an input string x, then Time(M,x) is defined as the number of steps in the computation of M on x before M halts. Time is undefined (i.e. equals infinity) if M does not halt on x. The *time complexity* of M is defined to be the integer function T_M where

$$T_M(n) = \max(\text{Time}(M,x): |x| = n)$$

for nonnegative integer n.
Space(M,x) is similarly defined as the number of tape squares used by M on x, and the *space complexity* S_M is defined by

$$S_M(n) = \max(\text{Space}(M,x): |x| = n)$$

However, in order to distinguish the space required for working as opposed to the space for the input string x, the machine is sometimes considered as having a read-only input tape, and Space(M,x) is defined as the number of writeable squares used by M on x.
It is also possible to define more general measures of complexity that share many of the common properties of time and space (*see* Blum's axioms).

An algorithm for which the complexity measure $T_M(n)$ or $S_M(n)$ increases with n no more rapidly than a polynomial in n is said to be *polynomially bounded*; one in which it grows exponentially is said to be *exponentially bounded*. Note that both these cases imply that the algorithm terminates.
See also complexity classes.

composition 1. (relative product) A method of combining *functions in a serial manner. The composition of two functions

$$f : X \rightarrow Y \text{ and } g : Y \rightarrow Z$$

is the function

$$h : X \rightarrow Z$$

with the property that

$$h(x) = g(f(x))$$

This is usually written as $g \circ f$. The process of performing composition is an *operation between functions of suitable kinds. It is *associative, and *identity functions fulfill the role of units.
If R denotes the set of real numbers and

$$f : R \rightarrow R, f(x) = \sin(x)$$
$$g : R \rightarrow R, g(x) = x^2 + 3$$

then $f \circ g$ is the function h:

$$h : R \rightarrow R, h(x) = \sin(x^2 + 3)$$

The idea of composition of functions can be extended to functions of several variables.
2. A subdivision of a positive integer n into parts $a_1, a_2, \ldots a_k$ in which the ordering is significant and in which

$$n = a_1 + a_2 + \ \ldots \ + a_k$$

where each a_i is a positive integer. It is thus similar to a partition (*see* covering) but in a partition the ordering is not significant. In general the number of compositions of n is 2^{n-1}.

composition table *See* Cayley table.

compression coding *Another name for* source coding.

computability *See* effective computability.

computable (Turing computable) *See* Turing machine, effective computability.

computable function A *function f, say, for which there exists an algorithm for evaluating $f(x)$ for any element x in the domain of f.

computational psychology A discipline lying across the border of *artificial intelligence and psychology. It is concerned with building computer models of human cognitive processes and is based on an analogy between the human mind and computer programs. The brain and computer are viewed as general-purpose symbol-manipulation systems, capable of supporting software processes, but no analogy is drawn at a hardware level. *Compare* cybernetics.

computer A device or system that is capable of carrying out a sequence of operations in a distinctly and explicitly defined manner. The operations are frequently numerical computations or data manipulations but also include input/output; the operations within the sequence may depend on particular data values. The definition of the sequence is called the program. A computer can have either a *stored program or *wired program. A stored program may exist in an alterable (*read-write or *RAM) memory or in a nonalterable (*ROM) memory. *See also* digital computer, analog computer.

computer-aided design (CAD) The application of computer technology to the design of a product, or the design itself. A computer-aided design uses as inputs both the appropriate technical knowledge of individuals who enter design criteria, edit results, and otherwise test and modify the design, and also accumulated information from libraries of standards for components, element sizes, regulations, etc., e.g. standard ICs for a digital design system, standard pipe lengths and fittings for a hydraulic or piping system.
Processing of the data from the inputs takes place in at least two phases:
(a) certain interactive programs are invoked by the technical designer during the

design process, these results being generally displayed on a VDU;
(b) programs are applied that may take considerable periods of running time to analyze tolerances, clearances, electrical characteristics, etc., the results of these runs being displayed back to the technical designer.
Output from a computer-aided design system consists of printouts of specifications and other information, and machine-readable files that are passed to *computer-aided manufacturing (CAM) systems and *computer-aided testing (CAT) systems. Examples of output to a CAM system are computer-produced artwork for printed circuit boards, or computer-produced tapes for automatic component insertion and board drilling.

computer-aided instruction (CAI) The original term for on-line use of a computer to administer instruction directly to one or more people. In many areas CAI has come to mean computer-based drill and practice; in other areas any computer-based tutorial, particularly one aimed at teaching the use of a particular computer or program, is referred to as CAI. *See also* computer-managed instruction, computer-based learning.

computer-aided manufacturing (CAM) A set of techniques which integrate various subtechniques that can be used in computer control or *process control for various forms of manufacturing. Computer-aided manufacturing implies the integration of all aspects of manufacturing systems within the factory, i.e. the use of computer techniques not only for process control but also for aspects such as automatic ordering of materials, predicting material usage, factory scheduling, inventory control, predicting machine changeover, and projecting manpower requirements. Computer-aided manufacturing is particularly important as it follows naturally from *computer-aided design. *See also* numerical control, computer-aided testing.

computer-aided testing (CAT) The application of computers to control either analog or digital test techniques to evaluate the quality of components and products. Computer-aided testing is used to check that the component parts, subassemblies, and full systems are within specified tolerances and also perform up to specification. Note that performance to specification may require that the unit or system operates under stressful conditions that would not be encountered in normal use. The parameters (test criteria) for computer-aided testing are often derived from *computer-aided design and *computer-aided manufacturing systems.

computer architecture *See* architecture.

computer-assisted instruction (CAI) *See* computer-aided instruction.

computer-based learning (CBL) Any use of computers to aid, define, or support any process involving human learning. It can include computer-based drill (use of repeated exercises), practice, and testing, as well as the use of computers to create a simulated environment that the student may explore. *See also* computer-managed instruction, computer-aided instruction.

computer family A group of (digital) computers that are successive generations of a particular computer system. They will tend to have similar but not identical *architectures.

computer graphics A mode of computer processing and output in which a significant part of the output information is in pictorial form. The information may range from a simple histogram or other plot of information to a complex map or engineering design annotated with alphanumerics and displayed in color. The output may be via a visual display terminal or as a permanent record via a printer/plotter or xy recorder. Suitable input devices include *data tablets and *light pens. The computer can be made to manipulate the information, e.g. straighten lines, move or

delete designated areas, expand or contract details, etc. (*see* windowing).
Probably the first successful graphics system was *Sketchpad*, an interactive system devised by Ivan Sutherland at MIT Lincoln Laboratory and published in 1963.

computer logic The basic organization, design, and wiring used to realize a particular computer *architecture. Someone involved with computer logic is therefore concerned with the design of building blocks or components, both logical and physical, and with the logic design involved in realizing a particular set of machine-code instructions; this may include the provision of facilities such as *microprogramming whereby the set of basic instructions can be altered.

computer mail *See* electronic mail.

computer-managed instruction (CMI) The use of computers (usually off-line) to produce lesson prescriptions based on student history and test performance. Components comprising each lesson unit are selected in accordance with learners' needs, as indicated by test performance on previous units, academic history, etc.

computer manager *See* data-processing manager.

computer network A *data network with computers at one or more of the nodes.

computer power A figure-of-merit for a computer system, sometimes defined in terms of performing a specific set of computations. It is described/measured by a number of methods: *add-subtract time, *cycle time, *throughput, and the results of *benchmarks are among the most common ones.

computer science The study of computers, their underlying principles and use. It comprises topics such as: programming, information structures; software engineering; programming languages; compilers and operating systems; hardware design and testing; computer system architecture; computer networks and interfacing; systems analysis and design; theories of information, systems, and computation; applicable mathematics and electronics; computing techniques (e.g. graphics, simulation, artificial intelligence techniques); applications; social, economic, organizational, political, legal, and historical aspects of computing.
It is not a science in the strict sense of being a discipline employing scientific method to explain phenomena in nature or society (though it has connections with physics, psychology, and behavioral science), but rather in the looser sense of being a systematic body of knowledge with a foundation of theory. Since however it is ultimately concerned with practical problems concerning the design and construction of useful systems, within constraints of cost and acceptability, it is far more a branch of engineering than it is a science.
Note that other branches of engineering have their theoretical foundations in separately named disciplines such as physics or chemistry; computer science, on the other hand, embraces both theoretical foundations and practical engineering. This idea that engineering can apply to the design and construction of mostly abstract (software) systems is new, and one that is not yet widely accepted.

computer-services manager *See* data-processing manager.

computer word *See* word.

concatenated code The effective compound code (comprising an inner code followed by an outer code) employed in a *concatenated coding system, or a code designed for use in such a system, either as the inner code or as the outer code.

concatenated coding systems *Communication systems in which messages are encoded by means of an *inner code* before being passed through a channel and then being decoded according to the inner

code; this entire inner encoder-channel-decoder system is itself regarded as a channel (it is hoped less noisy than the original channel), and therefore has a further encoder and decoder placed before and after it; these implement an *outer code*. Alternatively, such a system may be considered as a channel with a compound encoder before it and a compound decoder after it, the compound encoder and decoder implementing a *factorable code.
To a good approximation, the inner code should be designed to correct any *channel errors arising in the original channel, while the outer code should be designed to cope with decoder errors occurring in the inner decoder. Since these decoder errors tend to occur in bursts, the outer code is usually a burst-error-correcting code: the *Reed–Solomon codes are often used for this purpose. The inner code is often a *convolutional code.

concatenation of the *strings $u = a_1 \ldots a_m$ and $v = b_1 \ldots b_n$. The string

$$a_1 \ldots a_m b_1 \ldots b_n$$

It is variously denoted by

$$uv,\ u + v,\ u \,||\, v,\ u \,\&\, v$$

Concatenation is an *associative operation.
In *formal language theory, if u and v are two Σ-words (*see* word), their concatenation, uv, given as above, will also be a Σ-word. If Λ is the empty *word then for a word w

$$\Lambda w = w = w\Lambda$$

Since concatenation is associative, the set of all Σ-words, Σ*, forms a *monoid under concatenation, with identity Λ; this is the free monoid over Σ.
The concatenation of two sets of strings, say two languages, L_1 and L_2, is the set of strings L_1L_2 (a language) formed by the pairwise concatenation of elements of L_1 with L_2:

$$L_1L_2 = \{w_1w_2 \mid w_1 \in L_1,\ w_2 \in L_2\}$$

This also gives monoid structure – the identity is $\{\Lambda\}$.

concatenation closure *Another name for* Kleene star.

concentrator A communication device that combines input lines whose total *bandwidth is higher than that of the output line; the process is known as *concentrating* or *concentration*. A concentrator is used when the actual traffic of each of the input lines is below its potential traffic. It is possible for the concentrator to become overloaded and to lose data. A common method used by concentrators to combine (multiplex) the input lines is asynchronous *time division multiplexing. *See also* communication processor.

concurrency The progressing of two or more activities (processes, programs) in parallel. It is a term that describes the general topic of parallelism in computer systems, specifically *multiprocessing systems. Specification of concurrency, and the consequent problems of *interlock and *synchronization, requires special features in the programming language, and is a feature of the class of *real-time languages.
The usual method of describing parallelism is *Flynn's classification*, which does so in terms of parallelism in the *instruction stream and in the *data stream of a system. Thus there are four categories:
SISD, single instruction, single data;
SIMD, single instruction, multiple data;
MISD, multiple instruction, single data;
MIMD, multiple instruction, multiple data.
The first of these, *SISD*, is the conventional serial processor. The third of these, *MISD*, does not really occur in current systems. The other two are of most interest in multiprocessor systems. The *SIMD* is suited to operating upon data of the sort that exists in vectors and matrices by taking advantage of the inherent parallelism in that data. Thus the *array processor is one such system. Another is represented by the *supercomputer with parallel and different arithmetic units that *overlap

arithmetic operations. The *MIMD* system represents a wide range of architectures from the large symmetrical multiprocessor system to the small asymmetrical minicomputer/DMA channel combination.

concurrent programming A near-synonym for *parallel processing. The term is used both to describe the act of creating a program that contains sections to be executed in parallel as well as its subsequent execution.

condensation *See* connected graph.

P	F	F	T	T
Q	F	T	F	T
$P \longrightarrow Q$	T	T	F	T

Truth table for conditional

conditional A logic statement of the form

$$P \rightarrow Q \text{ or } P \supset Q, P \Rightarrow Q$$

that should be read as "if P is true then Q follows", although its meaning in logic only partly resembles its usage in English (*see* table).

conditional branch instruction A *branch instruction that is effective only if a specified condition holds, e.g. specified register contents zero, nonzero, negative, etc.

conditional transfer *Another name for* conditional branch instruction.

condition number A number that gives a measure of how sensitive the solution of a problem is to changes in the data. In practice such numbers are often difficult to compute; even so they can play an important part in comparing algorithms. They have a particularly important role in *numerical linear algebra. As an example, for the *linear algebraic equations

$$\boldsymbol{Ax} = \boldsymbol{b},$$

if $\boldsymbol{b}$ is changed to $\boldsymbol{b} + \Delta\boldsymbol{b}$ (simulating, for example, errors in the data) then the corresponding change $\Delta\boldsymbol{x}$ in the solution satisfies

$$\frac{\|\Delta \boldsymbol{x}\|}{\|\boldsymbol{x}\|} \leqslant \text{cond}(A)\, \frac{\|\Delta \boldsymbol{b}\|}{\|\boldsymbol{b}\|}$$

where $\text{cond}(A) = \|A\|\,\|A^{-1}\|$ is the condition number of A with respect to solving linear equations. The expression bounds the relative change in the solution in terms of the relative change in the data $\boldsymbol{b}$. The actual quantities are measured in terms of a vector norm (*see* approximation theory). Similarly the condition number is expressed in terms of a corresponding matrix norm. It can be shown that $\text{cond}(A) \geqslant 1$. If $\text{cond}(A)$ is large the problem is said to be *ill-conditioned* and it follows that a small relative change in $\boldsymbol{b}$ can lead to a large relative change in the solution $\boldsymbol{x}$; this means that any precision in the solution is spurious.

confidence interval A range of values about a *parameter estimate such that the *probability that the true value of the parameter lies within the range is some fixed value, α, known as the *confidence level.* The upper and lower limits of the range are known as *confidence limits*. Confidence limits are calculated from the theoretical *frequency distribution of the estimating function. The concept may be generalized to several parameters. A *confidence region* at level α contains the true values of the parameters with probability α.

configuration The particular hardware elements and their interconnection in a computer system for a particular period of operation. *See also* reconfiguration.

configuration management Ensuring throughout its lifetime that a product put to some usage is properly constituted for that usage – e.g. that the correct procedures have been followed in creating the product, that the appropriate version of each individual component has been selected, that any required tests have been performed, that the product represents a complete and consistent whole, and that all known problems in any way pertinent to the product have been properly considered. As an illustration, a relatively simple configuration management activity might ensure that the individual components of a software system are the appropriate ones for the particular hardware on which the system is to run. A rather more complex activity might be to assess the impact on all software systems of a newly discovered problem with some version of a compiler, and to initiate any necessary corrective action.

The problems of configuration management can be complex and subtle, and for many projects effective configuration management can be crucial to overall success. Approaches to configuration management fall into two broad classes. One approach attempts to retain control over the product as it evolves, so that configuration management is viewed as a continuous activity that is an integral part of product development. The other approach views configuration management as a separate activity; it is a distinct milestone when the product is first placed under configuration management, and each new revision of the product is subject to the configuration management process, but configuration controls are not imposed during periods of development.

configured-in, -off, -out Terms used to detail the *configuration of a system, or changes (*reconfigurations) therein.

confluent *See* Church–Rosser theorem.

congruence relation 1. An equivalence relation defined on the integers in the following manner. Let m be some given but fixed positive integer and let a and b be arbitrary integers. Then a is congruent to b modulo m if and only if $(a - b)$ is divisible by m. It is customary to write this as

$$a \equiv b \text{ (modulo } m)$$

One of the most important uses of the congruence relation in computing is in generating random integers. A sequence

$$s_0, s_1, s_2, \ldots$$

of integers between 0 and $(m - 1)$ inclusive can be generated by the relation

$$s_{n+1} \equiv as_n + c \text{ (modulo } m)$$

The values of a, c, and m must be suitably chosen.

2. An *equivalence relation R (defined on a set S on which a *binary operation $\circ$ is defined) with the property that whenever

$$x\,R\,u \quad \text{and} \quad y\,R\,v$$
$$\text{then } (x \circ y)\,R\,(u \circ v)$$

This is often referred to as the *substitution property*. Congruence relations can be defined for such *algebraic structures as certain kinds of *algebras, *automata, *groups, *monoids, and for the integers; the latter is the congruence modulo m of def. 1.

conjunction A logical expression of the form

$$a_1 \wedge a_2 \wedge \ \ldots \ \wedge a_n$$

where $\wedge$ is the *AND operation. A particular conjunction of interest is the *conjunctive normal form* (*CNF*) of a Boolean expression involving n variables, $x_1, x_2, \ldots, x_n$. Each a_i is of the form

$$(y_1 \vee y_2 \vee \ \ldots \ \vee y_n)$$

where $\vee$ is the *OR operation and y_i is equal to x_i or the complement of x_i. Reducing expressions to conjunctive normal form provides a ready method of determining the *equivalence of two Boolean expressions. *See also* propositional calculus. *Compare* disjunction.

conjunctive normal form (CNF) *See* conjunction.

connected graph A *graph in which there is a *path joining each pair of vertices, the graph being undirected. It is always possible to travel in a connected graph between one vertex and any other; no vertex is isolated. If a graph is not connected it will consist of several components, each of which is connected; such a graph is said to be *disconnected*.

If a graph G has e edges, v vertices, and p components, the *rank* of G, written $\rho(G)$, is defined to be

$$v - p$$

The *nullity* of G, written $\mu(G)$, is

$$e - v + p$$

$$\text{Thus } \rho(G) + \mu(G) = e$$

With reference to a directed *graph, a *weakly connected graph* is one in which the direction of each edge must be removed before the graph can be connected in the manner described above. If however there is a directed path between each pair of vertices u and v and another directed path from v back to u, the directed graph is *strongly connected.*

More formally, let G be a directed graph with vertices V and edges E. The set V can be partitioned into *equivalence classes $V_1, V_2, \ldots$ under the relation that vertices u and v are equivalent iff there is a path from u to v and another from v to u. Let $E_1, E_2, \ldots$ be the sets of edges connecting vertices within $V_1, V_2, \ldots$ Then each of the graphs G_i with vertices V_i and edges E_i is a *strongly connected component* of G. A strongly connected graph has precisely one strongly connected component.

The process of replacing each of the strongly connected components of a directed graph by a single vertex is known as *condensation.*

connectedness A measure of the extent to which a given graph is *connected. An undirected graph is k-connected if for every pair of vertices u and v there are at least k paths between u and v such that no vertex other than u and v themselves appear on more than one path. A *connected graph is 1-connected, a *biconnected graph is 2-connected.

connective A logical device used for the construction of more complex statements or expressions from simpler statements or expressions. Examples in everyday use are "and", "or", and "not". Connectives also occur in *Boolean algebra, *switching theory, *digital design, *formal logic, and in *programming languages. In all these cases they are used, often as operators, in the formation of more complex logical or Boolean expressions or statements from simpler components. These simpler components inevitably have a value that is either true or false. *Truth tables describe the effect or result of using a connective, given the truth of the simpler components.

connectivity of a *graph G. The minimum number of vertices (and associated edges) of G whose removal from G results either in a graph that is no longer *connected or in a trivial graph with a single vertex: at least k vertices must be removed from a graph with *k-connectivity*. The higher the connectivity the more edges there are joining vertices.

The quantity described above is sometimes called the *vertex connectivity* to distinguish it from the *edge connectivity*, which by analogy is the minimum number of edges whose removal from G results in a graph that is disconnected or trivial.

connectivity matrix *Another name for* adjacency matrix.

consistency A term that is usually used in the context of numerical methods for ordinary and partial differential equations. A formula derived from a *discretization is consistent if the local *discretization error has *order at least two with respect to the stepsize, h. Consistency is a necessary condition for convergence of a discretization formula (*see* error analysis).

console The workstation from which the operation of a computer system can be monitored and controlled. In current systems the console is usually a desk-height surface supporting a keyboard and one or more VDUs and reference documents. There may also be a number of other switches and indicators mounted on a panel. In early systems the control unit at the console was often a teleprinter. As systems became larger and more sophisticated the consoles first became more complex and then much simpler as the development of operating systems advanced. Some recent medium-sized systems do not have a console.

constant 1. A value that does not change. **2.** A value that is determined by its denotation, i.e. a *literal.

construct *See* language construct.

consumable resource Any resource that is, by its nature, usable on only a limited number of occasions. A punched card can only be punched once, although it may be read repeatedly, and must be regarded as consumable. *Compare* reusable resource.

contact bounce *See* debouncing.

content-addressable memory (CAM) *Another name for* associative memory. *See also* associative addressing.

context-free grammar A *grammar in which the left-hand side of each production is a single nonterminal, i.e. productions have the form

$$A \rightarrow \alpha$$

where α is a string of terminals and/or nonterminals. For brevity one writes

$$A \rightarrow \alpha_1 \mid \alpha_2 \mid .. .. \mid \alpha_n$$

to indicate the separate productions

$$A \rightarrow \alpha_1, A \rightarrow \alpha_2, .., .., A \rightarrow \alpha_n$$

As an example, the following generates a simple class of arithmetic expressions typified by $(a + b) \times c$:

$E \rightarrow T \mid T + E \mid (E)$
$T \rightarrow E \mid E \times T \mid a \mid b \mid c$

The *BNF notation used in defining the syntax of programming languages is simply a context-free grammar. The term itself was coined to contrast with *context-sensitive grammar.

context-free language (algebraic language) Any formal language generated by a *context-free grammar or, from another viewpoint, any formal language recognized by a *pushdown automaton. It is also the frontier of a regular *tree language.

context-sensitive grammar A *grammar in which each production has the form

$$\alpha A \beta \rightarrow \alpha \gamma \beta$$

where A is a nonterminal and α, β, and γ are arbitrary *words with γ nonempty. If γ was allowed to be empty then any type 0 language of the *Chomsky hierarchy could be generated. To derive the empty word, a production

$$S \rightarrow \Lambda$$

must also be included, with S not occurring in the right-hand side of any production. The term context-sensitive refers to the fact that A can be rewritten to γ only in the "context" $\alpha \ldots \beta$.
In a *length-increasing grammar* each production has a right-hand side at least as long as its left-hand side (apart possibly from $S \rightarrow \Lambda$). Clearly any context-sensitive grammar is length-increasing, but it can also be shown that any length-increasing grammar is equivalent to a context-sensitive one. *Compare* context-free grammar.

context-sensitive language Any formal language generated by a *context-sensitive grammar, or recognized by a *linear-bounded automaton.

continuation An approach to solving a mathematical problem that involves solving a sequence of problems with different parameters; the parameters are selected so that ultimately the original problem is solved. An underlying assumption is that the solution depends continuously on the parameter. This approach is used for example on difficult problems in *nonlinear equations and *differential equations. For example, to solve the nonlinear equations

$$\mathbf{F}(\mathbf{x}) = \mathbf{0},$$

let $x^{(0)}$ be a first approximation to the solution. Let α be a parameter $0 \leqslant \alpha \leqslant 1$, then define the equations

$$\hat{\mathbf{F}}(\mathbf{x},\alpha) = \mathbf{F}(\mathbf{x}) + (\alpha - 1)\mathbf{F}(\mathbf{x}^{(0)}) = \mathbf{0}$$

For $\alpha = 0$, $\mathbf{x}^{(0)}$ is a solution;
for $\alpha = 1$,

$$\hat{\mathbf{F}}(\mathbf{x},1) = \mathbf{F}(\mathbf{x}) = \mathbf{0},$$

which are the original equations. Hence by solving the sequence of problems with α given by

$$0 = \alpha_0 < \alpha_1 < \ldots < \alpha_N = 1$$

the original problem is solved. As the calculation proceeds each solution can be used as a starting approximation for the next problem.

continuous signal, system *See* discrete and continuous systems.

contradiction *See* tautology.

contrapositive of a conditional, $P \rightarrow Q$. The statement

$$\neg Q \rightarrow \neg P$$

where $\neg$ denotes negation. The contrapositive of a conditional is therefore equivalent to the original conditional. *See also* converse, inverse.

control bus A *bus that is dedicated to the passing of control signals.

control character *See* character set.

control circuitry Electric circuits within a computer or peripheral that regulate its operation.

control cycle *Another name for* fetch-execute cycle.

Control Data Corporation *See* CDC.

control design The design of a *control unit. Control units were originally designed with *random logic; they are now almost always designed with *microprogramming.

controlled sharing Making used resources available to more than one using resource through an *access control mechanism.

controller A subsystem that governs the functions of attached devices but generally does not change the meaning of the data that may pass through it. The attached devices are usually peripherals or communication channels. One of the functions of the controller may involve processing the data stream in order to format it for transmission or recording.

control line A conductor in a multiwire interface that conveys a control signal.

control memory *Another name for* microprogram store.

control stack A stack mechanism that contains an instruction sequence. It is part of the control unit in a computer with stack architecture. *See* stack processing.

control structure A syntactic form in a language, used to specify flow of control in a program, e.g.
repeat ⟨statements⟩ until ⟨condition⟩.

control unit (CU) The portion of a *central processor that contains the necessary *registers, *counters, and other elements to provide the functionality required to control the movement of information between the memory, the *arithmetic and logic unit, and other portions of the machine.

In the simplest form of the classical von Neumann architecture, the control unit contains a *program counter, an *address register, and a register that contains and decodes the *operation code. The latter two registers are sometimes jointly called the *instruction register*. This control unit then operates in a two-step *fetch-execute* cycle. In the fetch step the instruction is obtained (fetched) from memory and the decoder determines the nature of the instruction. If it is a *memory reference instruction the execute step carries out the necessary operation(s) and memory reference(s). In some cases, e.g. a *nonmemory reference instruction, there may be no execute step. When the instruction calls for *indirect addressing, an additional step, usually called "defer", is required to obtain the indirect address from the memory.

In more complex machines and *non von Neumann architectures, the control unit may contain additional registers such as *index registers, arithmetic units to provide address modifications, registers, *stacks, or *pipelines to contain forthcoming instructions, and other functional units. At present, most control units are microprogrammed (*see* microprogramming). Some exceptions are found in control units that have become powerful and complex; in supercomputers, for example, they may contain specialized hardware that allows for parallel processing of instructions which are issued sequentially.

control word 1. A word whose contents determine actions elsewhere; it may be used to control the use of a resource.
2. A word in a microprogram. *See* microinstruction, microprogramming.

convergence *See* error analysis.

conversational mode *See* interactive.

converse 1. of a conditional, $P \rightarrow Q$. The statement

$$\neg P \rightarrow \neg Q$$

where $\neg$ denotes negation. *See also* contrapositive, inverse.
2. of a binary relation. *Another name for* inverse.

conversion Any of a number of methods of mapping data or programs from one format into another. An example for data would be changing a number from binary to decimal representation. An example for a program would be conversion from assembly language into machine language representation.

convolution Mathematically, the operation of combining two functions, w and f, to produce a third function, g, such that

$$g_k = \sum_{i=0}^{k} w_i f_{k-i}$$

(or the corresponding continuous operation). This is envisaged as a transformation of an input function f to an output function g, by viewing f through a fixed window w.
In coding theory, f is considered as a *signal and w as the response of a *linear channel; g is then the effect upon that signal (regarded as a sequence of successive elements) brought about by the time response of the linear channel. The *channel time response* is the sequence of successive elements output by the channel in response to a signal that has one element of unit amplitude and all other elements zero. The input signal sequence and the channel time response are said to be *convolved.*
The inverse process is *deconvolution*: the convolved output sequence can be *deconvolved* with the channel time response sequence to restore the original input signal sequence.
See also feedback register, feed-forward register.

convolutional code A *linear error-correcting code, characterized by a $k \times n$ generator matrix,

$$G = (g_{ij}[x]),$$

whose elements $g_{ij}[x]$ are *polynomials whose highest degree, m, is called the *memory* of the code. The quantity

$$c = m + 1$$

is called the *constraint length* of the code. The convolutional encoder operates as follows. The input stream, regarded as the coefficients of a polynomial of arbitrary degree, is cyclically distributed (i.e. demultiplexed) among the inputs of k *shift registers, all of length c: the contents of the ith shift register is serially multiplied by each of the n polynomials $g_{ij}[x]$ (using n serial multipliers in parallel). Then n output streams are formed by summing the outputs of the jth multiplier on each register. These streams are cyclically multiplexed to form the output of the encoder. All this can be carried out to base q, for q prime; such codes are usually implemented in binary form ($q = 2$). In practice, the parameter k is normally equal to 1.
The main decoding algorithms for convolutional codes are *Viterbi's algorithm* and various *sequential algorithms, of which the most important are *Fano's algorithm* and the *stack algorithm*. Viterbi's is a maximum-likelihood algorithm.
Linear *block codes can be regarded as a special case of convolutional codes with $m = 0$ and $c = 1$. Convolutional codes are often specified by the parameters (n, k) or (n, k, c), although the simple phrase (n, k) code usually specifies a block code rather than a convolutional code.

Convolutional codes are of increasing importance as they become better understood theoretically, as better decoding algorithms are found, and as it becomes increasingly economical to provide programmable decoders, the decoding algorithms being best programmed in software owing to their complexity.

coprocessor A microprocessing element designed to supplement the capabilities of the primary processor. For example, several microprocessor manufacturers now offer coprocessors in their product lines that offer expanded mathematical processing abilities, including high-speed floating-point arithmetic and computation of trigonometric functions. The coprocessor extends the set of instructions available to the programmer. When the main processor receives an instruction that it does not support, it can transfer control to a coprocessor that does.
The variety of functions that could be implemented in a coprocessor is unlimited, and more than one coprocessor could be used in a system if the primary processor has been suitably designed. For instance, one coprocessor could provide high-speed math processing and another could provide database management primitives. An example of a coprocessor is the Intel 8087, which is a math chip designed to work with both the 8-bit-bus 8088 and 16-bit-bus 8086 processors.

copy To produce a replica of some stored information in a different part of the store or on a different storage device. This is often done to guard against loss or corruption of important records.

copyright The right to prevent copying. It is a negative right that can be exercised by a copyright owner if he chooses. Copyright protects the form in which an idea is expressed but not the idea per se. Computer programs are considered to be protected under the law of copyright as literary works in most countries that have copyright legislation. Hence a set of instructions given to a personal computer is given the same protection in law as a book of recipes – the use of the recipe or the instructions is not copyright infringement but the owner of the copyright can prevent the unauthorized copying of the literary work. The mere taking of an idea embodied in a copyright work (such as the use of some algorithms discovered from studying the source code of a computer program) is not copyright infringement (*but see* trade secrets). Some computer software houses feel that the protection granted to computer programs by the law of copyright is not sufficient (*see* patents).

CORAL A programming language loosely based on *Algol 60 and developed in the UK for military applications. Although described as a real-time language, CORAL has no built-in facilities for parallel processing, synchronization, interrupt handling, etc. These necessary facilities have to be provided in machine code, and for this purpose CORAL provides a macro facility and a convenient escape to assembler level. The most widely used version of the language is CORAL 66. It is expected that the use of CORAL will decline with the advent of *Ada.

core store A type of nonvolatile memory in which binary information is stored in an array of toroidal magnetic cores. The cores are made of a *ferrite material that has two stable magnetic states and can be switched from one to the other by imposing a sufficient magnetic flux; the flux is generated by electric currents in conductors threaded through the cores. The principle of the core store was discovered in 1949 by J. W. Forrester of MIT. Although widely used as main storage for processors from the mid-1950s to the late 1970s, core store has been displaced in modern processor design by *semiconductor memory.

coroutine A program component that allows structuring of a program in an unusual way. A coroutine resembles a *sub-

routine, with one important difference. A subroutine has a subordinate position relative to the main routine: it is *called* and then *returns*. Coroutines, however, have a symmetric relation: each can call the other. Thus a coroutine is *resumed* at a point immediately following its call of another coroutine; it never returns, but terminates its operation by calling (resuming) another coroutine.
Coroutines are not commonly found in high-level languages. They are particularly useful as a means of modeling concurrent activity in a sequential machine.

corrective maintenance *Another name for* remedial maintenance.

correctness proof *See* program correctness proof.

correlation A measure of a tendency for two or more *random variables to be associated. The formula for r, the sample *correlation coefficient* between two variables x and y, is

$$\frac{\Sigma(x_i-\bar{x})(y_i-\bar{y})}{\surd[\Sigma(x_i-\bar{x})^2\,\Sigma(y_i-\bar{y})^2]}$$

which varies between -1 and $+1$. Negative values or r indicate that y tends to decrease as x increases, while positive values indicate that x and y increase or decrease together. If the value of r is zero then x and y are *uncorrelated*.
Rank correlation measures the correlation between the ranks (or order numbers) of the variables, i.e. between the positions when the numbers are arranged in increasing order of magnitude.
Correlation does not imply causation. Variables may be correlated accidentally, or because of joint association with other unmeasured agencies such as a general upward trend with time. If the relationship is not linear the correlation coefficient may be misleading.

coset of a *group G that possesses a *subgroup H. The *subset of G comprising those elements that are mapped into H. The coset is the set of all x in G such that

$$x \circ H = \{x \circ h \mid h \in H\}$$
$$H \circ x = \{h \circ x \mid h \in H\}$$

where $\circ$ is the binary operation defined on G. A subset of the former kind is called a *left coset* of G modulo H or a left coset of G in H; the latter is a *right coset*. In special cases

$$x \circ H = H \circ x$$

for any x in G. Then H is called a *normal subgroup* of G. Any subgroup of an abelian *group is a normal subgroup.
The cosets of G in H form a partition of the group G, each coset showing the same number of elements as H itself. These can be viewed as the *equivalence classes of a *left coset relation* defined on the elements g_1 and g_2 of G as follows:

$$g_1 \rho g_2 \text{ iff } g_1 \circ H = g_2 \circ H$$

Similarly a *right coset relation* can be defined. When H is a normal subgroup the coset relation becomes a *congruence relation.
Cosets have important applications in computer science, e.g. in the development of efficient codes needed in the transmission of information and in the design of fast adders.

coset relation *See* coset.

COSMOS *Another name for* CMOS.

cost function A scalar measure of a complex situation, used for optimization. *See also* weighted graph.

countable set A *set that, in some sense, is no larger than the set of natural numbers. The elements of the set can be put into order and counted. Such a set is either *finite or *denumerable*; the elements of a denumerable set can be placed in a one-to-one correspondence with the set of natural numbers. The set of rational numbers can be shown to be countable but the set of real numbers is not countable.

counter A clocked digital electronic device whose output takes up one and one only of a number, *n*, of distinct states upon the application of each clock pulse. The output thus reflects the total number of clock pulses received by the counter up to its maximum capacity, *n*. All *n* states are displayed sequentially for *n* active transitions of the clock, the sequence then repeating. Since *n* clock pulses are required to drive the output between any two identical states, counters provide a "divide-by-*n* action" and are thus also known as *dividers*.
A counter whose output is capable of displaying *n* discrete states before producing an overflow condition can also be called a *mod-n counter* (or *modulo-n counter*), since it may be considered to be counting input pulses to a base of *n*. The value of *n* is normally an integer power of 2. Counters are generally formed by a cascaded series of clocked *flip-flops (*see* cascadable counter), each of which provides a divide-by-two action. For a counter consisting of *m* flip-flops, the maximum capacity of the counter will be 2^m since 2^m discrete output states are possible, i.e. *n* is equal to 2^m. These are known as *binary counters*.
Count lengths of other than integer multiples of two are possible. For example, a *decade counter* (or mod-10 counter) exhibits 10 separate and distinct states. To achieve this digitally requires a counter having at least four individual flip-flop elements, giving 2^4 or 16 possible output states; six of these states are prevented from occurring by a suitable arrangement of logic gates around the individual flip-flops. In *multimode counters* the number, *n*, of distinct states can be selected by the user.
See also ripple counter, synchronous counter, shift counter.

counting problem **1.** The task of finding the number of elements of some set with a particular property. Such counting problems are usually encountered in *combinatorics.
2. The task of counting the number of solutions to a problem. For example, to find the number of *spanning trees of a given graph, there is a formula in terms of the determinant of a certain matrix that is computable in *polynomial time. There are however other problems, like counting the number of *Hamiltonian cycles in a given graph, that are expected to be difficult since determining whether or not a graph has a Hamiltonian cycle is NP-complete (*see* P=NP question). Although it is possible to determine whether or not a graph has a perfect *matching* (a set of edges that do not meet each other but meet every vertex) in polynomial time, computing the number of such matchings can be done in polynomial time only if ***P*=*NP***. Such a problem is called *#P-complete.* The matching problem referred to is, in the bipartite case, the same as computing the permanent of 0–1 matrix, for which no good methods are known.

coupled A rather vague term, used to indicate that systems which might operate separately are actually being used in some form of cooperative mode. The term is applied to hardware units, as in *cross coupled*, where a pair of inverting gates are used to form a *latch circuit: the output of each gate serves as an input to the other. It is also applied to complete processors, as in *loosely coupled* and *tightly coupled* processors: there are substantial discrepancies in usage between different users of these terms, especially with respect to the precise overtone associated with the qualifying adverb.

covariance A measure of the joint variation of two random variables, analogous to variance (*see* measures of variation). If the variables are *x* and *y* then the covariance of *x* and *y* is

$$\Sigma(x_i - \bar{x})(y_i - \bar{y})$$

The *analysis of covariance* is an extension of the *analysis of variance in which the variables to be tested are adjusted to take account of assumed linear relationships with other variables. *See also* correlation.

covering 1. of a *set S. A finite set of *subsets of S whose *union is just S itself. The subsets, $A_1, A_2, \ldots, A_m$, are said to cover S. If the elements A_i for $i = 1, 2, \ldots, m$ are mutually *disjoint, then the covering

$$\{A_1, \ldots A_m\}$$

is called a *partition* of S.

2. A relationship between two elements of a partially ordered set S. If x and y are elements of S then y covers x if and only if $x<y$, and whenever $x \leqslant z \leqslant y$ for some element z in S, then either $x = z$ or $z = y$.

CPL *Abbrev. for* combined programming language. A language developed in the early 1960s at the Universities of Cambridge and London in the UK. Its aim, rather unusual for the time, was to provide a single language for all applications on a new computer, including those areas at that time universally thought to be the province of assembly language. Although it never came into general use, CPL is noteworthy for the fact that it anticipated many of the concepts that are now regarded as characterizing modern "advanced" languages, notably the control structures of *structured programming and the reference concept that forms a major feature of Algol 68. CPL was the direct precursor of *BCPL and thus an ancestor of *C.

CP/M *Trademark* An operating system intended for use on microprocessor-based systems that support a single user at any one time. The system includes file maintenance, facilities for inspecting and updating the contents of memory, and access to an assembler and compilers.

cps *Abbrev. for* characters per second. A rate of processing or transferring information.

CPU *Abbrev. for* central processing unit. *See* central processor.

CPU cycle Usually, the time required for the fetching and execution of one simple (e.g. add or subtract) machine instruction. It is one of many figures-of-merit for a computer system. *See also* computer power, add-subtract time, cycle.

CPU time (processor time) The time for which a process has been receiving service from the processor. *See also* system accounting.

crash A system failure that requires at least operator intervention and often some maintenance before system running can resume. The word is also used as a verb. *See also* recovery.

Cray Research A company formed in 1972 by Seymour Cray at which a series of high-speed scientific computers have been developed, including Cray-1 and Cray-2.

CRC *Abbrev. for* cyclic redundancy check, or for cyclic redundancy code.

critical path method (CPM) A project planning, management, and scheduling method that divides a project into activities, each with a statement of time and resources required, and their precedence dependencies. These activities are then connected in a graph that expresses the dependencies and the times. The *critical path* is defined as the path through the graph that requires the maximum time. Variations of this method allow for statistically distributed time and resources, time/resource tradeoffs, etc.

critical region A section of code that may only be executed by one process at any one time. *See also* critical resource, critical section, mutual exclusion.

critical resource A resource that can only be in use by at most one process at any one time. A common example is a section of code that deals with the allocation or release of a shared resource, where it is imperative that no more than one process at a time is allowed to alter the data that

defines which processes have been allocated parts of the resource.
Where several asynchronous processes are required to coordinate their access to a critical resource, they do so by controlled access to a *semaphore. A process wishing to access the resource issues a P operation that inspects the value of the semaphore; the value indicates whether or not any other process has access to the critical resource. If some other process is using the resource then the process issuing the P operation will be suspended. A process issues a V operation when it has finished using the critical resource. The V operation can never cause suspension of the issuing process but by operating on the value of the semaphore may allow some other cooperating process to commence operation.

critical section Part of a process that must be executed indivisibly. Originally it was thought that the indivisibility had to be absolute. Now it is considered that it is only necessary for the critical section to be uninterrupted by other critical sections of a particular set of processes, i.e. those among which there is *mutual exclusion.

cross compiler A *compiler for a high-level language that runs on one machine, producing code for a different machine. It is frequently used to produce code for microcomputers that are themselves too small to support a compiler.

cross coupling An interconnection between two *logic gates, permitting them to form a *flip-flop.

cross talk A signal that has leaked or "crossed" from one communication channel to an adjacent channel. This interferes with (causes errors on) the second channel. Cross talk is usually associated with physical communication channels, such as an RS232 connection.

CRT *Abbrev. for* cathode-ray tube.

cryogenic memory A type of memory operating at a very low temperature, usually that of liquid helium (about 4 K), by means of superconductivity and electron tunneling. *See* Josephson technology.

cryptanalysis Determination of the plain text of an encrypted message by any means that does not make use of knowledge of the encryption key. *See* encryption. *See also* decryption, cryptography.

cryptographic transformation *See* cryptography.

cryptography The protection of a message by either of two encryption methods, *code* or *cipher*, that transform plain text to cipher text. The first of these involves a one for one substitution of a cipher text code group for a plain text code group. The list of these substitutions is called a *codebook*; the codebook must be kept secret in order to protect the information.
A cipher process involves changing the plain text into cipher text by means of a *cryptographic transformation*, usually in such a way that each bit, character, or word of plain text is replaced by a bit, character, or word of cipher text. The cryptographic transformation is accomplished by a specific algorithm or device, which is normally in two parts. The first part consists of a known description of the algorithm or device; the second part is a *key*, a set of data that is used to particularize the algorithm or device for a specific usage.
The transformation from cipher text to plain text is called *decryption.

cryptology The science that embraces both *cryptography, the protection of information by encryption, and *cryptanalysis, the undoing of that protection without knowledge of the key.

CSMA/CD A *data link control protocol applicable to a broadcast network in which all stations can receive all messages (*see* broadcasting). A station can detect the presence of a transmitted message by sensing the carrier of the transmission. When a station wishes to send a message,

it first waits until no other station is transmitting (*carrier sense multiple access, CSMA*). When two or more stations try to send messages concurrently, *collisions* may occur since a station will not see another station's signal until after it has begun its own transmission. A *collision detection (CD)* mechanism detects the collision, causing the stations to terminate their current transmissions and try again later.
The CSMA protocol was developed by DARPA for use in satellite transmission systems. Collision detection was not possible until after the colliding messages had been completely sent by the ground stations, and returned to them by the satellite. When many stations have messages to send, collisions occur with increasing frequency until saturation is reached and no useful messages get through. Other protocols must be used to ensure recovery in this situation.
CSMA and CSMA/CD are forms of asynchronous *time-division multiplexing.

cumulative distribution function *See* probability distributions.

current address register *Another name for* instruction counter.

current instruction register (CIR) A register, usually in the control unit, that contains the information specifying the instruction that is being (or is about to be) performed. *See also* instruction format.

curried function A *function of one variable that is related to a function of several variables. Let f be a function of two variables, x and y. Then by considering x constant we obtain a function in y; this function depends on the value of x. We write

$$g(x)(y) = f(x,y)$$

where g is called a curried version of f. Note that $g(x)$ denotes a function rather than a plain value. Currying is often used in theoretical work to deal simply with functions of several variables, e.g. in the lambda calculus.

cursor A symbol on a display screen that indicates the active position, e.g. the position at which the next character to be entered will be displayed. The underline symbol is often used: it is made to blink or flash so that it is easily noticed and can be distinguished from an underline that is part of the text. Other symbols, such as a frame around the character space, are also used.

cut set of a *connected graph G. A set of edges whose removal produces a disconnected graph; no set with fewer elements would produce this effect. *See also* connectivity.

cut vertex (articulation point) of a *connected graph G. A vertex of G whose removal together with the removal of all edges incident to it results in the remaining graph being disconnected. The term can also be extended and applied to more general graphs. Then the removal of a cut vertex and all arcs incident to it increases the number of connected components of the graph. *See also* connectivity.

cybernetics A discipline concerned with control and communication in animal and machine. Cybernetics attempts to build a general theory of such systems, independent of their makeup, which could, for example, be electronic, organic, or clockwork. *Compare* computational psychology.

CYCLADES An early experimental *packet-switching network in France. The first hosts were connected in 1973. CYCLADES was composed of two parts: the *host computers and the *communication subnet CIGALE. CIGALE was a pure *datagram network, delivering individual packets without any sequencing or flow control. The host computers were responsible for providing reliable connections on top of the datagram service. *Compare* RCP.

cycle 1. (cycle time) An interval of time in which one set of events or phenomena is

completed. It is usually the time required for one cycle of the memory system – the time between successive accesses – of a computer, and is sometimes considered to be a measure of *computer power.
2. Any set of operations that is repeated regularly and in the same sequence. The operations may be subject to variations on each repetition.
3. (circuit) of a *graph. A path that starts and ends at the same vertex. A cycle is said to be *simple* provided no edge appears more than once, and is *elementary* if no vertex (other than the start) appears more than once. *See also* Euler cycle, Hamiltonian cycle.
4. A *permutation of a set that maps some subset

$$T = \{t_1, t_2, \ldots, t_m\}$$

of S in such a way that each t_i is mapped into t_{i+1}

$$(i = 1, 2, \ldots, m-1)$$

and t_m is mapped into t_1; the remaining elements of S are left unaltered by the permutation. Two cycles

$$(u_1\ u_2\ \ldots) \text{ and } (v_1\ v_2\ \ldots)$$

are disjoint provided the sets

$$\{u_1, u_2, \ldots\} \text{ and } \{v_1, v_2, \ldots\}$$

are disjoint. Every permutation of a set can be expressed uniquely as the *composition of disjoint cycles.

cycle index polynomial A formal polynomial associated with a *group of *permutations on a set, indicating the decomposition of the permutations into *cycles. Such polynomials occur for example in *switching theory.

cycle stealing (data break) *See* direct memory access.

cycle time *See* cycle.

cyclic access A mode of access to stored information whereby access can only be achieved at certain times in a cycle of events. A magnetic disk is an example of a device with cyclic access.

cyclic code A *linear code in which, given that v is a codeword, then so are all the cyclic shifts of v. For example, if

abcde

is a codeword in a cyclic code, then

bcdea
cdeab
deabc
eabcd

are also codewords.

cyclic redundancy check (cyclic redundancy code; CRC) The most widely used *error-detecting code. Extra digits are appended to each *block in order to provide a means of checking the data for errors that may have occurred, say, during transmission or due to recording and readback processes: the digits are calculated from the contents of the block on input, and recalculated by the receiver or during readback.
A CRC is a type of *polynomial code. In principle, each block, regarded as a polynomial A, is multiplied in the encoder by a generating *polynomial G to form AG. This is affected during transmission or recording by the addition of an error polynomial E, to form

$$AG + E$$

In the decoder this is divided by the same generating polynomial G to give a residue, which is examined to see if it is zero. If it is nonzero, an error is recorded and appropriate action is taken (*see* backward error correction). In practice, the code is made *systematic by encoding A as

$$Ax^r + R$$

where r is the degree of G and R is the residue on dividing Ax^r by G. In either case, the only errors that escape detection are those for which E has G as a factor: the system designer chooses G to make this as unlikely as possible. Usually, in the binary case, G is the product of $(x + 1)$ and a primitive factor of suitable degree.
A binary code for which

$$G = x + 1$$

is known as a *simple parity check* (or *simple parity code*). When applied across each character of, say, a magnetic tape record, this is called a *horizontal check*; when applied along each track of the record, it is called a *vertical check*. Simple checks (horizontal and/or vertical) are much less secure against *burst errors than a nontrivial CRC with *G* of degree (typically) 16. The term *longitudinal redundancy check (LRC)* usually refers to a nontrivial CRC, but may apply to a simple vertical check.

cylinder *See* disk drive.

D

DAC *Abbrev. for* digital-to-analog (D/A) converter.

D/A converter (DAC) *Short for* digital-to-analog converter. A device, usually in integrated-circuit form, that can accept a digital signal in the form of an *n*-bit parallel data word and convert it into an equivalent continuous or analog representation. Digital output signals from, say, a microprocessor may thus be converted into a form that is suitable for driving analog devices such as motors, meters, or bar graphs. The *resolution* of a D/A converter is a measure of the change in analog output for a change of one least significant bit in the input. *See also* A/D converter.

daisychain (bused interface) A means of connecting a number of devices to a *controller, or, used as a verb, to connect by this means. A cable is connected from the controller to the nearest of the devices and then a separate cable connects the first unit to the second and the process is repeated as required. This allows a single connector on the controller to serve a variable number of devices. It also reduces cable cost and eases installation when several devices have to be connected. The IEEE 488 interface is suitable for this sort of connection.

Daisychain connection is also used as a means to prioritize I/O interrupts. In this application there is active logic at the points of interconnection to ensure that the priority accorded to a device is directly related to its place in the chain. The device nearest to the controller has highest priority.

daisywheel printer A type of *serial *impact printer in which the font is formed on the end of spring fingers that extend radially from a central hub. The font carrier can be likened to the flower of the daisy and the spring fingers are often referred to as *petals*. The font carrier is rotated by a servosystem until the correct character is opposite the printing position and a single hammer impacts it against the inked ribbon and paper. The carriage on which are mounted the font and hammer – and usually the ribbon – is then moved to the next printing position in the line.

The daisywheel printer was introduced by Diablo Systems Inc. in 1972 and represented a considerable improvement in speed and reduction in mechanical complexity compared to the *golfball and other typewriters that were used as low-speed printers at that time. The speed was initially 30 characters per second with a repertoire of 96 characters. Developments led to speeds of 65 cps for average text. In 1982 Diablo introduced a machine that can have up to 192 characters on the type wheel; by overprinting it is possible to form a further 250 characters. This development partially overcomes the disadvantage – relative to *matrix printers – of the limited character set. Other developments have led to lower-cost but slower (12–20 cps) units that are competitive with conventional and golfball typewriters.

The print quality achieved by the daisywheel printer is equal to that of very good typewriters and they are used on word-processor systems for producing letters and documents. The print head and paper position can generally be incremented bidirectionally by control commands. This allows the features associated with typesetting, such as proportional spacing, justification, subscript and superscript characters, etc., to be achieved.

DARPA Defense Advanced Research Projects Agency, originally ARPA, Advanced Research Projects Agency. An agency of the US Department of Defense responsible for research and technical development in areas where no single service (Army, Navy, Air Force, Marine Corps) has a clear jurisdiction or interest. It is perhaps most famous for the network technology development that led to the *ARPANET.

DASD *Abbrev. for* direct-access storage device.

data *Information that has been prepared, often in a particular format, for a specific purpose. In computing the word has three particular connotations.

First, data as distinct from program instructions. The word is used to refer to all the operands that a program handles, as for instance the values of the constants and variables involved, or a data file as opposed to a program file. The latter distinction, however, depends on the context: source language instructions serve as data for a compiler, and the resulting object code is data for a link loader; but when execution begins the same object code is now the program.

Second, in the context of an individual program or suite of programs, the word data may be used in a more restricted sense to mean the input, as opposed to results (output), as for instance in data preparation or data vetting. (Results from one process are however almost invariably data for a subsequent one.)

Third, and far more recently, data is now often spoken of as distinct from text, voice, and image – and likewise data processing as distinct from word processing, voice processing, and image processing. This usage focuses on the highly formatted nature of data in traditional data-processing applications, as opposed to the much freer structure of natural language text, voice communication, and visual images.

data abstraction The principle of defining a *data type in terms of the operations that apply to objects of the type, with the constraint that the values of such objects can be modified and observed only by use of these operations. This application of the general principle of *abstraction leads to the concept of an *abstract data type. Data abstraction is of very considerable importance in modern programming, especially for the coarse structuring of programs. Such use yields several benefits. The abstract data type provides a natural unit for specification and verification purposes (*see* module specification). It provides some basis for high-level design, and is consistent with the principles of *information hiding. The specification of the data type in terms of available operations provides all the information needed to make use of the data type while leaving maximum freedom of implementation, which indeed can be changed if required without affecting the users. There is also the possibility of developing a "library" of useful data abstractions – stacks, queues, etc.

The typical implementation of an abstract data type within a program is by means of a multiprocedure module. This module has local data that can be used to represent a value of the type, and each procedure implements one of the operations associated with the type. The local data of the module can only be accessed by these procedures, so that the user of the data type can only access the operations and has no direct access to the representation. The implementer is therefore free to choose the representation, which remains "invisible" to the users and can be changed if required. Each instance of the abstract data type employs one instance of the local data of the module to represent its value.

Proper support for such multiprocedure modules demands that the concept be recognized by the programming language, which must, for example, allow for the clustering of modules and data and have scope rules reflecting the desired restrictions on access. The first language to provide such support was SIMULA with its CLASS. Many modern languages now offer a similar facility, e.g. the MODULE of Modula and the PACKAGE of Ada.

data acquisition *Another name for* data capture and/or data collection.

data aggregate A record in a file containing totals derived by summing values from other records in the file. The totals usually have some sensible meaning. *Compare* hash total.

databank A repository for data, usually covering some specific topic.

database A collection of interrelated data values of such a nature that they might be represented as a number of *files but not a single file. Depending upon the nature of the *database management system, these files may be integrated permanently into a single connected structure or integrated temporarily for each interrogation, known as a *query*. In its most technical sense the word database implies that any of the data may be used as key information to specify queries. In more common usage the word often means any accessible collection of information, and in that case only a limited set of the data values may be used to specify queries. *See also* database system, database language, data dictionary.

database administrator A person who controls the data structure and content of a database. The internal structuring of a database necessarily implies that certain forms of *transaction will proceed more efficiently than others. Part of the role of the database administrator is to ensure that the processing proceeds efficiently for the forms of transaction that occur in his organization. He will also be responsible for incorporating new items of data into the database *schema at the appropriate places and with appropriate links.

database language A general term that covers a number of languages that together define a database management system, the most important being the *data description language, the *data manipulation language, the stored data structure language (*see* data description language), and the *query language. The form of these languages will vary with the *database management system itself. The term is often used loosely to mean the database management system – in the same way as the name of a programming language is used to mean the compiler.

database management system (DBMS) An integrated software system that has facilities for defining the logical and physical structure of data in a *database and for accessing, entering, and deleting data. Increasingly, formal methods are used for the description of the data format and semantics.

The most common forms of database management system have traditionally been separated into *hierarchical (e.g. IMS), *network (e.g. CODASYL), and *relational (e.g. SQL/DS). There is an essential distinction between the first two systems and the latter. The first two permit a *transaction to "navigate" through the data in the system, working through several stages, in order to reach the required records; the records are then extracted, amended, or deleted, as required. A relational system operates in a different way; criteria that identify the required records are specified at the start of the transaction and the operations are carried out on the specified records without further interaction.

database system 1. *Short for* database management system.

2. A database management system together with its database. A database system is a complex form of *associative (i.e. content-addressable) memory. The items of

data within the database are primarily linked together in units, sometimes also called records. Data is retrieved by the process of specifying the values of some data items and causing the system to retrieve the values of some or all of the data items of a unit (or units) *matching those specified. For example, given an employee number the system may retrieve the employee's salary, the two data items being linked in a payroll unit.

data break (cycle stealing) *See* direct memory access.

data bus (data path) A group of signal lines used to transmit data in parallel from one element of a computer to another. The number of lines in the group is the *width* of the data bus, each line being capable of transferring one bit of information. In a mainframe the width of the data bus is typically equal to the word length, i.e. 32, 48, or 64 bits. In a microcomputer the width is typically 4, 8, or 16 bits. The data bus used to interconnect LSI components need not have the same width as is used on the chips themselves. For example, a processor with an internal data bus width of 16 bits could be designed to transmit information over an 8-bit-wide external data bus. Such processors are said to use a multiplexed data bus (*see* multiplexed bus). The wider the data bus, the higher the potential performance of the system, since more information is transmitted in parallel with a wider data bus. Narrower data buses in general degrade performance but are less costly to implement. A multiplexed data bus is often chosen to reduce the number of pins needed on an integrated circuit for the data bus.

data capture A process for achieving the extraction of relevant data while the related transaction or operation is occurring. An example is a supermarket checkout equipped with point-of-sale terminals. The transaction is primarily concerned with the sale to the customer but while the purchased items are being entered onto the bill it is usual for the machine to record, and thus capture, data that will allow calculation of stock movement and other information.
If the equipment for data capture is online to a computer system, it is part of a *data collection process and may be referred to as either data capture or data collection equipment.

data cartridge A *magnetic tape cartridge, commonly the 3M-type cartridge.

data chaining Arranging the format and content of *blocks of data so that each block contains the address of the next block of data in a sequence for that file. The blocks of data do not have to occupy contiguous locations and thus may be written to any available locations on a storage system. A block of data can be a member of more than one chain. The personnel file of a company may for instance be chained by factory number, by alphabetical order in the company and department, by age, and possibly by other attributes such as skills. With this type of file organization it is possible to hold one file of information but access it either in one of the predetermined orders or by defining a common attribute. Each chain has a key or home record with the first address.

data channel An information route and associated circuitry that is used for the passing of data between systems or parts of systems. In an interface that has a number of parallel channels the channels are usually separately dedicated to the passing of a single type of information, e.g. data or control information.

data cleaning The action of removing format errors and keying errors from data, usually achieved by a *data-vet program.

data collection The process of collecting data from distributed points at which it has been captured or input as a separate operation. Generally the equipment used for the process is connected to a host computer via a communication system; sometimes portable equipment is carried to each site for information to be input into its memory and then the equipment – or a disconnectable module containing the memory – is connected to the host system. *See also* data capture.

data communication equipment *See* DCE.

data communications The collection and redistribution of information (data) through communication channels. Data communications may involve the transmission and reception of data in analog or digital form. *Data sources* originate data while *data sinks* receive it.

data compaction *See* compaction.

data compression Any of many methods in *information theory whereby data can be coded or recoded in order to take advantage of *redundancy in that data. In ordinary alphabetic text the data size can be reduced by a factor of from 2 to nearly 5 by the use of such methods.

data concentrator *See* concentrator.

data contamination The alteration, maliciously or accidentally, of data in a computer system. *See also* data integrity.

data definition language (DDL) A notation for defining the form and structure of data. It is usually part of a programming language, e.g. PICTURE specifications in COBOL.

data description language (DDL) Loosely, the section of a *database management system concerned with the specification of the logical structure of the data; specifically, the language used for that purpose. In early database systems little distinction was made between the logical and physical structure of the data, and the DDL usually contained information concerning both. It is becoming increasingly common for these two aspects to be separated, and for the DDL to be restricted to the logical structure while information concerning the physical data structure is contained in a *data structure language*.

data dictionary (data dictionary/directory; DD/D) A structured description of a *database. It contains descriptions of the entities in the database, as distinct from the raw data held in the database itself. A basic data dictionary will contain the various schemes that apply to the database, information on the mapping of the database onto physical storage, data validation rules, and rules used to check for authorized access to the database. This basic information concerning the database is sometimes termed a *directory*. A more comprehensive data dictionary will also include cross-reference information, showing, for example, which programs access which data or which departments within an organization receive which reports.
Because it contains all pertinent information on the nature of the data in the database and its use, the data dictionary is of vital importance in a complete database system. It allows the database administrator to retain overall control of a database that is evolving and is accessed by a changing set of programs. Since the data dictionary is itself normally treated as a database, it can be regarded as a database about a database.

data encryption The *encryption of a data stream. *See* cryptography.

Data Encryption Standard (DES) A particular cryptographic transformation that has been adopted by the US Government for the protection of sensitive material. *See* cryptography.

data entry The process in which an operator uses a keyboard or other device to input data directly into a system. The term is sometimes misapplied to the process of (a) *data capture, where the input of data to the system is not the prime objective of the related activity, and (b) *data preparation, where data is being encoded prior to being entered into the system.

Direct data entry (DDE) is an on-line process in which data is entered into a system and written into its on-line files. The data may be entered by an operator at a keyboard (this is the usual meaning) or by a data capture device. *Compare* key to tape, key to disk.

data file A *file containing data, as opposed to a *program file.

dataflow machine A computer in which the primitive operations are triggered by the availability of operands. In a classical *von Neumann machine, there is the concept of sequential flow of control, and an operation (instruction) is performed as and when flow of control reaches that operation. By contrast, in a dataflow machine there is a flow of data values from the operations that produce those values to the operations that "consume" those values as operands, and an operation is triggered as soon as all its operands are available. Since the result of one operation can be an operand to many other operations, and hence can potentially trigger many operations simultaneously, there is the possibility of a high degree of parallelism.
Dataflow machines represent one of the major examples of *non von Neumann architecture, and are of considerable research interest. Traditional *imperative programming languages, which prescribe a particular flow of control, are poorly suited to dataflow machines; they are usually programmed in a *single-assignment language or a *declarative language.

Data General A company founded by several former employees of Digital Equipment Corporation (DEC), the prime individual being Edson DeCastro, who was the designer of the DEC PDP-5 and PDP-8 families. The company manufactures minicomputers and peripherals, and is one of the main competitors to DEC. The Data General machines go under the names of Nova, Eclipse, and some newer models.

datagram 1. A self-contained package of data that carries enough information to be routed from source to destination independently of any previous and subsequent exchanges. A *datagram service* transports datagrams on a "best-effort" basis. There is a nonzero probability that any datagram will be lost or damaged before reaching its destination. The order in which datagrams are submitted by the source is not necessarily preserved upon delivery. In some networks there is the possibility that a datagram may be duplicated and delivered to the destination more than once.
2. *See* SADT.

data hierarchy The structuring of data into sets, subsets, subsubsets, etc., so that the basic structure of the data is hierarchical. This hierarchy may be present in the logical specification, the physical specification, or both. *See also* hierarchical database system.

data independence A term implying that processing is described without reference to the way in which the data is represented: some level of implementation has been hidden from higher levels so as to render programming and usage more simple. Thus modern database systems attempt to provide data independence between the logical records as seen by the user and the physical records as stored within the system.

data integrity Resistance to alteration by system errors of data stored in a computer. It is a condition that denotes only authorized and proper alteration of data. It is a measure of the reliability of data read from magnetic media, in terms of the absence of undetected errors (*see* error rate). However the undetected error rate perceived by the host system may be worse than that arising at the magnetic tape or disk if undetected errors can arise, e.g. from the effect of noise on connecting cables where the interface concerned has insufficient error detection capability.

From a system point of view the undetected error rate of a peripheral may be inadequate: the system can improve on it by making additional provision for checking in software.

data link A physical connection between two or more devices (called *nodes* or *stations*) by a communication channel that appears "wire-like", i.e. bits arrive in the order sent. Coaxial cables, telephone lines, optical fibers, lasers, and even satellite channels can be data links. Data links are assumed to be susceptible to noise (i.e. have error properties) and have finite data rate and nonzero propagation delay.

data link control protocol A communication *protocol that converts noisy (error-prone) *data links into communication channels free of transmission errors. Data is broken into *frames, each of which is protected by *checksum. Frames are retransmitted as many times as needed to accomplish correct transmission. A data link control protocol must prevent data loss caused by mismatched sending/receiving capacities. A *flow control procedure, usually a simple sliding *window mechanism, provides this function. Data link control protocols must provide *transparent data transfer. *Bit stuffing or byte stuffing strategies are used to mask control patterns that occur in the text being transmitted. Control frames are used to start/stop logical connections over links. *Addressing may be provided to support several *virtual connections on the same physical link.

data link layer of network protocol function. *See* seven-layer reference model.

data logging A procedure that involves recording all data and interactions that pass through a particular point in a system. The point chosen is usually part of a communication loop or a data path to or from a device such as a keyboard and display on which data is transitory. If a system failure or an unexpected result occurs it is possible to reconstruct the situation that existed. Such logs are not generally archived [illegible] can be overwritten once the associated job has been completed.

data management A term normally used to refer to systems that offer users an interface that screens them from the majority of the details of the physical handling of the files, leaving them free to concentrate on the logical properties of the data.

data management system *See* database management system.

data manipulation language (DML) Loosely, the section of a *database management system concerned with the storage, deletion, accessing, and amendment of data; specifically, the language used for that purpose. The DML is usually embedded within some programming language and is usually associated with the older *hierarchical or *network database systems. In the case of *relational systems, the DML is effectively replaced by a *query language (e.g. SQL) and this query language may itself be embedded within one or more programming languages.

data mark *See* address mark.

data matrix A rectangular array of data variables, which may be numerical, classificatory, or alphanumeric. The data matrix forms the input structure upon which statistical procedures for *regression analysis, *analysis of variance, *multivariate analysis, *cluster analysis, or survey analysis will operate.

data medium A material having defined properties, including a physical variable that can be used to represent data. The defined properties ensure that the medium is compatible with devices that can record or read data on the medium. Examples of data media are *magnetic tape, *magnetic disks, *paper tape, and *optical disks, and also paper used for printer output.

data model A term used in a variety of situations in connection with data storage at either a logical or physical level but usually the former. It normally implies a formally defined structure within which the data may be represented.

Data Module The name used by IBM to refer to their removable, hermetically sealed disk pack, incorporating the read/write heads and carriage assembly, that was used with the 3340 *Winchester technology disk drive. The term data module is now used more generally and is interchangeable with disk pack and storage module.

data name A symbolic name chosen by the programmer to identify a data object when using a high-level language.

data network A communication network that is devoted to carrying computer information, as opposed to voice, video, etc. It consists of a number of nodes (stations) connected by various communication channels (circuits).

Datapac A Canadian *public packet network, operated by the Trans-Canada Telephone System (TCTS). It uses *X.25 to interface to hosts and *X.75 to connect to other public networks. Datapac was one of the world's first operational public packet networks based on the international CCITT standards.

data path *Another name for* data bus, although often used in a wider context to mean any logical or physical connection between a source and destination of digital or analog information.

Datapoint A company that was originally a manufacturer of simple terminals for computing machines; these terminals were often referred to as *glass teletypes*. In the late 1960s Datapoint elected to build a programmable terminal and for this purpose designed a base machine. They approached Intel to determine if this machine could be put onto a single chip. This chip design was Intel's original 8-bit processor, the 8008. It was never used by Datapoint because, although it performed all the functional requirements, it was too slow for their first intelligent terminal. Datapoint today puts out a number of computers and intelligent terminals that can be netted together to form fairly complex data-processing equipment.

data preparation The process of converting data into a machine-readable form so that it can be entered into a system via an available input device. The operation of *keypunch or *key-to-tape machines are examples. These machines are not usually connected to the system, but even in the case of machines specifically adapted to allow connection they do not interact with the system in the course of preparation. The process is being superseded by direct *data entry systems and *data capture.

data processing (DP) A term used predominantly in the context of industrial, business, governmental, and other organizations: within that context it refers (a) to a class of computer applications, (b) to a function within the organization.
While it is hard to generalize, data-processing applications may be characterized as those that store and process large quantities of data on a routine basis, in order to be able to produce (regularly or on request) information that is predictably needed by an organization's employees, by its customers or suppliers, by government, or by any other organization. Typical applications within this category include financial accounting, cost and management accounting, market research and sales forecasting, order processing, investment analysis, financial modeling, stock control, production planning and control, transport planning and control, payroll, and personnel records. *COBOL is at present the programming language used for almost all data-processing applications. Data-processing systems are normally long-lived (apart from the need to redesign/rewrite them periodically, they may well last as long as the host organiza-

tion), and they handle data that is large in volume and complex in organization (which leads to a major concern for the problems and costs of data capture and storage).

The data-processing function within an organization is that department responsible for the development and operation of application systems (largely of the types listed above) on behalf of other parts of the organization. Its tasks normally include systems analysis and design, program development and maintenance, database administration, computer operation, data preparation, data control, and network management. The data-processing department may not, however, be responsible for all data-processing applications within an organization (this is a live issue with the current diffusion of microcomputers and small business systems throughout some companies), and conversely it may have responsibility for some applications that are not usually thought of as data processing (e.g. industrial process control).

The term is a rather unfortunate one since all computing could be regarded as the processing of data (in at least one of the senses of that word). It is certainly used in contexts other than the one described above: for instance, scientific data processing means the fairly straightfoward processing of large quantities of experimental results, and personal data processing means an individual's use of a microcomputer to keep personal records.

The term has never seriously been used to refer to any applications other than computer-based ones, but it was recognized that a lot of clerical and unit-record tasks could be described as data processing. In order to exclude this possibility, the terms *automatic data processing (ADP)* or *electronic data processing (EDP)* were coined, and can still occasionally be encountered. The term *integrated data processing (IDP)* had some limited use, mainly in the 1960s, as it became clear that much of an organization's data was common to separately developed systems, and the effort was made to integrate or rationalize them; that effort has mainly been diverted into the growth of *databases and *database management systems.

data-processing manager (DPM) The executive responsible for the *data processing function in an organization, i.e. for organizing, planning, and directing the DP service in accordance with directives laid down by top management, usually in management services, administration, or finance. The DPM will participate in the formulation of DP policy and strategy, and will be responsible for ensuring that the most cost-effective hardware and software is procured, that applications systems appropriate to the organization's needs are developed, and that staff in the department have the necessary levels of technical competence. The reporting level of the DPM to senior management can be a significant determinant of the degree of success of an organization in employing DP.

Since the DP function involves computers, there may be a *computer manager* or *computer-services manager* to be responsible for the specifically computer-related aspects of this function.

data protection legislation Legislation that has been or is being introduced all over the world to protect personal data handled in computers. The aim of the legislation is to control the immense potential for misuse of information that arises when personal data is stored in computers. Once the data has been transcribed from paper files into a form that is easily readable and accessible by computers, it is an inexpensive and easy task for the data to be extracted from one record and correlated with personal data concerning the same person from another file. This results in a synergistic combination of information that is considered to be an infringement of *privacy.

To combat the fear of misuse of data, governments have introduced legislation that, among other things, makes the following requirements of organizations that maintain personal records on computers:
to declare and/or register the use for which the data is stored;
to provide the data subject with a right of access to data concerning himself on their computers;
to maintain a prescribed minimum level of electronic and physical security in their computer installation;
not to transmit personal data to any organization that does not have similar controls over misuse of data.
This last requirement has lead to fears that countries without data protection legislation on their statute books are losing contracts for the processing of data, since countries with such legislation can refuse to permit the export of data to countries where data is not adequately protected. For this reason companies that consider that the data protection fears are not borne out by real instances of misuse of data are nonetheless pressing for legislation.
In Europe a convention concerning misuse of data has been signed by all member countries of the Council of Europe and this will come into force by the mid-1980s. The OECD (Organization for Economic Cooperation and Development) has also drafted a convention of similar effect. The US has a Privacy Act that deals with data stored by government agencies, but it is thought by some in the legal profession that for constitutional reasons the US could not legislate to prohibit misuse of data along the lines required by the OECD and Council of Europe conventions. The debate is rapidly getting more complicated: third world countries are now finding that data protection legislation may enable them to create a nontariff barrier around indigenous data processing companies, and hence the issues are moving out of civil rights and into economics.

data reduction The transformation of a large volume of data into a smaller amount. Typically the input data to a particular transformation process will be *raw data obtained from some sensor, and the output data will be produced by sampling or some simple analysis.

data retrieval The process by which data is selected and extracted from a file, a group of files, or a database, following a search of the file(s) for specified keys.

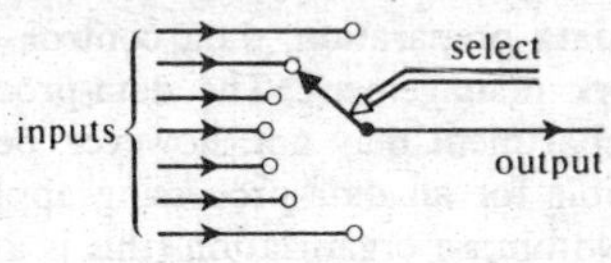

Data selector/multiplexer

data selector/multiplexer A logic circuit that may be considered as a single-pole multiway switch whose output is determined by the position of the switch wiper (*see* diagram). The wiper position is controlled by a select signal, normally digital, that indicates which of the inputs is to be connected to the output. In this way a number of channels of data may be placed sequentially on a time-shared output bus under the control of the select signal, a process known as *time-division multiplexing. Inputs to and outputs from a multiplexer may be in digital or analog form. *See also* decoder/demultiplexer.

data set 1. *Another name for* modem.
2. *Another name for* file.

data sheet A manufacturer's specification of the parameters of a device or integrated circuit, its functions, and its pin connections.

data sink *See* data communications.

data source *See* data communications.

data stream A sequence of data elements, often packed in some manner into a sequence of words having sizes different from the size of the data elements.

data structure (information structure) An aspect of *data type expressing the nature of values that are composite, i.e. not *atoms. The nonatomic values have constituent parts (which need not themselves be atoms), and the data structure expresses how constituents may be combined to form a compound value or selected from a compound value. Thus "date" regarded as a data structure is a set containing a member for every possible day, combined with operations to construct a date from its constituents – year, month, and day – and to select a desired constituent.
An implementation of a data structure involves both choosing a *storage structure and providing a set of procedures/functions that implement the appropriate operations using the chosen storage structure. Formally, a data structure is defined as a distinguished domain in an *abstract data type that specifies the structure. Computer solution of a real-world problem involves designing some ideal data structure, and then mapping this onto available data structures (e.g. *arrays, *records, *lists, *queues, and *trees) for the implementation.
Note that terms for data structures are used to denote both the structure and data having that structure.
See also dynamic data structure, static data structure.

data structure language *See* data description language.

data summarization *See* statistical methods.

data tablet A graphical input device that can generate digital signals (or in some cases analog signals) that represent the movement of a pen or pencil, frequently a specially adapted pen. The term was originally a tradename used by Sylvania to describe a product of this type, but it is now used generically. *See also* mouse.

data terminal equipment *See* DTE.

data transfer rate The rate at which data can be moved between devices. The average rate is determined by the capability of the read or write device but the instantaneous rate is determined by the capability of the interface or transmission path. *Buffer memories are used to achieve the change in rate. For typical magnetic tape operating at 800 bytes per inch and 75 inches per second the rate is about 60 kilobytes per second. Disk storage systems can have transfer rates in excess of 3 megabytes per second. Fast serial interfaces operate up to 50M bps.

data translation The process of converting data from the form used by one system into the form required by another.

data transmission The process of sending data (analog or digital measurements, coded characters, or information in general) from a sender to one or more receivers.

data transparency 1. A property of a communication system (network) such that the output data stream delivered is the exact bit sequence presented to the input of the system without any restriction or exception.
2. A property of a communication system such that the output data stream delivered provides an output bit sequence functionally equivalent to the input bit sequence, from which the exact input bit sequence can be derived.
The second definition implies that the communication system provides protocol translation between input and output devices whereas the first definition implies that there is a compensating translation. The second definition cannot be implemented in all cases since there are functions that are supported by some terminal devices but have no equivalent in others.

data type An abstract set of possible values that an instance of the data type may assume given either implicitly, e.g. INTE-

GER, REAL, STRING, or explicitly as, for example, in Pascal:

TYPE color = (red, green, orange)

The data type indicates a class of implementations for those values. *See also* abstract data type.

data validation The process of checking the expected characteristics of specific data. It is usually applied only to data that has recently been input to a system. Checks are made that there are the correct number of characters in each data field and that they are of the right type; for example, in a field defining a quantity they should be numerical characters and should lie within an expected range.

data-vet program A program that checks input data to verify that it conforms to given specifications and satisfies various consistency checks. It is used to prepare input for another program in contexts where the consequences of faulty input would be unacceptable.

data word A word that can only, or is expected only to, contain data.

datum An item of data: the smallest parcel of information that influences the outcome of a computation.

datum-limit register *Another name for* base-bound register.

daughter *Another name for* child, rarely used.

daughter board (daughter card) *See* mother board, printed circuit.

DBMS *Abbrev. for* database management system.

DC300, DC100 cartridges *See* magnetic tape cartridge.

DCE *Abbrev. for* data communication equipment. The side of an interface that represents the provider of a data communication in a standard such as RS232C or X.25. DCEs are usually analog or digital *modems. *Compare* DTE.

d.c. signaling *See* baseband networking.

DDC *Abbrev. for* direct digital control.

DDCMP *Abbrev. for* digital data communication message protocol. A *data link control protocol developed by Digital Equipment Corporation. It is similar to *SDLC and *HDLC but is character-oriented rather than bit-oriented. It allows a variety of data link characteristics: full duplex or half duplex, asynchronous or synchronous, switched or dedicated, point-to-point or multipoint, and serial or parallel. Data transparency is achieved using a data-length field rather than bit or byte stuffing techniques. Active NAKs are used for error control, in addition to timeouts.

DD/D *Abbrev. for* data dictionary/directory. *See* data dictionary.

DDE *Abbrev. for* direct data entry. *See* data entry.

DDL *Abbrev. for* data description language, data definition language.

deadlock 1. *Another name for* deadly embrace.

2. A specific form of *deadly embrace that arises in a *Petri net, in which some states of the net become forever inaccessible.

deadly embrace (deadlock) A situation that may arise when two (or more) separately active processes compete for resources. Suppose that process P requires resources X and Y and requests their use in that order, and that at the same time process Q requires resources Y and X and asks for them in that order. If process P has acquired resource X and simultaneously process Q has acquired resource Y, then neither process can proceed, each process requiring a resource that has been allocated to the other process. On larger systems containing more than two processes and more than two resources, it is still possible for deadlock to develop although its detection may be more difficult.

debouncing A technique whereby a device is made to pause after the initial detection of the closure of a switch or some other electrical contact in order to allow the reverbations of the contact, known as *contact bounce*, to die away. The contact is then sampled again to determine its final state. Debouncing is often used in connection with the reading of keyboards.

de Bruijn diagram (de Bruijn graph) *See* Good–de Bruijn diagram.

debugging The identification and removal of localized implementation errors – or bugs – from a program or system. By contrast, *testing seeks to establish whether bugs exist but does not isolate or remove them. Program debugging is often supported by a *debug tool*, a *software tool that allows the internal behavior of the program to be investigated. Such a tool would typically offer trace facilities (*see* trace program), allow the planting of *breakpoints* (i.e. points in the program at which execution is to be suspended so that examination of partial results is possible), and permit examination and perhaps modification of the values of program variables when a breakpoint is reached.

debug tool (debugger) *See* debugging.

DEC Digital Equipment Corporation, a company founded by two key individuals, Kenneth Olsen and Harlan Anderson, both formerly employees of MIT's Lincoln Laboratories. They originally founded the company to build transistorized digital circuit modules. Their first product, the PDP-1, was built to demonstrate the feasibility of building a full-fledged stored-program computer from these modules. This machine was unique in that it was the first machine with random-access core memory to be sold for under $100 000.

DEC was the first minicomputer manufacturer, and is today the largest minicomputer manufacturer in the world. It offers a full range of micros, minis (PDP series), medium-sized larger machines (VAX series), and mainframes (DEC systems). Though built to be operated as stand-alone systems, DEC machines have been popular with system designers, who integrate these machines into any number of large communication and other control systems. Perhaps DEC's most famous product is the PDP-11 minicomputer, which was made famous in the computer science community by the development of the *UNIX operating system and the *C programming language. These software products have contributed to the popularity of the PDP-11.

decade counter *See* counter.

decay time of a pulse. *See* pulse.

decidable *See* solvable.

decision gate An electronic *logic gate whose output indicates whether a logical relationship is either true or false. The following are examples: an equality *comparator, indicating when two binary numbers are equal; an *odd parity checker, indicating when a binary input has an odd number of ones; a *majority element, indicating when the binary inputs have more 1 entries than 0 entries.

decision problem The task of deciding in a finite number of steps whether a given problem has a solution. The problem may be deciding, for example, whether an element is a member of a set or deciding whether a logical expression is a tautology. When a decision can be so reached the resulting algorithm is called a *decision procedure* or an *effective procedure*. *See also* solvable.

decision procedure (effective procedure) *See* decision problem.

decision support system *See* management information system.

decision table A table that indicates actions to be taken under various conditions, the *decision* being the selection between the alternative actions. Typically a decision table has one row for each of the inputs to this decision and one column for each of the alternative actions. An entry in the body of the table then indicates the values of the input of the row for which it is permitted to select the action of the column. An action is thus selected only if all inputs have appropriate values. Normally the complete table covers all possible combinations of input values in such a way that application of the table always selects precisely one action (*see also* ELSE rule).

Decision tables have been used both for program specification and implementation, the latter being achieved by means of systems that can interpret (or generate an executable program from) the decision table format.

decision tree A *binary tree where every *nonterminal node represents a decision. Depending upon the decision taken at such a node, control passes to the left or right subtree of the node. A *leaf node then represents the outcome of taking the sequence of decisions given by the nodes on the path from the root to the leaf. *See also* bifurcation.

deck 1. *Short for* tape deck. *See* magnetic tape.
2. A number of punched cards that form a related collection.

declaration One of the two major kinds of element in a conventional program, the other being a *statement. A declaration introduces an entity for part of the program – its *scope* – giving it a name and establishing its static properties. Examples are declarations of variables, declarations of procedures, declarations of input/output ports or files.

declarative languages (nonprocedural languages) A class of programming languages. With a declarative language a program explicitly states what properties the desired result is required to exhibit but does not state how the desired result is to be obtained; any means of producing a result that displays the required properties is acceptable (*compare* imperative languages).

Since declarative languages are concerned with static rather than dynamic concepts (i.e. what rather than how), they do not depend on any inherent notion of ordering and there is no concept of flow of control and no *assignment statement. Ideally a program in a declarative language would consist solely of an unordered set of equations sufficient to characterize the desired result. However, for reasons of implementation and efficiency, the existing languages fall somewhat short of this, either in semantics or in style of use (or both). Declarative languages are not tied to the von Neumann model of computation and typically there is scope for employing a high degree of parallelism in obtaining the desired result.

See also functional languages, logic programming languages.

decoder 1. The means by which a decoding process is effected (*see* code). It may be implemented in hardware or software, the process being algorithmic in nature.
2. *See* decoder/demultiplexer.

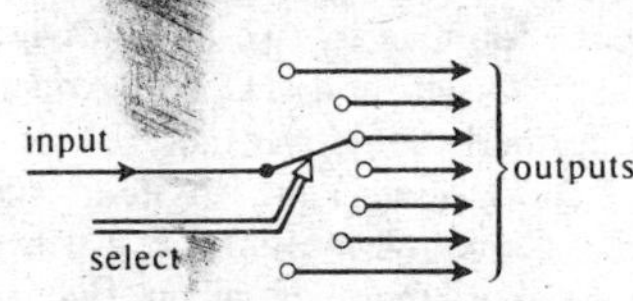

Decoder/demultiplexer

decoder/demultiplexer A logic circuit, usually an integrated circuit, that is capable of setting one of its 2^n output lines active, i.e. at logic 1, in response to an n-bit binary code present at its input. For an n-bit device, 2^n distinct elements of a code can be input.

A decoder/demultiplexer may be considered as a switch that directs data from a time-shared data bus to one of several possible outputs under the control of a select signal, which is normally digital; the select signal indicates which of the outputs is to be connected to the input (*see* diagram). Individual data channels may be recovered from a time-division multiplexed input bus provided that the scanning of the select signal is made synchronous with that of the multiplexer. The input to and outputs from a decoder/demultiplexer may be in digital or analog form. *See also* data selector/multiplexer.

decoder/driver An electronic device that is capable of accepting encoded data at its input and generating unencoded data at its output. The decoding process employed may conform to an agreed standard or be user-defined. The outputs of these devices are capable of directly driving external equipment such as *LCD- or *LED-type displays.

decoder error *See* channel error.

decoding The process of reconverting a coded message to the message from which it was encoded. *See* code.

decollator 1. A machine that can process multicopy printed output into separate stacks of copy and used carbon paper. It is normally done as an off-line activity and may be combined with a *burster that breaks the continuous forms at the perforations to give separate sheets.
2. A machine associated with card-based data processing systems that could separate a punched-card file into its constituent parts, i.e. header cards, which were frequently reused, and detail cards, which, once processed, were kept only for a short time. This facility was sometimes built into the collating machine. *See* collator.

decompiler A program that attempts to do for compiler output what a *disassembler does for assembler output, i.e. translate back from machine code to something resembling the source language. The task is difficult and not often attempted.

decomposition 1. In switching theory, the realization of an *n*-variable switching function as a composition of functions, each of which has less than *n* variables. Like other *minimizations, decomposition is facilitated by *Karnaugh maps.
2. In programming, the analysis of a problem into simpler subproblems. *See* program decomposition, modular programming.

deconvolution *See* convolution.

decryption Transformation of cipher text to plain text by use of a cryptographic transformation and the correct key, or by use of the correct codebook. *See* cryptography.

dedicated Committed entirely to a single purpose or device. For example, a computer system may be dedicated to the job of controlling an industrial machine tool. A dedicated device or resource may be idle for significant periods of time.

defect skipping A method by which a media defect on a magnetic disk *track is avoided such that no data is written in the vicinity of the defect. When a defect is detected, e.g. after the failure of attempts to write and check-read data at that position, the location of the center of the defect is written in the sector 0 header in terms of the number of bytes from the index point. The area of the defect is also treated such that a preamble pattern is written before, over, and after the defect. A synchronizing pattern is written after the preamble pattern so that normal data recording can be resumed on a subsequent pass. The defect skipping is invisible to the CPU operating software but it improves the economics of operation.

deferred addressing *Another name for* indirect addressing.

deferred approach to the limit (Richardson extrapolation) *See* extrapolation.

deflation *See* polynomial equation.

degree 1. of a vertex of a *graph. The number of edges incident with the vertex, i.e. that emanate from that vertex. In a directed graph, the *indegree* is the number of edges entering a vertex while the *outdegree* is the number leaving a vertex.
2. of a node in a *tree. The number of children of that node, i.e. the number of subtrees rooted at that node. More correctly, this is the *outdegree* of the node.
3. of a tree. The maximum degree of all the nodes in the tree.
4. of a polynomial. *See* polynomial equation, polynomial.

delay differential equations *Ordinary differential equations where the derivatives depend on values of the solution at the current value and several previous values of the independent variable. The simplest form is

$$y'(x) = f(x, y(x), y(x - \tau(x))),$$
$$a \leqslant x \leqslant b$$

where $\tau(x) \geqslant 0$. To determine a solution, $y(x)$ must be specified on an interval $a^* \leqslant x \leqslant a$ where a^* depends on the values taken by $\tau(x)$.
Most of the commonly used step-by-step methods for ordinary differential equations can be adapted to problems of this form, although they have not yet been developed to the same extent. It is necessary to incorporate an *interpolation scheme to approximate

$$y(x - \tau(x))$$

to a value that will not usually coincide with a previously computed approximation.

delay line An electronic device that produces a finite accurate time delay between a signal imposed on its input and the appearance of the same signal at its output. These devices may be used as short-term signal stores or to provide accurate delays in signal-processing circuits. In an *acoustic delay line* electrical signals are converted into a pattern of acoustic (sound) waves that travel through a medium between a transmitter and receiver.
Although delay lines are now rarely used as storage devices, an acoustic delay line memory was used in one of the first computers that had a stored program (EDSAC, 1949). Quartz crystals were used as transducers and the ultrasonic pulses were passed along a tube of mercury about 5 feet (1.5 meters) in length. The delay was approximately 1 millisecond but it enabled nearly 1000 pulses to be stored. Later acoustic memories used magnetostrictive transducers and nickel-iron wire, with the electrical signals converted into stress waves.

delete One of the basic actions performed on *sets that, when applied in the form

delete(el,S)

removes the element *el* from *S*; if *el* was not present in *S* the action has no effect on the membership of *S*. *See also* operations on sets.

deletion Removal or obliteration of a record or item of data. In a magnetic tape or disk, data is deleted by overwriting with new data or null characters. In paper tape files a character or block can be deleted by punching all holes in the row or block. The character represented by all holes is treated as a null.

delimiter A symbol that serves to mark the beginning or end of some programming construct, e.g. the semicolon that separates statements in Algol-like languages, the period that marks the end of a sentence in COBOL, the ENDIF that marks the end of an IF statement in FORTRAN 77.

delta PCM (ΔPCM) *See* pulse code modulation.

demand paging A method of dealing with a situation in which a process requires access to a *page of memory that has been written to backing store. Some systems attempt to forecast the pattern of demand for pages; other systems rely on demand paging in which no attempt is made to forecast the pattern of behavior, but pages are transferred from backing store into main memory on demand as required by the individual process.

demand reading, writing A process in which data is transferred directly between a processor and a storage device. This is a normal mode of operation for main memory but is sometimes applied to other devices.

demodulator A device that receives analog signals as input and produces digital data as output. Demodulators use the inverse of the methods used by *modulators, which encode data as analog signals. *See also* modulation, modem.

de Morgan's laws The two laws of a *Boolean algebra that provide a method of expressing the complement of a complex expression in terms of the complements of individual components:

$$(x \vee y)' = x' \wedge y'$$
$$(x \wedge y)' = x' \vee y'$$

The pair is self-dual. The term de Morgan's laws is often used to describe instances of these laws as they apply in particular cases, e.g. to sets or to logical expressions. The laws are named for Augustus de Morgan.

demultiplexer 1. In communications, a device that performs the reverse function to a *multiplexer.
2. A *combinational circuit that converts from n inputs to 1 of m outputs, where $m \leqslant 2^n$. *See also* decoder/demultiplexer.

dendrogram *See* cluster analysis.

denial of service (interdiction) Prevention of normal access to, or normal service by, a computer system without necessarily jeopardizing the information in the system. An example would be tying up a communication line or an I/O handler with bogus messages. This is one of the *threats to computer system security.

denotational semantics An approach to the *semantics of programming languages in which the meaning of a program in a particular language is given by a valuation function that associates with each well-formed syntactic construct of the language an abstract value, e.g. a number, truth value, or function. These valuation functions are compositional or recursive in nature: the value of a program is specified as a function of the values denoted by its syntactic subcomponents. A great deal of work in this area is currently directed at the semantics of parallel programs. This approach was initiated and developed by Christopher Strachey and Dana Scott.

density A measure of the amount of information in a given dimension of a storage medium. For magnetic tape it is the amount of information recorded per unit length of tape, usually in bits per inch or bits per millimeter. In general the number of flux reversals per inch (or per mm) is greater because of redundancy in the coding. The density is stated for a single track. A tape transport can often read tapes with different densities under program control.
The density of information on a disk is almost always a fixed number of bits per sector, sectors per track, and tracks per disk. The standard density for paper tape is usually 10 holes per inch on a single track.

denumerable set *See* countable set.

deposit To place a value in a register in a processor, or in a word in memory. On many microprocessor or mini systems this can be achieved by manual operations on the control panel of the system.

depth 1. of a node in a tree. The length of the unique path from the root of the tree to the node. Thus if a node A is the root node then its depth is zero, otherwise its depth is one greater than that of its parent.
In some texts, depth of a node is synonymous with *level of a node.
2. of a tree. The maximum depth of any node in a tree. The depth of a given tree

will have the same numerical value as the *height of that tree.

depth-balanced *See* balanced.

depth-first search A search of a directed *graph, and hence of a *tree, conducted as follows. An initial starting vertex u is selected and visited. Then a (directed) edge (u, v) incident upon u is selected and a visit is made to v. Let x be the most recent vertex visited. Select some unexplored edge (x, y) incident upon x. If y has not been previously visited, visit y and proceed from there. If y has been previously visited select another edge incident upon x. Having completed the search through all paths beginning at y, return to x and continue to explore the edges incident upon x.
Depth-first searches of graphs play an important part in the design of efficient *algorithms on graphs, in game theory, heuristic programming, and in artificial intelligence.
Compare breadth-first search.

deque *Derived from* double-ended queue. A linear *list where all insertions, removals, and accesses are made at the ends. *See also* stack.

derivation sequence In formal language theory, a sequence of *words of the form

$$w_1 \stackrel{*}{\Rightarrow} w_2 \stackrel{*}{\Rightarrow} \dots \stackrel{*}{\Rightarrow} w_n$$

(for notation *see* semi-Thue system). For a *context-free grammar, such a sequence is *leftmost* (or *rightmost*) if,

for each $1 \leq i \leq n$,

w_{i+1} is obtained from w_i by rewriting the leftmost (or rightmost) nonterminal in w_i. Such sequences exist for all derivable words.

derivation tree A way of indicating how a *context-free grammar derives a particular word. The *leaf nodes of the tree are terminals, the other nodes are nonterminals. For example, the tree in the diagram shows a derivation of *aabbcbb* from the grammar that is shown. Many different *derivation sequences can correspond to the same derivation tree.

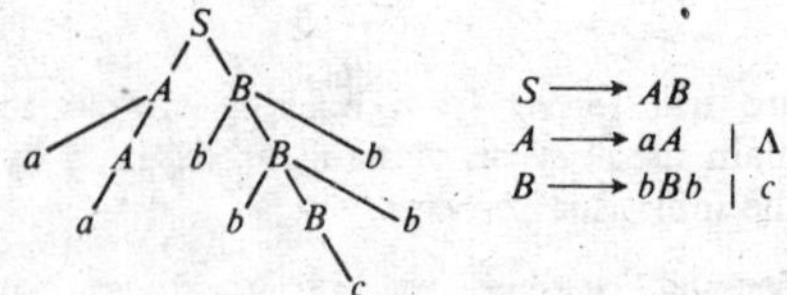

Derivation tree

derivative of a *formal language. The *left-derivative* of a Σ-language L, with respect to a Σ-word w, is

$$\{w' \mid ww' \in L\}$$

Similarly a *right-derivative* is

$$\{w' \mid w'w \in L\}$$

DES *Abbrev. for* Data Encryption Standard.

descendant of a node, A, in a tree. Any node, B, such that A is an *ancestor of B.

descriptor Stored information that describes how other information is stored, e.g. in an array, record, or file. By referring to the descriptor, a program can interpret the other data. *See also* file descriptor.

destructive read-out (DRO) *See* nondestructive read-out.

determinant A number associated with a *square matrix of numbers. The determinant of an $n \times n$ matrix A is denoted by $\det(A)$ or $|A|$ and given by

$$\sum_{\sigma} \operatorname{par}(\sigma)\, a_{1\sigma_1} a_{2\sigma_2} \dots a_{n\sigma_n}$$

where the sum is taken over all $n!$ *permutations

$$\sigma = \sigma_1\sigma_2 \dots \sigma_n$$

of the integers $1, 2, \dots, n$. par(σ), the parity of σ, is either $+1$ or -1 depending on whether σ is an even permutation or an odd permutation.

deterministic Denoting a method, process, etc., the resulting effect of which is entirely determined by the inputs and initial state. *See also* nondeterminism, statistical methods, pseudorandom.

deterministic language Any *context-free language recognized by a deterministic *pushdown automaton. An example of a simple nondeterministic language is the set of all palindromes over an alphabet with two or more letters. A language is deterministic if and only if it is LR(k) for some k (*see* LR parsing).

deterministic Turing machine *See* Turing machine. *See also* nondeterminism.

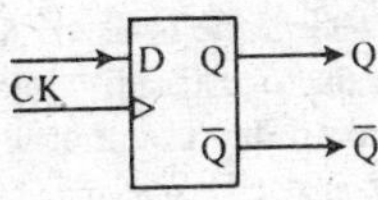

D flip-flop

D flip-flop A clocked *flip-flop having a single D input (*see* diagram). The flip-flop Q output will take on the current state of the D input only when a given transition of the clock signal occurs between its two logic states, i.e. from low to high voltage level (*positive-edge triggered*) or from high to low level (*negative-edge triggered*).

diagnostic routine A routine within a program that is entered as a result of some error condition having been detected, and serves to analyze the cause of that error or to provide information that is subsequently used for such analysis. A typical diagnostic routine might attempt to isolate the cause of the error to a particular hardware or software subsystem, or simply record the values of the major data objects at the time that the error occurred.

diagonalization A proof technique in recursive function theory that is used to prove the unsolvability of the *halting problem: in the establishment of this it is assumed (for the sake of argument) that there is an effective procedure for testing whether programs terminate. Under this assumption the method of diagonalization allows a contradiction to be derived. From this it is deduced that there is no such effective procedure.

The technique was developed by Cantor to prove that the *cardinality of the real numbers is greater than the cardinality of the integers. In this application the real numbers are enumerated in the form of a grid. A real number is then constructed along the diagonal of the grid that is not part of the original enumeration.

diagonal matrix A square matrix A in which $a_{ij} = 0$ if $i \neq j$. The *inverse of a diagonal matrix, if it exists, is particularly easy to calculate and is itself diagonal.

DIAM A database research system, the structure of which was important in database research and development. It was proposed in a series of papers by Mike Senko of IBM but was not developed (or intended) as a commercial system.

dichotomizing search *Another name for* binary search, rarely used.

dictionary Any data structure representing a set of elements that can support the insertion and deletion of elements as well as test for membership. *See also* data dictionary.

difference equations Equations that have the same general form as *recurrence relations; however, the term also refers to situations in which the solution is not determined recursively from initial conditions. Difference equations play a large part in numerical computation. The equations are sometimes expressed in terms of differences of function values rather than function values themselves. The standard difference representations are:

forward difference,

$$\Delta f(x) = f(x + h) - f(x)$$

backward difference,

$$\nabla f(x) = f(x) - f(x - h)$$

central difference,

$$\partial f(x) = f(x + \tfrac{1}{2}h) - f(x - \tfrac{1}{2}h)$$

Difference equations arise in the application of the *finite difference method.

differential equations Equations for one or more unknown functions involving derivatives of those functions. The equations describe changes in a system, usually modeling some physical or other law. Except in simple cases the solution cannot be determined analytically. *See* ordinary differential equations, partial differential equations.

differential PCM (DPCM) *See* pulse code modulation.

digital Operating by, responding to, or otherwise concerned with the use of digits (i.e. discrete units) to represent arithmetic numbers, approximations to numbers from a continuum, or logical expressions/ variables. *See also* discrete and continuous systems.

digital cassette A particular form of *magnetic tape cartridge.

digital circuit An electronic circuit that responds to *digital signals and produces digital signals as its output.

digital computer A computer that operates on discrete quantities (*compare* analog computer). All computation is done within a finite number system and with limited precision, associated with the number of digits in the discrete numbers. The numerical information is most often represented by the use of two-state electrical phenomena (on/off, high voltage/low voltage, current/no current, etc.) to indicate whether the value of a binary variable is a "zero" or a "one". Usually there is automatic control or sequencing (through a *program) of operations so that they can be carried through to completion without intervention. *See also* discrete and continuous systems.

digital data transmission Digital data uses discrete discontinuous signals to represent its meanings. In a DC (direct current) transmission system, different voltage (or current) values are used to represent the values 0 and 1. A digital transmission has a very low error rate and can be sent at very high speeds. Weak signals can be regenerated with low probability of cumulative error. Since all signals are made up of 0s and 1s, signals from many sources can be readily multiplexed using digital techniques. *See* multiplexing.
Digital data can also be transmitted over AC transmission lines. Since DC signals are blocked out by AC transmission lines, a different technique is used. AC lines use analog signals to transmit data; to transform digital data to analog signals a *modulator is used. *See also* modulation.

digital design (logic design) The design of circuits and systems whose inputs and outputs are represented as discrete variables. These variables are commonly binary, i.e. two-state, in nature. Design at the circuit level is usually done with *truth tables and *state tables; design at the system level is done with *block diagrams or *digital design languages.

digital design language A higher-order language, often called a *register transfer language, used to facilitate the description and manipulation of digital systems and their interconnection. *See also* digital design, hardware description.

Digital Equipment Corporation *See* DEC.

digital filtering The employment of *digital signal processing techniques to effect the *filtering of a signal.

digital logic A methodology for dealing with expressions and *state tables containing discrete (usually two-state) variables: in this sense the term is synonymous with *Boolean algebra (*see also* multiple-valued logic). The term is also applied to the hardware – components and circuits – in which such expressions and tables are implemented. *See also* digital design, combinational circuit, sequential circuit.

digital signal A waveform or signal whose voltage at any particular time will be at any one of a group of discrete levels, generally two; a two-level signal is sometimes called a *binary digital signal* or *binary signal.* In binary logic circuits, in which only two discrete voltage levels are used, one level will correspond to logic 1 (true), usually the high level, and the other will correspond to logic 0 (false).

digital signal processing The branch of *signal processing that uses digital systems to operate on signals. The advantages of digital over analog signal processing are that memory is more easily employed (so that time may be re-run in different speeds and directions) and that a wider range of arithmetic operations and algorithmic complexity is possible; the main advantage, however, is that the possible precision is arbitrarily high. The main disadvantage is that in some instances digital techniques are slower than analog techniques. Many specialized digital devices have been developed that retain the advantages but nevertheless operate at high speed, at the cost of flexibility.

digital sorting *Another name for* radix sorting.

digital system Any system handling digital (discrete) *signals. *See* discrete and continuous systems.

digital-to-analog converter *See* D/A converter.

digitization The process of quantizing a *signal and representing it in digital form. *See also* quantization, discrete and continuous systems, digitizer, A/D converter.

digitizer (quantizer) An electronic device that can convert an analog, i.e. continuous, signal into a signal having values that are identical to the analog signal only at discrete instants of time. The action is analogous to observing, i.e. *sampling, the analog signal and holding its value until the next observation time. The output signal thus consists of a number of steps between specified levels (*see* diagram).

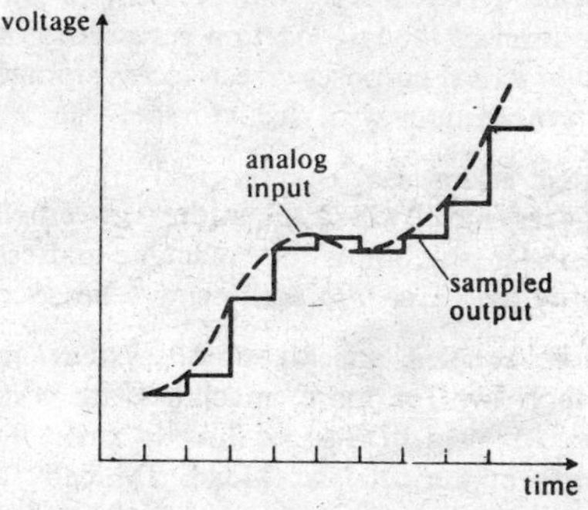

Digitizer

digitizing pad A digital *data tablet.

digraph *Short for* directed graph. *See* graph.

DIL *A UK acronym for* dual in-line package.

dimension (dimensionality) of an *array. The number of subscripts needed to locate any element in the array.

diminished radix complement *Another name for* radix-minus-one complement.

diminishing increment sort *Another name for* Shell's method.

diode An electronic device, generally of semiconductor material, that has two terminals and is capable of allowing current flow in one direction only. The terminals are called the *anode* and *cathode*. The diode presents a very low (high) impedance when a *forward bias (*reverse bias) is applied.

diode-transistor logic *See* DTL.

DIP *An acronym for* dual in-line package.

direct-access storage device (DASD) One of a class of storage devices that can access storage locations in any order: a sequential search is not required and the access time to read or write to a particular location is relatively independent of the position of the last location accessed. For all practical purposes direct-access storage is synonymous with disk storage.

direct addressing The "normal" mode of addressing in which the address specified in the instruction is the *machine address to be used. *See also* addressing schemes.

direct-coupled machines A system in which two (or more) machines are connected by a high-speed link in order to perform the total workload. Typically a small machine, the *master*, deals with file editing, job submission, and all scheduling. Larger jobs that would take too long to process on this small machine are passed to a larger machine, the *slave*, for processing, the results being returned to the user via the small machine. *See also* master-slave machine.

direct data entry (DDE) *See* data entry.

direct digital control (DDC) Control of a process by a digital computer, the information being supplied to the process as (appropriately timed) sequences of digits. *See* numerical control.

directed graph (digraph) *See* graph.

directed set A *set X, say, with the property that every finite subset of X has an *upper bound that is in X itself.

directed tree *See* tree.

directive A component of a program in assembly language that controls the subsequent assembly but does not of itself cause a machine instruction to be generated. Examples are
generate absolute/relative code;
request a page-feed in the listing;
start a new segment;
allocate space for constants or variables.

direct memory access (DMA) A method whereby I/O processes can obtain access to the CPU's memory while a program is running. This is accomplished by permitting the I/O controller or channel that has been previously instructed to move a block of data to or from the memory to temporarily take control of the memory for (usually) one *memory cycle, thus allowing a single word (or group of words if the memory is so organized) to be read or written. The method is therefore also referred to as *cycle stealing*. The timing requirement is normally that of the slower external device and is prompted by the ability of that device to receive or provide desired data, hence the alternative synonym *data break*.

directory A means of locating data items, usually files. A directory can be regarded as establishing a set of links between named data items and their locations in a *direct-access storage device. In many systems the directories are highly structured; their organization reflects the relationships between various categories of file. For example, the directory may allow one user to have other subordinate users, and permit controlled access by these subordinate users to their own and others' files. *See also* data dictionary.

direct product (product group) of two *groups G and H with group *operations ρ and τ respectively. The group consisting of the elements in the *Cartesian product of G and H and on which there is a binary operation $\circ$ defined as follows:

$$(g_1,h_1) \circ (g_2,h_2) = (g_1 \rho g_2, h_1 \tau h_2)$$

The identity of this group is then just (e_G,e_H), where e_G and e_H are the identities of groups G and H respectively. The inverse of (g,h) is then (g^{-1},h^{-1}).
These concepts can be generalized to deal with the direct product of any finite number of groups on which there are specified group operations.

disable 1. To make a device inactive. **2.** To suppress the action of an interrupt.

disarm To put a device into a state that is still serviceable but requires a preparatory action before it can be used.

disassembler A program that attempts to translate machine code back into assembly language as an aid to debugging. A simple disassembler operates on onc instruction at a time, translating the operation code to the appropriate mnemonic, displaying register references and addressing modes in the symbolic form used in the assembly language, and converting addresses into hexadecimal or symbols. More ambitious disassemblers try to show the structure of the program by replacing branch destinations with alphanumeric symbols, and placing the corresponding symbol as a label in the appropriate position in the program.

disconnected graph *See* connected graph.

discrete and continuous systems Systems by which *signals are recorded, communicated, or displayed may represent the data in discrete form (e.g. as integers) or in continuous form (as "real" numbers). An important classification results from the choice of discrete or continuous representation of the amplitude, and of discrete or continuous representation of the time at which the amplitude occurred. *Analog computers employ physical quantities that are approximations to continuous representations. Discrete representations of both time and amplitude are required by *digital computers.

The question of whether the signal (or its source) is intrinsically discrete or intrinsically continuous is unresolvable: any experiment to determine this would require infinite *bandwidth (or infinite time) and infinite *signal-to-noise ratio, and so would be impossible in practice. All that is in question is whether a discrete or continuous representation is more convenient, or useful, or appealing.

Signals that appear intuitively to be continuous-time or continuous-amplitude, but for which a discrete-time or discrete-amplitude representation is preferred, are said to have been *time-quantized* or *amplitude-quantized*. Time quantization is either adequate or inadequate according to *Nyquist's criterion. Time-quantized signals are said to be *sampled*, and the systems that handle them are called *sampled-data systems*. Amplitude quantization worsens the signal-to-noise ratio, an effect describable as the introduction of *quantization noise.

Time and amplitude must both be quantized for processing by digital computers (or by other digital devices), which operate at finite speeds on finite amounts of data held to finite precisions. The same physical constraints operate, although in a different way, to limit the extent to which analog computers (or other analog devices) can approximate to the continuous representation of signals.

See also quantization.

discrete channel A communication *channel whose input and output each have an alphabet of distinct letters, or, in the case of a physical channel, whose input and output are *signals that are discrete in time and amplitude (*see* discrete and continuous systems). The size of the alphabet, or the number of amplitude levels, is usually finite.

The *discrete memoryless channel (DMC)* has the property that its treatment of a symbol input at a certain time does not depend on the symbols input, or its treatment of them, at any earlier time.

The *discrete channel with memory (DCM)* has the property that its action depends on its inputs at a number of earlier times.

See also Shannon's model, channel coding theorem.

discrete Fourier transform *See* Fourier transform.

discrete signal *See* discrete and continuous systems.

discrete source A source of information whose output has an alphabet of distinct letters or, in the case of a physical source, whose output is a *signal that is discrete in time and amplitude (*see* discrete and continuous systems). The size of the alphabet, or the number of amplitude levels, is usually finite, although for mathematical analysis it may conveniently be regarded as infinite.

The *discrete memoryless source (DMS)* has the property that its output at a certain time does not depend on its output at any earlier time.

The *discrete source with memory (DSM)* has the property that its output at a certain time may depend on its outputs at a number of earlier times: if this number is finite, the source is said to be of *finite order*, otherwise it is of *infinite order*. DSMs are usually modeled by means of *Markov chains; they are then called *Markov sources*.

An *ergodic source* has the property that its output at any time has the same statistical properties as its output at any other time. Memoryless sources are, trivially, always ergodic; a source with memory is ergodic only if it is modeled by an ergodic Markov chain.

See also information theory, Shannon's model, source coding theorem.

discrete structure A *set of discrete elements on which certain operations are defined. Discrete implies noncontinuous and therefore discrete sets include *finite and *countable sets but not uncountable sets such as the real numbers. The term discrete structure covers many of the concepts of modern algebra, including integer arithmetic, *monoids, *semigroups, *groups, *graphs, *lattices, *semirings, *rings, *fields, and *subsets of these.

discrete system *See* discrete and continuous systems.

discretization The process of replacing a problem defined on a continuum, say an interval [0,1], by an approximating problem on a finite set of points, say nh,

$$n = 0,1,2, \ldots ,N,$$
$$\text{where } h = 1/N$$

Examples arise in many branches of numerical analysis, principally ordinary and partial differential equations where the *finite-difference method is the common form of discretization. For the ordinary differential equation

$$y' = f(x,y),$$
$$0 \leqslant x \leqslant 1,\ y(0) = y_0,$$

a simple discretization is given by *Euler's method*:

$$(1/h)(y_{n+1} - y_n) = f(x_n,y_n)$$

where

$$x_n = hn,\ n = 0,1, \ldots ,N,$$
$$h = 1/N$$

and y_n denotes the approximation to the true solution $y(x)$ at the point x_n. *See also* discretization error.

discretization error (truncation error) The error in a numerical method that has been constructed by a process of *discretization. It results from the discretization of a "continuous" problem, where it is assumed that all arithmetic is done exactly, and is of fundamental importance in methods for differential equations. A distinction is made between global and local errors. For example, in Euler's method (*see* discretization) y_n is the approximation to the solution $y(x)$ at x_n. The *global discretization* (or *truncation*) *error* is given by

$$y_n - y(x_n)$$

(Some authors take the maximum of this expression over $n = 0,1, \ldots ,N$.) The *local discretization* (or *truncation*) *error* is the amount by which the true solution of the differential equation fails to satisfy the discretization formula, i.e.

$$y(x_{n+1}) - y(x_n) - hf(x_n,y(x_n))$$

This quantity can be regarded as a first measure of the accuracy of the formula. It can be estimated at each step of the integration and provides a means of indirectly controlling the global discretization error. These definitions can be extended to other methods and beyond.

discriminant analysis *See* multivariate analysis.

disjoint A term applied to two sets that have no element in common, i.e. such that the *intersection of the sets results in the *empty set. A number of sets are said to be *mutually disjoint* if each pair is disjoint.

disjunction A logical expression of the form

$$a_1 \vee a_2 \vee \ \ldots \ \vee a_n$$

where $\vee$ is the *OR operation. A particular disjunction of interest is the *disjunctive normal form* of a Boolean expression involving n variables, $x_1, x_2, \ldots, x_n$. Each a_i is then of the form

$$(y_1 \wedge y_2 \wedge \ \ldots \ y_n)$$

where $\wedge$ is the *AND operation and each y_i is equal to x_i or the complement of x_i. Reducing expressions to disjunctive normal form provides a ready method of determining the *equivalence of two Boolean expressions. *See also* propositional calculus. *Compare* conjunction.

disjunctive normal form *See* disjunction.

disk An item of storage medium in the form of a circular plate. These devices are at present (1983) almost always *magnetic disks, in which the information is stored via *magnetic encoding. *See also* optical disk, magneto-optic disk storage.

disk cartridge A data storage medium in the form of an assembly containing a single rigid *magnetic disk permanently housed within a protective plastic cover. The term has been used to refer to a *disk pack, but conventionally this is no longer the case. The cartridge was introduced by IBM in 1964.

The cartridge, according to its type, may be loaded vertically onto its drive (*top-loading*), or horizontally from the front (*front-loading*). Either way the cartridge hub, to which the disk is clamped, centers onto the drive spindle and is magnetically clamped. The cover contains apertures to allow fixing of the cartridge to the drive, and a door that the drive opens to allow insertion of the magnetic heads. Once loaded, the disk can rotate clear of the covers. On some types the hub has a notch that is sensed by a transducer on the drive and signals the start of each recording track. Additionally, a set of equispaced notches may be present to signal the start of sectors within tracks; their presence and number depend on the requirements of the drive controller. On other types, this information, together with track spacing information, is prerecorded on one of the two surfaces, the *servosurface.*

Disk cartridges have storage capacities up to 15 megabytes, depending on track density, bit density, and disk size. Disk diameters range from 14″ to about 3″ (356–76 mm). *See also* exchangeable disk store.

disk drive (disk unit) A peripheral device with read/write heads and associated electronics that can store and retrieve data from *magnetic disks – either a single disk or *disk cartridge or a *disk pack. The term can also be applied to devices operating with *optical disks.

In a magnetic disk drive the data is recorded on one or both sides of a disk in a set of concentric tracks, which are usually subdivided into *sectors. The read/write heads of the disk drive are mounted on arms that can be moved, by means of an *actuator, to position the heads accurately over the required track. As the disk rotates, the sectors on that track are made accessible. In the case of a drive with a disk pack it is usual for the read/write heads to have a common actuator. The time required to access related records can then be minimized by arranging that the records form a notional *cylinder* by writing them to the same track number on different disk surfaces.

In a *fixed disk drive* the storage medium is permanently attached within the device, but in an *exchangeable disk store the disk or disk pack may be removed and replaced by another containing different files. *See also* floppy-disk drive, disk format.

diskette, diskette drive *Other names for* floppy disk, floppy-disk drive.

disk file A set of related records held on a storage disk. The term is sometimes misapplied to refer to a *disk drive together with its *disk or *disk pack and the data it holds.

disk format The *format of information recorded on magnetic disk, allowing a system to recognize, control, and verify the data. There are two levels at which formats are defined.
(a) The way in which the data stream is divided into separately addressable portions, called *sectors, with *address marks and data marks to differentiate between the different types of information within the sector, and with a *cyclic redundancy check or *error-correcting code also provided.
(b) The way in which the binary information is encoded as a pattern of magnetic flux reversals.
Since recordings on disks are made as a bit serial stream on a single track at a time, special provision has to be made to allow the reading system to maintain synchronization. This is achieved by the *encoding format*, which either includes *clock pulses or encodes the data in such a way that there cannot be a case where there is a succession of eight or more bit cells without a magnetic flux transition occurring. The read electronics can maintain synchronization for short periods without transitions. The common methods of encoding are as follows.
Frequency modulation (FM; F2F) is a form of self-clocking recording. The beginning of each bit cell is marked by a clock pulse recorded as a change in the direction of the magnetic flux. If the cell is to represent a binary 1 a second pulse or transition is written at the center of the cell, otherwise there is no further change until the start of the next cell. If the frequency of the clock is F then a stream of 1s will result in a frequency of $2F$ (hence F2F recording). In this form of recording the minimum separation between transitions is half of one cell and the maximum is one cell.
In *modified frequency modulation (MFM)* a binary 1 is always represented by a transition at the center of a bit cell but there is not always a transition at the boundary of the cell. A transition is written at the start of a bit cell only if it is to represent a binary 0 and does not follow a binary 1. Thus the minimum separation between transitions is one cell and the maximum is two cells. For the same spacing of flux transitions the MFM method allows twice as many bits to be encoded in a unit distance; it is thus sometimes referred to as a *double-density recording.*
Modified modified frequency modulation (M^2FM) is a modified form of MFM that deletes flux transitions between two 0s if they are followed by a 1.
Run-length limited encoding is a form of *NRZ (nonreturn to zero) recording in which groups of data are mapped onto larger groups before recording. A frequently used method known as *GCR (group code recording)* breaks the data stream into groups of four bits and maps these onto five bit groups. Because of the resulting redundancy, the five bit groups can be selected to limit the number of consecutive 0s and thus control the maximum spacing between flux transitions. Other similar codes are *EIR (error indicating recording)*, a form of four to six mapping that uses only the groups with odd parity, i.e. three or five 1s, and *3PM (three-phase modulation)*, which has a minimum sequence of two 0s and a maximum of eleven.
See also formatter.

disk pack A form of data storage medium consisting of an assembly of identical 14″ diameter rigid *magnetic disks that are mounted coaxially and equally spaced. A similar nonrecording protective disk is fitted above the top recording disk with another one below the bottom recording disk. The whole assembly is rigidly clamped together, and is designed for dynamic stability at its intended rotational speed on the *disk drive, which can be up to 3600 revolutions per minute. Disk packs are designed to be compatible with

disk drives, mechanically and magnetically, and most types are the subjects of international standards. The whole pack, when not mounted on the drive, is contained within sealed plastic covers, in two parts, which help to ensure that the pack is protected from damage, dust, and contamination. The bottom cover is removed before mounting the pack on the drive; the top cover can only be removed when the pack has been mounted.
The mechanical interface with the disk drive is via an axial lockshaft in the pack, having a female thread engaging the male spindle of the drive. On some types, a notch on the periphery of the bottom protective disk is sensed by a transducer on the drive and signals the start of each recording track. Additionally, a set of equispaced notches may be present to signal the start of *sectors within tracks; their presence and number depend on the requirements of the drive controller. On other types, this information, together with track spacing information, is prerecorded on a surface reserved for this purpose, the *servosurface*.
Storage capacities range from 30 to 300 megabytes, over the range of track densities up to 400 tracks per inch, recording densities up to 6000 bits per inch, and pack sizes of 5 to 12 disks. Disk packs were introduced by IBM in 1963.

disk unit *Another name for* disk drive.

dispatcher *Another name for* low-level scheduler. *See* scheduler.

dispersion *See* measures of variation.

display 1. To make information visible in a temporary form.
2. The device that enables information, either textual or pictorial, to be seen but not permanently recorded.
There are many types of display device but the most widely used is the *cathode-ray tube. Although domestic TV receivers can be used as computer-driven displays, it is usual to have specially designed units if there are to be periods of prolonged use by one operator. Under such conditions it is necessary to optimize the screen characteristics and provide a sharper and more stable image to avoid unnecessary fatigue. *See also* VDU.
Other display technologies that are used in association with computer systems are:
(a) *plasma displays, which for displaying small amounts of information – up to 240 characters – are an attractive alternative to cathode-ray tubes, although large displays are more expensive;
(b) *LED (light-emitting diode) displays, which are generally only used when up to 40 characters are to be displayed;
(c) *LCDs (liquid crystal displays), which are used in clocks and watches but have also been demonstrated in larger forms suitable for information display, although these are not yet widely adopted;
(d) *electroluminescent displays*, which are beginning to be used in portable computers.

display processor A specialized *I/O processor used to mediate between a file of information that is to be displayed and a display device. It reformats the information as required and provides the information in accordance with the timing requirements of the display system.

distributed array processor *See* array processor.

distributed database A *database in which the data is contained within a number of separate subsystems, usually in different physical locations. If the constituent subsystems are essentially similar, the system is said to be *homogeneous*, otherwise it is said to be *heterogeneous*. Distributed database systems may vary very considerably. At one extreme is the type where the complete system was conceived, designed, and implemented as a single entity; such systems exist within large commercial organizations and are usually homogeneous. At the other extreme is the case where a number of existing systems, originally planned as isolated systems, continue in their normal operation but in addition are loosely linked to provide a larger distributed system over the whole; in this instance the system is often heterogeneous. Distributed database systems are currently an active topic for database research and development, largely because of the availability of national and international communication facilities.

distributed file system A simple version of a distributed database system in which individual files may be accessed at remote sites but where the sites do not have facilities to process queries that involve cross-file connection.

distributed processing The organization of processing to be carried out on a *distributed system. Each process is free to process local data and make local decisions. The processes exchange information with each other over a data communication network to process data or to read decisions that affect multiple processes.

distributed system Any system in which a number of independent interconnected computers can cooperate. *See* distributed processing.

distribution *See* frequency distribution, probability distributions.

distribution counting sort A sorting algorithm that stores, for each sortkey, the number of records with the given sortkey (thus anticipating that keys might not be unique). With this information it is possible to place the records correctly into a sorted file. The algorithm is useful when the keys fall into a small range and many of them are equal.

distributive lattice A *lattice L, with meet and join operations $\wedge$ and $\vee$ respectively, in which the two *distributive laws hold for all elements in L. Since these laws are self-duals, the principle of *duality continues to hold for distributive lattices.

distributive laws The two self-dual laws

$$x \wedge (y \vee z) = (x \wedge y) \vee (x \wedge z)$$
$$x \vee (y \wedge z) = (x \vee y) \wedge (x \vee z)$$

that are satisfied by all elements x, y, and z in a *Boolean algebra possessing the two operations $\wedge$ and $\vee$. In the first law the operation $\wedge$ is said to be distributive over the operation $\vee$, and vice versa for the second law.

divide and conquer sorting A sorting algorithm that is similar to *radix sorting but works from the most significant digit of the sortkey down to the least significant.

divider *See* counter.

DL/1 The *data manipulation language of *IMS.

DMA *Abbrev. for* direct memory access.

DME *Trademark, acronym for* direct machine environment. A system offered by ICL as a means of using the microcode capabilities of their 2900 range of machines to allow users to run ICL 1900 series software, including the GEORGE operating system. Originally offered as an interim product for users migrating from 1900 to 2900 systems, DME is sufficiently attractive to be used as a main operating environment.

DML *Abbrev. for* data manipulation language.

documentation All material that serves primarily to describe a system and make it more readily understandable, rather than to contribute in some way to the actual operation of the system. Documentation is frequently classified according to purpose; thus for a given system there may be requirements documents, design documents, and so on. In contrast to documentation orientated toward development and maintenance of the system, user documentation describes those aspects of the system that are of interest to the eventual users.

document processing The machine processing (reading, sorting, etc.) of documents that are generally readable both by

people and machines, e.g. bank checks, vouchers from credit card transactions, and accounts from public utilities. In addition to the printed information for human interpretation, there is also some encoding that is machine-readable and may be in an *OCR or *MICR font.
The documents are frequently referred to as *turnaround documents* since the person receiving them "turns them around" and returns them to the system to complete a transaction.

document reader A machine for reading documents that are encoded in a way that is readable by person and machine. *See also* document processing.

document sorter A device that can read information encoded on documents and place them into separate stacks related to that code. Bank checks are processed in this way. Speeds up to about 1600 documents per minute are available (1982). *See also* document processing.

do loop A counting loop in a program, in which a section of code is obeyed repeatedly with a counter taking successive values. Thus in FORTRAN,

```
      DO 10 I = 1,100
            ⟨statements⟩
   10 CONTINUE
```

causes the ⟨statements⟩ to be obeyed 100 times. The current value of the counter variable is often used within the loop, especially to index an array. There are many syntactic variants: in Pascal and Algol-related languages the same basic construct appears as the *for loop*, e.g.

```
for 1 := 1 to 100 do
   begin
     ⟨statements⟩
   end
```

This kind of loop is a constituent of almost all programming languages (except APL, which has array operations defined as operators in the language).
See also do-while loop.

DOL system *See* L-system.

domain 1. *See* function, relation, category. *See also* range.
2. *Another name for* complete lattice.

dominator A vertex x_i on a graph G is a dominator of vertex x_j, relative to vertex x_k, if every path from x_j to x_k traverses x_i. This is used in flow analysis for code optimization.

do-nothing instruction *Another name for* no-op instruction.

dope vector A vector of data used to assist in accessing the elements in an *array. The dope vector contains
(a) the address of a fixed element in the array – this may be the first element present or the element that has all subscripts equated to zero;
(b) the number of subscripts associated with the array, i.e. its dimensionality;
(c) the *stride* associated with each subscript position, i.e. the number of stored elements that must be skipped over when a subscript's value is changed by 1.
The position in memory of an element is found by taking the inner product of the strides with the differences between the actual subscript values and those that correspond to the fixed element referred to in (a), and adding to this the address of the fixed element.

DOS *Trademark, acronym for* disk operating system. The original DOS written by IBM for the series-700 computers was one of the first major operating systems to be offered by a mainframe manufacturer, and was introduced shortly after the still more primitive system, *OS. DOS gave users the ability to construct files on disks that held images of punched cards and that could serve as the input to programs; similarly output ultimately destined for printers was *spooled into temporary disk files. The user was responsible for much of the management of these files, and had to contend with details of their physical location on disk and with their creation and disposal.

dot matrix printer A printer that creates each character from an array of dots that are usually formed by transferring ink by mechanical impact. It may be a *serial printer, printing a character at a time, or a *line printer.

The serial printer has a print head containing typically 7 or 9 electromagnetically operated styluses. In a *wire printer* the styluses are steel or tungsten wires that are constrained by a guide at the printing tip. The styluses may also be short rods rigidly attached to a pivoting armature. The head is mounted on a carriage that is moved along guides so that it travels parallel to the paper and the position of the line to be printed. The styluses are selectively operated to build up alphanumeric characters and other shapes from a matrix of small dots, printed so that they almost touch. Alphanumeric characters of data-processing quality are built up on a matrix of 7 or 9 dots high by 4 or 5 dots wide. These usually have voids and scalloped edges, which can however be removed by making repeated passes of the head along the same line but printing the dots in a slightly different place on each pass: the dots can thus be made to overlap in both horizontal and vertical lines. More recent designs of printers have 18 or 24 styluses and can produce characters that more closely resemble ordinary typewritten quality. The generally available speed range is 100–400 characters per second (cps) for print of data-processing quality, and up to 100 cps for a higher-quality character.

A widely adopted design for dot matrix line printers is to have a row of spring fingers that span the line to be printed. Such printers operate at 200–600 lines per minute.

Enhancements of dot matrix printers include the ability to print in seven colors. Ribbonless printers in which the ink is fed directly to the styluses are also available.

double buffering A form of *buffering in which two buffers are used. On output the program can be filling one buffer while the device empties the other; the buffers then exchange roles. A similar technique is used for input.

double complement of a *set S. The *complement of the set S', where S' itself is just the complement of S; the double complement of S is thus S itself. In logic double complement implies *double negation* of an element x, say, i.e. x itself.

double-density recording *Another name for* modified frequency modulation. *See* disk format.

double-length arithmetic *See* double precision.

double negation *See* double complement.

double precision The use of double the usual number of bits to represent a number. Arithmetic performed on double-precision numbers is called *double-precision* (or *double-length*) *arithmetic*. For floating-point numbers, most computers use the same number of bits for the exponent in single-length and double-length forms. Consequently, if the length of a single-precision number is l bits, p of which are used for the mantissa, then the mantissa of a double-precision number occupies $(p + l)$ of the $2l$ bits. Occasionally, *multiple precision*, i.e. more than double precision, may be available. Some computers implement double precision in hardware; higher precision is almost always achieved by software.

doubly linked list (two-way linked list; symmetric list) A *linked list where each item contains links to both its predecessor and its successor. This makes it possible to traverse the list in either direction. The flexibility given by double linking must be offset against the overhead of the storage and the setting and resetting of the extra links involved.

do-while loop A form of programming loop in which the condition for termination (continuation) is computed each time around the loop. There are several variants on this basic idea. For example, Pascal has

```
while ⟨condition⟩ do
   begin
      ⟨statements⟩
   end
```

and also

```
repeat
   ⟨statements⟩
until ⟨condition⟩
```

The first is a *while loop* and the second is a *repeat-until* loop. Apart from the obvious difference that the first specifies a continuation condition while the second specifies a termination condition, there is a more significant difference. The while loop is a *zero-trip* loop, i.e. the body will not be executed at all if the condition is false the first time around. In contrast, the body of a repeat-until loop must be obeyed at least once.
Similar constructs are found in most languages, though there are many syntactic variations. *See also* do loop.

downline The direction from a central or controlling node to a remote node in a hierarchical network, or (sometimes) the direction away from the current node without respect to hierarchical ordering.
The word is often used as a verb: to downline or to *downline load*, i.e. to send programs or data from a central or controlling node to a remote node in a network. The remote node may not have the facilities to store the programs or data permanently, in which case the downline load would be necessary each time the remote node is restarted. When the remote node does have permanent storage facilities, downline loading may be used to supply newer versions of programs or data to the remote node.
Compare upline.

down operation *Another name for* P operation. *See* semaphore.

downtime The percentage of time that a computer system is not available for use.

DP *Abbrev. for* data processing.

DPCM *Abbrev. for* differential PCM. *See* pulse code modulation.

DPM *Abbrev. for* data-processing manager.

driver 1. A routine within an operating system that handles the individual peripheral units on the computer system. Of necessity a driver routine is required to deal with the intimate details of the construction of each unit and of its real-time behavior. Consequently at least some of the driver will often need to be written in a machine-oriented programming language. **2.** An electronic circuit, often available in the form of a logic gate, that is capable of providing large currents or voltages to other circuits connected to the driver's output. These devices are often used to place signals onto bus lines, hence the term *bus driver*.

DRO *Abbrev. for* destructive read-out. *See* nondestructive read-out.

drop-in In magnetic recording technology (disk and tape), the presence among the signals read from the device of one or more bits that had not been deliberately written there. This is the result of a fault condition, often imperfect erasure of data previously on the medium, and will generally be a problem only in interrecord gaps (elsewhere it will be dealt with by the same means provided for *drop-out): magnetic tape and disk systems normally have means of identifying and coping with this problem.

drop-out In magnetic recording technology (disk and tape), the loss of one or a sequence of bits due to a fault condition, most frequently a flaw in the recording medium. Magnetic tape and disk systems employ some form of redundancy to detect and frequently correct the resulting data errors.

drum *See* magnetic drum, drum printer, plotter.

drum plotter *See* plotter.

drum printer A type of *solid-font *line printer in which the font is etched or engraved on the outer surface of a cylinder that extends across the full width of the line to be printed. This font carrier, referred to as a *drum* in the US, is more generally known as a *barrel* in the UK with the printer then referred to as a *barrel printer*. This was the first type of computer output printer to use the "hit-on-the-fly" principle, used on *chain printers and current band and train printers, and it was a significant change from the mechanically intensive printers that preceded it. The first commercially available machine was introduced by Shepard in about 1955.

dry run Execution of a program in a manner analogous to a *production run, but for purposes of checking that the program behaves correctly rather than for producing useful results. The results of execution are compared with expected results; any discrepancies indicate an error of some sort that must be investigated before the program is put into production usage.

DSPACE *See* complexity classes.

DTE *Abbrev. for* data terminal equipment. The side of an interface that represents the user of the data communication services in a standard such as RS232C or X.25. DTEs are usually computers or computer terminals. *Compare* DCE.

DTIME *See* complexity classes.

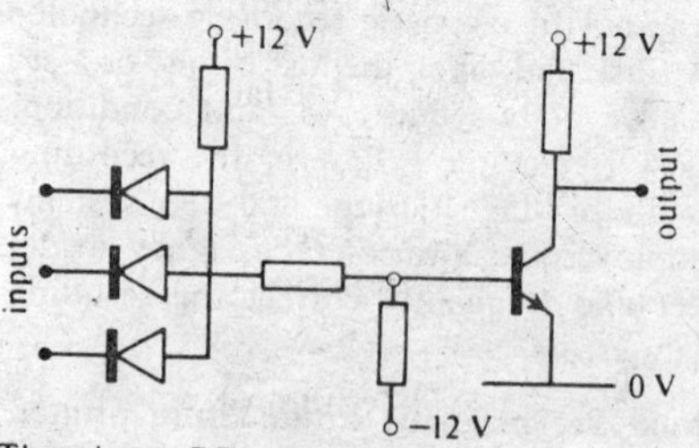

Three-input DTL NAND gate

DTL *Abbrev. for* diode-transistor logic. An early form of *logic family, normally produced in integrated-circuit form, whose principal switching components consist of semiconductor diodes and transistors. The equivalent circuit of a three-input DTL *NAND gate is shown in the diagram. Each input is fed to a diode and the output is taken from the collector of a *bipolar transistor. When all inputs are at logic 1, current can flow to the base of the transistor so driving it into saturation. As a result the collector voltage falls to logic 0.

D-type flip-flop *See* D flip-flop.

dual *See* duality.

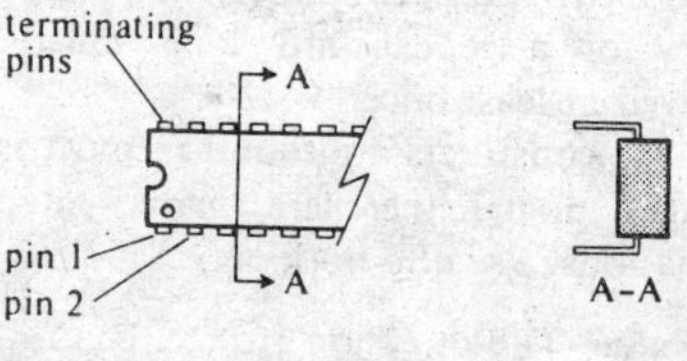

Dual in-line package

dual in-line package (DIP; DIL) A circuit that is fabricated on a single silicon chip and is encapsulated in such a way that the external connections are made accessible by means of two parallel rows of terminating pins perpendicular to the edges of the package. The package acts to protect and carry the chip and is often rectangular in shape, the terminations then being along the two longer edges (*see* diagram). The number of terminations and hence the package size is a function of the number of external connections to the chip.

duality The property exhibited by the laws and rules of *set algebra, the *propositional calculus, and *Boolean algebra that each law or rule has a *dual* law or rule, constructed by the simultaneous replacement of each occurrence of 0 by 1, 1 by 0, $\vee$ by $\wedge$, and $\wedge$ by $\vee$. Such a pair of laws or rules is then said to be *self-dual*. Thus

*de Morgan's laws, for example, are self-dual.
If a law or rule contains the *partial ordering ≤ inherent in any lattice, then in obtaining duals this should be replaced by ≥ and vice versa; thus inequalities should be reversed.

dual port memory A memory that is capable of receiving two concurrent access requests. Depending upon the internal memory organization, responses may or may not be simultaneous. Close-coupled *multiprocessor systems use these memories.

dual processor A *multiprocessor system with two central processors. Use of this term sometimes implies a two-processor system in which one processor is redundant so that the total system has a very high level of reliability.

dummy instruction (dummy) An item of data in the form of an *instruction that is inserted in the *instruction stream but is not intended to be executed.

dump 1. In a system handling large numbers of users' files stored on magnetic disks, one of the periodic records of the state of the disks that are made on magnetic tape in order to protect against accidental overwriting or machanical failure of the disks.
2. A printed version of the contents of system memory taken when a system crash has occurred. In principle it is possible to determine the immediate cause of a system crash by studying the dump and determining the reason for any inconsistencies in its contents. In practice this may be difficult even with the assistance of dump analysis software.
3. To take a dump (defs. 1 or 2).

dump check A copy of the contents of all the workspace associated with a job or process. If the job or process subsequently fails, it can be restarted at the point at which the dump check was taken. Note that the status of peripheral devices allocated to the job or process must be considered as constituting part of its workspace.

dump point *See* checkpoint.

duplex (full duplex) A connection between two endpoints, either physical or logical, over which data may travel in both directions simultaneously. *See also* half duplex, simplex, return channel.

duty cycle For pulsed or square-wave signals, the ratio of pulse duration to pulse spacing, often expressed as a percentage. A square wave signal normally has a 50% duty cycle, i.e. pulse duration is equal to the time between pulses.

DX-2 An X.25-based *public packet network of Japan. It first became operational in 1979.

dyadic Having two operands.

dyadic operation (binary operation) defined on a set S. A function from the domain $S \times S$ into S itself. Many of the everyday arithmetic and algebraic operations are dyadic, e.g. the addition of two integers, the union of two sets, and the conjunction of two Boolean expressions. Although basically functions, dyadic operations are usually represented using an infix notation, as in

$$3 + 4,\ U \cup V,\ P \wedge Q$$

A symbol, such as $\circ$, can be used to represent a generalized dyadic operation.
When the set is finite, *Cayley tables and sometimes *truth tables are used to define the meaning of the operation.

Dyck language A concept used in *formal language theory. Let Σ be the alphabet

$$\{a_1, \ldots, a_n, b_1, \ldots, b_n\}$$

The Dyck language over Σ is the set of all strings that can be reduced to the empty string Λ by "cancellations" of the form

$$a_i b_i \rightarrow \Lambda$$

For example,

$$\Sigma = \{(,)\}$$

gives the Dyck language of all balanced parenthesis strings. An important theorem characterizes the *context-free languages as those representable as the homomorphic image (*see* homomorphism) of the intersection of a Dyck language and a *regular language.

dynamic Capable of changing or of being changed. With reference to operating systems, the implication is that the system is capable of changing while it continues to run. As an example, the total amount of memory available may be defined by the contents of a word within the operating system. If this word can be altered without stopping the system and reloading a fresh copy of the operating system, then it is possible to alter dynamically the total amount of memory on the system.
With reference to programming, the adjective is applied to operations that take place while a program is running, as compared with those that take place during the compilation phase. For example, dynamic arrays are allocated space while the program is running.
Compare static.

dynamic allocation An allocation that is made dynamically, i.e. while the system is running, rather than statically at the time of first initiating the system.

dynamic data structure A data structure whose organizational characteristics may change during its lifetime. The adaptability afforded by such structures, e.g. linked lists, is often at the expense of decreased efficiency in accessing elements of the structure. Two main features distinguish dynamic structures from *static data structures. Firstly, it is no longer possible to have all structural information in a *header; each data element will have to contain information relating it logically to other elements of the structure. Secondly, using a single block of contiguous storage is often not appropriate, and hence it is necessary to provide some storage management scheme at run-time.

dynamic memory A form of *volatile semiconductor memory in which stored information is degraded with time. The most common example is dynamic *RAM (random-access memory) where the logic state to be entered in each cell is stored as a voltage on the small capacitance associated with the gate of the MOS output transistor for the cell. The voltage decays away with time because of leakage currents in the cell, and so it must be *refreshed (i.e. recharged) periodically by external circuitry.

dynamic programming The mathematical theory and planning of multistage decision processes; the term was introduced by Richard Bellman in 1957. It may be regarded as a branch of *mathematical programming or *optimization problems formulated as a sequence of decisions. Applications are very varied, including engineering problems and company planning.

E

EAROM *Acronym for* electrically alterable read-only memory. A form of semiconductor memory in which it is possible to change the contents of selected memory locations by applying suitable electrical signals. Normally these changes are infrequent and the device bears more similarity to a *ROM than to a *RAM.

Easyload *Trademark*. *See* magnetic tape cartridge.

EBCDIC (extended binary coded decimal interchange code) An 8-bit *character encoding scheme used primarily on the IBM 360–370 series. *See* character set.

EBNF *Abbrev. for* extended BNF.

echo The reflection of transmitted data back to its source. For example, characters typed on the keyboard of a data terminal (connected to a computer) will not appear on the display of the terminal unless they are echoed. The echoing may be done locally by the terminal itself, by a modem, or by an intervening communication processor. Echoing may also be done by the computer to which the terminal is attached. If the terminal itself echoes the characters, it is often said to be in *half-duplex mode*, although the term *local-echo mode* would be more accurate. In full-duplex character-at-a-time transmission, echoing is generally done at the computer, thus permitting certain application programs, such as editors, to determine whether or not incoming characters should be echoed. Half-duplex and/or line-at-a-time transmission generally implies local echoing.

echo check A way of establishing the accuracy achieved during the transfer of data over a data link, computer network, etc. When the data is received it is stored and also transmitted back to its point of origin in the transmission loop where it can be compared with the original data.
The term is also applied to other circumstances in which a transmitted signal directly causes a return signal. For example, in some line printers the sharp rise in the current waveform of an electromagnet drive pulse, which occurs when the armature impacts, is sometimes used to verify that the intended event has occurred.

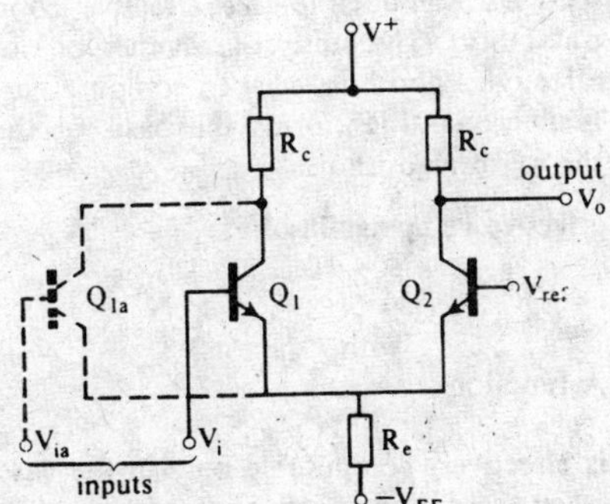

Two-input ECL OR gate

ECL *Abbrev. for* emitter-coupled logic. A high-speed *logic family available in the form of integrated circuits based on *bipolar transistors. The fast switching speeds are achieved by means of a design that avoids driving the transistors into saturation.
The basic circuit element is based on a difference amplifier, as shown in the diagram (ignoring dashed lines). In this symmetrical circuit the combined emitter current flowing through the resistor R_e is substantially constant. If the voltage V_i is equal to V_{ref} then each transistor, Q_1 and Q_2, conducts by the same amount and the output is at V_{ref}. If V_i is increased above V_{ref} by more than about 0.1 volts, Q_1 will be turned on while Q_2 turns off. As a result V_o increases to V^+. Similarly if V_i is decreased below V_{ref} by more than about 0.1 volts, V_o will decrease to some value largely determined by V_{EE}, R_e, and R_c.
By placing transistors in parallel with Q_1, as shown by the dashed lines, an ECL *OR gate is produced. Additional buffering is required on the gate output to provide the correct voltage swings for subsequent gate inputs.
ECL provides the highest speed of any logic family but its power dissipation is high and the output voltage swing is small.

Eclipse *See* Data General.

ECMA European Computer Manufacturers' Association, founded in 1961 and based in Geneva with members in nine European countries. Its aims are "to promote, in the general interest and in collaboration with national and international organizations, all ways and means destined to facilitate and standardize the utilization of data processing systems."

edge A connection between two vertices of a *graph.

edge board A *circuit board that is a modular part of a larger circuit. The term *edge card* is often used synonymously but is sometimes considered smaller than an edge board. Connections between this module and other modules are made through a printed-circuit pattern on the edge of the board that mates with an *edge connector. The edge connector normally contains the wiring that ties all modules together.

edge card *See* edge board.

edge connector A multiway socket whose contacts are arranged according to a standard pattern. The socket is capable of accepting a standard-sized *circuit board having contact areas that are formed along its edge and can mate with corresponding contacts in the socket. Connections to various points on the circuit board may then be made indirectly via the socket. *See also* backplane.

edge-triggered flip-flop *See* flip-flop, D flip-flop.

Edison A programming language for designing reliable real-time programs for multiprocessor systems. Edison is *block-structured and includes modules, concurrent statements, and when statements.

editor *See* link editor, text editor.

EDP *Abbrev. for* electronic data processing. *See* data processing.

EDS *Abbrev. for* exchangeable disk store.

EDSAC *Acronym for* Electronic Delay Storage Automatic Calculator. A machine designed in 1946 by M. V. Wilkes of Cambridge University, inspired by the stored-program concept being taught in the US by von Neumann and others. The design was notable for using acoustic *delay lines for memory. The EDSAC began operations in May 1949, becoming the second computer (after the *Manchester Mark I) that was operational using the stored-program concept. *See also* EDVAC.

EDVAC *Acronym for* Electronic Discrete Variable Automatic Calculator. The third electronic computer, originally commissioned from the University of Pennsylvania's Moore School by the US Army in 1944 while the *ENIAC was still under construction, but not operational until 1952. In 1945 John von Neumann prepared a proposal for the EDVAC that described the logical design of a computer with a "stored program", where the instructions to the machine would be stored in substantially the same fashion as the data. Although there is some disagreement as to whether von Neumann or the team of Mauchly and Eckert originated the stored-program concept, this was its first written documentation. Regardless of its origin, the stored-program model that formed the basis of the EDVAC design motivated all subsequent machine designs. *See also* EDSAC, Manchester Mark I.

EEROM *Acronym for* electrically erasable read-only memory. A form of semiconductor memory in which the entire contents can be erased by subjecting the device to suitable electrical signals. After erasing, the device can be reprogrammed. This procedure may be repeated hundreds of times without damaging the device.

effective address A direct address that has been developed by one of the *addressing schemes such as augmenting, relative addressing, or indexing. *See also* machine address.

effective algorithm An algorithm that is effectively computable (*see* effective computability). The study of whether or not effective algorithms exist to compute particular quantities forms the basis of the theory of algorithms.

effective computability Let

$$\mathbf{N} = \{0,1,\ldots\}$$
$$\mathbf{N}^k = \mathbf{N} \times \ \ldots \ \times \mathbf{N}$$
$$\text{(with } k \text{ factors)}$$

A function

$$f: \mathbf{N}^k \rightarrow \mathbf{N}$$

is effectively computable only in the case when there is an *effective procedure* (i.e. an algorithm) that correctly calculates f. An effective procedure is one that meets the following specifications. Firstly, the procedure must consist of a finite set of "simple" instructions (i.e. a program) and there must be no ambiguity concerning the order in which the instructions are to be carried out (*see* Turing machine). Secondly, if the procedure is given a k-tuple x in the domain of f, then after a finite number of steps, the calculation must terminate and output $f(x)$; if the procedure is given a k-tuple not in the domain of f it must not output a value.

effective enumeration *See* enumeration.

effective procedure *See* effective computability, decision problem.

EFTS *Abbrev. for* electronic funds transfer system.

EIA Electronics Industries Association, a US legislation-oriented information, education, and lobbying group made up of manufacturers of electronic equipment.

eigenfunctions *See* eigenvalue problems.

eigenvalue problems Problems that arise frequently in engineering and science and fall into two main classes. The standard (matrix) eigenvalue problem is to determine real or complex numbers,

$$\lambda_1, \lambda_2, \ldots \lambda_n \text{ (eigenvalues)}$$

and corresponding nonzero vectors,

$$x_1, x_2, \ldots, x_n \text{ (\textit{eigenvectors})}$$

that satisfy the equation

$$Ax = \lambda x$$

where A is a given real or complex $n \times n$ matrix.

By analogy the continuous eigenvalue problem is to determine similar eigenvalues and corresponding nonzero functions (*eigenfunctions*) that satisfy the equation

$$Hf(x) = \lambda f(x)$$

where H is a given operator on functions f.

A simple example arising from a vibrating-string problem is

$$y''(x) = \lambda y(x),$$
$$y(0) = 0, y(1) = 0$$

where values of the parameter λ (eigenvalues) are required that yield nontrivial eigenfunctions $y(x)$ (i.e. $y(x) \not\equiv 0$). *Finite-difference methods applied to such problems generally lead to matrix eigenvalue problems.

eigenvectors *See* eigenvalue problems.

either-or operation *See* OR operation.

elapsed time The actual time between two events, measured by a "clock on the wall". *Compare* CPU time.

electrographic printer A term that embraces *electrostatic, *electrosensitive, and *electrophotographic printers.

electroluminescent display *See* display.

electronic data processing (EDP) *See* data processing.

electronic filing A computer-based system for the storage, cataloging, and retrieval of documents. It is central to the success of a comprehensive *office automation system in that it provides the basic object management required to create, manipulate, and delete "office objects", which may be text, graphics, complex reports, or any other information that may be stored in a computer system.

A comprehensive electronic filing system should give a high degree of security for the objects entrusted to it, both against computer failure and against unauthorized access, together with flexible methods of organizing these objects. It should also provide shared access to community items while preserving privacy for confidential items.

Objects in an electronic filing system will generally be stored on magnetic disk or tape; some systems use microfilm techniques for bulk storage of items. Current systems generally allow the cataloging of "paper objects" that cannot be copied onto the computer system. This allows an easier transition to the computer-based system from an environment that previously relied on paper filing techniques.

electronic funds transfer system (EFTS) Generally, the use of computers in effecting payments between individuals and/or organizations. In some cases it is used to refer to advanced future systems in which debits and credits are made simultaneously with the transactions that give rise to them. In other cases its use covers all computer-based funds transfer systems, including long-established methods for check-clearance by banks.

Full-scale EFTSs cause particular anxiety to those who are concerned about the freedom and privacy of the individual in the information society, since they would enable very accurate profiles to be obtained of people's activities.

electronic mail (computer mail) Messages sent from one user of a computer system to one or more recipients (or the conveyance of such messages), the computer system being used to hold and transport messages. Sender and receivers need not be on-line at the same time, or even on the same computer, to communicate. Electronic mail is an important component of an office automation system.

The originator of a message creates a specially formatted message file by running a mail-sending program. The message may often be entered and modified using the general-purpose editor of the user's choice. Part of message entry is the acquisition of a list of recipients. When the message is complete, it is posted to a message transport system, which takes responsibility for delivering the message to recipients. This may involve passing the message through a *store-and-forward relay system when the sender and receiver are not connected to the same computer. At some later time the message is delivered into the recipient's incoming "mailbox". The recipient runs a program that retrieves incoming messages, allowing items to be filed, listed, etc. Frequently a single user-interface program is used both to send and receive messages.

Originally electronic mail was performed by using standard text hardcopy or CRT terminals. Newer systems support the composition and delivery of *multimedia mail*, which can combine text, graphics, voice, facsimile, and other forms of information in a single message. Other functions often performed by an electronic mail system include verification of a user's identity, expansion of named mailing lists into lists of recipients, and the location of a user on the basis of partial information (directory services).

electrophotographic printer A printer in which the required image is written by a beam of light onto a photoconductive drum or band that has a uniform electric charge over its surface. The action of the light beam causes local conductivity and allows the surface to assume the potential of the substrate. The charge pattern on the photoconductor is then developed by applying particles of pigment that carry an appropriate electrostatic charge: the toner particles are attracted to the image but are repelled by the background. The image is then transferred to paper by pressing the paper against the drum or band and applying an electric field. The toner is fixed to the paper by heat and/or pressure or by passing through a solvent vapor bath.

The principle is the same as that used in many office copiers and some recent designs of this type of printer can also function as a copier. In a copier the light image on the photoconductor drum is a projection of the original document via a lens system. In a printer the image is formed by a modulated light beam from a laser, the face of a display tube, an array of light-emitting diodes, or an array of photoelectric shutters.

This type of printer can yield very good print quality, forming its image as a fine matrix of dots. It can thus readily produce graphics and a wide variety of typestyles. There are over 40 electrophotographic printers available or at an advanced stage of development (1983), including machines that can print on both sides of the paper and can print in full color.

electrosensitive printer A type of printer that produces the required image by passing an electric current into the surface of specially prepared paper. The most common form uses paper with one surface coated first with a layer of carbon black and then with a fine coat of aluminum to give it a white appearance. The writing is done by a row of styluses that can be separately energized to pass sufficient electric current into the surface to vaporize the aluminum locally and expose the black undersurface. The styluses may be arranged as a small number (typically 7) that traverse along the line to be printed and print the characters serially, or as many as 400 may be arranged to span a distance of 4″. Such a printer can produce a copy of a display screen showing 25 lines of 80 characters in a few seconds and is compact enough to be built into the case of a VDU.

electrostatic printer A type of printer in which the required image is first written as a pattern of electrostatic charge, and is then made visible by bringing the pattern into contact with particles of pigment that carry a charge of opposite polarity. The pigment is only attracted to the charge pattern and is subsequently fused or bonded to the paper.

In some designs the charge pattern is applied by styluses directly to paper that has been specially treated. An alternative approach is to apply the pattern to a metal drum with a suitable coating such as aluminum oxide. The pattern is made visible by washing the paper or drum with a colloidal suspension of charged particles of pigment. The image on a drum is transferred to plain paper by pressure and the application of an electric field. The particles of pigment are very fine and thus penetrate the fibers of the paper and form a permanent image. A recent development in this technology is to apply the charge to the drum by the controlled projection of ions.

In some literature the term is used to refer to all printers in which an electrostatic image is formed as one of the steps in the process, including *electrophotographic printers.

electrostatic storage device An obsolete storage device in which the data was stored as a charge pattern within a *cathode-ray tube and could be read by a scanning beam of electrons. The data was not usually visible. One of the early designs was the *Williams-tube store*, named for F. C. Williams of the University of Manchester, UK, who led the development work; it was one of the earliest forms of random-access memory. Electrostatic storage gave a significant reduction in storage cost compared to the mercury *delay line memory that it superseded, but the information had to be frequently regenerated (rewritten) and was lost when power was removed. It was displaced in processor designs in the mid-1950s by *core stores.

element 1. of a set. *Another name for* member.

2. *See* logic element.

ELSE rule The last (usually rightmost) rule of an incomplete *decision table, i.e. a table that does not include all possible combinations of conditions. The ELSE rule defines the step set for all actions not satisfying the explicit rules of the decision table. A table with an ELSE rule is complete since all possible combinations are taken into consideration.

EMAS *Acronym for* Edinburgh multiaccess system. An operating system that was originally developed at the University of Edinburgh and is intended to support large numbers of interactive terminals. It is one of the earliest systems to be implemented almost entirely in a high-level language. A special implementation language, IMP, was devised for this purpose.

embedded computer system Any system that uses a computer as a component, but whose prime function is not that of a computer. One example is a weapons-guidance system. Another is a computer-controlled blood analyzer that uses a minicomputer or microcomputer to control various tests that are run on blood in order to produce an integrated printout of all test results.

embedded servo *See* actuator.

emitter-coupled logic *See* ECL.

empty list (null list) *See* list.

empty medium A *data medium that does not contain variable data but may have a frame of reference or preformatting. *Compare* virgin medium.

empty set (null set; void set) A *set with no elements. It is usually denoted by ø.

empty string (null string) A string whose *length is zero. It is commonly denoted by ε or Λ. The possibility of strings being empty is a notorious source of bugs in programs.

emulation The exact execution on a given computer of a program written for a different computer, accepting the identical data and producing the identical results. Emulation is formally defined as being achieved primarily by hardware; it is usually accomplished at the microprogram level. *See also* simulation, compatibility.

emulator Any system, especially a program or microprogram, that permits the process of *emulation to be carried out.

enable To selectively activate a device or function. When a number of devices are connected in parallel, selective operation can be achieved by an enabling action – such as a signal on a discrete line or a pattern of signals on the common line or lines – that will set only the desired device into a state in which it can receive further signals. *Compare* inhibit.

enable pulse A pulse that must be present to allow other signals to be effective in certain electronic logic circuits. Although the term is now used to describe an electronic logic function it was originally used in an analogous way in connection with *core stores, where the coincidence of two pulses is required to change the state of a core: one of the pulses is the write pulse and can be common to a number of cores; an enable pulse is simultaneously applied to a particular core and thus enables the write pulse to change the state of that core.

encapsulation *See* internetworking.

encoder 1. The means by which an encoding process is effected (*see* code). It may be implemented in hardware or software, the process being algorithmic in nature.
2. A logic circuit, usually an integrated circuit, that generates a unique *n*-bit binary word, indicating which of its 2^n input lines is active, i.e. at logic 1. A *keyboard encoder*, for example, may be required to generate a unique binary code indicating which key on the keyboard has been pressed.
If two or more of the device inputs can be active simultaneously then a *priority encoder* is required, which usually encodes only the highest-order data input.

encoding 1. The transformation of a message into an encoded form. *See* code.
2. The representation of symbols in some alphabet by symbols or strings of symbols in some other alphabet. A common example is *binary encoding.

encoding format *See* disk format.

encryption Transformation of plain text to cipher text by means of a cryptographic transformation and an associated key, or by means of a codebook. *See* cryptography.

end-around-carry A type of carry that is required when a *radix-minus-one complement representation of integers is used and two integers so represented are summed. If a carry is generated at the most significant end of the two numbers, then this carry must be added to the digit at the least significant end of the result to give the radix-minus-one complement representation of the sum.

end-around shift *Another name for* circular shift.

endomorphism A *homomorphism from one *algebraic structure G into another algebraic structure H, where the set of elements of G is a *subset of the elements of H.

endorder traversal *Another name for* postorder traversal.

end-to-end encryption The use of one *encryption to protect a transaction all the way from a user to the process being invoked in the destination computer system, and vice versa. *Compare* link encryption.

energizer A hardware or software mechanism that is used as an aid in testing the behavior of a subsystem. The intention is that the energizer should drive the subsystem in a way that simulates its actual application, and should at the same time analyze the responses from the subsystem in order to detect any erroneous behavior.

ENIAC *Acronym for* Electronic Numerical Integrator and Computer. The first general-purpose electronic calculator, designed and built by John W. Mauchly and J. Presper Eckert Jr. at the University of Pennsylvania's Moore School during the period 1943–46. Originally designed for the production of ballistic tables for the second world war, the machine was not completed until after the war ended. It was widely used for scientific computation until the early 1950s.

entropy A measure of the amount of information that is output by a source, or throughput by a channel, or received by an observer (per symbol or per second). Following Shannon (1948) and later writers, the entropy of a *discrete memoryless source with alphabet $A = \{a_i\}$ of size n, and output X at time t is

$$H(X) = \sum_{i=0}^{n-1} p(x_i) \log_b (1/p(x_i))$$

where

$$p(x_i) = \text{Prob}\,\{X_t = a_i\}$$

The logarithmic base b is chosen to give a convenient scale factor. Usually,

$b = 2$

$b = e = 2.71828 \ldots$

or

$b = 10$

Entropy is then measured in *bits*, in *natural units* or *nats*, or in *Hartleys*, respectively. When the source has memory, account has to be taken of the dependence between successive symbols output by the source.

The term arises by analogy with entropy in thermodynamics, where the defining expression has the same form but with a physical scale factor k (Boltzmann constant) and with the sign changed. The word *negentropy* is therefore sometimes used for the measure of information, as is *uncertainty* or simply "information".

entry 1. An item of data in a list or table. **2.** *Another name for* entry point.

entry point (entry) The instruction to which control is transferred when a subroutine is called.

entry time The time at which a process is started or restarted by the process scheduler.

Entscheidungsproblem *See* halting problem.

enumeration A list of items in order. Thus the items are organized in such a way that they can be counted, and for each nonnegative integer i within an appropriate range there is a unique item associated with it. An enumeration may be finite or infinite; when an infinite set is involved, the infinite set must be *countable. An enumeration is said to be *effective* if there

is an *algorithm for producing the enumeration.
Enumeration is used to define *types in languages of the Pascal and Jovial families. It also plays a significant role in *combinatorics where one might typically talk of an enumeration of *permutations or *combinations, of *binary trees, of *graphs, of *groups, etc.

EOB *Abbrev. for* end of block.

EOD *Abbrev. for* end of data. A code that is written into a serially accessed memory, such as a magnetic tape file, immediately after the last data record. It thus indicates the starting point for new records and is erased when they are added and then re-written in a new position.

EOF *Abbrev. for* end of file.

EOJ *Abbrev. for* end of job.

EOR *Abbrev. for* end of record.

EOT 1. *Abbrev. for* end of transmission. A character sequence on a data link indicating that the current transmitter has nothing further to send. Active stations on the data link return to their idle state and wait for a new series of messages.
2. *Abbrev. for* end of tape.

EOT marker *Short for* end of tape marker. A feature of a *magnetic tape by which the tape transport senses on the tape the end of the volume into which data can be or has been recorded. It is complementary to the *BOT marker, and is similarly defined by the standard pertaining to the type of tape.

epimorphism A *homomorphism that, when viewed as a *function, is a *surjection.

epoch The time interval between successive elements of a discrete-time signal, or between the discrete-time samples of a continuous-time signal (*see* discrete and continuous systems). Usually, for a given signal, the epochs are of a fixed size.

EPROM *Acronym for* erasable programmable read-only memory. A type of *PROM that is capable of being programmed a number of times by the user. The contents of EPROMs are generally erased, i.e. set to logic 0, by exposure to hard ultraviolet radiation. The EPROM may then be reprogrammed, i.e. selected elements set to logic 1, using a *PROM programmer.

equipotent *See* cardinality.

P	F	F	T	T
Q	F	T	F	T
$P \equiv Q$	T	F	F	T

Truth table for equivalence

equivalence 1. The logical connective combining two statements or formulas P and Q in such a way that the outcome is true if both P and Q are true or if both are false, as shown in the table. P and Q are said to be *equivalent*. The connective can be read as "if and only if" or "iff", and is usually denoted by one of the symbols

$$\equiv \quad \leftrightarrow \quad <-> \quad <=>$$

See also exclusive-NOR gate, propositional calculus.
2. A relationship between objects that are operationally or structurally indistinguishable, e.g. in *combinational circuits, *graphs, or *grammars. Equivalence is less strong than identity or equality but much more useful in practice. *See also* machine equivalence.

equivalence class A *subset of a set S (on which an *equivalence relation is defined) that consists of all the elements of S that are equivalent to each other, and to no other elements of S. An equivalence relation provides a partitioning (*see* covering) of a set into a number of mutually *disjoint equivalence classes.
The relationship "has the same surname as" defined on the set of people produces an equivalence class consisting of all those

with Jones as surname, another consisting of those with Smith as surname, and so on.

equivalence gate *See* exclusive-NOR gate.

equivalence relation A *relation that is *transitive, *symmetric, and *reflexive. The concept is a convenient generalization or abstraction of equality. It covers most notions of equals, equivalence, and similarity as defined between triangles, algorithms, Boolean expressions, algebraic structures, statements, etc. *See also* equivalence class, partial ordering.

equivalent binary digits For a given source alphabet, S, the number of equivalent binary digits is the minimum number of bits that need to be taken in a *block code to give at least as many codewords as there are symbols in S.

equivalent trees *Similar trees with the same data at corresponding nodes.

erasable programmable device *See* programmable device.

erase head *See* head, magnetic tape.

eraser An item of electronic equipment that can carry out the erasure process for an *EPROM. It often consists of an enclosed source of ultraviolet radiation, close to which the EPROM may be placed, and a timer.

erasure channel A communication *channel in which the effect of *noise is to cause the *decoder sometimes to be presented with an "error" symbol to decode. The decoder may then act in the knowledge that in such symbol positions the symbol actually transmitted is unknown: it is thus in a better position than when presented with an incorrect symbol but not the knowledge that it is incorrect (other than can be deduced by using an *error-detecting or *error-correcting code).

ergodic source *See* discrete source.

error analysis A term that when applied to *numerical analysis refers to the mathematical analysis that describes the various aspects of error behavior in numerical methods (or algorithms). *Convergence* of an algorithm is a fundamental requirement. Most algorithms result in the construction of a sequence of approximations. If this sequence tends more and more closely to the true solution of the problem, the algorithm is convergent. How fast the algorithm converges is important for its efficiency; some insight is provided by the *order of the method. Since most algorithms are terminated before convergence is reached, the size of the error after a finite number of steps must be estimated. How big the error is at most can be determined from an *error bound.* This must be reasonably "sharp", i.e. it must not grossly overestimate the error. How big the error is approximately is referred to as an *error estimate* and is usually determined from an asymptotic formula. Such estimates are widely used in step-by-step methods for *ordinary differential equations; here the stepsize, h, must be small enough for the estimate to be accurate.

In *numerical linear algebra *backward error analysis* has proved very successful in analyzing errors. In this approach it is shown that the numerical solution satisfies exactly a perturbed form of the original problem. Bounds for the perturbations are determined and these can be inserted into standard results, thus producing a bound for the error in the numerical solution. The approach can be applied to other areas.

error bound *See* error analysis.

error burst *Another name for* burst error.

error control The employment, in a computer system or in a communication system, of *error-detecting and/or *error-correcting codes with the intention of removing the effects of error and/or recording the prevalence of error in the system. The effects of errors may be removed by correcting them in all but a negligible proportion of cases. Error control aims to cope with errors owing to *noise or to equipment malfunction – in which case it overlaps with fault tolerance (*see* fault-tolerant system) – but not usually with the effects of errors in the design of hardware or software.

Error control is expensive: the balance between the cost and the benefit (measured by the degree of protection) has to be weighed within the technological and financial context of the system being designed.

error-correcting code A *code that is designed for *channel coding, i.e. for encoding information so that a decoder can correct, with a high probability of success, any errors caused in the signal by an intervening noisy channel.

Error-correcting codes may be *block codes or *convolutional codes, and in either case are employed in a *forward error-correction system. The most common error-correcting block codes are the *Hamming codes, *Bose–Chandhuri–Hocquenghem (BCH) codes, the *Reed–Solomon (RS) codes, the *simplex codes, and the *Golay (23, 12) code. Since errors may be corrected by detecting them and requesting retransmission, the process of error correction is sometimes taken to include *backward error-correction systems and, hence, *error-detecting codes.

See also Shannon's model, coding theory, coding bounds.

error-detecting code A *code that is designed for *channel coding, i.e. for encoding information so that a decoder can detect, with a high probability of success, whether an intervening channel has caused an error in the signal.

Error-detecting codes are usually *block codes, and are generally employed in a *backward error-correction system. The most common error-detecting codes are the *cyclic redundancy checks, of which the simple parity check is a technologically important case.

See also error-correcting code, Shannon's model, coding theory, coding bounds, Hamming distance.

error detection and correction Errors can occur in stored data, as data is transferred, or in the act of computation based on that data. They are detected by having some *redundancy in the data so that *redundancy checks can be performed, or by performing (logically) duplicative computational processes. Some detected data-transfer errors can be corrected by retransferring the data (e.g. from a magnetic tape in which the read process was affected by a transient error). Other errors require the use of *forward error correction features. Detected errors in computation are usually corrected by redundant computational units.

See also error control, error-correcting code, error-detecting code.

error diagnostics Information that is presented following the detection of some error condition and is mainly intended to assist in identifying the cause of the error. As an example, consider the compilation and subsequent execution of some program. *Syntactic errors* in the program, i.e. failure of the program to conform to the defined *syntax of the programming language, would normally be detected at compilation time, and the compiler would then generally produce error diagnostics to indicate both the location and the kind of error (unrecognized statement, undeclared identifier, etc.). At execution time certain kinds of *semantic errors* may be detected, i.e. improper behavior of a program that conforms to the defined syntax of the language. In this case the error diagnostics may be produced by some run-time system. *See also* error routine.

error estimate *See* error analysis.

error handling *Another term for* error management.

error management of magnetic tape. The procedure followed when an error is detected in data read by a tape transport, either in the course of a read operation or in the course of the read-while-write check associated with a write operation (*see* magnetic tape). The procedure is usually controlled by the host system software, but in buffered tape transports it may be partly or entirely *autonomous*, i.e. controlled by the *magnetic tape subsystem, which will usually either count error occurrences or notify the host of each one individually. Error management is carried out on a block-by-block basis.

Read error recovery usually consists of repeated attempts to read the *block containing the error, and this involves starting and stopping the tape for each attempt. Various physical parameters of the tape transport (including the direction of tape motion) may be varied for successive attempts. Typically the procedure allows for up to about 10 attempts, or *re-tries*, before the effort is regarded as irrecoverable (*see* error rate). Many *tape formats make provision for logical error recovery by redundant coding, which permits recovery without rereading the tape; this is attempted (either autonomously or with software assistance, depending on the particular format) before the main error recovery procedure is invoked.

Write error recovery is usually preceded by one or more attempts at read error recovery, since the error may have occurred in the read part of the read-while-write check; it is then usual to erase the block containing the error (which will be the last valid block on the tape, or at least in the file) and rewrite it, starting a predefined distance down the tape to avoid any flaw in the medium, and thus leaving an elongated interblock gap. This process will be repeated a predetermined number of times (typically five) before the error is regarded as irrecoverable.

Some recent tape format definitions, particularly for streaming cartridge tape, allow *on-the-fly write error recovery* where the block containing the error is not erased but simply repeated, without stopping the tape; in practice, timing considerations may require that two blocks are repeated. Block numbers in the block headers allow repeated blocks to be detected on reading.

The design of the error recovery procedure has an effect on the permanent *error rate, since the more attempts that are made at recovering an error – especially if the tape transport parameters are varied – the greater the chance that the recovery will succeed and the error be classified as transient rather than permanent. Thus the error rate quoted for a subsystem is valid only if the error recovery procedure prescribed by the hardware manufacturer is followed. Error rates and error recovery are also affected by block length.

error message *See* error routine.

error propagation A term that refers to the way in which, at a given stage of a calculation, part of the error arises out of the error at a previous stage. This is independent of the further *roundoff errors inevitably introduced between the two stages. Unfavorable error propagation can seriously affect the results of a calculation. The investigation of error propagation in simple arithmetical operations is used as the basis for the detailed analysis of more extensive calculations. The way in which uncertainties in the data propagate into the final results of a calculation can be assessed in practice by repeating the calculation with slightly perturbed data.

error rate 1. of a communication channel. The frequency with which errors or noise are introduced into the channel. Error rate may be measured in terms of erroneous bits received per bits transmitted. For example, one or two errors per 100 000 bits might be a typical rate for a narrowband point-to-point line. The distribution of errors is usually nonuniform: errors tend to come in bursts (*see* burst error). Thus the error rate of a channel may be specified in terms of percentage of error-free seconds. Frequently an error rate is expressed as a negative power of ten: an error rate of one bit per 100 000 would be expressed as an error rate of 10^{-5}.

Another method of presenting error rate is to consider the errors as the result of adding the data signal to an underlying error signal. The ratio of the strengths of the two signals – the *signal-to-noise ratio – is expressed in decibels.

2. of a *magnetic tape subsystem. A measurement of the proportion of errors occurring in data transfers to or from magnetic tape. It is usually expressed in terms of the average number of bytes or bits of data transferred per error, e.g. 1 error per 10^9 bytes, although it can also be useful to express the rate as the average time between errors for typical usage of the subsystem, e.g. 1 undetected error in 6 weeks at 10% duty cycle.

The error rates most frequently specified relate to the following.

A *transient* (or *recoverable) read error* occurs during reading and can be recovered by the error recovery procedure prescribed for the magnetic tape subsystem (*see* error management). A typical figure for ½″ tape is 1 in 10^9 bytes. Where the *tape format provides sufficient redundancy to allow some error to be recovered *on-the-fly*, i.e. without stopping the tape and re-reading the block, it is necessary to define also the *raw error rate*, which is the rate that would be perceived if on-the-fly error recovery was not applied.

A *permanent* (or *irrecoverable) read error* cannot be recovered by the prescribed error recovery procedure. A typical figure is 1 in 10^{11} bytes.

A *transient* (or *recoverable) write error* occurs during writing and can be recovered by the error recovery procedure prescribed. It is desirable, though not easy, to distinguish two components of this error rate: errors attributable to flaws in the media and to failings of the device (one reason for the difficulty is that these tend to interact). A typical figure, excluding media errors, is 1 in 10^8 bytes.

A *permanent* (or *irrecoverable) write error* cannot be recovered by the prescribed procedure. Again it is necessary to distinguish between media flaws and device errors: it is now usual not to give a figure for the latter but to regard each occurrence as a fault to be accounted for in the failure rate of the device (*see* hardware reliability).

An *undetected error* is an error that is not detected by the magnetic tape subsystem, presumably because of some inadequacy in the error check facilities defined by the format or in their implementation, or because of errors occurring outside the ambit of these facilities (*see* data integrity). A typical figure is 1 in 10^{13} bytes.

error recovery 1. The ability of a compiler to resume parsing of a program after encountering a syntax error.

2. *See* error management.

error routine Any routine within a program that is entered as a result of some error condition having been detected. The actions taken by such a routine will be dependent upon the reliability requirements that the program is expected to meet and upon the strategy for error analysis and recovery. A typical error routine might simply produce an *error message* (i.e. a message that reports the occurrence of an error) or it might attempt to diagnose the cause of the error or attempt to recover so that normal operation can continue.

escape character A control character that changes the meaning of a character or characters immediately following. It is like a temporary *shift character.

Ethernet Originally, an experimental *local area network, 3 megabits per second on coaxial cable with *CSMA/CD baseband signaling (*see* baseband networking). It was developed (1976) at Xerox PARC for linking personal computers. It was adopted (1980) by DEC, Intel, and Xerox as a standard communication medium, 10 megabits per second on coaxial cable with CSMA/CD baseband signaling. It effectively provides the two lower layers of the ISO/OSI *seven-layer reference model.

Euclidean norm (two-norm) *See* approximation theory.

Euclid's algorithm An algorithm for finding the greatest common divisor of two integers, *m* and *n*. If $m > n$ divide *m* by *n* and let *r* be the remainder. If $r = 0$ then *n* is the answer; otherwise apply the same algorithm to the integers *n* and *r*.

Euler cycle (Euler path) A *path in a directed *graph that includes each edge in the graph precisely once; thus it represents a complete traversal of the arcs of the graph. The concept is named for Leonhard Euler who introduced it around 1736 to solve the Königsberg (now Kaliningrad) bridge problem. He showed that for a graph to possess an Euler cycle it should be *connected and each vertex should have the same number of edges entering it as leaving it.

Euler's method *See* discretization.

Euronet A *packet switching network that was sponsored by the Commission of the EEC (European Economic Community) and became operational in 1979. Formally it is known as Euronet-Diane, where Diane stands for direct information access network for Europe. The partners in the project are: the major hosts in the EEC, offering on-line STI (scientific and technological information) interactive retrieval services; the EEC's *PTTs, building specifically for the project the European international data transmission network, which links the EEC countries; and the Commission of the EEC, sponsoring not only the project but common services for the on-line user.

even parity A property that holds when a group of binary values contains an even number of 1s. *See* parity.

event *See* relative frequency.

EVFU *Abbrev. for* electronic vertical format unit. *See* vertical format unit.

exception An error or fault condition that makes further execution of a program meaningless. If the programming language permits, occurrence of an exception will cause a break in the normal flow of control to an *exception handler*. Examples of exceptions are arithmetic overflow, read-error on external device, array element with index out of bounds, and unavailable storage.

excess-3 code An 8421 *code for which the weighted sum of the four bits in each codeword is three greater than the decimal digit represented by that codeword. For example, 9 is represented by 1100, the weighted sum of which is

$$8\times1 + 4\times1 + 2\times0 + 1\times0 = 12$$

excess factor *Another name for* bias. *See* floating-point notation.

excess-n notation (excess notation) *See* floating-point notation.

exchange in a network. *See* node.

exchangeable disk store (EDS) A storage medium that consists of a magnetic *disk pack or *disk cartridge that can be removed from its host system for library storage, and be replaced by another EDS of the same type. The store can be fitted to another host system having the same type of drive and means of recording and reading data. *See also* fixed and exchangeable disk store.

exchange selection *Another name for* bubble sort.

exclusive-NOR gate An electronic *logic gate whose output is logic 0 (false) only when any one of its inputs is logic 1 (true) and all the others are logic 0, otherwise the

inputs	A1	0	0	1	1
	A2	0	1	0	1
output B		1	0	0	1

Two-input EXNOR gate, circuit symbol and truth table

output is logic 1. It implements the logical operation of *equivalence and has the same *truth table. It is thus also known as an *equivalence gate*. Like the *exclusive-OR gate it can be used as a simple digital *comparator. The diagram shows the circuit symbol and truth table of a two-input gate.

inputs	A1	0	0	1	1
	A2	0	1	0	1
output B		0	1	1	0

Two-input EXOR gate, circuit symbol and truth table

P	F	F	T	T
Q	F	T	F	T
P XOR *Q*	F	T	T	F

Truth table for exclusive-OR operation

exclusive-OR gate An electronic *logic gate whose output is logic 1 (true) only when any one of its inputs is logic 1 and all the others are logic 0 (false), otherwise the output is logic 0. It therefore implements the logical *exclusive-OR operation and has the same *truth table; it is thus sometimes known as a *nonequivalence gate*. Like the *exclusive-NOR gate it can be used as a simple digital *comparator. The diagram shows the circuit symbol and truth table for a two-input gate.

exclusive-OR operation The logical *connective combining two statements, truth values, or formulas *P* and *Q* in such a way that the outcome is true if either *P* or *Q* (but not both *P* and *Q*) is true, as shown in the table. Since the outcome is true precisely when the operands are different, it is sometimes referred to as the *nonequivalence operation*. It can be represented in a variety of ways, the more common methods being XOR, xor, and $\not\vee$. *See also* OR operation.

execute To carry out an instruction or program. This includes interpreting machine instructions, performing subroutines, and applying functions to sets of parameters.

execute phase The time during a program run in which the target program is actually being executed.

execution states The various states in which a computer system may be operating; these states have differing degrees of ability or privilege attached to them. There may be two or more states. In the simplest case there is a *supervisor state* (or *executive state*) and a *user state*. With more than two execution states at different levels, differing degrees of privilege may be granted. These states can represent some of the used resources in an access matrix. *See* access control.

execute step The step in instruction execution that performs the operation(s) of the instruction and the associated memory references. *See* control unit.

execution time *Another name for* run time.

executive program An early name for a *supervisor. In current terminology an executive is not strictly speaking a program since the latter is usually taken to refer to one or more processes that are collaborating in order to achieve results on behalf of a single user. By contrast an executive is responsible for the supervision of many disjoint processes, which do not cooperate in any way.

executive state (supervisor state) *See* execution states.

exerciser A device or program used to test a subsystem. An example is a floppy-disk exerciser.

existential quantifier *See* quantifier.

exit point (exit) The point at which control leaves a subroutine.

EXNOR gate *Short for* exclusive-NOR gate.

EXOR gate *Short for* exclusive-OR gate.

expectation *See* measures of location.

experimental design A system of allocating treatments to experimental units so that the effects of the treatments may be estimated by *statistical methods. The basic principles of experimental design are *replication*, i.e. the application of the same treatment to several units, *randomization*, which ensures that each unit has the same probability of receiving any given treatment, and *blocking*, i.e. grouping of similar units, each one to receive a different treatment. *Factorial designs* are used to allow different types of treatment, or *factors*, to be tested simultaneously. *Analysis of variance is used to assess the significance of the treatment effects.

expert systems Computer programs built for commercial application using the programming techniques of *artificial intelligence, especially those techniques developed for problem solving, and involving the use of appropriate information acquired previously from human experts. *Knowledge engineering* is the subdiscipline of artificial intelligence concerned with building expert systems. Expert systems have been built for many purposes, including medical diagnosis, fault finding, mineral prospecting, and computer-system configuration.

exploratory data analysis (EDA) A term invented by J. W. Tukey to denote techniques for looking at numerical data with a view to discerning pattern. Exploratory data analysis is open-ended and makes few prior assumptions about the nature of any pattern that may be found. Graphical techniques are freely used. It can be contrasted with model-fitting techniques, which make highly specific prior assumptions. *Statistical methods contain aspects of both these processes.

exponent *See* floating-point notation.

exponentially bounded algorithm *See* complexity measure.

exponential space, time *See* complexity classes.

exponential waveform A nonrepetitive waveform that rises or falls exponentially from some initial value at some initial time, according to the logarithmic law

$$y(t) = e^{at}$$

For $a>0$ the waveform rises without bound with increasing time t; for $a<0$ the waveform decays to zero. One way in which logic signals can become corrupted as they travel through a system is for their switching edges to become exponentials.

exponentiation The *operation of raising to a power. Repeated multiplication of a quantity x by itself n times is written as x^n. When x is nonzero the value of x^0 is normally assumed to be 1.
Alternatively x^n can be defined inductively (*see* induction) in the following way:

$$x^0 = 1$$
$$x^n = x \times x^{n-1} \text{ for } n > 0$$

The concept of exponentiation can be extended to include exponents that are negative, fractional, or variable or are complex numbers. Exponentiation is an operation that is supplied in some form in most common programming languages (the significant exception being Pascal). It is also a fundamental part of the *floating-point notation for real numbers.

expression of requirements A statement of the requirements that some envisaged computer system (or program) is expected to meet. In order to define these requirements adequately, it is normally necessary for the expression of requirements to address not just the envisaged system but also the environment in which that system is to operate.

A good expression of requirements should be one of the earliest products of any system-development project, and for a project of significant size it is of crucial importance, not least because errors introduced at the requirements stage tend to be the most expensive to correct. Since it is the first reasonably complete description of any given system, its production presents several significant problems. In particular it may be necessary to obtain information from many individuals, none of whom have a full understanding of all aspects of the envisaged system. There may therefore be a need to resolve several confused, incomplete, and inconsistent views in order to produce a single coherent whole.

The expression of requirements is a primary vehicle for communication between the procurers of a system and its developers, and must therefore be understandable without specialist knowledge of computers or formal languages. A natural language expression of requirements is normally inadequate and more formal notations are usually adopted, often based on a graphical framework within which natural language can be used.

extended addressing Any of several methods that permit access to memory with *address space larger than the address space normally accessible in an instruction. *See* addressing schemes.

extended BNF (EBNF) A notation for defining the *syntax of a programming language, based on *BNF (Backus normal form). The main disadvantages of BNF are that repetition has to be expressed by a recursive definition, and options and alternatives require auxiliary definitions. For example, compare the definitions shown in BNF in Fig. 1 with the same definitions expressed in EBNF in Fig. 2: EBNF uses { . . . } to denote repetition, | to denote alternatives, (. . .) to group constituents, and [. . .] to denote options. The main difference is the notation for distinguishing between literals and syntactic variables. In BNF literals are plain and syntactic variables are marked using angle brackets; in EBNF syntactic variables are plain and literals are marked using quotation marks. This allows EBNF to define its own syntax.

```
<digit string> ::= <digit>|<digit><digit string>
<sign> ::= +|−
<unsigned number> ::= <digit string>|
                      <digit string>.
<number> ::= <unsigned number>|
             <sign><unsigned number>
```

Fig. 1 BNF notation

```
digit-string = digit {digit}
unsigned-number = digit-string[.]
number = unsigned-number|
         ("+"|"−") unsigned-number
```

Fig. 2 Extended BNF notation

extensibility The capability of a programming language to accept definitions of new constructs.

extensible addressing *See* addressing.

extensible language A programming language having the property of *extensibility.

extension of a source. In coding theory, the process of encoding several symbols at a time, or the results thereof. If the symbols of a *q-ary information source are taken r at a time, and the words of length r are treated (e.g. encoded) as if they were themselves symbols of an alphabet of size q^r, then this compound source is called the rth *extension* of the original source. *See also* source coding theorem.

extension field *See* polynomial.

external device A device that is subsidiary or peripheral to a computer system, usually a terminal or other remote device. In some I/O instructions the designation of an external device is made by specifying a (usually binary) number that distinguishes that device from all others. This number is often called the *external device address* although, strictly speaking, it is not an address in the true sense.

external fragmentation A form of *fragmentation that arises when memory is allocated in units of arbitrary size. When a large amount of memory is released, part of it may be used to meet a subsequent request, leaving an unused part that is too small to meet any further requests.

external interrupt An interrupt that is initiated by a device that is not part of the processor. Peripherals and communication connections are sources of external interrupts.

external node *Another name for* leaf node.

external path length of a tree. The sum of the lengths of all paths from the root to an external (i.e. a leaf) node.

external sorting *See* sorting.

external storage Any type of storage device that is connected to and controlled by a computer but is not integrated within it. Generally the devices are peripheral units such as tape transports or disk drives. An external storage device may be shared by more than one computer.

extrapolation The estimation of the value of a function (given other values of the function) at a point beyond the interval in which the data lies. One possible approach is to use the value of an *interpolation polynomial at this point. An important case arises when the data consists of approximations to the solution of a problem, for different values of a parameter controlling the magnitude of the acceptable error in the method used. A more powerful method can be constructed by extrapolating to the limiting case of the parameter, where the error is zero, using theoretical results giving the dependence of the error on the parameter. This is called *Richardson extrapolation* (or the *deferred approach to the limit*).

extrinsic semiconductor *See* semiconductor.

F

facsimile Systems that provide electronic transmission of ordinary documents, incuding drawings, photographs, and maps. The original document is scanned at the sending station, converted into an analog or digital representation, and sent over a communication channel to the receiving station, which constructs a duplicate image on paper; this image is referred to as a *facsimile*. Early facsimile systems were exclusively analog, but new systems have been designed that use digital techniques for data encoding and transmission.

factorable code An *error-correcting code that can be considered as the result of several coding stages, the output of each being encoded by the next. The constituent codes are the factors of the original compound code. *See* concatenated coding systems.

factor analysis *See* multivariate analysis.

factorial designs *See* experimental design.

fail-safe Denoting or relating to a computer system that does not make an error in spite of the occurrence of a single fault. *See also* fault-tolerant system.

fail-soft Denoting or relating to a computer system that can continue to provide a reduced level of service in spite of the occurrence of a single fault. The system is then said to be in a state of *graceful degradation*. *See also* fault-tolerant system.

failure A condition in which some portion of a computer system is unable to perform its prescribed function. The word *fault* is used as a synonym for failure but sometimes refers to the actual (physical) cause of the inability. *See also* fault-tolerant system.

failure recovery A procedure that allows for restart of a failed system in a way that either eliminates or minimizes the amount of incorrect system results. This usually requires the program that was running to have used a *checkpoint procedure.

fallback The *restarting of a process at a *checkpoint after correction of a fault. *See also* failure recovery.

fan-in The number of input lines (normally fixed) to a logic gate or logic device.

Fano coding (Shannon–Fano coding) *See* source coding.

Fano decoding The decoding of a *convolutional code by Fano's algorithm.

fan-out The maximum number of devices that can be safely driven by the output from a logic gate or logic device (which have only a limited ability to drive other devices from their output terminals). If the fan-out is exceeded the voltage levels corresponding to a logic 1 and a logic 0 become more similar and errors are more likely.

fast core A type of *core store that has a lower access time than the devices used for working store in the same processor.

fast Fourier transform (FFT) An algorithm that computes the discrete *Fourier transform accurately and efficiently on digital computers. FFT techniques have wide applicability in linear systems, optics, probability theory, quantum physics, antennas, and signal analysis.

father of a node. *Another name for* parent.

father file, father tape *See* file updating.

fault *See* failure.

fault detection Determination, normally by detection of a failure in a *check, that a fault (error) has occurred in a logic circuit, arithmetic circuit, or an information transfer.

fault diagnosis The task of determining where in a (repairable) computer system a fault has occurred and what the logical nature of that fault is.

fault-tolerant system A computer system that is capable of providing either full functionality (*fail-safe) or reduced functionality (*fail-soft) after a failure has occurred. Fault tolerance is usually provided through a combination of redundant system elements and error detection and correction procedures.

FCC Federal Communications Commission, the US regulatory commission for public communications. Its jurisdiction includes land line, cable, radio, and satellite communications. It is a party to international agreements on frequency allocation of the radio spectrum.

FDM *Abbrev. for* frequency division multiplexing.

feasibility study A study carried out prior to a development project in order to establish that the proposed system is feasible and can serve a useful purpose. Feasibility studies can be purely paper exercises or can involve the construction of experimental or prototype systems. Often a feasibility study will not address the entire scope of the proposed system, but will concentrate on specific areas or decisions where the feasibility is regarded as questionable or the potential risk is greatest.

feed **1.** A device for moving media, usually tape or cards, to a position at which the data can be read.
2. To cause data or media to be entered into a system or peripheral.

feedback queue A form of scheduling mechanism often used in multiaccess systems. Individual processes are allocated a *quantum of time on the processor. A process once started is allowed to run until it has exhausted its quantum, until it initiates a transfer on a peripheral device, or until an interrupt generated by some other process occurs. If the quantum is exhausted, the process is assigned a longer quantum and rejoins the queue. If the process initiates a transfer, its quantum remains unaltered and it rejoins the queue. If an externally generated interrupt occurs, the interrupt is serviced. Servicing the interrupt may free some other process already in the queue, in which case that process may be preferentially restarted.

feedback register (feedback shift register) A *shift register, generally consisting of several cells, in which the first cell has its input supplied by a combinational logic function of the parallel outputs of several cells and of a possible external input. An important case is the *linear feedback register* in which *linear logic is employed for the feedback function.

The linear feedback register has the effect of deconvolving the external serial input with the sequence of combinational coefficients (*see* convolution). If the external input is regarded as a *polynomial in which powers of the indeterminate denote succession in time, and if the combinational coefficients are regarded likewise as a second polynomial, then the linear feedback register has the effect of dividing the former polynomial by the latter. When used in coding or in digital signal processing, feedback shift registers may be binary or *q-ary and may be implemented in hardware or software.

When there is no external serial input, the linear feedback register can be used on its own to generate *m-sequences or, with parallel loading of the shift register with a source word, as an *encoder for *simplex codes; either of these applications requires that the feedback logic coefficients represent a *polynomial that is primitive. *See also* Good–de Bruijn diagram.

feed-forward (shift) register A *shift register, generally consisting of a number of cells, several parallel outputs of which are combined in a combinational logic function. An important case is the *linear feed-forward register* in which *linear logic is employed for the feed-forward function.

The linear feed-forward register has the effect of convolving the serial input to the register with the sequence of combinational coefficients (*see* convolution). If the input is regarded as a *polynomial in which powers of the indeterminate denote succession in time, and if the combinational coefficients are regarded likewise as a second polynomial, then the linear feed-forward register has the effect of multiplying these polynomials.

When used in coding or in digital signal processing, feed-forward registers may be binary or q-ary, and may be implemented in hardware or software.

Ferranti Ltd. Originally a company, now a group of companies, Ferranti plc., based in Manchester, UK. It has been a pioneer in electrical engineering, interest in the stored-program computer being aroused in the late 1940s by work at the University of Manchester. Its link with the university dates from 1948 and, on instructions from the government, it undertook to make a production version of the *Manchester Mark I. The Ferranti Mark I, delivered in 1951, was the world's first commercially available computer, and was followed by the Mark I Star (1953), Pegasus I and II (1956, 1959), and *Atlas (1963).

Ferranti's computer interests in the field of commerce were sold in 1963 to ICT (International Computers and Tabulators), ICT and EELM (English Electric Leo Marconi) merging in 1968 to form *ICL. Ferranti then concentrated on computers for use in industrial process control. In 1975 three divisions of Ferranti were amalgamated to form Ferranti Computer Systems Ltd. Since that time FCSL has expanded in the industrial, military, and commercial fields of application.

ferrite A sintered ferromagnetic material plus ceramic that combines the high magnetic permeablility of the former with the high electrical resistance of the latter. This means that ferrite can be used for magnetic cores in high-frequency and high-speed switching circuits in which iron losses are a problem. *See also* core store.

FET *Abbrev. for* field-effect transistor.

fetch-execute cycle (instruction cycle) The two steps of obtaining and executing an instruction. *See* control unit.

fetch protect Restriction of the memory reading privilege in a particular memory segment. *See* memory protection.

FF *Abbrev. for* flip-flop.

FFT *Abbrev. for* fast Fourier transform.

fiber optics transmission system A data communication system that uses *optical fibers* – special glass or plastic fibers – instead of copper wire. Information is carried by modulating light. The optical fibers are small, lightweight, and nonconductive. Cables made from optical fibers and other nonconductive materials may be used in military and industrial applications where ordinary conductive cables present a safety risk. Furthermore, since no electromagnetic radiation leaves the cable, and it is difficult to tap into an existing fiber-optic cable, fiber-optic transmissions are relatively secure.
There are three basic types of optical fibers in use: single-mode stepped index, multi-mode stepped index, and multimode graded index. They vary in how the optical density of the fiber varies from core to edge, which affects how light propagates down the cable. This leads to differences in transmission efficiency, and in the number of different light signals (wavelengths or polarizations) that may be present simultaneously.

Fibonacci search A searching algorithm that uses Fibonacci numbers in a way that is analogous to the use of powers of 2 in the *binary search.

Fibonacci series A sequence of numbers in which each number is the sum of the two preceding numbers, e.g.

$$0,1,1,2,3,5,8,\ldots$$

The *Fibonacci numbers* F_n are formally defined to be

$$F_0 = 0,\ F_1 = 1,$$
$$F_{n+2} = F_{n+1} + F_n,\quad n \geqslant 0$$

field 1. An item of data consisting of a number of characters, bytes, words, or codes that are treated together, e.g. to form a number, a name, or an address. A number of fields make a *record and the fields may be fixed in length or variable. The term came into use with punched card systems and a field size was defined in terms of a number of columns.
2. Normally a way of designating a portion of a word that has a specific significance or function within that word, e.g. an address field in an instruction word or a character field within a data word.
3. In mathematics, a commutative *ring containing more than one element and in which every nonzero element has an *inverse with respect to the multiplication operation.
Apart from their obvious relationship to arithmetic involving numbers of various kinds, fields play a very important role in discussion about the analysis of *algorithms. Results in this area mention the number of operations of a particular kind, and these operations are usually related to addition and multiplication of elements of some field.

field-effect transistor (FET) A semiconductor device having three terminals: *source*, *gate*, and *drain*. Current flow in a narrow conduction *channel* between drain and source is controlled by the voltage applied between gate and source, which can deplete the conduction channel of charge carriers. If the source and drain regions are composed of n-type semiconductor the conduction channel is n-type; these de-

vices are known as *n-channel* devices. Devices with p-type source, drain, and channel are called *p-channel* devices.
In the *junction FET* the channel is a composite part of the structure. In the *MOSFET the gate is insulated from the source and drain regions and the channel forms when the gate voltage is applied. Unlike the *bipolar transistor both types of FET require virtually no input current to the gate except a pulse to charge or discharge the output capacitance. Junction FETs have relatively slow *switching speeds compared with MOSFETs and bipolar transistors, and are therefore not used in logic circuits.

field-programmable devices *See* programmable devices, PLA.

FIFO or **fifo** *Acronym for* first in first out. *FIFO list* is another name for *queue.

file Generally, a collection of data, of any form, that is stored beyond the time of execution of a single job. A file may contain program instructions or data, which may be numerical, textual, or graphical information. In commercial data processing, a file is a set of similar or related records that are treated in the same way. For example, in a sales ledger application a file might consist of a set of customer name and address records.

file activity ratio The proporion of records in a file that are accessed over a given time period.

file descriptor Information that describes a file, giving details such as it s name, generation number, date of last access, expiry date, and the structure of the records it contains. It is normally stored as a header record at the front of the file, held on magnetic tape or on disk.

file directory *See* directory.

file maintenance Activities concerned with keeping data files accurate and complete. These include the writing of *backup copies, the deletion of superseded records, and the maintenance of a correct and efficient file structure. File maintenance may be distinguished from *file updating in that the former is not directly concerned with changing the values of data items relevant to users.

file management The allocation of logical files to physical storage devices, and the selection of a suitable organization for each file. Some functions of file management may be performed by an operating system.

file mark *See* tape mark.

file organization The technique used for organizing data records within a file. For files on direct-access storage devices, available file organizations will generally include *sequential*, *relative*, and *indexed* organization. A file's organization should be distinguished from the *access method by which records are selected for retrieval or storage: a file with indexed organization may usually be accessed either sequentially or randomly by a given application program, while a sequentially organized file can only be accessed sequentially. The records in a sequential file can be organized in logical sequence by a key field (key sequence) or in the physical sequence in which they are written in the file (entry sequence).

file processing The set of activities by which data is stored in and retrieved from files. Typically the activities are organized cyclically (e.g. daily, weekly, monthly), with data-processing operations within a cycle that access the contents of a file but do not change it, and a *file updating stage that marks the passage from one cycle to the next.

file protection The protection of files, and the data in files, from inadvertent or unauthorized alteration and deletion. This protection may be completely physical, as with the storage of file media in fire- and thief-proof locations, partly physical and partly logical, as with the provision of write permit rings on magnetic tape reels, or totally logical, as with the use of data and file retention periods in file header blocks.

file reel *See* magnetic tape.

file server *See* server.

file system The combination of physical data storage devices and operating system logic that permits the storage and retrieval of data within a computer system.

file transfer Movement of a file from one computer to another in a *network. The data may be moved either by opening a network connection directly to the destination, or by passing the data together with control information to a *message-switching file transfer relay. File transfer *protocols (FTPs) frequently encompass facilities to transform data between host-specific formats and a network standard form. This permits file transfer to take place between otherwise incompatible systems. Unfortunately different networks have developed different standards for file transfer. This has led to the development of internetwork file transfer protocols such as the *NIFTP (network independent file transfer protocol).

file updating Incorporating changes to the data in a file without altering its structure or significance. This is one of the most fundamental operations in data processing. The file to be updated is generally called the *master file, and frequently the changes to be introduced are collated together in a *transaction file. Before the introduction of disk stores the files were stored on magnetic tape, and the transaction file had to be sorted into the same order as the master file before updating began; on disk the master file may be organized so that it can be updated at random, in the order in which the transactions arise.
It is usual for the master file to retain the same name when updated, old and new files being distinguished by different *generation numbers* (or *version numbers*) associated with the file name. For security reasons at least one and often more generations preceding the current one are retained: a common procedure is to hold three generations of the file, referred to as *grandfather file*, *father file*, and *son file* – son being the current generation. When the files are on magnetic tape the terms *grandfather tape*, *father tape*, and *son tape* are used. *See also* file maintenance.

fill character *Another name for* ignore character.

filter 1. A program that processes a sequential stream of text, carrying out some simple transformation, e.g. condensing multiple spaces to single spaces, converting upper to lower case, counting words, etc.
2. A simple electric circuit or some more complicated device used in the process of *filtering.

filtering 1. The processing of a *signal (by a simple electric circuit or by some more complicated device) in such a way that the behavior of the signal is affected in either the *time domain* or in a *transform domain*. In time-domain filtering each element of the original signal is replaced by a sequence of elements, proportional in amplitude to the original signal but spaced in time; the sum (assuming linear fitering) of these sequences forms the new signal. In transform-domain filtering the elements of the original signal are not those of its amplitude but rather of its components under, for example, *Fourier analysis or *Walsh analysis; they are then spaced not in time but in *frequency or *sequency respectively. Many other transforms are also used.
Filtering, both in the time domain and in various transform domains, is of great importance in *multiplexing. A simple but very common example of filtering in the frequency (Fourier) domain is the use of resonant circuits to effect *low-pass, *band-pass, *high-pass, and *band-stop

functions; these are much used, e.g. in *data transmission lines and *modems.
2. *See* masking.

find One of the basic actions performed on *sets that, when applied in the form

find(el)

produces the set of which *el* is currently a member; if *el* is in no set or in more than one set the effect of the operation is undefined. *See also* operations on sets.

finite automaton *See* finite-state automaton.

finite-difference method A widely applicable *discretization method for the solution of *ordinary and *partial differential equations. In this approach all derivatives are replaced by approximations that involve solution values only, so in general the differential equation is reduced to a system of *nonlinear equations or *linear algebraic equations. For example, in the problem

$$y'' + by' + cy = d \quad 0 \leqslant x \leqslant 1,$$
$$y(0) = \alpha, y(1) = \beta,$$

where b, c, d, α, and β are given constants, the interval [0,1] is first divided into equal subintervals of length h; h is called the *stepsize* (or *mesh* or *grid size*). This gives the *mesh points* (or *grid points*) x_n,

$$x_n = nh,$$
$$n = 0,1, \ldots ,N+1,$$
$$h = 1/(N+1)$$

At interior mesh points the derivatives are now replaced by finite-difference approximations, e.g.

$$y'(x_n) \simeq (\tfrac{1}{2}h)[y(x_{n+1}) - y(x_{n-1})]$$
$$y''(x_n) \simeq (1/h^2)[y(x_{n+1}) - 2y(x_n) + y(x_{n-1})]$$

When combined with the boundary conditions these approximations result in a system of equations for approximations to $y(x_n)$, $n = 1, 2, \ldots, N$. Nonlinear differential equations yield a system of nonlinear equations.

finite-element method A widely applicable approach to solving *ordinary and particularly *partial differential equations and similar problems. The approach embraces several variants, principally *Galerkin's method* and the *Rayleigh–Ritz method.* The basic idea, however, is the same and involves approximating the solution of the problem by a linear combination:

$$u(x) = \sum_{j=1}^{n} c_j \phi_j (x)$$

The functions $\phi_1, \phi_2, \ldots, \phi_n$ are always chosen to be simple and are called *trial functions*. The success of the method is due in part to choosing these functions to be low-degree *splines. This in turn generally leads to a system of equations for the coefficients $c_1, c_2, \ldots, c_n$ that involves the treatment of sparse matrices, i.e. matrices in which a large proportion of the elements are zero; very efficient software can then be used.

In Galerkin's method the criterion for choosing the coefficients is that the amount by which $u(x)$ fails to satisfy the equation is in a certain sense small. The Rayleigh–Ritz method is a *variational method. The finite-element method can in general be regarded as a process in which a solution in an infinite-dimensional space is replaced by an approximation that lies in a finite-dimensional subspace.

finite field (Galois field) A (mathematical) *field with a finite number of elements. The number of elements must be of the form p^k where p is some prime number and k is a positive integer. Results concerning finite fields are of particular relevance in the areas of error detection and error correction.

finite-length arithmetic (fixed-length arithmetic) The approximation to real arithmetic in a computer. The term arises since the precision to which real numbers can be represented as floating-point numbers in a computer is limited by the length of the mantissa. *See* floating-point notation.

finite sequence (list) *See* sequence.

finite set A *set with a finite number of elements.

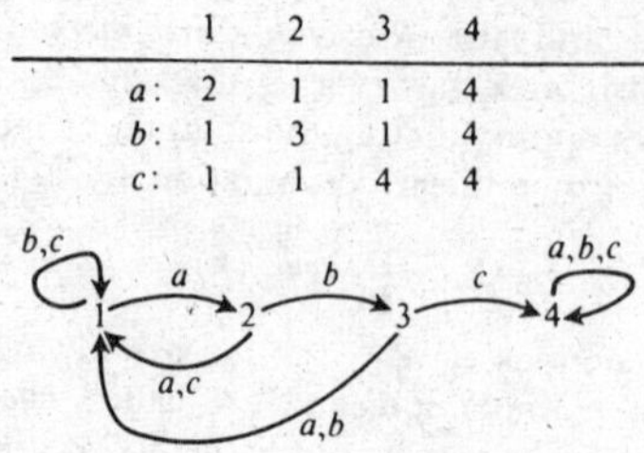

	1	2	3	4
a:	2	1	1	4
b:	1	3	1	4
c:	1	1	4	4

Equivalent transition table and diagram of an FSA

finite-state automaton (FSA; finite-state machine) A simple kind of *automaton. The input string is read once from left to right, looking at each symbol in turn. At any time the FSA has some internal *state*, which changes after each input symbol is read. The new state depends firstly on the symbol just read and secondly on the current state. An FSA is therefore determined by a function f from $I \times Q$ to Q, where I is the set of possible input symbols, Q is the set of states, and $I \times Q$ is the *Cartesian product of I and Q. Q must be finite, hence the name FSA.

The function f is called a *state transition function*. It is commonly represented either by a table or by a directed *graph, known respectively as a *state transition table* and a *state transition diagram*. The figure shows two equivalent representations in which

$$I = \{a,b,c\},$$
$$Q = \{1,2,3,4\}$$

In this example,

$$f(a,1) = 2,$$
$$f(c,4) = 4, \text{ etc.}$$

f extends to strings in the obvious manner: in the example,

$$f(bc,2) = 4,$$
$$f(aaa,3) = 1, \text{ etc.}$$

Let Q be divided into *accepting states* and *rejecting states*, and let q_0 be some member of Q (referred to as the *start state*). The *language recognized* by the FSA is the set of all w such that

$$f(w,q_0)$$

is an accepting state, i.e. the set of all strings that take the start state to an accepting state. For example, in the FSA shown in the figure let q_0 be 1 and let 4 be the only accepting state; the language recognized is then the set of all strings over $\{a,b,c\}$ that somewhere contain *abc* as a substring.

A generalization is to allow more than one state to which the FSA can move, for a given input symbol and current state. This gives a *nondeterministic FSA*. The input string is then accepted if there is some sequence of choices of moves leading to an accepting state. Such a machine can always be converted to a deterministic one recognizing the same language.

See also sequential machine, minimal machine.

FIPS *Acronym for* Federal Information Processing Standard. A publication (FIPS PUB) issued by the US National Bureau of Standards serves as the official source of information in the US federal government regarding standards issued by NBS.

Fire codes A family of *polynomial *block codes designed to correct *burst errors.

firmware System software that is held in read-only memory (*ROM). *See also* logic circuit.

first fit A method of selecting a contiguous area of memory that is to be allocated for a segment. The *free-space list is scanned in order of starting address, and the allocation made from the first free area whose size exceeds that of the request. Despite its apparent simplicity this algorithm has a number of desirable properties in terms of performance.

first generation of computers. The series of calculating and computing machines whose designs were started between 1940 (approximately) and 1955. These machines are characterized by electronic tube (valve) circuitry, and delay line, rotating, or electrostatic (Williams tube) memory.

The majority of them embodied the stored program concept. For the most part, first generation machines had primitive input/output, using punched paper tape, punched card, magnetic wire, magnetic tape, and primitive printers. Despite these seeming handicaps, impressive computations in weather forecasting, atomic energy calculations, and similar scientific applications were routinely performed on them.

Important first-generation development machines include the *Manchester Mark I, *EDSAC, *EDVAC, and *ENIAC while the earliest commercially available computers included the *Ferranti Mark I, *UNIVAC I, and *LEO.

first in first out *See* FIFO.

fixed and exchangeable disk store A disk drive in which part of the accessible data capacity is fixed and part is exchangeable in the form of a *data module.

fixed-base system *Another name for* fixed-radix system. *See* number system.

fixed disk drive *See* disk drive.

fixed head of a disk drive. A read/write head that cannot be moved relative to the center of the disk. A large number of these heads are usually incorporated into an assembly so that there is a "head per track", and such drives may be referred to by this expression. The advantage of a fixed head is that the average access time is reduced to the time for half a revolution since there is no track seek time required. Some drives have both fixed and moveable heads.

fixed-length arithmetic *Another name for* finite-length arithmetic.

fixed-length code A *code in which a fixed number of source symbols are encoded into a fixed number of output symbols. It is usually a *block code. (The term fixed-length is used in contrast to *variable-length, whereas block code can be contrasted with *convolutional code.)

fixed-point notation A representation of real numbers in which the position of the *radix point is fixed. The position of the point determines the absolute precision of the representation. If the point is fixed at the right-hand end of the number then all of the fixed-point numbers are integers. Due to a number of difficulties, fixed-point arithmetic is rarely used in a modern computer for calculations involving real numbers.

fixed-point theorem A theorem of recursive function theory that finds application in the *denotational semantics of programming languages. In particular it is used to provide the semantics of iteration and of recursive functions and procedures.

fixed-radix system (fixed-base system) *See* number system.

fixed word length computer A computer in which data is constrained to lie within words that are all of the same length. By extension the term is sometimes used to imply that all instructions also fit within one word. *Compare* variable word length computer.

flag A variable whose value indicates the attainment of some designated state or condition by an item of equipment or a program. The flag is subsequently used as a basis for conditional branching and similar decision processes.

flat addressing *See* addressing.

flatbed plotter *See* plotter.

flexible array An *array whose lower and/or upper bounds are not fixed and may vary according to the values assigned to it. *See also* string.

flexible disk cartridge In international standards, the formal name for flexible disk. *See* floppy disk.

flexi-disk *Another name for* floppy disk.

flip-flop (bistable; flop; FF) An electronic circuit element that is capable of exhibit-

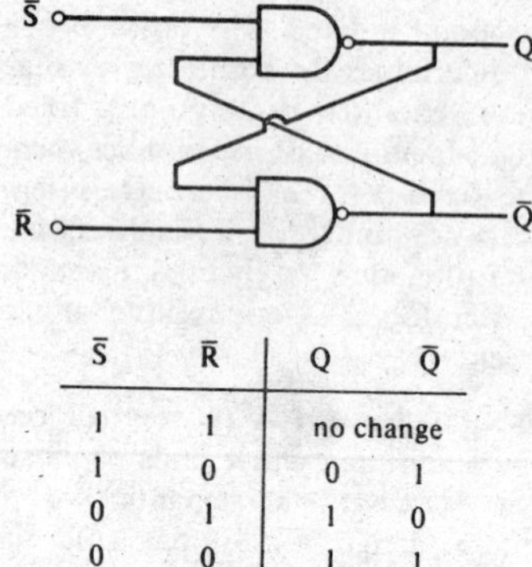

$\bar{S}$	$\bar{R}$	Q	$\bar{Q}$
1	1	no change	
1	0	0	1
0	1	1	0
0	0	1	1
		(disallowed)	

RS flip-flop, logic diagram and truth table

ing either of two stable states and of switching between these states in a reproducible manner. When used in *logic circuits the two states are made to correspond to logic 1 and logic 0. Flip-flops are therefore one-bit memory elements and are frequently used in digital circuits.

The simplest form is the *RS flip-flop*; an implementation using *NAND gates is shown in the diagram together with the flip-flop's truth table. A logic 1 on one of the two inputs either sets the Q output to logic 1 or resets Q to logic 0. Output $\bar{Q}$ is the logical complement of Q. When $\bar{R}$ and $\bar{S}$ are both logic 1 (which is equivalent to R and S both logic 0), Q does not change state. The situation of both $\bar{R}$ and $\bar{S}$ at logic 0 is ambiguous and is avoided in more complex flip-flop implementations (*see* JK flip-flop). The outputs of this (and other) flip-flops are not just functions of the inputs but depend on both inputs and outputs. The device is thus a simple *sequential circuit.

Extra logic gating may be included in the RS device, and in more complex flip-flops, to allow a clock signal to be input to the flip-flop, so producing a *clocked flip-flop* (*see* clock). The Q output will not then change state until an active edge of the clock pulse occurs (*edge-triggered device*) or a complete clock cycle has occurred (*pulse-triggered device*). Provision may also be made to set up a given output regardless of the state of the inputs.

Various forms of flip-flop are available to perform specific functions; these include JK *D, *T, and *master-slave flip-flops. Flip-flops are important as short-term memory devices in binary counting. The RS flip-flop is often considered to be the *universal flip-flop* since it forms the basic building block for more sophisticated implementations. The JK device is also considered to be universal since it is the most useful implementation and is available as a standard integrated-circuit package.

float An operator or function that converts a number in *fixed-point notation into an equivalent *floating-point form.

floating-point notation A representation of real numbers that enables both very small and very large numbers to be conveniently expressed. A floating-point number has the general form

$$\pm m \times R^e$$

where m is called the *mantissa*, R is the *radix (or base) of the number system, and e is the *exponent*.

The following format is typical of the floating-point representation used in computers. The first bit is a *sign bit*, denoting the sign of the mantissa. This is followed by a fixed number of bits representing the exponent, which is in turn followed by another fixed number of bits representing the magnitude of the mantissa. The exponent is often represented using *excess-n notation*, whereby a number, called the *characteristic* (or *biased exponent*), is stored instead of the exponent itself. To derive the characteristic for a floating-point number from its exponent, the *bias* (or *excess factor*) n is added to the exponent. For example, for an 8-bit characteristic, exponents in the range -128 to $+127$ are represented in excess-128 notation by characteristics in the range 0 to 255.

A nonzero floating-point number is *normalized* if the leading digit in its mantissa is nonzero.

floating-point operation The addition, subtraction, multiplication, or division of two floating-point operands to produce a floating-point result. *See also* floating-point notation, flops.

flop *Short for* flip-flop.

floppy disk (diskette; flexi-disk) A magnetic information storage medium consisting of a circular polyester substrate coated on one or both sides with magnetic oxide and enclosed within a stiff envelope, the inside of which is coated with a cleaning material. The envelope has a radial slot – or two slots for a double-sided floppy disk – through which the read/write heads of the *floppy-disk drive can contact the disk. A hole in the envelope and disk is provided so that a photosensor may be used to generate an index pulse once per revolution signal. In some types there are a number of holes, typically 32, in addition to the index hole and these are used to initiate writing of *sectors. A cutout on one edge of the envelope – the inner edge when inserted in the disk drive – can be blocked to prevent the drive from writing to the disk. The two most common sizes of floppy disk are 8″ and 5¼″ (210 mm and 133 mm) diameter, the latter sometimes being referred to as a *minifloppy*.

floppy-disk drive (diskette drive) A device that accepts flexible magnetic disks, i.e. *floppy disks, and reads or writes magnetic patterns that correspond to the data to be retrieved or stored. The data is encoded in one of the appropriate *disk formats. The floppy disk is put into the mechanism through a slot that is normally covered by a hinged flap or door. The mechanism automatically locates and clamps the disk and rotates it – usually at a speed of 360 rpm.

The read/write heads contact the disk through apertures in its cover. If the drive is configured for single-sided operation a resilient pad is pressed against the opposite face of the disk to hold it in contact with the read/write head. In double-sided devices the two heads are usually arranged so that they lightly clamp the disk between them. Some designs have the heads offset relative to one another and each has its own resilient pressure pad.

The floppy-disk drive was first introduced by IBM as a diagnostic software load device but it is now used extensively as a data storage device on small computing systems.

flops *Acronym for* floating-point operations per second. A commonly used measure of *computer power for very powerful computers (*supercomputers, *vector-processing computers) and *array processors. The rating of a computer, which in very powerful machines is usually in megaflops (million flops), must be qualified by a statement of the precision to which the operations are carried out.

flowchart A low-level graphical representation of the structure of a program, with emphasis on control flow and the primitive actions performed by the program rather than on the data structures employed by the program. It consists of a set of *boxes* of various shapes, interconnected by a set of directed *arcs*. The arcs indicate flow of control while the various box shapes indicate different kinds of action or decision. Within the boxes any notation can be employed to describe the action or decision; typical notations are pseudocode and natural language.

Flowcharts have been used extensively for many years but are now rather unpopular. For one reason they tend to obscure the structure of programs that follow the tenets of structured coding (*see* structured programming) and, more important, they ignore the topic of data structuring.

flow control Procedures used to limit the rate at which data is transmitted to the rate at which it can be received. There are two major classes of flow control: *end-to-end* and *hop-by-hop*. End-to-end flow control limits the amount of data according to the capacity of the final destination to absorb it, without regard to the path through the network taken by the data (which may vary from message to message). Hop-by-hop flow control limits the amount of data sent according to the capacity of each individual node and/or link on the path through the network. In this latter case, the path is usually constant for the lifetime of the connection between sender and receiver. *See also* window.

fluid logic (pneumatic logic) A means of implementing logic functions, not by the normal use of electronic circuitry but by the flow of incompressible fluids through tubing containing intersections and constrictions. The logic gates so formed are useful in situations in which high electromagnetic interference prevents the use of electronic components.

Flynn's classification *See* concurrency.

FM or **f.m.** *Abbrev. for* frequency modulation. *See* modulation.

folding A simple method of *hashing a key, in which the key is subdivided into several parts that are added together to give an address. The *folding ratio* is the ratio of the sizes of the domain of this hashing function to the size of its range.

footprint The area of front panel, desk, or floor space occupied by a peripheral device: thus if a cartridge tape drive is described as having an 8″ floppy footprint it will fit the same shape and size of panel opening as a standard 8″ floppy-disk drive.

foreground processing Processing that supports interaction in a system that supports both interactive and batch operations. *See also* background processing.

forest A directed *graph that is a collection of *trees. If the root is removed from a tree together with the arcs emanating from that root, the resulting collection of subtrees forms a forest.

for loop *See* do loop.

form A page of printer media. It may be a single sheet or a multipart set, i.e. a number of sheets interleaved with carbon paper or coated so that a single impact will produce similar marks on all sheets. The sheets are frequently joined to form a continuous web, with sprocket holes at the edges to allow automatic feeding through printers. The paper may be preprinted with headings, fixed information, and lines or boxes. Paper used for general-purpose listing is often preprinted with closely spaced groups of lines – a *stave* – to aid visual alignment.

formal language A finite or infinite subset of the set Σ^* of all Σ-words for some finite set of symbols Σ (*see* word). Σ is the *alphabet* of the language. This subset of Σ^* is referred to as a *language over* Σ or a Σ-*language*. Since, in the context of *formal language theory, languages are merely sets of strings, they are considered apart from any semantics they may have. Although infinite languages play an essential role, discussion is restricted to *recursively enumerable languages.

formal language theory The study of *formal languages, in particular the structure and representation of infinite classes of formal languages. Chief among the ways of representing formal languages are *grammars, *L-systems, and *automata.

The subject was initiated in 1956 by Noam Chomsky and arose out of the formalized study of natural languages. Additional applications and connections include: *parsing of programming languages, *effective computability, *complexity, theory of *semigroups, and genetic systems.

Typical issues investigated are decidability of properties of languages, *closure properties of language classes, and alternative ways of characterizing language

classes using for example *Dyck language. There are many significant open questions. For instance it is not known whether the *context-sensitive languages are closed under complementation, or whether equivalence of deterministic *pushdown automata is decidable.
The subject has been extended to include infinite strings, trees, and graphs.

formal logic The study of the analysis of propositions and of proofs, paying attention only to abstract symbols and form and paying no attention whatsoever to the meaning of the abstractions. *See also* symbolic logic.

format The defined structure of the pattern of information that is recorded on magnetic media, displayed on a VDU, or printed on a page. The word is also used as a verb: to put data into a predetermined structure or divide a storage medium, such as a disk into sectors, so that it is ready to receive data. *See* disk format, tape format, printer format, instruction format.

formatter 1. of a magnetic subsystem. The logic assembly that determines the *format of data recorded on magnetic media, and forms part of a device controller; the term is often misused to identify a magnetic device controller as a whole, including the logic controlling mechanism movements. The logic assembly is basically hardware but now often includes firmware executed in a dedicated microprocessor (which may perform all the controller functions and not merely those of the formatter). *See also* disk format, tape format.
2. (text formatter) A program that accepts text with embedded formatting instructions and produces a new version of the document with the specified margins, justification, pagination, etc.

form overlay The predetermined patterns of printed lines, logos, and fixed information that may be produced by a computer output printer in addition to the variable information. Many nonimpact printers and some impact matrix printers can print the form overlay concurrently with the variable data.

form stop A sensor on a printer that generates a signal to indicate that there is insufficient paper to allow printing to continue.

FORTH A programming language much in vogue among users of microcomputers. FORTH operands are held on a *stack, and programs take the form of strings in *reverse Polish notation. A vital feature of FORTH is that a symbol (a WORD) can be associated with any program string, and such a user-defined word can then be used in expressions on equal terms with the system words (operators). This makes FORTH a flexible *extensible language in which it is possible to define a customized language for, say, the control of a scientific instrument. The FORTH system is very compact; the interpreter and the dictionary containing the system-defined words can be fitted into 8K bytes.

FORTRAN or **Fortran** *Acronym for* formula translation. A programming language widely used for scientific computation. The first version of FORTRAN, FORTRAN I, was issued by IBM in 1956, to be succeeded by FORTRAN II in 1958. This in turn was succeeded by FORTRAN IV, also known as FORTRAN 66 when it was standardized by ANSI. This became the workhorse of the scientific world, although it has now been replaced by FORTRAN 77. The next version is expected in the middle-to-late 1980s, and is known as FORTRAN 8x.
FORTRAN programs use a notation strongly reminiscent of algebra (hence formula translation), and it is thus fairly easy for the scientist to specify his computation. The only data structure is the *array, which corresponds to the matrix commonly used in scientific calculations. FORTRAN II introduced the important idea of independent compilation of sub-

routines, making it possible to establish libraries of scientific subroutines. The efficient code produced by the early FORTRAN compilers did much to ensure the acceptance of high-level languages as a normal mode of use of computers.

forward bias The d.c. voltage required to maintain current flow in a *bipolar transistor or *diode or to enhance current flow in a *field-effect transistor. For example, a silicon diode will conduct current only if its anode is at a positive voltage compared to its cathode; it is then said to be *forward biased.* This voltage will be approximately 0.6 volts. *Compare* reverse bias.

forward error correction (forward error protection) Error correction that is accomplished by appending redundant data to actual data so that certain kinds of errors can be both detected and corrected. This differs from many error correction methods used in communications in that there is no request to resend the data (e.g. from a memory); there is thus no reverse message, hence the word forward. The nature of the redundancy is a function of the expected type of error. *See also* backward error correction.

Fourier analysis The analysis of an arbitrary waveform into its constituent sinusoids (of different frequencies and amplitudes). *See* Fourier transform. *See also* orthonormal basis.

Fourier series The infinite trigonometric series

$$\tfrac{1}{2}a_0 + \sum_{n=1}^{\infty} (a_n \cos nx + b_n \sin nx)$$

By suitable choice of the coefficients a_i and b_i, the series can be made equal to any function of x defined on the interval $(-\pi, \pi)$. If f is such a function, the *Fourier coefficients* are given by the formulas

$$a_n = (1/\pi) \int_{-\pi}^{\pi} f(x) \cos nx \, dx$$

$$(n = 0,1,2, \dots)$$

$$b_n = (1/\pi) \int_{-\pi}^{\pi} f(x) \sin nx \, dx$$

$$(n = 1,2, \dots)$$

Fourier transform A mathematical operation that analyzes an arbitrary waveform into its constituent sinusoids (of different frequencies and amplitudes). This relationship is stated as

$$S(f) = \int_{-\infty}^{\infty} s(t) \exp(-2\pi ift) \, dt$$

where $s(t)$ is the waveform to be decomposed into a sum of sinusoids, $S(f)$ is the Fourier transform of $s(t)$, and $i = \sqrt{-1}$. An analogous formula gives $s(t)$ in terms of $S(f)$, but with a normalizing factor, $1/2\pi$). Sometimes, for symmetry, the normalizing factor is split between the two relations.

The Fourier transform pair, $s(t)$ and $S(f)$, has to be modified before it is amenable to computation on a digital computer. This modified pair, called the *discrete Fourier transform* must approximate as closely as possible the continuous Fourier transform. The continuous time function is approximated by N samples at time intervals T:

$$g(kT),\ k = 0,1, \dots\ n-1$$

The continuous Fourier transform is also approximated by N samples at frequency intervals $1/NT$:

$$G(n/NT),\ n = 0,1, \dots\ N-1$$

Since the N values of time and frequency are related by the continuous Fourier transform, then a discrete relationship can be derived:

$$G(n/NT) = \sum_{k=0}^{N-1} g(kt) \exp(-2\pi ink/N)$$

fourth generation of computers. A designation covering machines that were designed after 1970 (approximately) and are characterized by use of integrated circuit technology and very large (more than one megabyte) main memory. In addition to these prominent characteristics, fourth generation systems nearly all have extensive support for networking. Other characteristics are essentially those of the *third generation. A proliferation of languages are available from most vendors. Systems to simplify the creation of certain classes of applications (e.g. IBM's CICS) have been introduced. This generation has also seen the introduction of database management systems for organizing and accessing large collections of interrelated data.

FPLA *Abbrev. for* field-programmable logic array. *See* PLA.

fractional part 1. The part of a number to the right of the radix point.
2. *Another name for* mantissa. *See* floating-point notation.

fragmentation The creation of many small areas of memory, which arises as memory is allocated to and then released by processes. The portions of unallocated memory tend to become so small that they fail to satisfy any request and so remain unused. *See also* external fragmentation, internal fragmentation.

frame 1. A single message or packet on a data link using a *data link control protocol such as HDLC, ADCCP, etc. The frame is the unit of error detection, retransmission, etc. A special pattern of bits – a flag – marks the beginning and ending of the frame. In the HDLC protocol, a flag is the 8-bit sequence

01111110

that when followed by any sequence of bits other than another flag denotes the beginning of a frame of data; the flag is maintained as a unique synchronizing sequence of bits since the rules of the protocol require that a 0 is automatically inserted by the sending equipment whenever it detects the presence of five 1s in the input data stream.
2. In general, a complete or self-identifying message in a data communication system.
3. A section of a recording on magnetic tape that comprises a single bit in each track.

Fredholm integral equation *See* integral equation.

freedom of information A catch phrase that has several meanings:
1. a lack of censorship – a state where there is no restriction on the recording of information or on the use of that information;
2. deregulation of the communications media – the removal of restrictions on the use of broadcasting frequencies and communication cables;
3. fair use of *copyright material – the right to impart news and information in western society;
4. the rights an American citizen has under the Freedom of Information Act to study almost any records concerning a government department;
5. technological transfer to third world countries – the rights of underprivileged people to high-technology information free of charge.
In this last case the difficulties in associating the concept of property to information, and the way in which the imparting of information leads to the creation of yet more information, are supporting arguments in favor of free or low-cost technological transfer.

free list *Another name for* available list.

free semigroup A *semigroup S consisting of words, i.e. strings of elements all of which reside in some alphabet A; the operation $\circ$ is that of *concatenation or juxtaposition between elements of S. Thus if

$$A = \{a, b, c\}$$

then $ab \circ aabb$ produces $abaabb$

S is the free semigroup generated by the alphabet A, whose elements are called the *generators* of S – the elements being free of interrelationships.

free-space list A list of unoccupied areas of memory in main or backing store. It is a special case of an *available list.

frequency The number of complete cycles of a periodically variable quantity, such as a pulse or wave, that occurs in unit time. It is measured in hertz.

frequency distribution A table of the number of occurrences of each of a set of classified observations. The occurrences might arise from the throw of dice, the measurement of a man's height in a particular range of values, or the number of reported cases of a disease in different groups of people classified by their age, sex, or other category.
It is usual practice to choose a fairly small number of categories so that the *relative frequencies within categories are not too small. If no definite upper or lower limits are known, all values above (or below) a certain value are grouped into a single category known as the *upper (*or *lower) tail.*
Frequency distributions may be summarized by computing *statistics such as the mean (or other *measures of location) and the standard deviation (or other *measures of variation), and sometimes measures of asymmetry or skewness and of compactness (i.e. the proportion of the sample in the center and in the tails).
The term frequency distribution is applied to observed data in a sample. In contrast, *probability distributions are theoretical formulas for the *probability of observing each event. Fitting probability distributions to observed frequency distributions is a fundamental *statistical method of data analysis.

frequency divider An electronic device that is capable of dividing the frequency of a given digital input pulse train by a fixed integer value, *n*. It often consists of an *n*-stage *counter, the output frequency at the *n*th stage of counting being an *n*th submultiple of the input frequency.

frequency division multiplexing (FDM) A form of *multiplexing in which the *bandwidth of the transmission medium is divided into logical channels over which multiple messages can be simultaneously transmitted. FDM is commonly used worldwide to combine multiple voice-grade telephone signals: 4000 hertz (Hz) is allocated for each channel, 3000 Hz per signal plus a 500 Hz *guard band* (unused frequency band) on either side of the signal. Each signal starts at DC, but the different signals are raised to different frequencies so that the signals do not overlap. Despite the guard bands, strong signal spikes at the edges of a channel can overlap into the next channel, causing noise interference.
See also broadband networking, time division multiplexing.

frequency function *See* probability distributions.

frequency modulation (FM, f.m.) *See* modulation. *See also* disk format.

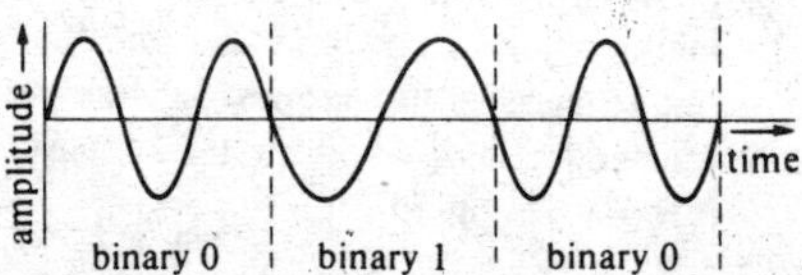

Frequency shift keying, 2 states

frequency shift keying (FSK) A method for representing digital data with analog signals by using a change in the frequency of the carrier to represent information. It is thus a type of *modulation. FSK with two frequencies, corresponding to the digital values 0 and 1 (*see* diagram) is the primary method used by low-speed *modems. *See also* digital data transmission.

front-end processor An *I/O processor that is used to format and/or process input data. The term is sometimes used to refer to a *communication processor. *Compare* back-end processor.

FSA *Abbrev. for* finite-state automaton.

FSK *Abbrev. for* frequency shift keying.

FTP *Abbrev. for* file transfer protocol. *See* file transfer.

Fujitsu A Japanese multiline manufacturing company of interest in the computer field in that, firstly, it was a prime investor in Amdahl Corporation in its formative stages, and, secondly, today manufactures IBM plug-compatible computers, i.e. computers that run IBM systems software.

full adder *See* adder.

full duplex *Another name for* duplex.

full subtractor *See* subtractor.

full text retrieval A form of information retrieval in which the full text of a document is stored, and retrieval is achieved by searching for occurrences of a given string in the text. This technique can be compared with the alternative of retrieving information by matching one of a set of predetermined keywords.

full tree A tree of *degree *m* and *level *k* in which every node at depth less than *m* has *m* children and thus, in particular, all leaf nodes are at depth *k*.

function (map; mapping; transformation) from one set *X* to another set *Y*. A *relation *R* defined on the *Cartesian product $x \times y$ in which for each element *x* in *X* there is precisely one element *y* in *Y* with the property that (x,y) is a member of *R*. It is then customary to talk about a function *f*, say, and to write

$$f : X \rightarrow Y$$

The unique association between elements *x* and *y* is denoted by

$$y = f(x) \text{ or } y = fx$$

X is called the *domain* of *f*, *Y* the *codomain* of *f*. Further, *y* is the *value* of *f* at the point *x* or the *image* of *x* under *f*. We say that *f* is a mapping or transformation between sets *X* and *Y* or that *f* maps *X* into *Y*, and that *f* maps *x* into *y*. When the domain *X* is the Cartesian product of *n* sets then *f* is a function of *n* variables. Otherwise it is a function of one variable.
Examples of functions are readily obtained from the mathematical equivalents of standard functions and operations typically supplied in programming languages. The usual trigonometric functions sin, cos, and tan are functions of one variable. The rule for converting from characters into their integer codes or equivalents is a function.
Functions are often represented pictorially as *graphs.
See also bijection, injection, surjection, operation, homomorphism.

functional languages (applicative languages) A class of programming languages, and a subclass of the *declarative languages, that is based on *lambda calculus or *recursion equations. Typically a program in a functional language consists of an unordered set of equations that characterize functions and values: functions are characterized by use of recursion, other functions, and values; values are characterized as functions of other values. Ultimately the complete set of equations is sufficient to characterize all functions and values in terms of the primitive functions and values provided by the language. The values that are characterized by the equations include the desired results, and these values are computed by executing the program.

functional partitioning A technique of system or program decomposition in which the primary criterion is that each identified module should contain only elements that all contribute to the achievement of a single goal. Thus each module should perform a single function in the broad sense of an identified job of work (the definition of which is both subjective and dependent upon the level of consideration). The technique is often associated with a general approach, termed *structured design*, that was developed by IBM in the early 1970s.

functional specification *See* module specification.

functional unit Any major component of a computing system, e.g. CPU, main memory, backing store unit, peripheral device.

function key A key on a keyboard that initiates an operation or inputs a code that will subsequently initiate an operation.

functor A *function that maps one *category into another. In computing terms a special functor represents mappings between mathematical concepts, such as *sets and *functions, and their implementation in a programming language; this is often called the *representation functor*. The idea generalizes to include mappings between different *abstract machines.

fusible link (fuse link) A physical link providing electrical continuity across an individual cell in the memory array of a *PROM. With this link intact the cell,when interrogated, will display a known *logic state. During programming this link can be destroyed, forcing the cell to take on the complementary logic state; this process is irreversible.
Fusible links are used in a similar manner in field-programmable logic arrays (*see* PLA).

fuzzy theory A branch of logic designed specifically for representing knowledge and human reasoning in such a way that it is amenable to processing by computer. Thus fuzzy theory is applicable to *expert systems, knowledge engineering, and *artificial intelligence.
The more traditional propositional and predicate logics do not allow for degrees of uncertainty, indicated by words or phrases such as fairly, very, quite possible. Instead of truth values such as true and false it is possible to introduce a multiple-valued logic consisting of, for example, the values true, not true, very true, not very true, more or less true, not very false, very false, not false, and false. Alternatively an interval such as [0,1] can be introduced and the degree of truth can be represented by some real number in this range. Predicates are then functions that map not into {true, false} but into these more general domains.
Fuzzy theory is concerned with the study of *sets and *predicates of this kind. There emerge such concepts as *fuzzy sets*, *fuzzy relationships*, and *fuzzy quantifiers*.

G

Galerkin's method *See* finite-element method.

gallium arsenide devices Semiconductor integrated-circuit devices that are implemented using gallium arsenide as the intrinsic *semiconductor material in preference to, say, silicon. Gallium arsenide has certain advantages over other semiconductor materials, in particular in the fabrication of optical and optically coupled devices such as light-emitting diodes and optoisolators.

Galois field *Another name for* finite field.

game theory A mathematical theory of decision-making by participants with conflicting interests in a competitive situation, originated by Emile Borel in 1921 and rigorously established by John von Neumann in 1928. The theory attempts to gain insights into economic situations by isolating these aspects, which occur in their simplest form in games of strategy.
In a two-player game, as defined by the theory, each participant has a choice of plays for which there are several possible outcomes, gains or losses, depending on the opponent's choice. An optimum strategy states the relative frequency with which a player's choices should be used, so as to maximize his average gain (or minimize his average loss). The problem of determining the optimum strategy can be formulated as a problem in *linear programming. Generalizations to *n*-person games are included in the theory.

gap on magnetic tape. Any gap between groups of signals recorded on magnetic tape, but usually the interblock gap (*see* block).

gap theorem A theorem in complexity theory that, like the *speedup theorem, can be expressed in terms of abstract complexity measures (*see* Blum's axioms) but will be more understandable in the context of time:
given any *total *recursive function

$$g(n) \geqslant n$$

there exists a total recursive function $S(n)$ such that

$$\text{DTIME}(S(n)) = \text{DTIME}(g(S(n)))$$

(*see* complexity classes). In other words there is a "gap" between time bounds $S(n)$ and $g(S(n))$ within which the minimal space complexity of no language lies.
This has the following counter-intuitive consequence: given two universal models of computation, say a Turing machine that makes one move per century and the other a very fast random-access machine capable of performing a million arithmetic operations per second, then there is a total recursive function $S(n)$ such that any language recognizable in time $S(n)$ on one machine is also recognizable within time $S(n)$ on the other.

garbage Information in a memory that is no longer valid or wanted. It is usually the result of *memory compaction operations. The removal of this superfluous information from the memory is known as *garbage collection* and is usually associated with memory compaction.

gate 1. *See* logic gate.
2. *See* field-effect transistor.

gateway A device or set of devices that interconnect two or more *networks, enabling data transfers to be made between them. When the networks offer similar services, a gateway may simply serve to route packets or messages from one network to another. When the networks differ (i.e. in packet size, connection service, etc.), a gateway performs extensive protocol translation services as well.
The word *bridge* is sometimes used to describe a gateway whose presence is invisible to hosts on the connected networks. The bridge receives all the packets that are addressed to hosts on other networks, and forwards them appropriately. Thus only the bridges need to have their routing tables changed when a host moves from one network to another, or when internetwork connectivity changes.
Within a particular protocol domain there may be a specific definition of the term gateway and the services that one provides. Many gateways participate in an intergateway status check and routing update protocol. Some gateways also provide secondary services such as current date and time, or host name to address conversion.
See also internetworking.

gather write The function of writing to memory a block of data comprising items of data that have been retrieved directly from scattered memory locations and/or registers.

Gaussian distribution *Another name for* normal distribution.

Gaussian elimination *See* linear algebraic equations.

Gaussian noise *Noise whose distribution of amplitude over time is *Gaussian.

GCD *Abbrev. for* greatest common divisor.

GCR *Abbrev. for* group code recording. *See* disk format, tape format.

generalized sequential machine *See* sequential machine. *See also* gsm mapping.

general-purpose computer (GP computer; GP) A computer that can be used for any function for which it can be conveniently programmed.

general-purpose interface bus (GPIB) *See* bus.

general recursiveness *See* Church's thesis.

generating polynomial *See* polynomial.

generation number (version number) *See* file updating.

generations of computers. An informal system of classifying computer systems, primarily according to the electronic technology used for their manufacture. *See* first generation, second generation, third generation, fourth generation.
Japan has plans to design and build a *fifth generation* of "intelligent" computers in the next decade.

generator 1. A program that accepts the definition of an operation that is to be accomplished, and automatically constructs a program for the purpose. The earliest example of this kind of program was the *sort generator*, which took a specification of the file format and the sorted order required, and produced a sorting program. This was followed by *report generators*, which constructed programs to print reports from files containing information in a specified format. The best-known program of this kind is *RPG II.
2. An element g of a *group G with the property that the various powers

$$g^0, g^1, g^2, \ldots$$

ultimately include all the elements of G. Such a group is said to be a *cyclic group*; it is also an abelian *group. Generators can also be defined for *monoids in a similar way.
The set of generators S of a group G is a subset of G having the property that every element of G can be expressed as a combination of elements of S. *See also* group graph.
3. *See* free semigroup.

generator matrix *See* linear code, convolutional code.

geodesic *See* reachability.

giga- (symbol: G) A prefix indicating a multiple of one billion, 10^9, or, loosely, a multiple of 2^{30}, i.e.

1 073 741 824

GIGO *Acronym for* garbage in garbage out, signifying that a program working on incorrect data produces incorrect results.

Gilbert–Varshamov bound The theorem that the maximum possible number, N, of codewords in a *binary *linear *block code is bounded by

$$N \geqslant \frac{2^n}{\sum_{r=0}^{d-1} \binom{n}{r}}$$

where the *code length is n digits, and the codewords are at a minimum *Hamming distance d. *See also* coding bounds, Hamming bound.

GINO *Acronym for* graphical input output. A package of FORTRAN subroutines for computer graphics. The GINO subroutines define a "language" for the production of elaborate graphics, including three-dimensional objects viewed in various projections. GINO separates the abstract description of the display from the device-dependent features of particular devices, and thus makes graphics programming largely machine-independent. GINO has provided a de facto graphics standard for many years, especially in the UK, but it is now being superseded by *GKS.

GKS *Abbrev. for* graphics kernel system. A (draft) International Standard for graphical input/output, based on the concept of a virtual input/output device containing a visible unit square that may be viewed in whole or in part by actual devices.

global A term used to define the scope of a *variable: global variables are accessible from all parts of a program. By contrast, *local* variables are accessible only in the program module within which they are defined.

global discretization error (global truncation error) *See* discretization error.

global optimization *See* optimization (in programming).

Gödel numbering of a formal system. A one-to-one mapping (i.e. an *injection) of the symbols, formulas, and finite sequences of formulas of the formal system onto some subset of the natural numbers. The mapping must be such that there is an algorithm that, for any symbol, formula, or finite sequence of formulas, identifies the corresponding natural number; this is the *Gödel number* of that object. There must also be an algorithm that, given any natural number, indicates whether it is the Gödel number of the object; if it is, the algorithm must identify the object.

Conferring Gödel numberings has the effect of permitting statements about elements in the nonnumeric system to be transformed into statements about natural numbers. Conversely, since much is known about natural numbers, it becomes possible to prove assertions about aspects of nonnumeric systems. The mapping was first used by the German mathematician Kurt Gödel.

Gödel's incompleteness theorems Two theorems put forward by Kurt Gödel in 1931. The first theorem (in one of its forms) states that the set of true sentences of arithmetic is not *recursively enumerable. (Actually a strengthening of the result tells us that the set of true sentences of arithmetic is not arithmetical – it does not lie in the hyperarithmetical hierarchy, at level ω.) Indeed, in any nontrivial mathematical system (i.e. one that contains arithmetic) it is possible to enunciate theorems that are true but that cannot be proven (or refuted) within the system. The second incompleteness theorem had consequences for the program of Hilbert in his work on the foundations of mathematics. Hilbert tried to devise a finitistic means of proving the consistency of mathematics. Gödel's second theorem established that Hilbert's consistency program could not be carried out. These theorems display the inherent limitations of formal systems.

Golay codes A family of *perfect *linear *error-correcting *block codes, of which the most important is the binary (23,12) Golay code. There is also a ternary (11,6) Golay code. Golay codes can be arranged to be *cyclic.

golfball printer A type of *serial *solid-font printer in which the characters of the typeface are molded onto a spherical carrier. The carrier is rotated about two axes to bring the required character opposite the paper, and is then struck against the paper and intervening ink ribbon. The mechanism was first devised as a typewriter but it was adapted to be driven as an output printer. The mechanism is complex and slow (about 10–12 cps) compared to that of a daisywheel printer (up to 60 cps) and is becoming obsolete.

Good–de Bruijn diagram (Good–de Bruijn graph) A directed *graph illustrating the possible succession of states of a *shift register. Each possible state of the shift register (indicated by its contents) is represented by a node in the graph; from each node a set of arcs lead to all its possible immediate successors. (Succession involves one clocking of the shift register, with some serial input.) If there are n cells in a *q-ary shift register, there will be q^n nodes, each with q arcs leading from it, and thus q^{n+1} arcs altogether.

When the serial input is some function of the current state, the behavior of the shift register is described by a Good–de Bruijn graph with some arcs deleted: such subgraphs are used in the study of *feedback registers.

Goppa codes A family of *linear *error-correcting *block codes. The most important classes of Goppa codes are the *Reed–Solomon codes and the binary *Golay (23,12) code. Goppa codes are not in general *cyclic.

GOTO statement A *branch instruction in a high-level language. It causes the normal flow of control to be broken by designating an explicit successor statement, usually identified by a label, e.g.

GOTO 99

⟨statements⟩
99: ...

Modern programming practice deprecates the use of GOTO since its use makes programs more difficult to follow, the flow of control being less visibly explicit. GOTO is, however, sometimes unavoidable, particularly in error situations where it is necessary to abort execution of a number of nested loops or procedures, when the language does not provide for exceptions.

GP *Short for* general purpose, general-purpose computer.

GPIB *Abbrev. for* general-purpose interface bus. *See* bus.

graceful degradation *See* fail-soft.

grammar One of the principal ways of specifying an infinite *formal language by finite means. Like a *semi-Thue system, a grammar consists of a set of rules (called *productions*) that may be used to derive one string from another by substring replacement. The strings of the specified language are obtained by repeated application of these rules, starting from some initial string. A grammar however has the additional feature that the alphabet is divided into a set T of *terminal symbols* and a set N of *nonterminal symbols*. While productions may be composed arbitrarily of terminals and nonterminals, the specified language contains strings of terminals only.

A grammar G can therefore be defined as comprising two sets of symbols T and N, a semi-Thue system over the union $T \cup N$, and a distinguished member S of N. The *language generated by* G is the set of all strings over T that can be derived from S by a sequence of substring replacements (*see* semi-Thue system); S is known as the *start symbol* or *sentence symbol*. As an example, let T be $\{b,c\}$, N be $\{S,A\}$ and let the productions be

(1) $S \rightarrow SA$
(2) $S \rightarrow A$
(3) $A \rightarrow bc$

Then, for instance, starting from S we can derive *bcbcbc* via the following sequence (among others):

SA – by production 1
SAA – by production 1
AAA – by production 2
bcAA – by production 3
bcbcA – by production 3
bcbcbc – by production 3

The language generated is

$\{bc, bcbc, bcbcbc, \ldots, \text{etc.}\}$

These are the only strings of *b*s and *c*s derivable from S. A string such as *SAbcA*, which is derivable from S but still contains nonterminals, is referred to as a *sentential form*.

This is the most general form of grammar. Typically however some restriction is placed on the form that productions may take (*see* regular grammar, context-free grammar, context-sensitive grammar). The syntax of programming languages is usually specified by context-free grammars; the example given above is context-free, although the language specified is regular.

A slightly different way of generating a language is by means of an *L-system. A different approach altogether is to define a machine that tests any string for membership of the language, i.e. an *automaton.

grandfather file, grandfather tape *See* file updating.

granularity A measure of the size of the *segments into which memory is divided for purposes of either *memory protection or *virtual-memory management.

graph 1. A nonempty but finite set of *vertices* (or *nodes*) together with a set of *edges* that join pairs of distinct vertices. If an edge *e* joins vertices v_1 and v_2, then v_1 and v_2 are said to be *incident* with *e* and the vertices are said to be *adjacent*; *e* is the unordered pair (v_1,v_2).

A graph is usually depicted in a pictorial form in which the vertices appear as dots or other shapes, perhaps labeled for identification purposes, and the edges are shown as lines joining the appropriate points. If direction is added to each edge of a graph, a *directed graph* or *digraph* is obtained. The edges then form a finite set of *ordered pairs of distinct vertices, and are often called *arcs*. In the pictorial representation, arrows can be placed on each edge. With no direction specified, the graph is said to be *undirected.*

Although helpful visually these representations are not suitable for manipulation by computer. More useful representations use an *incidence matrix or an *adjacency matrix.

Graphs are used in a wide variety of ways in computing: the vertices will usually represent objects of some kind and the edges will represent connections of a physical or logical nature between the vertices. So graphs can be used to model in a mathematical fashion such diverse items as a computer and all its attached peripherals, a network of computers, *parse trees, logical dependencies between *subroutines or nonterminals in a *grammar, *VLSI diagrams, and related items in *databases. *Trees and *lists are special kinds of graphs.

Certain variations exist in the definition of a graph. There is some dispute about whether one edge can join a vertex to itself, whether empty sets are involved, whether an infinite number of vertices and edges are permitted, and so on.

See also connected graph, network, weighted graph.

2. of a function f. The set of all *ordered pairs (x,y) with the property that $y = f(x)$. Often such a graph is represented by a curve.

graphics *See* computer graphics.

graphics characters *See* character set.

graph plotter *Another name for* xy plotter. *See* plotter.

Gray code A binary (n, n) *block code having the following properties:

(a) there are 2^n codewords, each of length n bits;

(b) successive codewords differ by the complementation of a single bit, i.e. the *Hamming distance between them is unity.

A Gray code can be conveniently represented by its *transition sequence*, i.e. the ordered list of bit positions that change when moving from one codeword to the next. Gray codes are used in encoding the positions of shafts, wheels, etc., in order to avoid the problems that would arise when several digits were supposed to change at the same time. They are also used to represent intensity or brightness levels.

gray-level array An array of numbers, each of which in a *Gray code represents the level of brightness in the corresponding area of a visual scene. The gray-level array might represent the output of a television camera or similar device.

gray scale A scale that assigns values to the range of gray tones that exist between black and white. The term is also used to refer to gradations between other extremes – in particular, levels of brilliance on a cathode-ray tube display. The information content and apparent resolution of a picture on a graphics display can be improved if the relative brilliance of each dot can be specified.

greatest common divisor (GCD) of two integers m and n. The largest integer, d, that exactly divides both m and n. If $d = 1$ then m and n are said to be *relatively prime*. For example, the GCD of 18 and 24 is 6; 21 and 25 are relatively prime.

greedy method An algorithm that, with a certain goal in mind, will attempt at every stage to do whatever it can, whenever it can, to get nearer to that goal immediately. In other words the method surrenders a possible longer-term advantage in favor of an immediate move toward the objective.

Greibach normal form A restricted type of *context-free grammar, namely one in which all productions have the form

$$A \rightarrow bC_1 \dots C_n$$

i.e. each right-hand side consists of a terminal followed by (zero or more) nonterminals. Any context-free language is generated by such a grammar, except that derivation of the empty string, Λ, requires the additional production

$$S \rightarrow \Lambda$$

One significance of this form is that it makes clear the existence of an equivalent *pushdown automaton: on reading b the PDA can pop A from the stack and push $C_1 \ldots C_n$.

Grosch's law The best known of many attempts to provide a measure of computer performance in terms of price, originally formulated by H. R. J. Grosch in 1953 as:

$$\text{performance} = \text{constant} \times \text{price}^2$$

Reliance on this law, which was approximately true at the time, led to the concept of "economy of scale", i.e. that large computers were less expensive per operation than small computers. Since that time other values of the exponent have been suggested: a good case can be made for the value 1 rather than 2. Current (LSI) technology has almost completely invalidated Grosch's law.

group A *set G on which there is defined a *binary operation $\circ$ (mapping $G \times G$ into G) that satisfies the following properties:
(a) $\circ$ is *associative;
(b) $\circ$ has an identity, i.e. there is a unique element e in G with the property that

$$x \circ e = e \circ x = x$$

for all x in G; e is called the *identity* of the group;
(c) *inverses* exist in G, i.e. for each x in G there is an inverse, denoted by x^{-1}, with the property that

$$x \circ x^{-1} = x^{-1} \circ x = e$$

These are the *group axioms*. It is sometimes assumed that G is *closed under $\circ$.
Certain kinds of groups are of particular interest. If the binary operation is *commutative, the group is said to be a *commutative group* or an *abelian group* (named for the Norwegian mathematician Niels Abel).
If there is only a finite number of elements n in the group, the group is said to be *finite*; n is then the *order* of the group. Finite groups can be represented or depicted by means of a *Cayley table.
If the group has a *generator then it is said to be *cyclic*; a cyclic group must be abelian.
The group is a very important *algebraic structure that underlies many other algebraic structures such as *rings and *fields. There are direct applications of groups in the study of symmetry, in the study of transformations and in particular *permutations, and also in error detecting and error correcting as well as in the design of fast adders.
Much of the work on group theory was carried out by Niels Abel and the French mathematician Évariste Galois. Groups were originally introduced for solving an algebraic problem. By group theory it can be shown that algorithmic methods of a particular kind cannot exist for finding the roots of a general polynomial of degree greater than four. *See also* semigroup.

group code *Another name for* linear code.

group code recording (GCR) *See* disk format, tape format.

group graph A directed *graph that represents a finite *group G; the vertices of the graph represent elements of the group and the edges represent *generators of the group. If edge E (representing generator g) joins vertices V and V' (representing group elements v and v' respectively) then

$$v \circ g = v'$$

where $\circ$ is the group operation. Each vertex of the group graph will have outdegree (*see* degree) equal to the number of generators of the group.

group mark A notation within a record that indicates the start or finish of a group of related fields. In the case of repeated fields, the group mark often indicates the number of repetitions of such fields.

Grzegorczyk hierarchy *See* hierarchy of functions.

gsm mapping *Short for* generalized sequential machine mapping. A function that is the response function of a generalized *sequential machine, and therefore generalizes the notion of *sequential function. Without constraining the machine to have a finite state-set, generalized sequentiality is equivalent to the following property of *initial subwords preservation*:
for all u,v in I^*, $f(uv)$ has the form $f(u)w$ for some w in O^*, where I^* and O^* are the sets of all input and output strings.

guard band *See* frequency division multiplexing.

gulp *Rare* Several, usually two, *bytes.

H

hacker *See* system hacker.

Hadamard codes *See* Hadamard matrices.

Hadamard matrices A family of matrices, a Hadamard matrix H of order m being an $m \times m$ matrix, all of whose elements are either $+1$ or -1, and such that

$$H H^{\mathrm{T}} = \lambda I$$

where H^{T} is the *transpose of H, I is the *identity matrix, and λ is a scalar quantity. They are usually written in "normalized" form, i.e. the rows and columns have been signed so that the top row and left column consist of $+1$ elements only. Hadamard matrices exist only for order $m = 1, 2$, or $4r$ for some r. It is conjectured, but not known, that they exist for all orders $m = 4r$.
The rows of any Hadamard matrix form an *orthonormal basis, from which property follows many of their applications in the theory of *codes, *digital signal processing, and statistical *sampling. When the order $m = 2^s$, they are called *Sylvester matrices*.
A Sylvester matrix has an equivalent matrix whose rows form a set of m-point *Walsh functions or, in a different arrangement, Paley functions. Various *linear *Hadamard codes* can be derived from a normalized Sylvester matrix in which $+1$ has been replaced by 0, and -1 by 1.

half adder *See* adder.

half duplex A connection between two endpoints, either physical or logical, over which data may travel in both directions, but not both simultaneously. An important parameter of a half-duplex connection is the *turnaround time*, i.e. the time it takes to reverse the roles of sender and receiver. *See also* duplex, simplex.

half subtractor *See* subtractor.

half word A unit of storage comprising half the number of bits in a computer's *word.

halt or **HALT** A program instruction that stops execution of the program. (It also appears as PAUSE and STOP in many languages.) Originally a halt instruction actually halted the processor (hence the name), but now it more often causes a *trap into the operating system so that the operating system can take over control and, for example, start another program.

halting problem (from the German **Entscheidungsproblem**) A decision problem that was investigated by Alan Turing. Suppose M is a *Turing machine and let x be an input to M. If we start the machine running two things might happen: after a finite number of steps the machine might stop, or it might run on forever. Is there any way to test which of these two situations will occur? This is the halting problem. In fact there is no effective procedure that, given any Turing machine and its input, will decide whether or not the calculation ever terminates.
The halting problem is said to be unsolvable or undecidable. It is one example of many unsolvable problems in mathemat-

ics and computer science. It has profound practical implications: if it were solvable it would be possible to write a "program tester" that, given (say) any Pascal program and its input, would print "yes" if the program terminated after a finite number of steps and "no" if it did not.

Hamiltonian cycle A *cycle of a *graph in the course of which each vertex of the graph is visited once and once only.

Hamming bound (sphere-packing bound) The theorem that the number, N, of codewords in a *binary *linear code is bounded by

$$N \leqslant \frac{2^n}{\sum_{r=0}^{e} \binom{n}{r}}$$

where the *code length is n digits, and the code is capable of correcting e errors. *See also* coding bounds, Gilbert–Varshamov bound.

Hamming codes A family of *binary *linear *perfect *error-correcting *block codes. They are capable of correcting any single error occurring in the block. Considered as (n, k) block codes, Hamming codes have

$$n = 2^m - 1, \quad k = n - m$$

where m characterizes the particular code. Where multiple-error-correcting abilities are required, Hamming codes may be generalized into *Bose–Chandhuri–Hocquenghem (BCH) codes. The code was discovered by R. W. Hamming in 1950.

Hamming distance (Hamming metric) In the theory of *block codes intended for error-detection or error-correction, the Hamming distance $d(\boldsymbol{u}, \boldsymbol{v})$ between two words $\boldsymbol{u}$ and $\boldsymbol{v}$, of the same length, is equal to the number of symbol places in which the words differ from one another. If $\boldsymbol{u}$ and $\boldsymbol{v}$ are of finite length n then their Hamming distance is finite since

$$d(\boldsymbol{u}, \boldsymbol{v}) \leqslant n$$

It can be called a distance since it is non-negative, idem-null, symmetric, and triangular:

$$0 \leqslant d(\boldsymbol{u}, \boldsymbol{v})$$
$$d(\boldsymbol{u}, \boldsymbol{v}) = 0 \quad \text{iff} \quad \boldsymbol{u} = \boldsymbol{v}$$
$$d(\boldsymbol{u}, \boldsymbol{v}) = d(\boldsymbol{v}, \boldsymbol{u})$$
$$d(\boldsymbol{u}, \boldsymbol{w}) \leqslant d(\boldsymbol{u}, \boldsymbol{v}) + d(\boldsymbol{v}, \boldsymbol{w})$$

The Hamming distance is important in the theory of *error-correcting codes and *error-detecting codes: if, in a block code, the codewords are at a *minimum Hamming distance d* from one another, then
(a) if d is even, the code can detect $d - 1$ symbols in error and correct $\frac{1}{2}d - 1$ symbols in error;
(b) if d is odd, the code can detect $d - 1$ symbols in error and correct $\frac{1}{2}(d - 1)$ symbols in error.
See also Hamming space, perfect codes, coding theory, coding bounds, Hamming bound.

Hamming metric *Another name for* Hamming distance.

Hamming radius *See* Hamming space.

Hamming space In coding theory, a mathematical space in which words of some given length may be situated, the separation of points in the space being measured by the *Hamming distance. The dimensionality of the space is equal to the number of digits in the words; the coordinate in each dimension is given by each successive digit in the words.
The *Hamming sphere* is the set of all words in Hamming space whose Hamming distance from some given word (the "center") does not exceed some given value (the *Hamming radius*).

Hamming sphere *See* Hamming space.

Hamming weight In coding theory, the number of nonzero digits in a word. It is numerically identical with the *Hamming distance between the word in question and the *zero word.

handle *See* bottom-up parsing.

handshake An arrangement for synchronizing two communicating devices, usually at low level. The handshake synchronizes the devices for the transfer of a unit of data.
For example, a *two-way handshake* begins when one of the communicating devices (the master) requires communication; it asserts a signal, or SYN. The other device (the slave) detects this signal and asserts a reply, SSYN. The two devices are now synchronized and can transfer data. The handshake is completed by one device removing its synchronizing signal, the other device detecting the change and removing its synchronizing signal. Another handshake can then take place.
Complications arise when more than two devices are involved. A *three-way handshake* is used in the IEEE 488 *bus (IEC 625, HP-IB).

handshaking A control procedure for transferring data across an interface. One side "shakes hands" with the other through a sequence of interlocking steps to transfer a unit of data.

hands off *See* hands on.

hands on A mode of operation of a system in which an operator is in control. The operator literally has hands on a keyboard and other switches to control the processes to be carried out by the system. The dependence on the capability of the operator to run a medium-size or large computer has been reduced by the introduction of supervisor programs or operating systems. When no operator intervention is required the mode of operation can be described as *hands off*.

hang-up 1. A state in which a program has come to an unexpected halt, e.g. because it is trying to read data from a device that is not connected to the processor.
2. In the context of time-sharing systems, the signal received by the program when a remote terminal breaks its connection ("hangs up the telephone").

hard copy A printed or otherwise permanent copy of data from a processing system.

hard disk (metallic disk) A magnetic recording medium consisting of an aluminum substrate coated or plated – usually on both sides – with a magnetic material. *See* magnetic disk. *Compare* floppy disk.

hard error A permanent error. *See* error rate.

hard-sectored disk *See* sector.

hardware The physical portion of a computer system, including the electrical/electronic components (e.g. devices and circuits), electromechanical components (e.g. a disk drive), and mechanical (e.g. cabinet) components. *Compare* software.

hardware circuitry *See* logic circuit.

hardware description An unambiguous method of describing the interconnection and behavior of the electrical and electronic subset of the computer hardware. There are a number of computer hardware description languages (CHDLs) that work at the register transfer level; the most well known are *AHPL* (a hardware programming language) and *CDL* (computer description language).

hardware reliability A statement of the ability of hardware to perform its functions for some period of time. It is usually expressed as MTBF (mean time between failures).

hardware security The use of hardware, e.g. *bounds registers or *locks and keys, to assist in providing computer security.

hardwired Denoting circuits that are permanently interconnected to perform a specific function, as distinct from circuits addressed by software in a program and therefore capable of performing a variety of functions, albeit more slowly.

Harvard Mark I The name given at Harvard University to the Automatic Sequence Controlled Calculator (ASCC), an electromechanical computer based on the ideas of Harvard's Howard H. Aiken. This machine, which followed a sequence of instructions on paper tape, was started in 1938; it was developed and built in collaboration with IBM engineers at their laboratories, and became operational at Harvard in 1944. It was donated by IBM to Harvard later that year. The Mark I was used by the US navy for ballistics and ship design.

hash function *See* hashing algorithm, hashing.

hashing A technique that is used for organizing tables to permit rapid *searching or *table look-up, and is particularly useful for tables to which items are added in an unpredictable manner, e.g. the symbol table of a compiler. Each item to be placed in the table has a unique *key*. To place it in the *hash table* a *hash function* is used, which maps the keys onto a set of integers (the *hash values*) that range over the table size. The function is chosen to distribute the keys fairly evenly over the table (*see* hashing algorithm); since it is not a unique mapping, two different keys may map onto the same integer.
In the simplest version of the technique, the hash value identifies a primary position in the table; if this is already occupied, successive positions are examined until a free one is found (treating the table as circular). The item with its key is inserted in the table at this position. To locate an item in the table a similar algorithm is used. The hash value of the key is computed and the table entry at this position is examined. If the key matches the required key, the item has been located; if not, successive table positions are examined until either an entry with a matching key is found or an empty position is found. In the latter case it can be concluded that the key does not exist in the table, since the insertion procedure would have placed it in this empty position. For the technique to work, there must be rather more table positions than there are entries to be accommodated. Provided that the table is not more than 60% full, an item can on average be located in a hash table by examining at most two table positions.
More sophisticated techniques can be used to deal with the problem of *collisions*, which occur when the position indicated by the hash value is already occupied; this improves even further the performance of the table look-up. Table look-up and insertion of new items can be interleaved, but if items are deleted from the table the space they occupied cannot normally be reused.

hashing algorithm An algorithm that, for a given key k, yields a function $f(k)$; this in turn yields the starting point for a *hash search* for the key k. The function f is called the *hash function*. A typical hash function is the remainder modulo p, where p is a prime,

$$f(k) \equiv k \pmod{p}$$

where k is interpreted as an integer. Another hash function uses a constant A and defines $f(k)$ as the leading bits of the least significant half of the product Ak. *See also* hashing.

hash P complete *See* counting problem.

hash search *See* hashing algorithm.

hash table *See* hashing.

hash total A number produced by adding together (or otherwise combining) corresponding fields over all the records of a file, when such a total does not have any external meaning but is used solely to verify the records in the file. The hash total can be recalculated when the file is examined again, and a change to the records of the file will probably show as a difference in the hash total.

hash value *See* hashing.

hazard A potential or actual malfunction of a *logic circuit during change(s) of state of input variables. Hazards result from the nonideal behavior of actual switching elements, e.g. noninstantaneous operation, turn-on time different from turn-off time. In the UK the word hazard is sometimes used as the equivalent of *race condition.

HDLC *Abbrev. for* high-level data link control. A *data link control protocol developed by ISO in response to IBM's *SDLC protocol, which is a subset of HDLC. CCITT defined a different subset of HDLC (*see* LAP) as the second (data link) layer of the *X.25 protocol.

head 1. The part of a peripheral mechanism that is in contact with the medium or very close to it and that is directly responsible for writing data or patterns onto the medium or for reading or erasing them. The word is most frequently used of a *magnetic head* in a *disk drive or tape transport (*see* magnetic tape), or a *print head* in a *serial printer.
2. The first item in a *list. *See also* list head.

headend *See* broadband coaxial system.

header Some coded information that precedes a more general collection of data and gives details about it, e.g. its length. The header of a data-structure representation is logically distinct from the data elements themselves and may serve several purposes:
(a) to hold global information about the whole structure, e.g. list length, array index bounds;
(b) to represent an empty structure;
(c) to provide links into the structure, e.g. pointers to first and last nodes in a list;
(d) to represent the entire structure in any other data structures of which it may be a part.

heap 1. An area of storage used for the allocation of data structures where the order of releasing the allocated data structure is random. *Compare* stack.
2. A *complete binary tree in which the value at each node is at least as large as the values at its children (if they exist).

heapsort A sorting algorithm developed by Williams and Floyd in 1964 and employing the ideas of *tree selection. It is more efficient for larger numbers of records but on average is inferior to *quicksort. However, the worst possible distribution of keys does not cause the efficiency of heapsort to deteriorate too much. The worst case for quicksort can then be worse. Some of the ideas of heapsort are relevant to *priority queue applications.

height 1. of a node in a tree. The length of a longest path from the node to a *leaf node.
2. of a tree. The maximum height of any node in a tree. The height of a given tree will have the same numerical value as the *depth of that tree.

height-balanced *See* balanced, AVL tree.

Hermite interpolation *See* interpolation.

hertz (symbol: Hz) The derived SI unit of *frequency. A periodic phenomenon has a frequency of one hertz if each cycle of the phenomenon repeats itself in a period of one second.

heuristic Employing a self-learning approach to the solution of a problem. The construction of a nonheuristic system directly reflects existing knowledge of some algorithm that can yield a solution to some problem. By constrast, a heuristic system has to be constructed so that it can acquire the knowledge needed to produce the required solution.
For example, in the absence of good known algorithms for the problem, heuristic methods have been used to control traffic routing in communications networks: feedback from the actual performance of the network is used to influence subsequent routing decisions, thereby maintaining satisfactory routing behavior despite changes in load or failures of network components. Heuristic techniques are also employed in *artificial intelligence to automate tasks for which no deci-

sion procedure is known or as a more efficient alternative to a decision procedure.

Hewlett-Packard A California-based electronics instrument, calculator, and computer manufacturer. HP is noted as the first manufacturer of a hand-held scientific calculator.

hex *Short for* hexadecimal.

hexadecimal notation The representation of numbers in the positional number system with base 16. The sixteen hexadecimal digits are usually represented by 0–9, A–F.

hex pad A *keypad with 16 keys that are labeled 0–9, A–F so that they correspond to *hedadecimal notation.

hidden-line algorithm An algorithm used in graph-plotting, etc., to determine which lines should not be visible when a three-dimensional surface is plotted.

hierarchical addressing *See* addressing.

hierarchical cluster analysis *See* cluster analysis.

hierarchical communication system An interconnection structure composed of several levels or groupings, each higher level covering a wider or more general area of operation than the next lower level. An example would be a data communication network for a large bank. Each branch office would have a *local area network (local loop) connecting the teller stations. Several branches would be tied into a data *concentrator connected to regional nodes. The regional nodes would be tied together by a national network. Thus ordered layer of communication facilities is employed.
Just as physical communication facilities may be organized hierarchically, so may communication *protocols be organized. The lowest levels deal with sending data over a single communication channel. Middle levels deal with shipping data from one computer to another over a series of data links. Higher levels deal with applications such as *TELNET and *electronic mail.
See also addressing.

hierarchical database system A *database management system in which there is a *data hierarchy whereby each record is "owned" by another record (its owner), and each member record type may be owned by only one owner record type. *Compare* network database system.

hierarchical memory structure *See* memory hierarchy.

hierarchy of functions A sequence of sets of functions $F_0, F_1, F_2, \ldots$ with the property that

$$F_0 \subseteq F_1 \subseteq F_2 \subseteq \ldots$$

(*see* subset). Typically the functions in F_0 will include certain initial functions; the sets of functions $F_1, F_2, \ldots$ are normally defined by combining initial functions in some way.
Hierarchies of *primitive recursive functions can be defined by letting F_i represent those functions that can be computed by programs containing at most i loops nested one within the other. Then

$$F_i \subseteq F_{i+1}$$

for all integers $i > 0$. The *union of all these sets includes all the primitive recursive functions and only those functions. Consequently the hierarchy is often called a *subrecursive hierarchy*. This same hierarchy can be expressed in a slightly different form, so resulting in the *Grzegorczyk hierarchy*.
In an attempt to circumvent problems caused by *recursion, Bertrand Russell invented a *theory of types*, which essentially imposed a hierarchy on the set of functions; functions at one level could be defined only in terms of functions at lower levels.
The study of hierarchies of functions dates from work of David Hilbert around 1926 on the foundations of mathematics. More recent interest stems from their applicability to computational *complexity.

high-level design (architectural design) *See* program decomposition, program design, system design.

high-level language A variety of programming language in which the *control and *data structures reflect the requirements of the programmer rather than the facilities actually provided by the hardware. A high-level language is translated into *machine code by a *compiler.

high-level scheduler *See* scheduler.

high-order language *Another name for* high-level language.

high-pass filter A *filtering device that permits only those components in the *Fourier transform domain whose frequencies lie above some critical value to pass through with little attenuation, all other components being highly attenuated.

highway *Another (UK) name for* bus.

hi res *Short for* high resolution. *See* resolution.

histogram A chart showing the *relative frequencies with which a measurable quantity takes values in a set of contiguous intervals. The chart consists of rectangles whose areas are proportional to the relative frequencies and whose widths are proportional to the class intervals. It can be used to picture a *frequency distribution.

Hitachi A large Japanese firm that manufactures a variety of products, among which is a line of computers that are plug-compatible with IBM equipment, i.e. will run the same software.

hit rate The fraction of references to one level of the *memory hierarchy that must otherwise be fulfilled in the less accessible levels within the hierarchy. Thus for a *cache memory the hit rate is the fraction of references that do not result in access to main memory. For a *page the hit rate is the fraction of references that do not result in a page turn.

HMOS A name applied by Intel Corp. to high-speed MOS technology, usually NMOS although it will be used in CMOS. HMOS implies both a short channel between source and drain, and also design (layout) rules that deal with minimum feature size of less than two micrometers.

hold time The time for which a signal must be held constant on a computer *bus such that a transfer of its value occurs between two devices sharing the bus. The hold time will normally be determined by the requirements of the device to which the transfer is being made (the listener), or it may be automatically set by the device sending the data (the talker).

Hollerith code A code for relating alphanumeric characters to holes in a punched card. It was devised by Herman Hollerith in 1888 and enabled the letters of the alphabet and the digits 0–9 to be encoded by a combination of punchings in 12 rows of a card.

holographic memory A storage device that records binary information in the form of holograms, which are produced (as interference patterns) on photographic or photochromic media by means of laser beams, and are read by means of low-power laser beams. The advantage of a hologram is the way in which the image is dispersed over the recording surface so that dust or scratches do not totally obscure data though they may reduce the contrast. Development of a mass store using this technology was done by RCA and Plessey Co. Ltd. in 1972 but it did not result in a commercially available product. In 1977 Holofile Industries announced a device developed from work done by TRW's Defence and Space Systems Group. It could store 200 million bits on a 4″ × 6″ fiche, but it was a read-only device and did not achieve widespread application.

homomorphic image of a formal language. *See* homomorphism.

homomorphism A structure preserving mapping between *algebraic structures including *algebras, *monoids, *groups, *rings, *fields, and even *graphs. Let G and H be two algebraic structures of the same type in the sense that G has a *binary operation $\circ$ defined on it and H has a binary operation $\cdot$ defined. G and H can be thought of as a pair of monoids or groups. Then

$$\phi : G \rightarrow H$$

is a homomorphism provided that it is a function from G into H and

$$\phi(g_1 \circ g_2) = \phi(g_1) \cdot \phi(g_2)$$

for all g_1 and g_2 in G. The idea can be extended to deal with more general algebras such as rings, fields, and graphs.

When homomorphisms exist, the two algebraic systems are said to be *homomorphic*. In some sense they are similar and share common properties. It is even possible to say that one algebraic system realizes another or one algebraic system simulates certain properties of another.

Since a homomorphism is a function it may also be an *injection, *surjection, or *bijection, and as such is known as a *monomorphism, *epimorphism, and *isomorphism respectively. *See also* endomorphism, automorphism.

In formal language theory, a homomorphism occurs between free monoids (*see* free semigroup, monoid). Let Σ_1 and Σ_2 be alphabets, and h a function from Σ_1 to Σ_2^*, i.e. h associates a Σ_2-word with each symbol in the set Σ_1 (*see* word). The function h can be extended to Σ_1^* thus:

$$h(a_1 \ldots a_n) = h(a_1) \ldots h(a_n)$$

i.e. the *concatenation of the strings $h(a_1)$, $\ldots$, $h(a_n)$. h then becomes a homomorphism from the free monoid Σ_1^* to the free monoid Σ_2^*. h is referred to as Λ-*free* if $h(a)$ is nonempty for all a.

h can furthermore be extended to a mapping on languages: if L is a Σ_1-language,

$$h(L) = \{h(w) \mid w \in \Sigma_1^*\}$$

$h(L)$ is called the *homomorphic image* of L. Similarly the *inverse homomorphic image*, $h^{-1}(L)$, of a Σ_2-language L is defined by

$$h^{-1}(L) = \{w \mid h(w) \in L\}$$

These mappings are also homomorphisms – between the monoids of languages over Σ_1 and over Σ_2.

Honeywell Corporation A company engaged generally in the design and manufacture of automation equipment and electronic systems, and whose subsidiary, Honeywell Information Systems, manufactures a line of primarily mainframe computers, with some minicomputers, for business and scientific computing.

hop *See* store-and-forward. *See also* flow control.

horizontal check *See* cyclic redundancy check.

horizontal microinstruction *See* microprogramming.

horizontal recording *See* magnetic encoding.

host computer (host) A computer that is attached to a *network and provides services other than simply acting as a *store-and-forward processor or communication switch. Host computers range in size from small microcomputers to large time-sharing or batch mainframes. Many networks have a hierarchical structure, with a *communication subnetwork providing *packet-switching services for host computers to support time-sharing, remote job entry, etc. A host computer at one level of a hierarchy may function as a packet or message switch at another. Sometimes host computers are divided into two classes: *servers*, which provide resources, and *users*, which access them.

housekeeping Actions performed within a program or system in order to maintain internal orderliness rather than to address the externally imposed requirements. For example, the housekeeping of a program often includes *memory management.

HPF *Abbrev. for* highest priority first. Where several processes are free to proceed, the *scheduler will initiate the process that has been assigned the highest priority.

HP–IB *See* bus.

hub polling *See* polling.

Huffman encoding A *binary encoding of the elements of a finite set, A,

$$A = \{a_1, a_2, \ldots, a_n\}$$

where each element a_i in A has an assumed probability, p_i, of occurring in a message. The binary encoding satisfies the *prefix property and is such that messages will have a minimum expected length. Thus an element a_i with a high probability of occurring in a message is encoded as a short binary string while an element with a low probability of occurring is encoded with a longer string. *See also* source coding.

hybrid computer A computer (system) that contains both a digital and an analog computer. The digital computer usually serves as the controller and provides logical operations; the analog computer normally serves as a solver of differential equations.

hybrid integrated circuit A complete electronic circuit that is fabricated on an insulating substrate using a variety of device technologies. The substrate acts as a carrier for the circuit and also has the interconnecting tracks between devices printed on it by multilayer techniques (*see* multilayer device). Individual devices, which comprise chip diodes, transistors, integrated circuits, and thick-film resistors and capacitors and which form the circuit function, are attached to the substrate and are connected together using the previously defined interconnecting tracks.

I

IA5 *Abbrev. for* International Alphabet, Number 5. An internationally agreed alphabet, specified by *CCITT. It consists of a subset of *ISO-7 in which characters that are "for national use" are either specified or not used at all.

IAL *Acronym for* international algorithmic language, the original name for the language later called Algol 58 and now obsolete. *See* Algol. *See also* JOVIAL.

IAS *Abbrev. for* immediate access store.

IAS (Institute for Advanced Study) computer The model for a class of computing machines designed by John von Neumann. The IAS machine was started at Princeton in 1946 and was completed in 1951. This machine used *electrostatic storage devices – cathode-ray tubes – as the main memory. Such tubes, called Williams tubes, could each store 1024 bits. Other computers modeled after the IAS computer included ORACLE, JOHNNIAC, ILLIAC I, MANIAC, and IBM 701.

IBG *Abbrev. for* interblock gap. *See* block.

IBM International Business Machines Corporation, the world's largest computer manufacturer. It was incorporated in 1911 as the Computing Tabulating Recording Company as a result of a merger of three companies, one of which had been Hermann Hollerith's Tabulating Machine Company, formed 1896. It adopted its present name in 1924. IBM produces a wide range of computers, from desk-top "personal" computers to 25–30 million instruction per second giants such as the 3081.

IBM system 360 IBM's famous *third generation computer family that used essentially the same architecture to span a wide range of performance and price objectives. The common architecture permitted upward mobility of users to larger versions of the same machine when their workload grew. Programs written for a smaller version of the 360 would run unchanged on the larger machines.

IBM system 370 IBM's fourth generation computer family. The 370 is very similar to the 360, but differs slightly in the instruction set and most markedly in the manufacturing techniques used (extensive microprogramming compared to the 360 family).

IC *Abbrev. for* integrated circuit.

ICL International Computers Ltd., a wholly British company and the largest computer system manufacturer in Europe. It was formed in 1968 by the merging of ICT (International Computers and Tabulators) and EELM (English Electric Leo Marconi), both of which were the results of earlier mergers of UK computer companies, including *Ferranti. ICL markets a complete range of computing equipment from personal computers to very large mainframes.

idempotent law The law satisfied by any *binary operation ∘ for which

$$x \circ x = x$$

for all elements x in the domain of ∘. *Union and *intersection of sets satisfy these laws. In a *Boolean algebra both of the binary operations are idempotent.

identification 1. The process of determining the identity of a user or a using process; it is necessary for *access control. Identification is usually accomplished by *authentication of an asserted identity. **2.** The process of determining how a control parameter influences a system.

identifier A string of characters used to identify (or *name) some element of a program. The kind of element that may be named depends on the programming language; it may be a variable, a data structure, a procedure, a statement, a higher-level unit, or the program itself.

identity burst *See* tape format.

identity element of a *set S on which some *binary operation ∘ is defined. An element e with the property that

$$a \circ e = e \circ a = a$$

for all elements a in S. It can be shown that e is unique. In normal arithmetic, 0 and 1 are the identity elements associated with addition and multiplication respectively. In a *Boolean algebra, 0 and 1 are the identities associated with the OR and the AND operations respectively.

identity function A *function

$$I : S \rightarrow S$$

with the property that

$$I(s) = s \text{ for all } s \text{ in } S$$

Such a function leaves every element in its domain unaltered. Identity functions are needed for such purposes as the definition of *inverses of functions.

identity matrix (unit matrix) A *diagonal matrix, symbol I, with each diagonal element equal to one.

idle time *See* available time.

IDP *Abbrev. for* integrated data processing. *See* data processing.

IEEE Institute of Electrical and Electronics Engineers, a US organization formed in 1963 by the merger of the IRE (Institute of Radio Engineers) and the AIEE (American Institute of Electrical Engineers). It has over 200 000 members world-wide; approximately 52 000 belong to the computer society subgroup of the IEEE.

IEEE 488 *See* bus.

if and only if statement A well-formed formula of the form

$$A \equiv B$$

where A and B are also appropriate well-formed formulas. *See* biconditional, propositional calculus.

iff *Short for* if and only if.

IFIP International Federation for Information Processing, founded in 1959 and coming into official existence in 1960 as the International Federation of Information Processing Societies. Its secretariat is in Geneva. It aims to "promote information science and technology, advance international cooperation in the field of information processing, stimulate research, development, and application of information processing, further dissemination and exchange of information in information processing, and encourage education in information processing." It has full members in 41 countries.

if then else statement The most basic conditional construct in a programming language, allowing selection between two alternatives, dependent on the truth or falsity of a given condition. Most languages also provide an *if* ... *then* construct to allow conditional execution of a single statement or group of statements. Primitive languages such as BASIC restrict the facility to a conditional transfer of control, e.g.
"IF A → 0 THEN 330"
which is reminiscent of the conditional jump provided in the order code of every CPU. *See also* conditional, propositional calculus.

ignore character (fill character) A character used in transmission to fill an otherwise empty position and whose value is thus ignored.

IH *Abbrev. for* interrupt handler.

I²L (IIL) *Abbrev. for* integrated injection logic. A semiconductor-device technology for a *logic family, fabricated using bipolar techniques. It is also called *MTL, merged transistor logic*. In I²L circuits the electrode areas of individual *bipolar transistors are merged into a single area, which is then common to each transistor. This permits a higher *packing density of individual devices in a single chip and a reduction in the complexity of chip fabrication. I²L is said to be capable of offering the low cost and low power consumption of *CMOS and the high speed of *TTL, but it is as yet a largely unproven technology.

ill-conditioned *See* condition number.

illegal character Any character not in the *character set of a given machine or of a given programming language.

illegal instruction An instruction that has an invalid *operation code. It is sometimes deliberately inserted in an instruction stream when debugging in order to have a program halt at a particular point.

ILLIAC IV An *array processor that was designed by Daniel Slotnick and used a 16-by-16 array of processing units (PUs), each interconnected to its four nearest neighbors. The array of PUs was regulated by a single processor that controlled the flow of instructions to the PUs. The ILLIAC IV was sponsored by ARPA and built by Burroughs Corporation. It became operable at the Ames Research Center of NASA in the early 1970s, and was finally dismantled in 1981.

image 1. A copy in memory of data that exists elsewhere.
2. *Another name for* picture. *See* picture processing.
3. *See* function.

image processing *Another name for* picture processing.

immediate access store (IAS) A memory device in which the access time for any location is independent of the previous access and is usually of the same order as the cycle time of the processor. Such devices are normally only used for main memory.

immediate addressing A method used to refer to data (often small constants or similar) that is located in an address field of an instruction. Strictly this is not a method of generating an address at all; it does provide a reference to the desired data in a way that is both compact and requires less memory reference time.

IMP *Acronym for* interface message processor. One of the switching computers that together form(ed) the *backbone network for the *ARPANET. The original IMPs were Honeywell 516 minicomputers with special interfaces for 56 kilobits per second leased lines. The current IMPs are BBN C/30 minicomputers; other minicomputers used include the Honeywell 316 and the Lockheed Sue (Pluribus IMP).

The primary function of the IMPs is to forward packets between the ARPANET hosts using 56 Kbps leased lines. Specially configured IMPs have, however, performed other functions in the ARPANET. The most important of these are the *TIPs* (terminal interface (message) processors). TIPs are IMPs with additional hardware and software to provide network access for asynchronous terminals at speeds up to 1200 baud. The TIP thus functions as a small host computer in addition to its packet-switching responsibilities as an IMP.

Other special IMP configurations include satellite IMPs with extra memory buffers for high-delay satellite links, IMPs with message encryption hardware for secure communication, and IMPs that run special control programs for high-bandwidth packet speech and video traffic.

impact printer Any device that makes use of mechanical impact to print characters onto paper. Typewriters come within this definition but the term is not usually applied to machines that are only operated through a keyboard. A character may be formed by impacting an inked ribbon against the paper with an engraved type character, or it may be built up from a number of dots printed by the impacts of separate styluses. *See* solid-font printer, dot-matrix printer.

imperative languages (procedural languages) A class of programming languages. With an imperative language a program explicitly states how the desired result is to be produced but does not explicitly define what properties the result is expected to exhibit – the result is defined only implicitly as whatever is obtained by following the specified procedure (*compare* declarative languages).

The procedure for producing the desired result takes the form of a sequence of operations, and thus with imperative languages the notions of flow of control and ordering of statements are inherent. Such a language is typically characterized by the presence of the *assignment statement, which, being destructive (the assigned value replaces the previous value of the variable), also depends on the notion of ordering. Imperative languages are closely associated with the von Neumann model of computation, and the majority of widely used languages – including COBOL, FORTRAN, Algol, and Pascal – are imperative.

implementation The activity of proceeding from a given design of a system to a working version (known also as an *implementation*) of that system, or the specific way in which some part of a system is made to fulfill its function. For example, a control unit may be implemented by random logic or by microprogramming; a multiplier may be implemented by successive additions and shifts or by a table look-up. Another example occurs in computer families, where different implementations may differ in the type of circuit elements used or in the actual parallelism (as opposed to logical parallelism) of the ALU.

With software, use of the term normally implies that all major design decisions have been made so that the implementation activity could be relatively straightforward. For many systems a number of important characteristics may not become bound until the implementation activity; examples include the programming language in which the system is written, the type of computer employed, the actual hardware configuration, or the operating system used. With such systems there may be a number of distinct implementation activities in order to provide several versions of the system, e.g. written in different languages or operating on different hardware.

implicant A *product term that covers at least one of the *standard sum of product terms in a *Boolean function, but will introduce no new (unwanted) standard sum of product terms.
A *prime implicant* is an implicant that includes a *standard product of a function that is not otherwise included.

implied addressing (inherent addressing) A type of *addressing scheme, the term referring to the fact that in many instruction formats the location of one or more operands is implied in the instruction name and is specified in the instruction description. An implied address is usually that of one of the machine registers.

impulse noise *Noise of large amplitude and some statistical irregularity, affecting an analog channel severely but (relatively) infrequently. In contrast, *white noise affects it (relatively) unseverely but continuously. Impulse noise affecting an analog channel carrying a binary signal usually causes *burst errors.

IMS *Trademark* A well-established *database management system provided by IBM. It was originally a *hierarchical system but has gained additional nonhierarchical features as a result of practical needs.

inactive Not running (pertaining to the state of a process).

incidence matrix A representation of a *graph *G* employing a *matrix in which there is a row for each vertex *v* of *G*. The entries on this row are just the vertices that are joined by an edge to *v*.

inclusive-OR gate *Another name for* OR gate.

inclusive-OR operation *Another name for* OR operation, making explicit the difference between this and the *exclusive-OR operation.

incompleteness theorems *See* Gödel's incompleteness theorems.

incremental compiler A compiler that compiles partial programs, and will compile additional statements for a previously compiled program, rather than recompiling the whole program. Incremental compilers are particularly useful for use in an interactive programming environment.

incremental plotter A device that can draw graphs and other line images when fed with digital data. The plotter forms the image by moving a pen or the paper or both in a succession of increments. The increments are typically 200 per inch for drum plotters and can be 500 per inch for flatbed plotters. *See also* plotter.

indegree *See* degree.

indeterminate system A logic system whose *logic states are unpredictable.

index 1. The mechanism, computer-oriented or otherwise, in which a data value is presented to an ordered list that contains not the desired value associated with the data item, but a location at which further searching for the data item should be continued. The index often does not contain all values of the data item presented but simply a limiting range that contains it, e.g. the page headings of a telephone directory.
2. The value held in an *index register.
3. (subscript) An integer value selecting a particular element of an *array.

indexed addressing (indexing) A method of generating an *effective address that modifies the specified address given in the instruction by the contents of a specified *index register. The modification is usually that of addition of the contents of the index register to the specified address. The automatic modification of index-register contents results in an orderly progression of effective addresses being generated on successive executions of the instruction containing the reference to the index register. This progression is terminated when the index register reaches a value that has been specified in an index-register handling instruction.

indexed file A *file whose organization uses an *index. The index may be separated from the file, as in the case of a book, or located within the file, as in the case of a telephone directory. An index may be based upon the data item on which the file is ordered, if the file is sequential. In this case it is usually called a *primary index* and the file is called an *indexed sequential file*. Alternatively, the index may be upon a data item that is not the one used for ordering and in that case it is known as a *secondary index*. *See also* file organization.

indexed sequential file *See* indexed file. *See also* file organization.

indexing *See* indexed addressing.

index register A register that can be specified by instructions that use *indexed addressing. An index register is usually controlled by one or more instructions with the ability to increment or decrement the register by a fixed amount, to test the register for equality with a specified value (often zero), and to jump to a specified location when equality is achieved.

indicator 1. A bit or bit configuration that may be inspected to determine a status or condition. Examples are an *overflow bit, a device status, any portion of the *program status word.
2. A visual, sometimes aural, indication of the occurrence of a specific status or condition, e.g. system running (halted), undefined instruction.

indirect addressing A method of addressing in which the contents of the address specified in the instruction (which may itself be an *effective address) are themselves an address to be used to provide the desired memory reference. Two memory references are thus needed to obtain the data.
One use of indirect addressing is to supply a way of circumventing short address field limitations since the first memory reference provides a full word of address size. Another use is as a pointer to a table. Since an operand is not available at the usual time in the fetch-execute cycle, completion of that cycle must be deferred until the operand is finally available. Indirect addressing is thus sometimes referred to as *deferred addressing*.

induction A process for proving mathematical statements involving members of an ordered set (possibly infinite). There are various formulations of the principle of induction. For example, by the *principle of finite induction*, to prove a statement $P(i)$ is true for all integers $i \geqslant i_0$, it suffices to prove that
(a) $P(i_0)$ is true;
(b) for all $k \geqslant i_0$, the assumption that $P(k)$ is true (the *induction hypothesis*) implies the truth of $P(k+1)$.
(a) is called the *basis* of the proof, (b) is the *induction step*.
Generalizations are possible. Other forms of induction permit the induction step to assume the truth of $P(k)$ and also that of

$$P(k-1),\ P(k-2),\ \ldots,\ P(k-i)$$

for suitable i. Statements of several variables can also be considered. *See also* structural induction.

industry standard formatter interface *See* magnetic tape subsystem.

inequality A *binary relation that typically expresses the relative magnitude of two quantities, usually numbers though more generally elements of a partially ordered set (*see* partial ordering).
The inequalities defined on the integers usually include
$<$ (less than)
$\leqslant$ (less than or equal to)
$>$ (greater than)

$\geqslant$ (greater than or equal to)
$\neq$ (not equal to)
A similar set of inequalities is usually defined on the real numbers; such inequalities can produce errors when used in programming languages because of the inherent inaccuracies in the way real numbers are usually represented (*see* floating-point notation).
The term inequality is often applied to any comparison involving algebraic expressions and using the above symbols. A special case is the *triangle inequality*:

$$|a + b| \leqslant |a| + |b|$$

where | | denotes the absolute value function.

inference The formal method of reasoning that underlies logical deduction. Rules of inference provide the means whereby a logician or a theorem-prover program (*see* theorem proving) may use previous results, theorems, or axioms to derive new results. *See also* propositional calculus, predicate calculus.

inference rules *See* program correctness proof, propositional calculus.

infix notation A form of notation in which operators appear between their operands, as in

$$(a + b) * c$$

Infix notation requires the use of brackets to specify order of evaluation, unlike prefix and postfix notation, i.e. *Polish notation and *reverse Polish notation respectively.

information Formally, collections of symbols. This is the sense in terms such as *information processing, *information technology, or *information theory. Symbols in turn may be defined as patterns that carry meaning, which therefore serves as an alternative definition of information.
A piece of information may be regarded from three main viewpoints.
(a) From the human behavioral viewpoint, some purpose underlies the creation of a piece of information, and some effect (observed action or inferred state of mind) may follow from its receipt.
(b) From the analytical, linguistic viewpoint, a piece of information may be described in terms of what it refers to, its meaning, and its structure.
(c) From the physical, engineering viewpoint, a piece of information may be described in terms of its physical manifestation – the medium that carries it, the resolution and accuracy with which it is inscribed, the amount that is output, conveyed, or received, etc.
The following operations may be performed on information: create, transmit, store, retrieve, receive, copy (in the same or a different form), process, destroy.
The patterns that constitute information may be created in a great diversity of forms including: light, sound, or radio waves; electric current or voltage; magnetic fields; marks on paper. In principle any conceivable material structure or energy flow could be used to carry information.
The scale of our use of information is one of the most important distinctions between the human species and all others, and the importance of information as an economic commodity is one of the most important characteristics of the "post-industrial" civilization, which we are often said now to be entering.

information destination *See* Shannon's model.

information hiding A principle, used when developing an overall *program structure, that each component of a program should encapsulate or hide a single design decision. The principle was first expounded by David Parnas, who advocated an approach to program development in which a list is prepared of design decisions that are particularly difficult or likely to change; individual components or modules are then defined so that each encapsulates one such decision. The interface to each module is defined in such a way as to

reveal as little as possible about its inner workings.
This approach leads to modules that are readily understood and can be developed independently. More important, it also leads to programs that are easy to change, with many desired changes requiring modification of only the inner workings of a single module.

information management system In popular usage, a term that is synonymous with *database management system. In more technical usage, the phrase database management system is usually taken to mean a system whose contents are well described and that carries out transactions within a formally defined syntax and semantics. The information management system is a larger concept with a broader, more complex, and less formally defined interface to its users. It will normally offer many more facilities and a database system will be one of the components that it contains.

information processing The derivation of information objects from other information objects by the execution of algorithms. Processing is one of the fundamental operations that can be performed on *information. It is the principal operation by which the amount and variety of information is increased.
The term has related meanings outside the computing field. It is used in psychology, for instance, and may also be used to refer to clerical operations.

information retrieval *See* information storage and retrieval.

information source *See* Shannon's model.

information storage and retrieval Information storage is the activity of recording information for subsequent use, usually on backing store, e.g. magnetic disk or tape. Storage is one of the fundamental operations that can be performed on *information. It is the principal operation by which information is retained over a period of time.
Information retrieval is the activity of retrieving stored information, and is another of the fundamental operations that can be performed on information. The term information retrieval has a related but distinct meaning in the field of librarianship, where it refers to techniques (such as keywords and indexes) for locating text and/or references on a specified topic. In this sense the information store is usually (though not invariably) held on a machine-readable medium and accessed by computer.
The term *information storage and retrieval (ISR)* refers not only to the activities of information storage and information retrieval, but also to the techniques involved – of which there are many. Storage and retrieval are intimately linked. Information is only stored in order that it may be subsequently retrieved; it may only be retrieved in ways that have been allowed for at storage time. ISR embraces all methods for labeling stored information in order to enable it to be accessed later, whether these are in the context of data-processing files/databases, textual files, graphic databases, etc.

information structure *Another name for* data structure.

information system A computer-based system with the defining characteristic that it provides information to users in one or more organizations. Information systems are thus distinguished from, for example, real-time control systems, message-switching systems, software engineering environments, or personal computing systems.
The term could have a very much wider meaning than that suggested, considering the range of meaning of the words *information and *system. It could, for instance, be broadened to include all computer-based systems, or further broadened to include many non-computer-based systems. Thus, within the domain of computer-based systems, the more specific term

organizational information system is sometimes used.
Information systems include *data processing applications, *office automation applications, and many *expert system applications. When their primary purpose is to supply information to management, they are commonly called *management information systems (MIS).
The following are among the more important characteristics of information systems, and make their design and construction particularly difficult.
(a) Their environment is complex, not fully definable, and not easily modeled.
(b) They have a complex interface with their environment, comprising multiple inputs and outputs.
(c) The functional relationships between inputs and outputs are structurally, if not algorithmically, complex.
(d) They usually include large and complex databases (or, in future, knowledge bases).
(e) Their "host" organizations are usually highly dependent on their continuing availability over very long periods, often with great urgency attending their initial provision or subsequent modification.

information technology (IT) Mankind has handled *information for thousands of years; early technologies to help him do so included the abacus and printing. The last three decades or so have seen an amazingly rapid development of such technology, spearheaded by the computer; more recently, cheap microelectronics have permitted the diffusion of this technology into almost all aspects of daily life and an almost inextricable cross-fertilizing and intermingling of its various branches. The term information technology was coined, probably in the late 1970s, to refer to this nexus of modern technology, electronic-based, for handling information. It incorporates the whole of computing and telecommunication technology, together with major parts of consumer electronics and broadcasting. Its applications are industrial, commercial, administrative, educational, medical, scientific, professional, and domestic.
The advanced nations have all realized that developing competence in information technology is important, expensive, and difficult; some are attempting to define national programs of research and education to stimulate development. The fundamental capabilities that are usually recognized to be essential comprise VLSI circuit design and production facilities, and a common infrastructure for the storage and transmission of digital information (including digitized voice and image as well as conventional data and text). Major research problems include improved systems and software technology, advanced programming techniques (especially in so-called knowledge-based systems), and improved man-machine interfaces.

information theory The study of information by mathematical methods. Informally, information can be considered as the extent to which a message conveys what was previously unknown, and so is new or surprising. Mathematically, the rate at which information is conveyed from a source is identified with the *entropy of the source (per second or per symbol). Although information theory is sometimes restricted to the entropy formulation of sources and channels, it sometimes includes coding theory, in which case the term is used synonymously with *communication theory.

INGRES *Trademark* A *relational database system originally developed by M. Stonebraker at Berkeley, California, and now marketed commercially.

inherent addressing *Another name for* implied addressing.

inherently ambiguous language A context-free language that has no nonambiguous grammar (*see* ambiguous grammar). An example is the set

$$\{aibjck \mid i = j \text{ or } j = k\}$$

inhibit To prevent the occurrence of an event, e.g. to use a logic gate to inhibit another signal. *Compare* enable.

initial algebra An *algebra A, from the *category C of algebras, with the property that for every algebra B in C there is a unique *homomorphism h such that

$$h : A \rightarrow B$$

All initial algebras are isomorphic. Initial algebras play an important role in specification techniques for describing *abstract data types.

initialization The act of assigning initial values to variables before the start of a computation. Many programming languages provide a facility for specifying initial values when a variable is first declared.

initial-value problem *See* ordinary differential equations, partial differential equations.

injection (one-to-one function) A *function with the property that distinct elements in its domain are mapped onto distinct elements in the codomain. Formally,

$$f : X \rightarrow Y$$

is an injection if

$$f(x_1) = f(x_2) \quad \text{implies} \quad x_1 = x_2$$

A common use of injections is to map or include elements of some smaller set, such as the set of integers, into a larger set, such as the set of real numbers.

ink jet printer A printer that forms the required image by projecting droplets of ink onto the paper. The technique has been used for a number of years in the printing and labeling industry. Although there have been devices for use in the data-processing environment since the late 1960s, the IBM 6640 (1976) was the first ink jet machine to achieve widespread use.

The *pulsed jet printer* has one or more columns of nozzles mounted in a head that can traverse along the line to be printed. Each nozzle ejects a single drop of ink onto the paper. The line of characters is printed as a matrix array of the drops of ink. With a single column of jets, speeds up to 400 characters per second have been achieved. Printers with larger numbers of nozzles offer higher resolution or multicolor capability.

One design of the *continuous stream printer* has a print head with a single nozzle that emits a jet of ink. The ink jet is made to break up into a constant-velocity stream of droplets of uniform size. Just prior to its separation from the jet each droplet receives an electric charge. In the ballistic flight toward the paper the droplets pass between electrode plates and each droplet is therefore deflected. The deflection is generally used to position the dot along the vertical axis of the printed character and the head is moved to give horizontal placement. Print speeds of 100 cps are achieved.

in-line program A program that has been written sequentially, without loops. When *control units were simpler, such a program required more memory but executed in less time since there were no counters to increment and test. As these functions became part of the control unit in the form of *index registers and associated instructions, these time savings lost importance. The procedure is still valuable in simpler computers, specifically low-end microcomputers.

inner code *See* concatenated coding system.

inorder traversal *Another name for* symmetric order traversal.

input 1. The process of entering data into a processing system or a peripheral device, or the data that is entered.
2. A signal that is applied to an electrical circuit, such as a logic circuit.
3. To enter data or apply a signal.

input area The area of main memory that is currently allocated to hold incoming data. The processing system will usually retrieve data from the input area and transfer it to a working area or register before it is processed. The result of the processing may be written to an *output area. Subroutines are usually organized so as to replenish the input area from a source such as an input peripheral or communication line and clear the output area by transfer to backing store.

input assertion *See* program correctness proof.

input device Any device that transfers data, programs, or signals into a processor system. Such devices provide the man-to-machine interface, the keyboard being the most common example. Early computers also used punched paper tape and cards but these are becoming obsolete. Current devices include *data tablets, *data collection terminals, speech recognition units, magnetic *card readers, and *document readers.

input-limited process A process whose speed of execution is limited by the rate at which input data is available or obtained.

input/output (I/O) The part of a computer system or the activity that is primarily dedicated to the passing of information into or out of the central processing unit. An important function of most I/O equipment is the translation between the host processor's signals and the sounds, actions, or symbols that are understood or generated by people. In some cases it may be translation between two types of machine-readable signals, as when a card or paper-tape reader reads the data encoded as holes and translates it into the particular data code required by the processor. *See also* I/O.

inquiry station A terminal from which information can be retrieved from a *database. Generally the terminal has a display and a keyboard, but there may also be ancillary devices such as a *badge reader. The user makes the inquiry via the keyboard either in the form of a question in plain text or by indicating a selection from a menu on the display. The display will show a series of possible selections that successively narrow the field of search. An inquiry station may also update information as the result of an action arising from an inquiry. An airline booking terminal is an example of an inquiry station. *See also* interrogation.

inscribe To encode a document by printing information that is readable by both a person and a machine.

insert 1. One of the basic actions performed on *sets that, when applied in the form

$$insert(el, S)$$

adds the element el to the set S. If el is already in S the operation has no effect on the membership of S. *See also* operations on sets.
2. One of the basic actions performed on *lists, that places a new element into a list, not necessarily at one end or the other.

instantaneously decodable *See* prefix codes.

instantiation A more defined version of some partially defined object.

instruction (instruction word) The description of an operation that is to be performed by a computer. It consists of a statement of an operation to be performed and some method of specifying the operands (or their locations) and the disposition of the result of the operation. Instructions are often divided into classes such as *arithmetic instructions, *logic instructions, and *I/O instructions. They may or may not be of fixed length. The set of operations available in a particular computer is known as its *operation code or order code. *See also* instruction format.

instruction counter (current address register; program counter) A counting *register that normally increments one memory address at a time and is used to obtain the program sequence (i.e. the sequence of instructions) from sequential memory locations. This counter will have its contents changed by branch instructions.

instruction cycle *Another name for* fetch-execute cycle. *See* control unit.

instruction format An instruction word is normally made up of a combination of an *operation code and some way of specifying an *operand, most commonly by its location or *address. Some operation codes deal with more than one operand; the locations of these operands may be specified using any of the many *addressing schemes.

Classically, the number of address references has been used to specify something about the architecture of a particular computer. In some instruction formats and machine architectures, the number of operand references may be fixed; in others the number is variable. In the former case descriptions of formats include *one-address*, *two-address*, *three-address*, and (now rarely) *four-address*. An example (symbolically) of a one-address instruction is

add x   i.e.
 add contents of address x
 to contents of accumulator;
 sum remains in accumulator.

An example of a three-address instruction is

add x,y,z   i.e.
 add contents of address x
 to contents of address y;
 sum is placed in location z.

In some cases the last address is the address of the next instruction to be executed. The ability to specify this address was important when rotating (drum) main memories were prominent. Thus a two-address instruction such as

add x,y   i.e.
 add contents of address x
 to contents of address y;
 sum is placed at address y,

may become

operation code	address
5	13

Simple one-address instruction

operation code	select partial word	destination register	index register	index register increment	indirect addressing	address
6	4	4	4	1	1	16

Complex one-address instruction

operation code	register containing one operand	index register	base address register	address (as modified by index and base) of second operand
8	4	4	4	12

Complex two-address instruction using registers and memory

Instruction formats

add x,y,z i.e.
add contents of address x
to contents of address y;
sum is placed at address y;
next instruction is taken
from address z.

The latter may be called either a three-address instruction or a *two-plus-one-address* instruction. In a similar way the term *one-plus-one address* instruction represents a one-address instruction together with the address where the next instruction is to be found. In these two cases the instructions do not come from sequential addresses; an instruction counter, if present, is bypassed.

In early computers instruction formats were forced into a fixed word size, that of the computer. An instruction format consisted of two fields: one containing the operation code and the other containing the address(es). As additional features of address modification became available, it was necessary to add special bit positions in the instruction word to specify functions such as *indirect addressing, use of *index registers, use of base registers in *relative addressing, etc. Still other bits were sometimes used to allow for reference to parts of a data word; this was usually as fractions of the word, as character positions, more recently as byte positions.

As registers became common, distinct operation codes were used to refer to register locations; these locations could be specified in many fewer bits than normal addresses, and variable-length instruction formats were developed.

The figure shows three examples of possible/typical instruction formats.

instruction register *See* control unit.

instruction repertoire *Another name for* instruction set.

instruction sequencing The order in which the instructions in a program are carried out. Normally the sequence proceeds in a linear fashion through the program, and the address of the instructions is obtained from the program counter in the *control unit. This sequence is interrupted when a *branch instruction is executed; at such a time the address of the branch instruction is inserted into the program counter and the process continues.

instruction set (instruction repertoire) The totality of *instructions that a computer is capable of performing. The list of all the *operation codes and the permitted *addressing schemes pertinent to each.

instruction stream The sequence of *instruction words from memory to the control unit.

instruction word *Another name for* instruction.

integer multiplication and division Multiplication of an n-place (n-digit) integer by an m-place integer gives at most an $(m + n)$-place product.

Division of an $(m + n)$-place integer by an n-place integer gives at most an $(m + 1)$-place quotient and an n-place remainder.

integer programming *See* mathematical programming.

integral domain *See* ring.

integral equation Any equation for an unknown function $f(x)$, $a \leq x \leq b$, involving integrals of the function. An equation of the form

$$f(x) = \int_a^x K(x,y)\, f(y)\, \mathrm{d}y + g(x)$$

is a *Volterra equation* of the second kind. The analogous equation with constant limits

$$f(x) = \int_a^b K(x,y)\, f(y)\, \mathrm{d}y + g(x)$$

is a *Fredholm equation* of the second kind. If the required function only appears under the integral sign it is a Volterra or Fredholm equation of the first kind; these are more difficult to treat both theoretically and numerically. The Volterra equation can be regarded as a particular case of the Fredholm equation where

$$K(x,y) = 0 \text{ for } y > x$$

Fredholm equations of the second kind occur commonly in boundary-value problems in mathematical physics. Numerical techniques proceed by replacing the integral with a rule for *numerical integration, leading to a set of *linear algebraic equations determining approximations to $f(x)$ at a set of points in $a \leqslant x \leqslant b$.

integrated circuit (IC) An implementation of a particular electronic-circuit function in which all the individual devices required to realize the function are fabricated on a single *chip of semiconductor, usually silicon. The individual devices normally consist of semiconductor diodes and transistors.

In *MOS integrated circuits* the active devices are *MOSFETs, which operate at low currents and high frequencies. A very large number of MOSFETs can be packed together on one silicon chip, i.e. MOS circuits have a high packing density. They also consume very little power. The development of MOS technology has allowed extremely complex functions to be performed on a single chip.

In *bipolar integrated circuits* the components are *bipolar transistors and other devices that are fabricated using the p-n junction properties of semiconductors. Compared with MOS circuits, bipolar circuits have higher operating speeds but have the disadvantages of high power consumption and low packing density. They are also less simple to fabricate than MOS circuits.

The improvement in the fabrication technology of integrated circuits has made possible the construction of a huge number of components on a single chip. These may be combined on the chip to make a wide variety of digital and analog circuits. The complexity of a digital circuit produced on a single chip is usually described in terms of the number of *transistors involved, or sometimes of the number of *logic gates. This leads to the following differentiation:

*VLSI, very large-scale integration;
*LSI, large-scale integration;
*MSI, medium-scale integration;
*SSI, small-scale integration.

Digital integrated circuits are often represented by their logic function rather than their electronic function in order to ease their understanding. *See also* hybrid integrated circuit.

integrated data processing (IDP) *See* data processing.

integrated injection logic *See* I^2L.

integrated services digital network *See* ISDN.

integration testing *See* testing.

integrity Resistance to alteration by system errors. A user who files data expects that the contents of his files will not be changed by system errors in either hardware or software. Since such errors inevitably will occur from time to time, the prudent system manager maintains a system of protective *dumps, organized in such a way that there always exists a valid copy of a recent version of every file on the system. For this to be possible, the manager must run system utilities that operate at such a level of privilege that they bypass the normal checks present to maintain the *privacy and *security of users' files. The dump utilities must be able to read the users' files in order to make copies, and must have write access to the users' files in order to reinstate a recent version of a file lost or corrupted by system error. Thus the system for maintaining the integrity of a user's files automatically represents a weakening of the systems for maintaining privacy and security.

integro-differential equation Any equation for an unknown function involving integrals and derivatives of the function. Many different types can arise and there is no straightforward classification. The initial-value problem (*see* ordinary differential equations) given by

$$f'(x) = F\left(x, f(x), \int_a^x K(x,y)f(y)\,dy\right)$$

$$f(a) = f_0$$

also contains features common to Volterra integral equations (*see* integral equation). Boundary-value problems and equations involving partial derivatives also occur in practice.

Intel A US manufacturer of semiconductors, notable for being one of the first suppliers of 1K dynamic RAM chips. It is reputed to be the first manufacturer of microprocessors, the 4004 and the 8008.

intelligent copier A machine that combines the capabilities of an office copier and a page printer. It can usually generate printed output in a variety of type styles and sizes.

intelligent terminal A device with some processing capability, by means of which information may be transferred to and from a larger processing system. The device is often a combination of a display and keyboard with at least one built-in microprocessor to provide facilities such as editing and prompts for the operator. Modern application terminals for banking, retail, and industrial data collection are other examples of intelligent terminals.

interactive A word used to describe a system or a mode of working in which there is a response to operator instructions as they are input. The instructions may be presented via an input device such as a keyboard or light pen, and the effect is observable sufficiently rapidly that the operator can work almost continuously. This mode of working is thus sometimes referred to as *conversational mode*. An interactive system for multiple users will achieve the effect by time sharing. *See also* multiaccess system.

interactive graphics A property of a system that enables it to produce and amend pictorial information in response to inputs from an operator at a terminal. Although interactive graphics systems are not yet widely used by comparison with interactive alphanumeric systems, they are growing rapidly in importance as an aid to understanding data. A number of packages are becoming available that allow numerical data to be presented in a variety of forms, e.g. pie charts, histograms, and cartesian or polar graphs. *See also* computer graphics.

interblock gap (IBG) *See* block.

interdiction *Another name for* denial of service.

interface 1. A common boundary between two systems, devices, or programs.
2. The signal connection and associated control circuits that are used to connect devices. *See also* standard interface.
3. Specification of the communication between two program units. For example, if a procedure does not refer to nonlocal variables, its interface is defined by the parameter list. Careful definition of interfaces makes it possible to use a program without knowledge of its internal working, and is a vital part of the design of a system that is to be implemented by a team of programmers.
4. To provide an interface.
5. To interact.

interior node *Another name for* nonterminal node.

interior path length of a tree. The sum of the lengths of all paths from the root to an interior (i.e. a nonterminal) node.

interleaving A technique for achieving *multiprogramming in a relatively simple system without a supervisor program. Each of the programs that are to be run concurrently are broken down into segments that are then linked up into a single program. The function of each segment and the order of linking is arranged so that maximum use is made of processor time. A segment that initiates a transfer to a peripheral, i.e. a relatively slow task not requiring processor activity, is linked to a segment of some other program for which processor activity is required. A multiplexer channel interface will interleave transfers from several slow peripherals.

interlock A hardware or software method of coordinating and/or synchronizing multiple processes in a computer. Such a method can be used, for example, in the situation in which a certain process should not begin until another process is completed. A common interlock method uses *flags to do this. Another typical situation is one in which requests for some service, e.g. memory access, arrive simultaneously. A hardware interlock procedure will force the requests to become sequential, usually according to a predefined rule.

intermediate assertion *See* program correctness proof.

intermediate storage Any part or type of storage that is used for holding information between steps in its processing.

internal fragmentation A form of *fragmentation that arises when allocations are made only in multiples of a subunit. A request of arbitrary size must be met by rounding up to the next highest multiple of the subunit, leaving a small amount of memory that is allocated but not in use. Internal fragmentation is reduced by reducing the size of the subunit; such a reduction increases *external fragmentation.

internal sorting *See* sorting.

internet protocol (IP) **1.** The *DARPA internet protocol, which links defense-research centers in the US and Europe using underlying networks such as the *ARPANET, satellite networks, and many different *local area networks. Host addresses use a 32-bit field, which is broken into one, two, or three octets of network numbers, with the remainder of the 32-bits being used for addressing within networks. The IP protocol provides a uniform *datagram network service on top of a heterogeneous underlying network.
2. The Xerox internet protocol, which provides *datagram network service on top of heterogeneous underlying networks, using a 32-bit network address and a 48-bit host address that is independent of the network.
See also internetworking.

internetworking Connecting several computer *networks together to form a single higher-level network. There are two basic approaches: *encapsulation* and *translation*. The junctions between networks are called *gateways, and their functions depend on which internetworking approach is taken. When encapsulation is used, a new protocol layer (or layers) is defined; this provides uniform semantics for services such as *datagram packet switching, *electronic mail, etc. When a message is entered into the internetwork, it is wrapped (encapsulated) in a network-specific protocol (local network datagram headers, or virtual circuits). The encapsulated packet is sent over the network to a gateway, which removes the old network-specific encapsulation, adds a new set of network headers, and sends the packet out on another network. Eventually the message reaches its destination, where it is consumed.
When protocol translation is used, messages are sent on a local network using the protocols and conventions of that network. A gateway receives the message and transforms it into the appropriate message on another network; this may involve interpreting the message at multiple protocol levels.
The encapsulation approach provides a uniform set of semantics across all networks, while the translation approach results in unanticipated problems due to subtle differences between protocols. The

encapsulation approach generally requires that new software be written for all hosts on all networks, while the translation approach requires new software only in the gateways.

interpolation A simple means of approximating a function $f(x)$ in which the approximation, say $p(x)$, is constructed by requiring that

$$p(x_i) = f(x_i),\ i = 0,1,2, \ldots ,n$$

Here $f(x_i)$ are given values $p(x_i)$ that fit exactly at the distinct points x_i (*compare* smoothing). The value of f can be approximated by $p(x)$ for $x \neq x_i$. In practice p is often a polynomial, linear and quadratic polynomials providing the simplest examples. The process is also widely used in the construction of many numerical methods, for example in *numerical integration. In addition the idea can be extended to include matching of $p'(x_i)$ with $f'(x_i)$; this is *Hermite interpolation*.

interpreter A language processor that analyzes a line of code and then carries out the specified actions, rather than producing a machine-code translation to be executed later.

interpretive language A programming language that is designed for or suited to interpretive implementation. In extreme cases, it is a language that can only be implemented by means of an *interpreter. Some languages are more conveniently interpreted but most can be compiled. BASIC is often interpreted on small computers, but the language does not make this essential. Thus the decision whether to compile or interpret is usually a property of the implementation rather than the language.

interquartile range *See* measures of variation.

interrogation The sending of a signal that will initiate a response. A system may interrogate a peripheral to see if it requires a data transfer. The response is normally a status byte. When a number of devices are interrogated in a sequence the process is called *polling. Interrogation terminals are more generally called *inquiry stations.

interrupt A signal to a processor indicating that an *asynchronous event has occurred. The current sequence of instructions is temporarily suspended (interrupted), and a sequence appropriate to the interruption is started in its place. Interrupts can be broadly classified as being associated with one of the following.
(a) Events occurring on peripheral devices. A processor having initiated a transfer on a peripheral device on behalf of one process may start some other process. When the transfer terminates, the peripheral device will cause an interrupt. *See also* interrupt I/O.
(b) Voluntary events within processes. A process wishing to use the services of the operating system may use a specific type of interrupt, a *supervisor call* (SVC), as a means of notifying the *supervisor.
(c) Involuntary events within processes. A process that attempts an undefined or prohibited action will cause an interrupt that will notify the supervisor.
(d) Action by operators. An operator wishing to communicate with the supervisor may cause an interrupt.
(e) Timer interrupts. Many systems incorporate a timer that causes interrupts at fixed intervals of time as a means of guaranteeing that the supervisor will be entered periodically.
See also interrupt handler.

interrupt handler (IH) A section of code to which control is transferred when a processor is interrupted. The interrupt handler then decides on what action should be taken. For instance, a *first level interrupt handler (FLIH)* is the part of an operating system that provides the initial communication between a program or a device and the operating system. When an interrupt occurs, the current state of the system is stored and the appropriate

FLIH is executed: it leaves a message for the operating system and then returns, restoring the system to its original state and allowing the original task to continue as though nothing had happened. The operating system will periodically check for new messages and perform the appropriate actions.

interrupt I/O A way of controlling input/output activity in which a peripheral or terminal that needs to make or receive a data transfer sends a signal that causes a program interrupt to be set. At a time appropriate to the priority level of the I/O interrupt, relative to the total interrupt system, the processor enters an interrupt service routine. The function of the routine will depend upon the system of interrupt levels and priorities that is implemented in the processor.

In a single-level single-priority system there is only a single I/O interrupt – the logical OR of all the connected I/O devices. The associated interrupt service routine polls the peripherals to find the one with the interrupt status set.

In a multilevel single-priority system there is a single interrupt signal line and a number of device identification lines. When a peripheral raises the common interrupt line it also sets its unique code on the identification lines. This system is more expensive to implement but speeds the response.

In a single-level multiple-priority system the interrupt lines of the devices are logically connected to a single processor interrupt in such a way that an interrupt from a high-priority device masks that of lower-priority devices. The processor polls the devices, in priority order, to identify the interrupting device.

A multilevel multiple-priority system has both the property of masking interrupts according to priority and of immediate identification via identification lines.

interrupt mask A means of selectively suppressing interrupts when they occur so that they can be acted upon at a later time. *See also* masking.

interrupt priority An allocated order of importance to program interrupts. Generally a system can only respond to one interrupt at a time but the rate of occurrence can be higher than the rate of servicing. The system control may arrange *interrupt masks to suppress some types of interrupt if a more important interrupt has just occurred.

interrupt vector *See* vectored interrupts.

intersection 1. of sets. The set that results from combining elements common to two sets S and T, say, usually expressed as

$$S \cap T$$

$\cap$ is regarded as an *operation on sets, the *intersection operation*, which is *commutative and *associative. Symbolically

$$S \cap T = \{x \mid x \in S \text{ and } x \in T\}$$

When two sets S and T intersect in the empty set, the sets are *disjoint. Since the intersection operation is associative, it can be extended to deal with the intersection of several sets.

2. of two graphs, G_1 and G_2. The graph that has as vertices those vertices common to G_1 and G_2 and as edges those edges common to G_1 and G_2.

intersegment linking The links between the *segments of a (large) program. Where segments are separately compiled it is necessary to provide a mechanism for transferring control out of one segment and into another, usually by introducing a specific type of labeled statement that identifies the point at which a segment can be entered, and whose value can be made accessible to other segments when the program is link-edited.

interval timer A digital circuit that is used to determine the time interval between an initial trigger pulse and subsequent *logic states that appear after a predetermined delay.

into function *See* surjection.

intrinsic semiconductor (i-type semiconductor) *See* semiconductor.

invariant A property that remains TRUE across some transformation or mapping. In the context of *program correctness proofs, an invariant is an assertion that is associated with some program element and remains TRUE despite execution of some part of that element. For example, a *loop invariant* is an assertion that is attached at some point inside a program loop, and is TRUE whenever the attachment point is reached on each iteration around the loop. Similarly a *module invariant* is associated with a given module, and each operation provided by the module assumes that the invariant is TRUE whenever the operation is invoked and leaves the invariant TRUE upon completion.
Note that invariants cannot accurately be described as TRUE AT ALL TIMES since individual operations may destroy and subsequently restore the invariant condition. However the invariant is always TRUE between such operations, and therefore provides a static characterization by which the element can be analyzed and understood.

inventory *See* pattern.

inverse 1. (converse) of a binary *relation R. A derived relation R^{-1} such that

whenever $x\ R\ y$
then $y\ R^{-1}\ x$

where x and y are arbitrary elements of the set to which R applies. The inverse of "greater than" defined on integers is "less than".
The inverse of a function

$$f: X \rightarrow Y$$

is (if it exists) another function, f^{-1}, such that

$$f^{-1}: Y \rightarrow X$$

and

$$f(x) = y \text{ implies } f^{-1}(y) = x$$

It is not necessary that a function has an inverse function.
Since for each monadic function f a relation R can be introduced such that

$$R = \{(x,y) \mid f(x) = y\}$$

then the inverse relation can be defined as

$$R^{-1} = \{(y,x) \mid f(x) = y\}$$

and this always exists. When f^{-1} exists (i.e. R^{-1} is itself a function) f is said to be *invertible* and f^{-1} is the *inverse* (or *converse*) *function*. Then, for all x,

$$f^{-1}(f(x)) = x$$

and for all y,

$$f(f^{-1}(y)) = y$$

To illustrate, if f is a function that maps each wife to her husband and g maps each husband to his wife, then f and g are inverses of one another.
2. *See* group.
3. of a *conditional $P \rightarrow Q$. The statement $Q \rightarrow P$.

inverse homomorphic image *See* homomorphism.

inverse matrix For a given $n \times n$ matrix of numbers, A, if there is an $n \times n$ matrix B for which

$$AB = BA = I$$

where I denotes the *identity matrix, then B is the inverse matrix of A and A is said to be *invertible* with B. If it exists, B is unique and is denoted by A^{-1}.

inverted file A file provided with a secondary *index on one or more of its data items (fields). In the case where indexes exist for all the data items of the record, the file is said to be *fully inverted*.

A B

input A	0	1
output B	1	0

Inverter circuit symbol and truth table

inverter (negator) An electronic *logic gate, fabricated in integrated-circuit form, that inverts the signal it receives so that a logic 1 (true) is converted to logic 0 (false) and vice versa. It therefore implements the logical *NOT operation. The diagram shows the circuit symbol and *truth table.

invertible matrix *See* inverse matrix.

involution operation Any *unary operation f that satisfies the law

$$f(f(a)) = a$$

for all a in the domain of f. The law is known as the *involution law*. It is satisifed by the elements of a *Boolean algebra where the unary function is the process of taking a complement. Taking complements of sets and negation in its different forms also satisfy the law, as does the principle of *duality as it applies in Boolean algebras.

I/O *Abbrev. for* input/output.

I/O buffering The process of temporarily storing data that is passing between a processor and a peripheral. The usual purpose is to smooth out the difference in rates at which the two devices can handle data.

I/O bus A *bus, or signal route, to which a number of input and output devices can be connected in parallel.

I/O channel *See* channel.

I/O control Either the hardware that controls the transfer of data between main memory and peripheral devices, or the part of the system software that in turn controls that hardware.

I/O device Any unit of a system that is the entry and/or exit point for information. Such devices, which are a type of peripheral unit, are the link between the system and its environment. *See also* input device, output device.

I/O file A file used to hold data that will be or has been transferred between backing store and an external peripheral such as a line printer or card reader.

I/O instruction One of a class of *instructions that describes the operations concerned with input and output.

I/O-limited Denoting a process that is either *input-limited, *output-limited, or both.

I/O mapping A technique used primarily in microprocessing whereby peripheral devices are interfaced to a processor whose architecture supports input and output instructions. An I/O mapped device is assigned one or more of the processor's I/O port addresses, and data and status information are transferred between the processor and the peripheral device using the processor's input and output instructions. *Compare* memory mapping.

IOP *Abbrev. for* I/O processor.

I/O port *See* port.

I/O processor (IOP) A specialized computer that permits autonomous handling of data between I/O devices and a central computer or the central memory of the computer. It can be a programmable computer in its own right; in earlier forms, as a *wired-program computer, it was called a *channel controller*. *See also* direct memory access.

I/O register A *register, perhaps one of several, used during the process of exchanging data between I/O devices and the main computer. An I/O register often has the ability to compose smaller units, such as bytes or characters, into units of machine-word size, or to perform the reverse decomposition.

I/O supervisor A more specific term than *I/O control, referring almost invariably to the appropriate software within the operating system.

I/O switching A means of selecting one out of several alternative hardware routes to a particular peripheral device, with consequent benefits either in system throughput or reliability.

IP *Abbrev. for* internet protocol.

IPL 1. *Abbrev. for* initial program load. The action of loading the operating software into a "cold" machine.
2. *Abbrev. for* information processing language. In the early days of research into artificial intelligence the need for special-purpose languages capable of manipulating *dynamic data structures was recognized. IPL-I to IPL-V were a series of *list-processing languages developed to meet this need. They have long been obsolete.

irrecoverable error of magnetic tape. *See* error rate.

irreducible polynomial *See* polynomial.

irreflexive relation A *relation R defined on a set S and having the property that $x\ R\ x$ does not hold for any x in the set S. Examples are "is son of", defined on the set of people, and "less than", defined on the integers. *Compare* reflexive relation.

ISDN *Abbrev. for* integrated services digital network. A proposed international all-digital communication network that will carry voice, video, facsimile, and computer data, plus other services, using common underlying facilities and interfaces. The ISDN is envisioned as a single system capable of handling all PTT/common-carrier communication traffic. As currently proposed, ISDN is based on 64 kilobit per second digital and circuit-switched communication networks.

ISO International Standards Organization, the body by which international standards are established for everything from data-processing equipment to machine screw sizes. It was founded in 1946 and its members comprise national standards bodies in over 70 countries. It is of interest in the area of information processing in that it establishes the standard link protocols, coding standards, machine-readable media-interchange standards, etc., that are required to make it possible for data to be communicated electronically between equipment of various manufacturers and from various countries.

ISO-7 An internationally agreed character code (ISO 646-1973), using 7 bits for each character. The code includes certain positions designated for national use, to allow different countries to include special characters for letters with diacritical marks, or currency symbols, etc. The US version is *ASCII, which is normally used in computing.

isolation Any of many kinds of separation of a computer system so that users and their processes and the system protection controls are kept within distinct boundaries in order to improve or to attain system security. Isolation requires extra hardware and/or software overhead.

isomorphism A *homomorphism that, when viewed as a function, is a *bijection. If

$$\phi : G \rightarrow H$$

is an isomorphism then the algebraic structures G and H are said to be *isomorphic* and so exhibit the same algebraic properties. *Isomorphic trees* are *trees that are isomorphic as directed graphs.

ISO/OSI reference model A general architecture proposed by the International Standards Organization for communication systems, allowing open system interconnection. *See* seven-layer reference model.

ISR *Abbrev. for* information storage and retrieval.

IT *Abbrev. for* information technology.

iteration 1. The repetition of a numerical or nonnumerical process where the results from one or more stages are used to form the input to the next. Generally the recycling of the process continues until some preset bound is achieved, or the process result is constantly repeated. Such an *iterative process* is the basis of many nu-

merical methods for a wide variety of areas of numerical mathematics, for example in *numerical linear algebra, solution of *ordinary and *partial differential equations and of *integral equations, and in nonlinear *optimization. Ideally for practical use one should design iterations that will converge to the correct solutions from poor starting estimates, employing few iterative cycles and with rapid convergence in the vicinity of the result. *Newton's method is an iterative method of fundamental importance.
An iterative process is *m-step* if the new value is derived from *m* previous values; it is *m-step, sequential* if the new value depends upon the last *m* values, i.e.

$$x^{(k+1)} = G_k(x^{(k)}, \ldots, x^{(k-m+1)})$$

The iteration is *stationary* if the function G_k is independent of k, i.e. the new value is calculated from the old values using the same formula. For example,

$$x^{(k+1)} = \tfrac{1}{2}(x^{(k)} + 1/x^{(k)})$$

is a stationary, one-step iteration.
2. of a formal language. *See* Kleene star.

J

Jackson method A proprietary brand of *structured programming, developed by the British consultant Michael Jackson specifically for use in *data processing. He observed that the inputs and outputs of programs could be defined in terms of particular data structures, which are mostly static and easier to define than programs. He then proposed that programs should be constructed by a systematic method based on data structure diagrams. Two main problems arise. First, it may not be possible to combine the separate data structure diagrams involved in a program because of what are called *structure clashes*; this is solved by a form of program decomposition called *inversion*. Second, error handling is not accommodated by the simple method, and gives rise to a technique called *backtracking*, which is programmed by using *assertions and the notation posit/quit/admit.
Jackson method is used in conjunction with Cobol and PL/I. Translators exist to convert from textual equivalents of Jackson data-structure diagrams into the required target language. It is claimed that the same code will always be produced from a given data specification.

JCL *Abbrev. for* job-control language.

J	K	Q	$\bar{Q}$
0	0	Q_n	$\bar{Q}_n$
0	1	0	1
1	0	1	0
1	1	$\bar{Q}_n$	Q_n

JK flip-flop, truth table and symbol

JK flip-flop A clocked flip-flop that has two inputs, J (set) and K (reset), and two outputs Q and $\bar{Q}$. The truth table for this device is shown in the diagram, along with the circuit symbol. Q_n represents the state of the Q output prior to the current active transition of the clock. The ambiguous condition of J and K both being true, logic 1, causes the device to "toggle", i.e. change to the complementary logic state, on active transitions of the clock signal. The JK flip-flop is the most useful type of flip-flop and is available as a standard integrated-circuit package. *See also* flip-flop.

job A set of programs and the data to be manipulated by these programs. The word also means the execution of the set of programs. In its simplest form a job may consist of loading a binary program and then executing this program using supplied data. In more complex forms whole series of steps may be taken, certain of which may be contingent on the outcome of earlier steps. The complete description of a job is written in a *job-control language.

job-control language (JCL; command language) A language used to write the sequence of commands that will control the running of a job. In a normal programming language the objects manipulated and the operations applicable to these objects correspond to variables within the original problem. In a JCL the objects manipulated are such things as complete programs, or the input and output streams for these programs. Most JCLs incorporate features to control the sequence in which actions will be performed, including some form of conditional statement.

job file A file containing in some suitable intermediate form one or more jobs awaiting execution. The jobs are commonly presented as JCL statements that may be preprocessed so as to eliminate the more blatant errors of syntax or other detectable errors before being appended to the job file.

job mix The set of jobs actually being executed within a multiprogramming system at any one time. *See* scheduler.

job monitoring The control of the jobs running within a system. The term is almost synonymous with *job scheduling.

job scheduling Selecting jobs for execution. *See* scheduler.

job step A single identifiable execution of a program on its data within a job. A typical job step will load a program module and execute it with appropriate data from files, producing output in files suitable for passing on to the next job step. Each job step will also produce an indication as to whether or not its outcome was successful.

job stream A sequence of jobs awaiting processing.

join operator *See* lattice.

Josephson junction A junction between two metals that exhibits controllable electron tunneling properties at cryogenic temperatures. First reported by Brian Josephson in 1962, it is a superconducting device that can act as an extremely fast electronic switch with very low power dissipation. *See* Josephson technology.

Josephson (junction) technology A computing technology based on superconductivity and electron tunneling between metals. These effects occur at extremely low temperatures, on the order of 4 K; such temperatures are obtained by immersing the whole system in liquid helium. Logic circuits and nonvolatile memories can be made out of the technology, which has the potential for ultrafast switching speeds and very low power dissipation (*see* Josephson junction). This combination of properties offers the potential of extremely fast computers that can be realized within minimum linear dimensions and that do not have the heat-transfer problems of VLSI silicon devices. As switching speeds become measured in picoseconds, system linear dimensions must be reduced accordingly. (One nanosecond is the order of 10 cm on a transmission line.)

journal tape The record produced in an *audit trail. It was once usually a magnetic tape.

JOVIAL *Acronym for* Jules' own version of international algorithmic language. A programming language designed by Jules Schwarz of System Development Corporation for military command-and-control systems. It was based on the international algorithmic language (IAL), otherwise known as *Algol 58, suitably extended for its purpose. JOVIAL was implemented on a number of military computers, and is still in use for military projects in the US.

jump instruction *Another name for* branch instruction.

junction The area of contact between two *semiconductor materials having different electrical properties, or between a semiconductor and a metal. Junctions play a fundamental role in semiconductor devices. The most frequently used is the *p-n junction*, which is formed between n-type and p-type *semiconductors. A p-n junction has rectifying properties as a result of the potential barrier built up across the junction by the diffusion of electrons from the n-type to the p-type material.

justify To move the bit pattern stored in a register so that either the least or most significant bit is at the appropriate end of the register. This is analogous to the similarly named process used in typesetting and word-processing systems to achieve uniform vertical edges to pages or columns of print. Some serial printers used with word-processing systems have a built-in justify facility. The space between words and/or letters is increased until the printed line fills the distance between the margins.

K

K or k *Symbols for* kilo-.

Karnaugh map (Veitch diagram) A graphical means for representing Boolean or logical expressions so that the manner in which they can be simplified or minimized is made apparent. It may be regarded as a pictorial form of *truth table or as an extension of the *Venn diagram. The method was proposed by E. W. Veitch and modified slightly by M. Karnaugh. The Karnaugh maps for expressions involving one, two, three, and four variables are shown in the diagram. When $n = 2$, for instance, the 00 square represents the term $a'b'$ (where $'$ denotes negation), the 11 square represents ab, and so on.

Terms that differ in precisely one variable can be combined. Such terms will appear as groups of adjacent squares on a Karnaugh map and so can readily be identified. For example, the terms abc and abc' can be combined since

$$abc \vee abc' = ab$$

These two terms should each occupy one square on the $n = 3$ map and appear side by side, i.e. share a common edge. However, so too should the $a'b'c$ and the $ab'c$ squares. This complication can be overcome by stipulating that the two edges marked with dashes should be identified or joined together, i.e. the Karnaugh map for $n = 3$ should be drawn on one side of a ring of paper. When $n = 4$ the situation is even more complex: the two edges marked with dashes are identified, as are the dotted edges. The map can then be viewed as drawn on the outside of a torus. Karnaugh maps are useful for expressions of perhaps up to six variables. When $n > 6$, the maps become unwieldy and too complex. Alternative methods of simplification, such as the Quine–McCluskey algorithm, are then preferable.

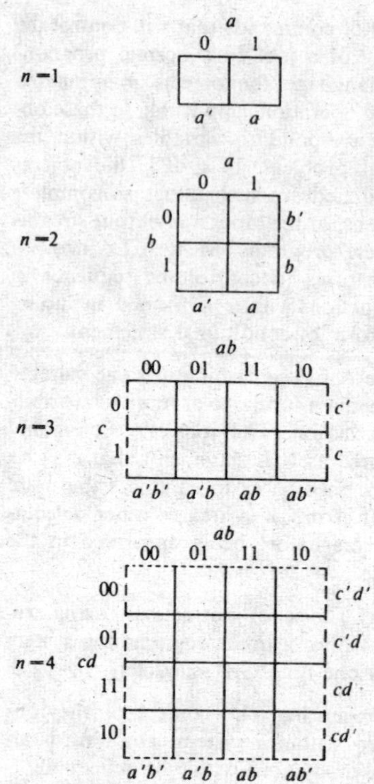

Karnaugh maps

k-connectivity *See* connectivity, connectedness.

kernel The lowest layer into which a large operating system is subdivided, each layer dealing with some aspect of the system hardware. The kernel is responsible for allocating hardware resources to the processes that make up the operating system and to the programs running under the operating system. It is the only part of an operating system that needs to be proved correct by rigorous program verification: the principal approach to providing the degree of security required in a computer system has been that of designing a secure kernel.
Nucleus is a near-synonym for kernel and tends to be used where the effects are achieved by a mixture of normal programming and microcoding. The microprogram is written in such a way as to complement the functions achieved by the normal code, with a gain in running speed.

key 1. A value used to identify a member of a set. Usually the elements of the set are records (*n*-tuples), in which one of the fields holds the key. Variations allow multiple key fields or any field to be used as a key.
2. A value used to establish authority to access particular information. *See* locks and keys.
3. A value used as a basis for encryption. *See* cryptography.
4. *See* keyboard.

keyboard An array of keys that may be captioned buttons or marked areas on a plane, each of which can cause a discrete signal or action when pressed with a finger. In current systems the operation of the key is detected and turned into a coded electrical signal; in the past mechanical coupling was used to allow depression of keys to directly punch a pattern of holes in a punch card or paper tape, or to print a character.

keyboard encoder *See* encoder.

keyed sequential access method An access method for use with a *sequential file. Each data record is accessed in its key or relative-record sequence, relative to the previously accessed record.

keypad A limited but compact form of keyboard, sometimes hand-held, with a small number, often 12 or 16, of captioned buttons or pressure-sensitive areas on a plane. It is used in conjunction with data collection equipment or as a means of entering limited information such as a personal identification number (PIN).

keypunch A *card punch that is controlled from a keyboard.

key sorting A form of *address table sorting in which the sortkey is placed with the addresses.

key to disk A data entry system in which the data entered by a number of keyboard operators is accumulated on a magnetic disk. The data is often verified by comparing it with data entered by a second operator working from the same original document. The small computer that routes the data from the operator to the correct file on the disk can also be used to carry out *data validation and produce statistics on operator productivity.

key to tape A data entry system in which the data entered by each keyboard operator is written to a magnetic tape. The data is verified by having a second operator read and enter data from the same source document on a machine that has been set to compare the keyboard input with the data already on the tape.

keyword A symbol in a programming language that has a special meaning for the *compiler or *interpreter. For example, keywords in BASIC include LET, IF, THEN, PRINT. The keywords guide the analysis of the language, and in a simple language each keyword causes activation of a specific routine in the language processor. *See also* keyword parameter.

keyword parameter A parameter of a subroutine, procedure, or macro that is identified by name rather than by its position in the parameter list, e.g.

SORT(INPUT = FILE A,
OUTPUT = SYSPRINT)

kilo- (symbol: K or k) A prefix indicating a multiple of 1000 (10^3) or, loosely, a multiple of 2^{10} (i.e. 1024). In computing it is used for instance in the context of memory size, e.g. 256 kilowords (or 256K words).

Kimball tag *See* punched tag.

Kleene closure *Another name for* Kleene star.

Kleene-plus *See* Kleene star.

Kleene star (star closure; Kleene closure; iteration) An operation on *formal languages that gives for any language L the language L^*, defined by

$$\{\Lambda\} \cup L \cup LL \cup LLL \cup \ldots$$

where Λ is the empty word. Thus a *word w is in L^* if and only if it has the form

$$w_1 w_2 \ldots w_n$$

with each w_i in L, i.e. is a *concatenation of words in L.

L^+, the *Kleene-plus* of L, is defined by

$$L \cup LL \cup LLL \cup \ldots$$

Thus L^+ comprises the nonempty strings of L^*.

Kleene's theorem on *regular expressions. A theorem in *formal language theory proposed by S. C. Kleene and stating that a language is definable by a regular expression if it is recognized by a *finite-state automaton. A regular expression equivalent to a finite-state automaton can be found by solving a set of simultaneous linear equations (*see* linear grammar, Arden's rule).

k lookahead *See* LR parsing, LL parsing.

knapsack problem A common example of an integer programming problem: a knapsack has volume V and there are an unlimited number of each of N different items. For $i = 1, \ldots, N$ one unit of item i has known volume V_i and known value m_i. Integer numbers of the various items may be put into the knapsack and the objective is to pack as much value as possible into the knapsack without exceeding the total volume V.

knot *See* spline.

knowledge engineering *See* expert systems.

Kraft's inequality When an instantaneously decodable code is to be formed from an alphabet of q letters, with the ith codeword being λ_i letters in length, Kraft's inequality

$$\sum_{i=1}^{n} q^{-\lambda_i} \leqslant 1$$

is a necessary and sufficient condition for such a code to be constructable with n codewords. In a code with no codewords remaining for allocation, the equality sign operates. *See also* prefix codes.

L

label 1. (tape label) A short file on a magnetic tape containing the name and characteristics of either the entire tape or the data file immediately following. A *labeled tape* starts with a *volume label*, and each data file on the tape has a preceding *header label and a following *trailer label.

2. (statement label) A numeric or alphanumeric identifier associated with a line or statement in a program and used in other parts of the program to refer to that statement.

lambda calculus A formalism for representing functions and ways of combining functions. Together with its variable-free equivalent, *combinatory logic*, it was invented around 1930 by the logicians Church, Schonfinkel, and Curry. Examples:

$\lambda x.x$ denotes the *identity function*, which simply returns its argument;
$\lambda x.c$ denotes the *constant function*, which always returns c regardless of what argument it is applied to;
$\lambda x.f(f(x))$ denotes the composition of the function f with itself, i.e. the function that, for any argument x, returns $f(f(x))$.
Much of the power of the notation derives from the ability to represent higher-order functions. For example,

$$\lambda f.\lambda x.f(f(x))$$

denotes the (higher-order) function that, when applied to a function f, returns the function obtained by composing f with itself.
In addition to being a mere notation, the λ-calculus comprises rules for transforming λ-expressions into equivalent ones. The most important is the rule of *β-reduction*, by which an expression of the form

$$(\lambda x.e_1)(e_2)$$

can be simplified; for example,

$$(\lambda x.f(x,x))(a)$$

β-reduces to $f(a,a)$
In combination with a few primitive functions, the λ-calculus provides yet another way of defining the set of all effectively computable functions on the nonnegative integers – it is thus in that sense equivalent to the *Turing machine and to *recursive functions, etc.
In recent years the lambda calculus has taken on a somewhat different role in computer science. It has had a profound influence on the design of a whole class of programming languages (e.g. LISP, PAL, POP-2). Moreover, the mathematical theory developed to provide the first set-theory model of the lambda calculus has formed the mathematical basis for the so-called *denotational semantics of programming languages.

LAN *Abbrev. for* local area network.

language *See* programming language, formal language.

language construct A syntactic structure or set of structures in a language for a particular class of operations. An example is a loop construct.

LAP *Acronym for* link access protocol. The second-layer (data link layer) protocol that is a subset of *HDLC and is used in *X.25-based networks in setting up channels between *DTE and *DCE. An alternative protocol, *LAPB*, developed after LAP, allows the DTE/DCE interface to operate in "balanced mode".

large-scale integration *See* LSI, integrated circuit.

laser printer An *electrophotographic printer in which a laser is used as the light source.

last in first out *See* LIFO.

latch An electronic device that can store temporarily a single bit of data. It can be considered as a simple type of *flip-flop. The storage is controlled by a *clock signal, a given transition of which fixes the contents of the latch at the current value of its input. The contents will remain fixed until the next transition of the clock.

latency The time taken for the start of a given sector of data on a storage disk or drum to reach the read/write head. The time is measured from the instant that the head settles at the track within which the sector lies. The average latency is the time for half a revolution of the disk or drum. *See also* seek time.

lattice An *algebraic structure, such as a *Boolean algebra, in which there are two *binary operations that are both *commutative and *associative and satisfy the *absorption and *idempotent laws. The two binary operators, denoted by $\wedge$ and $\vee$, are called the *meet* and the *join* respectively.
An alternative but equivalent view of a lattice is as a set L on which there is a *partial ordering defined. Further, every pair of elements has both a greatest *lower

bound and a least *upper bound. The least upper bound of $\{x,y\}$ can be denoted by $x \vee y$ and is referred to as the *join* of x and y. The greatest lower bound can be denoted by $x \wedge y$ and is called the *meet* of x and y. It can then be shown that these operations satisfy the properties mentioned in the earlier definition, since a partial ordering $\leqslant$ can be introduced by defining

$$a \leqslant b \text{ iff } a \vee b = a$$

Lattices in the form of Boolean algebras play a very important role in much of the theory and mathematical ideas underlying computer science. Lattices are also basic to much of the approximation theory underlying the ideas of *denotational semantics.

LBA *Abbrev. for* linear-bounded automaton.

LCD *Abbrev. for* liquid-crystal display. A device incorporated into many digital watches, calculators, some small computers, instruments, etc., in order to display numerical and alphabetical characters. The display comprises groups of segments from which individual characters can be formed. Each segment consists of a normally transparent anisotropic liquid sandwiched between two transparent electrodes. Application of an electric field across the electrodes causes the reflectivity of the liquid to change and the segment becomes opaque. Individual segments can therefore be selectively darkened to form a character. The digits and some letters are typically produced from groups of seven segments. Unlike *LED displays, LCDs do not generate their own light and thus require external illumination; they do however have a lower current drain than other forms of *display.

LCM *Abbrev. for* least common multiple.

LDU decomposition *See* LU decomposition.

leader A blank section of a tape, preceding recorded information, that is needed for threading the tape into a reading device.

leadless A "raw" semiconductor chip that is functionally complete except that it is unencapsulated and has no output leads affixed to the contact pads of the device. Leadless devices may be supplied by a manufacturer when, for example, they are to be used to produce *hybrid integrated circuits.

leaf *Short for* leaf node.

leaf node (terminal node; tip node; external node) Any node of a tree with no descendants and hence of *degree zero.

least common multiple (LCM) of two integers m and n. The smallest integer p such that m divides p exactly and n divides p exactly. For example, the LCM of 9 and 6 is 18.

least significant character In a *string where the position of a character determines its significance, the character at the end of least significance. Such a string is normally written with the least significant position on the right. For example, the *least significant digit (LSD)* and the *least significant bit (LSB)* contribute the smallest quantity to the value of a digital or binary number.

least squares approximation *See* approximation theory.

least squares, method of A method of estimating *parameters in a model by minimizing the sum of squares of differences between observed and theoretical values of a variable. If

$$y_i,\ i = 1, \ldots, n,$$

is a sample of n observations, and μ_i is a set of theoretical values corresponding to a set of unknown parameters, θ, and a set of known associated observations, x_i, then the criterion to be minimized with respect to variations in θ is the sum of squares,

$$\Sigma(y_i - \mu_i)^2$$

The values of θ at which the minimum occurs are known as *least squares estimates*. The method of *weighted least squares* is used when each observation is associated with a weight, w_i (*see* measures of location), and the criterion to be minimized is

$$\Sigma w_i(y_i - \mu_i)^2$$

See also likelihood, regression analysis.

LED display A device used in some calculators, digital watches, etc., to display numerical and alphabetical characters. It consists of an array of *light-emitting diodes*, LEDs, which are semiconductor diodes that emit light when a *forward bias is applied; the color of the light is usually red. LEDs are small, cheap, and have relatively low current and voltage requirements and long life. Their power requirements are, however, significantly higher than those of *LCDs. In an LED display these diodes are arranged in such a way that by selectively illuminating individual ones in the array, simple characters are formed on the display. Seven diodes suffice to display the digits and some letters. *See also* display.

Lee distance (Lee metric) In the theory of *block codes intended for error detection or error correction, a distance measure analogous to the *Hamming distance but modeling more accurately a *linear *q-ary channel, such as the phase-modulated carrier used in *modems. When $q = 2$ or $q = 3$, the Lee and Hamming distances are the same.

left-linear grammar *See* linear grammar.

left shift *See* shift.

left subtree *See* binary tree.

left-to-right precedence A simple form of *precedence hierarchy, used in APL, in which operators are taken in the order in which they appear in the expression. Each operator takes everything to the right as its right operand, thus

$$a * b + c$$

evaluates as

$$a * (b + c)$$

Note that, paradoxically, left-to-right precedence actually causes operators to be applied in right-to-left sequence.

length 1. of a sequence. The cardinality of the domain of the sequence. Thus the sequence

$$a_1, a_2, \ldots, a_n$$

has length n.

2. of a string. The upper bound of the string, hence the number of elements in the string.

3. of a vector. The number of elements in the vector.

length-increasing grammar *See* context-sensitive grammar.

LEO A line of computers, and a company, of historic importance in the British computing industry. J. Lyons & Co (a large firm in the catering industry) initiated in 1947 a project to build a computer to mechanize clerical functions in their own offices. (This decision was almost simultaneous with a similar decision in the US by Eckert and Mauchly, which led to UNIVAC 1.) The project was led by T. R. Thompson, a mathematician, and J. Pinkerton, an electrical engineer. The machine they built, which was christened LEO (Lyons Electronic Office), had the same basic architecture as *EDSAC but had double the amount of mercury delay line memory and (for that time) very extensive and sophisticated input/output facilities, enabling I/O to proceed simultaneously with processing. The machine was fully operational, executing routine jobs for Lyons, at the end of 1953.

In 1954, LEO Computers Limited was founded. The company traded until 1963, when it was merged with the computing division of English Electric. During that time it sold eleven LEO IIs (enhanced versions of LEO I) and about fifty LEO IIIs. LEO III was an extremely advanced commercial machine for its time: it had a microprogrammed instruction set, standard I/O interfaces, a full-scale multiprogramming operating system, and a full-scale high-level programming language (CLEO).

letter (in formal language theory) *See* word.

letter distribution *See* Parikh's theorem.

letter-equivalent languages *See* Parikh's theorem.

level of a node in a tree. A numerical value equal to one greater than the *depth of the same node. The level of the root node is thus one; the level of any other node is one greater than that of its parent. In some texts, the term level is used as a synonym for depth.

lexical analyzer (scanner) The part of a *compiler that breaks up the input into meaningful units, e.g. names, constants, reserved words, operators. The lexical analyzer will also remove redundant characters, e.g. spaces, and may deal with character-set mappings, e.g. replacing upper-case letters by the equivalent lower-case letters. The units recognized by the lexical analyzer are called *tokens*, and are output in some conveniently coded form for subsequent processing by the compiler.

lexicographic order The order of words in a dictionary, given the order of letters in the alphabet. In general, let a set S be *well-ordered by relation $<$, and for $n > 0$ let T be a set of n-tuples

$$(x_1, x_2, \dots, x_n)$$

of elements x_j in S. Then the ordering relation $<$ over such n-tuples can be defined so that

$$(x_1, \dots, x_n) < (y_1, \dots, y_n)$$

iff $x_1 < y_1$ or there is some k, $1 \leq k \leq n$, for which

$$x_i = y_i \text{ for } 1 \leq i < k$$
$$x_k < y_k$$

The set T is in lexicographic order if the n-tuples are sorted with respect to this relation. The concept can be extended to strings whose lengths may be different. The order would then be that in which words are placed in a dictionary.

lexicographic sort Any sorting algorithm for putting n-tuples into *lexicographic order.

library, library program *See* program library.

life-cycle *See* software life-cycle.

LIFO or **lifo** *Acronym for* last in first out. *LIFO list* is another name for *stack. A stack implemented in hardware is sometimes referred to as a *lifo*.

light-emitting diode (LED) *See* LED display.

light pen A penlike input device that is used with a cathode-ray tube display. It can be used to point to areas of the screen and thus indicate a selection from a displayed list, or it can be used to draw shapes. The light pen has a photosensor at the tip that responds to the peak illumination that occurs when the CRT scanning spot passes its point of focus. The display system correlates the timing of the pulse from the photosensor with the timing of the display scan to determine the position of the light pen.

When the light pen is used to draw shapes, the difficulties of parallax – due to thickness of the screen – and the lack of a fine point at the tip of the pen are overcome by use of a tracking cross. The display system generates a fine-line tracking cross and positions it so that its intersection is central in the field of view of the light pen. As the light pen is moved across the screen the tracking cross follows it closely and the path of the intersection point is stored in the display file. A switch – usually on the pen – is used to indicate the intended start and finish points of a stroke.

likelihood The *probability that an observation belongs to a *probability distribution with *parameters θ, considered as a function of the parameters rather than of the observation.

The method of *maximum likelihood*, originated by R. A. Fisher, estimates *parameters in statistical models by maximizing the likelihood of observing the data with respect to the parameters of the model. The values taken by the parameters at the maximum are known as *maximum likelihood estimates*. This method is computationally equivalent to the method of *least squares when the distribution of the observations about their theoretical means is the *normal distribution.

Lindenmeyer system *See* L-system.

linear algebraic equations (simultaneous equations) A problem in *numerical linear algebra that requires the solution of n equations in the unknowns $x_1, x_2, \ldots, x_n$ of the form

$$Ax = b$$

where A is a square $n \times n$ matrix. The solution obtained by computing the inverse matrix and forming $A^{-1}b$ is less accurate and requires more arithmetical operations than elimination methods. In *Gaussian elimination* multiples of successive equations are added to all succeeding ones to eliminate the unknowns $x_1, x_2, \ldots, x_{n-1}$ in turn. Properly used, with row interchanges to avoid large multiples, this leads to a solution that satisfies exactly a system close to the one given, relative to the machine precision. The accuracy of the solution, which can be cheaply estimated, depends on the *condition number of the problem. Many other methods are used to deal with matrices of special form. Very large systems where the matrix A has predominantly zero entries occur in the solution of *partial differential equations. Elimination methods tend to fill in the zeros causing storage problems and iterative methods are often preferred for such problems.

linear array *Another name for* one-dimensional array, i.e. for a *vector. *See also* array.

linear-bounded automaton (LBA) A *Turing machine M such that the number of tape cells visited by M is bounded by some linear function of the length of the input string. Of equivalent power is the smaller class of Turing machines that visit only the cells bearing the input string. The *context-sensitive languages are precisely those recognized by such Turing machines.

For arbitrary Turing machines, a nondeterministic one always has an equivalent deterministic one. It is still unknown whether this is the case for linear-bounded automata.

linear channel A transmission channel in which the information *signal and the *noise signal combine additively to form the output signal. In a *q-ary linear channel, with a finite number, q, of amplitudes, the signals add modulo-q; in the binary case ($q = 2$), this has the same effect as an *exclusive-OR operation between the signals.

linear codes In coding theory, codes whose encoding and decoding operations may be expressed in terms of linear operations. The term is usually applied to certain *error-correcting codes in which the encoding operation involves a *generator matrix* and the decoding operation involves a *parity-check matrix*. Linear codes are, therefore, also called *parity-check codes*. A particular linear code forms a commutative *group that has the zero codeword as its identity. In the case of linear (n, k) *block codes, the generator matrix is $k \times n$ and the parity-check matrix is $(n - k) \times n$; the elements of both matrices are elements of the base field (this being $\{0, 1\}$ for *binary codes). *See also* convolutional code.

linear grammar A *grammar in which each production contains at most one nonterminal in its right-hand side. Such a grammar is *right-linear* if a nonterminal can only occur as the rightmost symbol, i.e. if each production has one of the forms

$$A \rightarrow w$$
$$A \rightarrow wB$$

where A and B are nonterminals and w is a string of terminals. A *left-linear grammar* can be similarly defined:

$$A \rightarrow w$$
$$A \rightarrow Bw$$

The right- and left-linear grammars generate precisely the *regular languages.

The word linear relates to an analogy with ordinary algebra. For example, a right-linear grammar such as

$$S \rightarrow aS|abT|abcT|abcd$$
$$T \rightarrow S|cS|bcT|abc|abcd$$

corresponds to the simultaneous linear equations

$$X = \{a\}X \cup \{ab,abc\}Y \cup \{abcd\}$$
$$Y = \{\Lambda,c\}X \cup \{bc\}Y \cup \{abc,abcd\}$$

where X and Y are sets of strings and Λ is the empty string. *Union and *concatenation play roles analogous to addition and multiplication. The smallest solution to the equations gives the language generated by the grammar. *See* Arden's rule.

linear independence A fundamental concept in mathematics. Let

$$x_1, x_2, \ldots, x_n$$

be m-component vectors. These vectors are linearly independent if for some scalars $\alpha_1, \alpha_2, \ldots, \alpha_n$,

$$\sum_{i=1}^{n} \alpha_i x_i = 0$$

implies

$$\alpha_1 = \alpha_2 = \ldots = \alpha_n = 0$$

Otherwise the vectors are said to be *linearly dependent*, i.e. at least one of the vectors can be written as a linear combination of the others. The importance of a linearly independent set of vectors is that, providing there are enough of them, any arbitrary vector can be represented uniquely in terms of them.

A similar concept applies to functions $f_1(x), f_2(x), \ldots, f_n(x)$ defined on an interval $[a,b]$, which are linearly independent if for some scalars $\alpha_1, \alpha_2, \ldots, \alpha_n$, the condition,

$$\sum_{i=1}^{n} \alpha_i f_i(x) = 0$$

for all x in $[a,b]$,

implies

$$\alpha_1 = \alpha_2 = \ldots = \alpha_n = 0$$

linear list *See* list.

linear logic A system of *combinational and possibly *sequential circuits in which the combinational component comprises *exclusive-OR gates only. This is sometimes referred to as *strongly linear logic* in order to distinguish it from *weakly linear logic* in which *inverters are permitted.

In nonbinary (q-valued) systems, the EX-OR gates are generalized to modulo-q adders and subtractors.

linearly addressed memory (two-dimensional (2-D) memory) *Obsolete* A *core-memory organization in which coordinate addressing is not used. All the cores for a given word are switched simultaneously by current in a single wire. This organization uses one less wire, permitting smaller cores, and allows higher switching current, leading to overall faster operation.

linearly dependent *See* linear independence.

linear programming A technique in *optimization, pioneered by George B. Dantzig, that is widely used in economic, military, and business-management decisions. It deals with the problem of finding nonnegative values of the variables $x_1, x_2, \ldots x_n$ that satisfy the constraints

$$a_{i1}x_1 + a_{i2}x_2 + \ldots + a_{in}x_n = b_i,$$
$$i = 1,2, \ldots ,m$$

and minimize the linear form

$$c_1x_1 + c_2x_2 + \ldots + c_nx_n$$

Maximizing problems and problems with inequality constraints or unrestricted variables can be converted to this form. An optimum solution (if any exist) is known to be a *basic feasible solution*, which is one that satisfies the constraints and has at most m positive x_i values.

Computationally such problems are solved by the *simplex method*, which starts at a basic feasible solution and searches the set of such solutions in such a manner that the value of the linear form is nonincreasing. An important recent advance is the algorithm developed by N. Z. Shor and L. G. Khachian. In theory this is significantly faster than the simplex method but it is as yet uncertain whether this can be realized in practice.

linear recurrence A relationship that defines the next term in a sequence in the form of sums and differences of multiples of earlier terms in the sequence. For example,

$$a_{r+1} = 2a_r + 1$$
$$b_{r+1} + 2b_r - b_{r-1} = 0$$

See also recurrence.

linear regression model *See* regression analysis.

linear structure (totally ordered structure) A collection of items ordered by a single property so that each item, except possibly for the first or last, has a unique "predecessor" and a unique "successor". It is the most commonly used structure and appears under a variety of names depending on storage representation and its intended use. Linked representations are normally called *lists while sequential representations are called *arrays.

line discipline *Another name for* line protocol.

line finder Any computer program that detects lines in a *gray-level array. The line finder might look for the boundaries of regions of similar gray-level, or for a bar of similar gray-levels, etc.

line printer A computer output device that produces a line of print per cycle of its operation. The number of character positions in a line generally ranges from 80 to 160, and lines are printed at rates from 150 to 3000 lines per minute. A complete line of information has to be assembled in a buffer memory within the machine before it can start printing. When a line of print has been completed a paper-feed system moves the paper so that the position for the next line of print is opposite the printing mechanism.

The paper to be printed is usually supplied as a continuous web of up to 2000 forms divided by perforations. To ensure positive control of the forms, the margins are punched with holes that engage on the tractors of the printer's paper-feed system.

line protocol (line discipline) A formally specified set of possible bit sequences that will guarantee that two ends of a communication link will be able to pass information between them in an understandable way. A number of standards have been devised for the implementation of such protocols, including *SDLC and *BISYNC protocols (originally developed by IBM) and *HDLC and *ADCCP (developed by standards organizations as an outgrowth of the efforts of a number of manufacturers).

line switching The most common form of concentration (*see* concentrator), used to connect *n* transmitting devices to *m* receiving devices, where *n* is much greater than *m*. Buffering of data is done by the input devices if the transmission medium is busy.

link 1. (pointer; reference) When a field of an item A in a data structure contains the address of another item B, i.e. of its first word in memory, it contains a link to B. Two items are *linked* when one has a link to the other. *See also* linked list.

2. (line) A path for communication that may be physical (as in a circuit) or either physical or logical (as in a channel).

link editor (linkage editor) A utility program that combines several separately compiled modules into one, resolving internal references between them. When a program is assembled or compiled, an intermediate form is produced into which it is necessary to incorporate library material containing the implementation of standard routines and procedures, and to add any other modules that may have been supplied by the user, possibly in other high-level languages. The final stages of *binding references within the original program to storable address forms appropriate to the hardware is performed by the link editor. *See also* link loader, loader.

linked list (chained list) A *list representation in which items are not necessarily sequential in storage. Access is made possible by the use in every item of a *link that contains the address of the next item in the list. The last item in the list has a special *null link* to indicate that there are no more items in the list.

link encryption The *encryption of communication link(s) individually in a computer network. *Compare* end-to-end encryption.

link layer of network protocol function. *See* seven-layer reference model. *See also* X.25.

link loader A utility program that combines all the separately compiled modules of a program into a form suitable for execution. *See also* link editor, loader.
2. (line) A path for communication that may be physical (as in a circuit) or either physical or logical (as in a channel).

link testing Testing of a group of modules to ensure that the modules operate correctly in combination. It is normally performed after the individual modules have been tested in isolation and prior to the integration testing that is performed for the complete system.

liquid-crystal display *See* LCD.

LISP *Acronym for* list processing. A programming language designed for the manipulation of nonnumeric data. The basic data structure is a *list whose elements are either atomic symbols or lists. An unusual feature of LISP is that programs are also expressed as lists, i.e. the programs and the data they manipulate have an identical structure. Pure LISP is a *functional language, having no assignment operator. LISP is very widely used in *artificial intelligence research.

list A finite ordered *sequence of items $(x_1,x_2, \ldots x_n)$, where $n \geq 0$. If $n = 0$, the list has no elements and is called the *null list* (or *empty list*). Unless stated otherwise, the items in a list can be arbitrary in nature. In particular it is possible for an item to be another list, in which case it is known as a *sublist*. For example, let L be the list

(A,B,(C,D),E)

then the third item of L is the list (C,D), which is a sublist of L. If a list has one or more sublists it is called a *list structure*. If it has no sublists it is a *linear list*. Certain items of a list are often of particular interest, in particular the first item, or *head* of the list. The two basic representation forms for lists are sequentially allocated lists and *linked lists, the latter being of greater flexibility.

list head In many list representations, special header cells that are added to a list and possibly any sublists to aid management and traversal algorithms.

listing *Short for* program listing.

list insertion sort *See* list sorting.

list processing A programming technique for dealing with data structures that consist of similar items linked by pointers (*see* linked list). In list processing, each data item contains at most two pointers. By contrast, in *plex processing, data items may contain an arbitrary number of items.

list sorting A form of sorting that utilizes a *link field in each record. The links are manipulated so that each link points to the following record in the sorted file to form a straight linear *list. An insertion sort that utilizes link fields is a *list insertion sort*.

list structure *See* list.

literal A word, symbol, or number that describes or defines itself rather than something it might represent, i.e. its value is determined by its denotation. A variable in a Boolean expression, appearing in uncomplemented or complemented form, is a literal.

LL parsing The most powerful *top-down parsing technique that proceeds without backtracking, LL standing for *L*eft-to-right *L*eftmost derivation sequence. In general an LL parser uses a k-symbol lookahead, where k is an integer $\geqslant 1$, to effect parsing decisions. For most practical purposes, however, k is taken to be 1. An LL parser may be implemented as a *pushdown automaton or by the method of recursive descent (*see* top-down parsing). In the former method a stack is used to store that portion of a leftmost *derivation sequence that has not been matched against the input string. Initially the start symbol of the grammar is pushed onto an empty stack. Subsequently, if the top element of the stack is a terminal symbol it is matched against the next symbol in the input string. If they are the same then the stack symbol is popped and the input marker advanced, otherwise there is an error in the input string. If the top stack symbol is a nonterminal A, say, it is removed from the stack and replaced by the right-hand side symbols of a production with left-hand side A. The right-hand side symbols are pushed onto the stack in right-to-left order. Thus if the production is

$$A \rightarrow XYZ$$

the first symbol to be stacked is Z, then Y, and finally X. The choice of a production is made by consulting a parsing table that contains an entry for each combination of nonterminal symbol and k-symbol lookahead. Parsing is successfully completed when the input is exhausted and the stack is empty.

A grammar that can be parsed using this technique is said to be an *LL(k) grammar*. Not all grammars are LL(k); in particular any grammar that uses left recursion is not LL(k) for any value of k.

load and go A method of operation, now obsolete, in which program loading together with a possible compiling or assembling is followed immediately by the program's execution phase.

load and store A method of operation, now obsolete, in which program loading together with a possible compiling or assembling is concluded by storage of the object code.

loader A utility program that sets up an executable program in main memory ready for execution. This is the final stage of the compiling/assembly process. *See also* link editor, link loader.

local A term applied to variables that are accessible only in a restricted part of a program, typically in a procedure or function body. By contrast, *global* variables are accessible throughout a program. The use of local variables can help to resolve naming conflicts, and may lead to a more efficient use of memory.

local area network (LAN) A communication network linking a number of stations in the same "local" area, variously defined as the same building, a radius of one kilometer, or a single plant. Local area networks generally provide high-speed (100K bps to 100M bps) data communication services to directly connected computers. *Gateways are used to connect local networks to each other, or to longer-distance communication networks. Due to limited distance, controlled environments, and (usually) homogeneous implementation, local networks have very low error rates and can utilize simplified data communication protocols. *See also* wide area network.

local discretization error (local truncation error) *See* discretization error.

local-echo mode *See* echo.

local optimization (peephole optimization) *See* optimization (in programming).

location *Another name for* address.

location operator An operator in a programming language that yields the address of its operand.

lock (lock primitive) An indivisible operation that allows a process to ensure that it alone has access to a particular resource. On a single-processor system the indivisible nature of the operation can be guaranteed by turning off interrupts during the action, ensuring that no process switch can occur. On a multiprocessing system it is essential to have available a *test-and-set instruction that, in a single uninterruptible sequence, can test whether a register's contents are zero, and if they are will make the contents nonzero. The same effect can be achieved by an exchange instruction. *See also* unlock, semaphore.

lockout A mechanism for arranging controlled access to a shared resource. *See* lock, semaphore.

locks and keys A system of *memory protection in which segments of memory are assigned identification numbers (the locks) and authorized users are provided the numbers (the keys) by the operating system. This provision is done by a privileged process in some location, such as a *program status word, not accessible to the user.

logarithmic search algorithm *Another name for* binary search algorithm.

logic 1. The science of reasoning, proof, thinking, or inference. In *mathematical logic* the investigation involves mathematical methods taken from algebra or the theory of algorithms. The two most common systems are *propositional calculus and *predicate calculus.
2. *See* digital logic.

logical 1. Involving or used in logic.
2. Conceptual or virtual, or involving conceptual entities, as opposed to physical or actual.

logical connective *See* connective.

logical data type 1. A data type comprising the values *true* and *false*. *See* logical value.
2. Loosely, an *abstract data type.

logical encoding The representation of symbols in a source alphabet by strings of logical values. It is hence equivalent to binary encoding.

logical operator, logical operation *See* logic operation.

logical shift *See* shift.

logical value (Boolean value) Either of the two values *true* and *false* that indicate a truth value. Although a single bit is the most obvious computer storage structure that can be applied to logical data, larger units of store, such as a byte, are frequently used in practice since they can be addressed distinctly.

logic analyzer An electronic instrument that monitors the *logic states of digital systems and stores the results for subsequent display. The storage of data is initiated in the analyzer by the recognition of preset "trigger states" as these arise in the system under test. *Synchronous* analyzers sample data at intervals determined entirely by the external system. *Asynchronous* analyzers sample at intervals determined internally by the analyzer.

logic card A printed circuit board that is of a standard size and carries a number of digital logic devices in a circuit arrangement capable of fulfilling a specific function. The board will, in general, also carry a standard connector by means of which power and ground connections are provided and control and data signals may be transferred to and from a standard *bus.

logic circuit An electrical circuit concerned with logical systems. The term *logic device* is often used synonymously. A logic circuit is required to produce specified binary outputs as a result of specified binary inputs. This may be accomplished by using *logic gates, producing what is called *hardware circuitry*. Alternatively the inputs may be associated with the address lines of a *ROM and the outputs with the data lines of a ROM; this is called *firmware circuitry*.

Hardware circuitry constructed from integrated-circuit packages on circuit boards requires two types of wiring. The first type carries the logical information between gates. The second type provides the power for the individual chips. The process of locating the power paths so that they do not interfere with the logic paths is called *power routing*.

Logic circuitry may be mathematically analyzed using *Boolean (or switching) algebra. In this representation the binary 1 is associated with the *identity element and the logic 0 is associated with the null element, i.e. zero.

See also combinational circuit, sequential circuit, digital logic, multiple-valued logic.

logic design *Another name for* digital design.

logic device *See* logic circuit.

logic diagram A diagram that displays graphically, by interconnection of *logic symbols, the digital design of a *logic circuit or system.

logic element A small part of a digital *logic circuit, typically a *logic gate. Logic elements can be represented by *operators in symbolic logic.

logic family A range of electronic devices that is made by the same manufacturing technique and provides a number of logic functions. The range includes *logic gates, *flip-flops, and *counters. Families in common use are *ECL, *TTL, and *I^2L, which are all based on *bipolar transistors, and the *NMOS and *CMOS families, which are based on *MOSFETs.

Logic families vary as regards *switching speed, *propagation delay, and power dissipation, although developments in the fabrication technology of the different families often improve these characteristics. A member of a logic family whose output changes state typically within a few nanoseconds (10^{-9} seconds) is considered a high-speed logic device. These devices are also characterized by short propagation delays, also in the order of a few nanoseconds. *See also* logic circuit.

logic function *Another name for* Boolean function.

logic gate A device, usually but not exclusively electronic, that implements an elementary logic function; examples include *AND, *OR, *NAND, and *NOR gates, and *inverters. There are typically between two and eight inputs and one or two outputs. In order to represent the two *logic states, true and false, in electronic logic gates, the input and output signals are held at either of two different voltage levels; a high voltage level usually represents true (logic 1) and a low level false (logic 0).

Each type of logic gate has a *logic symbol that conveys its logic function but does not indicate the electronic circuitry involved. The use of these symbols in circuit diagrams simplifies the understanding of a complex logic circuit and means that technological advances in electronics need not be taken into account.

Logic gates based on *fluid logic have been successfully used and optical logic gates, triggered by light, have recently been demonstrated. *See also* logic circuit, digital logic, multiple-valued logic.

logic instruction An instruction that performs one of the class of *logic operations on one or more specified operands. These operations may apply to a single variable as in complementation, or more generally are defined on two variables. *See also* Boolean algebra.

logic level 1. In a *combinational circuit, the maximum number of logic gates between any input and any output. The logic

level represents a measure of delay time through such a circuit.
2. Either of the two voltage levels used in a binary *logic gate.

logic operation An operation on *logical values, producing a Boolean result (*see also* Boolean algebra). The operations may be *unary or *binary, and are denoted by symbols known as *operators*. In general there are 16 logic operations over one or two operands; they include *AND, *OR, *NOT, *NAND, *NOR, *exclusive-OR, and *equivalence.
Logic operations involving more than two operands can always be expressed in terms of operations involving one or two operands. Those involving two operands can be expressed in terms of other operations involving one or two operands.
Logic circuits are fabricated for the implementation of logic operations on their input signals. The inputs may be words (or bytes), and the logic operation is applied to each bit in accordance with Boolean algebra.

logic probe An item of electronic test equipment that is capable of displaying the logic state – true (logic 1), false (logic 0), or undefined – of a digital signal applied to its input probe. It is generally used to check the operation of individual devices within a digital logic circuit.

logic programming languages A class of programming languages, and a subclass of the *declarative languages, that is based on *symbolic logic. Ultimately the objective is to program in "pure" logic, but this has not yet been achieved. The most widely used logic programming language is *PROLOG, which is based on the Horn clause subset of logic but includes certain "impure" features in order to provide a practical language.
Logic programming languages are important because of their declarative nature, their potential power and flexibility, and their suitability for execution on highly parallel architectures.

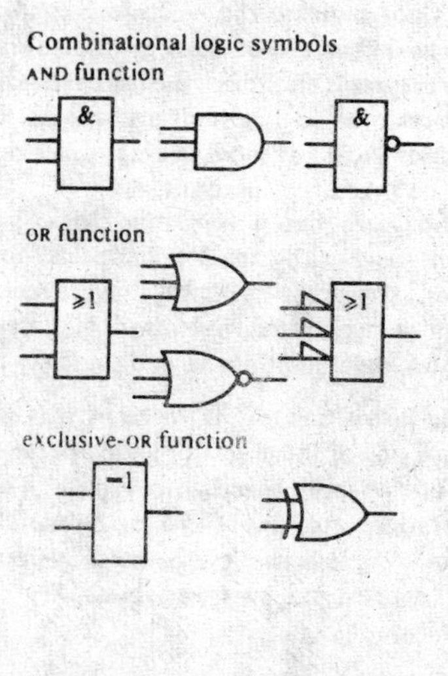

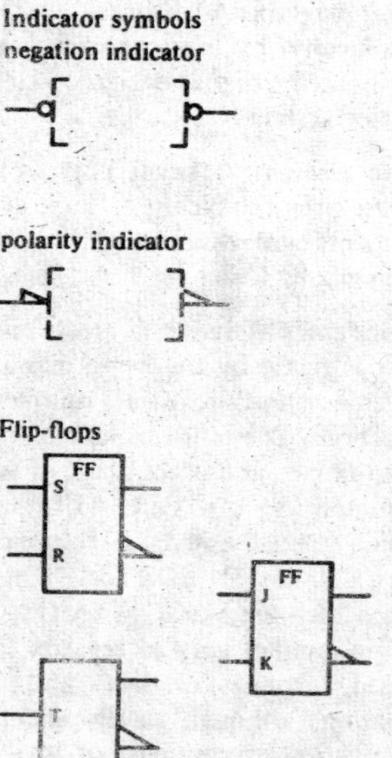

Commonly used logic symbols

logic state The logical sense, true or false, of a given binary signal. A binary signal is a *digital signal that has only two valid values. In physical terms the logical sense of a binary signal is determined by the voltage level or current value of the signal, and this in turn is determined by the device technology. In *TTL circuits, for example, a true state is represented by a logic 1, approximately equal to +5 volts on a signal line; logic 0 is approximately 0 volts. Voltage levels between 0 and +5 volts are considered undefined.
Since only two logic states, logic 1 and logic 0, are possible, the techniques of *Boolean algebra may be used to analyze digital circuits involving binary signals. The term positive logic is applied to circuits where logic 1 is assigned to the highest voltage level; in negative logic circuits a logic 1 is indicated by the lower voltage level.

logic symbols A set of graphical symbols that express the function of individual *logic gates in a *logic diagram. The most common symbols are those for the simple Boolean functions and for flip-flops, as shown in the diagram.

login (logon) The process by which a user identifies himself to a system. The terms are also used as verbs: log in, log on, or *sign on*. A system with many registered users will require each user to log in, and to produce some form of *authentication (such as a password) before allowing the user access to system resources. The login activity will also open an *accounting file for the session.

logoff (logout) The process by which a user terminates his session. The terms are also used as verbs: log off, log out, or *sign off*. By logging off, the user ensures that all the system resources that have been used during the session are accounted for, and any temporary files created during the session are deleted.

logon or **log on** *See* login.

logout or **log out** *See* logoff.

longitudinal redundancy check (LRC) *See* cyclic redundancy check.

lookahead *Short for* carry lookahead.

look-up table *See* table look-up.

loop 1. A sequence of instructions that is repeated until a prescribed condition, such as agreement with a data element or completion of a count, is satisfied. *See also* do loop.
2. A configuration of a *local area network that consists of nodes connected serially in a ring topology. *See* ring network.
3. (local loop) The (twisted pair) connection from a switching exchange to the subscriber terminal.

loop invariant *See* invariant.

loosely coupled *See* coupled.

lower bound of a set S on which the *partial ordering $<$ is defined. An element l with the property that $l < s$ for all s in S. Also l is a *greatest lower bound* if, for any other lower bound h, $h < l$.
Since numerical computing demands the truncation of infinite arithmetic to finite arithmetic, the computation of greatest lower bounds of real numbers, indeed of any limit, can only be achieved to a machine tolerance, usually defined to be machine precision: the smallest epsilon eps, such that

$$1.0 - \text{eps} < 1.0$$

See also array, upper bound.

low-level language A variety of programming language in which the control and data structures directly reflect the underlying machine architecture.

low-level scheduler (dispatcher) *See* scheduler.

low-pass filter A *filtering device that permits only those components in the *Fourier transform domain whose frequencies lie below some critical value to pass through with little attenuation, all other components being highly attenuated.

lpm *Abbrev. for* lines per minute, one of the terms used to describe the rate of output of line printers.

LR parsing A *bottom-up parsing technique, LR standing for *L*eft-to-right *R*ightmost derivation sequence. Originally developed by D. E. Knuth, it is the most powerful left-to-right, no backtracking parsing method for *context-free grammars.

An LR parser consists of a pushdown stack, a parsing table, and a driving routine. The driving routine is the same for all grammars. The stack is manipulated by the driving routine using the information contained in the top stack element and the next k symbols in the input stream (called the *k lookahead*); k is an integer $\geqslant 0$, but for most practical purposes $k = 1$. The stack consists of a string

$$s_0X_0s_1X_1 \ldots s_nX_ns_{n+1}$$

where each X_i is a symbol of the input grammar and each s_i is called a *state*.

The parsing table is indexed by pairs (s,a) where s is a state and a is the lookahead. Each entry in the table has two parts: (a) an action, which may be shift, reduce p (for some production p), accept, or error, and (b) a state, called the *goto state*. When the action is shift, the next input symbol and goto state are pushed onto the stack (in that order). When the action is reduce p the top $2l$ elements of the stack will spell the right-hand side of p but with goto states interspersed, where l is the length of this right-hand side. These $2l$ elements are popped from the stack and replaced by the left-hand side of p and the new goto state. This operation corresponds to adding a new node to the *parse tree for the input string. The accept action is only encountered when the start symbol S is the only symbol on the stack (i.e. the stack contains s_0Ss_1 for some states s_0 and s_1) and the lookahead is the end-of-input symbol. It signifies that parsing has been successfully completed. On the other hand an error entry in the parse table indicates an error in the input string.

A grammar that can be parsed by an LR parser using k-symbol lookahead is called an *LR(k) grammar*. The power of the LR parsing method comes from the fact that the LR(1) grammars properly include other grammar types like precedence grammars and LL(1) grammars (*see* LL parsing). This and its efficiency make it a popular choice of parsing method in *compiler-compilers. If a grammar is not LR(1) this will be evidenced as multiply defined entries in the parsing tables called *shift-reduce conflicts* or *reduce-reduce conflicts*.

Many different parsing tables may be constructed for one grammar, each differing in the number of states it defines. The so-called *canonical LR table* tends to be too long for practical purposes and it is commonly replaced by an *SLR* (simple LR) or *LALR* (lookahead LR) table. A grammar that is LR(1) may not however be SLR(1) or LALR(1).

LSD, LSB *Abbrevs. for* least significant digit, least significant bit.

LSI *Abbrev. for* large-scale integration, i.e. integrated-circuit fabrication technology that allows in the range of 10 000 to 100 000 transistors to be integrated on a single chip. *See* integrated circuit.

L-system (Lindenmeyer system) A way of generating infinite sets of strings. L-systems are similar to *grammars with the crucial difference that, whereas for grammars each step of derivation rewrites a single occurrence of a nonterminal, in an L-system all nonterminals are rewritten simultaneously. An L-system is therefore also known as a *parallel rewriting system*. L-systems were first defined in 1968 by Lindenmeyer as a way of formalizing ways in which biological systems develop. They now form an important part of *formal language theory.

The subject has given rise to a large number of different classes of L-systems. The simplest are the *DOL systems*, in which all symbols are nonterminals and each has a single production. For example, with productions

$$A \rightarrow AB$$
$$B \rightarrow A$$

one derives starting from A the sequence
A AB ABA ABAAB ABAABABA ...
This is called the *sequence* of the DOL-system, while the set of strings in the sequence is called the *language*. The *growth-function* gives the length of the ith string in the sequence; in the example this is the Fibonacci function.
Note that the productions form a *homomorphism – in this example from $\{A,B\}^*$ to itself. A DOL-system consists therefore of an alphabet Σ, a homomorphism h on Σ^*, and an initial Σ-word w. The sequence is then

$$w\, h(w)\, h(h(w))\ \ldots$$

The letter D in DOL stands for deterministic, i.e. each symbol has just one production. An *OL-system* can have many productions for each symbol, and is thus a *substitution rather than a homomorphism. Other classes are similarly indicated by the presence of various letters in the name: T means many homomorphisms (or many substitutions); E means that some symbols are terminals; P means that no symbol can be rewritten to the empty string; an integer n in place of O means context-sensitivity – the rewriting of each symbol is dependent on the n symbols immediately to the left of it in the string.

LU decomposition A method used in *numerical linear algebra in order to solve a set of linear equations,

$$Ax = b$$

where A is a square matrix and b is a column vector. In this method, a lower *triangular matrix L and an upper *triangular matrix U are sought such that

$$LU = A$$

For definiteness, the diagonal elements of L may be taken to be 1. The elements of successive rows of U and L may easily be calculated from the defining equations. Once L and U have been determined, so that

$$LUx = b,$$

the equation

$$Ly = b$$

is found by *forward substitution*. Thereafter the equation

$$Ux = y$$

is found by *backward substitution*. x is then the solution to the original problem.
A variant of the method, the method of *LDU decomposition*, seeks lower and upper triangular matrices with unit diagonal and a diagonal matrix D, such that

$$A = LDU$$

If the matrix A is *symmetric and positive definite, there is an advantage in finding a lower triangular matrix L such that

$$A = L\,L^{\mathrm{T}}$$

This method is known as *Cholesky decomposition*; the diagonal elements of L are not, in general, unity.

M

M *Symbol for* mega-.

MAC A project at Massachusetts Institute of Technology to introduce the first practical *multiaccess system. The name is an acronym derived from machine-aided cognition (expressing the broad project objective) and multiple-access computer (describing its major tool). The system incorporated not only a new approach to operating systems, but also introduced novel forms of highly interactive compilers and of terminals. *See also* MULTICS.

machine Usually, a real – or imagined – computer (*see also* virtual machine, abstract machine, Turing machine), which may or may not be sequential and deterministic. In formal language theory it may imply a *sequential machine.

machine address (absolute address; actual address) A unique number that specifies a unique location within the *address space where an operand is to be found/deposited. It generally specifies a memory location but in some cases specifies a machine register or an I/O device. In the case of a binary machine, it is an n-bit number specifying one of 2^n locations. The result of calculating an *effective address is usually a machine address.

machine code The *operation code of a particular machine, and hence, by association, code specific to a particular machine.

machine equivalence The property describing two usually abstract machines that can simulate one another. Machines M_1 and M_2 are said to be equivalent if M_1 can simulate M_2 and M_2 can simulate M_1. *See* machine simulation.

machine-independent A term applied to software that is not dependent on the properties of a particular machine, and can therefore be used on any machine. Such software is also described as *portable*.

machine intelligence *See* artificial intelligence.

machine language Strictly, the written representation of machine code. The term is also used as a synonym for machine code.

machine-oriented language *See* MOHLL.

machine simulation The process whereby one machine M_1 can be made to behave like a second machine M_2. Formally, let there be *functions g and h that perform encoding and decoding roles respectively:

$$g : M_1 \rightarrow M_2, \quad h : M_2 \rightarrow M_1$$

g encodes information for machine M_1 and produces corresponding information for machine M_2; h is the *inverse function. Machine M_2 is said to *simulate* machine M_1 if it is possible to specify an *algorithm such that, when given a program P_1 for M_1, it produces a corresponding program P_2 for M_2; further the effect of P_1 on M_1 should be equivalent to the effect of

applying function g
then executing P_2 on M_2
then applying function h

Machine simulation of this kind is generally discussed in relation to idealized abstract machines, such as *Turing machines, which are free from physical limitations. *See also* machine equivalence.

machine word *See* word.

macro *Short for* macro-instruction. An instruction in a programming language (almost always but not necessarily *assembly language) that is replaced by a sequence of instructions prior to assembly or compiling. A *macro-assembler* permits the user to define macros, specifying the macro-instruction form, its arguments, and a replacement text (otherwise called the *body* of the macro), and then allows macro-instructions to be interspersed among the assembly code. On encountering a macro-instruction the assembler replaces it by the macro body, substituting the parameters provided in the places marked in the macro body. The macro thus provides a mechanism for inserting a particular body of text at various places in a program (and is thus the same thing as an open *subroutine, though this nomenclature is obsolete).

A *macro-processor* provides similar facilities, though not in combination with an assembler. It accepts macro definitions and then reads arbitrary text in which *macro calls* (i.e. instances of a macro name) can occur. Text is copied to the output until a macro name is encountered: when this happens the arguments (parameters) are found and the macro call is replaced by the macro body in the output stream, with appropriate substitution of the parameters.

macro-assembler *See* macro.

macro-generator *Another name for* macro-processor. *See* macro.

macro-instruction *See* macro.

macro-processor (macro-generator) *See* macro.

magnetic bubble memory A type of digital memory in which data is represented by magnetic bubbles that are made to move through a stationary planar medium; the bubbles are tiny circular areas (stable magnetic domains) in which the medium is magnetized in the reverse direction to the rest of the medium. Bubble memory thus differs from magnetic tape and disk stores, in which the medium moves and the data bits are stationary with respect to it. It belongs to the class of *magnetic domain memory* but is the only form in current use.

In the commonest form the medium is a thin layer of complex garnet, deposited epitaxially on a substrate of a simpler garnet. A pattern of metal shapes is deposited on the surface of the epitaxial layer. The preferred direction of magnetization of the epitaxial layer is perpendicular to its plane, in either direction. When a suitable biasing magnetic field is applied perpendicular to the layer, magnetic bubbles can form, magnetized in the opposite sense to this field. If an additional magnetic field is applied in the plane of the layer the bubbles will move through the layer, the pattern of metal shapes influencing the way in which they move. Usually this field is made to rotate regularly, typically at 100,000 revolutions per second, and the metal shapes are arranged in regular rows so that each bubble moves one step through the pattern for each cycle of rotation. Means are provided for inserting bubbles at the entry to the pattern and detecting their arrival at the exit; the device therefore acts as a shift register.

A typical bubble device stores one megabit of data. There is usually only one input point and one output point per device so that data flow is serial. However, within the device it is usual to divide the data path into a series of parallel loops, with means of distributing the data stream between them, so that the access time to a particular item of data is only a fraction of the time taken to fill the whole device with data. Typically the data rate is 100 kilobits per second and the access time 30 milliseconds. A number of such devices can be used together to provide a greater total capacity, and if required these can be arranged so that several are accessed in parallel to give a higher data rate.

The performance and cost per bit of bubble memory is intermediate between that of semiconductor memory and magnetic disk. It is nonvolatile (if the bias field is provided by permanent magnets, which is usual) and resistant to cosmic rays and similar particles. Having no moving parts it is more rugged than disk memory. Bubble memory has found limited application where these properties are of value, e.g. in portable computer terminals and in satellites. However the initial promise of the technology (pioneered by Bell Telephone Laboratories) has not been realized in full since manufacturing costs have proved higher than expected.

magnetic card A data medium consisting of a card that is partly or completely coated on one side with ferromagnetic film on which data can be encoded and read (*see* card reader). The credit card is one example, the encoding being restricted to a single strip that can contain three tracks. Other sizes of card have been used as interchangeable media in data-processing and word-processing applications. The most widely used example of a word-processing application is the IBM magnetic card. In the late 1960s a number of mass storage devices were designed in which large magnetic cards were filed and retrieved automatically. These were superseded by *automated tape libraries and *magnetic disk stores.

magnetic cell A *memory element in which two different states of its magnetic flux pattern are used to represent binary values. The element may be a ferromagnetic core, part of a perforated ferromagnetic plane, or the intersection of two coated wires, and it can store a single bit of information.

magnetic disk A storage medium in the form of a circular plate coated on one or both sides with a magnetic film. The disk substrate may be rigid, in which case it is usually made of an aluminum alloy, or it may be flexible, in which case it is usually a polyester. The coating may be a compound of ferric oxide in a binder or a thin metallic plating of an alloy such as cobalt/nickel or cobalt/chrome. Metallic coatings have advantages in being homogeneous, having a better hysteresis loop shape, and allowing storage densities 10 times that achievable with conventional ferric oxide coatings. Flexible disks (i.e. *floppy disks) with oxide coating provide low-cost lightweight media that can be handled in a normal office environment. Magnetic disks used in computer peripheral equipment range in diameter from 3″ to 36″ (76–914 mm). *See also* disk pack, disk cartridge, disk drive, magnetic encoding, disk format.

magnetic drum The earliest form of rotating magnetic storage device, used in some of the first computers at a time when random-access store was volatile, bulky, and expensive. The drum therefore formed the main memory of some of these machines, the random-access stores being used only as registers. Although random-access store developed rapidly it was still relatively expensive and the drum was retained as a local backing store on some computers. Magnetic disk, when introduced, took over a large part of the backing store function. Drums remained in use however on certain systems that required faster access than was generally provided by disk, but today they are obsolete apart from a few special applications.

A magnetic drum consists of a cylinder whose curved surface is coated with a suitable recording medium, either metal or iron oxide. On the *head-per-track drum* the drum rotates past a number of fixed read/write heads, one for each track of recorded information. On the *moving-head drum* the drum rotates past a single head or small group of heads that can be moved axially to access any track. The latter was rapidly superseded by disk stores but the head-per-track drum survived: track selection requires only electronic switching between heads rather than movement of the head so that such drums have much shorter access times than disk stores.

magnetic encoding The method by which binary data is recorded on magnetic media. In *horizontal recording* on magnetic disks, tapes, and cards, magnetic domains in the media are aligned along the direction of the applied magnetic field with either north or south pole leading: each domain is a tiny bounded region in which the magnetic moments of the component atoms are aligned, and it therefore behaves like a magnet. The domains are arranged end to end along a track, which may be either a concentric ring on a disk or run the length of a tape or card. There may not be a one-to-one relationship between the binary information of the data and the orientation of the magnetic domains. *See* disk format, tape format.

In 1975 Shun-ichi Iwasaki published his work on *vertical recording* methods. The magnetic domains are oriented through the thickness of the magnetic film and have either a north or a south pole at the exposed surface. The magnetic material is usually a vacuum-deposited film of metal such as an alloy or combination of cobalt and chromium over a layer of permalloy. Linear densities as high as 200,000 bits per inch have been demonstrated. Vertical recording can thus yield an increase of at least 25 times and possibly 100 times the bit density achievable by current horizontal recording techniques.

magnetic head *See* head.

magnetic-ink character recognition *See* MICR.

magnetic media The various types of media on which data recording is effected by writing a magnetic pattern onto the magnetizable surface of the medium. The term distinguishes these types of media from others that use different recording techniques, e.g. optical disks, punched cards, and paper tape. *See* magnetic tape, magnetic tape cartridge, magnetic disk, disk cartridge, disk pack, floppy disk, magnetic drum.

magnetic tape 1. An information storage medium consisting of a magnetic coating on a flexible backing in tape form. The coating usually consists of fine particles of iron oxide suspended in an inert binder, and the backing is usually polyester. Data is recorded by *magnetic encoding of tracks on the coating according to a particular *tape format.

Magnetic tape is wound on *reels* (or *spools*), sometimes contained within a *cartridge or *cassette. To use magnetic tape, the reel containing the tape – the *file reel* – is placed on a peripheral device known as a *tape transport*. (This device is also called a *magnetic tape unit (MTU)*, *tape drive*, *tape deck*, and *tape mechanism*.) The tape transport is capable of moving the tape from the file reel, past one or more magnetic heads, and winding it onto a *take-up reel*; the latter may be associated, detachably or not, with the transport or alternatively be contained in the cartridge or cassette.

An electrical signal is applied to the *write head* to record information as a magnetic pattern on the tape (*see also* write ring); in most cases the tape passes first over an *erase head* to erase any signal previously written on the tape. As the tape passes over the *read head* the magnetic pattern induces an electrical signal that can be processed electronically to recreate the signal that was recorded. Sometimes a single *read/write head* is provided, with its connections switched so that it can be used for either reading or writing; more often two separate heads – or two gaps and windings in the same head – are used, and this permits a *read-while-write check* to be made by reading and checking information as soon as it has been recorded (*see* error management).

The most common dimensions for an individual magnetic tape – a *volume* – are ½ inch wide and 2400 feet long, wound on a 10½ inch diameter reel; 1200 and 600 ft lengths of ½″ tape, on 8½″ or 7″ reels, are less frequently used, and occasionally a thinner plastic backing is used to allow 3600 ft to be wound on the standard 10½″ reel. Various other widths and lengths of tape are used, generally in some form of cartridge.

The most important uses of magnetic tape in computer systems are as follows.

(a) Data interchange. There are international standards for the format of data recorded on magnetic tape (*see* tape format); it is the most widely used medium for the interchange of data between separate computer systems, including those of different makes, and also between systems and off-line peripherals such as printers.

(b) Backup of magnetic disk memory, particularly fixed disks.

(c) Software distribution.

(d) Input, when the tape is written by a key-to-tape system. Tape is now rarely used in this way.

(e) Serial processing. Although this function was once very important, the use of magnetic disk memories has made it obsolescent.

Magnetic tape was introduced for computer use in the 1950s, when it was already widely used for audio and instrumentation purposes. It largely superseded punched tape and punched cards although these remained in use for limited applications. The demise of magnetic tape as a computer medium has often been predicted but its use is likely to continue at least through the 1980s.

2. A term sometimes used by software and systems people to mean *magnetic tape subsystem.

magnetic tape cartridge (tape cartridge) A casing containing one or more reels carrying a volume of *magnetic tape, so arranged that it can be loaded on a suitable tape transport for access without the tape being handled by the operator. There are many forms of tape cartridge, some containing both the file reel and the take-up reel (*see* magnetic tape) and some the file reel only. The term is also used to describe a file reel without a separate casing but with some other provision, such as a special leader to protect the tape and avoid the need for the operator to touch it.
The best-known forms of tape cartridge are as follows.
(a) The *autoload* or *Easyload cartridge*, introduced by IBM and consisting essentially of a collar clamped around the periphery of a standard 10½″ reel of ½″ wide magnetic tape. Its purpose is to facilitate *autothreading of tape on suitably equipped tape transports. The reel can be removed from the cartridge for use on other transports.
(b) The *DC300 cartridge*, introduced by 3M and consisting of a metal and plastic casing containing two small reels of ¼″ wide magnetic tape. The cartridge is used in a transport whose heads protrude through a window in the cartridge to make contact with the tape as it passes from one reel to the other. Variants of this cartridge carry 300, 450, or 600 feet of tape in similar housings. It is usual for the drive to record several tracks of data on the tape, one at a time (i.e. serially); a number of different *tape formats are used and at least one of these is now defined by an ANSI Standard. This type of cartridge, and the similar but smaller *DC100* type, is used mainly on small computers in an office environment.
(c) The *digital cassette*, based on the standard audio cassette developed by Philips and made to similar dimensions though with more precision. The plastic casing contains two small reels of tape 0.15″ wide, in various lengths, and is used in a transport whose heads protrude through a window in the cartridge to make contact with the tape. The tape is moved by direct contact with a capstan against which it is pressed by a pinch roller, both being part of the transport; the transport also connects mechanically to the hubs of both reels to control the winding and unwinding of the tape. Cassette tape is now used mainly on hobbyist computers and these often use standard audio cassettes and decks rather than the higher-quality digital variety.
(d) Various designs of cartridge containing a relatively short length of wide tape on a single reel, used in *automated tape libraries.
(e) Cartridges consisting of small (typically 3″ or 4″ diameter) reels of ½″ tape without an outer casing, but with a tough protective leader slightly wider than the tape so that it gives full protection when wound onto the reel.

magnetic tape subsystem A subsystem provided in order to enable a host system to obtain access to data on magnetic tape. The subsystem consists of one or more tape transports (*see* magnetic tape) and a device controller that incorporates a *formatter. The device controller has an interface by which it is connected to the host. Some manufacturers specify their own proprietary interface, but several use a common interface specification, originally developed by Pertec, which has informally become recognized as the *industry standard formatter interface*.

magnetic tape unit (MTU) *Another name for* tape transport. *See* magnetic tape.

magnetographic printer A type of printer in which the required image is first written on a band or drum of magnetic recording material as a pattern of closely spaced magnetic poles. The image is then developed by brushing it with a pigment that is also ferromagnetic and thermoplastic. The image is transferred and bonded to paper by applying pressure and/or heat.

magneto-optic disk storage A storage technique that uses the magneto-optic effect to store and retrieve data. The current technique, still in a development stage (1983), uses a laser beam to demagnetize a point on a magnetic film by heating it above its Curie temperature. Initially a unidirectional magnetic field is induced in the film. To write on the disk the laser beam and a magnetic field are applied to a small area and thus small regions (domains) of opposite polarity to the main field can be generated. To read the information the disk is scanned by polarized light from a low-power laser. The plane of polarization of the light reflected from a magnetized surface is rotated according to the direction of the magnetic field – the Kerr effect. This rotation can be detected and the original binary signal can be reproduced. The technique has potential for recording densities many times higher than that achievable by either conventional or vertical *magnetic encoding.

mag tape *Short for* magnetic tape.

mailbox A repository – often secure – for documents or data that have been transmitted via an *electronic mail system. For documents there are usually a number of mailboxes associated with a printer and they are similar in principal to the sorter pockets on large office copiers. Information for an addressee can be sent via a communication line to an electronic mail station where it may be printed out and automatically put into the mailbox designated in the address. The addressee will access the data via his own terminal by sending his unique identifying code.

mainframe 1. Generally, the combination of central processor and primary memory of a computer system. The term excludes the I/O, backing store, etc., and is sometimes used synonymously with central processor.
2. Any large computer system.

main memory (main store; main storage) The storage that is closely associated with the processor of a computer system and from which the program instruction and data can be directly retrieved and to which the resulting data is written prior to transfer to *backing store or *output device. In modern machines this is usually a *semiconductor memory but in somewhat earlier machines *core stores were used. The majority of storage activity takes place in the main memory but the backing store has usually the larger capacity. *See also* memory hierarchy.

main program The section of a program that is entered first and from which program units and procedures are called. It is the outermost block of a block-structured program.

main store, main storage *Other names for* main memory.

maintenance 1. The performance of *preventive or *remedial maintenance in order to prevent incipient hardware faults or to correct a hardware fault that has occurred.
2. *See* program maintenance.

majority element (majority gate) A logic element with an odd number of inputs, and whose output agrees with the majority of the inputs. *See also* threshold element.

malfunction The occurrence of a fault, usually a hardware fault.

management information system (MIS) An *information system whose prime purpose is to supply information to management. The early concept of an MIS, commonplace in the 1960s and early 1970s, was that systems analysts would determine the information requirements of individual managers in an organization, and would design systems to supply that information routinely and/or on demand.
Decision support systems form a new class of MIS, giving managers much greater independence in their use of computer-based information. They depend on the

union of office information systems (including personal computing facilities for managers, operated by themselves) with more conventional database and data-processing systems. They assume that managers will be able to build and access their own personal databases, as well as accessing the corporate databases, and that they will be able to formulate their own access enquiries without depending on specialist intermediaries.

Manchester coded *Another term for* phase encoded. *See* tape format.

Manchester Mark I The world's first operational stored-program computer, running its first program in June 1948. It was designed by T. Kilburn and F. C. Williams at the University of Manchester, UK, commencing in 1946. Several improvements were added and the first realistic problem to be solved by the machine was achieved in April 1949, shortly before *EDSAC began operations. It became the world's first commercially available computer when marketed by *Ferranti Ltd in 1951 as the Ferranti Mark I. The effectiveness of the machine was due to its use of *electrostatic (Williams tube) storage.

Mann Whitney U-test *See* nonparametric techniques.

mantissa (fractional part) *See* floating-point notation.

manual control Control of computer-system or subsystem operation by an operator who may intervene at arbitrary times or at times specified in the running program.

map 1. (mapping) *See* function.
2. *See* memory map.
3. *See* Karnaugh map.

map method A procedure for minimizing Boolean functions using a *Karnaugh map.

mapping 1. (map) *See* function.
2. *See* memory mapping, I/O mapping, bit mapping.

marginal check (marginal test) *See* preventive maintenance.

mark 1. An electrically positive state of a communication line. The negative state is called *space*.
2. A line drawn on specially formatted cards or forms that are used with *mark sensing or *mark reading equipment.
3. *See* tape mark.

marker on a magnetic tape. *See* BOT marker, EOT marker.

Markov chain A sequence of discrete random variables such that each member of the sequence is probabilistically dependent only on its predecessor.

Markov source *See* discrete source.

mark reading (mark scanning; optical mark reading) A method for data input in which marks made on preformatted documents are sensed by photoelectric means. The marks are interpreted as either characters or values according to their position on the form. This provides an efficient type of data input in applications in which there are relatively few answers to a limited number of questions. No further data preparation activity or machines are required since the reader can be connected directly to the system.
The mark reading document is often printed on 80 column punch card stock for ease of automatic handling. Some punch card readers are designed to read punchings and/or marks. The accuracy of placement of pen or pencil marks cannot be as precise as the punchings so it is usual to provide no more than 40 columns for sensing the marks, i.e. each mark can cover the space of two columns of punching. Special readers are available to handle larger documents. The documents are printed on paper, and information to the user as to where the marks should be put and what significance they will have is

usually printed in a color that will not be detected by the photoelectric sensors. Machine-readable timing marks are preprinted along the edge of the document.

mark scanning *Another name for* mark reading.

mark sensing A method for data input in which electrically conductive marks, usually made with a soft graphite pencil on a preformatted card or form, are electrically sensed. This method has been displaced by the more reliable method of *mark reading in which the marks are detected photoelectrically.

mark-space ratio *See* pulse train.

masking 1. (filtering) A logical operation carried out on a byte, word, or field of data in order to modify or identify a part of it. A bit pattern – the same length as the item to be masked – is generated and stored in a register as a *mask*. By use of the appropriate operation, e.g. subtract, logical AND, logical OR, the mask can be used to suppress bits in the data, or set them to zero, etc. The process is used for purposes such as identifying the presence of high-priority bits in a status byte or resetting interrupts.
2. The use of a chemical shield, the *mask*, to determine the pattern of interconnects in an integrated circuit. Read-only memories (*ROMs) and programmable logic arrays (*PLAs) are customized for their particular applications by the masking process.

mask-programmable device *See* programmable devices, ROM.

mass storage An on-line backing store system capable of storing larger quantities of data (sometimes an order of magnitude more) than conventional backing store. The quoted capacity of mass storage has increased with advances in technology: in the early 1960s a megabyte of storage came in this category; in the early 1980s the term applies to devices such as the IBM 3850 automated tape library that can store up to 472 billion bytes (gigabytes) of data.

master file (primary file) A file of records containing a cumulative history or the results of accumulation. It is updated in each file-processing cycle and carried forward to the next cycle.

master record The current relatively permanent record that is usually held on the *master file and updated by a *transaction file record.

master-slave flip-flop A type of clocked *flip-flop consisting of master and slave elements that are clocked on complementary transitions of the clock signal. Data is only transferred from the master to the slave, and hence to the output, after the master-device outputs have stabilized. This eliminates the possibility of ambiguous outputs, which can occur in single-element flip-flops as a result of *propagation delays of the individual logic gates driving the flip-flops.

master-slave system A system that has more than one processor and in which one of the processors is designated as being the *master* and all other processors are *slaves*. The master processor is capable of actions that the slaves cannot perform, usually in connection with resource scheduling and the initiation of peripheral transfers. This approach means that the problems of *synchronization are greatly reduced, since only the master processor can be active in what might otherwise be *critical regions. It has the drawbacks of introducing an artificial asymmetry between processors, and of causing delays when processes that might be able to proceed are in fact delayed since the only available processors do not have the necessary privileges.

master tape A magnetic tape volume that is used in a data-processing operation without any change to its contents. It may contain a *master file, or part of one. A master tape is usually protected by a *write ring, or some equivalent mechanical device, by which the operator can protect the tape from being erased or overwritten even though this is commanded by the host.

The term master tape was also used in connection with paper tape.

matching The basic mechanism of an *information management system or *database management system whereby desired records are identified by comparing the values in fields of the records with data values provided: the determining data item values are presented, *matched* against data items within files in the database, and files of associated data items are output. The matching may be exact, i.e. two strings of characters matched character by character. Alternatively, some other matching rule may be applied. Where the value of a field is to be ignored in matching, the matching rule may be given using a *joker symbol* that matches anything. Matching mechanisms are usually present in the facilities provided by operating systems for *file management.

mathematical logic *See* logic.

mathematical programming A wide field of study that deals with the theory, applications, and computational methods for *optimization problems. An abstract formulation of such problems is to maximize a function f (known as an *objective function*) over a constraint set S, i.e.

$$\text{maximize } f(\boldsymbol{x}),\ \boldsymbol{x} \in S \subseteq \boldsymbol{R}^n,$$

where $\boldsymbol{R}^n$ denotes the space of real n-component vectors $\boldsymbol{x}$,

$$\boldsymbol{x} = (x_1, x_2, \ldots, x_n)^T$$

and f is a real-valued function defined on S. If S consists only of vectors whose elements are integers, then the problem is one of *integer programming*. *Linear programming treats the case of f as a linear function with S defined by linear equations and/or constraints. Nonlinear objective functions with or without constraints (defined by systems of *nonlinear equations) give rise to problems generally referred to as optimization problems.

Mathematical-programming problems arise in engineering, business, and the physical and social sciences.

matrix A two-dimensional *array. In computing, matrices are usually considered to be special cases of n-dimensional arrays, expressed as arrays with two indices. The notation for arrays is determined by the programming language. The two dimensions of a matrix are known as its *rows* and *columns*; a matrix with m rows and n columns is said to be an $m \times n$ matrix.

In mathematics (and in this dictionary), the conventional notation is to use a capital letter to denote a matrix in its entirety, and the corresponding lower-case letter, indexed by a pair of subscripts, to denote an element in the matrix. Thus the i,jth element of a matrix A is denoted by a_{ij}, where i is the row number and j the column number.

A deficient two-dimensional array, in which one of the dimensions has only one index value (and is consequently elided), is a special kind of matrix known either as a *row vector* (with the column elided) or *column vector* (with the row elided). The distinction between row and column shows that the two dimensions are still significant.

matrix inversion A numerical method by which the *inverse matrix of a given matrix is produced.

matrix multiplication The multiplication of two matrices A and B according to the rule

$$c_{ij} = \sum_{k=1}^{n} a_{ik} b_{kj}$$

matrix norm *See* approximation theory.

matrix printer A printer that forms the character or shape to be printed from an array of dots. The dots can be formed on paper by a stylus impacting an inked ribbon, by separate drops of ink ejected from a nozzle, or by one of the other nonimpact technologies in which dots are formed by changing the color of the media by heating (thermal printer), etching or burning (electrosensitive printer) or by ink adhering to an electric charge or magnetic pole pattern (electrographic and magnetographic printers).

A significant advantage of matrix printers over *solid-font printers is the ability to accommodate a very large repertoire of character shapes and styles and also to print the ideograms of oriental languages and script characters of Arabic. Diagrams and pictures can also be reproduced. When the term is used in reference to a single type of printer it generally means an *impact printer or *dot matrix printer.

matrix-updating methods *See* optimization.

maximum-length sequence *See* m-sequence.

maximum-likelihood decoding A strategy for decoding an *error-correcting code: it chooses the *codeword most likely to have been transmitted, given the word that has been received.

maximum likelihood, method of *See* likelihood.

maxterm (standard sum term) A sum (OR) of *n* Boolean variables, uncomplemented or complemented but not repeated, in a Boolean function of *n* variables. With *n* variables, 2^n different maxterms are possible. The complement of any maxterm is a *minterm. *See also* standard product of sums.

MDR *Abbrev. for* memory data register.

Mealy machine *See* sequential machine.

mean *See* measures of location.

mean deviation *See* measures of variation.

means/ends analysis A technique used in *artificial intelligence for forming plans to achieve goals. A plan consists of a sequence of actions. The sequence is put together by comparing the goals that each action achieves (the means) with the goals that must be achieved (the ends).

measures of location Quantities that represent the average or typical value of a *random variable (*compare* measures of variation). They are either properties of a *probability distribution or computed *statistics of a sample. Three important measures are the *mean*, *median*, and *mode*.

The *mean* of a sample of *n* observations, denoted by $\bar{x}$, is

$$\sum_i x_i/n$$

The mean of a probability distribution, denoted by μ, is

$$\Sigma\ x.p(x)$$

for a discrete distribution and

$$\int x.f(x)\,dx$$

for a continuous distribution; it is also called the *expectation* of *x*, denoted by *E*(*x*).

A *weighted mean* is used when members of a sample are known with different reliability. To each observation x_i corresponds a *weight* w_i, and now $\bar{x}$ is

$$\Sigma\ (w_i\,.\,x_i)/\Sigma\ w_i$$

If each observation is the mean of *w* observations, the formulas for the weighted and unweighted means agree.

The *median* is the value of *x* exceeded by exactly half the sample or distribution. The median of a distribution is the value for which the cumulative distribution function, *F*(*x*), equals 0.5 (*see* probability distributions).

The *mode* is the most commonly occurring value. For distributions in which the frequency function, *f*(*x*), has one or more local maxima, each maximum is called a mode.

These measures may be illustrated on the following sample of eight values of x:

1,1,1,2,3,3,5,7

The mean is 2.875, the median is 2.5, and the mode is 1.

measures of variation Quantities that express the amount of variation in a *random variable (*compare* measures of location). Variation is sometimes described as *spread* or *dispersion* to distinguish it from systematic trends or differences. Measures of variation are either properties of a *probability distribution or sample estimates of them.

The *range* of a sample is the difference between the largest and smallest value. The *interquartile range* is potentially more useful. If the sample is ranked in ascending order of magnitude two values of x may be found, the first of which is exceeded by 75% of the sample, the second by 25%; their difference is the interquartile range. An analogous definition applies to a probability distribution.

The *variance* is the expectation (or mean) of the square of the difference between a *random variable and its mean; it is of fundamental importance in statistical analysis. The variance of a continuous distribution with mean μ is

$$\int (x-\mu)^2 f(x)\,\mathrm{d}x$$

and is denoted by σ^2. The variance of a discrete distribution is

$$\Sigma\,(x-\mu)^2 \,.\, p(x)$$

and is also denoted by σ^2. The sample variance of a sample of n observations with mean $\bar{x}$ is

$$\Sigma\,(x_i-\bar{x})^2 \,/\, (n-1)$$

and is denoted by s^2. The value $(n - 1)$ corrects for *bias.

The *standard deviation* is the square root of the variance, denoted by σ (for a distribution) or s (for a sample). The standard deviation has the same units of measurement as the mean, and for a *normal distribution about 5% of the distribution lies beyond about two standard deviations each side of the mean. The standard deviation of the distribution of an estimated quantity is termed the *standard error*.

The *mean deviation* is the mean of the absolute deviations of the random variable from the mean.

mechanical verifier A system that provides automated assistance to the production of a *program correctness proof. Typically such a system consists of two distinct parts: a *verification condition generator* and a *theorem prover*. The former is responsible for generating the theorems that must be proven in order to demonstrate that *preconditions and *postconditions are consistent with the semantics of the statements to which they relate. The theorem prover is then responsible for proving these verification conditions.

Different mechanical verifiers vary considerably in their capabilities. A relatively simple system might require that assertions giving all relevant information are attached between every pair of successive statements (simple or compound), and would present any nontrivial verification conditions to the user for manual proof; this system is sometimes called an *assertion checker*. A more sophisticated mechanical verifier requires only major assertions to be attached prior to verification (perhaps only the input assertion and output assertion) and is able to generate its own intermediate assertions as necessary. Further, the theorem prover is capable of proving complex verification conditions, perhaps presenting only the occasional lemma to the user for confirmation.

median *See* measures of location.

medium *See* data medium. The plural form is *media*, although this is often used as a singular form.

medium-scale integration *See* MSI, integrated circuit.

meet operator *See* lattice.

mega- (symbol: M) A prefix indicating a multiple of one million (10^6) or, loosely, a multiple of 2^{20}, i.e.

1 048 576

In computing it is used for instance in the context of storage capacity, e.g. 400 megabytes (or 400M bytes).

member (element) of a *set S. An object x that is in S, usually denoted by $x \in S$. One of the basic actions that can be performed on sets is asking whether or not an object is in a set. *See also* operations on sets.

memory A device or medium that can retain information for subsequent retrieval. The term is synonymous with *storage* and *store*, although it is most frequently used for referring to the internal storage of a computer that can be directly addressed by operating instructions. *See* main memory, cache memory, semiconductor memory, memory hierarchy, memory management.

memory compaction (block compaction) Any of several methods used to relocate information blocks in main memory in order to maximize the available free space in the memory. *See also* storage allocation.

memory cycle 1. The complete sequence of events for a unit of memory to go from a quiescent state through a read and/or write phase and back to a quiescent state. **2.** The minimum length of time that is required between successive accesses (read or write) to a memory. *See also* cycle.

memory data register (MDR) A *register used for holding information (either program words or data words) that is in the process of being transferred from the memory to the central processor, or vice versa.

memory dump A representation, which can be read by a person, of the contents at some time of some part of the main memory of a computer system. A variety of representation formats might be employed, but typically these would all be relatively low-level – e.g. purely numeric or assembler-code format. A memory dump is normally taken for *postmortem purposes.

memory element A device that stores one item of information: if it has q stable states it is said to be *q-ary, and if $q = 2$ it is said to be binary. It is usually implemented electronically, sometimes with the assistance of the magnetic, optical, or acoustic properties of a storage medium. In practice, most memory elements are binary. In fast computer circuitry, the *flip-flop is the most common type of memory element.

Memory elements are employed specifically in computer memories and generally in *sequential circuits. A memory element is any smallest part of such a system that possesses more than one stable state. For example, a binary *shift register contains four flip-flops and has 16 states, but each of its four memory elements has only two states; a similar ternary shift register would have 81 states, but would still consist of four memory elements, each having three states.

memory fill An aid to program debugging in which every location in the memory is filled with a predetermined character before being overwritten by the incoming program.

memory guard A form of hardware *interlock used in some systems to control access to memory that is currently involved in a peripheral transfer. At the time of initiating the transfer the channel sets an indication that the buffer area is associated with the transfer; this indication is cleared by the channel on completion of the transfer. Any attempt to access the buffer area (other than by the channel) will suspend the process attempting to access the buffer until the transfer has been completed.

memory hierarchy For physically different kinds of memory, there are significant differences in the time to access the contents of a particular location in a memory, the volume of information that can be stored, and the unit cost of storing a given amount of information. To optimize its use and achieve greater efficiency and economy, memory is organized in a number of levels in a hierarchy arranged as follows:

1. A single word held in each register of the processor; typically a word contains 4 bytes. (This is sometimes not considered as memory.)
2. Groups of words within the cache; typically a single cache entry will hold 8 words (say 32 bytes).
3. Words within the main memory; groups of words are transferred between the main memory and the cache.
4. Blocks of words held on permanently connected backing store. There are two sublevels:
(a) pages of memory held on a swapping device – complete pages are transferred between their backing store home and a page frame in main memory;
(b) complete files held on disk storage in the file store system.
5. Complete files backed up onto removable disks or magnetic tape within the file store system.

unit		realized as	access time	cost, $	capacity	cost/bit
processor register	L	row of ECL flip-flops	0.5 ns	10	32 bits	30 c
	M	row of MOS inverters	5 ns	0.1	16 bits	1 c
cache	L	bipolar RAM	50 ns	5k	32 kbyte	2 c
	M	(not found)				
main memory	L	MOS RAM	500 ns	10k	1 Mbyte	0.1 c
	M	MOS RAM	500 ns	10k	1 Mbyte	0.1 c
swapping device	L	head/track disk	10 ms	50k	10 Mbyte	.05 c
	L	or bulk RAM	100 μs	50k	10 Mbyte	.05 c
	M	(not found)				
disk	L	Winchester	25 ms	20k	500 Mbyte	4 mc
	M	floppy disk	100 ms	500	1 Mbyte	6 mc
magnetic tape	L	6250 bpi mounted	100 s	10k	100 Mbyte	0.1 mc
	L	ditto unmounted	1000 s	10	100 Mbyte	1 μc
	M	cassette mounted	100 s	500	1 Mbyte	5 mc
	M	ditto unmounted	1000 s	1	1 Mbyte	10 μc

Rows prefixed by L refer to a larger system
Rows prefixed by M refer to a micro system

Memory hierarchy

At the time of writing (1982) the table indicates typical access times and unit costs for memory in each of these categories. Not all systems have all levels, and there are anomalous situations such as large slow core memories that back up main memories. *See also* memory management.

memory management Control of the *memory hierarchy of a system as a whole, or control of allocation at a fixed level within the memory hierarchy. In the former case information stored within the system is shuttled between one realization of memory and another, the objective being to maintain maximum *hit rate in each form of memory. This movement may be controlled by
(a) voluntary user action, e.g. copying a file from disk to memory in order to edit it;
(b) system software, e.g. transfer of a page between swapping device and memory when a page fault occurs;
(c) system hardware, e.g. movement of a set of words from memory to cache when a word within the set is accessed.
At a given level of the hierarchy the operating system will control what fraction of that level is to be allocated to each process. This can clearly only occur where control is by system software, and refers most particularly to the allocation of memory to a process, or to the allocation of space on the swapping device. Movement between disk and magnetic tape is often separately treated as archiving. *See also* storage protection.

memory map A schematic presentation of the use to which memory is being put, often presented as a byproduct during the compilation of a program. The memory map may be useful in the diagnosis of faults in the compiled program.

memory mapping A technique for managing peripheral devices, used on many microprocessor systems and on some smaller miniprocessor systems. The control registers of the peripheral device appear to the processor as words in memory whose contents can be written and read using the normal store and fetch operations.

memory protection Any of many methods for controlling access to or use of memory. This control may be to prevent inadvertent user-interference, to provide for system security, or both.
A mechanism for controlling the types of access permitted to an area of memory is known as a *memory protect*. In virtual memory systems it may be possible to assign certain areas as being capable of designated modes of access; for example, an area that is known to contain only the code of shared subroutines may be designated as having "execute only" access, and can only be read during the instruction-fetch phase of executing an instruction. The permitted mode of access may differ for different processes. Definition of memory areas may use *bounds registers; fixed memory areas may be controlled by *locks and keys; individual words may be controlled by *tags.
A violation of the memory protection system usually leads via an interrupt to a forced process termination.

memory reference instruction An *instruction that has one or more of its operand addresses referring to a location in memory, as opposed to one of the CPU registers or some other way of specifying an operand location.

memory-to-memory instruction An instruction that transfers information from a memory and returns it to a memory. The information may be modified during the transfer (e.g. incremented); the information may or may not be returned to the same location. The term is also used to refer to an instruction that transfers information between levels of a *memory hierarchy. Transfers may be word by word or block transfers.

menu A displayed list from which a choice can be made. The list of options may be displayed with a single code opposite each. The selection may then be made by keying the single code. The method provides a simple way of guiding a user through a complex situation by presenting a sequence of simpler decisions. Although a visual display and keyboard are frequently used for this purpose, other arrangements, such as visual displays with touch-sensitive screens or light pens and arrays of touch-sensitive LEDs, are available.

mergeable heap Any data structure representing a set of ordered elements that can support the insertion and deletion of elements as well as the set operation of union and the calculation of the minimum elements in a set. *See also* operations on sets.

merged transistor logic (MTL) *Another name for* integrated injection logic. *See* I^2L.

merge exchange sort *Another name for* Batcher's parallel method.

message 1. A collection of data of arbitrary length that is communicated through a *message switching system. A message could be a few bits, a file, or even a database.
2. *Another name for* packet. *See* packet switching.
3. *See* Shannon's model (of a communication system).
4. A specially formatted document sent in an *electronic mail system.
5. To send a message in an electronic mail system.

message authenticator *See* authentication code.

message queueing The process of storing a message in a node of a *message switching network until sufficient resources are available for the message to be forwarded to the next node along the path to its destination.

message switching 1. A data-switching strategy that requires no physical path to exist between sender and receiver before communication can take place. Message switching passes *messages via relays, called *switching offices*, in a *store-and-forward network. Each switching office receives a message, checks it for errors, and retransmits it to the next switching office on the route to the destination. Because of the large buffers and variable delays of message switching, most computer networks use *packet switching or *circuit switching techniques for their underlying network components, and add message switching functions (such as *electronic mail and *file transfer protocol) at higher levels.
2. *An informal name for* packet switching.

meta-assembler An *assembler that accepts a description of the assembly language to be recognized.

metacompiler A *compiler that accepts the *metalanguage description of a language and generates a compiler for it, i.e. a *compiler-compiler.

metalanguage A language used to describe a programming language.

metallic disk *Another name for* hard disk.

MFM *Abbrev. for* modified frequency modulation. *See* disk format.

M²FM *Abbrev. for* modified modified frequency modulation. *See* disk format.

MICR *Abbrev. for* magnetic ink character recognition. A process in which data, printed in ink containing ferromagnetic particles, is read by magnetic read heads. The shape of the characters resembles those of normal typescript but each generates a unique signal as it is scanned by the read head. The most common application is for encoding numbers on bank checks. There are two standardized fonts: the E13B and CMC7. The E13B font is very rectangular in appearance and some parts of the vertical limbs may be thickened to accentuate the difference in the generated wave form. This font is widely used in the

US and the UK. The CMC7 font has the character shape sliced into seven vertical strips with the six intervening spaces either wide or narrow. Each of the numerical symbols and the four special symbols is coded with a combination of two wide and four narrow spaces.

micro 1. (symbol: μ) A prefix to a unit, indicating a submultiple of one millionth, 10^{-6}, of that unit, as in microsecond.
2. *Short for* microcomputer or microprocessor.

microcircuit An *integrated circuit, generally one performing a very complex function. An example is a *microprocessor comprised of arithmetic logic unit, control circuits, registers, program counter, and some memory, all within a single integrated circuit.

microcode A sequence of *microinstructions, i.e. the program code in a microprogrammed *control unit. *See* microprogramming.

microcomputer 1. A single LSI chip containing all the logic elements needed for a complete computer system, in contrast to a *microprocessor, which requires additional support chips.
2. A computer system that utilizes a *microprocessor as its central control and arithmetic element. More sophisticated microcomputers may utilize a number of microprocessors. The capability of the system is determined not only by the characteristics of the microprocessor employed but also by the amount of memory included, types of peripheral devices, quality of design, expandability, etc. Until recently microcomputers were rather limited in capability, being of interest primarily for games and hobbyists. They are now serious problem-solving tools. As microprocessors become still more powerful and peripheral devices become more cost-effective, microcomputers will continue to encroach on the domain of minicomputers and the distinction between them will blur, if not disappear.

microcontroller 1. An LSI microprocessor designed specifically for use in device control, communication control, or process-control applications. A typical microcontroller chip might have a relatively short word length, a rich set of bit-manipulation instructions, and lack certain arithmetic and string operations found on general-purpose microprocessors.
2. A microprocessor-based device or system designed for control applications.

Microdata A US manufacturer of minicomputers. The Microdata computers are notable in that they were some of the earliest machines that were microprogrammable and could (in theory) be modified by the user.

microinstruction One instruction in a microprogram that specifies some of the detailed control steps needed to perform an *instruction. *See* microprogramming.

microprocessor A semiconductor chip, or chip set, that implements the *central processor of a computer. Microprocessors consist of, at a minimum, an *arithmetic and logic unit and a *control unit. They are characterized by speed, word length (internal and external), *architecture, and *instruction set, which may be either fixed or microprogrammed. It is the combination of these characteristics and not just the cycle time that determines the performance of a microprocessor.
Most microprocessors have a fixed instruction set. Microprogrammed processors have a control store containing the microcode or firmware that defines the processor's instruction set; such processors may either be implemented on a single chip or constructed from *bit-slice elements.
The processor's architecture determines what register, stack, addressing, and I/O facilities are available, as well as defining the processor's primitive data types. The

data types, which are the fundamental entities that can be manipulated by the instruction set, typically include bit, nibble (4 bits), byte (8 bits), word (16 bits), and, on the latest microprocessors, double words (32 bits). Note that a word is usually defined as the number of bits in the processor's internal data bus rather than always being 16 bits. Instructions generally include arithmetic, logical, flow-of-control, and data movement (between stacks, registers, memory, and I/O ports). With some microprocessors, *coprocessors can be added to the system in order to extend the range of data types and instructions supported, e.g. floating-point numbers and the set of arithmetic operations defined on them.

The first microprocessor, the four-chip set Intel 4004, appeared in 1971 accompanied by considerable debate about its utility and marketability. It was the outcome of an idea proposed by Ted Hoff of Intel Corp. for a calculator that could implement a simple set of instructions in hardware but permitted complex sequences of them to be stored in a read-only memory (ROM). The result of his proposal was a design for a four-chip set consisting of a CPU, *ROM, *RAM, and a *shift-register chip, the chip design proceeding in 1970 under the direction of Federico Faggin, later the founder of Zilog, Inc. The Intel 4004 had a 4-bit data bus, could address 4.5K bytes of memory, and had 45 instructions. Its 8-bit counterpart, the Intel 8008, was introduced in 1974 and its improved derivative, the Zilog Z-80, in 1976. By this time there were over 50 microprocessors on the market.

Current (1983) microprocessors include the Zilog Z8000, Motorola 68000, Intel 8086, National 16000, as well as the older Texas Instruments 9900 and Digital Equipment Corporation LSI-11. All of these chips use a 16-bit-wide external data bus. Still higher performance microprocessors using 32-bit external data buses are now beginning to appear. Examples include the Intel iAPX-432, Bell Lab's Bellmac-32, and a chip set from Hewlett-Packard.

microprogramming A method of accomplishing the *control unit function by describing the steps in that function as a sequence of operations that are much more elementary than *instructions. In this method of designing and building a control unit, an additional memory, commonly called a *microprogram store*, contains a sequence of *microinstructions*. A number of microinstructions will be required to carry out an ordinary machine instruction, thus the microprogram store should be faster – have a shorter *cycle time – than the normal fast memory.

Microinstructions are usually classified as either *horizontal* or *vertical*. In a horizontal microinstruction most of the bit positions have a one-to-one correspondence with specific control functions. Horizontal microinstructions provide explicit control of functions at particular points within the CPU. For example, a particular bit in the microinstruction would call for a specific register to be cleared at a specific clock time. A vertical microinstruction generally contains highly coded fields describing elementary operations to be performed by certain elements of the control unit and *arithmetic and logic unit, and the sources and destinations of information passing between these units. In such a microinstruction, a field, say of three bits, might be decoded to indicate which of eight registers is to be one source of an operation to be performed in an ALU. Other fields would define the operation and any other necessary sources. Horizontal microinstructions will in general contain more bits, or be wider, hence the word horizontal. Vertical microinstructions, although containing fewer bits, require more decoding.

Some microprogrammed control units go through two levels of microprogramming. The first level consists of addresses of horizontal microinstructions. The second lev-

el is the used or useful subset of all horizontal microinstructions. This provides for more efficient use of a horizontal microprogram memory at the expense of two memory references per microinstruction execution. In this form of microprogramming the first memory has been called the microprogram store and the second memory has been called the *nanoprogram store*.
Almost all control units are now microprogrammed. This permits a more orderly and flexible approach to control unit design and permits changes in a control unit by changing the memory contents. Most microprogram stores are made with *ROM. These memories are generally faster and are potentially less prone to errors. Other microprogram stores, usually called *writeable control stores (WCS)*, are made with *RAM. These provide greater ease of change of control unit function; in some cases users are permitted or encouraged to "build" specialized instructions. Some microprogrammed control units have a mixture of ROM and RAM microprogram stores. These permit special microprograms to be loaded for maintenance and diagnostic purposes.
The only control units that are not now microprogrammed are those in some of the *supercomputers where it is found that hardwired control can provide faster operation than several microinstruction executions.

microprogram sequencer The part of a microprogrammed control unit that provides the equivalent of a *program counter at the microprogram level. *See* microprogramming.

microprogram store (control memory) The memory that contains a microprogram. It may be fixed (ROM) or alterable (writeable control store). *See* microprogramming.

microsequence A sequence of *microinstructions, i.e. a microprogram or a portion thereof. *See* microprogramming.

middleware Products that in some sense occupy a position between hardware and software. In particular where microcoded systems are used, the actual microcode is sometimes spoken of as middleware.

milli- (symbol: m) A prefix to a unit, indicating a submultiple of one thousandth, 10^{-3}, of that unit, as in millisecond.

MIMD processor *Short for* multiple instruction (stream), multiple data (stream) processor. *See* concurrency.

min *Abbrev. for* minimum. **1.** A *unary operation applied to a language L and defined in such a way that $min(L)$ is the set of strings in L that have no proper *prefixes that are also in L.
2. One of the basic actions performed on a set on whose elements a *total ordering $\leqslant$ is defined; when applied in the form $min(S)$ it produces the smallest element of the set S with respect to $\leqslant$.

minicomputer (mini) Originally, a computer that physically went within a single equipment cabinet, i.e. on the order of a few cubic feet. Compared with larger computers, minicomputers were and still are cheaper and slower, with smaller memory and usually shorter word length. The word minicomputer is no longer used very specifically. It predates the term *microcomputer and the boundary between these two classes of device is unclear.

minifloppy (minidiskette) *See* floppy disk.

minimal machine To any *finite-state automaton or *sequential machine there corresponds a unique (up to isomorphism) minimal machine that recognizes the same language (in the case of finite automata) or has the same response function (in the case of sequential machines). This is true for infinite as well as finite state-sets.
There are two ways in which a state q may be "redundant": it is either "inaccessible" in that there is no input string that takes the start-state to q, or else it is equivalent to another state q' in that the subsequent

behavior of the machine is the same whether it is in state q or q'. In a minimal machine all inaccessible states have been dropped and all equivalent states have been merged. There is a simple algorithm that will give the minimized version of any machine. *See also* Myhill equivalence, Nerode equivalence.

minimax procedure A procedure usually used in *approximation theory in order to find an approximating function, often a polynomial, that has the smallest maximum error on a given interval.

minimization 1. The process of manipulating a logical expression and thereby transforming it into a simpler but equivalent expression with the same truth table. In practice this commonly means reducing the number of *logic gates, number of gate inputs, or number of *logic levels in a *combinational circuit that realizes the logical expression. Minimization methods include use of *Karnaugh maps and algebraic manipulation (often computer-aided).
2. *See* optimization.
3. A process whereby a new *function can be obtained from an old function using the *minimization* or *μ-operator*, which is defined as follows. Let g be a function of $n+1$ variables taking nonnegative integer values and having the integers as its range. Then

$$\mu_y(g(x_1,x_2, \ldots ,x_n,y) = 0)$$

produces the least nonnegative integer y for which

$$g(x_1,x_2, \ldots ,x_n,y) = 0$$

for the fixed $x_1, x_2, \ldots x_n$. Of course, such a y may not exist. If y does exist a new *partial function f of n variables can be defined from g by applying the μ-operator:

$$f(x_1, \ldots ,x_n) = \mu_y(g(x_1, \ldots ,x_n,y) = 0)$$

Otherwise $f(x_1, \ldots x_n)$ is undefined.
To illustrate the use of minimization, let f be defined as follows:

$$f(x) = \mu_y(|2y - x| = 0)$$

Then $f(x) = x/2$ when x is even.

minimum-access code A form of programming for early computers with magnetic-drum storage. It was also known as *optimum programming*. In programs for this kind of machine, each instruction specifies the address of its successor, and it is desirable to place instructions in addresses so chosen that they are available under the reading heads when required. Since the execution time of instructions varies, it was necessary to work out how far the drum would rotate during execution of an instruction: this then determined the optimum position of its successor. Since this address might already be occupied, obtaining an optimal (or nearly optimal) distribution of instructions on the drum was extremely difficult.
The most widely used machine of this kind was the IBM 650; the success of the machine was largely due to the SOAP assembler, which produced near-optimal code positioning without any special effort on the part of the programmer.

minimum-cost spanning tree *See* spanning tree.

minterm (standard product term) A product (AND) of n Boolean variables, uncomplemented or complemented but not repeated, in a Boolean function of n variables. With n variables, 2^n different minterms are possible. The complement of any minterm is a *maxterm. *See also* standard sum of products.

mips *Abbrev. for* million instructions per second.

MIS *Abbrev. for* management information system.

MISD processor *Short for* multiple instruction (stream), single data (stream) processor. *See* concurrency.

mixed-base system *See* number system.

mixed logic A *digital design that includes both *positive and *negative logic.

mixed-radix system *See* number system.

mnemonic code A simple form of *assembly language: the name arises from the use of mnemonic abbreviations for operation codes, e.g. LDA for "load accumulator".

mode 1. A term used in many contexts concerning the operation and use of a computer system. For example: conversational mode refers to interactive computer use; interpretive mode refers to a way of executing a language; there are addressing modes in instruction descriptions.
2. *See* measures of location.

modem *Short for* modulator and demodulator. A device that can convert a digital bit stream into an analog signal suitable for transmission over some analog communication channel (*modulation), and can convert incoming analog signals back into digital signals (*demodulation). Modems are used to connect digital devices across analog transmission lines. Most modems are designed to match specific national or international standards so that data communication equipment from one manufacturer can talk to that of another.

modifier bits Usually a small subset of bits (i.e. bit locations) in an instruction word, used to provide some additional specification of the way in which the operation code and/or operand addresses are to be used or interpreted. *See* instruction format.

mod-n counter (modulo-n counter) *See* counter.

Modula A programming language that is a development of *Pascal. Modula was designed as a research exercise to demonstrate that operating systems can be written entirely in a high-level language. Its successor, Modula-II, is the sole programming language for the Lilith personal computer system.
Modula is used for *concurrent programming, and like *Ada it includes facilities for describing parallel computations together with their interaction and synchronization. Its name derives from the fact that a program is made up of *modules* – collections of procedures that can store variables and have a controlled interface with other modules.

modular arithmetic (residue arithmetic) Arithmetic based on the concept of the *congruence relation defined on the integers and used in computing to circumvent the problem of performing arithmetic on very large numbers.
Let $m_1, m_2, \ldots, m_k$ be integers, no two of which have a common factor greater than one. Given a large positive integer n it is possible to compute the remainders or residues $r_1, r_2, \ldots, r_k$ such that

$$n \equiv r_1 \pmod{m_1}$$
$$n \equiv r_2 \pmod{m_2}$$
$$\ldots$$
$$n \equiv r_k \pmod{m_k}$$

Provided n is less than

$$m_1 \times m_2 \times \ \ldots \times m_k$$

n can be represented by

$$(r_1, r_2, \ldots, r_k)$$

This can be regarded as an internal representation of n. Addition, subtraction, and multiplication of two large numbers then involves the addition, subtraction, and multiplication of corresponding pairs, e.g.

$$(r_1, \ldots, r_k) + (s_1, \ldots, s_k) = (r_1 + s_1, \ \ldots, r_k + s_k)$$

Determining the sign of an integer or comparing relative magnitudes are less straightforward.

modular counter *See* cascadable counter.

modular programming A style of programming in which the complete program is decomposed into a set of components, termed *modules*, each of which is of manageable size, has a well-defined purpose, and has a well-defined interface to the outside world. Since the only alternative – that of completely monolithic programs – is untenable, the point is not whether programs should be modular but rather what criteria should be employed for their decomposition into modules. This was raised by David Parnas, who proposed that one major criterion should be that of *information hiding. Prior to this, decomposition had typically been performed on an ad-hoc basis, or sometimes on the basis of "stages" of the overall processing to be carried out by the program, and only minor benefits had been gained. More recently there has been great emphasis on decomposition based on the use of *abstract data types; such a decomposition can remain consistent with the principles of information hiding.

modulation The process of varying one signal, called the *carrier*, according to the pattern provided by another signal. The carrier is usually an analog signal selected to match the characteristics of a particular transmission system. Modulation signals and techniques may be combined to produce composite signals carrying many independent channels of information (*see* multiplexing).

The primary types of modulation are as follows:

(a) *Amplitude modulation (AM)* – the strength or amplitude of the carrier signal is varied. This form of modulation is not often directly used in computer communication.

(b) *Frequency modulation (FM)* – the frequency of the carrier is varied. This technique is often used by *modems. *See also* frequency shift keying.

(c) *Phase modulation (PM)* – the phase of the carrier wave is varied. This technique is often used together with amplitude modulation in high-speed modems. *See also* phase shift keying.

(d) **Pulse code modulation (PCM)* – an analog signal is encoded as a series of pulses in a digital data stream. This technique is used by *codecs.

(e) *Spread-spectrum modulation (SSM)* – the carrier wave is frequency modulated by the analog or digital data signal in conjunction with a third or code signal. This technique is used by *packet radio networks for military applications.

The term shift keying, as in frequency shift keying, denotes specialized modulation techniques in which the modulating signal is digital rather than analog.

modulator A device that translates a digital signal into an analog signal: the modulator uses the digital signal as a pattern that determines the wave shape that the analog signal will have. A *demodulator performs the reverse transformation to recover the original digital signal. *See also* modulation, modem.

module *See* modular programming, module specification.

module invariant *See* invariant.

module specification A precise statement of the effects that a software module is required to achieve. It can be employed both by the implementer of the module, since it gives a definitive statement of the requirements that are imposed on the module, and by users of the module, since it gives a precise statement of what the module provides. A good module specification makes no commitment as to how the module's effects are achieved.

A variety of techniques have been developed for module specification. A *functional specification* identifies the operations that the module makes available and provides an individual specification for each operation, typically in the form of an input-output specification describing the mapping that the operation provides from a set of input values to a set of output values. In the typical case where a module has local data, a simple functional specification will need to refer to this local data when specifying each individual operation. This tends to obscure the specification, and also violates the principle that a specification should state what a module does but not how this is done.

The state machine model technique developed by Parnas treats the module as a *finite-state machine and distinguishes operations that can observe the state of the machine from those that can alter the state of the machine. The specification is given by indicating the effect of each operation that can change the state on the result of each operation than can observe the state. This technique therefore avoids the need to refer to the module's local data.

The same applies to the technique of *algebraic specification*, largely due to Guttag and Horning. With this technique, which is tailored to the specification of *abstract data type modules, the specification is given in two parts – a syntactic specification and a set of equations. The syntactic specification states the names, domains, and ranges of the operations provided by the module. Each equation specifies the net effect of some sequence of operations (or perhaps a single operation), and the complete set of equations must be sufficient to specify the effects of all operations under all conditions.

Because of the need for precision, module specifications are best given in some formal *specification language*. A variety of such languages have been developed, many drawing heavily on first-order *predicate calculus. Specific examples include the SPECIAL language of the HDM system, which adopts the finite-state machine approach, and the language used by the AFFIRM system, which employs algebraic specification techniques.

module testing (unit testing) *See* testing.

modulo *m* (mod *m*) *See* congruence relation, modular arithmetic.

modulo-*n* check *Another name for* checksum.

MOHLL *Acronym for* machine-oriented high-level language. A programming language with the control structures of the typical high-level language (if-then, while-do, etc.), whose data types and structures map onto the underlying machine architecture. Thus such a language will allow variables of type bit, byte, word, etc. These languages, also known simply as *machine-oriented languages*, provide an alternative to assembly language for systems programming at the hardware-interface level. Well-known examples are *Babbage and *PL/360. *Compare* POL.

monadic Having one operand.

monadic operation (unary operation) defined on a set S. A *function from the domain S into S itself. The *identity function is a monadic operation. Other examples are the operations of *negation in arithmetic or logic and of taking *complements in set theory or in *Boolean algebra. Although basically functions, monadic operations are frequently represented using a special notation, e.g. $\neg A$ or A' or $\bar{A}$. When the set S is finite, a *truth table can be used to define the meaning of the operation.

monic polynomial *See* polynomial.

monitor 1. A device that is used for checking the progress and operation of a system. A visual display and keyboard may be used in the roles of both a control console and a monitor. Visual display screens without keyboards may be used as remote monitors to allow the status of the system to be observed from remote locations.

2. *Another name for* supervisor, or even a complete operating system.

3. A programming construct devised by Hoare to allow controlled sharing of resources by otherwise asynchronous processes, and involving the provision of controlled passing of variables between the processes.

monoid A *semigroup that possesses an *identity element, e. If S is a semigroup on which there is defined a binary operation $\circ$, then

$$x \circ e = e \circ x = x$$

for all elements x in S. Monoids play an important role in various areas of computing, especially in the study of *formal languages and *parsing.

monomorphism A *homomorphism that, when viewed as a function, is an *injection.

monostable (one-shot) A digital circuit that has only one stable output state. It is constructed in such a way that it may be triggered by an externally generated signal to produce a single pulse. The time duration of the pulse is specified by the choice of external components, usually a capacitor. The requirements for retriggering are also under the control of the user.

Monte Carlo method A method for studying mathematical or physical problems by *stochastic processes. A probabilistic model is constructed, corresponding to the mathematical or physical problem, and random samples are taken within the model. By taking more samples, a more accurate estimate of the result is obtained. The method is commonly used to calculate two- or three-dimensional integrals.

Moore machine *See* sequential machine.

morphism *See* category.

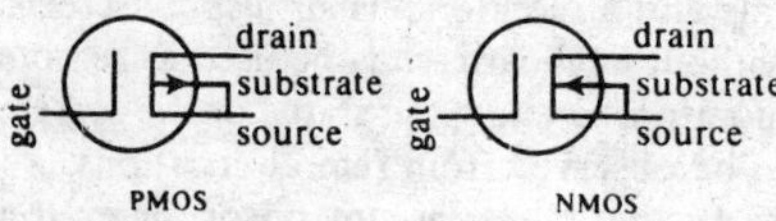

MOSFET circuit symbols

MOSFET (MOS transistor) *Acronym for* metal oxide semiconductor field-effect transistor. A type of *field-effect transistor that has an insulating layer of oxide, usually silicon dioxide, separating the gate from the drain-source conduction channel in the semiconductor. In an *NMOS* the channel is formed between n-type source and drain by negative charge carriers (i.e. electrons). In a *PMOS* the channel is formed between p-type source and drain by positive charge carriers (i.e. holes). The circuit symbols are shown in the diagram. MOSFETs require no gate input current, other than a pulse to charge or discharge their input capacitance. They can operate at higher switching speeds and lower currents than *bipolar transistors.

MOS integrated circuit *See* integrated circuit.

MOS transistor *Another name for* MOSFET.

most significant character The character in the most significant position in a number, word, signal, etc. Common examples are the *most significant digit (MSD)* and the *most significant bit (MSB)*, which contribute the greatest quantity to the value of a digital or binary number.

mother *Another name for* parent, rarely used.

mother board A *printed circuit that in general will carry all the major functional elements of a computer system, e.g. the CPU, memory, keyboard, etc., and may thus act as a stand-alone unit. The board's functions may be enhanced by the addition of modular elements, known as *daughter boards*, that perform specific activities such as memory extension or disk control and that communicate to the mother board via sockets onto a standard bus. *See also* backplane.

Motorola A US communications firm primarily devoted to automobile and other forms of mobile wireless communications and entertainment radios. Motorola entered the semiconductor field in the late 1950s and is now a major US manufacturer of VLSI design chips. The Motorola 6800 was an also-ran behind the Intel 8080. However, the Motorola 68000 is one of the high-performance 16-bit processors and is being widely used.

mouse *Informal* A device that is moved by hand to indicate a precise position on a digital *data tablet. The device has a transparent panel engraved with a fine cross and has several switches arranged

under the finger tips. The data tablet and associated processor can correlate the function indicated by the switches with the precise position of the cross intersection. The near-hemispherical shape and trailing cable suggest similarity to an animal mouse.
Variants are available that rely on wheels to be friction-driven from a table surface and generate a train of pulses proportional to the distance moved. Such devices can be used without a data tablet by observing the indicated position on the screen.

movement file *Another name for* transaction file.

moving-average methods *See* time series.

MPU *Abbrev. for* microprocessor unit, the primary control and arithmetic element of a microcomputer system. *See* microprocessor.

MSD, MSB *Abbrevs. for* most significant digit, most significant bit.

m-sequence A periodic sequence of symbols generated by a linear *feedback shift register whose feedback coefficients form a primitive *polynomial. A *q-ary register (with q prime) whose generating polynomial is of degree n will have period $q^n - 1$, provided that the initial state is nonzero, and its contents will proceed through all the nonzero q-ary n-tuples. The termwise modulo-q sum of two m-sequences is another m-sequence: the m-sequences (of a given generating polynomial), together with the zero sequence, form a *group.
The term is short for maximum-length sequence. It is so called because the generating shift register only has q^n states, and so such a register (with arbitrary feedback logic) cannot generate a sequence whose period exceeds q^n. But with linear logic the zero state must stand in a loop of its own (*see* Good–de Bruijn diagram) and so the period of a linear feedback register cannot exceed $q^n - 1$. This period, which can be achieved when and only when the polynomial is primitive, is therefore the maximum that can be achieved.
m-sequences have many useful properties. They are employed as *pseudorandom sequences, *error-correcting codes (as they stand, or shortened, or extended), and in determining the time response of linear channels (*see* convolution). *See also* simplex codes.

MSI *Abbrev. for* medium-scale integration, i.e. integration in the range of 100 to 10 000 transistors on a single chip. *See* integrated circuit.

MTBF *Abbrev. for* mean time between failures. A figure of merit for system reliability.

MTL *Abbrev. for* merged transistor logic. *See* I^2L.

MTS *Acronym for* Michigan terminal system. An operating system that was developed at the University of Michigan in the late 1960s, and is specifically intended to offer interactive computing to large numbers of users, each carrying out relatively straightforward tasks.

MTU *Abbrev. for* magnetic tape unit. *See* magnetic tape.

mu-law (μ-law) encoding *See* pulse code modulation.

multiaccess system A system allowing several users to make apparently simultaneous use of the computer. Each user has a terminal, typically a keyboard plus VDU display, and is connected via a multiplexer or front-end processor to the main system. As individual users type their commands, the system will multiprogram among the several users of the system, each command being processed as it is received. *See also* time sharing.

multiaddress *Short for* multiple-address.

Multibus *Trademark* A flexible bus structure designed by Intel Corp. and now used in many commercial microprocessor systems. It is capable of supporting both 8-

and 16-bit processors and 20-bit addresses, allowing up to one megabyte of physical address space. The bus supports master-slave and multi-master configurations, with *handshaking to permit devices of different speeds to communicate. Up to 16 masters can share Multibus resources. Multibus boards are approximately 12″ wide by 6.75″ high (about 30 by 17 cm). Electrical interfacing is via two adjacent card edge connectors, one of 43/86 pins and the other a 30/60 pin connector.

multicasting *See* broadcasting.

MULTICS *Trademark* A *multiaccess operating system designed in project *MAC to provide a MULTiplexed Information and Computing Service. The MULTICS system makes extensive use of "rings" of hardware protection of access to memory in order to achieve management of a very large virtual memory. Users operating on files move their entire file into memory in order to operate on it. The MULTICS system was implemented on specially commissioned hardware constructed by GEC and the entire project was later taken over by Honeywell Computer Systems.

multidimensional array An *array of dimension greater than one.

multidrop line A single communication line that connects multiple stations – terminals or computers. Typically, one station will use *polling to coordinate access to the line and prevent collisions (multiple stations transmitting at once). A control protocol such as *BISYNC or *SDLC is used. *See also* multipoint connection. *Compare* point-to-point line.

multilayer device An electronic device that is fabricated by a technique that involves the deposition of a number of layers of conductive track onto an insulating substrate, the individual layers being separated by a layer of insulating material. Interconnections are made to the various conductive layers by means of holes in the insulating material. The technique is used, for example, to produce compact multilayer circuit boards for hybrid integrated circuits and to fabricate multilayer CMOS integrated circuits.

multilevel memory A memory system containing at least two memory subsystems with different capacity and access-time attributes. *See* memory hierarchy.

multilevel security A mode of operation in which various levels of security are provided for users and processes concurrently. There is an implied *compartmentalization in this type of operation. Since some of the users have the lowest level of access rights, there is a further implication that a number of these users may or will deliberately attempt to violate security safeguards.

multilinked Having a *link to several distinct data structures. For example, a *sparse matrix is frequently held so that each element belongs to two separate linear lists corresponding to a row list and a column list. A multilinked structure is sometimes called a *multiple chain*.

multimedia mail *See* electronic mail.

multimode counter *See* counter.

multiple-address machine A computer whose *instruction format specifies (for at least some instructions) more than one operand address.

multiple assignment A form of *assignment statement in which the same value is given to two or more variables. For example, in Algol,

$$a := b := c := 0$$

sets a, b, c to zero.

multiple chain *See* multilinked.

multiple precision (multiprecision) *See* double precision.

multiple regression model *See* regression analysis.

multiple-valued logic (multivalued logic; nonbinary logic) Digital logic for use in *logic circuits that are designed to handle more than two levels (voltages, etc.). In q-valued logic there are q levels and each *memory element (flip-flops, etc.) can exist in q different states. The classification of logic circuits into *combinational and *sequential circuits applies to multiple-valued logic exactly as it does to binary logic.

There is much interest currently in *ternary logic* ($q = 3$) and, to a somewhat lesser extent, in *quaternary logic* ($q = 4$). Such logics promise reduced numbers of logic gates, memory elements, and – perhaps most significantly – interconnections. Ternary logic is simple to implement in *CMOS technology, and is likely to become important in the design of *VLSI circuits. Its increased logical richness is shown by the fact that there are 16 possible two-input binary gates, but 19 683 such ternary gates (ignoring degeneracies in both cases).

multiplexed bus A type of bus structure in which the number of signal lines comprising the bus is less than the number of bits of data, address, or control information being transferred between elements of the system. For example, a multiplexed address bus might use 8 signal lines to transmit 16 bits of address information. The information is transferred sequentially, i.e. time-domain multiplexed, with additional control lines being used for sequencing the transfer.

multiplexer **1.** A device that merges information from multiple input channels to a single output channel. *See* multiplexing.
2. A *combinational circuit that converts from 1 of m inputs to n outputs, where $m \leq 2^n$. *See also* data selector/multiplexer.

multiplexer channel *See* channel.

multiplexing The process of combining multiple messages simultaneously on the same physical or logical transmission medium. There are two main types: *time division multiplexing (TDM) and *frequency division multiplexing (FDM). In TDM a device is allocated specific time slots in which to use the transmission medium. FDM divides the transmission medium into channels of smaller *bandwidth to which the user has exclusive rights. FDM and TDM can be combined to provide devices with time slots of logical channels.

multiplier A specific part of an *arithmetic and logic unit that is used to perform the operation of multiplication. It is not always explicitly present in an ALU; for example, a multiplication can be accomplished by a sequence of additions and shifts under the direction of the *control unit.

multiply connected Denoting a node in a communication network that has links, circuits, or channels to more than one of its neighbors. If one link fails, the node may still communicate using the remaining links.

multipoint connection A connection of a number of terminals in parallel, analogous to a *multidrop connection. Sometimes the terms are used synonymously, although multidrop strictly implies that the connections are all served from a common connection point (node), whereas multipoint implies that connections are made through a series of (analog) bridging connections where some or all of the terminals are served by different common carrier offices interconnected by communication trunks.

multipoint line A data communication link that connects more than two parties – stations, nodes, etc. Individual stations are identified by unique addresses. A *data link control protocol is used to determine which station has the right to transmit on the line, and which station(s) should be receiving.

multiprecision (multiple precision) *See* double precision.

multiprocessing system (multiprocessor; multiunit processor) A system in which more than one processor may be active at any one time. While the processors are actively executing separate processes they run completely asynchronously. However it is essential to provide synchronization between the processors when they access critical system resources or critical regions of system code. A multiprocessing system is also a *multiprogramming system.

multiprocessor *Another name for* multiprocessing system.

multiprogramming system A system in which several individual programs may be active. Each active program implies a running process, so there may be several processes, but only one process runs at any one time on any particular processor. It is perfectly feasible to run a multiprogramming system containing only one processor; a *multiprocessing system, containing several processors, will also be a multiprogramming system.

multiset *Another name for* bag.

multitape Turing machine A *Turing machine that has a finite number of tapes, each tape having a tape head that can move independently. Such machines have the same computational power as single-tape Turing machines. Consider a multitape Turing machine T. If for no input word of length *n* does T scan more than L(*n*) cells on any tape then T is said to be an *L(n) tape-bounded Turing machine*. If for no input word of length *n* does T make more than T(*n*) moves before halting then T is said to be a *T(n) time-bounded Turing machine.*

multitasking The concurrent execution of a number of tasks, i.e. of a number of jobs or processes. *See* parallel processing.

multithreading A form of code that uses more than one process or processor, possibly of different types, and that may on occasions have more than one process or processor active at the same time. *See also* single threading, threading.

multiunit processor *Another name for* multiprocessing system.

multiuser system A system that is (apparently) serving more than one user simultaneously, i.e. a *multiprogramming or *multiprocessing system.

multivalued logic *See* multiple-valued logic.

multivariate analysis The study of multiple measurements on a sample. It embraces many techniques related to a range of different problems.

*Cluster analysis seeks to define homogeneous classes within the sample on the basis of the measured variables. *Discriminant analysis* is a technique for deciding whether an individual should be assigned to a particular predefined class on the basis of the measured variables. *Principle component analysis* and *factor analysis* aim to reduce the number of variables in the study to a few (say two or three) that express most of the variation within a sample.

Multivariate *probability distributions define probabilities for sets of random variables.

multivibrator An electronic oscillator that consists of two resistor-capacitor amplifier stages that interact in such a way that the amplifier's outputs are complementary and exhibit two stable mutually exclusive states, i.e. fully on and fully off. The circuit can be made to oscillate continuously, producing a square wave (astable mode), produce single pulses (monostable mode), or change state on application of an external trigger (bistable mode). *See also* flip-flop.

multiway search tree of degree *n*. A generalization of a *binary search tree to a tree of degree *n* where each node in the ordered tree has $m \leqslant n$ children and contains $(m-1)$ ordered key values, called subkeys. For some given search key, if the key is less than the first subkey then the first subtree (if it exists) is searched for the key; if the key lies between the ith and $(i+1)$th subkey, where

$$i = 1,2, \ldots, m-2$$

then the $(i+1)$th subtree (if it exists) is searched; if the key is greater than the last subkey then the mth subtree (if it exists) is searched. *See also* B-tree.

mu operator *See* minimization.

mutual exclusion A relationship between processes such that each has some part (the *critical section) that must not be executed while the critical section of another is being executed. There is thus exclusion of one process by another. In certain regions of an operating system, for example those dealing with the allocation of nonsharable resources, it is imperative to ensure that only one process is executing the relevant code at any one time. This can be guaranteed by the use of *semaphores: at entry to the critical region of code a semaphore is set; this inhibits entry to the code by any other process until the semaphore is reset as the last action by the process that first entered the critical region.

MUX *Short for* multiplexer.

MVS *Trademark, acronym for* multiprogramming with a variable number of processes. An operating system commonly used on large IBM or IBM-compatible processors.

Myhill equivalence An *equivalence relation arising in *formal language theory. If L is a language over Σ (*see* word) then its Myhill equivalence is the relation $=_M$ on Σ^* defined as follows:

$$u =_M u'$$

if, for all w_1,w_2 in Σ^*,

$$w_1uw_2 \in L \text{ iff } w_1u'w_2 \in L$$

Similarly (and more generally), if f is a function from Σ^* to any set, its Myhill equivalence is defined by:

$$u =_M u'$$

if, for all w_1,w_2 in Σ^*,

$$f(w_1uw_2) = f(w_1u'w_2)$$

See also Nerode equivalence.

An important fact is that L is *regular iff $=_M$ is of finite index (i.e. there are finitely many *equivalence classes). Indeed, L is regular iff it is a union of classes of any equivalence relation of finite index. In addition $=_M$ is a *congruence on Σ^*, i.e.

$$u =_M u' \text{ and } v =_M v' \text{ implies}$$
$$uv =_M u'v'$$

The equivalence classes therefore can be *concatenated consistently and form a *semigroup. This is in fact the semigroup of the *minimal machine for L (or f).

N

NAK *Short for* negative acknowledgment. *See* acknowledgment.

name A notation for indicating an entity in a program or system. (The word can also be used as a verb.) The kinds of entity that can be named depend on the context, and include variables, data objects, functions, types, and procedures (in programming languages), nodes, stations, and processes (in a data communication network), etc. The name denotes the entity, independently of its physical location or address. Names are used for long-term stability (e.g. when specifying a node in a computer program) or for their ease of use by humans (who recognize the name more readily than an address). Names are converted to addresses by a process of *name lookup*.

In many languages and systems, a name must be a simple identifier, usually a textual string. In more advanced languages, a name may be composed from several elementary components according to the rules of the language.

NAND gate An electronic *logic gate whose output is logic 0 (false) only when all (two or more) inputs are logic 1 (true), otherwise it is logic 1. It thus implements the logical *NAND operation and has the same *truth table. The diagram shows the usual circuit symbol of a two-input gate (which implies by the small circle that it is equivalent to an *AND gate whose output has been inverted) and the associated truth table.

A1, A2 → B

inputs	A1	0	0	1	1
	A2	0	1	0	1
output B		1	1	1	0

Two-input NAND gate, circuit symbol and truth table

P	F	F	T	T
Q	F	T	F	T
$P \mid Q$	T	T	T	F

Truth table for NAND operation

NAND operation The logical *connective combining two statements, truth values, or formulas *P* and *Q* in such a way that the outcome is true only if either *P* or *Q* or both is false (*see* table). The NAND operation may be represented by the *Sheffer stroke*, |, or by Δ. $P|Q$ is just the negation of $P \wedge Q$, hence the name (*see* AND operation).
The NAND operation is of particular significance to computer designers since any Boolean expression can be realized by an expression using only the NAND operation. In practical terms, circuits can be built using only *NAND gates.

nano- (symbol: n) A prefix to a unit, indicating a submultiple of one billionth, 10^{-9}, of that unit, as in nanosecond.

nanoprogram store *See* microprogramming.

narrowband *See* bandwidth.

natural binary-coded decimal (NBCD) *See* binary-coded decimal.

NBCD *Abbrev. for* natural binary-coded decimal. *See* binary-coded decimal.

NCP *Abbrev. for* network control protocol. A transport layer protocol that was designed for the *ARPANET and provides error-free sequenced *simplex connections across a subnet that is assumed to be perfectly reliable (the ARPANET *IMPs). Full *duplex communication is achieved with paired NCP connections.
NCP connections are established and terminated with a simple two-message exchange between the connected entities. Data *sequencing and *acknowledgment are provided by the underlying subnet. *Flow control is supported with an allocate and "give-back" strategy expressed as two quantities: number of messages and number of total bits. NCP also provides a connection "interrupt" signal and a reset function to purge the connection. In addition NCP provides a system-wide echo function plus error reports regarding erroneous or unexpected control messages and header parameters.
NCP is not suitable for unreliable subnets, and has no provision for carrying additional connection parameters such as military security level. The DARPA internetworking project developed the *TCP protocol to replace NCP.

NCR National Cash Register, a US manufacturer originally making only cash register equipment. It entered the computer business in the mid-1950s, and has produced various sizes of business systems that would now be classified as being in the minicomputer range.

NDRO *Abbrev. for* nondestructive readout.

negation 1. In arithmetic, the operation of changing the sign of a nonzero arithmetic quantity; the negation of zero is zero. Negation is usually denoted by the minus sign.
2. In logic, the application of the *NOT operation on a statement, truth value, or formula.

negative acknowledgment (NAK) *See* acknowledgment. *See also* backward error correction.

negative logic 1. A logic system in which the normal meanings of the binary signal levels are interchanged, e.g. high voltage equals logic 0, low voltage equals logic 1.
2. A logic system in which all the Boolean variables and Boolean functions behave as though they were complements.
Compare positive logic.

negator *Another name for* inverter.

negentropy *See* entropy.

Nerode equivalence An *equivalence relation, $=_N$, arising in *formal language theory. It is defined analogously to the *Myhill equivalence by the weaker properties:
for a language L over Σ,
$$u =_N u'$$
if, for all w in Σ^*,
$$uw \in L \text{ iff } u'w \in L$$
for a function f,
$$u =_N u'$$
if, for all w in Σ^*,
$$f(uw) = f(u'w)$$
Although coarser than the Myhill equivalence, it is finite only if the latter is. Unlike the latter, it gives only a right congruence:
$$u =_N u' \text{ implies } uv =_N u'v$$
and thus does not give rise to a *semigroup. The number of *equivalence classes is the number of states in the *minimal machine for L.

nested blocks, nested scopes *See* block-structured languages.

nesting A feature of language design in which constructs can be embedded within instances of themselves, e.g. nested loops:

```
while b1 do
begin
      while b2 do
      begin
          ...
      end;
end;
```

Nesting of blocks in Algol-like languages provides an elegant, though not entirely practicable, control over the scope of *identifiers, since identifiers are local to the innermost level of nesting at which they are declared. *See also* block-structured languages.

nesting store *Another name for* stack, implemented in hardware.

network 1. In communications, a rather loosely defined term applied to a system that consists of terminals, nodes, and interconnection media that can include lines or trunks, satellites, microwave, medium- and long-wave radio, etc. In general, a network is a collection of resources used to establish and switch communication paths between its terminals. *See also* local area network, wide area network, network architecture, packet switching, message switching.
2. In electronic circuitry, an interconnection of various electrical elements. A *passive network* contains no active (amplifying or switching) three-terminal elements such as transistors; a *linear network* is a passive network that contains no nonlinear elements such as diodes.
3. In mathematics, a *connected directed *graph that contains no cycles. Interconnections involving objects such as telephones, logic gates, or computers could be represented using a connected but not necessarily directed graph.

network architecture The design and implementation of a communication network with respect to its communication disciplines and its interconnection topology. Network architecture deals explicitly with the encoding of information, its transmission, *error control and *flow control, techniques for *addressing subscribers on the network, analysis of network performance under abnormal or degraded conditions (such as missing communication lines or improperly functioning switching nodes), etc. Examples of generalized network architectures are OSI (*open systems interconnection, an architecture propounded by the ISO) and SNA (systems network architecture, proposed and supported by IBM).

Interconnection topology is also considered a part of network architecture. There are three generic forms of topology: *star*, *ring*, and *bus*. Star topology consists of a single hub node with various terminal nodes connected to the hub; terminal nodes do not interconnect directly. By treating one terminal node as the hub of another star, a *tree-like* topology is obtained. In ring topology all nodes are on a ring and communication is generally in one direction around the ring; some ring architectures use two rings, with communication in opposite directions. Various techniques (including time division multiplexing, token passing, and ring stretching) are used to control who is allowed to transmit onto the ring. Bus topology is noncyclic, with all nodes connected; traffic consequently travels in both directions, and some kind of arbitration is needed to determine which terminal can use the bus at any one time. *Ethernet is an example. Hybrids that mix star and ring topologies have been employed.

A special area of network architecture is involved with the necessary disciplines required of some of the newer network architectures (*see* ring network, token ring, CSMA/CD).

network database system A *database management system based on the concept of ownership: member records are "owned" by owner records, and each member record type may have a number of owner record types. *Compare* hierarchical network system.

network delay In a *packet switching network, generally the transit time through a network measured from the time of entry of the last bit of a packet on an input node to the delivery of the first bit of the same packet at the destination node. Although network delay is an important measure of relative performance of one packet network versus another, it is important to realize that the delay as defined does not include the delays associated with necessary buffers at the input/output nodes. For long packets that are input and output at relatively low data rates, the buffer delay often exceeds the network delay by a substantial amount.

network front end An auxiliary processor or system attached to another computer specifically to connect that computer to a network. The goals of a network front end are to improve overall performance by doing network-related tasks that would be expensive on the main computer, and to convert the standard interfaces and protocols used by the external network into a form better suited to the local system's internal operation (and vice versa). A network front end may also be used to multiplex a single network interface among several computers, in which case the network front end may be considered a *gateway or bridge.

network interconnection *See* internetworking.

network layer of protocol function. *See* seven-layer reference model. *See also* X.25.

network topology *See* network architecture.

network virtual terminal (NVT) *See* TELNET. *See also* virtual terminal.

Newton's method An iterative technique for solving one or more *nonlinear equations. For the single equation

$$f(x) = 0$$

the iteration is

$$x_{n+1} = x_n - f(x_n)/f'(x_n),$$
$$n = 0,1,2, \ldots$$

where x_0 is an approximation to the solution. For the system

$$f(x) = \mathbf{0},$$
$$\boldsymbol{f} = (f_1, f_2, \ldots, f_n)^T,$$
$$\boldsymbol{x} = (x_1, x_2, \ldots, x_n)^T,$$

the iteration takes the mathematical form

$$\boldsymbol{x}_{n+1} = \boldsymbol{x}_n - J(\boldsymbol{x}_n)^{-1} f(\boldsymbol{x}_n),$$
$$n = 0,1,2, \ldots$$

where $J(x)$ is the $n \times n$ matrix whose i,jth element is

$$\partial f_i(x)/\partial x_j$$

In practice each iteration is carried out by solving a system of linear equations. Subject to appropriate conditions the iteration converges quadratically (ultimately an approximate squaring of the error occurs). The disadvantage of the method is that a constant recalculation of J may be too time-consuming and so the method is most often used in a modified form, e.g. with approximate derivatives. Since Newton's method is derived by a linearization of $f(x)$, it is capable of generalization to other kinds of nonlinear problems, e.g. boundary-value problems (*see* ordinary differential equations).

NIFTP *Abbrev. for* network independent file transfer protocol. An *internetworking protocol developed in the UK to transfer files across multiple networks. *See* file transfer.

nine's complement *See* radix-minus-one complement.

(n, k) code *See* block code.

NMOS A type of *MOSFET.

no-address instruction An instruction that does not require the designation of an operand address, e.g. "complement the accumulator". *See* implied addressing.

node 1. A substructure of a hierarchical data structure that cannot be further decomposed, e.g. a vertex in a *graph or *tree.

2. A computer used at the connection points (nodes) of a communication network for the purpose of monitoring and/or switching communications. The node may be separate from the *host computer(s). Nodes can also be called *stations*, and in many X.25 networks the switching nodes are known as *exchanges*.

noise Any signal that occurs in an electronic or communication system and is considered extraneous to the desired signal being propagated. Noise can be introduced, for example, by external disturbances and may be deleterious in a given system since it can produce spurious signals, i.e. errors.

The *noise immunity* is a measure of the magnitude of external disturbances that a digital circuit can tolerate without producing errors. Logic values are represented electronically by two different voltage levels. Any noise introduced into logic circuitry by external disturbances is added (or subtracted) from the real digital logic signal. The *noise margin* is the maximum noise voltage that can be added or subtracted from the logic signal before a threshold voltage for a logic state is passed. *See also* impulse noise, white noise, Gaussian noise.

noise immunity *See* noise.

noiseless coding In communication theory, the use of a code to improve the efficiency of a *communication system in which *noise is absent or negligible. Noiseless coding is thus generally the same as *source coding. Note that the process of coding is itself usually noiseless: there is no need for encoders or decoders to introduce noise, so the term noiseless coding is not used to imply the absence of such noise.

noise margin *See* noise.

noise sequence *See* pseudonoise sequence.

noise source *See* Shannon's model.

noisy mode A method of operation that is sometimes used when normalizing a floating-point number. If the mantissa is shifted *m* bits to the left during normalization, then in noisy mode the digits generated to fill the *m* rightmost bits in the normalized mantissa are not necessarily zeros.

NOMAD A commercial *database management system by NCSS that supports both hierarchies and relations.

nonbinary logic *Another name for* multiple-valued logic.

nondestructive read-out (NDRO) The process of reading a memory device in such a manner that the contents of the memory are not altered. The reading of most integrated-circuit devices is nondestructive.
In some types of computer memory, especially magnetic cores, *destructive read-out (DRO)* occurs, i.e. whenever a memory location has a read operation, the contents of the location are destroyed. Therefore each reading must be immediately followed by a rewriting of the contents of the location in order to preserve them. These operations are not generally under the control of the programmer.

nondeterminism A mode of computation in which, at certain points, there is a choice of ways to proceed: the computation may be thought of as choosing arbitrarily between them, or as splitting into separate copies and pursuing all choices simultaneously. The precise form of nondeterminism depends on the particular computational formalism.
For example, a nondeterministic *Turing machine will have a choice of moves to make for a given internal state and tape symbol being read. After a choice has been made, other choice-points will be encountered. There is therefore a *tree of possible different overall computations, with the *nonterminal nodes representing choice-points. If, for example, the algorithm performs some kind of "search", then the search succeeds if at least one sequence of choices (path through the tree) is successful. Many algorithms are expressed most conveniently in this way; nondeterminism also arises naturally in connection with *concurrency.
Nondeterminism is important in the field of *complexity: it is believed that a nondeterministic Turing machine is capable of performing in "reasonable time" computations that could not be so performed by any deterministic Turing machine.

nonequivalence gate *Another name for* exclusive-OR gate.

nonequivalence operation *Another name for* exclusive-OR operation.

nonerasable programmable device *See* programmable device.

nonhierarchical cluster analysis *See* cluster analysis.

nonimpact printer A printer in which the image is formed without use of mechanical impact. *Ink jet, *thermal, and *electrographic printers are examples of this type.

nonlinear equations In general, a problem that requires the determination of values of the unknowns $x_1, x_2, \ldots, x_n$ for which

$$f_i(x_1,x_2, \ldots ,x_n) = 0,$$
$$i = 1,2, \ldots ,n$$

where $f_1, f_2, \ldots, f_n$ are given algebraic functions of n variables, i.e. they do not involve derivatives or integrals. This in both theory and practice is a very difficult problem. Such systems of equations arise in many areas, e.g. in numerical methods for nonlinear *ordinary and *partial differential equations. When $n = 1$ the single equation can be solved by a variety of effective techniques (all involving *iteration); the case of *polynomial equations can give rise to complex solutions. For systems of equations, *Newton's method and principally its many variants are widely used. For cases of extreme difficulty where, for example, only poor starting approximations are available, methods based on the idea of *continuation can be of value.

nonlinear regression model *See* regression analysis.

nonmemory reference instruction An instruction that can be carried out without having to obtain an operand from, or return a result to, memory. Immediate and branch instructions are examples.

nonparametric techniques *Statistical methods that make no assumptions about the precise form of the *frequency distribution from which the data are sampled. They are mainly of use for hypothesis testing using the information in the rank order within each sample. For example, the *Mann Whitney U-test* may be used to test whether two samples are drawn from the same distribution, and the *rank correlation coefficient* may be used to test whether two variables are independent.
These methods can be contrasted with *parametric techniques*, which require specific models with *parameters to be estimated.

nonpreemptive allocation An allocation that does not preempt a resource from a process to which it is already allocated. *Compare* preemptive allocation.

nonprocedural language *Another name for* declarative language.

nonreturn to zero *See* NRZ, tape format.

nonsingular matrix A square matrix, A, of numbers whose *determinant is nonzero. A is nonsingular if and only if it is invertible (*see* inverse matrix).

nonterminal (nonterminal symbol) *See* grammar.

nonterminal node (interior node) of a tree. Any node that is not a terminal node (i.e. a leaf node) and hence has one or more children.

nonvolatile memory A type of memory whose contents are not lost when power to the memory is removed. *ROM, *PROM, and *core store are examples. *Compare* volatile memory.

non von Neumann architecture Any computer architecture in which the underlying model of computation is radically different from the classical von Neumann model (*see* von Neumann machine). A non von Neumann machine may thus be without the concept of sequential flow of control (i.e. without any register corresponding to a "program counter" that indicates the current point that has been reached in execution of a program) and/or without the concept of a variable (i.e. without "named" storage locations in which a value may be stored and subsequently referenced or changed).
Examples of non von Neumann machines are the *dataflow machines and the *reduction machines. In both of these cases there is a high degree of parallelism, and instead of variables there are immutable bindings between names and constant values.
Note that the term non von Neumann is usually reserved for machines that represent a radical departure from the von Neumann model, and is therefore not normally applied to multiprocessor or multicomputer architectures, which effectively offer a set of cooperating von Neumann machines.

no-op instruction (pass instruction; do-nothing instruction) An instruction that causes no action to take place in the computer except for consumption of time and instruction storage space. There are several uses for this instruction including time adjustment of a program, filling out program space in a system where instruction boundaries do not always coincide with word boundaries, and replacement of unwanted instructions without having to recompute all other program addresses.

inputs				
A1	0	0	1	1
A2	0	1	0	1
output B	1	0	0	0

Two-input NOR gate, circuit symbol and truth table

P	F	F	T	T
Q	F	T	F	T
$P \downarrow Q$	T	F	F	F

Truth table for NOR operation

NOR gate An electronic *logic gate whose output is logic 1 (true) only when all (two or more) inputs are logic 0 (false), otherwise it is logic 0. It thus implements the logical *NOR operation and has the same truth table. The diagram shows the usual circuit symbol of a two-input gate (which implies by the small circle that it is an inclusive *OR gate whose output has been inverted) and the associated truth table. *See also* exclusive-NOR gate.

norm *See* approximation theory.

normal distribution (Gaussian distribution) An important *probability distribution for data in the form of continuous measurements. The frequency function is given by

$$(2\pi\sigma^2)^{-1/2}\exp[-\tfrac{1}{2}(x-\mu)^2/\sigma^2]$$

The distribution is symmetric about the mean μ, and its variance is σ^2. The range of x is infinite $(-\infty, \infty)$. Many sampling distributions tend to the normal form as the sample size tends to infinity.

normal form A term applied to relations in a *relational database. A relation is said to be in normal form if it satisfies certain defined constraints. Codd's original exposition of the relational model of data defined three normal forms, but two further normal forms have since been defined. The importance of normal forms is that certain *relational operators require the data to be in a particular normal form in order to guarantee successful execution.

normalize *See* floating-point notation. *See also* orthonormal basis, orthogonal functions.

normal subgroup *See* coset.

NOR operation The logical *connective combining two statements, truth values, or formulas P and Q in such a way that the result is true only if both P and Q are false (*see* table). The NOR operation is the dual of the *NAND operation (*see* duality). It may be represented by the *Pierce arrow*, $\downarrow$, or by ∇. $P \downarrow Q$ is just the negation of $P \vee Q$, hence the name (*see* OR operation).
The NOR operation is of particular significance to computer designers since any Boolean expression can be expressed using the NOR operation alone. In practical terms, circuits can be built using only *NOR gates.

notch filter *See* band-stop filter.

not-equivalence gate *Another name for* exclusive-OR gate.

NOT operation A logical *connective with just one operand. When applied to a statement, truth value, or formula P, the outcome is false if P is true, and vice versa, i.e. it produces a negation. It can be denoted in a variety of ways, e.g.

not P, $\neg P$, $\sim P$, P', $\bar{P}$

Nova *See* Data General.

NP, NP-complete, NP-hard *See* P=NP question.

NRZ *Abbrev. for* nonreturn to zero. A way of encoding binary signals that aims to achieve the highest possible data transfer rate for a given signal frequency. The name is derived from the principle of operation, i.e. the signal line does not return to zero – make any transition – between a succession of 1 bits. The method was first used for communications signaling in which there was always a 1 bit at the start of a character and thus there was a predictable and acceptable short interval over which the sending and receiving devices had to maintain synchronism independently.

Many variants of the basic principle have been derived to overcome synchronization problems that occur at high speeds and long bit streams, one of which is *NRZI, nonreturn to zero inverted.* (This should not be confused with NRZ1, nonreturn to zero one (or mark) – *see* tape format.) NRZI is a form of encoding used for magnetic recording in which a 1 bit is always indicated by a magnetic flux transition, regardless of direction. Zeros do not give rise to transitions and thus a long sequence of zeros could exceed the capability to maintain synchronism. For this reason it cannot be used in single bit stream recording such as that used on a disk, but can be used in multitrack systems such as magnetic tape provided that choice of parity ensures that there is at least one transition per character and the skew between tracks is small compared to the pitch of transitions. *See also* disk format, tape format.

NRZI 1. (more correctly **NRZ1**) *Abbrev. for* nonreturn to zero one, or mark. *See* tape format.
2. *Abbrev. for* nonreturn to zero inverted. *See* NRZ.

NSPACE, NTIME *See* complexity classes.

***n*-tuple** *See* ordered pair, Cartesian product.

n-type semiconductor *See* semiconductor.

nucleus *See* kernel.

null character A special character in a *character set, denoting nothing, and usually (as in ASCII and EBCDIC) represented by zero.

nullity of a graph. *See* connected graph.

null link *See* linked list.

null list (empty list) *See* list.

null matrix (zero matrix) A square matrix, all the elements of which are zeros.

null set *Another name for* empty set.

null string *Another name for* empty string.

number cruncher *Informal name for* supercomputer.

number system Although early number systems were not positional, all of the number systems most commonly used today are *positional systems*: the value of a number in such a system is determined not just by the digits in the number but also by the position in the number of each of the digits. If a positional system has a *fixed radix* (or *fixed base*) R then each digit a_i in any number

$$a_n a_{n-1} \ldots a_0$$

is an integer in the range 0 to $(R - 1)$ and the number is interpreted as

$$a_n R^n + a_{n-1} R^{n-1} + \ldots + a_1 R^1 + a_0 R^0$$

Since this is a polynomial in R, such numbers are sometimes called *polynomial numbers*. The decimal and binary systems are both fixed-radix systems, with a radix of 10 and 2, respectively.

Fractional values can also be represented in a fixed-radix system. Thus,

$$.a_1 a_2 \ldots a_n$$

is interpreted as

$$a_1 R^{-1} + a_2 R^{-2} + \ldots + a_n R^{-n}$$

In a *mixed-radix* (or *mixed-base*) *system*, the digit a_i in any number

$$a_n a_{n-1} \ldots a_0$$

lies in the range 0 to R_i, where R_i is not the same for every *i*. The number is then interpreted as

$$(\ldots ((a_n R_{n-1}) + a_{n-1}) R_{n-2} + \ldots + a_1) R_0 + a_0$$

For example, 122 days 17 hours 35 minutes 22 seconds is equal to

$$(((((1\times 10) + 2)10 + 2)24 + 17)60 + 35)60 + 22 \quad \text{seconds}$$

numerical analysis A branch of mathematics dealing with the numerical solution of problems formulated and studied in other branches of mathematics. Numerical analysis now plays an important part in engineering and in the quantitative parts of pure and applied science.
The tasks of numerical analysis include the development of appropriate *numerical methods together with the provision of a suitable *error analysis. On the practical side it involves the writing of efficient and reliable computer subroutines for a wide variety of problems.

numerical code A code whose target alphabet contains only digits and/or strings of digits, e.g. a binary code.

numerical control The application of digital computer techniques to the control of a manufacturing process. The concept has been applied primarily to various kinds of machine tools such as milling machines, metal-cutting lathes, welding machines, and some specialized machines. The machines are controlled by numerical specification of parameters such as position, where the numbers are usually calculated beforehand by a computer and recorded on a medium such as punched paper tape. In the computer field, standard numerically controlled machines are used for drilling holes in printed circuit boards and for inserting components into a printed circuit board. *See also* computer-aided manufacturing.

numerical differentiation The problem of approximating the derivative of a function using values of the function. An obvious approach is to use the derivative of an *interpolation polynomial. Such estimates involve differences of function values, and loss of potential accuracy occurs, due to *cancellation, if the data values are at points too close together.

numerical integration (quadrature) The problem of approximating definite integrals using values of the integrand. The range of integration is divided into subintervals and a quadrature rule, typically derived by integrating an *interpolation polynomial, is used on each interval. An example is the *trapezium rule*:

$$\int_{x_i}^{x_{i+1}} f(x)\,\mathrm{d}x \simeq \tfrac{1}{2}h(f(x_i)+f(x_{i+1})),$$

$$h = x_{i+1} - x_i$$

The overall accuracy of the quadrature rule can be checked by refining the subdivision and comparing the results obtained. *Adaptive quadrature* routines use finer subdivisions in the sections of the range where $f(x)$ changes more rapidly. Some quadrature rules give as a byproduct an estimate of the error.

numerical linear algebra A subject that deals with two important problems. The first is solving the *linear algebraic equations

$$A\boldsymbol{x} = \boldsymbol{b}$$

given the square matrix A and the column vector $\boldsymbol{b}$. The majority of computational scientific problems involve or can be approximated to the solution of linear systems. A related problem is the solution of overdetermined systems where A has more rows than columns. Here there are good theoretical reasons for computing $\boldsymbol{x}$ to minimize the norm

$$\|A\boldsymbol{x} - \boldsymbol{b}\|_2$$

(*see* approximation theory).
The second problem is to determine the eigenvalues λ_k and the eigenvectors $\boldsymbol{x}_k$ such that

$$A\boldsymbol{x}_k = \lambda_k\boldsymbol{x}_k$$

(*see* eigenvalue problems). The methods used here have mainly been developed since about 1960.
The accuracy of solutions to these problems is easily influenced by small de-

tails of implementation and it is very desirable to make use of the high-quality software that is available.

numerical methods Methods designed for the constructive solution of mathematical problems requiring particular numerical results, usually on a computer. A numerical method is a complete and unambiguous set of procedures for the solution of a problem, together with computable error estimates (*see* error analysis). The study and implementation of such methods is the province of *numerical analysis.

numerical stability *See* stability.

Nyquist interval The time interval between successive samples of a continuous-time band-limited signal that is being sampled at the Nyquist rate. *See* Nyquist's criterion.

Nyquist rate *See* Nyquist's criterion.

Nyquist sampling The process of *sampling a continuous-time band-limited channel at, or possibly more frequently than, the Nyquist rate. *See* Nyquist's criterion.

Nyquist's criterion The statement that when a continuous-time *band-limited channel is to be sampled, the *sampling process may or may not cause information to be lost according to whether the sampling rate, ν, is less than, greater than, or equal to twice the *bandwidth, W.

If $\nu = 2W$, sampling is said to occur at the *Nyquist rate*.

If $\nu < 2W$, *sub-Nyquist sampling* is said to take place, and some information will be lost; this may be quite acceptable in certain cases.

If $\nu > 2W$, *super-Nyquist sampling* occurs; it cannot cause any more information to be extracted than sampling at the Nyquist rate.

Super-Nyquist sampling (at somewhat over the Nyquist rate) is, however, commonly employed to allow a margin of safety since there may be some doubt about the actual value of the bandwidth. There is no harm in it, if it is convenient, but the samples taken at a super-Nyquist rate will not be independent of one another.

See also discrete and continuous systems.

O

object architecture (object-oriented architecture) An architecture in which everything (processes, files, I/O operations, etc.) is represented as an *object*. Objects are *data structures in memory that may be manipulated by the total system (hardware and software); they provide a high-level description that allows for a high-level user interface. Objects have descriptors that are referred to variously as *names*, *pointers*, and *labels*. These descriptors also provide information as to the type of object and a description of capabilities that apply to the particular object. Object architecture systems can thus be considered as an extension or generalization of *capability architecture systems, and have the same ability to provide a basis for protection and computer security.

Examples of object architecture systems are the IBM System 38, the Carnegie-Mellon experimental C.mmp/Hydra, and the Intel iAPX 432.

object code The output of a *compiler.

object language The language in which the output of a *compiler or *assembler is expressed.

object-oriented architecture *Another name for* object architecture.

object-oriented language A programming language for an object-oriented programming system. In such a system the concept of procedure and data, which is embodied in conventional programming systems, is replaced by the concepts of *objects* and *messages*: an object is a package of information and a description of its manipulation, and a message is a specification of one of an object's manipulations. Unlike a procedure, which describes how manipulations should be carried out, a message merely specifies what the sender wants done, and the receiver determines exactly what will happen. The most fully developed object-oriented language is Smalltalk.

object program Like object code, the output of a *compiler. The object program is the translation into *object language of the *source program.

OCR *Abbrev. for* optical character recognition. A process in which a machine scans, recognizes, and encodes information printed or typed in alphanumeric characters. The first devices, marketed around 1955, could only recognize a limited repertoire of characters that had to be produced in a font that was optimized for machine recognition but was still recognizable by people. By the mid-1970s OCR A font and OCR B font were the dominant fonts and were close to a normal letter-press appearance. By 1982 there were at least six types of machine available that could sense and encode a typewritten or printed page provided that it was in one of the seven popular typewriter fonts. In some instances printed information intended for *MICR (magnetic ink character recognition) is read by optical recognition techniques, as with some check readers associated with bank teller terminals.

octal notation The representation of numbers in the positional number system with radix 8. The octal digits are denoted by 0–7. Any octal number may be simply converted into its binary equivalent, and any binary number into its shorter octal equivalent.

octet Eight contiguous bits; an eight bit byte. The term is used instead of byte to prevent confusion in cases where the term has preexisting hardware associations, as in machines with 7 bit bytes, 9 bit bytes, 12 bit bytes.

odd-even check *Another name for* parity check.

odd parity A property that holds when a group of binary values contains an odd number of 1s. *See* parity.

office automation The application of computers to office tasks. This may involve the use of *electronic filing systems, *word processing systems, *computer graphics systems, and *electronic mail or *teleconferencing systems.

off-line Not on-line. A peripheral device that is accessible to the system or to system users is said to be on-line. If the device is not accessible it is off-line. The device may still be physically connected, but the system supervisor informed that the device is not to be used.

offspring *Another name for* child.

OMR *Abbrev. for* optical mark reading. *See* mark reading.

one-address instruction *See* instruction format.

one-level store The original term used for what is now called *virtual memory. The term arose from the fact that although the memory in use was found on units at different levels within the *memory hierarchy, the user saw all his memory at a single level of accessibility.

one-pass program A program that requires only one linear forward scan of its input data.

one-plus-one address instruction *See* instruction format.

one's complement *See* radix-minus-one complement.

one-shot *Another name for* monostable.

one-to-one function *Another name for* injection.

one-to-one onto function *Another name for* bijection.

one-way linked list *Another name for* singly linked list.

on-line 1. Connected to the system and usable. *See also* off-line.
2. In automaton theory, describing an automaton that, having read the first *k* symbols of the input string, has already produced the first *k* symbols of the output string. The concept of being on-line is analogous to the initial subwords-preserving property of *gsm-mappings.

O notation, o notation *See* order.

on-the-fly error recovery *See* error management, error rate.

onto function *Another name for* surjection.

op-amp *Short for* operational amplifier.

op code *Short for* operation code.

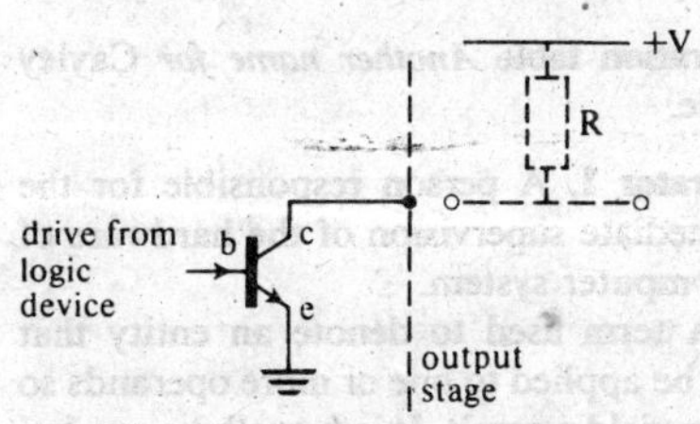

Open-collector device

open-collector device A particular implementation of an electronic logic device in which the output of the device is formed by the open-circuit collector termination of the output transistor (*see* diagram). The device's output is thus active-low and a *pull-up resistor is required to establish the active-high state. These devices are used to drive loads with high supply voltages or to implement *wired-logic buses.

open shop A method of running a computing facility such that the design, development, writing, and testing of computer programs is carried out by the problem originator and not by specialist computing staff. *Open shop operation* is the operation of a computing system by the writer or user of a program and not by specialist computer operators. *Compare* closed shop.

open subroutine *Obsolete name for* in-line *subroutine, usually provided by a *macro.

open system interconnection (OSI) A concept whereby communication-oriented computer equipment with different protocols can be interconnected by means of a data network. The principal methods being developed are those of the major computer vendors (especially IBM) and of the International Standards Organization (ISO). The term open system interconnection is specifically related to the efforts of the ISO and its *seven-layer reference model.

operand 1. In general, a quantity or function upon which a mathematical or logical operation is performed.
2. The information (number, data, quantity) that is found at an address specified in an *instruction word, or is produced as the result of an instruction and whose destination is specified in the instruction word. *See also* instruction format.

operating system (OS) The set of software products that jointly controls the system resources and the processes using these resources on a computer system.

operation A *function from some domain S^m into S itself, where S is some set specific to the function. Such a function is usually referred to as an m-ary or m-adic operation over S; m being some positive integer. The most common operations are the *binary (or dyadic) operations that map $S \times S$ into S and the *unary (or monadic) operations that map S into S. *See* Cartesian product. *See also* logic operation, operations on sets.

operational amplifier (op-amp) A very high gain voltage amplifier having a differential input, i.e. its output voltage is proportional to (and very much greater than) the voltage difference between its two inputs. Operational amplifiers usually have feedback circuits of resistors and/or capacitors connected between their output and inputs. These circuits make op-amps operate as voltage amplifiers with a gain precisely defined by the values of the resistors, or else enable them to perform mathematical operations, such as integration, or signal-conditioning functions, such as filtering.

operational semantics An approach to the *semantics of programming languages that uses the concept of an "abstract machine" that has a state and some primitive instructions. The machine is defined by specifying how the components of the state are changed by each of the instructions. The abstract machine is not meant to be a model of any realistic machine; it is meant to be simple enough so that the language can be unambiguously defined. No misunderstanding should arise with respect to its set of primitive instructions, or order code (elsewhere called *operation code). The semantic description of the programming language specifies a translation into this code. Unlike *denotational semantics there is no guarantee that the meaning of a whole program will be a function of the meanings of its parts. Examples of this approach include the Vienna Definition method used to define PL/I.

operation code (op code; order code) 1. The portion of the *instruction word that specifies the operation to be performed by the instruction. *See* instruction format.
2. The set of such portions available for a particular computer, and defining the repertoire of operations it can perform.

operation register The part of the *control-unit instruction register that contains the *operation code.

operations on sets The simple *operations that can be performed on sets are those of *union, *intersection, and *complement, and possibly *set difference. Using these it is possible to create new sets from existing sets. Certain other actions that have to be performed on sets are sometimes considered as operations, although they do not conform to the strict definition of the word. These include the actions *find, *insert, *delete, *split, and *min.

operations research (operational research; OR) The study of some human operation or set of operations by quantitative means. It is usually conducted with the aid of computer modeling; models may be hypothesized and fitted to experimental data, or experimental data may be analyzed to derive a model. Once a model is available, the effects of changes in the operations under study can be developed and predicted in a quantitative way.

operation table *Another name for* Cayley table.

operator 1. A person responsible for the immediate supervision of the hardware of a computer system.
2. A term used to denote an entity that can be applied to one or more operands so as to yield a result. It is (usually) a symbol representing an operation to be carried out, as opposed to a *variable, which represents a data value.

optical character recognition *See* OCR.

optical disk A storage device that uses a laser to record digital data as microscopic marks in concentric or spiral tracks, and reads the data via photoelectric sensors. A double-sided disk 12″ (305 mm) in diameter can store over 2 *gigabytes.
Philips demonstrated a prototype device in 1980 but neither they nor other potential vendors expect to have a commercial product before 1983. An important feature of some approaches is that the disks are not erasable while in others the disks can be erased and rewritten.

optical font A printing font or style of character specially designed to be accurately read by reading machines and by people. The most widely used are OCR A and OCR B and they are defined in internationally recognized standards. Although reading machines are available that can process a wide variety of fonts, provided that they are clearly printed, lower cost machines and lower error rates can be achieved if the specialized optical fonts are used. *See also* OCR.

optical mark reading (OMR) *See* mark reading.

optimal binary search tree A *binary search tree constructed to be of maximum expected efficiency for a given *probability distribution of search data.

optimization The process of finding the best solution to some problem, where "best" accords to prestated criteria. The word is used in a number of contexts.

1. In mathematics the word is generally used to describe the theory and practice of maximizing, or minimizing, a function (known as an *objective function*) of several variables that may be subject to a set of constraints. The special case of a linear objective function is the subject of *linear programming. The case of nonlinear objective functions, with or without constraints, is treated in a quite well-developed field. The unconstrained optimization problem (usually expressed as *minimization*) is:

$$\text{minimize } f(\boldsymbol{x})$$

where $f(\boldsymbol{x})$ is the given objective function of n real variables,

$$\boldsymbol{x} = (x_1, x_2, \ldots, x_n)^T$$

A necessary condition for a minimum is that

$$\partial f / \partial x_i = 0, \; i = 1, 2, \ldots, n$$

which is a system of *nonlinear equations. *Newton's method can be applied, but in practice this technique has been extensively modified to improve computational efficiency. *Matrix-updating methods* are a broad class of methods that involve a sophisticated means of computing approximations to the matrices required in Newton's method.

For constrained problems, $\boldsymbol{x}$ must also satisfy a system (possibly nonlinear) of equations or inequalities. Some of the ideas and methods for unconstrained problems can be suitably modified to handle the constraints.

Optimization problems are widespread in control theory, chemical engineering, and many other fields.

2. In programming the word is usually applied to part of the code-generation phase of a *compiler, denoting production of object code that is in some sense optimal, i.e. making best use of the resources provided by the target machine, or at least using these resources in a manner that is not blatantly wasteful. Programs can be space-efficient in the sense of occupying minimal storage, or time-efficient in the sense of executing in the minimum time. Compiler optimization is usually directed toward generating time-efficient programs, and takes two forms. *Global optimization* seeks to reorder the sequencing of a program so as to eliminate redundant computations (moving invariant operations outside loop bodies, coalescing loops, etc.). *Local (peephole) optimization* seeks to adapt the code to exploit particular features of the machine architecture and to remove local mishandling such as loading a register with a value that it already contains.

optimum programming *Another name for* minimum-access code.

optoelectronics An increasingly important technology concerned with the generation, processing, and detection of optical signals that represent electrical quantities. Major areas for application of this technology include communications, where electrical signals may be transmitted along fiber-optic cables (*see* fiber optics transmission system) and where two unconnected electrical circuits may exchange

signals by means of an optical link yet remain electrically isolated; these latter devices are called *optoisolators*. The technology is also being used to implement logical gating functions employing lasers and liquid crystals (*see* LCD), the advantages being high speeds of operation.
Optical signals may be generated from electrical signals using *LEDs. Detection of optical signals is often achieved using *phototransistors*, i.e. *bipolar transistors whose base drive is made dependent on incident light.

optoisolator *See* optoelectronics.

Oracle One of the UK's two *teletext systems.

order 1. A means of indicating the way a function varies in magnitude as its argument tends to some limits, usually zero or infinity. More precisely if there is some constant K such that

$$|f(x)| \leqslant K\,\phi(x)$$

for all $x \geqslant x_1$, then we say that $f(x)$ is order $\phi(x)$ as x tends to infinity, and we write

$$f(x) = O(\phi(x))$$

For example,

$$100x^2 + 100x + 2 = O(x^2) \quad \text{as } x \to \infty$$

If

$$\lim_{x \to a} f(x)/g(x) = 0$$

then we write

$$f(x) = o(g(x))$$

For example,

$$x = o(x^2) \quad \text{as } x \to \infty$$

Both these notations are statements about maximum magnitude and do not exclude f from being of smaller magnitude. For example,

$$x = O(x^2)$$

is perfectly valid, but equally

$$x = O(x)$$

If

$$\lim_{x \to a} f(x)/g(x) = \text{const. } k \neq 0$$

then we write

$$f(x) \simeq k\,g(x) \quad \text{as } x \to a$$

For example,

$$10x^2 + x + 1 \simeq 10x^2 \quad \text{as } x \to \infty$$

The term order and the O notation is used in numerical analysis, particularly in *discretization methods. In *ordinary differential equations, if h denotes the step size, then a method (or formula) has order p (a positive integer) if the global *discretization error is $O(h^p)$. This means that as the step size h is decreased, the error goes to zero at least as rapidly as h^p. Similar considerations apply to *partial differential equations. High-accuracy formulas (order up to 12 or 13) are sometimes used in methods for ordinary differential equations. For reasons of computational cost and stability, low-order formulas tend to be used in methods for partial differential equations.
2. *Another name for* operation code.
3. of a matrix. *See* square matrix.
4. of a finite group. *See* group.

order code *Another name for* operation code.

ordered pair A pair of objects in a given fixed order, usually represented by

$$(x,y) \text{ or } \langle x,y \rangle$$

for objects x and y. Two ordered pairs are said to be equal if and only if the first elements of each pair are equal and the second elements are equal. Typical situations in which ordered pairs are used include discussion of points in the Cartesian plane or complex numbers.
The idea can be extended to cover ordered triples, such as

$$(x_1,x_2,x_3)$$

and indeed ordered n-tuples, such as

$$(x_1,x_2, \ldots x_n)$$

ordered tree *See* tree.

ordering relation A relation that is *reflexive, *antisymmetric, and *transitive. The relation "less than or equal to" on integers is an ordering relation. *See also* partial ordering. *Compare* equivalence relation.

order statistics A branch of statistics that uses not the numerical value of an observation but its ranking relative to other observations. The *r*th *order statistic* of a sample of *n* observations is simply the *r*th smallest variate value in the sample. Examples of statistical tests for ordering include: the median test, the sign test, Cochran's test, the Wald-Wolfowitz "runs test", the Mann-Whitney test, the Wilcoxen test, the Kruskal-Wallis test, and the Friedman test.

ordinary differential equations *Differential equations that involve one independent variable, which in practice may be a space or time variable. Except in simple cases the solution cannot be determined analytically and approximation methods are used.

Numerical methods are mainly developed for equations involving first derivatives only, written in the form

$$y' = f(x,y),\ a \leqslant x \leqslant b,$$

where $\boldsymbol{y}$ and $\boldsymbol{f}$ are s-component vectors with component functions

$$y_i(x),$$
$$f_i(x, y_1(x), y_2(x), \ldots, y_s(x))$$

Equations involving higher derivatives can be equivalently written in this form by introducing intermediate functions for the higher derivatives.

In general, s conditions must be imposed to determine a particular solution. If the values $\boldsymbol{y}(a) = \boldsymbol{y}_0$ are specified, it is an *initial-value problem*. These problems can be solved directly using step-by-step methods, such as *Runge-Kutta methods, which determine approximations at a set of points in $[a,b]$. The problem is a *boundary-value problem* if the s conditions are given in terms of the component functions at a and b. In general, such problems require iterative methods, such as the *shooting method. However, if $\boldsymbol{f}$ is linear in $\boldsymbol{y}$, *finite-difference methods can be advantageous. Excellent software has been developed for both types of problem.

An area of particular interest in many applications is the solution of *stiff equations*. A stiff system possesses solutions that decay very rapidly over an interval that is short relative to the range of integration, and the solution required varies slowly over most of the range. To allow large steps in the slowly varying phases, it is necessary to use special methods, such as the implicit *trapezoidal rule*:

$$x_{n+1} = x_n + h$$
$$y_{n+1} = y_n + \tfrac{1}{2}h(f(x_{n+1}, y_{n+1}) + f(x_n, y_n))$$

At each step a system of equations has to be solved for $\boldsymbol{y}_{n+1}$, using very often a modification of *Newton's method. More straightforward explicit methods rapidly lead to catastrophic error growth unless the stepsize h is prohibitively small. These problems are still the subject of very active research interest.

organizational information system *See* information system.

inputs					
	A1	0	0	1	1
	A2	0	1	0	1
output B		0	1	1	1

Two-input OR gate, circuit symbol and truth table

P	F	F	T	T
Q	F	T	F	T
$P \vee Q$	F	T	T	T

Truth table for OR operation

OR gate An electronic *logic gate whose output is logic 0 (false) only when all (two or more) inputs are logic 0, otherwise it is logic 1 (true). It therefore implements the logical *OR operation and has the same *truth table. The diagram shows the usual circuit symbol and the truth table for a two-input gate. The device is more correctly called an *inclusive-OR gate* since the condition of both inputs true generates a true output. *See also* exclusive-OR gate.

OR operation (inclusive-OR operation; either-or operation) The logical *connective combining two statements, truth values, or formulas P and Q in such a way that the outcome is true if either P or Q or if both P and Q is true (*see* table). The latter outcome distinguishes the OR from the *exclusive-OR operation. The OR operation is usually denoted by $\vee$ and occasionally by $\bar{+}$. It is one of the binary operations of *Boolean algebra and is both *commutative and *associative.

One way of implementing the OR operation (e.g. in LISP) is to test P first, and then evaluate Q only if P is false. The resulting operation is noncommutative; in some languages there is a distinct notation for this.

When it is implemented as a basic *machine code instruction, OR usually operates on pairs of bytes or pairs of words. In these cases the OR operation defined above is normally applied to pairs of corresponding bits.

orthogonal analysis *See* orthonormal basis.

orthogonal basis *See* orthonormal basis.

orthogonal functions Let

$$f_1(x), f_2(x), \ldots, f_n(x)$$

be a set of functions defined on the interval (a,b); also let $w(x)$ be a given positive function (a *weight function*) on (a,b). The functions $f_i(x)$,

$$i = 1,2, \ldots ,n$$

are said to be orthogonal with respect to the interval (a,b) and weight function $w(x)$, if

$$\int_a^b w(x)\, f_i(x)\, f_j(x)\, dx = 0,$$

$$i \neq j, \quad i,j = 1,2, \ldots ,n$$

If, for $i = j$,

$$\int_b^a w(x)\, f_i^2(x)\, dx = 1,$$

$$i = 1,2, \ldots ,n$$

then the functions are said to be *orthonormal*.

A similar property is defined when (a,b) is replaced by the set of points

$$x_1, x_2, \ldots, x_N$$

and the integral is replaced by a sum,

$$\sum_{k=1}^{N} w(x_k)\, f_i(x_k)\, f_j(x_k) = 0,$$

$$i \neq j$$

Orthogonal functions play an important part in the approximation of functions and data.

orthogonal list A two-dimensional orthogonal list has list cells that are linked symmetrically to both left and right horizontal neighbors and up and down to vertical neighbors. This idea can be generalized to higher dimensions and suggests an efficient representation for *sparse matrices.

orthogonal memory *See* associative memory.

orthonormal analysis *See* orthonormal basis.

orthonormal basis The set of orthonormal functions employed in calculating the terms of a transform of the kind exemplified by the *Fourier transform and the Walsh transform (*see* Walsh analysis): the orthonormal basis of the Fourier transform consists of the imaginary exponential functions, and that of the Walsh transform consists of the *Walsh functions.

In order to calculate the terms of a transform effectively, the basis functions must be *orthogonal but need not also be normal (orthonormal). Such a non-normalized basis is called an *orthogonal basis*. The calculation of the transform terms is correspondingly called *orthonormal analysis* or *orthogonal analysis*. Such analysis is only possible if there are sufficient functions in the set to form a basis: such a set is called a *complete set of functions*.

orthonormal functions *See* orthogonal functions.

OS *Abbrev. for* operating system. The abbreviation was used as the name for a specific operating system (OS/360) introduced by IBM, but is now used generically.

oscilloscope An item of electronic test equipment that can display a wide variety of waveforms of electrical signals. It does this effectively by "plotting" the amplitude variations of the signal with time on a display device, normally a *cathode-ray tube. The electron beam of the CRT is deflected horizontally so that the display is scanned linearly in a preset time period. Vertical beam deflections, derived from the input signal, are then superimposed on the display, the horizontal and vertical deflections being synchronized by means of trigger circuits. *See also* storage oscilloscope.

OSI *Abbrev. for* open system interconnection.

outdegree *See* degree.

outer code *See* concatenated coding system.

output 1. The result of data processing activity when it is presented external to the system, or the process of presenting the data externally. The output from a computer can be in a form for use by people, e.g. printed or displayed, or it may be ready for input to another system or process, when it may be encoded magnetically on a tape or disk or punched into a card or paper tape.
2. A signal that is obtained from an electrical circuit, such as a logic circuit.
3. To produce a result or signal.

output area The area of main memory that is allocated for storage of data prior to transfer to an output device. *See also* input area.

output assertion *See* program correctness proof.

output device Any device that converts the electrical signals representing information within a computer into a form that can exist or be sensed outside the computer. Printers and visual displays are the most common type of output device for interfacing to people, but voice is becoming increasingly available. Devices such as card or tape punches or magnetic tape transports are really types of intermediate or backing store but are sometimes referred to as output devices.

output-limited process A process whose speed of execution is limited by the rate at which output data can be accepted.

overflow The condition that arises when the result of an arithmetic operation exceeds the size of the number allotted for receipt of that result, or the amount by which the result exceeds the allotted number.

overlap A form of parallelism in which events that are not mutually dependent take place concurrently in order to increase computer performance, e.g. fetching a second instruction while a first instuction is being executed. When there is overlap between portions of arithmetic operations (i.e. when the portions are *overlapped*), the process is usually called *pipelining.

overlay A section of code that is loaded into memory during the execution of a program, overwriting what was previously there. The loading of an overlay is under the explicit control of the programmer, and should not be confused with *paging. In general several overlays are loaded into the same area of memory, "overlaying" the code already residing in that part of memory. Overlays can be thought of as a form of voluntary memory management.

overwrite To destroy information in a memory location by writing in new information.

P

P *See* P=NP question.

pack 1. To store compactly in order to reduce the amount of memory required to hold the same data. There are several ways of doing this, for example by storing several bytes in one word or by replacing multiple occurrences of a character or word by a triplet consisting of
(a) a special code indicating the start of a triplet;
(b) a single instance of the replicated character or word;
(c) a count of the number of times the character or word occurs.
2. *Short for* disk pack.

package *See* application package.

packed decimal An economical method of storing decimal digits represented as binary-coded decimals (BCD), using only four bits per digit. Thus two decimal digits may be stored in one *byte. This is only slightly less compact than storing a number in binary, and avoids decimal-to-binary conversion. *See also* character encoding.

packet A group of bits of fixed maximum size and well-defined format that is switched and transmitted as a composite whole through a *packet switching network. Any message that exceeds the maximum size is partitioned and carried as several packets.

packet assembler/disassembler *See* PAD.

packet layer protocol *See* X.25.

packet radio A transmission method that makes use of radio broadcast signals carrying *packets of data. There is no assurance that only a single transmitter is active at a time, so it is necessary to have a convention for the action to be taken when packets "collide". Logically, packet radio is essentially equivalent to bus architecture networks that are used in some local network architectures. *See* CSMA/CD.

packet switched data service A data communication service offered to the public by some *PTTs and *common carriers. *See* public packet network.

packet switching A technique by which communication resources are allocated dynamically to multiple communicating entities. Messages between entities are partitioned into segments with a fixed maximum size. The segments, or *packets*, are passed through a *store-and-forward switching network until they reach their destination (or are discovered to be undeliverable). The packets are reassembled, if necessary, into complete messages when they reach their destination. Packet switching, as it applies to electronic communication, was first proven feasible by the development of the *ARPANET in 1969.
A *packet switching network* may provide a variety of levels of service, depending upon the sophistication of the underlying communication technology and the requirements of the network's customers. The simplest packet switching networks provide only *datagram service, which is unordered unreliable delivery of packets. Other networks may provide only reliable individually flow-controlled *virtual connections. The decision between datagrams, virtual connections, or other modes of operation can be made independently for the internal operation of a packet switching network, and the interface that it presents to its customers.

packing density 1. A measure of the number of electronic devices per unit area contained on one *integrated circuit.
2. A measure of the amount of information in a given dimension of a storage medium.

PAD *Acronym for* packet assembler/disassembler. A translating computer that provides access for asynchronous character-at-a-time terminals to a synchronous *packet switching network.

padding A filler used to extend a string or record to some prescribed length. *See also* block.

page The unit of interchange between memory and swapping device involved in a *paging system. The number of words or bytes in a page is usually fixed for a given system and is almost invariably an exact power of 2. The term *page frame* is used as an alternative name for page, but is more particularly used to apply to the copy of a page that is held on the swapping device.

page frame *See* page.

page printer A type of printer that prints a complete page of output in one cycle. It is generally a *nonimpact printer in which the printing process requires continuous movement of the paper. The information for one page of output is usually accumulated within a buffer in the printer before the printing process is started. *Compare* line printer, serial printer.

page table A table within a computer that contains a mapping between logical page addresses and physical page addresses. In many systems the table is supported in a fast-acting memory area. *See* paging.

paging A method of managing *virtual memory. The logical address is subdivided into two fields: the low-order bits indicate a word or byte within a *page and the high-order bits indicate a particular page. Active pages are held in main memory and a page that is not active may be transferred out to the *swapping device. An associative memory indicates the physical location within memory of those pages that are present. For pages that are not in memory the associative memory will contain a pointer to the backing-store home for that particular page. When reference occurs to a page, an interrupt is generated if the page is not in main memory and the operating system will transfer the relevant page from the swapping device into main memory.

paging drum The *swapping device used to hold the images of *pages no longer held in main memory in a *paging virtual management system. Paging drums typically are designed to have a relatively small capacity, low latency, and very high transfer rate.

paper slew (*UK name*: **paper throw**) A rapid and continuous movement of the paper in a line printer such that the space of several line pitches occurs without printing. In high-performance line printers the slew rate may be 75 inches per second (190 cm/s).

paper tape A data medium in the form of a continuous tape of paper with uniform width and thickness and specified physical attributes; other materials of greater durability or strength are also found, e.g. laminates of paper and polyester. All these forms can be referred to as *punched tape* or *punch tape*, although the former term is sometimes reserved for tape on which data has been recorded.

Data is encoded by punching patterns of holes on the tape. Generally a data character is punched as a coded set of holes across the tape at standard pitch. One-inch wide tape will accommodate characters of up to 8 bits. A longitudinal set of holes or hole positions at a fixed distance from the reference edge of the tape is known as a *track*: 1″ tape can therefore be 8-track while narrower tapes can be 5-track or 7-track.

In addition to the data tracks, a full track of smaller-diameter holes is always punched. Historically these originated as feed holes that were compatible with the sprocket feed of the tape punch and reader. Later higher-speed readers were friction-driven but the sprocket holes had become an essential feature for synchronization. In most tapes the center line of a feed hole is in line with that of data holes (*center feed tape*) but in some implementations it is in advance of the data holes (*advance-feed tape*). The data and feed holes are now sensed optically, thus the optical characteristics of the material are now part of the specification. The tape is normally in the form of a *reel* wound onto a core of standardized dimensions.

Punched tape was in use for data communication purposes (telex) prior to its use for computer input/output. Initially the 5 bit International Telegraph Alphabet encoded in 5 tracks on 11/16″ wide tape was used, but as I/O usage began to generate a significant market, 6, 7, and 8 bit codes were introduced and the tape width was increased to 1″.

Punched tapes have largely been superseded by other forms of media for data storage, interchange, and program loading in data processing. They are still widely in use for programmed control of industrial equipment, and on some computer printers the preprogrammed control of the continuous paper through the printer is by tape loops (*see* vertical format unit).

paper tape I/O A means of entering data into and extracting it out of a processor system using punched paper tape as the medium. Although punched cards were used for data processing before computers were available, paper tape I/O was adopted for many of the early computers: *tape punches* and *tape readers* were already in use for telex and were lower in cost than punched card equipment.

Early tape readers operated at about 10 characters per second (cps) by moving the tape in discrete steps, and sensed the holes by pressing a row of pins against the tape. The next generation of machines moved the tape continuously and sensed the holes via star-shaped wheels that rotated only when the points engaged a punched hole. Photoelectric sensing allowed speeds of up to 1500 cps to be achieved by 1975. There have been higher-speed readers but they were not able to stop within a character pitch. Tape punches as fast as 300 cps have been available but 110 cps was the more usual speed for volume output. Paper tape was widely used for program input, typesetting, and machine control and still has some use in these applications.

paper throw *UK name for* paper slew.

PAR *Acronym for* positive acknowledgment and retransmission. *See* backward error correction.

parallel access Access to a storage device in which a number of bits are transferred simultaneously rather than sequentially. For example, access to semiconductor memory almost invariably yields a number of bytes in parallel; by contrast access to the contents of a disk is usually serial in nature.

parallel adder A binary adder that is capable of forming sum and carry outputs for addend and augend words of greater than one bit in length by operating on corresponding pairs of addend and augend in parallel, i.e. at the same time. Parallel adders require a short settling time to allow carries to be propagated between subsequent stages of addition. *See also* adder, serial adder.

parallel algorithm An algorithm designed to run "efficiently" on a *parallel computer such as the Cray-1 and CDC Cyber 205 (pipeline computers) or the ICL DAP (distributed array processor). A parallel algorithm may involve a greater number of arithmetic operations than a serial counterpart. It is designed, however, so that many arithmetic operations are independent and can be performed in parallel, i.e. simultaneously.

parallel arithmetic Operation upon more than one bit or digit of a number at the same time.

parallel computer A computer that is capable of *parallel processing.

parallel in parallel out (PIPO) A term used to describe a *shift register that can be loaded in parallel and also read in parallel, in addition to which (by implication) data can enter and leave the device serially.

parallel input/output (PIO) A method of data transfer between devices, typically a computer and its peripherals, in which all the bits associated with a character or byte are presented to the interface simultaneously on separate conductors. There are usually other parallel conductors to carry the control signals. PIO is frequently used since it is compatible with the format used within the processor and enables high rates of data transfer to be achieved. When connection over any significant distance has to be made, the cost of the conductors and the associated drive circuits becomes significant and it is then preferable to convert to a *serial input/output.

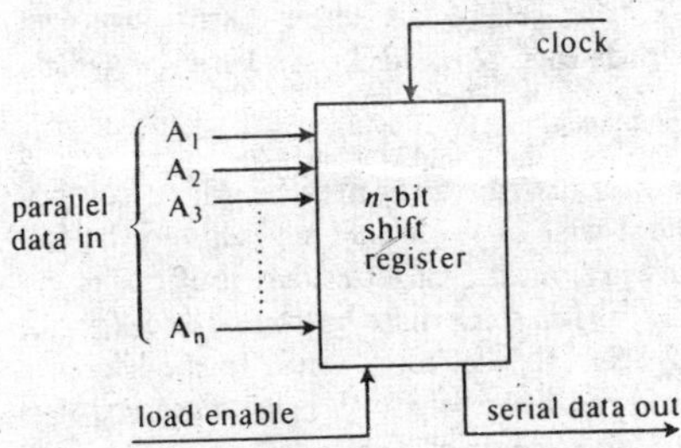

Parallel in serial out

parallel in serial out (PISO) A term used to describe a class of digital device that can accept parallel *n*-bit data words and convert them into serial sequential *n*-bit data streams. These devices often consist of an *n*-bit *shift register that is parallel loaded with the data word (*see* diagram). This data is then clocked out of the register in serial form. *Compare* serial in parallel out.

parallel processing A term applied rather loosely to a number of rather similar concepts but with important detailed differences. The essence of parallel processing is that more than one particular process is active at any given instant; however the term is often applied to a situation in which a large number of processes are potentially active but at any one instant only one is active. Strictly speaking the term parallel processing should only be applied where more than one processor is active among a group of processes at any one instant. In practice it is seldom used with this accurate connotation. *See also* concurrent programming.

parallel rewriting system *See* L-system.

parallel running *Another term for* parallel processing.

parallel shooting method *See* shooting method.

parallel transfer To transmit multiple units of information concurrently. For example, if two computers connected by eight wires wish to communicate an 8 bit unit of information, the sending computer would present all eight bits at the same time, one bit per wire. The receiving computer would accept the bit from the wires, and recreate the 8 bit unit. Thus an 8 bit parallel transfer would have occurred. *Compare* serial transfer.

parameter 1. Information passed to a subroutine, procedure, or function. The definition of the procedure is written using *formal parameters* to denote data items that will be provided when the subroutine is called, and the call of the procedure includes corresponding *actual parameters*. *See also* parameter passing.
2. A quantity in a function or mathematical model whose value is selected or estimated according to the circumstances. Parameters should be distinguished from *constants*, which are fixed for all uses of the function or model, and *variables*, which are the actual recorded measurements involved in the function or model.

Many properties of functions and mathematical models can be deduced from their structural characteristics without reference to particular values; such properties include continuity, differentiality, and linear independence. A function or model for a specific purpose may be formulated by first establishing the appropriate structure (e.g. polynomial, differential equation of a certain form) in which particular values are not yet determined; such values are parameters of the function or model. Various techniques can then be used to find the most suitable value or range of values for the parameters when considering the observed set of data.
For simple models, such as elementary *probability distributions, parameters may be estimated from the *statistics of the sample, such as the mean and the variance. General principles of estimation, in which the criterion is the agreement between model and data, lead to procedures that may require iterative computing to obtain estimates; important examples are the method of *least squares and its generalization, the method of maximum *likelihood.
The *probability distribution of a parameter estimate is often required, and it is usual to compute its standard deviation, known as its standard error (*see* measures of variation), its *correlation with other parameter estimates, and its confidence limits where appropriate (*see* confidence interval).

parameter passing The mechanism used to pass *parameters to a procedure (subroutine) or function. The most common methods are to pass the value of the actual parameter, or to pass the address of the memory location where the actual parameter is stored. The latter method allows the procedure to change the value of the parameter, whereas the former method guarantees that the procedure will not change the value of the parameter. Other more complicated parameter-passing methods have been devised, notably *call-by-name* in Algol 60.

parametric techniques *See* nonparametric techniques.

parent (father) A node A is the parent of node B in a *tree if B is the root of one of the subtrees of the tree rooted at A.

parenthesis-free notation *See* Polish notation, reverse Polish notation.

Parikh's theorem A theorem in formal language theory that concerns the nature of *context-free languages when order of letters is disregarded.
Let the alphabet Σ be the set $\{a_1, \ldots, a_n\}$. The *letter distribution*, $\phi(w)$, of a Σ-word w is the n-tuple

$$\langle N_1, \ldots, N_n \rangle$$

with N_i the number of occurrences of a_i in w. The *Parikh image*, $\phi(L)$, of a Σ-language L is

$$\{\phi(w) \mid w \in L\}$$

i.e. the set of all letter-distributions of words in L. L_1 and L_2 are *letter-equivalent* if

$$\phi(L_1) = \phi(L_2)$$

Letter distributions may be added component-wise as vectors. This leads to the following: a set S of letter distributions is *linear* if, for some distributions d and $d_1, \ldots, d_k$, S is the set of all sums formed from d and multiples of d_is. S is *semilinear* if it is a finite union of linear sets.
Parikh's theorem now states that if L is context-free $\phi(L)$ is semilinear. It can also be shown that $\phi(L)$ is semilinear if and only if L is letter-equivalent to a *regular language. Hence any context-free language is letter-equivalent to a regular language – although not all such languages are context-free.

parity A function that is computed to provide a check on a group of binary values (e.g. a word, byte, or character) by forming the modulo-2 sum of the bits in the group. The generated sum, a redundant value, is called the *parity bit*. The parity bit is 0 if the number of 1s in the original

group was even. The parity bit is 1 if the number of 1s in the original group was odd.
The parity computation just defined will cause the augmented group of binary values (the original group plus the parity bit) to have an even number of 1s; this is called *even parity*. In some cases, hardware considerations make it desirable to have an odd number of 1s in the augmented group, and the parity bit is selected to cause the total number of 1s to be odd; this is called *odd parity*. *See also* parity check.

parity bit *See* parity.

parity check (odd-even check) The computation, or recomputation for verification, of a parity bit to determine if a prescribed parity condition is present. *See* parity. *See also* checksum.

parity-check code, parity-check matrix *See* linear code.

parser (syntax analyzer) *See* parsing.

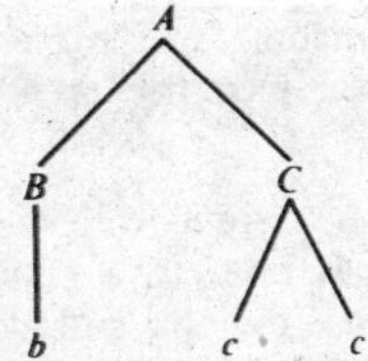

Parse tree

parse tree (syntax tree) A tree defining the syntactic structure of a sentence in a *context-free language. The interior nodes are labeled by nonterminals of the context-free *grammar; the descendants of a node labeled by *A*, say, spell from left to right the right-hand side of some production having left-hand side *A*. The leaf nodes of a parse tree may be terminals or nonterminals. If all the leaves are terminals then they spell from left to right a sentence of the language.
An example of a parse tree is shown in the diagram. It is assumed that the grammar in question has productions

$$A \to BC,\ B \to b,\ C \to cc$$

Note that it is conventional for the top of the tree to be its root and the bottom to be its leaves.
An early stage in compiling a program usually consists of generating a parse tree in which the constructs that make up the program are expressed in terms of the *syntax of the programming language.

parsing (syntax analysis) The process of deciding whether a string of input symbols is a sentence of a given language and if so determining the syntactic structure of the string as defined by a *grammar (usually *context-free) for the language. This is achieved by means of a program known as a *parser* or *syntax analyzer*. For example, a syntax analyzer of arithmetic expressions should report an error in the string

$$1 - + 2$$

since the juxtaposition of the minus and plus operators is invalid. On the other hand the string

$$1 - 2 - 3$$

is a valid arithmetic expression with structure specified by the statement that its subexpressions are

$$1,2,3 \text{ and } 1-2$$

(Note that 2−3 is not a subexpression.)
The input to a syntax analyzer is a string of tokens supplied by a *lexical analyzer. Its output may be in the form of a *parse tree or a *derivation sequence. *See also* bottom-up parsing, top-down parsing, precedence parsing.

partial correctness, proof of. *See* program correctness proof.

partial differential equations Differential equations that involve two or more independent variables, which in practice are often space and time variables. Because more than one independent variable is present, the "derivatives" that occur are partial derivatives. Such equations are widespread in science and model physical phenomena; they also arise frequently in the form of systems of equations. Simple examples in space and time are given by the heat conduction (or diffusion) equation,

$$\partial u/\partial t = \alpha\partial^2 u/\partial x^2$$

and the wave equation,

$$\partial^2 u/\partial t^2 = \beta\partial^2 u/\partial x^2$$

where α and β are physical constants. Steady-state phenomena in two space variables are typified by Laplace's equation,

$$\partial^2 u/\partial x^2 + \partial^2 u/\partial y^2 = 0$$

Appropriate initial and boundary conditions must be specified for these equations. The majority of partial differential equations that arise in practice require numerical techniques for their solution, the most successful and widely used being *finite-difference and *finite-element methods.

partial function Roughly, a *function

$$f : S \rightarrow T$$

that holds for only a proper *subset of S. Strictly, if the subset over which it holds is R, then

$$f : R \rightarrow T$$

is a function. However it may be more convenient to work with S rather than with R. The set U,

$$U = S - R,$$

is nonempty, and f has no value (or rather has the *undefined value*) at points in U; f is then said to be *undefined* on U and *defined* for all elements in the subset R of S, i.e. in S but not in U.

Partial functions arise naturally in computing. When recursive definitions of functions are given, the definition can sometimes loop for certain parameters. Definitions of functions can also give rise to overflow or exceptional situations. In these cases it is convenient to talk about partial functions. *Compare* total function.

partially ordered set *See* partial ordering.

partial ordering (partial order) A *relation defined between elements of some *set and satisfying certain properties, discussed below. It is basically a convenient generalization of the usual comparison operators, such as $>$ or $<$, that are typically defined on the integers or the real numbers. The generalization also captures the essential properties of the set operations such as "is a subset of", the alphabetic ordering of strings, and so on.

Two different but equivalent definitions of a partial ordering are possible. The first, denoted by $\preccurlyeq$, is a generalization of the usual $\leqslant$ operation in which $\preccurlyeq$ must be a *transitive, *antisymmetric, and *reflexive relation defined on the set S. The second definition, denoted by $\prec$ is a generalization of the usual $<$ operation in which $\prec$ must be a transitive, *asymmetric, and *irreflexive relation defined on S. A set with a partial ordering defined on it is called a *partially ordered set* or sometimes a *poset*.

partial recursive function A *function that can be obtained from certain initial functions by a finite number of applications of *composition, *recursion, and *minimization. In general it may not be defined for certain values of its parameters and so is a *partial function. The initial functions used are normally the *zero function, *successor function, and *projection functions. *See also* primitive recursive function.

partition 1. The term used in some operating systems to refer to a static area of memory for use by jobs, and also applied by association to the jobs executed in that area.

2. of a set. *See* covering.

Pascal A programming language in very common use. Pascal was designed as a tool to assist the teaching of programming as a systematic discipline. To that end it incorporates the *control structures of *structured programming – sequence, selection, and repetition – and *data structures – arrays, records, files, sets, and user-defined types. It is an austere language, with a minimum of facilities, but what is provided is so well suited to its task that the language is in practice more powerful than its more elaborate competitors.

Pascal was relatively easy to implement on a variety of machines since the Pascal compiler was written in Pascal. Used first as an educational tool, Pascal became a more-or-less standard language for the teaching of computer science. Later it spread into the microcomputer world, particularly in the form of the UCSD p-System. In addition to the standard form of Pascal (ISO-Pascal), enhanced versions are used for system development by a number of manufacturers.

Pascal-Plus A derivative of *Pascal, providing facilities for *concurrent programming.

pass The movement of a complete magnetic tape, or just the part on which information is recorded, past the read position.

passband A range of frequencies with a lower limit and an upper limit, such that all frequencies between these limits (but not necessarily excluding other frequencies) are passed, with little attenuation, by a filter or a channel. *See also* bandwidth, band-pass filter, filtering.

pass instruction *Another name for* no-op instruction.

passive star A network topology in which the outer nodes connect to a single central node. The central node does not process the message in any way but simply connects the transmission paths between the outer nodes. The central node is unlikely to fail due to its passive operation. It is thus unlikely that the entire network will be disabled during normal operation. *See also* active star, star network, network architecture.

password A commonly used means of *authentication. When a user attempts to *log in he will be required to state his password, and the value he supplies will be compared with that held by the system. If the values do not agree, the user will not be allowed to log in. As an added precaution many systems allow a user to change the value of the password dynamically.

patch 1. *Informal* A change to a program – usually to correct some error – that is introduced in a manner that emphasizes convenience and speed of change rather than security, and is intended to effect only a temporary repair. Even where a program is written in some high-level language, the patching might be carried out in machine-code terms on the compiled version of the program. Often during testing a series of minor errors will be corrected by patching in order to permit testing to continue without the delay of recompilation. Subsequently the corresponding changes will all be incorporated into the program source text at a single compilation.

2. *See* patchboard.

patchboard (plugboard) A matrix of sockets that can be interconnected manually by means of *patchcords*, i.e. cables with plugs attached to each end. Thus one socket can be *patched* to another. Patchcords are used to make temporary connections between devices, to program *analog computers, and to connect different peripheral devices to computer lines.

patchcord *See* patchboard.

patent A government grant to an inventor assuring him/her the exclusive right to exploit or sell the invention for a limited period. Patent protection is not available to computer programs in Europe although programs can be patented in the US if they comply with the originality and other requirements in the US Patent Act. Inventive hardware is patentable in Europe and this leads to a serious flaw in the law; the same task can be performed by both software and hardware yet the former is excluded from protection under the law by a clause in the European Patent Convention. The question of whether a program that performs the same task as a piece of patented hardware infringes the patent in the hardware has not yet been decided in Europe, nor has it been decided whether a PROM is a piece of software or hardware.

path A route between two vertices of a *graph, passing along edges and, in the case of a directed *graph, with attention paid to the direction along the edges. More formally there is a path between vertices V_0 and V_k if each pair

$$(V_i, V_{i+1}), i = 0,1 \ldots, k-1$$

is an edge of the graph and, in the case of a directed graph, is suitably directed.
In typical applications, the existence of paths between vertices indicates physical connections between them or perhaps logical connections or dependencies. *See also* cycle.

pattern An *equivalence class associated with a special kind of *relation defined on functions. Let

$$F = \{f | D \rightarrow A\}$$

be a set of functions mapping elements from some domain D into some set A, which can be regarded as an alphabet. With each function f in F is associated a *weight* $w(f)$, defined as the formal multiplication of all the images $f(x)$ under f. In effect $w(f)$ describes the number of occurrences of the different images in A.
An equivalence relation can then be defined between two functions of F in such a way that equivalent functions have equivalent weights, though the reverse is not in general true. The patterns of F are the equivalence classes that emerge from this equivalence relation.
The weight of a pattern is just the weight of any member of that pattern; the weight of the equivalence class $[f]$ containing f is just $w(f)$. The formal sum of the weights $w(f)$ taken over all the equivalence classes in F gives the *pattern inventory* of the set F. An important theorem due mainly to George Pólya indicates the close link between pattern inventory and *cycle index polynomial.
These ideas are often applied in *combinatorics and *switching theory. For example, a pattern inventory can indicate the number of essentially different wiring diagrams or logic circuits needed to realize the different possible logic functions.

pattern inventory *See* pattern.

pattern recognition The process of detecting the presence of a specified pattern in a *signal, or assigning a probability to its possible presence. For example, visual pattern recognition involves the identification of two-dimensional patterns in a *gray-level array. The specification of one of more patterns is done either analytically, or, more usually, by the provision of *templates*, which are model patterns for comparison. Pattern recognition employs the techniques of *digital signal processing, *picture processing, and *artificial intelligence.

PCB *Abbrev. for* printed circuit board. *See* printed circuit.

PCM *Abbrev. for* pulse code modulation.

PDA *Abbrev. for* pushdown automaton.

PDL *Abbrev. for* program design language.

PDP series A family of machines manufactured by *DEC.

PE *Abbrev. for* phase-encoded. *See* tape format.

peek To examine the contents of an absolute memory location from a high-level language, usually by means of a function of this name whose argument is the address in question. *Compare* poke.

peephole optimization *See* optimization (in programming).

penetration A method of testing and improving computer system security by attempting to breach the system; successful penetration is followed by the adjustment of the existing system in order to accommodate security provisions to counter the *threat. Results of penetration studies provide guidelines for better design of secure computer systems.

perfect codes *Error-correcting codes in which the Hamming spheres surrounding the codewords entirely fill the *Hamming space without overlap. These spheres all have radius *e*, where the code can correct *e* errors, and their centers (codewords) are separated from each other by a distance of $(2e + 1)$; thus the spheres have no points (words) in common where they touch, but their surfaces are separated by unit distance with no points between them. Perfect codes attain the *Hamming bound exactly.
The only *binary *linear perfect codes are the *repetition codes, the *Hamming codes, and the (23,12) *Golay code.

performance analysis and evaluation Recording and analyzing information on the dynamic behavior of a system. Normally the intention is to ensure that use of resources, typically processor time or real time, is within desired bounds, or to reduce the system's use of such resources.
There are many techniques for attempting to characterize the performance (sometimes performance per unit cost) of a system. There is no satisfactory way of obtaining such a characterization from a system description; the characterization will, of necessity, be application-dependent. As a result, a principal method of performance evaluation is running *benchmark programs to compare different systems or system *configurations. *Simulation methods are also used in determining the effects of system configurations. *See also* performance monitoring.

performance monitoring Measurement, by direct observation or by programmed processes, of activity at various points in a computer system to find out where bottlenecks and delays are taking place. Results are used for system *reconfiguration in order to improve overall performance.

peripheral Any device, including I/O devices and backing store, that is connected to a computer.

peripheral interface adapter (PIA) A set of electronic circuits fitted to a processor or a peripheral to achieve compatibility between the interfaces. The interface offered by the vendor of a peripheral may not be appropriate for direct connection to a given system for several reasons: the system manufacturers may have designed a unique interface to prevent the connection of unauthorized peripherals, or the interface fitted may have been optimized for low cost and short cable length, e.g. parallel input/output, and thus be incompatible with a peripheral interface optimized for long lines or network connection. Many vendors of peripheral equipment provide space and power within their equipment to accommodate a PIA, which may be available as an option or may be designed and manufactured by the system supplier or user. In microprocessors the interface to peripherals is often provided via a PIA integrated into a single package. The device may provide control of bidirectional data flow, handling of interrupts, etc. The function may be altered by appropriate signals on its control inputs.

peripheral processor The name used in CDC systems for a special-purpose processor used to control peripheral units. (These processors go by a variety of names: on IBM systems they are referred to as *channels, and have a much more restricted order code than a CDC peripheral processor.) In all cases the essence of the peripheral processor is that its order code is specifically tailored to the requirements of transferring information between main memory and the peripheral device or devices controlled by the peripheral processor.

Perkin–Elmer Data Systems A US corporation, initially concerned only with optics, that became involved in computers with the purchase of the Interdata Corporation. They now manufacture small to large minicomputers, including some very high performance machines, and are also noted as manufacturers of low-cost CRT terminals.

permanent error of magnetic tape. *See* error rate.

permutation of a *set S. A *bijection of S onto itself. When S is finite, a permutation can be portrayed as a rearrangement of the elements of S. The number of permutations of a set of n elements is $n!$
A permutation of the elements of {1,2,3} can be written

$$\begin{pmatrix} 1 & 2 & 3 \\ 2 & 1 & 3 \end{pmatrix}$$

indicating that 1 is mapped into 2, 2 into 1, and 3 into 3. Alternatively the above can be written, using a *cycle notation, as (1 2); this implies that the element 3 is unaltered but that 1 is mapped into 2 and 2 into 1.
For collections of elements in which repeated occurrences of items may exist, a permutation can be described as a rearrangement of elements in which each element appears with the same frequency as before.

permutation group A *subgroup of the group that is formed from the set, S_n, of all *permutations of n distinct elements and on which is defined the binary operation of *composition of functions. The full group S_n is usually called the *symmetric group* and possesses $n!$ elements. Every finite group is isomorphic to some permutation group.

permutation matrix A square matrix in which each column contains precisely one nonzero element, which is equal to unity. If P is an $n \times n$ permutation matrix and x is a vector of n elements, the vector Px will be a *permutation of the elements of x.

personal computer A general-purpose single-user microcomputer designed to be operated by one person at a time. Personal computers range from cheap domestic or hobby machines with limited memory, program storage on cassette tape, and an ordinary TV as the display device, to extremely sophisticated machines with powerful processors, large-capacity disk storage, high-resolution color-graphics systems, and many other options. In scientific engineering and business environments the personal computer is a real alternative to a terminal connected to a time-sharing system, especially since communication ports allow transfers of data between the personal computer and other computers. The development of the personal computer is a consequence of the ratio of computing power to cost increasing to a point where it is no longer necessary for a computer to work continuously to be cost-effective.

PET A popular low-cost microcomputer manufactured by Commodore Computer Systems, now superseded by the VIC-20.

Petri net A model of a concurrent system that is expressed in a specific graphical notation and can be used to explore certain properties of the system. A Petri net consists of a set of *places*, a set of *transition bars*, and a set of directed edges. Each transition bar has an associated set of input places and an associated set of output places. A transition bar is linked to each of its input places by a directed edge from the place to the bar, and to each of its output places by a directed edge from the bar to the place. Typically a single place is an output place for one or more transition bars and an input place for one or more other transition bars.
The state of the concurrent system is represented by the presence of *tokens* at places, while transition bars represent possible changes of state. A transition bar can only *fire* (i.e. the change of state occur) when each of its input places holds at least one token. When a bar fires it removes one token from each of its input places and deposits one token at each of its output places. Thus the combination of the

input and output places for a transition bar represents both the conditions under which the change of state can occur and the effects of that state change.
The firing of a transition bar is an indivisible event and simultaneous firing of two or more bars is therefore not possible. When the state is such that two or more bars are candidates to fire, each candidate must be considered individually.
By starting from a token distribution that represents an initial state of the system and applying a straightforward procedure that yields all possible token distributions that can be reached from this starting distribution, it is possible to explore the possible states of the concurrent system and the ways in which these states can be reached. For example, both deadlock states and unproductive looping can be readily detected and in general it is possible to check that the behavior of the system is as expected.

phase of a regularly recurring (periodic) quantity. The stage or state of development of the quantity. It can be expressed, in the form of an angle, as the fraction of a cycle of the periodic quantity that has been completed, with respect to a fixed datum point. Two sinusoidally varying quantities of the same frequency can be *in phase* (reaching corresponding phases at the same time) or *out of phase*. In the latter case the difference in phase – the *phase difference* – is usually expressed as an angle.

phase-encoded (PE) *See* tape format.

phase modulation (PM) *See* modulation.

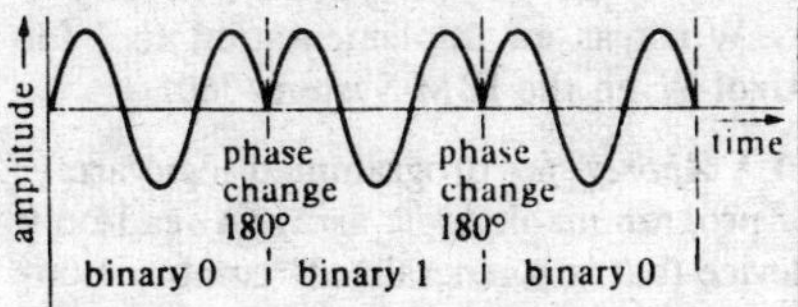

Phase shift keying, 2-phase modulation

phase shift keying (PSK) A method for representing digital data with analog signals by changing the phase of the analog carrier to represent the digital information (*see* diagram). It is a type of *modulation. There are two ways of detecting the phase information in a signal. *Fixed-reference PSK* assigns a meaning to each phase position. The *demodulator uses a signal source of the same frequency to compare with the incoming signal and detect its phase. *Differential PSK* assigns meaning to phase changes, e.g. a phase change of 180° could be taken to mean a 1, while no phase change means a 0. No comparison with another wave is needed in the demodulator.
The amount of information associated with a phase or phase change depends on the number of discrete phases that the carrier may assume. If the carrier may assume two phases then each phase or phase change represents a single bit. If four phases are used then each phase or phase change represents a different combination of two bits. The greater the number of discrete phases, the more difficult it is to generate, transmit, and detect the analog signal, thus the cost is higher.
See also digital data transmission.

phototransistor *See* optoelectronics.

physical Actual, or involving actual entities, as opposed to logical or conceptual.

physical layer of network protocol function. *See* seven-layer reference model. *See also* X.25.

PIA *Abbrev. for* peripheral interface adapter.

pico- (symbol: p) A prefix to a unit, indicating a submultiple of a millionth of a millionth, 10^{-12}, of that unit, as in picosecond.

picture 1. A description of one string by another string that denotes the properties of the string being described. For example, a three-digit number could be de-

scribed using the picture DDD where D denotes a digit.
2. (image) *See* picture processing.

picture processing (image processing) The analysis, generally by *digital signal processing techniques, of the information contained in *pictures* (or *images*). The original picture may be a drawing, photograph, scene, etc., which is digitized in such a way that it can be regarded as a two-dimensional array of data, i.e. as a two-dimensional spatial *signal whose amplitude represents the brightness at the position in the *space domain. Sometimes the amplitude is taken to include the color (hue and saturation). The process of spatial sampling of a scene is usually carried out by a TV camera or, for example, by a scanning electron microscope.
Each element of the two-dimensional array is called a *pixel* (picture element). The *definition* is the fineness of spatial sampling; it is expressed in terms of pixels, e.g. high definition is usually considered to be 1024 by 768 pixels. The amplitude is generally encoded by between three and eight bits for *gray scale (monochrome) or up to 16 bits for color.
Typical processing operations include contrast distortion, expansion of a specified range of brightness, bright outlining of objects, correction of over- or underexposure of portions of the picture, recognition (and perhaps counting) of predefined objects, and comparison of one picture with another. The last two of these operations are examples of *pattern recognition. Some of the more advanced operations make use of the concepts of *artificial intelligence. The development of picture processing has been prompted by applications such as satellite and unmanned spaceprobe observations, undersea exploration, medical physics, and industrial robotics.

Pierce arrow *See* NOR operation.

piggyback acknowledgment *See* acknowledgment.

PIO *Abbrev. for* parallel input/output.

pipeline processing A form of processing in which the time required to pass through some functional unit (e.g. a floating point ALU) of a computer system is longer than the intervals at which data may enter that functional unit, i.e. the functional unit performs its process in several steps. When the first step is completed, the results are passed to a second step that uses separate hardware; the first-step hardware is thus free to begin processing new data. This provides fast throughput for sequential processes, but at the expense of complicating the control unit, which must keep account of operations that are simultaneously in progress. The technique is commonly used in supercomputers, which require maximum performance, and in vector and array processors, which provide long orderly sequences of data as input to pipeline processors.

pipelining *Pipeline processing itself, or the use of pipeline processing.

PIPO *Abbrev. for* parallel in, parallel out. *See also* shift register.

PISO *Abbrev. for* parallel in, serial out. *See also* shift register.

pixel *Derived from* picture element. One of the elements in a large *array that is holding pictorial information. It contains data representing the brightness and possibly color of a small region of the image. *See also* picture processing.

pixelization (space quantization) *See* quantization. *See also* picture processing, discrete and continuous systems.

PL/1 *See* PL/I.

PL/360 The first machine-oriented high-level language (or *MOHLL), developed by Wirth as an implementation tool for Algol-W on the IBM System/360.

PLA *Abbrev. for* programmed logic array, or programmable logic array. A read-only device that is a generalized *combinational circuit and may include a *sequential circuit. By means of connections on a semiconductor device, the PLA usually provides a "programmable" *sum of products function that feeds an output register, and sometimes an internal register. When the internal register is used to provide part of the input variables, the PLA is a sequential circuit; otherwise it is a combinational circuit.

The product terms in the function can be thought of as representing values that are to be acted upon when they occur; thus the PLA is a form of fixed *associative memory or a specialized *table look-up device adapted to the situation when the truth table has sparse entries.

Since the PLA is made specific only by the interconnections, it represents a general-purpose building block that requires changes in only one or two steps of the production process to provide different functionality. PLAs can be programmed at the time of manufacture; alternatively they may be programmed by the user, and are then called *field-programmable*.

planar graph A *graph that can be drawn on paper (with points representing vertices and lines joining vertices representing edges) in such a way that edges intersect only at vertices.

plasma display A form of *display used in association with computer systems in which a red or orange light is provided by an electrical discharge through a gas. A matrix of cells in which discharge can be arranged is fabricated by bonding a sheet of perforated material between layers – one of which is transparent – on which there are electrodes and connecting tracks. They are frequently configured as rows of character-sized (5 × 7 or 7 × 9) groups of cells, but panels that have a continuous matrix over the whole area, and thus can display graphics, are available. For displaying small amounts of information – up to 240 characters – they are an attractive alternative to display devices incorporating a cathode-ray tube; large displays however are more expensive.

platter The metallic substrate of a rigid magnetic disk.

PL/C, PL/CT *See* PL/I.

plex A *multilinked structure consisting of a collection of cells of various sizes linked together by pointers into essentially a connected directed *graph, possibly containing cycles. *See also* list processing.

PL/I A programming language developed by the IBM Corporation. PL/I was intended to replace all pre-existing programming languages, and incorporated features from COBOL, FORTRAN, and Algol 60. The resulting language is large and complex: it was not taken up by manufacturers other than IBM, and has had only limited acceptance among IBM users.

PL/I was adopted as a teaching language by a number of institutions, notably Cornell University who produced their own versions, PL/C and PL/CT. It was also used as a basis for the microcomputer languages *PL/M and *PL/Z.

PL/M A systems programming language for microcomputers in the Intel family. It is based on and bears a strong resemblance to *PL/I.

plotter An output device for translating information from a computer into pictorial or graphical form on paper or a similar medium. There are a wide variety of plotters to match the differing requirements for size, accuracy, speed, and other attributes such as color.

One of the simplest implementations of an *xy plotter* or *graph plotter* is a *flat-bed plotter*. One or more pens are mounted on a carriage that can be moved to precise positions on a bar that spans the width of the medium, i.e. the *x*-axis. The bar is mounted so that it can be moved precisely on tracks that lie parallel to the lengthwise edge of the medium, i.e. the *y*-axis. It is thus possible to move the pen to any point that lies within the available range of x and y coordinates. When drawing a diagonal line on an xy plotter the computer generally has to provide only the coordinates of the start and finish points, but when using an *xy recorder* it is necessary to send a succession of x and y increments.

Although large flatbed plotters are produced it is often preferable to use the *drum plotter* configuration for large drawings. The drum plotter has an arrangement similar to the flatbed plotter for moving the pen across the width of the medium, but the bar is fixed parallel to the axis of a drum. The medium is wrapped around part of the drum surface and is often wound onto take-up spools on either side of the drum axis. The medium has holes punched at its edges that engage with pintles on the drum and thus maintain registration with the rotation of the drum as it translates longitudinal axis coordinates.

plugboard *Another name for* patchboard.

plug compatible (plug-to-plug compatible) *See* compatibility.

PL/Z The family name for the systems programming languages provided by Zilog for the Z8000 microcomputer. PL/Z–SYS is a variant of *Pascal, while PL/Z–ASM is an assembly language.

PMOS A type of *MOSFET.

pneumatic logic *Another name for* fluid logic.

p-n junction *See* junction.

P=NP question One of the major open questions in theoretical computer science at present.

P is the class of formal languages that are recognizable in *polynomial time. More precisely a language L is in ***P*** if there exists a *Turing machine program M and a polynomial $p(n)$ such that M recognizes L and

$$T_M(n) \leqslant p(n)$$

for all nonnegative integers n, where T_M is the time complexity of M (*see* complexity measure). It is generally accepted that if a language is not in ***P*** then there is no algorithm that recognizes it and is guaranteed to be always "fast".

NP is the class of languages that are recognizable in polynomial time on a nondeterministic *Turing machine.

Clearly

$$\boldsymbol{P} \subseteq \boldsymbol{NP}$$

but the question of whether

$$\boldsymbol{P} = \boldsymbol{NP}$$

has not been solved despite a great amount of research.

A language is said to be *NP-hard* if any language in ***NP*** can be polynomially reduced to it, even if the language itself is not in ***NP***.

Contained in ***NP*** is a set of languages *NPC*, said to be *NP-complete*. A language L_1 is in *NPC* if every language L_2 in ***NP*** can be polynomially reduced to L_1, i.e. there is some function f such that

(a) $x \in L_1$ iff $f(x) \in L_2$

(b) $f(x)$ is computable in time bounded by a polynomial in the length of x.

It can be shown that if any NP-complete language is also in ***P*** then ***P = NP***.

A wide variety of problems occurring in computer science, mathematics, and operations research are now known to be NP-complete. As an example the problem of determining whether a Boolean expression in conjunctive normal form (*see* conjunction) can be satisfied by a truth assignment was the first problem found to be NP-complete; this is generally referred to as the *satisfiability* (or *CNF satisfiability*) *problem*. Despite considerable effort none of these NP-complete problems have been shown to be polynomially solvable. Thus it is widely conjectured that no NP-complete problem is polynomially solvable.

PN sequence *Short for* pseudonoise sequence.

pocket sorting *Another name for* radix sorting.

pointer *Another name for* link.

point-of-sale system A system in which *point-of-sale terminals* are used as input to a digital computer. A point-of-sale terminal is a specialized cash register, credit-card recording system, or ticket dispenser that causes all information on the transaction to be relayed to a central computer. Some point-of-sale systems include credit validation. Better stock, cash, and credit control are maintained by having the data entered into a computer as soon as it is available at the point of sale. Point-of-sale systems are also useful in monitoring petty theft of cash and merchandise.

point-to-point line A dedicated communication link that joins only two nodes in a network. *Compare* multidrop line.

Poisson distribution The basic discrete *probability distribution for data in the form of counts of random events. If each event occurs with the same probability and the mean frequency of events is μ, the probability that exactly r events will occur is

$$e^{-\mu}\mu^r/r!$$

The Poisson distribution is discrete, taking the values $r = 0, 1, 2, \ldots$ and it can be obtained as a limiting case of the *binomial distribution as n tends to infinity while np is held fixed. The mean and variance of the Poisson distribution both equal μ.

poke To modify the contents of an absolute memory location from a high-level language, usually by means of a procedure of this name whose two arguments are the address in question and the value to be deposited there. *Compare* peek.

POL *Acronym for* problem-oriented language. A programming language whose control structures and (in particular) data structures reflect in some measure the characteristics of a class of problems, e.g. commercial data processing or scientific computation. By contrast, the structures of a machine-oriented language reflect the internal structure of the underlying machine.

Polish notation (prefix notation) A form of notation, invented by the Polish mathematician Jan Lukasiewicz, in which each operator precedes its operands, e.g.

$a + b$ is expressed as $+ab$

If all operators take exactly two operands, or if each operator has a specific number of operands, then no brackets are required since the order of evaluation is always uniquely defined; the notation can then be described as *parenthesis-free*. *See also* reverse Polish notation.

polling The process by which one station on a *multidrop line (the primary station) addresses another station (a secondary station), giving the secondary station access to the communication channel. The secondary station is then able to send status information and/or data to the primary. The primary station resumes control of the line and may send data of its own or poll another station.

Polling is a form of *time division multiplexing. The precise polling strategy used depends upon the application. In *roll-call polling* the primary station addresses each secondary station in turn. Some stations may be addressed more often than others if their response-time requirements or traffic loads are heavier. *Hub polling* is used to minimize line turnaround delays on *half duplex multidrop lines. The primary station polls the station at the opposite end of the line, which transmits any data it has and polls the next closest station. This process is repeated until control reaches the primary station again. Since data is flowing in one direction only, from the outermost nodes toward the primary station, the only turnaround delays occur when the primary station wishes to transmit.

Polling is not suitable for situations where the response delay time is fairly large, as is the case in satellite transmission systems.

polynomial A formal power series, i.e. a sum of multiples of powers of an independent variable known as the *indeterminate* (often written as x, s, or t), e.g.

$$3x^4 + 7x^2 + 2x + 5$$

or, in general,

$$p(x) = \sum_{i=0}^{\infty} a_i x_i$$

The coefficients (a_i) are elements of some algebraic system, S, having appropriate addition and multiplication operations; the expression is then described as a polynomial over S. For example, if the coefficients are all integers, the polynomial is said to be over the integers. If $a_r \neq 0$ but $a_i = 0$ for all $i > r$, then r is called the *degree* of the polynomial, usually written

$$r = \deg(p)$$

If $a_r = 1$, the polynomial is *monic*.

Arithmetic on polynomials consists primarily of addition, subtraction, and multiplication of polynomials; in some cases division, factoring, and taking the greatest common divisor are also important operations.

Addition and subtraction are done by adding or subtracting the coefficients of like powers of x.

Multiplication is done by the rule

$$(a_r x^r + \ldots a_1 x + a_0)(b_s x^s + \ldots b_1 x + b_0)$$
$$= (c_{r+s} x^{r+s} + \ldots c_1 x + c_0)$$

where

$$c_k = a_0 b_k + a_1 b_{k-1} + \ldots a_{k-1} b_1 + a_k b_0$$
$$a_i, b_j = 0 \quad \text{for } i > r, j > s$$

In coding theory, much use is made of polynomials over the *ring of integers modulo q, for some integer $q > 1$. Such polynomials themselves form a commutative *ring with an identity. More particularly, coding theory employs polynomials over the *field of integers modulo p, for some suitable prime number p. (For binary systems, $p = 2$.) These polynomials can be multiplied and divided; in general, they may be factorized. A polynomial (over a field) that can be factorized is said to be *reducible*; otherwise it is *irreducible*. When divided by another, a polynomial over a field gives a unique quotient and remainder. Every such polynomial can be uniquely factorized into irreducible factors.

The set of polynomials (over a field), modulo a given monic irreducible polynomial (over the same field), itself forms a field; this is called an *extension field* of the original *base field* of coefficients (which were integers modulo p). Extension fields of this kind are fundamental to much of coding theory.

The extension field of polynomials modulo G, over the integers modulo p, contains p^g elements, where g is the degree of G. G is called the *generating polynomial* of the extension field. A polynomial that is an element of this field is said to be *primitive* if and only if it does not exactly divide the polynomial $x^c - 1$ (over the field of integers modulo p) for any c less than $p^g - 1$.

polynomial codes A family of *linear *error-correcting or *error-detecting codes whose encoding and decoding algorithms may be conveniently expressed in terms of *polynomials over a base field (and therefore easily implemented in terms of *shift registers with *linear combinational logic).

polynomial equation An equation of the form

$$p_n(x) = a_n x^n + a_{n-1} x^{n-1} + \ldots + a_0 = 0$$

Such equations have n solutions, called *roots*, which in general are complex. If the given coefficients a_i are real the complex roots occur in conjugate pairs. It is quite common for some of the roots to be very sensitive to small changes in the coefficients, i.e. to have a large *condition number. The number n is called the *degree* of the polynomial.

A single root α may be found by an iteration such as *Newton's method. The polynomial

$$p_{n-1}(x) = p_n(x)/(x - \alpha)$$

has the same roots as p_n except for α; it may be used to determine the other roots. The process of calculating p_{n-1} is known as *deflation*, and is used after each root is found; thus the polynomials used are of progressively lower degree. Deflation depends on the roots being accurate. If an approximate root is used, the deflated polynomial will have inaccurate coefficients, and possibly very inaccurate roots. To minimize deterioration of the successive polynomials used, it is important to determine each root to the greatest possible precision and, where feasible, to determine the roots in increasing order of magnitude.

polynomial interpolation *See* interpolation.

polynomially bounded algorithm *See* complexity measure.

polynomial number A number in a fixed-radix system. *See* number system.

polynomial space A way of characterizing the *complexity of an algorithm. If the space complexity (*see* complexity measure) is polynomially bounded, the algorithm is said to be executable in polynomial space. Many problems for which no *polynomial time algorithms have been found, nevertheless can easily be solved in an amount of space bounded by a polynomial in the length of the input.

Formally ***PSPACE*** is defined as the class of formal languages that are recognizable in polynomial space. Defining ***P*** and ***NP*** as the classes of languages recognizable in polynomial time and recognizable in polynomial time on a nondeterministic Turing machine, respectively (*see* P = NP question), it can be shown that ***P*** is a subset of ***PSPACE*** and that ***NP*** is also a subset of ***PSPACE***. It is not known, however, whether

$$NP = PSPACE$$

although it is conjectured that they are different, i.e. that there exist languages in ***PSPACE*** that are not in ***NP***.

Many problems associated with recognizing whether a player of a certain game (like GO) has a forced win from a given position are *PSPACE-complete*. In a similar manner to NP-completeness (*see* P = NP question) this means that such languages can be recognized in polynomial time only if

$$PSPACE = P$$

Such problems can thus be considered to be even harder than NP-complete problems.

polynomial time A way of characterizing the *complexity of an algorithm. If the number of elementary operations required to apply the algorithm to data of length *n* increases with *n* no more rapidly than a polynomial in *n*, the algorithm is said to be executable in polynomial time. *See also* complexity measure, P = NP question.

pooling block An area of memory used to contain many short records that are to be transferred to or from a device for which the access time is long compared with the actual transfer time. *See also* buffer.

pop *See* stack.

POP-2 A programming language developed by the University of Edinburgh (UK) for research in *artificial intelligence. POP-2 provided the facility to manipulate the linked data structures characteristic of *LISP, but retained a more familiar procedural structure, and was thus more accessible to programmers raised in the Algol environment of the time.

P operation (down operation) *See* semaphore.

population *See* sampling.

port 1. (I/O port) A connection point with associated control circuitry that allows I/O devices to be connected to the internal bus of a microprocessor. Generally the port can be switched to input or output and is often associated with a *peripheral interface adapter. The PIA has connections compatible with the I/O port on one side and one or more interfaces to suit various peripherals on the other. It also allows longer connection cables to be used.

2. Loosely, an interconnection to a communication network on either the network or the *DTE (computer) interface.

portable 1. *Another word for* machine-independent.
2. A word applied to software that can readily be transferred to other machines, although not actually *machine independent.

poset *Short for* partially ordered set. *See* partial ordering.

POS expression *Short for* product of sums expression.

positional system *See* number system.

position-independent code *Another name for* relocatable program.

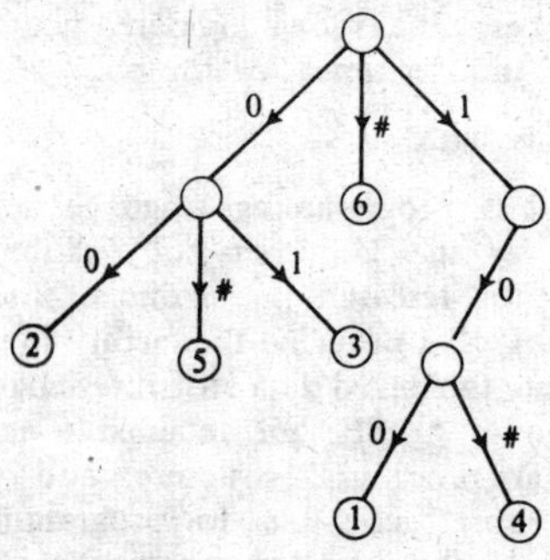

Position tree for 10010#

position tree Let $\alpha = a_1a_2 \ldots a_n$ denote a string, or *word, in the set of all Σ-words, Σ*, and let # be in the alphabet Σ. Then the position tree, T(α), for α# is a tree whose edges are labeled with elements of

$$\Sigma \cup \{\#\}$$

and is constructed according to the following rules:
(a) T(α) has $(n + 1)$ leaves labeled 1,2,..., $n + 1$ (*see* diagram);
(b) the sequence of labels on the edges of the path from the root to the leaf labeled i is the *substring identifier for position i in α#.

positive acknowledgment *See* acknowledgment. *See also* backward error correction.

positive logic A logic system in which all the Boolean variables and Boolean functions behave as described. *Compare* negative logic.

post To update a record or file.

Postal, Telegraph, and Telephone administration *See* PTT.

postcondition of a statement S in some program. An *assertion that characterizes the state of the program immediately after execution of S. The postcondition is expressed in terms of properties of certain program variables and relationships between them. Where a program text is annotated by attaching assertions, a postcondition is attached immediately after the statement to which it relates. *See also* precondition, program correctness proof.

postedit *See* postprocessor.

postfix notation *Another name for* reverse Polish notation.

postmortem Analysis of the cause of some undesired system behavior, based upon information recorded at the time that the undesired behavior was detected. For example, *abnormal termination of a program might result in a record of the state of the program at the time of termination, and this record might subsequently be used for postmortem analysis of the reason for termination.

postorder traversal (endorder traversal) A tour of the nodes of a binary tree obtained by using the following recursive algorithm: visit in postorder the left subtree of the root (if it exists); visit in postorder the right subtree of the root (if it exists); visit the root of the tree. *Compare* preorder traversal, symmetric order traversal.

postprocessor A program that performs some operations on the output of another program, typically formatting the output for some device or filtering out unwanted items. This operation is often called a *postedit*.

Post-production system An approach to *effective computability on strings of symbols, formulated by E. L. Post. A *Post-production* is a string rewriting rule. A set of strings is said to be *Post-generable* if there exists a finite set of axioms (strings) and a finite set of Post-productions Σ such that each string in the set can be obtained from the axiom set by some finite derivation, where each step in the derivation is sanctioned by an application of some production in Σ. It turns out that the class of Post-generable sets is exactly the class of *recursively enumerable sets (on some fixed alphabet).

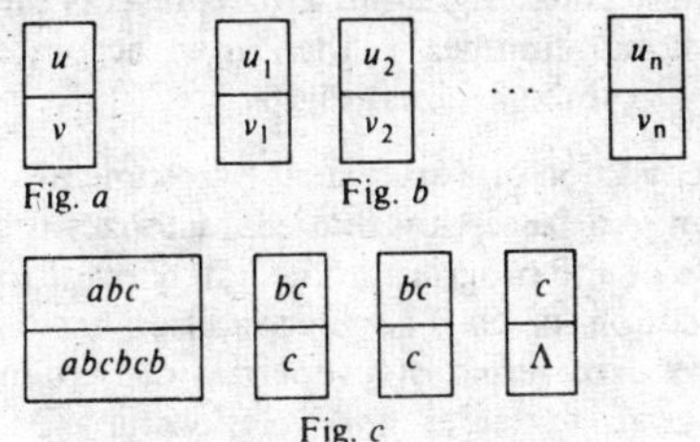

Post's correspondence problem

Post's (correspondence) problem A well-known algorithmically unsolvable problem. Given a finite set of "dominoes" of the form shown in Fig. *a*, with *u* and *v* being *strings, the question is whether or not one can form a sequence, as shown in Fig. *b*, such that reading all the *u*s in order gives the same string as reading all the *v*s. Fig. *c* shows such a sequence, where Λ is the empty string. Even though there are only finitely many different dominoes given, there is an infinite supply of duplicates for each one; the same domino can thus be used more than once in the sequence. Dominoes cannot be inverted.

Depending on the dominoes given, it is sometimes obvious that the answer to the question is "no". However there is no algorithm that can discover this in all cases.

power-fail recovery A method of dealing with the effects of a loss of the incoming power supply. The system is equipped with a power line monitor, which detects any long-term deviation in the supply-line voltage from acceptable limits, and causes a *power-fail interrupt* when deviations occur. The service routine for this interrupt stores the *process descriptors for all processes in *nonvolatile memory and then halts all activity. When the supply-line voltage is restored, the system restarts and can reinstate all processes from the previously stored process descriptors.

power-limited channel A physical transmission channel whose rate of throughput of energy is limited to some value. *See* signal-to-noise ratio, channel coding theorem.

power of the continuum *See* cardinality.

power routing *See* logic circuit.

power set of a *set *S*. The set of all *subsets of *S*, typically denoted by 2^S. It can be described as

$$\{A \mid A \subseteq S\}$$

The number of elements in the power set of *S* is 2^N, where *N* is the number of elements in *S*.

pragma 1. A statement in a programming language that is intended to convey information to a particular implementation, and can be ignored in other implementations of the language.

2. A statement in a programming language that provides information that may assist the compiler in translating the program, but can be ignored without affecting the correct working of the program.

precedence hierarchy The rules determining the order in which operations are carried out, if this is not defined unambiguously by brackets. For example, in most languages the expression

$$a * b + c$$

will be evaluated by doing the multiplication first, and brackets would be used to enforce the alternative order thus:

$$a * (b + c)$$

There is no consensus about precedence hierarchies in languages. *See also* left-to-right precedence.

precedence parsing A *bottom-up parsing technique that exploits precedence relations on the symbols of the grammar to decide when a string of symbols may form a handle. Two precedence parsing techniques, *operator precedence* and *simple precedence*, are in common use.

In simple precedence three relations, $<\cdot$ $\cdot>$ and $\doteq$, are defined on the symbols (terminal and nonterminal) of the *grammar. If

$$X <\cdot Y,\ X \doteq Y, \text{ or } X \cdot> Y$$

then, respectively, X is said to yield precedence to Y, have the same precedence as Y, or take precedence over Y. Note that these relations are not symmetric. By inserting the precedence relations between symbols in a sentential form and then regarding the $<\cdot$ and $\cdot>$ symbols as matching brackets, a handle is determined as the leftmost string delimited by $<\cdot$ at its left end and $\cdot>$ at its right end.

Operator precedence differs from simple precedence in that the three precedence relations are defined on just the terminal symbols of the grammar. Furthermore the grammar must satisfy the property that nonterminals on the right-hand side of a production must always be separated by at least one terminal.

Arithmetic expressions provided the original motivation for operator precedence since conventionally multiplication takes precedence over addition. Simple precedence is a generalization of operator precedence. Both methods are limited in the scope of their application to grammars for which at most one precedence relation exists between any ordered pair of symbols. In addition the right-hand side of productions must be unique.

precision The number of digits to which numbers are represented. For example, if p bits are allocated to the mantissa in the representation of floating-point numbers used in a particular computer, then in that computer floating-point numbers have p bits of precision. In general, the precision of floating-point numbers is proportional to their value (i.e. relative) whereas the precision of fixed-point numbers is absolute (independent of the value).

It is important not to confuse the term precision with accuracy. For example, the number

3.142 8571

has eight-decimal digit precision, irrespective of what it represents. If this number represents 22/7 then it is also accurate to eight decimal digits but if it represents the irrational number π then it is accurate only to three decimal digits.

precondition of a statement S in some program. An *assertion that characterizes the state of the program immediately prior to execution of S. The precondition is expressed in terms of properties of certain program variables and relationships between them. Where a program text is annotated by attaching assertions, a precondition is attached immediately before the statement to which it relates. For a consistent annotation the precondition of S must be implied by the *postcondition of any statement whose execution can immediately precede execution of S. *See also* program correctness proof, weakest precondition.

predicate A *function from some domain to a truth value. If the domain comprises n variables

where $n = 0,1,2, \ldots$

the function is called an n-place predicate. In the special case where $n = 0$, the predicate is a *statement*. Predicates are the fundamental building blocks of the *predicate calculus.

predicate calculus A system of inference that is a generalization of the quantified or

extended *propositional calculus, obtained by introducing generalized *functions and *predicates. As well as the notation of the propositional calculus, the predicate calculus makes use of symbols that represent both function constants and function variables (the latter can be qualified by the quantifiers ∀ or ∃); symbols can also be used to represent predicate constants and predicate variables.
The possibility of function variables and predicate variables gives what is commonly known as the *second-order predicate calculus*. An important and simpler subset is the *first-order predicate calculus*, which does not make use of either function variables or predicate variables.
The generality of the predicate calculus can be illustrated by introducing the concept of a *term*: each constant or variable (where permitted, i.e. in second-order predicate calculus) is a term; if $t_1, t_2, \ldots t_n$ are terms then so is each

$$f(t_1,t_2, \ldots t_n)$$

where f is a function constant or variable (where permitted). In addition, if A is some well-formed formula then

if A then t_1 else t_2

is a term.
The concept of an atomic formula can be redefined so that as well as the items used in the propositional calculus it includes:
(a) each $p(t_1,t_2, \ldots ,t_n)$, where p represents a predicate constant or variable (where permitted);
(b) items of the form $(t_1 = t_2)$.
(It is implicit in this discussion that the predicate calculus admits the existence of the equality operator and the conditional operator *if-then-else*.) With these added facilities, the well-formed formulas, defined using BNF notation (*see* propositional logic), become much more complex.

predicate transformer A function that maps predicates to predicates. Specifically, the predicate transformer for some statement S is a function that maps some predicate R into the *weakest precondition of S with respect to R. The term was introduced by Dijkstra in 1975 in conjunction with a calculus for the derivation of programs; this provides for development of a program to be guided by the simultaneous development of a total correctness proof for the program. *See* program correctness proof.

predictive PCM *See* pulse code modulation.

preemptive allocation An allocation that removes a resource from one process and transfers it to another. When a process requests use of a resource, the appropriate resource controller will at some stage assign the resource to the process. A resource such as a processor is used for a period of time, during which no other process can use the resource. If during this period of use a second process becomes available to run, the processor scheduler may preempt the processor and transfer it to the second higher-priority process.
A more important type of preemptive allocation arises when a nonsharable resource, such as a tape transport, has been allocated to a process but not yet used by it. If a second process requests a tape transport then use of the transport may be denied the first process, and the transport preempted for use by the second process.

prefix of a string α. Any string β where α is the *concatenation $\beta\gamma$ for some string γ. Thus in coding theory, a word is said to be a prefix of another word if the former word matches the first symbols of the latter. *See also* prefix codes.

prefix codes Codes in which no codeword is a *prefix of any other codeword. The idea is usually applied to *variable-length codes. A prefix code has the property that, as soon as all the symbols of a codeword have been received, the codeword is recognized as such. Prefix codes are therefore said to be *instantaneously decodable*. (They are of necessity *uniquely decodable.)

prefix notation *Another name for* Polish notation.

prefix property The property exhibited by a *binary encoding of a set A whereby no code for any element of A is a *prefix of a code for some other element of A.

preorder traversal A tour of the nodes of a binary tree obtained by using the following recursive algorithm: visit the root of the tree; visit in preorder the left subtree of the root (if it exists); visit in preorder the right subtree of the root (if it exists). *Compare* postorder traversal, symmetric order traversal.

preprocessor A program that performs modifications to data in order that the data conforms to the input requirements of a standard program, such as a compiler or a statistical package.

presentation layer of network protocol function. *See* seven-layer reference model.

Prestel The UK *videotex system.

prestore To store, in advance, data needed by a program, or storage of such data.

pretty printer A program that takes a text file and produces a listing or copy of that file in a format that conforms to some set of conventions for textual layout. Pretty printers are most commonly employed to format the source text of high-level language programs; by performing syntax analysis the pretty printer can produce a layout in which indentation is used to give a simple visual indication of program structure.

preventive maintenance Maintenance performed on a regular basis, and intended to prevent failures or to detect incipient failures. An example of the former is routine lubrication and cleaning of devices that have moving magnetic media. An example of the latter is a *marginal check* in which electrical parameters may be varied to induce failures in marginally performing circuits. *Compare* remedial maintenance.

primary file 1. *Another name for* master file.
2. The file that controls the order in which RPG II records are to be selected for processing.

primary index *See* indexed file.

primary memory *Another name for* main memory, specifically the form used as the medium for storing instructions and data that are currently undergoing processing by a CPU.

prime implicant *See* implicant.

primitive Not capable of being broken down into simpler form. The term is used for example with reference to actions requested by a process via supervisor calls, especially the use of P and V operations (*see* semaphore).

primitive data type A *data type, such as integer, real, Boolean, and character, that is made available to the user by the basic hardware. More complex data structures are built up from the primitives, usually by software.

primitive element An element α of a *finite field F whose various powers,

$$\alpha^0\ (=1),\ \alpha,\ \alpha^2,\ \alpha^3,\ \ldots$$

will ultimately include all the nonzero elements of F. Every finite field contains such an element.

primitive polynomial *See* polynomial.

primitive recursive function A *function that can be obtained from certain initial functions by a finite number of applications of *composition and *recursion. The initial functions are normally the *zero function, *successor function, and *projection (or generalized identity) functions, where all functions are defined on the nonnegative integers.
The arithmetic functions of addition and multiplication are examples of primitive recursive functions. Indeed many of the functions that can be evaluated by a computer are primitive recursive.
The term primitive recursive can also be applied firstly to sets whose *characteris-

tic function is primitive recursive and secondly to sets of functions that operate on strings of characters or on lists. In the latter case the definition is analogous to that given above, the successor function adding an element to the string or list. *See also* recursive function.

principal component analysis *See* multivariate analysis.

printed circuit A physical realization of an electronic circuit design in which the connections between the terminals of individual components are formed from copper conductors laminated onto a flat supporting sheet of an insulating material such as fiber glass. The conductor pattern is normally printed and etched onto the sheet and components are then attached to the copper "lands" by hand or dip soldering. The supporting sheet plus circuit is known as a *printed circuit board (PCB)*.
In a typical modular-type construction, a printed circuit is connected via a socket to interconnected *backplane wiring. Smaller modular elements that connect to the printed circuit (but not the backplane) are called *daughter boards*.
Double-sided PCBs are commonly produced. These consist of an insulating sheet with a circuit on each side, with interconnections possible between the two circuits. Multilayer printed circuits are also fabricated (*see* multilayer device).

printer An output device that converts the coded information from the processor into a readable form on paper. There are many types, varying in method, speed, and quality of printing: there are *serial printers, *line printers, and *page printers, and these may be *solid-font or *matrix printers. The technology involved may or may not use mechanical impact to transfer ink (*see* impact printer, nonimpact printer).

printer format The *format for printed output, defining the character and line spacing and the areas of the page where printing will occur. In most *line and *serial printers the pitch of characters and lines is selected by switches or is not variable. The format aspect that is often different for each job involves the lines on which printing is not required; this is controlled by a *vertical format unit. Recent designs of serial and *page printers allow the host system to control all aspects of the format by the use of control codes.

printout The output of a printer. Usually it is a stack of fanfolded paper prior to any bursting or trimming operations.

print server *See* server.

prioritize To put into an order according to the relative urgency or importance. In a multiprogramming environment the programs should be prioritized so that urgent jobs are not delayed by background processing tasks. Program interrupts should be similarly treated. *See also* interrupt priority.

priority Relative importance or urgency. Priority is the quality of having precedence, i.e. requiring early attention, and can be quantified by numerical value, used to determine the order in which several requests for a resource are satisfied. In the situation where several otherwise identical processes are free to run, the one with the highest priority will be run next, hence the term *priority processing*. A *priority interrupt* in a system will be dealt with ahead of standard interrupts that may be awaiting a response. In data transmission a field is allocated to the holding of a code that indicates the relative urgency of the associated message. *See also* interrupt priority.

priority encoder *See* encoder.

priority queue A linear *list where each insertion specifies a priority number as well as the element to be inserted, and each removal or access takes the earliest of the elements with highest priority.

privacy of data. Protection against unauthorized reading. There are two concepts.

1. Protection of data about an individual or corporate entity. Where data can be determined to refer to a specific person, or in some cases to a specific organization, there may exist a legal right to limit access to that data and, in many cases, associated rights to guarantee accuracy and completeness. This form of privacy exists only for data about an identifiable individual, and exists to protect the rights of the individual to whom the data refers. *See* data protection legislation.

2. Protection of data owned by an individual or corporate entity. Where data is deemed to be in some sense the property of someone (or some group) there may exist a right to limit access to that data. This form of privacy exists for data belonging to someone, and exists to protect the rights of the owner of the data. *See* trade secrets. *See also* integrity, security.

privileged instructions Instructions that can only be issued when a computing system is operating in one of the high, or the highest, *execution states.

probability A number between 0 and 1 associated with an event (*see* relative frequency) that is one of a set of possible events: an event that is certain to occur has probability 1. The probability of an event is the limiting value approached by the relative frequency of the event as the number of observations is increased indefinitely. Alternatively it is the degree of belief that the event will occur.

The concept of probability is applied to a wide range of events in different contexts. Originally interest was in the study of games of chance, where correct knowledge of probability values allowed profitable wagers to be made. Later the subject was studied by insurance companies anxious to predict probable future claims on the basis of previously observed relative frequencies. Today probability theory is the basis of statistical analysis (*see* statistical methods).

The *probability calculus* is the set of rules for combining probabilities for combinations of events, using the methods of symbolic logic applied to sets.

See also probability distributions.

probability calculus *See* probability.

probability distributions Theoretical formulas for the *probability that an observation has a particular value, or lies within a given range of values.

Discrete probability distributions apply to observations that can take only certain distinct values, such as the integers 0, 1, 2, . . . or the six named faces of a die. A probability, $p(r)$, is assigned to each event such that the total is unity. Important discrete distributions are the *binomial distribution and the *Poisson distribution.

Continuous probability distributions apply to observations, such as physical measurements, where no two observations are likely to be exactly the same. Since the probability of observing exactly a given value is about zero, a mathematical function, the *cumulative distribution function*, $F(x)$, is used instead. This is defined as the probability that the observation does not exceed x. $F(x)$ increases monotonically with x from 0 to 1, and the probability of observing any value between two limits, x_1 and x_2, is

$$F(x_2) - F(x_1)$$

This definition leads, by differential calculus, to the *frequency function*, $f(x)$, which is the limiting ratio of

$$F(x + h) - F(x) \text{ to } h$$

as h becomes small, so that the probability of an observation between x and $(x + h)$ is $h.f(x)$. The most important continuous distribution is the *normal (or Gaussian) distribution.

Probability distributions are defined in terms of *parameters, whose values determine the numerical values of the probabilities.

problem definition A precise statement of some problem to be solved, with the emphasis on providing a complete and unambiguous definition of the problem rather than an easy introduction to it. *Compare* problem description.

problem description A self-contained overview of some problem to be solved, perhaps with accompanying information on constraints that the solution must respect, possible approaches to the solution, etc. *Compare* problem definition.

problem-oriented language *See* POL.

procedural abstraction The principle that any operation that achieves a well-defined effect can be treated by its users as a single entity, despite the fact that the operation may actually be achieved by some sequence of lower-level operations (*see also* abstraction). Procedural abstraction has been extensively employed since the early days of computing, and virtually all programming languages provide support for the concept (e.g. the SUBROUTINE of Fortran, the **procedure** of Algol, Pascal, Ada, etc.).

procedural language *Another name for* imperative language.

procedure A section of a program that is identified by *name. A procedure usually carries out some well-defined operations on data specified by *parameters. It can be *called from anywhere in a program, and different parameters can be provided for each call.
The term procedure is generally used in the context of high-level languages; in assembly language the word *subroutine is more commonly employed.

procedure-oriented language A programming language that enables a program to be specified by defining a collection of *procedures. These procedures may call each other, and are called by the main program (which can itself be regarded as a procedure).

process A stream of activity. A process is defined by its code, i.e. the ordered set of machine instructions defining the actions that the process is to take, the contents of its workspace, i.e. the set of data values that it can read, write, and manipulate, and its *process descriptor, which defines the current status of any resources that are allocated to the process.

process control Use of a dedicated computer (known as a *process controller*) to control a specific industrial or manufacturing process. Information (sensed) from that process is used as a source of data; computations made upon that data determine control signals to be sent to the process.
In general there are two forms of process control: *continuous* and *discrete*. Continuous process control is involved with the manufacturing of some form of continuous product, primarily chemicals, e.g. the automatic control of a catalytic cracker for petroleum distillation. Although chemicals may be manufactured in batches, this is still considered a continuous process since the variables that control the process can be varied continuously. Discrete control is concerned with the manufacturing of individual (discrete) items, e.g. the welding of two parts to form a larger assembly. Discrete process control is very closely allied to what is now referred to as *applied robotics*. *See also* numerical control, computer-aided manufacturing.

process descriptor A set of information that defines the status of resources allocated to a process. When a system contains a number of processes, any of which may be active at any one time, there will be for each process a descriptor defining the status of that process. Within the descriptor the *ready* indicator shows whether the particular process is able to proceed, or whether it must await the completion of some other activity before it can be executed by the CPU. For processes that are unable to run, the process descriptor will indicate the reason for which that process is *suspended* and will contain pointers to relevant queues and semaphores. The rocess descriptor will also contain a copy of the contents of the processor registers that are to be reinstated when the process is restarted. When a process is running, the process descriptor will contain information (the *resource descriptor*) on the resources allocated to the process and on the permissible operations on these resources.

processor A computer, usually/often the *central processor. *See also* microprocessor, I/O processor, communication processor.

processor allocation The measure of the amount of processor resource that is available to a process. Normally the allocation will be expressed as a time, or as a number of instructions to be executed.

processor status word (PSW) A word that describes fully the condition of a processor at each instant. It indicates which classes of operations are allowed and which are forbidden, and the status of all interrupts associated with the processor. It will also contain the address of the instruction currently being executed and in many cases contains the address of the word that holds the next instruction to be executed. *See also* program status word.

processor time (CPU time) The time for which a process has been receiving service from the processor. *See also* system accounting.

product group *Another name for* direct product.

production *See* semi-Thue system, grammar.

production-rule system A coherent set of rules, each of which identifies a condition of applicability and an action to be taken when the rule is applicable. Such a system may be interpreted by a repetition of the following operations: all rules whose conditions are satisfied are found, one of them is selected, and its action is carried out. Such systems have been extensively used in *computational psychology and in the building of *expert systems.

production run Execution of a program in the normal way to produce useful results. *Compare* dry run.

productive time *See* available time.

product of sums expression (POS expression) A *Boolean function expressed as a product of sum terms, i.e. as an AND of OR terms containing uncomplemented or complemented variables. An example is

$$f = (x \vee y) \wedge (x' \vee z')$$

The function is also realizable as the NOR of a group of NOR terms. *See also* standard product of sums, sum of products expression.

product term A product (AND) of Boolean variables, uncomplemented or complemented. *See also* sum of products expression.

profiling Production of a histogram (or equivalent) concerning some aspect of a system. For example, an *execution profile* for a program might show the proportion of time spent in each individual procedure during a run of the program, while a *statement profile* might show the distribution of the statements in a program between the different kinds of statement provided by the language.

program A set of statements that can be submitted as a unit to some computer system and used to direct the behavior of that system. A *procedural program* gives a precise definition of the procedure to be followed by the computer system in order to obtain the required results. By contrast, a *nonprocedural program* specifies constraints that must be satisfied by the results that are produced but does not specify the procedure by which these results should be obtained; such a procedure must be determined by the computer system itself.

program compatibility A measure of the degree to which programs can effectively be used together in a common environment. Factors affecting program compatibility include machine and operating system dependencies, and the structure of the data that are read and written by the programs.

program control Control of a computer's functioning by a sequence of instructions that comes from a memory and is called the program.

program correctness proof A formal mathematical demonstration that the *semantics of a program are consistent with some specification for that program (*see* program specification). There are two prerequisites to the provision of such a proof: there must be a formal specification for the program, and there must be some formal definition of the semantics of the programming language. Such a definition may take the form of a set of axioms to cover the semantics of any simple statement in the language, and a set of *inference rules* that show how the semantics of any compound statement, including a complete program, can be inferred from the semantics of its individual component statements (simple or compound).

For a typical sequential program written in some *imperative (procedural) language, the program specification can conveniently be given in the form of two *assertions: an *input assertion* and an *output assertion*. These are expressed in terms of properties of certain program variables and relationships between them. The proof then consists of a formal demonstration that the semantics of the program are consistent with the input and output assertions; this demonstration is of course based upon the formal definition of the semantics of the programming language. Interpreted operationally, the assertions characterize program states and the proof shows that if execution of the program is initiated in a state for which the input assertion is "true" then the program will eventually terminate in a state for which the output assertion is "true".

This kind of proof is known as a *proof of total correctness.* Historically, however, such a proof has often been resolved into two parts: first, a *proof of partial correctness*, which shows that if the program terminates then it does so in a state for which the output assertion is "true", and second, a *proof of termination*, which shows that the program will indeed terminate (normally rather than abnormally).

A common approach to the proof of partial correctness begins by attaching the input and output assertions to the program text at the very beginning and very end respectively. Further assertions, called *intermediate assertions*, are attached to the program text both before and after every statement (simple or compound). The assertion attached immediately before and immediately after a statement are known respectively as the *precondition and *postcondition of that statement.

The proof of partial correctness consists of a formal demonstration that the semantics of each statement in the program, whether simple or compound, are consistent with its precondition and postcondition. This demonstration can begin at the level of the simple statements and then proceed through the various levels of compound statement until eventually it is demonstrated that the semantics of the complete program are consistent with its precondition and postcondition, i.e. with the input assertion and the output assertion. The semantics of an individual statement are shown to be consistent with its precondition and postcondition by applying to the precondition and postcondition the appropriate axiom or inference rule for that statement. This yields a theorem, called a *verification condition*, that must be proved using conventional mathematics in order to demonstrate the required consistency.

Note particularly that the overall proof of correctness is achieved not by consideration of execution histories, but rather by treating the program as a static mathematical object to which certain axioms and inference rules apply.

The central problem with such a proof is the devising of the intermediate assertions. This requires a full appreciation of the design of the program and of the semantics of the programming language. Often the key lies in finding appropriate intermediate assertions to attach inside the various loops in the program, i.e. loop *invariants. Devising intermediate assertions for some arbitrary program is often extremely difficult and a constructive approach, in which program and proof are developed together, is definitely preferable.

In order to present a proof of termination it is necessary to demonstrate first that the program does not suffer from abortive termination and second that the program does not endlessly repeat some loop. A demonstration of the former may become very complex, e.g. it may be necessary to demonstrate that arithmetic overflow will not occur. A demonstration that the program will eventually exit from some loop can be based on a *well-ordered set. For example, suppose that for some loop an expression E can be found such that the loop can be shown to terminate immediately if the value of E is negative. Further suppose that the value of E can be shown to decrease on each iteration around the loop. It then follows that the loop must terminate.

Proofs of correctness do not offer a complete solution to the problems of software reliability in practical systems. The sheer size and complexity of proofs presents many difficulties that are only partly alleviated by *mechanical verifier systems. Issues such as the limitations of computer arithmetic, indeterminacy, and parallelism all present additional problems. It may be very difficult to develop a specification against which to verify a program, and impossible to demonstrate that this specification is itself "correct" in that it properly reflects the intentions of the developers.

Work on proofs of correctness has made a major contribution to software engineering in that many advances in the understanding of programming languages, principles, and methods have their origins in this work. In addition the scope for practical applications of program proofs is growing and the formal approach to program correctness is of increasing significance.

program counter (instruction counter; current address register) A counting *register that normally increments one memory address at a time and is used to obtain the program sequence (i.e. the sequence of instructions) from sequential memory locations. This counter will have its contents changed by branch instructions.

program decomposition The breaking down of a complete program into a set of component parts, normally called modules. The decomposition is guided by a set of design principles or criteria that the identified modules should reflect. Since the decomposition determines the coarse structure of the program, the activity is also referred to as *high-level* or *architectural design*. *See also* modular programming, program design.

program design The activity of progressing from a specification of some required program to a description of the program itself. Most phase models of the *software life-cycle recognize program design as one of the phases. The input to this phase is a specification of what the program is required to do. During the phase the design decisions are made as to how the program will meet these requirements, and the output of the phase is a description of the program in some form that provides a suitable basis for subsequent implementation.

Frequently the design phase is divided into two subphases, one of coarse *architectural design* and one of *detailed design*. The architectural design produces a description of the program at a gross level; it is normally given in terms of the major components of the program and their interrelationships, the main algorithms that these components employ, and the major data structures. The detailed design then refines the architectural design to the stage where actual implementation can begin.

program design language (PDL) A language, used for expressing program designs, that is similar to a conventional high-level programming language but emphasizes structure and intention rather than the ability to execute programs expressed in the language. PDLs are often employed in conjunction with *structured programming. When not executable they are termed *pseudocode.

Typically the formal syntax of a PDL would cover data definition and overall program structure. Facilities in the latter area would include the basic control-flow constructs – sequential, conditional, and iterative – plus those for the definition and invocation of subroutines. These facilities would be used to define the overall framework of the program, but individual actions within the framework would be expressed using pseudocode – natural English or a more formal semantically rich language. Correspondingly, the PDL facilities for data definition may be expected to be richer than those of a typical programming language, encompassing a broader range of basic types and a more extensive set of data-structuring facilities. A wide variety of PDLs have been defined; normal practice is to select one that is well-matched to the target programming language.

program development system A computer system that provides support to the program development phase of a software project. A typical program development system employs a simple database (or perhaps just a basic filing system) as a repository for information, and offers *software tools for editing of program source texts, compiling, link loading, and debugging. Usually some form of command-language interpreter is also available; this may have been produced specifically for the program development system, or may have been inherited from the underlying operating system. *Compare* software engineering environment.

program file A *file containing a program, as opposed to a *data file.

program library A collection of programs and packages that are made available for common use within some environment; individual items need not be related. A typical library might contain compilers, utility programs, packages for mathematical operations, etc. Usually it is only necessary to reference the library program to cause it to be automatically incorporated in a user's program.

program listing (source listing; listing) An output produced by a *compiler, consisting of the source program neatly laid out and accompanied by diagnostic information and error messages.

programmable devices 1. Devices under the control of a *stored program obeyed by a *fetch-execute cycle. *See* computer, central processor.

2. Integrated circuits whose action is determined by the user either until reprogrammed (*erasable programmable devices*) or for the life of the device (*nonerasable programmable devices*). Erasable devices are usually implemented by the storage of static electric charges, whereas nonerasable devices either employ *fusible links or have their structure determined at the final masking stage of manufacture.

Static charge or fusible-link devices are called *field-programmable*, since they may be programmed by the user "in the field"; masked devices are called *mask-programmable*, implying programmability only at the time of manufacture. This terminology is common for *programmed logic. In the case of read-only memory the same distinction often appears as "programmable"

(*PROM) and, by implication, "non-programmable" (*ROM).

programmable logic array *See* PLA.

programmable ROM *See* PROM.

program maintenance All technical activities related to a given program following its release for operational usage. Such activities are not limited to the correction of errors but may also include modification of the program to meet changing operational requirements, amendments to the program documentation, upgrades to the program, and so on. Because of the range of these activities, some models of the *software life-cycle view program maintenance as simply being iteration that occurs after, rather than before, release of the system for operational use. For many programs the maintenance activities account for more than half of the total life-cycle costs.

programmed I/O A way of controlling input/output activity in which the processor is programmed to interrogate a peripheral or a number of peripherals to see if they are ready for a data transfer. When a number of peripherals are involved the interrogation process is called *polling. *Compare* interrupt I/O.

programmed logic In general, *programmable devices that are more complicated (logical) than read-only memories, including programmed logic arrays (*see* PLA), programmed gate arrays (PGAs), programmed-array logic (PAL), and uncommitted logic arrays (ULAs).

programmed logic array *See* PLA.

programmer unit *Another name for* PROM programmer.

programming In the broadest sense, all technical activities involved in the production of a *program, including analysis of requirements and all stages of design and implementation. In a much narrower sense it is the coding and testing of a program from some given design. This narrower usage is most common in the context of commercial programming, where a distinction is often drawn between systems analysts, who are responsible for analysis of requirements and design, and programmers, who are responsible for implementaton and testing.

programming language A notation for the precise description of computer programs or algorithms. Programming languages are *artificial* languages, in which the *syntax and *semantics are strictly defined. Thus while they serve their purpose they do not permit the freedom of expression that is characteristic of a natural language.

programming standards A set of rules or conventions that constrain the form of the programs that are produced within an organization. Such rules may range in scope from those that address the high-level design and decomposition of the program to *coding standards*, which govern the use of individual constructs provided by the programming language.

programming support environment *See* software engineering environment.

programming theory A general term for a number of interrelated and rapidly developing subjects concerned broadly with the application of formal mathematical methods to the study of programming concepts. Principle areas are: *semantics of programming languages, *program correctness proof; *program transformation, *program specification, and programming methodology.

program proving *See* program correctness proof.

program specification A precise statement of the effects that an individual program is required to achieve. It should clearly state what the program is to do without making any commitment as to how this is to be done. For a program that is intended to terminate, the program specification can take the form of an input-output specification that describes the desired mapping from the set of input values to the set of output values. For cyclic programs, which are not designed to terminate, it is not possible to give a simple input-output specification; normal practice is to focus attention on the individual functions performed by the program during its cyclic operations.

For both terminating and cyclic programs a variety of notations have been employed for program specifications, ranging from natural language with embedded equations and tables to formal notations such as those based upon first-order *predicate calculus. *See also* software specification.

program status word (PSW) A collection of information that permits an interrupted process to resume operation after the interrupt has been handled. The information is held in the *program status register*, and usually contains the value of the program counter and bits indicating the status of various conditions in the ALU such as overflow and carry, along with the information on supervisor privileged status. *See also* processor status word.

program structure The overall form of a program, with particular emphasis on the individual components of the program and the interrelationships between these components. Programs are frequently referred to as either *well structured* or *poorly structured*. With a well-structured program the division into components follows some recognized principle such as *information hiding, and the interfaces between components are explicit and simple. By contrast, with a poorly structured program the division into components is largely arbitrary (or even nonexistent), and interfaces are implicit and complex. At a finer level, a well-structured program employs appropriate data structures and program units with a single entry point and a single exit point (*see* structured programming, def. 2), while a poorly structured program has arbitrary data structures and flow of control.

program testing Checking by means of actual execution whether a program behaves in the desired manner. The program is executed and supplied with test data, and the way in which the program responds to this test data is analyzed. *Compare* program correctness proof.

program transformation The study of systematic ways of transforming a program into another program that has some desirable property and is equivalent to the original program (or, if not equivalent, has a meaning bearing a simple relation to that of the original).

Often the aim of such transformation is to produce a more efficient program. It is widely felt that much of the complexity of programming results from the need to produce efficient programs, and that it is therefore desirable to begin with a simple (yet inefficient) program and then transform it to an efficient (but complicated) one. Such transformations may be carried out by hand, by machine, or by a mixture of the two.

Other aims of transformation include expressing certain *language constructs in terms of others (*transformational semantics*). Also, developing algorithms by transformation can serve to verify their correctness, to elucidate their structure, and to provide a classification of the space of possible algorithms.

program unit (subprogram) A constituent part of a large program, and in some sense self-contained.

program verification Any method that will ensure that a program will do exactly what it is supposed to do. *See also* program correctness proof.

projection function The function U_i^n that extracts the ith coordinate from an ordered n-tuple (*see* ordered pair). More formally

$$U_i^n(x_1, x_2, \ldots x_n) = x_i$$

See also primitive recursive function.

PROLOG A *logic programming language, widely used in artificial intelligence. The basic element of PROLOG programs is the *atom*, which expresses a simple relationship among individuals, the latter being named (in the simplest sense) either by constants or by variables. Examples of atoms are
"Mary is the sister of Jane", where Mary and Jane are both constants;
"Adam is an ancestor of *x*", where Adam is a constant and *x* is a variable.
A program in PROLOG consists of a collection of (Horn clause) sentences, where each sentence is either a simple assertion or an implication. The former consists of a single atom, while the latter takes the form
"A if B1 and B2 and ... and Bn"
where the conclusion A and the conditions B1 ... Bn are all atoms. An example of an implication is
"*x* is a grandfather of *y* if *x* is the father of *z* and *z* is a parent of *y*"
A PROLOG program is invoked by presenting a *query* in the form of a collection of atomic conditions
"A1 and A2 and ... and An"
Execution of the program then determines a set of values for the variables of the query such that the truth of the query then follows from the assertions and implications of the program (assuming that such a set of values exist).
PROLOG has been selected as the basis for the Japanese "fifth generation" computers.

PROM *Acronym for* programmable read-only memory. A form of semiconductor read-only memory, *ROM, whose contents are added by a separate process after the device has been manufactured. This process of programming the PROM is accomplished by means of a device known as a *PROM programmer. In general the programming process involves the destruction of *fusible links within the PROM and is irreversible, i.e. the contents of the memory cannot be altered. Certain PROMs, including *EPROMs, can however be reprogrammed numerous times.

PROM programmer (programmer unit) An item of equipment that establishes the correct conditions for the programming of a *PROM device and thus allows the user to program the PROM. The programming process often requires the physical destruction of fusible links within the PROM using relatively high voltage pulses, hence the jargon terms PROM zapping, blowing, blasting, and burning. Such equipment may be capable of programming a number of different types of PROM and/or *EPROM devices.

prompt A short message, sent from a process to a user, indicating that the process expects the user to present fresh data. The prompt frequently has some mnemonic content indicating the type of data expected.

PROM zapping *Jargon* The process of programming a *PROM using a *PROM programmer.

propagation delay The time required for a change in the input to a *logic gate or *logic circuit to produce a change in the output. It is usually very brief. It is inherent in any gate or circuit, being caused by unavoidable delays in transistor switching.

proper ancestor *See* ancestor.

proper subset, subgroup, subgraph *See* subset, subgroup, subgraph respectively.

propositional calculus A system of *symbolic logic, the study of which is known as *propositional logic*. There are many alternative but equivalent definitions, one of the more useful for the computer scientist being given below.
The only admissible terms of the propositional calculus are the two symbols *T* and *F* together with logical propositions that are denoted by small letters; these sym-

$$\langle wff \rangle ::= \langle atf \rangle \mid (\sim \langle wff \rangle) \mid ((\langle wff \rangle \vee \langle wff \rangle) \mid ((\langle wff \rangle \wedge \langle wff \rangle) \mid ((\langle wff \rangle \supset \langle wff \rangle) \mid ((\langle wff \rangle \equiv \langle wff \rangle) \mid (\text{IF } \langle wff \rangle \text{ THEN } \langle wff \rangle \text{ ELSE } \langle wff \rangle)$$

Fig. 1 Class of wffs in BNF notation, used in propositional calculus

$$\frac{\Gamma \rightarrow A \text{ and } \Gamma \rightarrow B}{\Gamma \rightarrow A \wedge B}$$

$$\frac{\Gamma \rightarrow A \wedge B}{\Gamma \rightarrow A} \qquad \frac{\Gamma \rightarrow A \wedge B}{\Gamma \rightarrow B}$$

Fig. 2 Rule of inference for $\wedge$

bols are basic and indivisible and are thus called *atomic formulas*.

The propositional calculus is based on the study of *well-formed formulas* or wffs for short. Common wffs of the form

$$(\sim A), (A \vee B), (A \wedge B),$$
$$(A \supset B), (A \equiv B),$$
$$(\text{IF } A \text{ THEN } B \text{ ELSE } C)$$

are formed from appropriate wffs A, B, and C using logical *connectives; they are called respectively *negation*, *disjunction*, *conjunction*, *implication*, *equivalence*, and *conditional*. If $\langle atf \rangle$ denotes the class of atomic formulas, then the class of wffs, $\langle wff \rangle$, can be described in *BNF notation (*see* Fig. 1).

Proofs and theorems within the propositional calculus should be conducted in a formal and rigorous manner: certain basic axioms can be assumed and certain *rules of inference* must be followed. In particular these rules must provide some formal method of dealing with the various connectives.

The rules of inference are stated using a form such as

$$\frac{\alpha}{\beta}$$

The rule should be interpreted to mean that on the assumption that α is true, it can be deduced that β is then true. (This notation is used in computing circles though logicians often use a notation such as $\alpha \vdash \beta$.) In writing the rules it is convenient to employ a notation such as

$$\Gamma, A \Rightarrow B$$

Γ is some set of wffs whose truth has been established; A and B are some other wffs highlighted for the purposes of the rule; $\Rightarrow$ denotes implication (to avoid confusion with the symbol $\supset$). For example, the rules for the introduction and elimination respectively of the $\wedge$ connective are shown in Fig. 2.

An *extended* or *quantified* propositional calculus is formed by the introduction of the universal and existential *quantifiers, $\forall$ and $\exists$. To the previous definition of well-formed formula are added the rules that if A is a valid wff and v is a variable whose values may be only T or F then

$$(\forall v)A \quad \text{and} \quad (\exists v)A$$

are both valid wffs. There are also additional rules of inference for quantifiers.

protected location A memory location that can only be accessed by an authorized user or process. *See also* memory protection.

protection domain A set of access privileges to protected resources. Where many processes coexist, each process having differing access permission to a number of protected resources via some form of key, it may be convenient to group together a set of such keys in order to provide a single process with access to the resources that it requires. Access control can then be manipulated independent of the processes concerned. The protection domain is either the set of keys, or equivalently, the set of resources to which the keys give access.

protocol Any agreement that governs the procedures used to exchange information between cooperating entities. The agreement usually includes how much information is to be sent, how often it is sent, how to recover from transmission errors, and who is to receive the information. In general, a protocol definition will include definitions of message formats, sequencing rules concerning messages, and interpretation rules concerning messages transferred in proper sequence. *See also* seven-layer reference model.

protocol hierarchy *See* hierarchical communication system.

protocol translation *See* internetworking.

pseudocode A program-like but informal notation containing natural-language text, used to describe the functioning of a procedure or program. Usually the control flow is expressed in programming terms,

if . . . then . . . else,
repeat . . . until,
etc.,

while the actions are elaborated as narrative prose. Used mainly as a design aid, it is superior to flow diagrams since it allows the structure of a program to appear explicitly and facilitates top-down design. *See also* program design language.

pseudoinstruction (pseudo-operation; directive) An element in an assembly language that is similar to an instruction but provides control information to the assembler as opposed to generating a particular instruction. Examples are:

generate absolute code/generate relative addresses;
start a new segment;
allocate space for constants or variables.

pseudolanguage A notation resembling a programming language, used for program design. Pseudolanguage is an effective substitute for the *flowchart: unlike a programming language it is not necessary to have a compiler to convert it into executable code. A pseudolanguage usually incorporates the control-flow primitives of a programming language, but combines these with a narrative prose description of the computation to be carried out, e.g.

while not end-of-file
deal with the next character

pseudonoise sequence (PN sequence) A sequence of symbols with *pseudorandom properties intended to simulate *noise. Most commonly *m-sequences are used.

pseudorandom Mimicking randomness. A *deterministic process, which cannot in principle be random, may nevertheless exhibit any number of the properties of randomness to any desired degree (by appropriate design), and so may serve as a surrogate random process; it is then called pseudorandom.

pseudorandom numbers *See* random numbers.

PSK *Abbrev. for* phase shift keying.

PSL/PSA *Abbrev. for* problem statement language/problem statement analyzer. A computerized system that can be used for the development and analysis of an *expression of requirements and to provide assistance during system design. The expression of requirements is maintained in a computer database: PSL is the input language to this database while PSA is the management system and report generator for the database.

The basic database model consists of objects that may have properties and may be interconnected by means of relationships.

The types of object and relationship are predefined within PSL, there being more than 20 kinds of object and more than 50 kinds of relationship. The objects and relationships are concerned with various aspects of the system for which requirements are being expressed: system input/output flow, system structure, data structure, data derivation, system size and volume, system dynamics, system properties, and project management. PSA permits the analysis of the database and the production of various kinds of report, e.g. on database modifications, database content, and on unused data objects or breaks in information flow.

PSL/PSA was developed by Daniel Teichroew on the ISDOS project at the University of Michigan. The system has been implemented on a wide range of computers and has been used extensively by many organizations.

PSPACE, PSPACE-complete *See* polynomial space.

PSS *Abbrev. for* packet switch stream. The *public packet network of the UK's PTT, British Telecom; it offers a national packet switched data service and has been available since 1981. It uses the *X.25 interface protocol, providing full duplex working at a range of speeds up to and including 48 000 bps; it can also provide intercommunication between data terminal equipment operating at different speeds. Connections to other public packet networks can be made.

PSW *Abbrev. for* processor status word, program status word.

PTIME *See* polynomial time.

PTT *Short for* Postal, Telegraph, and Telephone administration. The national governmental entity that provides communication services in many countries. *Public packet networks are offered by these carriers as an extension to their existing telegraph and telephone services. PTTs usually hold a national monopoly on communication services, and private competition is not allowed. Traditional PTT data communication offerings include dedicated lines at low-speed (up to 300 bps), voice-grade (300 to 9600 bps), and wideband (anything above 9600 bps) capacities. More recently, PTTs have initiated national and international packet switching service based on the *X.25 protocol. PTTs participate in the development and adoption of international standards through organizations such as the CCITT and ISO. *See also* common carrier.

p-type semiconductor *See* semiconductor.

public key system A system used in *cryptography in which the enciphering key is made public but the deciphering key is kept secret.

public packet network (public data network) A network providing *packet switching services to public customers. In most countries the public packet networks are offered by the national *PTT, a governmental organization; public packet networks in the US are offered by *common carriers licensed by the FCC. Most public packet networks are based on the *X.25 interface protocol and related CCITT standards. Examples of public networks are *Telenet, *Tymnet, *PSS, *Transpac, and *Datapac.

pull-up resistor A resistor that is connected between the power-supply line and a logic line and ensures that the line is normally pulled up to the supply potential. *Open-collector logic devices may be connected to the logic line and each device is then capable of pulling the line low, i.e. to ground.

pulse A transient change in voltage, current, or some other normally constant physical parameter. This transient consists of a fixed-amplitude geometrically defined transition, followed, after a fixed time, by an opposite and often equal amplitude transition.

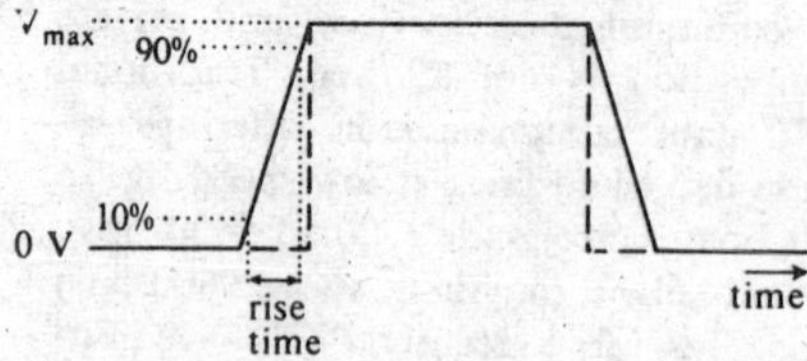

Rectangular voltage pulse

For rectangular pulses the transitions should in theory be stepwise, i.e. instantaneous. In reality however they require a finite time in which to occur. For transitions from low to high voltage, current, etc., a convenient measure of this time is the *rise time*, defined as the time required for the pulse amplitude to rise from 10% to 90% of its maximum value (*see* diagram). The *decay time* is an analogous measure for high to low transitions and is defined as the time required for the pulse amplitude to decay from 90% to 10% of its maximum value.
The time interval between the rising and falling edge of a rectangular pulse is called the *pulse width*. The *pulse height* is the amplitude of a pulse, usually its maximum to minimum voltage, current, etc., ignoring any short-duration spikes or low-amplitude ripple superimposed on the main pulse. *See also* ringing.

pulse code modulation (PCM) A technique used by *codecs to convert an analog signal into a digital bit stream. The amplitude (usually) of the analog signal is sampled (8000 samples per second for voice-quality telephone lines with 4000 Hz bandwidth), and a digital code is selected to represent the sampled value. The digital code is transmitted to the receiving end, which uses it to generate an analog output signal. Encoding techniques may be used to reduce the amount of data that is transmitted between the sender and the receiver, based on known characteristics of the analog signal. For example, *mu-law (μ-law) encoding* converts the analog signal to a digital code based on the logarithm of its value, rather than on a linear transformation.
Differential PCM (DPCM) transmits the difference between the current sample and the previous sample. DPCM assumes that the difference requires fewer bits than the signal amplitude.
Delta (Δ) PCM is a version of DPCM in which a single bit is used for each sample, representing a signal change of plus or minus one unit. A constant signal is represented as a series of plus or minus transitions.
Predictive PCM extrapolates from the previous few samples what the next sample should be, and transmits the difference between the actual value and the predicted value.
See also modulation.

pulse generator A circuit or instrument that generates a sequence of *pulses, usually (but not necessarily) of uniform height, width, and repetition rate or frequency.

pulse height *See* pulse.

pulse repetition rate (pulse repetition frequency) of a *pulse train. The average number of pulses that occur per second, expressed in hertz.

pulse shaping Alteration of the shape of a *pulse. Usually pulse-shaping circuits receive pulses that are distorted and convert them into rectangular pulses; sometimes they incorporate a *monostable circuit to set the output pulse width.

pulse stretcher An electronic device that is often included in logic circuitry in order to extend the duration of very short input pulses. This ensures that the pulses are of adequate length, i.e. they are of the minimum duration required for reliable processing by the circuitry. A *monostable is often used for this purpose.

pulse train A repetitive series of *pulses, separated in time by a fixed and often constant interval. The duration of each pulse and its amplitude are also often made constant. This type of waveform may be defined by its *mark-space ratio*, i.e. the ratio of pulse duration, t_1, to pulse separation, t_2, and by its *pulse repetition rate, which is given by

$$1/(t_1 + t_2)$$

pulse-triggered flip-flop *See* flip-flop.

pulse width *See* pulse.

pumping lemmas Two theorems in formal language theory that express necessary conditions for languages to be *regular or *context-free:

If language L is regular, there exists an integer n such that,
for any *word z in L, $|z|>n$,
there exist u,v,w with
$z = uvw$, v nonempty, $|vw|\leqslant n$,
such that:

$$uv^kw \in L, \text{ for all } k\geqslant 0$$

If language L is context-free, there exist integers p and q such that,
for any z in L, with $|z|>p$,
there exist u,v,w,x,y with
$z = uvwxy$, v and x nonempty, $|vwx|\leqslant q$,
such that:

$$uv^kwx^ky \in L, \text{ for all } k\geqslant 0$$

punch card *Another name for* punched card, sometimes used to refer to a card that has not yet been punched.

punched card (punch card) A rectangular paper card, typically 0.007″ (0.178 mm) thick, into which data has been – or can be – encoded by punching holes that are sensed by a *punched card reader. Punched cards were used extensively for input, output, and file storage of data on early computer systems and are still used for data input.

The cards are of a uniform size and are notionally divided into a number of *columns* that are parallel to the short edge and a number of *rows* – usually 12 – parallel to the long edge. The 80 column card, 7.375″ by 3.25″ (18.73 by 8.25 cm) in size, was the most common type; each column is divided into 12 positions at which holes can be punched, a particular combination of holes in a column representing a specific character. Other types of card have also been devised with as few as 21 columns and as many as 160. The last type of punched card to be widely used was the 96 column IBM card.

Prior to the development of computers a variety of machines were available that enabled the various activities of data processing, e.g. sorting, collating, and listing or tabulating, to be carried out using data files composed of punched cards. Stout cards with holes punched in them were used by Jacquard to control the weaving of patterns on a loom in about 1800. Charles Babbage saw the possibility of using punched cards to control his *Analytical Engine, conceived in the 1830s.

In the 1880s Herman Hollerith, a statistician at the US Census Bureau developed a machine that electrically sensed holes punched in cards and could sort and accumulate totals; the machines were used in the 1890 census. In 1896 Hollerith formed his own company, which was later to become IBM.

punched card reader A machine that can sense data encoded on a card as a pattern of punched holes and convert it into a series of binary codes. The reader may be designed so that a stack of punched cards may be placed in the input hopper and the machine will pick the cards singly and in sequence and enter them into a track. The card is driven at a constant speed between a light source and 12 photocells, which sense the light that passes through the punchings; the card is then deposited in a stacker. There may be provision for an additional stacker to receive cards that could not be read correctly.

The electronics associated with the reader mechanism converts the signals from the 12 photocells into appropriate 6 or 8 bit binary codes and either transmits them via an interface or puts them into an internal buffer for subsequent transmission. If the

cards are read column by column by 12 photocells, the machine is referred to as a *serial card reader*; these generally operate at speeds between 150 and 2000 cards per minute. If the card is moved along the track such that it passes beneath the read head row by row, the machine is referred to as a *parallel card reader*.
Static card readers used in some data collection require the card to be inserted manually. It is then gripped and held while sensing takes place. The sensing may be photoelectric or mechanical, the mechanical sensing system having an array of probes associated with switches. The array is pressed against the card and in those cases where the probe passes through a hole the associated switch remains made. Where the card is not punched the probe is pushed back against a spring and a switch contact is broken.

punched tag A small card that is encoded with a pattern of holes and attached to a product in a shop or factory. When the product is sold or moves to a different part of the factory the tag – or part of it – is removed and fed into a machine that senses the holes. The data thus captured is a valuable aid to stock and production control. The most prominent punched tag system in retail applications is the *Kimball tag*.

punched tape *See* paper tape.

punch tape *See* paper tape.

pure BCD *Another name for* natural BCD. *See* binary-coded decimal.

push *See* stack (def. 1).

pushdown automaton (PDA) A *finite-state automaton augmented by a *stack of symbols that are distinct from the symbols in the input string. Like the finite-state automaton, the PDA reads its input string once from left to right, with acceptance or rejection determined by the final state. After reading a symbol, however, the PDA performs the following actions: change state, remove top of stack, and push zero or more symbols onto stack. The precise choice of actions depends on the input symbol just read, the current state, and the current top of stack. Since the stack can grow unboundedly, a PDA can have infinitely many different configurations – unlike a finite-state automaton.
A *nondeterministic PDA* is one that has a choice of actions for some conditions. The languages recognized by nondeterministic PDAs are precisely the *context-free languages. However not every context-free language is recognized by a deterministic PDA.

pushdown stack, pushdown list *Other names for* stack (def. 1).

pushup stack, pushup list *Other names for* queue. *See also* stack (def. 2).

Q

***q*-ary (*q*-valued)** Having q values, where q is a positive integer not less than 2. In *logic circuits, the treatment of q values is called *multiple-valued logic, or binary logic for $q = 2$. In coding theory, some codes are restricted to the binary case; others can operate with arbitrary q or with q a prime number. Throughout switching and coding theory, the binary case is by far the most important. *See also* polynomial.

QL *Abbrev. for* query language.

quadrature *Another name for* numerical integration.

quality assurance *See* software quality assurance.

quality control The use of sampling, inspection, and testing methods at all levels of system production to produce defect-free hardware and software.

quantifier One of the two symbols ∀ or ∃ used in the extended *propositional

calculus and the *predicate calculus. ∀ is the *universal quantifier* and is read "for all". ∃ is the *existential quantifier* and is read "there exists". One or more variables must immediately follow a quantifier; they are called *bound variables*. These must be followed by a predicate, which may contain variables known as *free variables*. The whole quantified predicate states the truth value of the predicate concerning the free variables (if any). i.e. eliminating the bound variables.
In either case the quantification refers to all possible values of the bound variables, within the domains of those variables in the predicates. The universal quantifier means that the predicate is true for all such values. The existential quantifier means that the predicate is true for at least one such value.

quantization The process of constructing a discrete representation of a quantity that is usually regarded as continuous (*see* discrete and continuous systems). For example, the measurement of the amplitude of a *signal at discrete intervals of time, when the signal occurs over continuous time, is called *time quantization*, or *sampling*; the measurement of the brightness of picture elements (*pixels) in a space-continuous picture is called *space quantization*, or *pixelization*.
The term quantization without the predication of time or space usually refers to the quantization of amplitude; the same applies to *digitization, which is nearly synonymous with quantization.

quantization noise The effective continuous noise power, the addition of which to a continuous signal has the same effect as the amplitude *quantization to which the signal is subjected (*see* discrete and continuous systems). The effect of time *quantization may also be described by the addition of noise, but in a more complex way. *See also* Nyquist's criterion.

quantizer *Another name for* digitizer.

quantum The amount of time allocated to an individual process in a *time-slicing process-management system. *See also* scheduling algorithm.

quasi- Seemingly; mimicking. It is a combining form used sometimes in computing in place of pseudo-, as in quasi-random numbers or quasi-instruction.

quaternary logic *See* multiple-valued logic.

Qube A US *videotex system.

query language (QL) The section of a *database management system (DBMS) that provides facilities for the interrogation of the *database. The power and complexity of a query language varies widely from one DBMS to another. A query language designed to access the database directly from a terminal is known as an *interactive query language (IQL)*. *See also* query processing.

query processing 1. The processing of *transactions against a *file or against a *database where information is abstracted but the contents of the file or database are unchanged. Modern database systems usually have an associated *query language instead of, or in addition to, a *data manipulation language for this purpose.
2. The process of translation from the specification of the query in the query language to executable commands.

queue (FIFO list; pushup stack; pushup list) A linear *list where all insertions are made at one end of the list and all removals and accesses at the other. Like a pushdown *stack, a queue can be implemented in hardware as a specialized form of addressless memory, and is most commonly used for speed buffering between a real-time data input/output stream and a form of memory that requires start/stop time.

queue management A queue is characterized by the way in which customers (i.e. processes) join it in order to wait for service, and by the way in which customers already in the queue are selected for servicing. Both of these activities are controlled by the *queue manager*.

queuing theory The study of systems in which customers, arriving at random and requiring varying periods of service, may have to wait in order to be served. From the number of service points and the *probability distributions of arrival times and service times, the distribution of the length of queue and the waiting time before service may be predicted.
Queuing theory has important applications in any system liable to congestion, where the costs of improved service may be balanced against the costs of congestion.

quibinary code *Another name for* biquinary code.

quickersort An algorithm published in 1965 by R. S. Scowen using a method similar to *quicksort. It repeatedly splits the array to be sorted into parts such that all elements of one part are less than all elements of the other, with a third part in the middle consisting of a single element.

quicksort A form of sorting by exchanging due to C. A. R. Hoare. By comparing sortkeys from the two extremes of the file, and alternately working up the file from the bottom until an exchange is necessary and then working down the file from the top, the original problem can be reduced to two smaller problems. The same process is then applied to each part, and is further repeated until the problems are trivially small. *See also* heapsort.

quiesce To render inactive or quiescent.

***q*-valued** *See* *q*-ary.

R

race condition (race) A condition in *sequential circuits in which two or more variables change at one time. In practice, i.e. with nonideal circuits, there is a possibility of incorrect operation under such a condition. *See also* hazard.

racking *See* scroll.

radix (base) The number of distinct digits in a fixed-radix *number system. These digits represent the integers in the range zero to one less than the radix. *See also* binary system, hexadecimal notation, octal notation.

radix complement (true complement) For an integer represented in a fixed-radix *number system, a number formed by adding one to the *radix-minus-one complement of the given integer. For example, in the decimal system the *ten's complement* of 0372 is 9628 (i.e. 9627 + 1); in the binary system the *two's complement* of 1100 is 0100 (i.e. 0011 + 1). *See also* complement number system.

radix exchange A form of sorting by exchanging that is applicable to binary computers. Instead of comparing two sortkeys, individual bits are compared, starting with the most significant bit. The file is then split into two subfiles, one with keys having 0 as first bit, the other with 1 as first bit. The process continues on the first subfile, comparing the second bits, and similarly on the second subfile, and so on until the file is sorted.

radix-minus-one complement (diminished radix complement) For an integer represented in a fixed-radix *number system, a number formed by replacing each digit d in the integer by its *complement*, i.e. by

$$(R - 1 - d)$$

where R denotes the radix of the system. For example, in the decimal system the *nine's complement* of 0372 is 9627; in the binary system the *one's complement* of 1100 is 0011. *See also* complement number system, radix complement.

radix notation *See* radix point.

radix point A symbol, usually a dot, used to separate the integral part from the frac-

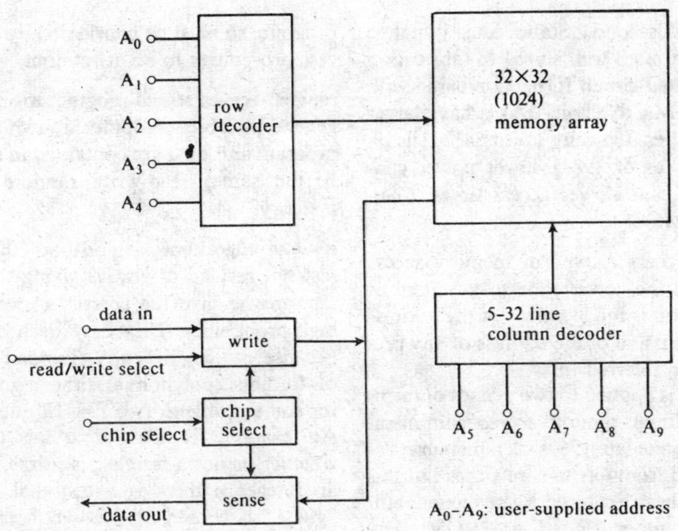

Typical organization of a RAM

tional part of a number expressed in a *radix notation*, i.e. in the notation used in a positional *number system.

radix sorting (digital sorting; pocket sorting) A sorting algorithm in which the file is first sorted on the least significant digit of the sortkey, then the next least significant until in the final pass a sort is made on the most significant digit. The algorithm is best implemented using *linked lists. *See also* divide and conquer sorting.

ragged array A two-dimensional array where the numbers of elements in each row (or column) are not equal: such arrays are described as *row-ragged* (or *column-ragged*). A ragged array is usually represented using an *access vector or a vector of pointers, each pointer referring to a row (or column) of the ragged array.

RAM *Acronym for* random-access memory. A semiconductor *read-write memory device in which the basic element consists of a single cell that is capable of storing one bit of information. Large-capacity memories are formed as two-dimensional arrays of these cells. An individual cell is identified uniquely by row and column addresses, which are derived by decoding a user-supplied address word. A typical organization is shown in the diagram. Each cell in a RAM is thus independent of all other cells in the array and can be accessed in any order and in the same amount of time, hence the term *random access. Since RAM devices are read-write memories, data can be both read from and written to the cells in the array. RAM is usually *volatile memory and is used for temporary storage of data or programs.

RAM devices can be classified as *static* or *dynamic*. Static RAMs are fabricated from either bipolar or MOS components (*see* bipolar transistor, MOSFET); each cell is formed by an electronic *latch whose contents remain fixed until written to. Dynamic RAM cells, which comprise MOS devices, utilize the charge stored on a capacitance as a temporary store; due to leakage currents, the cell contents must be *refreshed at regular intervals, typically every millisecond. Static and dynamic RAMs are both well suited to fabrication in integrated-circuit form. Compared with static RAMs, dynamic RAMs have larger cell densities, typically up to 64K cells on one chip (as of 1982), lower power consumption, but slower access times. *Compare* ROM.

random access A type of memory access for which the access time to any item of information is independent of the address of that item and of the address of any previous item referred to.
The term is applied to two classes of memory. The first is random-access main memory. Until the late 1960s such memory was fabricated from ferrite-core stores but this type has been replaced by semiconductor memory, either *RAM or *ROM. Any word, or byte, in random-access main memory is accessible in a fixed time, typically on the order of 0.1–1 microsecond.
The term random-access memory is also used to describe memory implemented using magnetic disk or drum, for which the access time contains two components: a seek time necessary to locate the appropriate track and a latency necessary to allow the information in that track to become available under the read/write heads. Typical seek times are in the range 10–30 milliseconds. The latency is usually quoted as one half the time for a complete revolution of the device, say 8 milliseconds.

random-access device A peripheral such as a magnetic disk on which data can be read in a different order from that in which it was written. *See* random access.

random-access memory *See* RAM. *See also* random access.

random-access method An *access method in which data records are accessed in a sequence determined dynamically: the selection of a record need have no relationship with the record selected previously. The ordering is determined by the application program, so must be considered by the access procedures to be at random.

random-access stored-program machine A general-purpose computer in which the program and data are contained in (usually the same) read-write random-access memory.

random algorithms Algorithms that are fast but instead of always giving the correct answer give the correct answer with high probability. They have been devised because of the difficulty (impossibility?) of finding *polynomial time algorithms for some problems (*see* P=NP question).
An example is that of trying to test whether or not a number is prime. Given an integer n there is a test that uses a "guess" i, chosen at random between 1 and n, that takes $O(\log_2 n)$ time to perform. If the test is successful n is known to have factors; on the other hand if n has factors then the test will be successful for at least half of the integers in the range 1 to n. Thus if the test fails k times it can be said that n is prime

with probability $1 - 2^{-k}$

Several other examples of problems amenable to a similar approach have now been found. However, all such examples are either already known to be solvable in polynomial time anyway (although the random algorithms are an order of magnitude faster) or like prime-testing, under suspicion of so being.

random logic A term generally used to describe a relatively nonuniform digital logic circuit. For example, a control unit will contain random logic; an ALU, having a regular structure, will not.

random numbers Numbers that are drawn using a random *sampling technique from a set of permissible numbers. True random numbers are difficult to obtain, and programs using them are difficult to debug. Special devices to generate random numbers are required in machines such as

ERNIE, which selects the winners of the British premium bond scheme.
Attempts to produce random numbers using the arithmetic properties of a computer result in *pseudorandom numbers*, since in principle the numbers generated depend on their predecessors. Frequently, however, pseudorandom numbers suffice for the purpose intended. Many methods for their generation have been proposed over the years, one of the earliest being the *middle square method* proposed by von Neumann: the previous random number is squared and the middle digits extracted from the result to form the next number in the sequence. More successful methods are based upon the linear congruential method in which a sequence of numbers is generated using the formula

$$X_{n+1} = aX_n + c \pmod{m}$$

for particular choices of a, c and m.
Pseudorandom numbers are used in a number of applications: in *Monte Carlo methods of numerical integration, to sample a large set and so gain insight into the set, and to simulate natural phenomena such as the collision of nuclear particles.

random sampling *See* sampling.

random variable A quantity that may take any of a prescribed set of values with *relative frequency determined by its *probability distribution.

range 1. of a binary *relation R, a subset of $S_1 \times S_2$, say. The *subset of S_2 consisting of all elements to which some element of S_1 is related. If R is the relation "is the wife of" defined from men to women, the range of R is the set of married women.
Since a *function is a special kind of relation, the range of

$$f: X \rightarrow Y$$

can be written as

$$\{y \mid y \in Y \text{ and } y = f(x) \text{ for some } x \text{ in } X\}$$

2. *See* measures of variation.

rank 1. The number of linearly independent rows or columns of a matrix of numbers.
2. of a graph. *See* connected graph.

rank correlation *See* correlation.

rank correlation coefficient *See* nonparametric techniques.

RAPPORT *Trademark* A *relational database system marketed in the UK by Logica, Ltd.

raster-mode graphic display (raster graphics) A method of presenting graphical or pictorial images in which the desired shape is built up by means of a succession of parallel movements of the pen of a plotter or the spot on a VDU, in a similar manner to a television picture, i.e. without each line being traced as a continuous movement of the pen or spot.

raster scan A mode of exploration or reproduction of an image in which an electron beam is made to trace a succession of adjacent parallel lines. The most common example of this is the way in which a television picture is written on the screen.

rate 1. of a code. For any (n, k) *block code or *convolutional code, the value defined as

$$R = k/n$$

It is a measure of "efficiency" in the sense that the more *redundancy there is in the code, the lower the rate. On the other hand, high redundancy may bring about greater efficiency in detecting or correcting errors. Thus the rate measures only one aspect of the overall efficiency.
2. *See* data transfer rate.

rational language *Another name for* regular language.

raw data Data in the form in which it reaches a computer system from the outside world: data that has not been vetted for correctness, nor sorted into any sequence, nor processed in any other way.

raw error rate of magnetic tape. *See* error rate.

Rayleigh–Ritz method *See* finite-element method.

RCP *Abbrev. for* Rescau à Commutation par Paquets. An experimental network that was run by the French PTT, beginning in 1974, and served as a testbed for the public packet network *Transpac. RCP pioneered individually flow-controlled virtual connections over the interface between the backbone network and the network hosts. This prevents any one connection from consuming an unfair portion of network or host's communication resources, and was an important contribution to the development of the *X.25 interface protocol. *Compare* CYCLADES.

reachability A concept from graph theory concerned with whether there is a *path between two vertices in a directed *graph. Vertex V is said to be *reachable* from vertex U provided that there is a path from U to V. There may be several different paths from one vertex to another, the shortest being called a *goedesic*. The set of points that can be reached from a given vertex V is called the *reachable set* of V.
A directed graph is *unilaterally connected* when, for any pair of vertices, at least one vertex is reachable from the other.

reachability matrix *Another name for* adjacency matrix.

read To sense and retrieve (or interpret) data from a form of storage or input medium. The word is often used to qualify the meaning of a noun, as in read head.

read and restore cycle *Another name for* regenerative read.

reader A device for holding or moving a data medium and sensing the data encoded on it. *See* punched card reader, card reader, document reader.

read error *See* error rate. *See also* error management.

read head *See* head, magnetic tape.

read instruction A program step that causes data to be retrieved from a defined storage location and written into a register or buffer.

read-only memory *See* ROM.

read out To copy words or fields from a specified location in an internal memory of a computer into an external storage or display device. Both the operation and the copy are referred to as *read-out*.

read time The period between the availability of the first and last bits of data concerned in a single read instruction. It does not include any latency or waiting time or any regenerative action that may be associated with a destructive read operation.

read-while-write check *See* magnetic tape.

read/write head A magnetic *head that can read, write, and erase data encoded as polarized patterns on magnetic disk, tape, or drum. *See* disk drive, magnetic tape.

read-write memory A type of memory that, in normal operation, allows the user to access (read from) or alter (write to) individual storage locations within the device. The choice of read or write operation is normally determined by a read/write signal applied to the device. *RAM devices are typical read-write memories. *Compare* ROM.

real-time clock A clock that runs regardless of whether processes that refer to the clock are running or not. The clock may take two forms, either as a peripheral device that can be read by a process when the process chooses, or as a source of interrupts that occur at precisely determined intervals. A real-time clock measures *elapsed time. *See also* relative-time clock.

real-time language A programming language designed for programming systems in which the response time of the computer to stimuli is time critical. For instance, if a computer is controlling an elevator, then the computer must be able to respond quickly to the movements of the cage. *Ada, *Modula, *CORAL 66, and RTL-2 are real-time languages.

real-time system Any system in which the time at which output is produced is significant. This is usually because the input corresponds to some movement in the physical world, and the output has to relate to that same movement. The lag from input time to output time must be sufficiently small for acceptable timeliness. Timeliness is a function of the total system: missile guidance requires output within a few milliseconds of input whereas scheduling of steamships requires responses measured in days. Real-time systems are usually considered to be those in which the response time is of order milliseconds; interactive systems are those with response times of order seconds and batch systems are those with response times of hours or days. Examples of real-time systems include process control, embedded computer systems, point-of-sale systems, and computer-aided testing.

recognize (accept) *See* automaton.

reconfiguration The process of redefining and in some cases reconnecting the units of a multiple-unit computer system. This procedure may be accomplished automatically, manually, or by a combination of both. The purpose may be to provide different system functionality or continued operation after the failure of one unit. If done automatically the latter case would represent a *fail-soft situation. *See also* configuration.

reconstitute To rebuild, generally used to denote the recovery process necessary to restore a system to an operational state after some error. It usually involves resorting to a backup state and running appropriate programs.

record 1. A collection of data relating to one subject, i.e. a composite data object, in which the individual components or fields may be of different types.
2. A collection of data handled together in transfers to and from peripheral devices. Files held on backing store are frequently treated as sequences of records. The collection of data transferred as a unit is called a *physical record.* In contrast, the collection of data relating to one subject is then called a *logical record.* The number of logical records in a physical record is the *blocking factor.*
A peripheral device that handles data in fixed-size units, such as a card reader, card punch, or line printer, is known as a *unit-record device.*
3. A *data structure in which there are a number of named components, not necessarily of the same type. It may have variants in which some of the components, known as *variant fields*, are absent; the particular variant for a given value would be distinguished by a discriminant or *tag field. The record is widely recognized as one of the fundamental ways of aggregating data (another being the *array) and many programming languages now offer direct support for data objects that take the form of records. Such languages permit operations upon an entire record object as well as upon its individual components.
4. *Another term for* write, used particularly when writing the value of data that may change or disappear.

recoverable error of magnetic tape. *See* error rate.

recovery The process of restoring normal operation after the occurrence of a fault. *See* failure recovery, power-fail recovery.

recurrence A statement describing some quantity such as $f(n)$ (where f is some *function and n is a positive integer) in terms of values of $f(m)$, where m is a nonnegative integer smaller than n; initial values such as $f(0)$ or $f(1)$ can be assumed to be defined. The concept can be extended to include functions of several variables. A recurrence will then involve defining $f(m,n)$, say, in terms of $f(m',n')$ where in some sense (m',n') is smaller than (m,n); again initial values can be assumed. The numbers in the *Fibonacci series can be defined by a recurrence.

In general, a recurrence can be considered as an equation connecting the values of the function at a number of related points. It has the form

$$g(n, f(n), f(n-1), \ldots, f(n-k)) = 0$$
$$n = k, k+1, \ldots, N$$

Assuming initial values for $f(0), f(1), \ldots, f(k-1)$, values for other points n can be calculated.

Equations of this type arise naturally in the *discretization of continuous problems, and in a slightly different form, known as a *difference equation, appear repeatedly in *combinatorics.

recursion The process of defining or expressing a function, procedure, language construct, or the solution to a problem in terms of itself, so producing a *recursive function, a *recursive subroutine, etc.

In recursive function theory a more formal and rigorous use of the term recursion is employed; all variables take values in the set of nonnegative integers and this same set is the *range of the various functions. Recursion is then the process of defining a function f of $(n+1)$ variables in the following manner:

$$f(x_1,x_2, \ldots ,x_n,0) = g(x_1,x_2, \ldots ,x_n)$$
$$f(x_1,x_2, \ldots ,x_n,y+1) =$$
$$h(x_1,x_2, \ldots ,x_n,y,f(x_1, \ldots , x_n,y))$$

where g and h are two other functions of n and $(n+2)$ variables respectively. *See also* primitive recursive function.

recursion theorem A variant of the *fixed-point theorem of recursive function theory.

recursive descent parsing *See* top-down parsing, LL parsing.

recursive function 1. A *function that is defined in terms of itself, e.g. *Ackermann's function.

2. (general recursive function; total recursive function) A *partial recursive function that is also a *total function.

Recursive functions are used in computer science to study *effective computability and *computable functions. *See also* recursion.

recursive list (self-referent list) A *list that contains itself as a sublist element or is a sublist element of one of its sublists.

recursively enumerable set A subset A of a set B is said to be recursively enumerable, relative to B, if there is an effective procedure that, given an element b in B, will output "yes" if and only if b is an element of A. If b is not in A then, in general, the procedure will never terminate. This is a weaker notion than that of a *recursive set. A set can be recursively enumerable without being recursive. The set of *Ada programs that terminates (for a given input) is recursively enumerable (with respect to the class of all Ada programs) but it is not recursive.

recursive relation A *relation whose *characteristic function is recursive.

recursive set A *set whose membership is defined by a general *recursive function. In principle, it is a subset of a larger set over which a *characteristic function is defined, that function being generally recursive. For example, the set of programs in a particular language is recursive in the larger set consisting of all strings that can be made up from the basic alphabet of symbols defined for that language. Thus it can be decided whether or not a given string of the symbols is actually such a program by use of a general recursive function. This must be so since one task of a compiler is to determine whether or not such a string of symbols constitutes a syntactically well-formed program. *See also* recursively enumerable set.

recursive subroutine A *subroutine that calls itself. Such a self-referential call must occur as one branch of a conditional statement, otherwise there would be an infinite series of calls. As an example, a recursive subroutine to calculate factorial (n) would call itself to calculate factorial ($n - 1$), unless $n = 1$ when the value 1 will be returned.

reducible polynomial *See* polynomial.

reduction machine A machine that evaluates expressions by successively reducing all component subexpressions until only simple data values remain. Evaluation is achieved by expression substitution. For each expression that is not a simple data value, a set of rules define what should be substituted when that expression appears. The machine operates by matching each subexpression of the expression currently being evaluated with its appropriate rule, and substituting as specified by that rule. This process of expression substitution continues until only simple data values remain, representing the value of the original expression.

All subexpressions can be matched and substituted concurrently, and thus there is the potential for a high degree of parallelism. A major objective of reduction machines is to exploit this parallelism.

Reduction machines represent one of the major examples of *non von Neumann architecture, and are of considerable research interest. Traditional *imperative programming languages are wholly unsuited to reduction machines, so *declarative languages are employed.

redundancy The provision of additional components in a system, over and above the minimum set of components to perform the functions of the system, for purposes of *reliability or *robustness. For example, with *triple modular redundancy* three components are deployed in parallel, all performing the same function. Their outputs are compared, and when one component produces a different result from the other two, this item is assumed to be faulty and is ignored. Redundancy covers not only the incorporation of duplicate or triplicate hardware for backup in case of *failure, but also the inclusion of excess symbols in messages sent through communication systems in order to combat the effects of noise (*see* error-correcting code, error-detecting code).

redundancy check A check made with redundant hardware or information that can provide an indication that certain errors have occurred. *See* redundancy, cyclic redundancy check.

Reed–Muller codes (RM codes) A family of *binary *cyclic (2^m, k) *error-correcting *block codes.

Reed–Solomon codes (RS codes) An important and practical family of *linear *error-correcting *block codes, especially suited to the correction of *burst errors. They can be regarded as a generalization of *Bose–Chandhuri–Hocquenghem (BCH) codes, and as a special case of *Goppa codes. RS codes can be arranged to be *cyclic.

reel *See* magnetic tape, paper tape.

re-entrant program A program whose instructions are invariant, hence it can be used again without being reloaded. Re-entrant programs consist of logically separate code and data segments, and two instances of such a program can share the same code.

reference *Another name for* link.

reference file A file that will remain relatively unchanged over a comparatively long period of time, so that other files can refer to records in it.

reflexive closure *See* transitive closure.

reflexive relation A *relation R defined on a set S and having the property that

$$x \; R \; x$$

for all elements x in S

The relation "is the same age as" defined on the set of people is reflexive. *Compare* irreflexive relation.

refresh (regenerate) 1. To replenish the charge on the storage capacitors used in *dynamic memory cells and other similar devices. Some devices are provided with internal circuitry that automatically refreshes dynamic cells whenever these cells are read. The word refresh is also used as a noun.
2. To repeat at regular intervals the display of digital information on a cathode-ray tube or television monitor in order that the display can appear continuous.

regenerate *Another term for* refresh.

regenerative memory A type of memory, not widely used in modern computing systems, in which the content has to be regularly rewritten to avoid depreciation. Such devices frequently store information as a train of pulses circulating in a loop that includes a read and a write transducer. For continued storage the output of the read transducer is connected to the write transducer, and thus the depreciation of the signal that occurs during its passage around the loop is corrected at the start of each pass. Some types of semiconductor memory are regenerative in that they need a *refresh cycle to prevent loss of data.

regenerative read (read and restore cycle) A type of read operation in which the data extracted from a storage location is also written back into that location. In some types of memory, e.g. core store, the process of sensing the state of the storage element is destructive, i.e. will cause the state to change, and thus provision for regenerative read has to be made if the data is to be retained at that location.

register A group of (usually) *bistable devices that are used to store information within a computer system for high-speed access. A register of n bistables can store a word of length n bits, which can represent any n bits of information. Different interpretations can be given to the bit configuration stored in the register, e.g. the configuration could represent an instruction, a binary number, an alphanumeric character, etc. A register is often the same size as the computer word; it may also be byte- or character-size or some other size as required. Some registers can behave as *counters as well, or they may behave as *shift registers.

register optimization In a compiler, the allocation of machine registers to variables and intermediate quantities in such a way as to minimize the number of occasions on which a register has to be stored and later reloaded.

register transfer language Any of several higher-order languages used to specify or design a system comprising a number of interconnected *registers. *See* digital design language.

regression analysis A statistical technique that is concerned with fitting relationships between a dependent variable, y, and one or more independent variables, $x_1, x_2, \ldots,$ usually by the method of *least squares.
A *linear regression model* is one in which the theoretical mean value, μ_i, of the observation y_i is a linear combination of independent variables,

$$\mu = \beta_0 + \beta_1 x_1 + \ldots + \beta_k x_k$$

when k x-variables are included in the model. The multiples $\beta_0, \beta_1, \ldots \beta_k$ are parameters of the model and are the quantities to be estimated; they are known as *regression coefficients*, β_0 being the *intercept* or *constant term*. A model with more than one x-variable is known as a *multiple regression model*.
Nonlinear regression models express μ as a general function of the independent variables. The general functions include curves such as exponentials and ratios of polynomials, in which there are parameters to be estimated.
Various procedures have been devised to detect variables that make a significant contribution to the regression equation, and to find the combination of variables that best fits the data using as few variables as possible. *Analysis of variance is

used to assess the significance of the regression model.

regular event *Another name for* regular language.

regular expression An expression built from finite *formal languages (i.e. finite sets of strings) using the operations of *union, *concatenation, and *Kleene star. For example, the following two regular expressions each denote the set of all strings of alternating *a*s and *b*s:

$$\{a,\Lambda\}\ \{ba\}^*\ \{\Lambda,b\}$$

$$\{ba\}^* \cup \{a\}\{ba\}^* \cup \{ba\}^*\{b\} \cup \{a\}\{ba\}^*\{b\}$$

where Λ is the empty string. A language is *regular if and only if it is representable by a regular expression. Thus the class of regular languages is the smallest one that contains all finite languages and is closed under concatenation, union, and star – the so-called *regular operations*. These three operations correspond to "sequence", "choice", and "iteration" in structured iterative programs.

regular grammar A *grammar in which each production has one of the forms

$$A \rightarrow b$$

$$A \rightarrow bC$$

where b is a terminal and A,C are nonterminals. Like the right-linear and left-linear grammars (*see* linear grammar) regular grammars generate precisely the *regular languages.

regular language (regular set; rational language) A language recognized by a *finite-state automaton. Of the language classes commonly studied, the class of regular languages is the smallest and mathematically the simplest. Its importance is shown by the existence of several alternative definitions; for some of them *see* regular grammar, linear grammar, regular expression, Myhill equivalence, Nerode equivalence, tree grammar.

regular operations *See* regular expression.

regular representation A representation of a *group as a particular set of transformations.

regular set *Another name for* regular language, since in formal language theory a language is simply a set of strings.

relation (defined on sets $S_1, S_2, \ldots S_n$) A *subset R of the *Cartesian product

$$S_1 \times S_2 \times \ \ldots \ \times S_n$$

of the n sets $S_1, \ldots, S_n$. This is called an n-ary relation. When a relation R is defined on a single set S the implication is that R is a subset of

$$S \times S \times \ \ldots \ \times S \ (n \text{ terms})$$

The most common situation occurs when $n = 2$, i.e. R is a subset of $S_1 \times S_2$. Then R is called a *binary relation* on S_1 to S_2 or between S_1 and S_2. S_1 is the *domain* of R and S_2 the *codomain* of R. If the *ordered pair (s_1,s_2) belongs to the subset R, a notation such as

$$s_1 \, R \, s_2 \quad \text{or} \quad s_1 \, \rho \, s_2$$

is usually adopted and it is then possible to talk about the relation R or ρ and to say that s_1 and s_2 are related.

An example of a binary relation is the usual "is less than" relation defined on integers, where the subset R consists of ordered pairs such as (4,5); it is however more natural to write $4 < 5$. Other examples include: "is equal to" defined on strings, say; "is the square root of" defined on the nonnegative reals; "is defined in terms of" defined on the set of subroutines within a particular program; "is before in the queue" defined on the set of jobs awaiting execution at a particular time.

The *function is a special kind of relation. *Graphs are often used to provide a convenient pictorial representation of a relation.

Relations play an important part in theoretical aspects of many areas of computing, including the mathematical foundations of the subject, databases, compiling techniques, and operating systems. *See also* equivalence relation, partial ordering.

relational database A form of database specification based upon the mathematical concept of a *relation. The mathematical nature of the concept is, however, not necessary to its appreciation and the database may be regarded as composed of a number of rectangular tables, each expressing one relation. Unlike *network or *hierarchical database models, the relational system is structured at the time each query is posed rather than at the time the database is established. The structuring is achieved by the combination of relations using *relational operators.
Because of the run-time structuring, the relational database concept has received widespread acceptance since it is more amenable to ad hoc queries than the older, statically structured database systems. Particular examples of relational systems are INGRES, SQL/DS, and RAPPORT, but most large manufacturers now provide some relational system in their standard software.

relational operator 1. An operator representing a comparison between two operands that returns a truth value, e.g. "equals", "less than".
2. An operator that combines several relations into one. For example, if *R* is the relation between employee number and employee's salary, and *S* is the relation between employee number and employee's department, a relational operator (join) can combine these to give the relation between employees' departments and employees' salaries (to find the departmental salary totals).
Relational operators are often presented to the user in a more palatable manner in an associated *query language.

relative addressing Usually either of two ways to expand a short specified address. The first is *self-relative addressing* where the specified address is added to the address of the instruction (generally the current contents of the program counter) that contains the self-relative reference to produce a direct address. The second is *base addressing* in which the specified address is added to the contents of a *base register* containing a base address to produce a direct address. *See also* addressing schemes.

relative complement *Another name for* set difference.

relative frequency The number of occurrences of a particular event, E, divided by the total number of observed events. An *event* is a particular instance of a class of observations, such as the result of the throw of dice, the recording of a man's height, or the survival of a patient given a particular treatment. Relative frequency should be distinguished from *probability. For example, the probability that a fair coin when tossed lands heads up is 0.5, whereas the relative frequency in a particular run of 100 tosses might be 47/100 or 0.47.
The set of relative frequencies for all the events that are possible is called a *frequency distribution. It may be displayed graphically as a *histogram.

relatively prime *See* greatest common divisor.

relative product *Another name for* composition.

relative-time clock A free-running clock that raises an interrupt at regular intervals, often associated with the period of the incoming supply of electricity. These interrupts allow the supervisory system to track the passage of real time, and also guarantee that if a process does not call the supervisor explicitly, the supervisor will nevertheless be entered.

release Transfer of a system from the development stages into wider usage, e.g. into operational use. *See also* software lifecycle.

reliability 1. The ability of a computer system to perform its required functions for a given period of time. It is often quoted in terms of percentage of *uptime, but may

be more usefully expressed as MTBF (mean time between failures). *See also* hardware reliability, repair time.
2. of software. *See* software reliability.

relocatable program 1. (position-independent code) A program that can be moved anywhere in memory since it does not contain any absolute memory addresses.
2. A program that can be loaded anywhere in memory, in which all memory addresses are expressed relative to an origin at the start of the program, and the compiler/assembler produces a table of all such memory references so that the loader can update them at load time.

remedial maintenance (corrective maintenance) Maintenance that is performed after a fault, in hardware or software, has been found, in order to correct that fault. *Compare* preventive maintenance.

remote A term used to describe a process or system that uses a communication link, as in remote job entry, remote sensing, and remote data-access facilities.

remote job entry (RJE) A system by which a communications link is used to submit work from an input device and to receive results on a printer or other output medium. Strictly RJE refers only to the entry of jobs, but the term is commonly applied to cover both input and output. Early computer systems had all their input/output devices in the same room or at best in a room adjacent to the computer mainframe. In the early 1960s the introduction of long-distance telecommunications made it possible to site card readers and line printers at a distance from the computer center. It was this that led to the concept of remote job entry.

remote message processing A near-obsolete term denoting the handling of interactive terminals over data transmission links.

remote sensing The technique whereby sensors located remotely from a computer are used to produce inputs for a digital system. These inputs are then transmitted either by wire or radio techniques to the computer. An example is the use of digital thermometers and humidity detectors in large buildings: the sensors transmit their readings to a central computer that optimizes energy use by regulating heat and air conditioning.

repair time The (sometimes average) time required to diagnose and repair a computer failure, either hardware or software. In combination with MTBF (mean time between failures) it provides a figure-of-merit for system *reliability and/or *uptime.

repeat-until loop *See* do-while loop.

repertoire *Short for* instruction repertoire. *See* instruction set.

repetition codes A trivial family of *cyclic *perfect *error-correcting *block codes, in which the codewords are formed merely by repeating the message words r times. Considered as (n, k) codes (*see* block code), these codes have $n = rk$ for some k.

report generator *See* generator, RPG.

requirements analysis The analysis that is necessary for the production of an *expression of requirements.

rerun To run a program again, usually due to a machine malfunction. (The word is also used as a noun.) Some languages allow the programmer to specify restart points: at such points a memory image is preserved so that in the event of a rerun the program does not need to be restarted from scratch.

rescue dump A copy of the workspace associated with a process, taken with a view to allowing the process to be restarted following a system failure. *See* dump.

reset (clear) To set a register or counter to the all-zero state.

resident Permanently present in main memory, as opposed to transient material that is loaded from disk when required.

residue arithmetic *Another name for* modular arithmetic.

residue check *Another name for* checksum.

resistor-transistor logic *See* RTL.

resolution 1. The amount of graphical information that can be shown on a visual display. The resolution of a display device is usually denoted by the number of lines that can be distinguished visually. The resolution of a computer-graphics system is also defined by the number of displayable lines, or alternatively, by the number of points or pixels (picture elements) that can be displayed in the vertical and horizontal directions. Computer graphics systems are now capable of over 7000 lines of resolution. This is generally described as a *high resolution*, or *hi res*. Many microcomputer manufacturers however have adopted the term high resolution to describe the highest resolution their particular system can achieve. This is typically on the order of 200 (vertical) by 400 (horizontal) points.
2. *See* A/D converter, D/A converter.
3. A rule of inference in *predicate calculus, used to deduce a new logical formula from two old ones. It has been used extensively in the automatic derivation of mathematical theorems since it is an efficient alternative to traditional rules of inference.

resource Any of the component parts of a computer system and the facilities that it offers. All computer systems must include one or more processors, which actually manipulate the stored information, some form of memory in which to store both instructions for the processors and data awaiting manipulation, and input/output devices capable of reading information from the outside world and writing results to the outside world.

resource allocation Either the act of making a resource available to a process, or the amount of a particular resource that has been allocated. The context almost invariably makes clear which meaning is intended. The amount allocated in the second form of usage may either be a period of time if the entire resource is allocated, as with a processor, or it may be a number of subunits in the case of a resource, such as memory, that is made up of a large number of essentially identical subunits, of which some are allocated to the process.

resource descriptor *See* process descriptor.

response function *See* sequential machine.

response time Usually the elapsed time between an action by a computer-system user and the receipt of some form of response or feedback from the system.

restart To set running again after a temporary halt. The term (also used as a noun) applies particularly to the situation in which a transient hardware error has caused the entire operating system (and all the processes running under its control) to halt. In such cases it is often found that only processes that were actively running at the time of the error have suffered damage. The damaged processes must be *aborted, but all other processes can be restarted since the resources allocated to them are unaltered, and their *process descriptors are still an accurate reflection of their behavior up to the time of the system error.

restore To reset to an earlier value. For example, when a process is about to be *restarted on a processor, the contents of the working registers of the processor must be restored to the values they last held when the process was previously running.

restriction of a *relation *R* or *function *f*. A relation or function obtained by restricting the domain of *R* or *f*. If "is the son of" is a relation defined on all the males in a certain country, a restriction would be this same relation defined on the males of a particular city.

return channel In a *duplex transmission channel, it is sometimes the case that the main channel operates only in one direction (i.e. *simplex), but that a channel of much lower capacity (and much lower cost) operates in the opposite direction: this is the return channel. It is chiefly used for monitoring the main channel, and for notifying the transmitter of errors detected by the receiver on the main channel. *See also* backward error correction.

return instruction An instruction used to effect the return to the regular program from a *subroutine or an *interrupt. A return instruction must restore the *program counter to the correct value; in the case of a return from interrupt, certain status bits must also be restored. *Compare* call instruction.

reusable resource A resource, such as a CPU or tape transport, that is not rendered useless by being used. A magnetic tape or disk can be used often indefinitely and are to be regarded as reusable resources. *Compare* consumable resource.

reversal function The *function $r : L \rightarrow L$, where L denotes strings of characters from some *alphabet, defined in such a way that r reverses the order of the elements in its parameter. If & denotes *concatenation of strings, then

$$r(s) = s$$

if s is null or a single character and

$$r(s \,\&\, t) = r(t) \,\&\, r(s)$$

The idea can be extended to include reversing of items in a *list, of items in some *sequence, or of items in an arbitrary one-dimensional *array. Reversal is an *involution operation.

reverse bias The applied d.c. voltage that prevents or greatly reduces current flow in a diode, transistor, etc. For example, a negligible current will flow through a diode when its cathode is made more positive than its anode; the diode is then said to be *reverse biased*. *Compare* forward bias.

reverse Polish notation (RPN; postfix notation; suffix notation) A form of notation, invented by the Polish mathematician Jan Lukasiewicz, in which each operator follows its operands. Thus, for example,

$a + b$ is written $ab+$

$a + b * c$ is written $abc*+$

If each operator has a specific number of operands (e.g. if all operators take exactly two operands), then no brackets are required since the order of evaluation is always uniquely defined; the notation can then be described as *parenthesis-free*.

The importance of RPN is that an expression in this form can be readily evaluated on a *stack. Thus translation to RPN, followed by stack evaluation, is a simple but effective strategy for dealing with arithmetic expressions in a programming language. *See also* Polish notation.

rewriting system *See* L-system.

Richardson extrapolation (deferred approach to the limit) *See* extrapolation.

right-linear grammar *See* linear grammar.

right shift *See* shift.

right subtree *See* binary tree.

ring 1. An *algebraic structure R on which there are defined two *binary operations, normally denoted by + (addition) and or juxtaposition (multiplication). With respect to addition, R is an abelian *group,

$$\langle R, + \rangle$$

i.e. + is *commutative and *associative. With respect to multiplication, R is a *semigroup,

$$\langle R, \cdot \rangle$$

i.e. · is associative. Further, multiplication is *distributive over addition.

Certain kinds of rings are of particular interest:

(a) if multiplication is commutative the ring is called a *commutative ring*;

(b) if $\langle R, \cdot \rangle$ is a *monoid, the ring is called a *ring with an identity*;

(c) a commutative ring with an identity, and having no nonzero elements x and y with the property that $x \cdot y = 0$, is said to be an *integral domain*;
(d) a commutative ring with more than one element, and in which every nonzero element has an inverse with respect to multiplication, is called a *field.
The different identity elements and inverses, when these exist, can be distinguished by talking in terms of additive identities (or zeros), multiplicative identities (or ones), additive inverses, and multiplicative inverses.
The concept of a ring provides an algebraic structure into which can be fitted such diverse items as the integers, polynomials with integer coefficients, and matrices; on all these items it is customary to define two binary operations.
2. *Another name for* circular list, but more generally applied to any list structure where all sublists as well as the list itself are circularly linked.

ring counter *See* shift counter.

ringing A damped oscillation that occurs in many electrical circuits when signals change rapidly, and is due often to unwanted capacitance and inductance in devices and connecting wires.

ring network A network constructed as a *loop of unidirectional links between stations. It generally uses a bit-serial medium such as twisted pairs or coaxial cable. A master clock may be used to tell each station when to read and write bits, or the timing information may be encoded into the data as long as certain restrictions are met to prevent the ring from overflowing. Each station receives messages on its incoming link. Address and control information is present at the beginning of the message. Based on this information and the control procedure being used on the ring, the station must make two decisions: whether or not to make a copy of the message in its local memory, and whether to pass the message on via its outgoing link or delete the message from the ring. If a station determines that no message is being received on its incoming link, then it may have the option of inserting a message on its outgoing link.
Several different control structures have been used on ring networks:
(a) *daisychain* – dedicated wires pass control information from station to station;
(b) *control token* – a special bit pattern identifies control information: a station, upon receiving the control token, may insert a message into the ring and reissue the token;
(c) *message slots* – a series of "slots" are continuously transmitted around the ring: a station detecting an unused slot may mark it "in use" and fill it with a message;
(d) *register insertion* – a station loads a message into a shift register, then inserts the register into the ring when the ring is idle or at the end of any message; the register contents are shifted onto the ring. When the message returns to the register, the register may be removed from the ring.

ripple-carry adder (ripple adder) *See* adder.

ripple counter An n-stage binary *counter that is formed from n cascaded *flip-flops. The clock input to each of the individual flip-flops, with the exception of the first, is

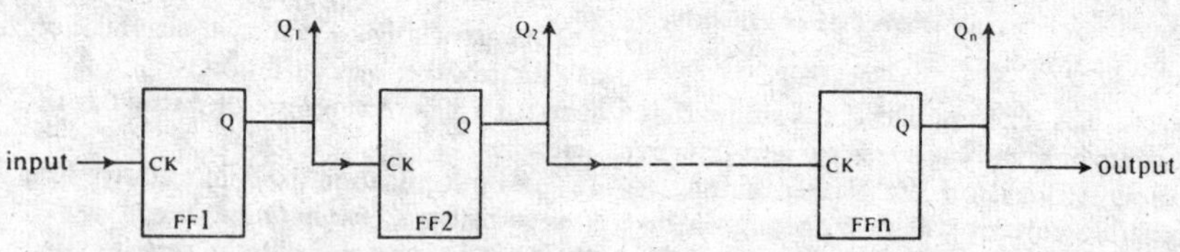

Ripple counter

taken from the output of the preceding one (*see* diagram). The count thus ripples along the counter's length due to the *propagation delay associated with each stage of counting. *See also* cascadable counter, synchronous counter.

rise time of a pulse. *See* pulse.

risk assessment The attempt to make a quantitative determination of risk in a computer system, based on the probability of *threats to security, the cost of security losses, and the cost of the associated countermeasures.

RJE *Abbrev. for* remote job entry.

RM code *Short for* Reed–Muller code.

robotics A discipline lying across the border between *artificial intelligence and mechanical engineering. It is concerned with building *robots*: programmable devices consisting of mechanical manipulator(s) and sensory organ(s), which are linked to a computer. Most robots in current industrial use have very little (if any) sensory capability and follow a fixed but reprogrammable sequence of instructions. The main goal of robotics research in artificial intelligence is to provide the robot with an artificial eye, typically a television camera, and to use visual perception to guide a mechanical arm in a flexible manner. *See also* process control.

robustness A measure of the ability of a system to recover from error conditions, whether generated externally or internally, e.g. a robust system would be tolerant to errors in input data or to failures of internal components. Although there may be a relationship between robustness and reliability, the two are distinct measures: a system never called upon to recover from error conditions may be reliable without being robust; a highly robust system that recovers and continues to operate despite numerous error conditions may still be regarded as unreliable in that it fails to provide essential services in a timely fashion on demand.

roll back To restart at a *checkpoint.

roll-call polling *See* polling.

roll-in roll-out A method of handling memory in a system dealing with a number of simultaneously active processes. When a process becomes active, all its associated workspace and code is brought into main memory. As soon as the process is unable to continue for any reason, typically because the user associated with the process is providing input, the entire workspace and code of the process is copied out onto backing store, retaining only a small buffer capable of receiving input from the user. When the user ceases his input and the process is able to continue running, the workspace and code are rolled back into main memory. When the process requires to output results to the user or is awaiting further input from the user, it is rolled out onto backing store. *See also* swapping.

ROM *Acronym for* read-only memory. A *nonvolatile semiconductor memory device used for the storage of data that will never require modification: the memory contents are permanently built into the device during its manufacture according to a specially created pattern or mask. It is thus sometimes called *mask ROM* to distinguish it from programmable ROM, i.e. *PROM. Although it is possible only to read data from the memory locations of a ROM, the locations can be accessed in any order and in the same length of time. Hence ROM is a *random-access device. *Compare* RAM, read-write memory.

romware Software (machine instructions) stored more-or-less permanently in a *ROM, *PROM, *EPROM, *EEROM, *EAROM, etc.

root of a tree. The unique node in the tree with no parent. *See* tree.

rooted tree *See* tree.

rotation position sensor A feature of some disk drives that allows the central processor to be made aware that a required sector is about to come under the read head of the drive.

roundoff error The error caused by truncating numbers in a calculation, usually necessitated because registers in a computer can only hold numbers of a fixed length, say *t* binary digits. Arithmetical operations on such numbers often give results requiring more than *t* digits for their representation, which must then be reduced to *t* digits for further calculation. The nearest *t*-digit approximation may be used (rounding) or digits after the *t*th may be dropped (chopping or truncation). The repeated reduction to *t* digits can cause systematic buildup of error in certain types of calculation.

round robin A method of allocating CPU time in a multiuser environment. Each user is allocated a small amount or quantum of processor time. Once a user has exhausted his quantum, control passes to the next user. The round robin scheduler bears many resemblances to the *feedback queue, which can be thought of as a refinement of the simple round robin scheduler.

route The path used to move information from one place to another. In a packet switching network it is the list of nodes that a particular packet or class of packets is to follow or has followed.

routine *Another name for* subroutine, used usually in combinations, as in input routine.

routing The procedure used to determine the *route taken by a packet in a packet switching computer network. Routing may be *fixed* (computed once at system starting or session initiation) or *dynamic* (recomputed periodically or on a packet-by-packet basis). Routing may be centralized or *distributed* (computed by different nodes independently).

row-major order One way of mapping the elements of a two-dimensional array onto a vector. If a two-dimensional array, $\boldsymbol{A}$, with m rows and n columns is mapped in row-major order onto a vector $\boldsymbol{b}$ with mn elements then

$$a_{ij} = b_k$$
$$\text{where } k = n(i-1) + j$$

See also column-major order.

row-ragged *See* ragged array.

row vector *See* matrix.

RPG *Acronym for* report program generator. A programming language used in commercial data processing for extracting information from files. The input to an RPG consists of a description of the file structure, a specification of the information required, and of its layout on the page. From this information, the RPG constructs a program to read the file, extract the desired information, and format it in the required manner. The best-known example is RPG II.

RPN *Abbrev. for* reverse Polish notation.

RS232C interface A standard interface that is used in the US and covers the electrical connection between data communication equipment, such as a *modem, and data terminal equipment, such as a computer or computer terminal. The RS232C interface standard was developed by the EIA (Electronic Industries Association) and is essentially equivalent to the CCITT's *V.24 interface.

In 1975 the EIA introduced two new specifications in order to upgrade system capabilities; these are the RS423 interface, which closely resembles RS232C, and the RS422 interface, both of which allow higher transmission rates.

RS code *Short for* Reed–Solomon code.

RS flip-flop (SR flip-flop) *See* flip-flop.

RTL *Abbrev. for* resistor-transistor logic. An early *logic family, usually produced in integrated-circuit form, whose principal

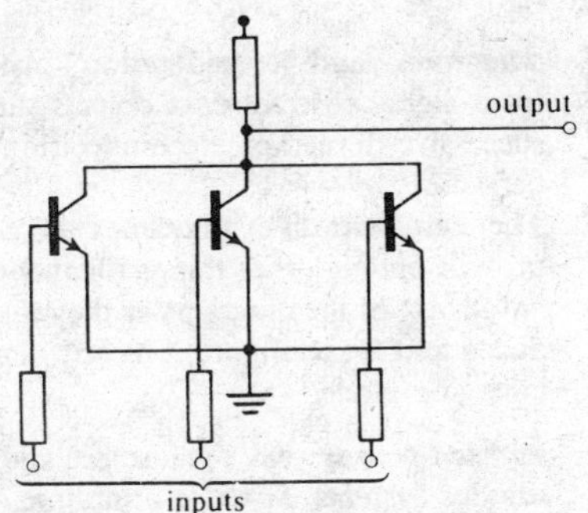

RTL positive NOR gate

component parts consist of integrated resistors and *bipolar transistors.

The diagram shows the equivalent circuit of an RTL positive *NOR gate. The output is at a high voltage (logic 1) only if all the inputs are low (logic 0). If any input is high, the associated transistor will be driven into saturation and the output voltage will be low (*see* bipolar transistor).

Despite its low power dissipation, RTL is now little used since it has a relatively slow switching speed and small *fan-out.

rule of inference *See* propositional calculus, inference.

Runge–Kutta methods A widely used class of methods for the numerical solution of *ordinary differential equations. For the initial-value problem

$$y' = f(x,y),\ y(x_0) = y_0,$$

the general form of the m-stage method is

$$k_i = f(x_n + c_i h,\ y_n + h \sum_{j=1}^{m} a_{ij} k_j)$$

$$i = 1,2, \ldots ,m$$

$$y_{n+1} = y_n + h \sum_{i=1}^{m} b_i k_i$$

$$x_{n+1} = x_n + h$$

The derivation of suitable parameters a_{ij}, b_i, and c_i requires extremely lengthy algebraic manipulations, except for small values of m.

Some early examples were developed by Runge and a systematic treatment was initiated by Kutta about 1900. Recently, significant advances have been made in the development of a general theory and in the derivation and implementation of efficient methods incorporating error estimation and control.

Except for stiff equations (*see* ordinary differential equations), explicit methods

$$\text{with } a_{ij} = 0,\ j \geqslant i$$

are used. These are relatively easy to program and are efficient compared with other methods unless evaluations of $f(x,y)$ are expensive.

running (active) Currently being executed, usually on a CPU. The *process descriptor for a process that is running will contain an indication that this is the case. Clearly, once the process becomes suspended for any reason, the "running" bit in the process descriptor will be reset.

run time (execution time) The time at which a program is executed, in contrast to the time at which it may have been submitted, loaded, compiled, or assembled.

Russell's paradox A contradiction originally formulated by Bertrand Russell and phrased in terms of *set theory. Let T be the set of all sets that are not members of themselves, i.e.

$$T = \{S \mid S \notin S\}$$

Then it can be shown that T is a member of T if and only if T is not a member of T. The paradox results from certain kinds of recursive definitions. It arises for example in the following situation: the barber in a certain town shaves everyone who does not shave himself; who shaves the barber?

S

SADT *Trademark, abbrev. for* structured analysis and design technique A method for modeling complex problems and systems; developed by Douglas Ross in the mid-1970s. Although SADT is a general-purpose modeling tool, it is particularly effective for requirements definition for arbitrary systems problems and is widely used for this purpose in the software engineering field. SADT can be viewed as having three main parts: a set of methods that can assist an analyst in gaining an understanding of a complex system, a graphical language that can be used to record and communicate that understanding, and administrative guidelines that contribute to the orderly progress of the analysis and early detection of problems.

The methods of SADT are based upon several concepts. Top-down decomposition allows information to be dealt with at progressive levels of detail. Model-building both assists understanding and permits communication of that understanding. Adoption of a variety of complementary viewpoints allows all relevant aspects of a system to be considered while limiting consideration at any time to one well-defined topic. The dual "things" and "happenings" aspects of any subject are used to reinforce understanding and promote consistency. Review and iteration procedures ensure the quality of the model that is developed.

The graphical language of SADT consists basically of boxes and arrows that are used to construct SADT diagrams. The language is concerned only with the structured decomposition of the subject matter, and any other language (e.g. natural language) can be used within the boxes and to label the arrows. A single SADT diagram may model either processes or data. A diagram that models processes, called an *actigram*, uses boxes to show the individual processes and uses arrows to show data flows between processes, any constraints that apply, and the mechanisms for carrying out the processes. The arrows entering and leaving a box serve to bound the context of the process, and this can then be decomposed on further actigrams through successive levels of detail to any level required. Similarly the corresponding data decomposition is presented in *datagrams* and consideration proceeds from highly abstract data objects through successive levels of decomposition and definition.

The administrative guidelines of SADT provide among other things for independent review of the diagrams as they are produced and for configuration control of the emerging model.

sampled-data system *See* discrete and continuous systems. *See also* sampling.

sampling 1. (time quantization) A process by which the value of an analog, or continuous, signal is "examined" at discrete fixed intervals of time. The resulting *sampled value* will normally be held constant until the next sampling instant, and may be converted into a digital form using an *A/D converter for subsequent processing by a computer.

The *rate* at which a given analog signal is sampled must be a certain minimum value, dependent upon the maximum frequency of the analog signal; this ensures that none of the information in the analog signal is lost. The sampling rate may also affect the stability of an analog system if the system is to be controlled by a computer. *See also* Nyquist's criterion.

2. The act of selecting items for study in such a way that the measurements made on the items in the sample will provide information about similar items not in the sample. Items can be people, machines, periods of time, fields of corn, games of chance, or whatever is being studied. *Sample size* is the number of items included in the sample. If the variance of the measurement (*see* measures of variation) is approximately known, the variance of its mean in a sample is the population variance divided by the sample size. This formula can then be used to indicate an appropriate sample size.

A *population* is a complete set of items about which information is required. It must be defined before selecting the sample or results may be ill-defined. The sample is the basis for inference about *probability distributions of measurements on the population. Problems of sampling include avoidance of *bias and selection of enough samples to ensure adequate precision.

Random sampling is the process that results in each item having the same probability of inclusion in the sample. Items may be selected with the aid of tables of random numbers or with mechanical devices such as cards or coins.

Systematic sampling selects items in some regular manner. It is valid when the order in which items are encountered is irrelevant to the question under study, but can be an unintentional source of bias.

sanitation The erasure of sensitive material from memory systems and memory media.

satellite computer A computer that forms part of a computing system but is generally much less capable than the mainframe. It is located at a distance from the main system and serves auxiliary functions such as remote data entry or printing. It is now often nearly synonymous with *terminal.

satisfiability The property exhibited by any logical expression or well-formed formula for which it is possible to assign values to variables in such a way that the expression or formula is true. *See also* propositional calculus, predicate calculus, P = NP question.

satisfiability problem *See* P = NP question.

saturation of a transistor. *See* bipolar transistor.

sawtooth waveform A periodic repetitive waveform that is constrained to lie between a maximum and a minimum value. Between these limits the waveform alternately rises and falls linearly with time. The slope of the falling edge of the waveform is made very much steeper than that of the rising edge, and the waveform thus appears as a repetitive series of linear ramps. *Compare* triangular waveform.

S-100 bus A popular microcomputer *bus in which each *logic card has a 100-contact edge connector on the bottom (50 contacts on each side). It is derived from the *backplane used in the original Altair 8080-based microcomputer, but has been expanded to accommodate 16-bit processors, multiple processors, a 24-bit address space, and *direct memory access. It is currently being considered for standardization by the IEEE (IEEE-696). Most S-100 logic cards measure approximately 5″ by 10″ (127 by 254 mm) but the proposed standard permits a double-height card of 10″ by 10″. The S-100 bus is unusual in that it utilizes distributed power regulation, i.e. unregulated voltages (+8, +16, and −16) are supplied to the bus, and each logic card is responsible for regulating the voltages that are required for it. A wide variety of microprocessors has been interfaced to the S-100 bus.

scaling The adjustment of values to be used in a computation so that they and their resultant are within the range that can be handled by the process or equipment. The scaling factor is reapplied to correct the result before output or – if this is not possible – it is output as a qualifier with the result.

scanner *Another name for* lexical analyzer.

scatter read A process in which data from a single record may be collected into (or for the process of *scatter write* written into) several noncontiguous areas of memory.

scheduled maintenance Periodic *preventive maintenance.

scheduler The code responsible for controlling use of a shared resource. Access to a shared resource must be subject to two requirements. It is essential to ensure that any process about to be granted use of a resource will not itself suffer damage, and that it will not cause damage to other processes. This can be thought of as establishing the correctness of the scheduling.

Quite separately from this, where it is feasible to allow any of several processes to access a resource, then it is necessary to make a choice between them. This choice will generally have a bearing on the efficiency with which system resources are utilized, and is determined by the *scheduling algorithm.

When used without further qualification, the word scheduler refers to controlling the use of the processors. Scheduling of jobs is usually carried out in two stages. The *high-level scheduler* collects together a particular job mix that is to be executed at any one time, according to criteria that are thought to allow the system to be optimally used. The scheduling among these jobs on a very fine time scale is the province of the *low-level scheduler* (or *dispatcher*), which thus allocates processors to processes.

scheduling algorithm The method used to determine which of several processes, each of which can safely have a resource allocated to it, will actually be granted use of the resource. The algorithm may take into account the priority of the user associated with the process, the requirement to maintain high utilization of system resources, and deadlines for the job.

For example, in a priority *time-slicing system, the processes awaiting execution are organized in several queues with the higher-priority queues having a smaller time *quantum. Whenever a processor becomes available for scheduling, the oldest process that is free to run in the highest-priority queue is started.

If this process runs to the end of its quantum without generating an interrupt then it will be rescheduled into a lower-priority queue with a larger quantum. If, before the quantum has expired, the process generates an interrupt then it will be returned either to the same queue or possibly to a higher-priority queue with a shorter quantum. If the process is itself interrupted by some external event that allows the rescheduling of a higher-priority process (with a shorter quantum) then again the interrupted process is returned to the queue from which it originated.

The net effect is that low-priority processes, with long quanta, are likely to be interrupted by the completion of input/output transactions on behalf of higher-priority processes, which will thus be freed for further processing.

schema (*plural*: schemata) The formal description of the data structuring in a *database, at some level of abstraction. A complex database system will have a number of schemata corresponding to various user descriptions, the conceptual logical description, and the physical description. *See also* ANSI-SPARC schemata, subschema.

Schmitt trigger A discrete or integrated circuit whose output has two stable states, i.e. two sustainable values of output voltage, to which it is driven by the movement of its input voltage past two well-defined trigger values. A rise in input voltage above one trigger level causes the output to switch to one state. A fall in input voltage below the other trigger level causes the output to switch to the other state.

Logic signals become corrupted as they travel through a system; the switching edges become *exponentials, *ringing can occur, and *noise may be added. Feeding such a signal through a Schmitt trigger restores the rising and falling edges to a fast transition between the voltages corresponding to the 0 and 1 logic states.

Schonhage algorithm An algorithm that multiplies large numbers very rapidly, based on the ideas of *modular arithmetic. *See* Chinese remainder theorem.

Schonhage–Strassen algorithm A development of the *Strassen algorithm that was published in 1970 and avoids the explicit use of complex numbers. It multiplies two n-bit numbers in steps of

$$O(n\log n \log\log n)$$

Schottky TTL A relatively fast bipolar *logic family, normally produced in integrated-circuit form, whose internal configuration is similar to normal *TTL except that *Schottky transistors* are used. These transistors can be considered as equivalent to a normal *bipolar transistor with a *Schottky diode* connected across the base-collector junction. The Schottky diode is a semiconductor-metal diode that has a low cut-in voltage (*forward bias voltage drop), typically 300 millivolts, compared with 600 mV for other common semiconductor diodes. It also has a relatively high switching speed. In Schottky TTL the low cut-in voltage of the diode limits the base-collector voltage to about 400 mV, which prevents the transistor falling into saturation. This results in faster switching times for the transistors constructed in this way.

scissoring (windowing) Processing the stored data of a large image so that part of it can be displayed. The visible *frame* or *window* formed by the process can be moved to allow examination of the entire stored image. Some graphics terminals have hardware "frame scissoring", but this is only effective when the complete image can be contained in the display file.

scope *Short for* nested scope. *See* block-structured languages, declaration.

scratch To delete a work file.

scratch file 1. *Another name for* work file.
2. A file, usually on magnetic disk or tape, that is used to store data produced as the output of a program and that may then be held permanently.

scratchpad A type of semiconductor memory that usually has small capacity but very fast access. It is used for temporary storage of intermediate results or other information that is required during the course of a computation.

screen 1. *Short for* visual display screen. The surface of a cathode-ray tube on which information can be displayed. The word is used more specifically than *display, which can also refer to devices using panel technologies such as plasma, electroluminescent, and liquid crystal displays.
2. To select and display information in response to an instruction or an inquiry.

screen editor *See* text editor.

scroll To move the information displayed on a screen or panel toward the top or bottom of the display area: as information disappears at one edge new information becomes visible at the other edge, or alternatively space is provided for the entry of new data. The scrolling action is perceived as a smooth movement. In some displays the movement is in discrete increments of one line pitch and this is referred to as *racking*. Scrolling is technically more difficult to achieve but eases simultaneous reading.

SDLC *Abbrev. for* synchronous data link control. A *data link control protocol developed and used by IBM, and based on the use of *frames to delimit message boundaries. Only link-layer functions are provided; there is no dependence upon characteristics of data structures of the devices that are communicating.
The frame format consists of an 8-bit flag, an 8-bit address, an 8-bit control field, a variable-length information field, a 16-bit frame check sequence, and another 8-bit flag. The information field carries "user" data and may be any length, although implementations of the protocol often limit it to a multiple of 8 bits in length.
The flag character is

01111110

*Bit stuffing is used to provide data transparency. Whenever a contiguous string of five 1 bits is encountered in the outgoing user data, the sender inserts a 0 bit. When the receiver encounters five contiguous 1 bits in the incoming bit stream, it examines the next one or two bits. If the first bit following (i.e. the 6th bit) is a 0 then it is removed and the user data is accepted.

If the 6th bit is a 1 and the 7th bit is a 0, then a flag is accepted and the frame terminated. If both the 6th and 7th bits are 1, then a protocol violation has been detected and the frame is aborted. In the idle state, continuous 1s are sent for 15 bit times.
The address field permits 254 station addresses. Address 0 is reserved for testing, and address 1 means that the frame is directed to all stations on the link.
The link endpoints (stations) are assigned primary or secondary roles. A primary station initiates link activation, directs link use among multiple stations, performs error recovery, and directs link deactivation. The secondary stations may share receiving addresses but have unique sending addresses.
The control field is used by a primary to carry control information and acknowledgments, and to poll receivers. The control field is used by secondaries for the same functions as for primaries, and also to indicate "final frame", i.e. to return control to the primary. In addition there is a special mode in which stations may be configured on a single unidirectional loop. Positive *acknowledgments are used with retransmission in the case of link errors. Acknowledgments are encoded modulo-8. ACKs may be piggybacked; a single frame may acknowledge up to seven previous frames in the reverse direction, as well as carrying user data in its own direction.

search and insertion algorithm *See* searching.

searching The process of locating information in a *table or *file by reference to a special field of each record, called the *key*. The goal of the search is to discover a record (if any) with a given key value. There are many different algorithms for searching, principally depending on the way in which the table or file is structured.
If a record is to be inserted in the file, and it is important to ensure that keys are unique, then a search is necessary: the insertion may take place as soon as the search has discovered that no existing record has the new key. Such an algorithm is known as a *search and insertion algorithm*. *See also* table look-up, sequential search algorithm, binary search algorithm, breadth-first search, depth-first search, trie search.

search tree *See* binary search tree, multiway search tree.

secondary access A method by which a record can be accessed using one or more secondary index items or keys in the record, i.e. items that do not uniquely identify the record. This means of access is often desirable or even necessary and a variety of file structures exist to support it.

secondary file When a large number of files are being processed, any file other than the *primary file.

secondary index *See* indexed file.

secondary memory *Another name for* backing store.

second generation of computers. Machines whose designs were started after 1955 (approximately) and are characterized by both vacuum tube (valve) and discrete transistor logic. They used magnetic core main memory. By this time a wider range of input/output equipment was beginning to be available, with higher-performance magnetic tape and the first forms of online storage (magnetic drums and early magnetic disks). Models of such on-line storage devices include magnetic drums in the UNIVAC LARC and 1105, and early disks in the IBM 1401–1410. During the second generation, initial efforts at *automatic programming produced B0, Commercial Translator, FACT, FORTRAN, and Mathmatic as programming languages, these in turn influencing the development of the *third generation languages – COBOL and later versions of FORTRAN. *See also* Atlas.

sector A subdivision of a track on a magnetic disk that represents the smallest portion of data that can be modified by overwriting. Each sector has a unique address, which contains the location of the track and the sector number. In order to read an address or data the drive decoding electronics must be synchronized to the data stream. To achieve this a special pattern, the *preamble*, is written. Following the preamble comes the *address mark or data mark as appropriate.
A disk may be *soft-sectored* or *hard-sectored*. In soft-sectoring the size and position of the sectors is determined by the control electronics and software: disk drives generate an index signal once per revolution of the disk, and when this is received from the drive unit all the sectors of a track are written in one continuous operation. On a hard-sectored disk the start of each sector is related to a sector signal generated by the disk drive and is positively related to the position of the disk. Hard sectoring can achieve higher packing of sectors since it is not necessary to have large intersector gaps to accommodate speed variations.

security Protection against unauthorized alteration of stored data. A user who files data may require that only other users who have been explicitly authorized to do so may alter the contents of his file. The concepts of integrity, privacy, and security are interlinked. *See* integrity.

security certification Some form of certification by an external authority that a computer system is appropriately secure for the anticipated uses and against the anticipated *threats.

seek time The time taken for a particular track on a storage disk or drum to be located. Typical seek times are in the range 10–30 milliseconds. *See also* latency.

segment 1. Originally, a clearly identifiable set of data, or code, that was moved between backing store and main memory under the control of the user. Later the term was applied to a set of data, still clearly visible to the user, that was managed by the operating system as part of the *virtual-memory system. A segment differs from a *page in that its size is not fixed, and the user has a measure of direct control over its management.
2. Part of a program. The word is usually used in the context of storage allocation, as in code segment, data segment.

SEL Systems Engineering Lab, a US manufacturer of minicomputers. The SEL computers are noted for their extremely high speed: the SEL 832 is still one of the fastest large minicomputers on the market.

select 1. To initiate an action or enable a data path.
2. To choose one of several possible control paths at a particular point in a program. The selection is usually made by a *case statement*, though if there are only two alternatives an *if then else statement can be used.

selector 1. A device that can switch a signal path or initiate some other action on receipt of a predetermined signal. The actioning signal can be on the path to be switched or from a separate path. Multicontact relays were extensively used as selectors in combination with patchboards to program tabulators and similar equipment.
2. A punched card machine that can extract cards from a file when it detects coincidence between a pattern of code set on its switches or patchboard and the pattern of code in a designated field of the card.
3. *Short for* selector channel. *See* channel.

selector channel *See* channel.

self-adapting process (self-learning process) An *adaptive process that can be "trained" on representative data to provide a best model for that data and that can "recognize" similar data. *See also* artificial intelligence.

self-checking code A method of encoding data that permits detection, and possibly correction, of cases where the encoded values become corrupted, e.g. due to data transmission errors. This is achieved by selecting encoded values in such a way that minor corruption does not lead to a different legitimate encoded value but rather to an illegal value. The corruption can thus be detected and, dependent upon the level of redundancy, perhaps corrected.

self-compiling compiler A compiler that is written in the language it compiles. Such a compiler makes it relatively easy to transfer a language to another machine, since the compiler can be compiled on a machine on which it has already been implemented.

self-defining A term applied to a programming language, implying that the compiler for the language can be written in the language. *See* self-compiling compiler.

self-dual *See* duality.

self-extending A term applied to a programming language, denoting the ability to add new features to the language by writing programs in that language.

self-learning process *Another term for* self-adapting process.

self-organizing system A computing system that is capable of developing information and structure out of sets of natural data that are presented to it. *See also* artificial intelligence.

self-referent list *Another name for* recursive list.

self-relative addressing *See* relative addressing.

semantic error A programming error that arises from a misunderstanding of the meaning or effect of some construct in a programming language. *See also* error diagnostics.

semantic network A means of representing relational knowledge as a labeled directed *graph. Each vertex of the graph represents an object and each label represents a relation between objects. Access and updating procedures traverse and manipulate the graph.

semantics That part of the definition of a language concerned with specifying the meaning or effect of a text that is constructed according to the *syntax rules of the language. *See also* denotational semantics, operational semantics, axiomatic semantics.

semaphore A special-purpose *data type introduced by Edsger Dijkstra (1965). Apart from creation, initialization, and annihilation, there are only two operations on a semaphore: *wait* (*P operation* or *down operation*) and *signal* (*V operation* or *up operation*). The letters P and V derive from the Dutch words used in the original description.

A semaphore has an integer value that cannot become negative. The signal operation increases the value by one, and in general indicates that a resource has become free. The wait operation decreases the value by one when that can be done without the value going negative, and in general indicates that a free resource is about to start being used. This therefore provides a means of controlling access to *critical resources by cooperating sequential processes.

semiconductor A material, such as silicon or germanium, whose electrical conductivity increases with temperature and is intermediate between metals and insulators. In pure semiconductors this effect is due to the thermal generation of equal numbers of negative charge carriers (electrons) and positive charge carriers (holes). These materials are called *intrinsic* or *i-type semiconductors*.

The introduction of specific types of impurity atoms into a pure semiconductor can significantly increase its conductivity:

donor impurities, which belong to group 5 of the periodic table, greatly increase the number of conduction electrons and produce an *n-type semiconductor*; *acceptor impurities*, which belong to group 3, greatly increase the number of holes and produce a *p-type semiconductor*. These materials are called *extrinsic semiconductors*. The conductivity of an extrinsic semiconductor depends on the type and the amount (or *doping level*) of impurity present.

Semiconductors of different conductivity – n-type, p-type, highly doped n- and p-type, i-type – can be brought together to form a variety of *junctions, which are the basis of semiconductor devices used as electronic components. The term semiconductor is frequently applied to the devices themselves.

semiconductor memory (solid-state memory) Any of various types of cheap compact memory device, normally produced in *integrated-circuit form, that are used for storing binary data patterns in digital electronic circuits. They consist internally of arrays of *latches constructed of semiconductor devices such as *bipolar transistors or *MOSFETs. The memory *capacity of a single chip is increasing by a factor of four every few years: the 64K (kilobit) chip of dynamic *RAM is now on the market and the 256K chip should be available in 1984/85.

semigroup A very simple *algebraic structure comprising a *set S on which there is defined an *associative operation denoted by $\circ$ (*compare* group). The operator $\circ$ is assumed to take operands from the set and produce results that are also in S. When the set S is finite a semigroup can be described by giving the *Cayley table of the operation $\circ$; otherwise it can be described by giving a rule for $\circ$.

Examples of semigroups include: strings with the operation of *concatenation (joining together); the set of $n \times n$ matrices together with the operation of multiplication; the integers and the operation of choosing the maximum (or minimum) of two elements. The set of integers together with subtraction does not constitute a semigroup.

Semigroups play a major role in the theory of *sequential machines and *formal languages. If M is a sequential machine then any input string induces a function over the state-set of M. The set of all such induced functions forms a *semigroup of the machine* under function *composition (*see* Myhill equivalence, Nerode equivalence). Semigroups are also used in certain aspects of computer arithmetic. *See also* free semigroup, transformation semigroup, monoid.

semiring A *set S (containing a 0 and a 1) on which there are defined two *binary operations that are denoted by $+$ and $\cdot$ and that obey certain properties: the set S, regarded as a set with a zero on which the operation $+$ is defined, is a *monoid; the set S, regarded as a set with a unit on which $\cdot$ is defined, is a monoid; the operation $+$ is *commutative; the operation $\cdot$ is *distributive over $+$. A semiring is said to be *unitary* if the operation $\cdot$ possesses a unit. A semiring is *commutative* if the operation $\cdot$ is commutative.

The set of polynomials in x whose coefficients are nonnegative integers constitutes an example of a semiring (which is not a ring), the two operations being addition and multiplication. Other uses of semirings occur in *fuzzy theory. *See also* ring, closed semiring.

semi-Thue system An important concept in formal language theory that underlies the notion of a *grammar. It was defined and investigated by Axel Thue from about 1904. A semi-Thue system over the alphabet Σ is a finite set of ordered pairs of Σ-words:

$$\{\langle l_1,r_1\rangle, \ldots ,\langle l_n,r_n\rangle\}$$

Each pair $\langle l_i,r_i\rangle$ is a rule, referred to as a *production*, with *left-hand side* l_i and *right-hand side* r_i; it is usually written

$$l_i \rightarrow r_i$$

Let u and v be Σ-words, and $l \rightarrow r$ be a production, then the word ulv is said to *directly derive* the word urv; this is written

$$ulv \Rightarrow urv$$

So w directly derives w' if w' is the result of applying a production to some substring of w. If

$$w_1 \Rightarrow w_2 \Rightarrow \ldots \Rightarrow w_{n-1} \Rightarrow w_n,$$

then w_1 is said to *derive* w_n; this is written

$$w_1 \overset{*}{\Rightarrow} w_n$$

So w derives w' if w' is obtained from w by a sequence of direct derivations.

As one example, let Σ be $\{a,b\}$ and let the productions be

$$\{ab \rightarrow ba,\ ba \rightarrow ab\}$$

then *aabba* derives *baaab* by the sequence

$$aabba \Rightarrow ababa \Rightarrow baaba \Rightarrow baaab$$

It is clear that w derives any permutation of w.

As a second example, with productions

$$\{ab \rightarrow ba,\ ba \rightarrow \Lambda\}$$

w derives Λ (the empty word) if and only if w has the same number of *a*s as *b*s.

The question of whether w derives w' is algorithmically undecidable.

sender-receiver terminal A term applied to teletype terminals, defining whether the teletype was a receive only (RO), a keyboard-driven terminal that could both send and receive (KSR), or a terminal that was also equipped with paper-tape reader and punch for automatic send-receive (ASR).

sense To determine the condition or content of a signal or storage location. When used in reference to a storage location the word has the same meaning as read.

sense switch A switch that can be manually set and interrogated by an instruction. This device and associated instruction(s) are rarely seen in modern computers.

sensitivity analysis Investigation of the degree to which the behavior of a system is affected by a change in the value of some (explicit or implicit) parameter or variable, or by a combination of changes. For example, a simple analysis might determine how the performance of a system is impacted by changing the number and sizes of the storage buffers that are allocated to that system.

sentence symbol (start symbol) *See* grammar.

sentential form *See* grammar.

sentinel A *datum that indicates some important state, usually in the context of input or output. For example, an end-of-data sentinel means all the data has been read.

separator A symbol that separates statements in a programming language, e.g. the semicolon in Algol-type languages.

sequence 1. A *function whose domain is the set of positive integers (or sometimes the set of nonnegative integers). The image set can thus be listed $s_1, s_2, \ldots$ where s_i is the value of the function given argument i. A *finite sequence* (or *list*) is a function whose domain is

$$\{1,2, \ldots ,n\} \text{ for } n \geqslant 1$$

and hence whose image set can be listed

$$s_1, s_2, \ldots, s_n$$

2. The listing of the image set of a sequence. Hence it is another name for *string.

sequence control register A part of the *control unit that causes the steps of the fetch and execute processes to occur in the correct sequence/timing.

sequence generator A digital logic circuit whose purpose is to produce a prescribed sequence of n-bit binary outputs. A binary *counter is a special type of sequence generator. Sequence generators are useful in a wide variety of coding and control applications.

sequencer A logic circuit that produces outputs that are intended to provide coordination stimuli for other logic circuits. The exact timing and sequence of these control outputs is dependent on the sequencer circuitry and may depend on a set of input control signals provided by external devices.

sequencing 1. The procedure by which ordered units of data (octets or messages) are numbered, transmitted over a communications network (which may rearrange their order), and reassembled into the original order at their destination.
2. Proceeding through a program in its ordinary order, normally from sequential memory locations. *See also* loop.

sequency The number of positive-going zero crossings (and therefore half the total number of zero crossings) that the amplitude of a *signal makes per unit time, or, in the case of a spatial signal (a picture), per unit of distance. The term is used mainly with regard to signals capable of taking only one positive and one negative value of amplitude, especially the simple case of +1 unit and −1 unit. Although the amplitude is usually discrete, the time (or space) coordinate may be regarded as discrete or continuous, depending on the application and the mathematical methods to be employed.
The term was originally applied to *Walsh functions. In the case of Walsh functions, or any similar functions which are periodic but in which there are several zero crossings per period at unequal intervals, the number of zero crossings per period is called the *normalized sequency*.
Many concepts such as *bandwidth, and processes such as *filtering, which were originally defined in terms of *frequency, can equally well be defined in terms of sequency. The sequency formulation is often handled more simply and more rapidly by discrete devices such as computers.
See also discrete and continuous systems.

sequential access A method of access in which the order in which blocks are to be accessed is always the same. The order in which the blocks are initially written is the same as the order in which they are subsequently read.

sequential algorithm In general, any algorithm executed sequentially, but, specifically, one for decoding a *convolutional code.

sequential circuit (sequential machine) A *logic circuit whose outputs at a specified time are a function of the inputs at that time, and also at a finite number of preceding times. In practice, any physically realizable sequential circuit will have a finite transit time, or delay, between the inputs changing and the outputs changing (one or more of these inputs may be clock signals); the intention of the term sequential is to include not only *combinational circuits but also (explicitly) *memory elements such as flip-flops. Analysis and synthesis of sequential circuits is facilitated by *state diagrams.

sequential file A file whose organization is sequential. *See* file organization.

sequential file organization *See* file organization.

sequential function Let I and O be alphabets. A function f from I^* to O^* (*see* word) is sequential if it is the response function of a *sequential machine. Often, though not always, there is the implication that the machine has finitely many states. In this sense therefore sequential function is to function as *regular language is to language, since the regular languages are those recognized by finite-state automata.

sequential machine 1. A *finite-state automaton with output (in some contexts including machines with infinite state-set). Thus there is a function f from the *Cartesian product $I \times Q$ to the product $Q \times O$, with Q a set of states and I, O finite sets of input and output symbols respectively. Suppose, for example,

$$a,q_0 \mapsto q_1,x$$
$$b,q_1 \mapsto q_1,y$$
$$c,q_1 \mapsto q_2,z$$

Then, if the machine is in state q_0 and reads a, it moves to state q_1 and outputs x, and so on. Assuming the starting state to be q_0, it can be seen for example that the input string *abbbc* is mapped to the output string *xyyyz*. This mapping from the set of all input strings to the set of all output strings, i.e. I^* to O^*, is called the *response function* of the machine. The function f comprises a *state-transition function* f_Q from $I \times Q$ to Q and an *output function* f_O from $I \times Q$ to O.

What is described here is sometimes called a *Mealy machine* to distinguish it from the more restricted *Moore machines*. In a Moore machine, the symbol output at each stage depends only on the current state, and not on the input symbol read. The example above is therefore not a Moore machine since

$$f_O(b,q_1) = y$$

whereas

$$f_O(c,q_1) = z$$

Any Moore machine can be converted to an equivalent Mealy machine by adding more states.

A *generalized sequential machine* is an extension of the notion of sequential machine: a string of symbols is output at each stage rather than a single symbol. Thus there is a function from $I \times Q$ to $Q \times O^*$. *See also* gsm mapping.

2. *Another name for* sequential circuit.

sequential search algorithm The most simple searching algorithm in which the keys are searched sequentially from the top of the file until a match is found.

sequential transducer A nondeterministic version of a generalized *sequential machine.

serial access A method of access to data in which blocks are read from the storage medium in the physical order in which they occur, until the required item is reached.

serial adder A binary *adder that is capable of forming sum and carry outputs for addend and augend words of greater than one bit in length. The individual bits of the addend and augend, starting with the least significant bit, are presented in sequence, together with a carry, to the adder, which then forms sum and carry outputs. The carry must then be stored so that it can be used with the next most significant pair of input bits. The overall result of the summation is stored in, for example, a *shift register, at the completion of each stage of addition. The diagram shows a typical circuit with the addend and augend initially loaded into the addend and accumulator registers.

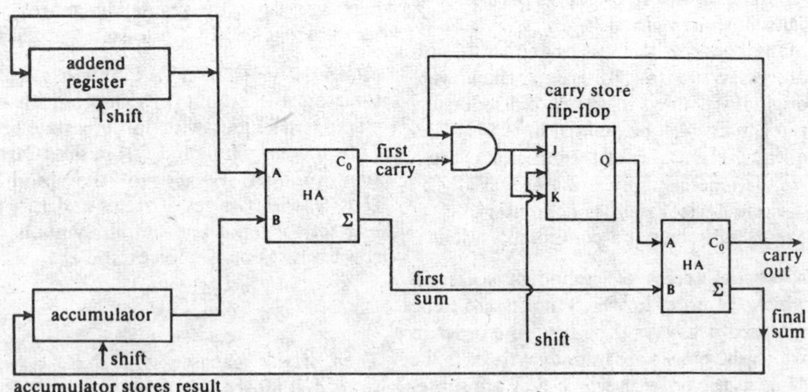

Serial adder

A serial adder affords a saving in component count when compared with a *parallel adder, but is generally slower.

serial arithmetic Operation upon one bit or digit of a number at a time.

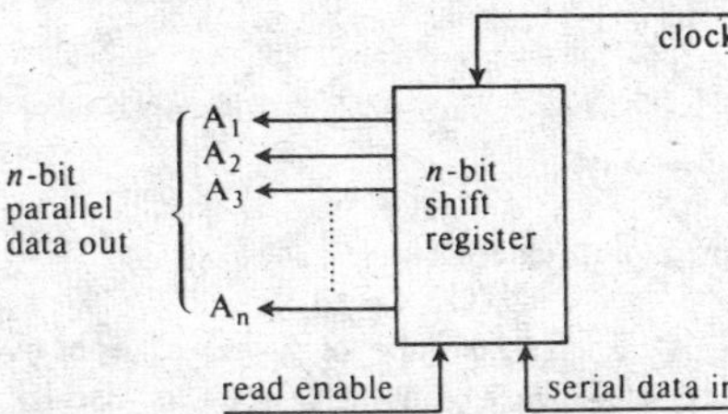

Serial in parallel out

serial in parallel out (SIPO) A term used to describe a class of digital device that can accept serial sequential *n*-bit data streams and convert them into parallel *n*-bit data words. These devices often consist of an *n*-bit *shift register that is serial loaded with *n* bits of data from the input stream under the control of an external clock (*see* diagram). The *n*-bit data word can then be read in parallel form from the shift register. *Compare* parallel in serial out.

serial input/output (SIO) A method of communicating data between devices, typically a computer and its peripherals, the individual data bits being sent sequentially. Integrated-circuit devices known as *UARTs can be used to implement the transmitter and receiver required for such a scheme. *See also* parallel input/output.

serial in serial out (SISO) A term used to describe a *shift register that, by implication, cannot be loaded in parallel and cannot be read in parallel: data can only enter or leave the device serially.

serial interface A connection point through which information is transferred one digital bit at a time. The rate may be high, e.g. 10 megabits per second as in Ethernet, or as slow as 110 bits per second via an RS232C interface. The term is sometimes applied to interfaces such as the RS232C and RS422 in which the data is transferred serially via one path, but some control signals can be transferred simultaneously via parallel paths.

serial-parallel A combination of serial and parallel processing; for example, a decimal string is often processed as 4 bits in parallel, and successive 4-bit units are processed serially.

serial printer A printer that prints one character at a time in the sequence in which they appear in the line of text. The sequence may be taken from left to right, or it may be in alternate directions for alternate lines thus avoiding an unproductive carriage-return movement. All serial printers have an arrangement in which a print head moves parallel to the paper and along the line to be printed. The print may be formed by impacting an inked ribbon against the paper, as in the case of *dot matrix and *daisywheel printers, or by one of the nonimpact marking technologies such as *ink jet or *thermal printers. In some designs the productivity is increased when printing other than complete lines by arranging for the head to move at high speed when passing blank areas. The direction in which the line is to be printed is also optimized.

The speed of a serial printer appears slow compared to the equivalent character per second rate for a *line printer printing full lines. However, the serial printer's ability to print short lines more quickly improves its performance on applications with short lines, such as addresses and amounts on preprinted forms. A 200 cps serial printer can print some types of consumer bills at a rate equivalent to 600 lines per minute.

serial process A process in which stages in the process are executed in a strictly serial manner, one stage completing before the next starts, and with only one stage active at any one instant.

serial programming *See* single threading.

serial transfer To transmit information as sequential units. For example, if two computers connected by a single wire wish to communicate an 8-bit unit of information, the sending computer would transmit each of the eight bits in sequence over the wire, while the receiving computer would reassemble the sequential bits into the original 8-bit units. Thus an 8-bit serial transfer would have occurred. *Compare* parallel transfer.

server A node on a network, usually a *local area network, that provides service to the terminals on the network through managing an expensive shared resource. The following are examples.
A *file server* manages a set of disks and provides storage and archival services to computers on the network that may not have their own disks;
A *printer server* provides printing in hard copy – often high-quality printing at very high speed – so that each terminal or computer on the network need not have its own printer;
A *communication server* provides connection to other communications media, including other local area nets or the public networks, i.e. it is a *gateway.

service bit A bit in an *X.25 *packet that indicates whether the packet is formatted to contain primarily data or control information.

service engineering Any maintenance, *preventive or *remedial.

service routines The collection of programs and subroutines that forms part of every computer system and provides a variety of generally useful functions, including file copying and deleting, text preparation, and program cross referencing.

servosurface *See* disk pack, disk cartridge, actuator.

session layer of network protocol function. *See* seven-layer reference model.

set 1. A collection of distinct objects of any sort. The objects in the set are called its *members* or *elements*. An element can occur at most once in a set and order or arrangement is unimportant. If x is a member of the set S it is customary to write

$$x \in S$$

If x is not a member of S this can be expressed as

$$x \notin S$$

and is equivalent to

$$\text{NOT } (x \in S)$$

i.e. $\in$ and $\notin$ can be regarded as operators. When any element in set S is also in set T, and vice versa, the two sets are said to be *identical* or *equal*.
A *finite set* has a fixed finite number of members and a notation such as

{Ada, Algol, Cobol, PL/I}

is possible; the members are separated by commas and here are just the names of various programming languages. When the number of elements is not finite, the set is said to be *infinite* and explicit enumeration of the elements is not then possible.
Infinite and finite sets can be described using a *predicate or statement such as $p(x)$ that involves x and is either true or false, thus

$$\{x \mid p(x)\}$$

This is read as "the set of all elements x for which p(x) is true", the elements being characterized by the common property p. Examples of sets described in this way are (letting R be the set of real numbers):

$$\{(x,y) \mid x \in R, y \in R \text{ and } x + y = 9\}$$

$$\{n \mid n \text{ is a prime number}\}$$

$$\{l \mid l \text{ is the name of a language}\}$$

There is an implicit assumption here that there is some algorithm for deciding whether $p(x)$ is true or false in any particular case.
The idea of a set is fundamental to mathematics. It forms the basis for all ideas involving *functions, *relations, and indeed any kind of *algebraic structure. Authors

differ considerably in the way they define sets. A mathematical logician will distinguish carefully between classes and sets, basically to ensure that paradoxes such as *Russell's paradox cannot occur in sets. However, the informal definition is adequate for most purposes.
See also operations on sets.
2. Any data structure representing a set of elements. One example is a *characteristic vector.
3. To cause the condition or state of a switch, signal, or storage location to change to the positive condition.

set algebra The *algebra that consists of the *set of *subsets of some *universal set U together with the associated operations of *union, *intersection, and *complement. The set of subsets associated with set algebra is sometimes described as the *power set of U.

set difference The *binary operation between two sets S and T, say, resulting in the set $S - T$ consisting of those elements that are in S but not in T. Formally

$$S - T = \{s \mid s \in S \text{ and } s \notin T\}$$

Set difference is a generalization of the idea of the *complement of a set and as such is sometimes called the *relative complement* of T with respect to S. The *symmetric difference* between two sets S and T is the *union of $S - T$ and $T - S$.

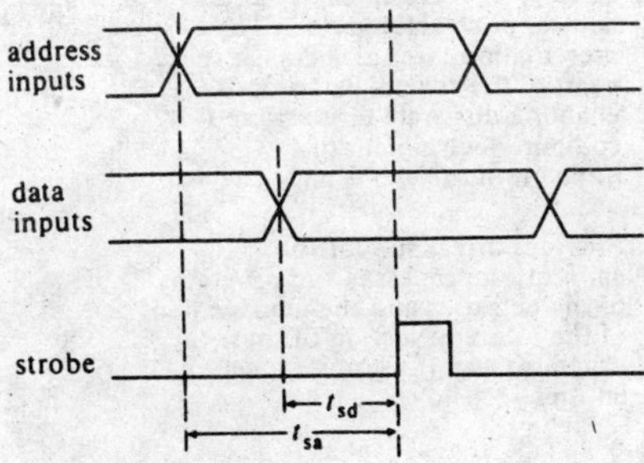

Set-up time

set-up time The period of time during which binary data must be present or "set up" at the input to a digital device before the device enters or samples the data. It is commonly specified for memory devices, for which the timing diagram shown might be typical. The rising edge of the strobe pulse enters data into the memory.

seven-layer reference model A model for communication protocols that is being proposed by the International Standards Organization (ISO) with the goal of allowing *open system interconnection between computer equipment with differing protocol standards. The ISO effort has concentrated initially on a structure (model) for digital communication protocols and not on the protocols themselves. The fundamental idea behind the effort has been the decision that protocol function can be divided into seven separate categories or layers, each of which is connected to a single higher and lower layer (except for the lowest and highest layers). Networks that are expected to exhibit open connectability should thus have a relatively simple implementation. The names of the layers together with an outline of their basic functions are given in the table.
The seven-layer model has not yet resulted in a complete set of protocols for each layer. In fact, there will undoubtedly be a collection of protocols that will be implemented for each layer. It is the intention of the seven-layer open interconnection philosophy to provide a "model" into which various protocols can be fitted as they are developed, rather than attempting to build a universal set of protocols. Whereas there is considerable merit in the objectives of the seven-layer model, it is clear that there will be many difficult peer-layer protocol interconnection questions that will have to be answered as the number of protocols increase at each layer.
Even so, there has been real progress made toward standardization at the lower

SEVEN-LAYER REFERENCE MODEL

Layer	Layer Name	Functional Description
1	Physical Layer	Provides mechanical, electrical, functional, and procedural characteristics to establish, maintain, and release physical connections.
2	Data Link Layer	Provides functional and procedural means to establish, maintain, and release data lines between network entities (e.g. terminals and network nodes).
3	Network Layer	Provides functional and procedural means to exchange network service data units between two transport entities (i.e. devices that support transport layer protocols) over a network connection. It provides transport entities with independence from routing and switching considerations.
4	Transport Layer	Provides optimization of available communication services (supplied by lower-layer implementations) by providing a transparent transfer of data between session layer entities.
5	Session Layer	Provides a service of "binding" two presentation service entities together logically and controls the dialogue between them as far as message synchronization is concerned.
6	Presentation Layer	Provides a set of services that may be selected by the application layer to enable it to interpret the meaning of the data exchanged. Such services include management of entry exchange, display and control of structured data. The presentation layer services are the heart of the seven-layer proposal, enabling disparate terminal and computer equipment to intercommunicate.
7	Application Layer	Provides direct support of application processes and programs of the end user and the management of the interconnection of these programs and the communication entities.

ISO/OSI seven-layer reference model

three layers under the auspices of the ISO and CCITT, resulting in *packet switching standards for public data networks. Recently there has been progress at the upper four layers for certain types of applications, specifically for *file transfer. In addition, there have been presentation layer (layer 6) standards proposed for *videotex applications by a number of organizations.

seven-segment display *See* LCD, LED display.

S-gate *Another name for* ternary threshold gate.

Shannon–Fano coding (Fano coding) *See* source coding.

Shannon–Hartley law *See* channel coding theorem.

Shannon's diagram of a *communication system. A diagram illustrating *Shannon's model of such a system, embodying the source, encoder, channel, noise source, decoder, and destination of information.

Shannon's model of a *communication system. A widely accepted model, set down by Claude Elwood Shannon in 1948, that has an *information source* sending a *message* to an *information destination* via a medium or mechanism called the *channel*. According to Shannon, "the fundamental problem of communication is that of reproducing at one point either exactly or approximately a message selected at another point."

In general, the channel will distort the message and add *noise to it. In order to avoid the distortion, and to reduce the effect of the noise to any desired degree, an *encoder is placed between the source and the channel, and a *decoder is placed between the channel and the destination. Now, the source sends the *transmitted message*, which is encoded as the *transmitted signal*; this is sent through the channel. It emerges as the *received signal*, which is decoded to give the *received message*; this arrives at the destination.

The channel is considered to have a *noise source* that inputs "information" in addition to that in the transmitted signal. The aim of the encoder and decoder is to make the received message resemble, as closely as required, the transmitted message, in spite of the "information" from the noise source.

See also source coding theorem, channel coding theorem.

Shannon's theorems *See* source coding theorem, channel coding theorem.

shared logic system A term sometimes used to refer to a system where several terminals share a CPU simultaneously.

shared memory The use of the same portion of memory by two distinct *processes, or the memory so shared. Shared memory is used for interprocess communication and for purposes, such as common subroutines, that lead to compactness of memory.

Sheffer stroke *See* NAND operation.

Shell's method (diminishing increment sort) A sorting algorithm proposed by Donald Shell in 1959 and published as *shellsort*. It is a variant of *straight insertion sort that allows records to take long leaps rather than move one position at a time. It does this by sorting each group $G^{(i)}_j$ of records a distance h_i apart within the file. (The $G^{(i)}_j$ are *disjoint and together contain all the information in the file.) This is repeated for a decreasing sequence of values h_i, and consequently increasing number of groups $G^{(i)}_j$, finally ending with $h_i = 1$.

shellsort *See* Shell's method.

shift 1. To change the interpretation of characters. The term is commonly met on normal typewriters as a change from lower to upper case.

2. Any complete set of characters obtainable without shifting. Hence *change shift* is a synonym for shift (def. 1).
3. The movement of a bit pattern in a bit string. A *left shift* of m ($<n$) bits will move the bit pattern in a string

$$b_1b_2 \ldots b_n$$

leftward, giving

$$b_{m+1} \ldots b_n? \ldots ?$$

Similarly, a *right shift* of m bits converts

$$b_1b_2 \ldots b_n$$

$$\text{to } ? \ldots ?b_1b_2 \ldots b_{n-m}$$

The bits that are introduced (shown here as question marks) and the use of the bits that are shifted off the end of the string depend on the kind of shift: *arithmetic*, *logical*, or *circular*. In an arithmetic shift the bit strings are regarded as representations of binary integers; if the leading m bits that are lost are all zero, a left shift of m bits is equivalent to multiplication by 2^m and a right shift can be interpreted as integer division by 2^m. In logical shifts the bits introduced are all zero. In circular shifts the bits shifted off at one end are introduced at the other.

shift character Any character used in a stream of characters to change *shift. *Compare* escape character.

shift counter A *synchronous counter that consists of clocked *flip-flops arranged as a *shift register. Data is propagated from left to right (or from right to left) between the flip-flops by the application of a clock or count pulse. Counting is achieved by setting the contents of the shift register to logic 0 (or logic 1) and loading the leftmost (rightmost) flip-flop with a logic 1 (logic 0). An m-bit counter, which has m flip-flops, will then require m clock pulses to shift this 1 (or 0) to the rightmost (leftmost) flip-flop. The position in the register of the 1 (or 0) thus acts as a count of the number of pulses received since application of the load.
The counter may be made to count continuously by arranging that the output of the rightmost (leftmost) flip-flop sets the input of the leftmost (rightmost) flip-flop. The counter is then known as a *ring counter*.

shift instruction An instruction specifying that the contents of a shiftable register (occasionally concatenated registers) are to be shifted either to the left or to the right a specified number of register positions. *Shifts can be circular or they can be open at both ends. In the latter case there is usually a specification of what happens to bits being shifted out of the register (often they are discarded) and

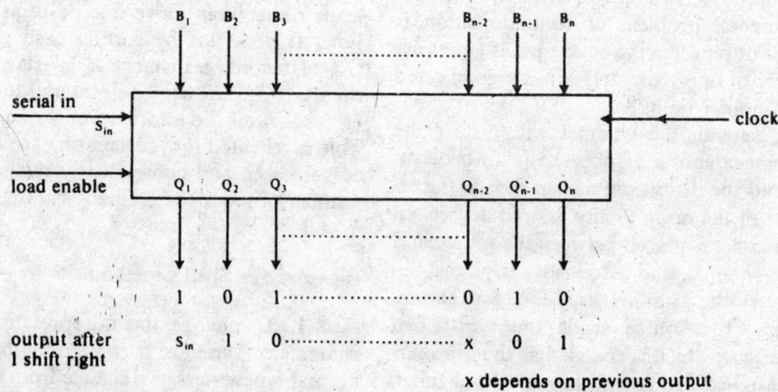

An n-bit shift register

what bits are to be shifted into the register (most often 0s).

shift keying *See* modulation, frequency shift keying, phase shift keying.

shift-reduce parsing *Another name for* bottom-up parsing.

shift register A *register that has the ability to transfer information in a lateral direction. It is an n-stage clocked device whose output consists of an n-bit parallel data word (*see* diagram). Application of a single clock cycle to the device causes the output word to be shifted by one bit position from right to left (or from left to right). The leftmost (or rightmost) bit is lost from the "end" of the register while the rightmost (or leftmost) bit position is loaded from a serial input terminal. The device may also be capable of being loaded with parallel n-bit data words, these then being shifted out of the device in serial form. *See also* serial in parallel out, parallel in serial out, parallel in parallel out, serial in serial out.

Shift registers with parallel outputs, and with combinational logic fed from those outputs (*see* combinational circuit), are of great importance in *digital signal processing, and in the encoding and decoding of *error-correcting and *error-detecting codes. Such registers may be implemented in hardware or in software, and may be binary or *q-ary. (Hardware implementation is usually convenient only for binary and sometimes ternary logic.) *See* feedback register, feed-forward (shift) register, Good–de Bruijn diagram.

shooting method An iterative method for the solution of boundary-value problems in *ordinary differential equations. Consider the problem

$$y'' = f(x,y,y'),\ y(a) = \alpha,\ y(b) = \beta$$

Let $y(x;t)$ denote the solution of this differential equation from initial conditions

$$y(a) = \alpha,\ y'(a) = t$$

This solves the above problem if $F(t) = 0$ where

$$F(t) = y(b;t) - \beta$$

The equation $F(t) = 0$ is solved iteratively, usually by some variant of *Newton's method. Each iteration therefore requires the numerical integration of an initial-value problem.

The method is applicable to all types of boundary-value problems, whatever the form of the boundary conditions. Apart from the problem of obtaining good estimates to start the iteration, difficulties can arise due to severe *error propagation in the integration of the initial-value problem. A useful improvement is to guess the missing conditions at both ends of the range, matching the two solutions so defined at an interior point. In difficult cases estimates and matching can be used at several interior points to reduce error propagation; this is known as the *parallel-shooting method.*

shortest-path algorithm An algorithm that is designed essentially to find a *path of minimum length between two specified vertices of a *connected *weighted graph. A good algorithm for this problem was given by E. W. Dijkstra in 1959.

sibling (brother; sister) Either of two nodes in a *tree that are both children of the same parent.

sifting technique *Another name for* straight insertion sort.

sigma language (Σ-language) *See* formal language.

sigma tree (sigma term; Σ-tree; Σ-term) *See* tree language.

sigma word (Σ-word) *See* word.

sign A means used to distinguish between positive and negative numbers. In a computer there are a number of ways of representing the sign of a number, each of which makes use of a single bit called the *sign bit*. The most obvious way of representing positive and negative integers in computer words is by means of the *signed-magnitude* (or *sign-and-magnitude*) *repre-*

sentation. Here, the leftmost bit in a word is used to denote the sign (0 for + and 1 for –) and the remaining bits in the word are used to represent the magnitude of the integer. It is more usual, however, for a computer to use the two's complement representation of integers. *See* radix complement, complement number system.

signal A form of data that is usually envisaged as a sequence of values of a scalar quantity – the *amplitude* – recorded (i.e. measured, tabulated, or plotted) against time. The amplitude is most often, but by no means always, an electric potential. *See also* discrete and continuous systems, space domain.

signal conditioning *Filtering a continuous signal.

signal operation *See* semaphore.

signal processing The processing of *signals by means of hardwired or programmable devices, the signals being regarded as continuous or discrete and being approximated by analog or digital devices accordingly (*see* discrete and continuous systems). *Filtering and *picture processing are examples of signal processing. *See also* digital signal processing.

signal-to-noise ratio The ratio of the *signal power to the *noise power in a physical transmission channel; it is often measured in decibels (dB). The definition is best applied to statistically well-behaved noise such as *white *Gaussian noise.

signature analysis A method of determining the location and/or nature of a fault in a digital system by input of test sequences of binary digits and inspection of the resulting output sequences (signatures) of binary digits. The theory is that of *sequential circuits.

sign bit *See* sign digit.

sign digit (signed field) A single digit used to indicate the algebraic sign of a number. If the binary system is being used, the sign digit is called a *sign bit*. *See also* sign, floating-point notation.

signed field *Another name for* sign digit.

signed-magnitude representation *See* sign.

sign off *Another term for* log off.

sign on *Another term for* log in.

silicon chip *See* chip.

silicon-on sapphire (SOS) circuitry A metal-oxide-semiconductor (MOS) technology in which a layer of single-crystal silicon is grown onto a synthetic sapphire substrate. The individual devices comprising a particular integrated-circuit function may then be fabricated on the silicon layer. Since the substrate is insulating, lower capacitances are achieved between parasitic devices and the substrate, with consequent improvements in switching speeds and packing densities of the devices. The substrate material is however more expensive to produce than silicon.

SIMD processor *Short for* single instruction (stream), multiple data (stream) processor. *See* concurrency.

similar trees Trees that have the same structure or shape. More formally, two trees are similar if they both comprise exactly one node or, if not, the corresponding subtrees of the two roots are equal in number and are pairwise similar. For ordered trees, the pairwise correspondence is that given by the ordering imposed upon the subtrees of the two trees.

simple parity check (simple parity code) *See* cyclic redundancy check.

simplex A connection between two endpoints, either physical or logical, that can carry data in only one direction with no possibility of data flow in the opposite direction. *See also* duplex, half duplex.

simplex codes A family of *linear *error-correcting or *error-detecting *block codes, easily implemented as *polynomial codes (by means of *shift registers). Considered as (n, k) codes (*see* block code), they have codeword length

$$n = q^k - 1$$

Binary simplex codes have a minimum *Hamming distance equal to 2^{k-1}. They can be regarded as *Reed–Muller codes shortened by one digit, and are identical with the *m-sequences of length $2^k - 1$, together with the *zero word.

simplex method *See* linear programming.

SIMULA A programming language based on Algol 60, with extensions to make it suitable for writing *simulation programs.

simulation Imitation of the behavior of some existing or intended system, or some aspect of that behavior. Examples of areas where simulation is used include communication network design, where simulation can be used to explore overall behavior, traffic patterns, trunk capacity, etc., and weather forecasting, where simulation can be used to predict likely developments in the weather pattern. More generally, simulation is widely used as a design aid for both small and large systems, and is also used extensively in the training of people such as airline pilots or military commanders. It is a major application of digital computers and is the major application of analog computers.

From an implementation viewpoint, a simulation is usually classified as being either discrete event or continuous. For a *discrete event simulation* it must be possible to view all significant changes to the state of the system as distinct events that occur at specific points in time; the simulation then achieves the desired behavior by modeling a sequence of such events, treating each individually. By contrast, a *continuous simulation* views changes as occurring gradually over a period of time and tracks the progress of these gradual changes. Clearly the choice between these two in any particular case is determined by the nature of the system to be simulated and the purposes that the simulation is intended to achieve.

Although the distinction between simulation and emulation is not always clear, an emulation is normally "realistic" in the sense that it could be used as a direct replacement for all or part of the system that is emulated. In comparison, a simulation may provide no more than an abstract model of some aspect of a system.

simulation language A programming language that is specialized to the implementation of simulation programs. Such languages are usually classified as either discrete event simulation languages or continuous simulation languages. *See* simulation.

simulator Any system that performs a *simulation. It is normally a system dedicated for some period to performing a specific simulation, as distinct from, say, the case where a simulation program is executed as a normal job on some general-purpose computer. Simulators often employ either special-purpose hardware or hardware components from the system that is simulated.

simultaneous equations A set of equations that together define an unknown set of values or functions. The term is normally applied to *linear algebraic equations.

single-address instruction An instruction that makes reference to only one operand location. *See also* instruction format, addressing schemes.

single-assignment languages A class of programming languages. These languages have the appearance of traditional *imperative languages in that they incorporate the *assignment statement and typical control flow constructs such as if statements and loops. They impose the limitation, however, that no variable may be assigned a value more than once. (Special provision must be made for assignment statements within loops.) This limitation significantly alters the nature of the assignment statement, which can then be viewed as statically associating a name with a value rather than as a dynamic destructive operation. This static nature allows the normal ordering restrictions of imperative languages to be relaxed, and assignment statements can be executed as soon as the expression on the right-hand side can be evaluated. Because of this property, single-assignment languages are closely associated with dataflow computing (*see* dataflow machine).

single-step operation Proceeding through the execution of a program either by single instructions or by single steps (clock times) within an instruction. This method is used during program and/or hardware debugging.

single threading A property of a body of code that activates more than one processor, but does so in such a way that at any one time no more than one processor is active. This results in what is termed *serial programming*. For example, code that initiates peripheral transfers may be so written that while a transfer is in progress the processor will not be active, and vice versa. *See also* multithreading, threading.

singly linked list (one-way linked list) A *linked list in which each item contains a single link to its successor. By following links it is possible to access the entire structure from the first item.

singular matrix A square matrix, *A*, of numbers whose *determinant is zero. *A* is singular if and only if it is not invertible (*see* inverse matrix).

sinking technique *Another name for* straight insertion sort.

SIO *Abbrev. for* serial input/output.

SIPO *Abbrev. for* serial in, parallel out. *See also* shift register.

SISD processor *Short for* single instruction (stream), single data (stream) processor. *See* concurrency.

SISO *Abbrev. for* serial in, serial out. *See also* shift register.

sister *Another name for* sibling, rarely used.

sizing Preparing an estimate of the likely size of a program or software system. This estimate may subsequently be used, for example, to determine the amount of memory required on a computer system that is to execute the program.

Sketchpad *See* computer graphics.

skew In a *sequential circuit, the arrival of a signal at two or more places at significantly different times, when it should have arrived at more nearly the same time. Skew is said to be present when the difference in arrival times is great enough to cause or threaten malfuction of the circuit; this difference (usually measured in nanoseconds) is called the amount of skew. Most commonly, concern is expressed about *clock skew*, which is the skew in *clock signals (for which the phenomenon has usually the most serious consequences). Skew may be caused by component malfunction, or bad physical construction, but most often by bad logic design of the circuit. *See also* race condition.

skewed tree (unbalanced tree) Any tree that is not *balanced.

skew-symmetric matrix A square matrix, *A*, such that

$$a_{ij} = -a_{ji}$$

for all a_{ij} in *A*.

skip sequential access method An *access method for use with a *sequential or *indexed file. Data records are accessed in key sequence, but there may be skips past unwanted records. The required record or collating position is derived from the sequential index.

slave machine (direct-coupled machine) A large processor used to handle large jobs in a *master-slave system.

slice of an array of dimension *n*. **1.** The array of lower dimension that is obtained by

fixing one or more of the indices of the n-dimensional array. For example, if A is a 3×4 two-dimensional array then the slice $A[2,]$ denotes the one-dimensional row vector comprising the second row of A while $A[,3]$ denotes the column vector comprising the third column.
2. (trim) The array that is obtained from a larger array of dimension n by restricting the range of an index. For example, if A is a 3×4 two-dimensional array then the 2×4 two-dimensional array comprising the first two rows only of A is a slice of A.

slice architecture *See* bit-slice architecture.

slot reader *See* card reader.

small-scale integration *See* SSI, integrated circuit.

smart card *Informal name for* chip card.

smart terminal *Informal name for* intelligent terminal.

smoothing A means by which a table of values $f(x_0), f(x_1), \ldots, f(x_m)$ at the distinct points $x_1, x_2, \ldots, x_m$, can be approximated (represented) by a function, say

$$\sum_{i=1}^{n} c_i \phi_i(x),$$

where $\phi_i(x)$, $i = 1,2, \ldots, n$, are chosen, and the coefficients c_i, $i = 1,2, \ldots, n$, are to be determined. Typically $m > n$. The objective is to choose a fit that reduces the effect of random errors in the data combined with producing a curve that is smooth (no rapid changes or oscillations) between the data points. This is generally referred to as smoothing. The smoothing is often achieved by using low-degree polynomials (with suitable $\phi_i(x)$) and the coefficients c_i are frequently determined by the least-squares criterion (*see* approximation theory). *Compare* interpolation.

SNA *Acronym for* systems network architecture. A *network architecture developed by IBM for use with large mainframe computers.

snapshot dump A *dump that shows the state of a program at some particular point in its execution. It is usually obtained during testing or debugging and indicates the point in the program that has been reached and the values of some subset of the program variables.

SNOBOL A programming language for the manipulation of character strings. It incorporates powerful pattern-matching and string-searching operators.

soft copy A nondurable form of data output, such as text or graphical information on a VDU or the output from an audio response unit.

soft error A transient error. *See* error rate.

soft keyboard A keyboard in which the function or code to be generated by each key can be allocated and changed by program control. Keyboards on terminals for applications such as industrial data collection or point-of-sale applications frequently have keyboards in which some keys – usually the numeric and certain essential functions – are hardwired and the others are soft keys. The soft keys may have a meaning that is allocated to them at the time of initial installation and remains unchanged, or they may have their meaning changed during the course of a single transaction.

soft-sectored disk *See* sector.

software A generic term for those components of a computer system that are intangible rather than physical. It is most commonly used to refer to the programs executed by a computer system as distinct from the physical hardware of that computer system, and to encompass both symbolic and executable forms for such programs. A distinction can be drawn between *systems software, which is an essential accompaniment to the hardware in order to provide an effective overall computer system (and is therefore normally supplied by the manufacturer), and *applications programs specific to the particular role performed by the computer within a given organization.

software engineering The entire range of activities used to design and develop software, with some connotation of "good practice". Topics encompassed include *requirements analysis and specification, *program specification, program development using some recognized approach such as *structured programming, systematic *testing techniques, *program correctness proofs, *software quality assurance, software project management, documentation, performance and timing analysis, and the development and use of *software engineering environments. Further, software engineering is generally expected to address the practical problems of software development, including those encountered with large or complex systems. Thus, while there is some emphasis on formal methods, pragmatic techniques are employed where necessary. In its entirety, software engineering addresses all aspects of the development and support of reliable and efficient programs for the entire range of computer applications.

software engineering environment (programming support environment) A computer system that provides support for the development, repair, and enhancement of programs, and for the management and control of these activities. A typical system contains a central database and a set of *software tools. The central database acts as a repository for all information related to a project throughout the lifetime of that project. The software tools offer support for the various activities, both technical and managerial, that must be performed on the project.
Different environments vary in the general nature of their databases and in the coverage provided by the set of tools. In particular, some encourage (or even enforce) one specific software engineering methodology, while others provide only general support and therefore allow any of a variety of methodologies to be adopted. All environments, however, reflect concern for the entire *software life-cycle (rather than just the program development phase) and offer support for project management (rather than just technical activities). These two features normally differentiate a software engineering environment from a *program development system.

software house A company whose primary business is to produce software or assist in the production of software. Software houses may offer a range of services, including hiring out of suitably qualified personnel to work within a client's team, consultancy, and a complete system design and development service.

software life-cycle The complete lifetime of a software system from initial conception through to final obsolescence. The term is most commonly used in contexts where programs are expected to have a fairly long useful life, rather than in situations such as experimental programming where programs tend to be run a few times and then discarded. Traditionally the life-cycle has been modeled as a number of successive phases, typically:

system requirements
software requirements
overall design
detailed design
component production
component testing
integration and system testing
release
operation and maintenance

Such a breakdown tends to obscure several important aspects of software production, notably the inevitable need for iteration around the various life-cycle activities in order to correct errors, modify decisions that prove to have been misguided, or reflect changes in the overall requirements for the system. It is also somewhat confusing to treat operation and maintenance as just another life-cycle phase since during this period it may be necessary to repeat any or all of the activities required for initial development of the system. There has therefore been a gradual movement toward more sophisticated models of the software life-cycle. These provide explicit recognition of iteration, and often treat the activities of the operation and maintenance period simply as iteration occurring after rather than before release of the system for operational use.

software package *Another name for* application package.

software prototyping Development of a preliminary version of a software system in order to allow certain aspects of that system to be investigated. Often the primary purpose of a prototype is to obtain feedback from the intended users; the requirements specification for the system can then be updated to reflect this feedback, and so increase confidence in the final system. Additionally (or alternatively) a prototype can be used to investigate particular problem areas, or certain implications of alternative design or implementation decisions.
The intention with a prototype is normally to obtain the required information as rapidly as possible and with the minimum investment of resources, and it is therefore common to concentrate on certain aspects of the intended system and completely ignore others. A prototype may for example be developed with no concern for its efficiency or performance, and certain functions of the final system may be entirely omitted. It must however be realistic in those aspects specifically under investigation.

software quality assurance (SQA) The process of ensuring that a software system and its associated documentation are in all respects of sufficient quality for their purpose. While a quality assurance team may be involved in all stages of a development project, there is typically a recognized quality assurance activity following completion of development and prior to release of the system for operational use. The checks performed by the quality assurance team (which should be independent of the development team) vary between organizations and also depend on the nature and purpose of the software system. However they typically include functional testing of the software, checks that *programming standards have been respected, that the program documentation is complete and of an adequate standard, and that the user documentation for the system is of the desired quality. The team would also probably explore the reliability of the software system, and attempt to ensure that the software system and its associated documentation are so organized as to promote system maintainability.
A standard for SQA plans is published by IEEE (Std 730 – 1981).

software reliability A measure of the extent to which a software system can be expected to deliver usable services when those services are demanded. Software reliability differs considerably from program "correctness" (*see* program correctness proof). Correctness is the static property that a program is consistent with its specification, while reliability is related to the dynamic demands that are made upon the system and the ability to produce a satisfactory response to those demands.
A program that is "correct" may be regarded as unreliable if, for example, the specification against which the program is shown to be correct does not capture all of the users' expectations of the program. Conversely, a program that is not completely correct may be regarded as reliable if the errors are insignificant, occur infrequently at noncritical times, or can simply be avoided by the users.

software specification A precise statement of the effects that the software component of a system is required to achieve. When

developing a system, production of the *system specification is typically followed by a period of preliminary investigation and high-level design. It is then possible to identify any necessary hardware components of the system and to produce the software specification for the software component.
A software specification should be detailed, focusing on what the software is to do rather than how this is to be done. The traditional use of natural language for this purpose is gradually being superseded by use of more formal notations. *See also* program specification.

software tool A program that is employed in the development, repair, or enhancement of other programs. Traditionally a set of software tools addressed only the essential needs during program development: a typical set might consist of a *text editor, *compiler, *link loader, and some form of *debug tool. Such a set concentrates solely on the program production phase and is that normally provided by a *program development system.
It is now recognized that software tools can assist in all activities of all phases of the *software life-cycle, including management and quality-assurance activities. Thus a comprehensive set would address such issues as requirements specification, design, validation, configuration control, and project management. Such tools would frequently form part of an integrated *software engineering environment.

solid-font printer Any type of *impact printer in which the complete shape of each character of the repertoire is engraved or molded onto a font carrier. The font carrier may be one of a number of forms including a molded ball or wheel, as in a *daisywheel printer, an etched band of metal, as in a *band printer, or a train of separate type slugs that are driven around a track, as in a *train printer. *Compare* matrix printer.

solid-state In general, formed on (or concerned with circuitry formed on) a single chip of semiconductor material, usually silicon, and therefore comprising *bipolar or *field-effect transistors.

solid-state memory *Another name for* semiconductor memory.

solvable A term that can be applied to a *predicate P(x) on the natural numbers if its *characteristic function, C_P, is computable (Turing computable – *see* Turing machine), where

$$C_P(x) \begin{array}{l} = 1 \text{ if } P(x) \text{ holds} \\ = 0 \text{ if } P(x) \text{ does not hold} \end{array}$$

Other terms for solvable are that
P(x) is recursively decidable;
P(x) has a recursive decision problem;
P(x) is recursively solvable;
P(x) is computable.
If P(x) is not solvable it is said to be *unsolvable* (or *undecidable*). *See also* recursion, recursively enumerable set.

son *Another name for* child.

son file, son tape *See* file updating.

SOP expression *Short for* sum of products expression.

sort generator *See* generator.

sorting The process of rearranging information into ascending or descending order by means of *sortkeys. Sorting may be useful in three ways: to identify and count all items with the same identification, to compare two files, and to assist in searching, as used in a *dictionary. An *internal sorting* method keeps the information within the computer's high-speed random-access memory; an *external sorting* method uses backing store.
There are a wide variety of methods: *see* bubble sort, bucket sort, cocktail shaker sort, comparison counting sort, distribution counting sort, heapsort, list sort, merge exchange sort, quicksort, quickersort, radix exchange sort, radix sort, shell-

sort, straight insertion sort, straight selection sort, tree selection sort.

sortkey (key) The information, associated with a record of information, that is to be compared in a *sorting process. It follows that the sortkeys must be capable of being ordered, i.e. two keys k_1 and k_2 are such that

$$k_1 < k_2, \quad k_1 = k_2, \quad \text{or } k_1 > k_2$$

sort merge *See* merge exchange sort.

source alphabet (source set) *See* code.

source code The form of a program that is input to a *compiler or *translator for conversion into equivalent object code.

source coding (compression coding; source compression coding) The use of *variable-length codes in order to reduce the number of symbols in a message to the minimum necessary to represent the information in the message, or at least to go some way toward this, for a given size of alphabet. In source coding the particular *code to be used is chosen to match the source (i.e. the relative probabilities of the symbols in the source alphabet) rather than any channel through which the message may ultimately be passed.
The main problem in source coding is to ensure that the most probable source symbols are represented by the shortest *codewords, and the less probable by longer codewords as necessary, the weighted average codeword length being minimized within the bounds of *Kraft's inequality. The most widely used methods for ensuring this are *Huffman coding* and *Shannon–Fano coding*; the former is more efficient for a given *extension of the source but the latter is computationally simpler. In either case, a large extension of the source may be necessary to approach the limiting compression factor given by the *source coding theorem.
See also Shannon's model. *Compare* channel coding.

source coding theorem In *communication theory, the statement that the output of any information source having *entropy H units per symbol can be encoded into an alphabet having N symbols in such a way that the source symbols are represented by codewords having a weighted average length not less than

$$H/\log N$$

(where the base of the logarithm is consistent with the entropy units). Also, that this limit can be approached arbitrarily closely, for any source, by suitable choice of a *variable-length code and the use of a sufficiently long *extension of the source (*see* source coding).
The theorem was first expounded and proved by Claude Elwood Shannon in 1948.

source compression coding *Another name for* source coding.

source compression factor The ratio of message lengths before and after *source coding (which is generally intended to make messages shorter). *See also* source coding theorem.

source language The language in which the input to a *compiler or *translator is written.

source listing *Another name for* program listing.

source program The original high-level language program submitted to a *compiler.

source set *Another name for* source alphabet. *See* code.

space complexity *See* complexity measure, polynomial space.

space-division switch Any switching mechanism that is based on the through connection of a set of input lines selectively to a set of output lines. Space division switches are implemented either by electromechanical means or by electronic means. Prior to the advent of time-division switching, all telephone and telegraph switching machines were implemented using a variety of space-division switching techniques, particularly Stroger (step-by-step) switches and crossbar switches.

space domain A term used to refer to a situation in which the amplitude of a *signal varies with position (usually in two dimensions, as in a picture) rather than with time. *See also* time domain, picture processing, filtering.

space quantization (pixelization) *See* quantization. *See also* picture processing, discrete and continuous systems.

spanning subgraph *See* subgraph.

spanning tree A *subgraph of a *connected graph G; this subgraph is a *tree and includes all the nodes of G. A *minimum-cost* spanning tree is a weighted spanning tree, formed from a *weighted graph, such that the real numbers assigned to each edge, when summed, total not greater than the corresponding sum for any other weighted spanning tree.

sparse matrix A matrix in which most of the elements are equal to zero.

special character *See* character set.

specification *See* module specification, program specification, software specification, system specification.

specification language *See* module specification.

spectral analysis *See* time series.

speed of a computer. A rather vaguely defined term that is often used to indicate the relative processing power of a given computer system, since the power of a computer is largely governed by the ability of the central processing unit to execute instructions rapidly. The CPU's speed is itself dependent on numerous factors such as word length, instruction set, technology of implementation, and memory access times. In general large mainframe computers are very much faster and hence more powerful than small minicomputers, which are in turn faster than microprocessors.

speedup theorem A theorem in complexity theory that, like the *gap theorem, can be expressed in terms of abstract complexity measures (*see* Blum's axioms) but will be more understandable in the context of time:

given any *total *recursive function $r(n)$, there exists a recursive language L such that for any Turing machine M recognizing L, say within time bound $S(n)$, there exists another Turing machine M′ that also recognizes L but within a time bound $S'(n)$ that satisfies

$$r(S'(n)) \leqslant S(n)$$

for all but a finite number of values of n. Thus for this language there can be no fastest program.

Sperry Univac One of the major US computer manufacturers. It produces a product-line that spans small business computers to very large scientific and data-processing machines. *See also* Univac.

sphere-packing bound *Another name for* Hamming bound.

spline In its simplest form a spline function (of degree n), $s(x)$, is a piecewise polynomial on $[x_1,x_N]$ that is $(n - 1)$ times continuously differentiable, i.e.

$$s(x) \equiv \text{polynomial of degree } n$$
$$x_i \leqslant x \leqslant x_{i+1},\ i = 1,2, \ldots ,N-1$$

These polynomial "pieces" are all matched up at points (called *knots*)

$$x_1 < x_2 < \ldots < x_N$$

in the interior of the range, so that the resulting function $s(x)$ is smooth. The idea can be extended to functions of more than one variable. Cubic splines provide a useful means of approximating data to moderate accuracy. Splines are often the underlying approximations used in *variational methods.

split One of the basic actions applicable to a set S on whose elements a *total ordering ≤ is defined; when applied in the form

$$split(a, S)$$

where a is a member of S, S is partitioned into two *disjoint sets S_1 and S_2: all the elements in S_1 are less than or equal to a and all those in S_2 are greater than a. *See also* operations on sets.

split screen A visual display screen in which the top and bottom areas of the screen face may be treated as separate screens for the purpose of data manipulation. The split is usually into two parts, not necessarily equal, but there may be more. One part may be used for entering data from the attached keyboard while the other part displays instructions or prompts. The entered data may be manipulated by *scrolling or erasing without affecting the other part of the screen.

spoofing *Jargon* A deliberate attempt to cause a user or resource to perform an incorrect action.

spool 1. The reel or former on which magnetic tape, paper tape, or printer ribbon is wound.

2. To transfer data intended for a peripheral device (which may be a communication channel) into an intermediate store, either so that it can be transferred to the peripheral at a more convenient time or so that sections of data generated separately can be transferred to the peripheral in bulk. Spooling is therefore a method of handling virtual input and output devices in a *multiprogramming system.

For simplicity consider the case of output. Normally a program wishing to output to a line printer will claim a printer, use it to produce its results, and then release the printer. In a multiprogramming environment this is a potent source of delay since the speed at which a printer operates is typically slow compared with the speed of the process driving the printer; it would therefore be necessary to provide a number of printers approximately equal to the number of processes active in the system.

Spooling is commonly used to overcome this problem. Output destined for a printer is diverted onto backing store. A process wishing to use a printer will be allocated an area of backing store, into which the results destined for the printer are written, and a *server process, which acts as a virtual printer and transfers information destined for the printer into the backing store area. When the process has no more data to send to the printer, it will inform the server process, which will terminate the information written into backing store. Subsequently a system utility will be used to copy the contents of the backing store for this process onto the printer. Similar arrangements can be established for dealing with the input to processes.

spread *See* measures of variation.

spread-spectrum modulation *See* modulation.

SQA *Abbrev. for* software quality assurance.

SQL/DS *Trademark* A *database package marketed by IBM, one component of which is a *relational database system. This system grew directly out of a research project, *system R*, at the San Jose Laboratory of IBM. *System R** is a *distributed database version of system R.

square matrix A matrix in which the number of rows is equal to the number of columns. An $n \times n$ matrix is sometimes called a matrix of *order n*.

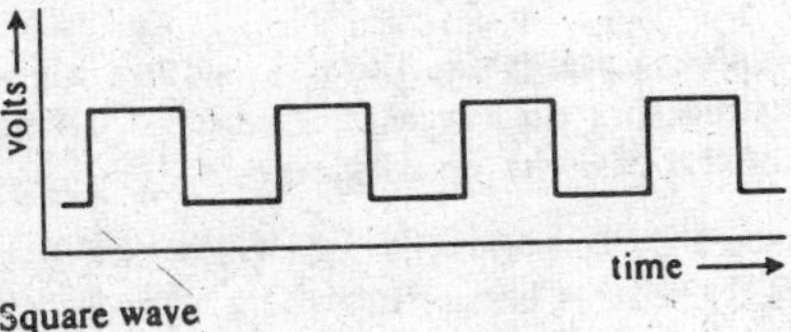

Square wave

square wave A signal consisting of alternate binary ones and zeros. The diagram shows how such a signal, when displayed on an *oscilloscope, may appear. A square wave can be considered as a *pulse train in which pulse separation is equal to pulse duration. When such a waveform is used to operate an electronic switch, it is described as a *switching waveform.

SR flip-flop *Another name for* RS flip-flop. *See* flip-flop.

SSI *Abbrev. for* small-scale integration, i.e. integration of generally less than 100 transistors on a single chip. *See* integrated circuit.

stability A multidiscipline term with a variety of (related) meanings. In *numerical analysis it is used with what appears to be a bewildering array of possible prefixes. There are, however, two important basic usages.

Given a well-defined numerical procedure it is important that roundoff errors do not seriously influence the accuracy of the results. This is referred to as *numerical stability* and depends on the *error-propagation properties of the procedure.

*Discretization methods for the solution of integral and differential equations are based on a subdivision of the region in which the solution is required. Stability here means that perturbations in the data (initial or boundary conditions) have a bounded effect on the solution obtained (ignoring roundoff error) for a given subdivision. The existence of a uniform bound on this effect over all sufficiently fine subdivisions is a necessary condition for the convergence of the method as the subdivision is refined.

stable sorting algorithm A sorting algorithm that preserves the relative ordering of records with equal sortkeys.

stack 1. (pushdown stack; pushdown list; LIFO list) A linear *list where all accesses, insertions, and removals are made at one end of the list, called the *top*. This implies access on a last in first out (LIFO) basis: the most recently inserted item on the list is the first to be removed. The operations *push* and *pop* refer respectively to the insertion and removal of items at the top of the stack. Stacks occur frequently in computing and in particular are closely associated with *recursion.

2. Loosely, a linear *list where accesses, insertions, and removals are made at one end or both ends of the list. This includes a pushdown stack, described above. When the earliest inserted item on the linear list is the first to be removed (first in first out, FIFO), it is a *pushup stack*, more properly known as a *queue. When insertions and deletions may be made at both ends, it is a double-ended queue, or *deque.

A stack may be implemented in hardware as a specialized kind of addressless memory, with a control mechanism to implement any of the insertion/removal regimes. *See also* stack processing.

stack algorithm In general, any algorithm that employs a *stack, but, specifically, one for decoding a *convolutional code.

stack architecture An architecture in which *stack processing is used.

stack frame In a *block-structured language, storage required by a block (procedure) is allocated on entry to the block and is de-allocated at the exit from the block. Since blocks are nested, storage can be allocated on a last in first out basis on a *stack, and the area of the stack containing data for a particular block is called the stack frame for the block.

stack manipulation *Another name for* stack processing.

stack processing (stack manipulation) Use of (almost always) a pushdown *stack implemented in hardware as memory for programs and data. This permits addressless instructions to be employed and makes programs more compact. Stack mechanisms are also used to provide a way of keeping track of multiple interrupts in which the stack serves as a way of "nesting" the interrupts so that those of lesser priority are pushed down until those of higher priority can be attended to.

staging A form of *spooling associated with the use of magnetic tape. The contents of a tape that is to be operated upon by a process may be staged onto magnetic disk. In this form, tape-winding time is virtually eliminated since it is possible to locate a particular part of the "tape" much more rapidly if it is entirely held on disk.

staircase waveform A waveform that is generally constrained to lie between maximum and minimum voltage values. Between these extremes the waveform can only take on discrete and constant values of voltage for fixed periods of time. The waveform thus consists of a number of small step changes in voltage level, hence the term staircase. The height of each step will normally be made constant but may be variable, as may the period of time over which the waveform resides at a given voltage level.

stand-alone Denoting a computer system or subsystem that is capable of operation without being connected to any other computer system or subsystem.

standard 1. A publicly available definition of a hardware or software component, resulting from international, national, or industrial agreement.

2. A product, usually hardware, that conforms to such a definition.

standard deviation *See* measures of variation.

standard error *See* measures of variation.

standard interface A point of interconnection between two systems or parts of a system, e.g. that between a processor and a peripheral, at which all the physical, electrical, and logical parameters are in accordance with predetermined values and are collectively used in other instances. An interface may be classed as standard on the basis of manufacturer, industry, or international usage. The I/O channels of a processor may be classed as standard interfaces because they are common to all processors of that type, or common to more than one type of peripheral – but they may be specific to a manufacturer. Some interfaces are de facto industry standards and can be used to connect devices from different vendors. The Centronics parallel interface for printers is an example of a manufacturer's interface for which compatible interfaces are available from a number of other printer manufacturers.

Some interfaces are standardized by agreement within trade associations or international committees. The *RS232C interface is used for connecting many types of relatively slow peripherals to processors or modems: the specification is published by EIA of Washington DC but it is also in close agreement with the series of recommendations issued by CCITT of Europe (*see* V.24).

standardization 1. The establishment of an international, national, or industrial agreement concerning the specification or production of components – electrical, electronic, or software – or equipment in general, or of procedures for the use or testing of equipment or software.

2. The act of committing an organization to use specific standards to meet particular needs whenever they arise within the organization. Typically an organization might standardize upon use of a specific compiler for some language, some specific application package, or a particular database management system.

standard product of sums One of the two canonical (i.e. standard or normal) forms of a *Boolean function, useful in comparing and simplifying functions. This form contains one *standard sum term, or maxterm, for each "zero" (false) entry in the *truth table for the expression. This form can be represented as the AND (product) of a group of ORs (the sum terms) of Boolean variables, uncomplemented or complemented. It can also be shown to be the NOR of a group of NORs of the identical variables. *Compare* standard sum of products.

standard product term (minterm) A product (AND) of n Boolean variables, uncomplemented or complemented but not repeated, in a function of n variables. With n variables, 2^n different standard product terms are possible. The complement of any standard product term is a *standard sum term, or maxterm.

standard subroutine A *subroutine for some common operation, e.g. reading a decimal number, made available as part of an assembly language programming system. The term is rarely used now.

standard sum of products One of the two canonical (i.e. standard or normal) forms of a *Boolean function, useful in comparing and simplifying functions. This form contains one *standard product term, or minterm, for each "one" (true) entry in the *truth table for the expression. This form can be represented as the OR (sum) of a group of ANDs (the product terms) of Boolean variables, uncomplemented or complemented. It can also be shown to be the NAND of a group of NANDs of the identical variables. *Compare* standard product of sums.

standard sum term (maxterm) A sum (OR) of n Boolean variables, uncomplemented or complemented but not repeated, in a function of n variables. With n variables, 2^n different standard sum terms are possible. The complement of any standard sum term is a *standard product term, or minterm.

STAR One of the early *vector processors, manufactured by CDC and unique on several grounds: it is one of the large machines built by CDC that was not designed by Seymour Cray (the architect was Jim Thornton); it was noted for having very wide words that can be processed in parallel; it was the first machine marketed that was aimed at very rapid processing of vectors.

star closure *See* Kleene star.

star-height The maximum depth to which the *Kleene-star operator is nested in a given *regular expression. The star-height of a *regular language L is the smallest star-height of any regular expression for L. There is no known algorithm for determining the star-height of a regular language. It is however known that there are regular languages of arbitrary star-height. If complement and intersection are allowed, the class of *generalized* regular expressions is obtained. For these it is not known if there are languages of star-height greater than one.

star network A simple network topology with all links connecting directly to a single central station. Star networks work well when traffic consists of multiple secondary nodes communicating with a single primary node, e.g. computer terminals connected to a time-sharing host.
The main disadvantages of a star network are:
(a) central switch failure disrupts the entire network;
(b) circuit failures between the central switch and the terminals result in loss of user communication (no alternate paths);
(c) the cost of having every user directly connected to the central site may be very high for geographically distant (dispersed) nodes;
(d) total communication capacity is often limited by the speed of the central switch.
The main advantage of a star network is that the design of the end terminals may be very simple. *See also* network architecture.

start symbol (sentence symbol) *See* grammar.

start time *Another name for* acceleration time.

starvation 1. *Jargon* A situation occurring when the rate at which a process can proceed is sharply reduced by its inability to gain access to a particular resource.
2. A situation arising in a *Petri net when the time between successive entries to a state can become indefinitely long.

state assignment The assignment of combinations of *state variables to the stable internal conditions – *states* – of a *sequential circuit in the synthesis (realization) process.

state diagram A graphical version of a *state table. *See also* finite-state automaton.

statement The unit from which a high-level language program is constructed: a program is a sequence of statements. It is analagous to an *instruction at the machine-code level. *See also* declaration.

statement label *See* label.

state table 1. A table describing the behavior of a *sequential circuit as a function of stable internal conditions – *states* – and input variables. For each combination of these, the next state of the circuit is specified together with any output variables.
2. *See* finite-state automaton.

state transition function, table, diagram *See* finite-state automaton.

state variable A (generally) binary variable describing the state of each memory element within a *sequential circuit.

static Not changing, or incapable of changing, with time. The term usually refers to a value that cannot be changed while the system continues to run but can only be reassigned by stopping and reloading the system. In contrast a *dynamic value can be reset while the system is running.

static allocation An allocation that cannot be changed while a process is running.

static data structure A data structure whose organizational characteristics are invariant throughout its lifetime. Such structures are well supported by high-level languages and familiar examples are *arrays. The prime features of static structures are
(a) none of the structural information need be stored explicitly within the elements – it is often held in a distinct logical/physical header;
(b) the elements of an allocated structure are physically contiguous, held in a single segment of memory;
(c) all descriptive information, other than the physical location of the allocated structure, is determined by the structure definition;
(d) relationships between elements do not change during the lifetime of the structure.
Relaxation of these features leads to the concept of a *dynamic data structure.

static dump A dump, usually of the workspace of a process, taken at a time when the process can be guaranteed to be inactive, such as at the end of a job step.

static RAM *See* RAM.

statistical analysis *See* statistical methods.

statistical methods Methods of collecting, summarizing, analyzing, and interpreting variable numerical data. Statistical methods can be contrasted with *deterministic methods, which are appropriate where observations are exactly reproducable or are assumed to be so. While statistical methods are widely used in the life sciences, in economics, and in agricultural science, they also have an important role in the physical sciences in the study of measurement errors, of random phenomena such as radioactivity or meteorological events, and in obtaining approximate results where deterministic solutions are hard to apply.
Data collection involves deciding what to observe in order to obtain information relevant to the questions whose answers are

required, and then making the observations. *Sampling involves choice of a sufficient number of observations representing an appropriate population. Experiments with variable outcomes should be conducted according to principles of *experimental design.
Data summarization is the calculation of appropriate *statistics (def. 2) and the display of such information in the form of tables, graphs, or charts. Data may also be adjusted to make different samples more comparable, using ratios, compensating factors, etc.
Statistical analysis relates observed statistical data to theoretical models, such as *probability distributions or models used in *regression analysis. By estimating *parameters in the proposed model and testing hypotheses about rival models, one can assess the value of the information collected and the extent to which the information can be applied to similar situations. *Statistical prediction* is the application of the model thought to be most appropriate, using the estimated values of the parameters.
More recently, less formal methods of looking at data have been proposed, including *exploratory data analysis.

statistical multiplexing A technique of *time division multiplexing of a number of subchannels onto a common wider-bandwidth channel, where the total *bandwidth required by the individual subchannels exceeds the bandwidth of the multiplex channel. Since the maximum rate required by any one channel is seldom used, due to breaks in transmission, this technique is possible through judicious use of buffering. In this system bandwidth is not allocated permanently to each subchannel but only as required.

statistical prediction *See* statistical methods.

statistics 1. Numerical data relating to sets of individuals, objects, or phenomena. It is also the science of collecting, summarizing, and interpreting such data.
2. Quantities derived from data in order to summarize the properties of a sample. For example, the mean of a sample is a statistic that is a *measure of location, while the standard deviation is a *measure of variation.

status of a process. *See* process descriptor.

status register *See* program status word.

stepper motor *See* actuator.

stepsize *See* finite-difference method.

stiff equations *See* ordinary differential equations.

stochastic matrix A matrix, much used for example in simulation, modeling, and communication theory, in which every row is a probability distribution, i.e. every element lies between 0 and 1, and the sum of the elements of each row is unity.

stochastic process A set of *random variables whose values vary with time (or sometimes in space). Examples include populations affected by births and deaths, the length of a queue (*see* queuing theory), or the amount of water in a reservoir. *Stochastic models* are models in which random variation is of major importance, in contrast to deterministic models. Stochastic processes give theoretical explanations for many *probability distributions, and underly the analysis of *time-series data.

storage (memory, store) A device or medium that can retain data for subsequent retrieval. *See* storage device. *See also* memory.

storage allocation 1. The amount of storage allocated to a process.
2. The act of allocating storage to a process. In a multiprogramming system it is necessary to control the use of storage to ensure that processes do not interfere with one another's workspace, except where they do so intentionally in order to cooperate. This represents one instance of the

resource control activities within the system.

storage device A device that can receive data and retain it for subsequent retrieval. Such devices cover a wide range of capacities and speeds of access. The semiconductor devices used as the *main memory for the processor may take only a few nanoseconds to retrieve data but the cost of storing each bit is very high by comparison with the devices used as *backing store, which may take milliseconds or even many seconds to retrieve data. *See also* memory hierarchy, memory management.

storage element *See* memory element.

storage hierarchy *See* memory hierarchy.

storage matrix of magnetic tape. *See* automated tape library.

storage oscilloscope An instrument that is used to measure fast nonrepetitive signals. It does this by capturing the signal on demand and continuing to display it until reset. This can be achieved in two ways: a digital storage oscilloscope samples the incoming signal, stores these samples, and displays them; other storage oscilloscopes use a special storage *cathode-ray tube that retains the image by mapping it as a charge pattern on an electrode behind the screen; the pattern then modulates the electron beam to give a picture of the captured signal.

storage pool Those areas of storage that are not allocated to processes and are used by the storage allocation system as the source from which to meet requests. When a process releases storage it will be returned to the pool for subsequent reallocation.

storage protection The mechanisms, both hardware and software, ensuring that processes access storage in a controlled manner. For storage in the high-speed levels of the *memory hierarchy, protection is implemented by hardware in order to maintain speed; for slower devices the protection may be entirely by software. In all cases, the intention is to ensure that the type of access made by a process to the storage is in accordance with that indicated when the storage was allocated to the process. For example, in a system with paged memory management a process may be granted access to an area of memory, but only for the purpose of executing the code in that page. Attempts to read from the page or to write to it would be prohibited by the (hardware) protection mechanism.

storage structure A mapping from one representation of a data item to another. Thus a date may be represented as a vector of three integers (with six permutations to choose from), directly as a string of characters, or, in more recent high-level languages, as a record with three selectors – day, month, and year. A good choice of storage structure permits an easy and efficient implementation of a given *data structure.

storage tube A vacuum tube that can receive and retain information. The data can be erased and new data entered as required. The data may be graphical and visible on the face of the tube or it may be retrieved as an electrical signal. *See also* electrostatic storage device.

store 1. *Another name for* storage, or memory, used especially in the UK.
2. To enter or retain information for subsequent retrieval.

store and forward A method in which information is passed from node to node in a communication network, pausing in each node until sufficient resources (e.g. bandwidth, buffer pools) are available for the next leg of the journey – called a *hop*. In computer networks the information being passed may be *messages or *packets, and may be self-contained with regard to the store-and-forward network (*datagrams), or may depend upon the maintenance of state information (*flow control, *routing paths, etc.) from previous messages or packets. A store-and-forward network is based upon the tradeoff between the cost of memory and computational resources in the store-and-forward nodes, and the cost of the transmission lines between the nodes. *See also* message switching, packet switching.

stored program A *program that is stored in the *memory of a computer. The execution of the program then requires the use of a *control unit – to read instructions from the memory at appropriate times and arrange to carry them out.
The memory used to store the program may be the same as or different from memory used to store the data. There are advantages in using the same (read-write) memory, allowing programs to be modified, but there are greater advantages in limiting opportunities for program modification, either by using physically read-only memory or by restricting access to the part of the memory containing programs.
The concept of program and data sharing the same memory is fundamental to what is usually referred to as a *von Neumann machine or a von Neumann architecture. Although there is some disagreement as to whether the stored-program concept was originated by John von Neumann or by the team of John W. Mauchly and J. Presper Eckert, the first documentation was written by von Neumann in 1945 in his proposal for the *EDVAC.

straight insertion sort (sifting technique; sinking technique) A sorting algorithm that looks at each sortkey in turn, and on the basis of this places the record corresponding to the sortkey correctly with respect to the previous sortkeys.

straight selection sort A sorting algorithm based upon finding successively the record with the largest sortkey and putting it in the correct position, then the record with the next largest key, etc.

Strassen algorithm An algorithm developed in 1968 by V. Strassen to multiply large numbers. It uses the properties of *Fourier transforms. *See also* Schonhage–Strassen algorithm.

stream 1. A flow of data characterized by relatively long duration and constant rate. When the rate is known ahead of time then communication resources may be reserved for the stream. For example, stream traffic may be carried using low-overhead synchronous *time division multiplexing (TDM), while other traffic on the same channel is carried by higher-overhead asynchronous TDM. This is particularly important in satellite transmission systems, where overhead differences between synchronous and asynchronous traffic are very great. It is also important in applications, such as packet speech, that require a low variation in *network delay.
2. To operate a tape transport in *streaming mode.

streamer *Informal name for* streaming tape transport.

streaming A mode of operation of a tape transport, introduced in 1978 by IBM, in which the length of magnetic tape passing the head while stopping and restarting exceeds the length of the interblock gap. After a stop, therefore, the tape has to be *repositioned* (i.e. backed up) in order to be in the correct position for the next start. The alternative to streaming mode is start/stop mode.
Streaming allows a tape transport with only moderate acceleration to handle tape at a considerably higher speed than it could in start/stop mode. However, the average data rate is only improved if substantial quantities of data (typically tens to thousands of kilobytes) are transferred between stops, because of the considerable repositioning time (typically 0.1–2 seconds). The most common application is disk *backup.

Streaming also allows the interblock gap to be very short, increasing the amount of data that can be stored on a given length of tape; this is not, however, compatible with the currently used international format standards.

streaming tape transport A tape transport capable of operating in *streaming mode, and of automatically repositioning the magnetic tape when it stops. Some versions are also capable of operating in start/stop mode at a lower tape speed (or with extended interblock gaps).
Streaming tape transports can use simpler, and hence cheaper and more reliable, mechanisms than those designed for start/stop mode at similar tape speeds. In particular, they usually operate without the *capstan and tape *buffers (tension arm or vacuum column) of conventional tape transports, tape motion and tension being controlled entirely from the reels.

stride *See* dope vector.

string 1. A *flexible one-dimensional array, i.e. a flexible vector, of symbols where the lower bound of the vector is fixed at unity but the upper bound, i.e. the string length, may vary.
2. Any one-dimensional array of characters.
In formal language theory a string is often referred to as a *word. *See also* sequence.

string manipulation The action of the fundamental operations on strings, including their creation, *concatenation, the extraction of *string segments, *string matching, their comparison, discovering their length, replacing *substrings by other strings, storage, and input/output.

string matching Searching within a string for a given substring.

string segment A *substring of a character string that can usually only be replaced by an array of the same size.

strongly connected *See* connected graph.

structural induction The principle of *induction defined as follows. Let S be a set on which the *partial ordering $\prec$ is defined and which contains no infinite decreasing sequences (where decreasing is defined by the ordering relation). If P is some *predicate and if the following two conditions hold.
(a) let a be a smallest element of S, i.e. there is no x in S such that $x \prec a$, then $P(a)$ is true,
(b) for each element s in S, if $P(x)$ is true for each x in S with $x \prec s$, and from this it follows that $P(s)$ is true,
then $P(s)$ is true for all s in S. Structural induction tends to be used in proving properties of recursive programs.

structure 1. of a program. *See* program structure.
2. *See* data structure, control structure, storage structure.

structured analysis 1. *See* structured systems analysis.
2. *See* SADT.

structured coding *See* structured programming (def. 2).

structured programming 1. A method of program development that makes extensive use of *abstraction in order to factorize the problem and give increased confidence that the resulting program is correct. Given the specification of a required program, the first step is to envisage some "ideal" machine on which to implement that program. This ideal machine should offer both an appropriate set of *data structures and an appropriate set of operations on those data structures. The required program is then defined as a program for the specified ideal machine.
By this means the original problem has been reduced to one of implementing the specified ideal machine, and this problem is itself tackled in the same way. A second ideal machine is envisaged, this machine being ideal for implementing the data structures and operations of the first

machine, and programs are produced to effect the implementation. This process continues until eventually a level is reached at which the specified data structures and operations of the ideal machine can conveniently be implemented directly in the chosen programming language. Thus the eventual program is based upon "levels of abstract machine", where the top-level machine is ideally suited to the specific application and the lowest-level machine directly executes the chosen programming language. The development process is not, however, simply one of "subroutinization", since both operations and data structures are refined simultaneously at each level.

The overall method of structured programming, which is largely due to E. W. Dijkstra, is heavily influenced by a concern for *program correctness. The intention is that at any level the implementation machine should be so well suited to the problem at hand that the programs for that machine will be small and simple. It should therefore be possible at each level to provide a convincing rigorous argument that the programs are correct.

2. (structured coding) An approach to *coding in which only three constructs are employed for governing the flow of control through the program. These three constructs allow for sequential, conditional, and iterative control flow. Arbitrary transfer of control (i.e. the *GOTO statement) is expressly forbidden. As a direct result, for each compound statement within the program there is precisely one entry point and one exit point, and reasoning about the program is thereby made easier.

structured systems analysis A specific technique for systems analysis that covers all activities from initial understanding of the problem through to specification and high-level design of the software system. The technique embodies four main concepts: dataflow diagrams, a data dictionary, data store structuring, and process logic representations.

The data-flow diagrams show the various processing elements in the system, the data flows between these processing elements, and the major stores of data within the system. The processing elements are described in nonprocedural terms, typically using natural language, and a processing element from one diagram may be decomposed onto further diagrams to show greater levels of detail. A data dictionary is used to record all the various data items in the system, the constraints upon these data items, and the processing elements by which they are accessed. As the decomposition proceeds so both the data stores and the actions of the processing elements are defined in more detail. The data store structuring techniques are based upon the relational model of data and show how each data store is accessed and organized. The algorithms employed by the processing elements are defined by use of process logic representations, typically *program design languages, *decision tables, or "structured" natural language.

Two similar versions of structured systems analysis were developed separately by Gane and Sarson and by De Marco. The technique is intended primarily for use in traditional DP system development.

structured variable (record) A variable in a programming language that is a composite object, being made up of components that are either simple data items or are themselves structured objects; these components are identified by *names.

stub A substitute component that is employed temporarily in a program so that progress can be made, e.g. with compilation or testing, prior to the genuine component becoming available. To illustrate, if it is required to test the remainder of a program before a particular procedure has been developed, the procedure could be replaced by a stub. Dependent upon circumstances, it might be possible for this stub always to return the same result, return values from a table, return an approximate result, consult someone, etc.

subgraph A portion of a *graph G obtained by either eliminating edges from G and/or eliminating some vertices and their associated edges. Formally a subgraph of a graph G with vertices V and edges E is a graph G' with vertices V' and edges E' in which V' is a subset of V and E' is a subset of E (edges in E' joining vertices in V'). If V' is a proper *subset of V or E' is a proper subset of E then G' is a *proper subgraph* of G. If all the vertices of G are present in the subgraph G' then G' is a *spanning subgraph* of G. *See also* spanning tree.

subgroup A subset T of a *group G on which the binary operation $\circ$ is defined; T contains the identity, e, of G, the inverse x^{-1} for any x in T, and the quantity $x \circ y$ for any x and y in T. For any group G the set consisting of e alone is a subgroup; so also is the group G itself. All other subgroups are *proper subgroups* of G.

sublist *See* list.

submatrix of a given matrix, A. Any matrix derived from A by deleting one or more of its columns and/or one or more of its rows.

subnet *Short for* communication subnetwork.

sub-Nyquist sampling *See* Nyquist's criterion.

subprogram *Another name for* program unit.

subrecursive hierarchy *See* hierarchy of functions.

subroutine A piece of code that is obeyed "out of line", i.e. control is transferred to the subroutine, and on its completion control reverts to the instruction following the *call. (The instruction code of the CPU usually provides *subroutine jump* and *return* instructions to facilitate this operation.) A subroutine saves space since it occurs only once in the program, though it may be called from many different places in the program. It also facilitates the construction of large programs since subroutines can be formed into libraries for general use. (The same concept appears in high-level languages as the *procedure.) In the early days of programming, what is now called a subroutine was known as a *closed subroutine*. This was in contrast with the *open subroutine*, which was a piece of code that appeared in several places in a program, and was substituted "in line" by the assembler for each call appearing in the program. The open subroutine was just a convenient shorthand for the programmer: the same facility is now known as a *macro.

subschema A definition of a subset of the contents of a *database, the whole database being defined by a *schema. The word is most usually employed in connection with *CODASYL-type databases. A subschema may be used for various purposes, e.g. to define a subset of the database to which access is available for a class of users, to simplify the view of the database to those who wish to view only a part of it, or to specify that for a *distributed database system only a particular part of it resides at a particular node.

subscript A means of referring to particular elements in an ordered collection of elements. For example, if R denotes such a collection of names then the ith name in the collection may be referenced by R_i (i.e. R subscript i). This printed form is the origin of the term but it is also used when the "subscript" is written on the same line, usually in parentheses or brackets:

R(i) or R[i]

See also array.

subscripted variable *Another name for* array.

subsemigroup A *subset T of a *semigroup S, where T is *closed under the binary operation $\circ$ defined on S. Let x

be an arbitrary element of S. Then the set consisting of

$$x, x \circ x, x \circ x \circ x, \ldots$$

i.e. all powers of x, is a subsemigroup of S.

subsequence 1. A *function whose domain is a subset of the positive integers and hence whose image set can be listed:

$$s_{i1}, s_{i2}, \ldots s_{im}$$
$$\text{where } i1 < i2 < \ldots < im$$

2. The listing of the image set of a subsequence. Hence a subsequence of a string $a_1a_2 \ldots a_n$ is any listing of the form

$$a_{i1}, a_{i2}, \ldots a_{im}$$
$$\text{where } 1 \leqslant i1 < i2 \ldots < im \leqslant n$$

See also sequence.

subset of a *set S. A set T whose members are all members of S; this is usually expressed as

$$T \subseteq S$$

A subset T is a *proper subset* of S if there is some element in S that is not in T; this is expressed as

$$T \subset S$$

substitution A particular kind of mapping on *formal languages. Let Σ_1 and Σ_2 be alphabets. For each symbol, a, in Σ_1 let $s(a)$ be a Σ_2-language. The function s is a substitution. A *homomorphism occurs where each $s(a)$ is a single word. s is Λ*-free* if no $s(a)$ contains the empty word.
The function s can be extended to map Σ_1-words to Σ_2-languages:

$$s(a_1 \ldots a_n) = s(a_1) \ldots s(a_n)$$

i.e. the *concatenation of the languages $s(a_1), \ldots, s(a_n)$. s can then be further extended to map Σ_1-languages to Σ_2-languages:

$$s(L) = \{s(w) \mid w \in L\}$$

$s(L)$ is called the *substitution image* of L under s.

substring of a string of symbols, $a_1a_2 \ldots a_n$. Any string of symbols of the form

$$a_ia_{i+1} \ldots a_j$$
$$\text{where } 1 \leqslant i \leqslant j \leqslant n$$

The *empty string is regarded as a substring of any string.

substring identifier Let $\alpha = a_1a_2 \ldots a_n$ denote a string in Σ^* and let $\# \notin \Sigma$. The substring identifier for position i in $\alpha\#$ is the shortest substring in $\alpha\#$ starting at position i that identifies position i uniquely. The existence of such a substring is guaranteed since

$$a_ia_{i+1} \ldots a_n\#$$

will always identify position i uniquely. *See also* position tree.

minuend	0	0	1	1
subtrahend	0	1	0	1
difference	0	1	1	0
borrow	0	1	0	0

Modulo-two subtraction

subtractor An electronic *logic circuit for calculating the difference between two binary numbers, the minuend and the number to be subtracted, the subtrahend (*see* table). A *full subtractor* performs this calculation with three inputs: minuend bit, subtrahend bit, and borrow bit. It produces two outputs: the difference and the borrow. Full subtractors thus allow for the inclusion of borrows generated by previous stages of subtraction when forming their output signals, and can be cascaded to form n-bit subtractors. Alternatively the subtract operation can be performed using two *half subtractors*, which are simpler since they contain only two inputs and produce two outputs.
Neither of these devices is commonly encountered since modulo-two subtraction is more conveniently accomplished using two's complement arithmetic and binary *adders.

subtree *See* tree.

successor function 1. The *function $SUCC$ that occurs in programming languages such as Ada or Pascal and produces the next element of an enumeration type. Typically

$SUCC(4)$ produces 5
$SUCC('A')$ produces 'B'

2. The *function

$$S : N \rightarrow N$$

for which $S(n) = n + 1$

where N is the nonnegative integers. S plays a crucial role in recursive function theory, particularly in the definition of *primitive recursive functions.

suffix of a string α. Any string β where α is the *concatenation $\gamma\beta$ for some string γ. *Compare* prefix.

suffix notation *Another name for* reverse Polish notation.

suite A set of programs or modules that is designed as a whole to meet some specified overall requirement, each program or module meeting some part of that requirement. For example, a single program suite might contain a program to initialize some database, a program that permits normal access to that database, a program that performs periodic major updates (such as at the end of each month), and a program that can recover the database after failure.

sumcheck *See* checksum.

sum of products expression (SOP expression) A *Boolean function expressed as a sum of product terms, i.e. as an OR of AND terms containing uncomplemented or complemented variables. An example is

$$f = (x \wedge y') \vee (x' \wedge z)$$

The function is also realizable as the NAND of a group of NAND terms. *See also* standard sum of products, product of sums expression.

sum term A sum (OR) of Boolean variables, uncomplemented or complemented. *See also* product of sums expression.

supercomputer Usually, a class of very powerful computers that are capable of performing over 10 megaflops (million floating point operations per second), hence the informal name *number cruncher*. Two families of commercially available supercomputers are the Cray-1, built by Cray Research Inc., and the Cyber 205, built by CDC. *Illiac IV, now dismantled, was the only supercomputer of its kind to be built.

superconducting memory A memory made using some form of *Josephson (junction) technology.

superconducting technology *See* Josephson (junction) technology.

super-Nyquist sampling *See* Nyquist's criterion.

supervisor (monitor; executive) The permanently resident part of a large operating system, dealing most directly with the physical components of the system as distinct from the virtual resources handled by most processes. Within the supervisor different parts handle different physical components (*see* kernel, memory management, I/O supervisor).

The term has also been used as another name for the entire operating system.

supervisor call (SVC) *See* interrupt.

supervisor state (executive state) *See* execution states.

support programs Programs that do not make a direct contribution to performing the primary function of a computer system but rather serve to assist in the operation of the system. A typical example is a program that serves to archive the contents of a filing system.

suppress To prevent the output or sensing of selected data or signals. *See also* zero suppression.

surjection (onto function) A *function whose *range and codomain coincide. If

$$f : X \rightarrow Y$$

is a surjection then for each y in the codomain Y there is some x in X with the property that

$$y = f(x)$$

A function that is not surjective is sometimes said to be *into*.

surveillance program A system program that monitors the use of a resource on behalf of system security.

suspended *See* process descriptor.

swapping A method of handling main memory by writing information to backing store during periods when it is not in use, and reading it back when required. *See also* paging, roll-in roll-out.

swipe reader *US; informal term for* slot reader. *See* card reader.

switch 1. An electronic or electromechanical device that is used to connect or disconnect an electric current to an electrical circuit. An electronic switch can present either an effective open circuit or closed circuit depending on the status of an applied "select" signal. These switches are often used to provide isolation between low- and high-voltage switching circuits or to allow remote control of electrical systems.
The word is also used as a verb, followed by a suitable preposition.
2. A type of branch with a choice of many places to which control may be passed. The destination of the branch is determined by the value of some variable. Most high-level languages have a means of doing this: Algol 60 has switch variables, FORTRAN has computed GOTOs, and several other languages, such as Algol 68, Pascal, and Ada, have case statements.
3. To undergo or cause to undergo *switching.

switching Any of various communication techniques that provide point to point transmission between dynamically changing data sources and sinks. *See also* packet switching, message switching, circuit switching.

switching algebra A term that is virtually synonymous with *Boolean algebra when applied to the analysis and synthesis of *logic (switching) circuits.

switching circuit *Another (largely obsolete) name for* logic circuit. Before the availability of low-cost electronic components, logic circuits were commonly implemented using relays and other switching devices. An AND function was implemented using a series connection of two switches; an OR function used a parallel combination of two switches.

switching speed (toggling speed) A measure of the rate at which a given electronic logic device is capable of changing the logic state of its output in response to changes at its input. It is a function of the delay encountered within the device, which in turn is a function of the device technology.

switching theory The theory of and manipulative methods for *switching algebra. It includes *Boolean-algebra and *state-table or *state-diagram methods of description, as well as *minimization methods.

switching waveform A waveform or signal that is capable of exhibiting one of two possible distinct states, often corresponding to logic 1 and logic 0, and that may be used to change the status of an active switching element between two distinct conditions such as on and off or open and closed.

Sylvester matrices *See* Hadamard matrices.

symbolic addressing An addressing scheme whereby reference to an address is made by some convenient symbol that (preferably) has some relationship to the meaning of the data expected to be located at that address. It serves as an aid to the programmer. The symbolic address is replaced by some form of computable/computed address during the operation of an assembler or compiler.

symbolic language A language in which the addresses of data, instructions, peripherals, etc., are represented by arbitrary *names rather than numerically.

symbolic logic The treatment of *formal logic involving the setting up of a formalized language. The *propositional calculus and *predicate calculus are two of the more common areas of interest.

symbol manipulation The manipulation of characters rather than numbers, as occurs in symbolic mathematics, text preparation, and finite-state automata simulation. *SNOBOL is a programming language that can be used for writing such programs.

symbol table A list, kept by a language *translator, of *identifiers in the source program and their properties. Before the translator processes any of the source program, the symbol table contains a list of predeclared identifiers; for example, the value of π or the largest integer that a system can hold might be associated with particular names by the translator. As translation proceeds, the translator will insert and remove symbols from the table as necessary. The properties of entries in the symbol table vary with both language and implementation.

symmetric difference *See* set difference.

symmetric function A *function $f(x_1,x_2, \ldots x_n)$ whose value is unaltered by any *permutation of its n variables. Such functions arise repeatedly in *switching theory.

symmetric group *See* permutation group.

symmetric list *Another name for* doubly linked list.

symmetric matrix A square matrix A such that $a_{ij} = a_{ji}$ for all a_{ij} in A. Thus a symmetric matrix is equal to its *transpose.

symmetric order traversal (inorder traversal) A tour of the nodes of a binary tree obtained by using the following recursive algorithm: visit in symmetric order the left subtree of the root (if it exists); visit the root of the tree; visit in symmetric order the right subtree of the root (if it exists). *Compare* postorder traversal, preorder traversal.

symmetric relation A *relation R defined on a set S and having the property that

whenever $x \; R \; y$
then $y \; R \; x$

where x and y are arbitrary elements of S. The relation "is equal to" defined on the integers is symmetric. *See also* antisymmetric relation, asymmetric relation.

symmetry group A *group consisting of all those *functions that transform a rigid plane figure into itself; the *binary operation on the elements of the group is that of *composition of functions. The larger and more complex a symmetry group the greater the symmetry associated with the underlying geometric figure.

synchronization A relationship between processes such that one process cannot proceed beyond a particular point until another process has reached a particular point. For example, when one process is writing data in a buffer to be read by another process, the two processes must be synchronized so that the reading process does not attempt to read the buffer beyond the point at which the writing process has written data in the buffer. Synchronization can be achieved by using a *semaphore.

synchronizer A storage device with a wide range of operating speeds that is used in an intermediate capacity when transferring data between devices that cannot operate at the same rate.

synchronous Involving or requiring a form of computer control operation in which sequential events take place at fixed times. This requires predetermination of the length of time required by each class/set of events; it requires no acknowledgment that preceding events have been completed. *Compare* asynchronous.

synchronous circuit An electronic logic circuit in which logical operations are performed under the control of and hence in synchronism with an externally generated clock signal.

synchronous counter A *counter consisting of an interconnected series of *flip-flops in which all the flip-flop outputs change state at the same instant, normally on application of a pulse at the counter input. These counters have advantages in speed over asynchronous *ripple counters, in which the output must propagate along the chain of flip-flops after the application of a pulse at the count input. *See also* cascadable counter, shift counter.

synchronous TDM *See* time division multiplexing.

syndrome In coding theory, a symbol vector (ordered set of symbols) generated at an intermediate stage of the decoding algorithm for an *error-correcting code. The syndrome depends only on the error pattern and not on the transmitted codeword. A further stage of the decoding algorithm will use the syndrome to correct the errors in the received message. The details of how the syndrome is found and how it is used, and indeed whether all the errors can be corrected, will depend on the particular error-correcting code that is being employed. If no errors occurred, the syndrome will usually be the *zero word.

syntactic errors *See* error diagnostics.

syntactic monoid of a formal language *L*. The *semigroup of the *minimal machine for *L*.

syntax The rules defining the legal sequences of elements in a language – in the case of a programming language, of characters in a program. The syntax rules define the form of the various constructs in the language, but say nothing about the meaning of these constructs. *See also* parsing.

syntax analysis *Another name for* parsing.

syntax analyzer (parser) *See* parsing.

syntax diagram A diagrammatic representation of the *syntax rules of a programming language; a pictorial equivalent of *BNF.

syntax-directed compiler A compiler that works from the *syntax rules of the language explicitly, and is therefore capable in principle of compiling another language if different parse tables are provided. In practice, syntax is less than half the story, and most of the work of the compiler writer goes into dealing with the *semantics, i.e. in defining the actions to be taken after a particular construct has been recognized in the program.

syntax tree *Another name for* parse tree.

system Anything we choose to regard (a) as an entity and (b) as comprising a set of related components. In computing the word is widely used with many shades of meaning. Most commonly, however, it may refer to a related set of hardware units, or programs, or both. The hardware contents of a computer room may be spoken of as "the system", and so may a range of manufacturer's equipment; in each case, the term may be broadened to include the basic software such as operating systems and compilers. A set of programs for a particular application (independently of the hardware and basic software on which it runs) may be referred to as a system; in this case the term may be broadened to include such things as documentation and manual procedures.

system accounting Recording the use of system *resources. On a *multiprogramming system the apportioning of the use of system resources among the active processes can only be done by the system. For resources such as processors, which are allocated in their entirety to an individual process for a large number of short intervals of time, the appropriate measure is found by recording the real time at the start and finish of each interval to give the length of each interval; accumulating these through the life of the process yields the processor time.

For resources such as memory, in which a number of subunits is allocated to the process (which will subsequently return them to the *resource allocation mechanism), the usually accepted measure is to determine the elapsed time for which the subunits are allocated to the process and to charge a "rent" for each subunit. For nonreusable resources the normal practice is to charge on a unit-cost basis for the amounts used.

In a bureau, which relies for its revenue on real money charges made to clients, the implementation of the accounting system is a nontrivial problem, especially in regard to decisions concerning spoilt work, or delays experienced by one client because of other clients' activities.

systematic code An (n, k) *block code in which every codeword can be separated into k *information symbols* and $(n - k)$ *check symbols*. The information symbols are identical with those of the source message before encoding. Thus the process of encoding a systematic code involves the insertion of $(n - k)$ check symbols into (i.e. among, before, or, most usually, after) the information symbols. The insertion positions must be the same for all the codewords in the code. Every *linear code can be arranged to be systematic.

system crash *See* crash.

system definition The document, or set of documents, that gives the most authoritative available description of some existing or envisaged system. The nature of the system definition document can vary considerably from project to project, or even during the lifetime of a single project. For example, a system definition prepared early in a development project (prior to system design) might contain an *expression of requirements for the system, the current development plan, estimates of development cost, and a cost/benefit analysis. By contrast, once development is complete, the system definition delivered with the system would be expected to contain a precise description of the actual behavior of the implemented system.

system design The activity of proceeding from an identified set of requirements for a system to a design that meets those requirements. A distinction is sometimes drawn between *high-level* or *architectural design*, which is concerned with the main components of the system and their roles and interrelationships, and *detailed design*, which is concerned with the internal structure and operation of individual components. The term system design is sometimes used to cover just the high-level design activity.

system generation The construction of a version of an operating system. Any large system is almost invariably constructed from a number of separate modules of code, each dealing with specific aspects of the system or with specific types of device Where it is known that a facility or device will not be supported, it is possible to omit the corresponding modules and to generate a version of the system that contains only modules that are known to be required. This is achieved during system generation.

system hacker A programmer who obsessively tinkers with system software, producing more or less useful additional features that tend to be badly documented and may have unfortunate side effects. Such programmers are often highly skilled and it is their virtuosity that leads them to omit essential safeguards.

system life cycle The phases of development through which a computer-based system passes. The term is primarily used in the context of *information systems, and gained common currency during the 1970s. Life cycle phases have been defined in very many different ways and in varying degrees of detail. Most definitions, however, recognize broad phases such as initial conception, requirements definition, outline design, detailed design, programming, testing, implementation, maintenance, and modification. Some include additional activities such as manual procedures design and staff training.

Most life cycle definitions arose as a result of analysis of the tasks of system development, with the objective of making those tasks more amenable to traditional techniques of management planning and control. In some cases, elaborate planning and control systems have been designed on the basis of the life cycle analysis, with highly formalized documentation and clearly defined managerial decision points.

system R, system R* *See* SQL/DS.

systems analysis The analysis of the role of a proposed system and the identification of a set of requirements that the system should meet, and thus the starting point for *system design. The term is most commonly used in the context of commercial programming, where those involved in software development are often classed as either systems analysts or programmers. The systems analysts are responsible for identifying a set of requirements (i.e. systems analysis) and producing a design. The design is then passed to the programmers, who are responsible for actual implementation of the system.

system security An (operating) system is responsible for controlling access to system resources, which will include sensitive data. The system must therefore include a certain amount of protection for such data, and must in turn control access to those parts of the system that administer this protection. System security is concerned with all aspects of these arrangements.

system specification A precise and detailed statement of the effects that a system is required to achieve. A good system specification gives a complete statement of what the system is to do without making any commitment as to how the system is to do it. Thus for these purposes the system is treated as a "black box" and the system specification constrains only the externally observable behavior, not the internal implementation.

A system specification is normally produced after an *expression of requirements, and is then used as the basis for *system design. The system specification typically differs from the expression of requirements in both scope and precision: the latter may cover both the envisaged system and the environment in which it will operate, but may leave many broad concepts unrefined.

Traditionally system specifications have taken the form of natural language documents. However both the need for precision and problems with the increasing size of specification documents are leading to the development of more formal notations.

systems programmer A latter-day harmless drudge.

systems programming Work carried out by systems programmers, i.e. the production of systems software. The boundary between systems programming and users' programming depends on the circumstances. For example, the writer of a compiler will be regarded as a user by the author of the nucleus, but is likely to be regarded as a systems programmer by the writer of a subroutine for locating the minimum of a function. The user of the minimization routine may regard all these three as systems programmers.

systems software The totality of software required to produce a system acceptable to end users.

systems theory The study of *systems per se, usually to find characteristics common to all systems or to classes of systems. Systems theorists may be most concerned

with the development of theory for its own sake (most often called *general systems theory*), or they may be more concerned with the applications of systems ideas within particular disciplines or problem areas in order to solve problems that are not amenable to traditional "reductionist" approaches. Systems theory has been called the study of organized complexity. There have been a number of attempts to categorize systems. Perhaps the simplest and most useful is by P. Checkland, who proposes four categories: natural systems, designed physical systems, designed abstract systems, and human activity systems. He also proposes four concepts that are central to systems thinking:
"the notion of whole entities which have properties as entities (emergent properties . . .); the idea that the entities are themselves parts of larger similar entities, while possibly containing smaller similar entities within themselves (hierarchy . . .); the idea that such entities are characterized by processes which maintain the entity and its activity in being (control . . .); and the idea that, whatever other processes are necessary in the entity, there will certainly be processes in which information is communicated from one part to another, at the very minimum this being entailed in the idea 'control'."

system tables The data that collectively defines the status of all resources and all processes within the system. Although such data may be represented as tables, it may be more conveniently represented internally as linked lists with pointers back to associated semaphore variables in some cases.

system testing *See* testing.

T

tab *Short for* tabulate, i.e. to lay out data, *and for* tabulation character, a control character used when laying out data to control the movement of a print or display mechanism.

table A collection of *records. Each record may store information associated with a key by which specific records are found, or the records may be arranged in an *array so that the index is the key. In commercial applications the word table is often used as a synonym for matrix or array.

table-driven algorithm An algorithm that uses *table look-up.

table look-up (TLU) A fast method of transforming one set of data values into another. The target data is stored in the form of a *table. In order to perform the transformation, a source datum is used to index into or search the table of target data. The resulting target datum is the result of the table look-up. *See also* hashing.

tablet *Short for* data tablet.

tag 1. To mark in some distinctive fashion any node in a data structure that has been traversed. Using this technique precautions can be taken against revisiting nodes, e.g. in a circular list.
2. *Short for* tag field. A field that is used to discriminate between variants of the same type.

tagged architecture A computer architecture in which extra data bits are attached to each word to denote the *data type, the function of the word, or both. Tagged architecture can represent a powerful form of *memory protection, and has formed a foundation for certain secure computer systems based on *hardware security.

tail of a list. **1.** The last item in a *list. **2.** The list remaining when the *head has been removed.

take-up reel *See* magnetic tape.

Tandem computer *Trademark* A particular *multiprocessor system (originally a *dual processor system, hence the name) that is intended to have ultrareliable system performance.

tape Either *magnetic tape or *paper tape, now normally the former if unspecified.

tape-bounded Turing machine *See* multitape Turing machine.

tape cartridge *Short for* magnetic tape cartridge (generally).

tape deck *Another name for* tape transport. *See* magnetic tape.

tape drive *Another name for* tape transport. *See* magnetic tape.

tape file A file recorded on magnetic tape.

tape format The format of information recorded on magnetic tape, allowing a system to recognize, control, and verify the data. There are two levels at which formats are defined.
(a) The format presented by the host system to the *magnetic tape subsystem. This consists of data, usually preceded and followed by *labels, and divided into sections (generally corresponding to files) by *tape marks and sometimes by additional labels; the sections of data are themselves divided into *blocks, although this is done for physical convenience and need have no logical significance.
(b) The format actually recorded, as a pattern of reversals of magnetization, on the tape by the magnetic subsystem.
To the magnetic tape subsystem, "data" means all the information – both logical data and labels – transferred to or from the host. Most magnetic subsystems require tape marks to be distinguished from the data stream. To this data the subsystem adds its own information block by block – often in a preamble to aid synchronization, a postamble to serve a similar purpose when reading in reverse, and check digits, though this varies between one standard format and another. The subsystem inserts an interblock gap (an area with no reversals of magnetization) between blocks, and writes tape marks where directed by the host; in many formats it precedes the first block on the tape by an *identity burst*, i.e. a special pattern of signals that tells the subsystem which of a number of possible formats is in use, and may also help the tape transport to optimize certain of its physical parameters.
A number of different formats (in the second sense) have been standardized as magnetic tape subsystems have developed: those currently used for data interchange use 9 tracks on ½″ tape. Three formats are in common use, all defined by ISO standards (and by corresponding ANSI and ECMA standards). They are as follows.
Nonreturn to zero (NRZ): the particular form standardized is *nonreturn-to-zero mark*, which is properly abbreviated *NRZ1* but much more widely known as *NRZI*. The density is 800 bits per inch (bpi) which, with typical block lengths, allows about 20 megabytes to be recorded on a 2400 foot reel of tape. Error detection is adequate but error correction facilities are crude, and the format, introduced in the 1950s, is now obsolescent.
Phase encoded (*PE*) format, introduced in the 1960s. The density currently standardized is 1600 bpi, and allows about 40 megabytes on a 2400 foot reel. Logical error detection is less powerful than for NRZ but electrical checks on signal waveforms are also used and a measure of on-the-fly error correction is possible. This format is reasonably simple to implement and is the one most widely used (1983) for data interchange; a 3200 bpi version has been proposed to ANSI as an additional standard.
Group code recording (*GCR*) format, introduced in the 1970s. The density standardized for 9-track ½″ tape is 6250 bpi: this refers to the density in terms of bits of logical data, but as this data is translated by the subsystem into a redundant code the actual density recorded on tape is higher. The format permits about 140 megabytes to be stored on a 2400 foot tape and the redundant coding allows excellent error detection and on-the-fly error correction.

The redundant coding does however need complex hardware.

There are further standard formats for ¼″ cartridge tape, with higher density standards under discussion, and also for cassette tape (though where personal computers use cassette tape it is generally not to this rather old standard). For all types of tape, further standards giving higher density are likely to be defined as the state of the art develops.

tape header A *header label written at the beginning of a volume of magnetic tape. *See also* label.

tape label *See* label.

tape library 1. An area in which reels of magnetic tape are stored when not actually in use on a tape transport. Each reel is normally stored in a protective case and is visibly labeled, in addition to any *label that may be recorded on the tape.

2. An *automated tape library.

tape mark A signal recorded on magnetic tape that does not represent data but is used to delimit sections of data – usually individual files, hence the alternative term *file mark*. The tape mark is written at the direction of the host system but its form is determined by the magnetic tape subsystem in accordance with the standard for the relevant *tape format. Most formats allow the tape mark to be recorded as a separate *block, but in formats that provide for the insertion of block headers by the subsystem it is usual for the tape mark to take the form of a flag in one of these headers.

If the subsystem encounters a tape mark during a read operation, the host system is informed. In most magnetic tape subsystems there is a *skip to tape mark* (or *tape-mark search*) command that causes the tape to be run to the next tape mark without transferring any data to the host; sometimes there is also a *multiple-skip* command containing a parameter *n*, which causes the tape to skip to the *n*th tape mark. Skip operations are sometimes performed at a higher speed than that used for reading.

It is conventional to write a double tape mark after the last file in a volume.

tape marker *See* BOT marker, EOT marker.

tape mechanism *Another name for* tape transport. *See* magnetic tape.

tape punch *See* paper tape I/O.

tape reader *See* paper tape I/O.

tape transport (tape drive; (magnetic) tape unit; tape deck; tape mechanism) A peripheral device that moves magnetic tape past sensing and recording heads. *See* magnetic tape.

tape unit *Another name for* tape transport. *See* magnetic tape.

target alphabet *See* code.

target program *Another name for* object program.

task 1. *Another name for* process.

2. *Another name for* job.

When each job consists of only one process, the above difference is not significant. The concurrent execution of a number of tasks is referred to as *multitasking*. *See also* parallel processing.

tautology A law of logic, in the form of a proposition, that describes a universal truth; no matter what values are assigned to the variables in the proposition the result is always true. An example from the *propositional calculus is

$$(P \vee Q)' = P' \wedge Q'$$

where $\vee$ and $\wedge$ are the *or* and *and* operators and P' is the negation of P. In the *truth table for a tautology the final result column contains only the value true. If the final column contains only the value false, then a *contradiction* has been identified.

TCP *Abbrev. for* transmission control protocol. The reliable connection-oriented protocol used by DARPA for their *internetworking research. TCP uses a three-way *handshake with clock-based sequence number selection to synchronize connecting entities and to minimize the chance of erroneous connections due to delayed messages. TCP uses positive acknowledgment with retransmission (*PAR), byte sequencing, and sliding window *flow control to provide duplex, ordered, error-free, guaranteed data transfer over established connections. Connections can be "gracefully" closed, i.e. without loss of in-transit data, with a three-way handshake of closing messages. *See also* NCP.

TDM *Abbrev. for* time division multiplexing.

teleconferencing A computer-based system enabling users to participate in an activity, such as the management of a complex project, despite being separated in space and/or time. Users will typically be provided with access to a computer terminal, which will allow them to communicate with other members of their team, often but not necessarily simultaneously. Data communication lines are used to transmit the conference information between participants. The system is controlled by a "manager" whose function is to organize the participants and allow them access to the conference and to transmit their inputs to other members. Some teleconferencing systems enable conference participants to "see" each other via television cameras and monitors connected to the system, but other systems use very simple terminals and can only communicate using the written word. Additional facilities may be provided to allow participants to vote on an issue, the votes being recorded automatically and tabulated. A conference log will be maintained by the system to keep a record of all activity in the conference, and can be displayed for reference by the participants.

Telenet A *public packet network that is owned by General Telephone & Electronics Corp. (GTE) and has been in operation since 1975. It is available in the US and some other countries and provides access to a large number of computer-based services. Telenet was developed from *ARPANET technology and has since evolved.

teleprinter (teletypewriter; typewriter terminal) A device that is similar to an electric typewriter but also has a signal interface by means of which it can receive messages for printing or can send messages that are generated on its keyboard. Teleprinters were developed for use on the telegraph and telex systems, operated at about 10 characters per second, and often had paper tape punch and reader units attached or integrated into the units. They were readily available by the time that there was a need for an I/O device to use as a control console for early computers. Visual displays and keyboards have superseded teleprinters in that role, but many are still used as interactive terminals.

teletex A means of medium- to high-speed text transmission using public switched data networks. It is expected to replace telex by about 1990. Transmission speeds can range from 2.4K bps (using *circuit switching) to 48K bps (using *packet switching), as against 50 bps for telex. Other important advantages are that it permits a much more extensive character set than telex, and permits line and paragraph formatting as in normal correspondence. It is expected that facsimile transmission capability will be incorporated into teletex. Teletex standards are the responsibility of *CCITT.

teletext A system for one-way broadcast transmission of information, primarily in text form but with primitive graphics capability, using spare television channel capacity and adapted domestic TV receivers. On a channel offering teletext, a number

of "pages" of information (up to about 100) are transmitted in a continuous cycle, concurrently with the normal TV signal and leaving it unaffected while the receiver is used for normal viewing. Having selected teletext mode on the control pad, it is then possible to select any page number; when the selected page next arrives in the transmission cycle, it is stored in local memory in the set and displayed indefinitely (until the user selects another page or exits from teletext mode).
Among countries in which teletext services are available are Australia, France (Didon and Antiope), West Germany (Bildschirmzeitung and – confusingly – Videotext), UK (Ceefax and Oracle), and US (Closed Captioning).
Compare videotex.

teletypewriter *Another name for* teleprinter.

Telidon A Canadian *videotex system.

TELNET *Acronym for* teletype network. The protocol developed for the *ARPANET to allow users on one host computer to connect to the time-sharing resources of another host. The TELNET protocol specifies a standard terminal type, the *network virtual terminal (NVT)*, including its character set (a modified form of ASCII) and standard control sequences for terminal functions such as "move to the next line". Standard control sequences are also defined for host functions such as "interrupt process". It is the responsibility of the programs at each end of the TELNET connection to perform a suitable mapping between the NVT's character set and control functions, and the conventions of the local system. Many of the parameters of the NVT can be modified through option negotiation, in which both ends of the TELNET connection must agree to a proposed change before it can take place.
The name TELNET is also used for similar protocols in networks other than the ARPANET.

template A structure specification. The term is a convenient means of differentiating the structure specification from the declaration of individual instances of the structure. The provision of template facilities allows a programmer to build his own data types.

ten's complement *See* radix complement.

tension arm *See* buffer.

tera- (symbol: T) A prefix indicating a multiple of one million million, 10^{12}, or, loosely, a multiple of 2^{40}, i.e.

1 099 511 627 776

terminal 1. A data input and/or output device that is connected to a controlling processor to which it is subservient and usually remote. There are a very wide range of terminal types. The *teleprinter is frequently used as a terminal by which a user can input queries or instructions and receive printed information, but *VDUs are becoming preferred. The information may be in the form of text or it may be mainly graphical. Terminals designed for a particular environment and business activity come under a general heading of *application terminals. If the terminal has a built-in capability to store and manipulate data it is classed as an *intelligent terminal; without this capability terminals are classed as dumb.
2. (terminal symbol) *See* grammar.

terminal node *Another name for* leaf node.

terminal symbol *See* grammar.

termination The end of execution of a process. A process that reaches a successful conclusion terminates normally by issuing a suitable supervisor call to the operating system. *See also* abnormal termination.

termination, proof of *See* program correctness proof.

term language *Another name for* tree language.

ternary logic *See* multiple-valued logic.

ternary selector gate (T-gate) A *combinational ternary logic gate that is important as a building block in the synthesis of ternary logic circuits (*see* multiple-valued logic). A T-gate has four inputs

$$\{a_0, a_1, a_2, s\}$$

and one output $\{t\}$, all of which can take values represented by elements of the set

$$\{0, 1, 2\}$$

The function of the T-gate is given by $t = a_s$. It thus acts as a ternary selector, the choice from

$$\{a_0, a_1, a_2\}$$

being selected by the value taken by the s input.

ternary threshold gate (S-gate) A *combinational ternary logic gate that is important as a building block in the synthesis of ternary logic circuits (*see* multiple-valued logic). An S-gate may have any number of inputs $\{a_i\}$ and one output $\{s\}$, all of which can take values represented by elements of the set $\{0,1,2\}$. The function of the S-gate is given by

$$\left.\begin{matrix} s=0 \\ s=1 \\ s=2 \end{matrix}\right\} \text{ iff } \sum_i (a_i - 1) \begin{cases} < 0 \\ = 0 \\ > 0 \end{cases}$$

The reason for the name S-gate is because the French for threshold is *seuil.* The S-gate should not be confused with the *ternary selector gate (T-gate). More complicated versions of the S-gate have been defined in various ways. *See also* threshold element.

test and set A single indivisible instruction that is capable of testing the value of the contents of a register and altering them. The instruction is used to implement more powerful indivisible operations (such as *lock, *unlock, or *semaphore operations) when the process executing the operation is capable of being interrupted and where the servicing of the interrupt may cause another process to be restarted.

test bed Any system whose primary purpose is to provide a framework within which other systems can be tested. Test beds are usually tailored to a specific programming language and implementation technique, and often to a specific application. Typically a test bed provides some means of simulating the environment of the system under test, of test-data generation and presentation, and of recording test results.

test data *See* testing.

test-data generator Any means for the automatic or semiautomatic production of data for use in the *testing of some system. Typically both valid and invalid input data for the system under test will be generated in order to test responses to both valid and erroneous inputs. Some generators effectively produce a pseudorandom data stream, recognizing only constraints on the formats of the data. More advanced generators might attempt to produce data that will give good test coverage.

testing Any activity that checks by means of actual execution whether a system or component behaves in the desired manner. This is achieved by one or more *test runs* in which the system is supplied with input data, known under these circumstances as *test data*, and the system's responses are recorded for analysis.

Tests can be categorized according to the conditions under which they are performed and the purposes they serve. *Module testing* (or *unit testing*) is performed on individual components in isolation. At the time that components are brought together to form complete subsystems or systems, *integration testing* is performed in order to check that the components operate together correctly. Integration testing typically pays particular attention to the interfaces between components. By contrast, *system testing* normally treats the complete system as a "black box" and investigates its behavior without concern for individual components or internal interfaces. *Acceptance testing* is normally under the control of the procurers of the system, and is designed to ensure that the system is suitable for operational use.

test run *See* testing.

Texas Instruments A US company originally founded to supply instrumentation and other technical support to the petroleum industry, primarily in the areas of well exploration and development. TI was one of the early semiconductor manufacturers, and became dominant in the fields of integrated circuits (including microprocessors), calculators, and minicomputers. It also manufactured a few large computers. It now produces a line of microcomputers.

text editor A program used specifically for entry and modification of data that is in a textual format. Such data may be a program written in a high-level language or a report or book written in a natural language.
Text editors form an essential part of the user interface of all interactive systems. They may be *line-oriented*, where the text is considered to be a series of lines separated by end-of-line markers, *character-oriented*, where the text is considered to be a stream of characters with any end-of-line or page markers counting as characters, or *screen editors*. With screen editors, the display screen forms a movable *window into the text, within which the cursor may be positioned at points where insertions, deletions, and other editing functions are to be performed.
There is a considerable overlap in function between text editors and *word processing systems.

text formatter *See* formatter.

text processing *Another name for* word processing.

T flip-flop An arrangement of a clocked *flip-flop in which the flip-flop's set (S) and reset (R) inputs are held at logic 1. For this condition the flip-flop's output will "toggle", i.e. change to the complementary logic state, on every active transition of the clock signal (*see* clock). The device acts as a divide-by-two *counter since two active transitions of the clock signal generate one active transition of the output.

T-gate *Another name for* ternary selector gate.

theorem proving The formal method of providing a proof in *symbolic logic. Each step in the proof will (a) introduce a premise or axiom; (b) provide a statement that is a natural consequence of previously established results using only legitimate rules of inference.
Such formal proofs are often long and tedious. Sophisticated programs known as *theorem provers* can be used to automate much of the process. *See also* mechanical verifier.

theory of types *See* hierarchy of functions.

thermal printer A type of printer in which the image is produced by localized heating of paper that has a very thin thermosensitive coating containing two separate and colorless components. When heated the color former melts and combines with the previously colorless dyestuff to make a visible mark. Various colors are possible but blue and black are the most common. Blue toning paper allows higher print speeds but the image fades with time and is not compatible with some photocopiers. Black toning paper requires higher temperatures and pressure at the print head – thus causing greater wear – but fades less quickly and has a longer shelf life. The printers can be either *serial or *line printers. *See also* thermal transfer printer.

thermal transfer printer A printer in which thermoplastic ink is transferred to paper from a donor roll or thin backing material by localized heating. This type of printer, introduced in 1982, is very quiet in operation, produces a good contrast image, and is mechanically simple in design. The print head is similar to that used in the earlier *thermal printers that use sensitized paper, but the heating elements are usually smaller and thus allow the formation of a better character shape.

The printers may be *serial or *page printers. The print head of the serial printer version can have 12 heating elements within the height of a character. The special ribbon is mounted on the carriage with the print head; after a mark has been made a new area of ribbon is presented between print head and paper. A speed of 100 characters per second has been achieved. The page printer can have a print head with as many as 1024 elements spanning an 8″ width. A donor film, the same size as the page to be printed, is laid over the paper and they are passed beneath the print head. Successive donor films of different colors can be used to print full-color pictures.

thin-film memory A memory device whose individual elements are formed by evaporating a thin film of a magnetic material onto a glass substrate. The status of each element may be interrogated (read) or changed (written to) by the application of a d.c. magnetic field parallel to the surface of the device. Large-capacity memories having many thousands of elements can be formed in a single operation using this process.

third generation of computers. Machines whose design was initiated after 1960 (approximately) and that exhibit the characteristics of integrated families of machines. The IBM 360 is the most important example of this characteristic. Defining generations in terms of hardware characteristics or construction technology is more difficult in the third generation due to the range of construction techniques employed in this period. Discrete transistors were used through most of this generation. Memory was almost exclusively *core store, although this generation saw the introduction of a *cache memory to speed up the overall machine operations. Most manufacturers introduced at least three members of a system family, architecturally similar but differing in price and performance.

The third generation saw the introduction of comprehensive operating systems that included support for *multiprogramming, *multiprocessing, and multiprocessors (e.g. IBM's 360/65mp, Sperry Univac's 1108, and the Burroughs B5000), and eventually *time sharing. With the advent of the third generation, system emphasis shifted to software. The third generation input/output was marked by

(a) the introduction of specialized high-performance printers;

(b) the true integration of communications technology with computers, thereby making it possible to have on-line terminals and data-entry terminals;

(c) the use of large on-line storage, larger fixed disks, and the appearance of the removable disk pack.

It was also during the third generation that punched paper tape almost completely vanished and punched cards lost their main emphasis as primary input/output media.

thrashing A phenomenon that may arise in *paging or other forms of *virtual-memory system. If the page-turning rate for a paging system becomes high, usually because the amount of real memory available for holding pages is small compared with the total *working set of all the processes currently active, then each process will find itself in a situation in which, on attempting to reference a page, the appropriate page is not in memory. In trying to find space to hold the required page the system is likely to move out onto backing store a page that will very shortly be required by some other process. As a consequence the paging rate rises to very high levels, the fraction of CPU cycles absorbed in managing page-turning overheads becomes very high, processes become blocked as they wait for page transfers to complete, and system throughput falls sharply.

One method by which thrashing may be alleviated is by an increase in the bandwidth between main memory and backing store, i.e. by providing sufficient interchange capacity to allow the thrashing to take place without inducing unduly long waits for paging-drum transfers. A more effective cure is to reduce the ratio between the total working-set size and the amount of space available for holding the active pages, thus increasing the hit rate on pages in memory, either by reducing the size of the working set or by increasing the amount of memory on the system.

threaded list A list in which additional linkage structures, called *threads*, have been added to provide for traversals in special orders. This permits bounded workspace, i.e. read-only traversals along the direction provided by the threads. It does presuppose that the list and any sublists are not recursive and further that no sublist is shared.

threading A programming technique used in some code generators in which the "code" consists of a sequence of entry points of routines. The threaded code is interpreted by executing an unconditional branch to the destination indicated by a word of the code; on completion the routine thus activated terminates by again executing an unconditional branch to the entry point indicated by the next code word. *See also* single threading, multithreading.

threat Any of many potential violations of computer operation and of the security of information contained in a computer system. Threats include *browsing, *denial of service, loss of information without knowledge that the information has been copied, and destruction of information. Threats may be accomplished by *penetration techniques, by wire tapping, and by many physical methods.

three-address instruction *See* instruction format. *See also* multiple-address machine.

three-dimensional array *See* array.

three-state output *Another name for* tristate output.

three-way handshake *See* handshake.

threshold element (threshold gate) A *logic element whose output is determined by comparing a weighted sum of inputs with a predetermined/prescribed threshold value. If the threshold is exceeded, the output is a logic 1; if not, the output is logic 0. If the number of inputs is odd, if the weights are all equal, and the threshold is equal to half of the number of inputs, then the threshold element behaves as a *majority element.

A system of threshold elements is described by or as *threshold logic*. *See also* ternary threshold gate.

throughput A figure-of-merit for a computer system in which some description of operating rate such as instructions-per-minute, jobs-per-day, etc., is used.

Thue-system A *semi-Thue system in which, for each production $l \to r$, the reverse production $r \to l$ is also present (as in the first example under semi-Thue system). Clearly then

$$w \Rightarrow w' \text{ iff } w' \Rightarrow w$$

tightly coupled *See* coupled.

time-bounded Turing machine *See* multitape Turing machine.

time complexity *See* complexity measure, P = NP question.

time division multiplexing (TDM) A method of sharing a transmission channel among multiple sources by allocating specific time slots to each source. Both synchronous and asynchronous TDM is used.

Synchronous TDM does not require identity bits to be included in a message since the receiving device knows which device is transmitting at all times. The two main methods used in synchronous TDM to identify when a device's time slot occurs are *polling and *clocking. Polling requires a central device to interrogate each sending device when its time slot occurs. Clocking requires each device to have a synchronized clock and a prearranged sending sequence known to all devices. Polling and clocking waste time slots if a device has no data to send. More refined methods require devices to reserve their time slots ahead of time or allow devices to use time slots of other devices if they were unused on the previous cycle.
Asynchronous TDM allows devices to send data as it is ready, without a prearranged ordering. Data must carry with it the identity of the sending device. Since devices may send data at the same time, collisions may occur, making the messages unreadable. Many networks that utilize asynchronous TDM use *CSMA/CD (carrier sense multiple access with collision detection) to sense when messages have collided and must be retransmitted.
TDM is used in *baseband networking, and may also be used on channels of a *broadband networking system.
See also multiplexing, frequency division multiplexing.

time division switch An all-electronic switching system based on *time division multiplexing principles: an input digitized signal from a source is connected to an output trunk by assigning a group of bits from the input data stream to a time slot in a high-speed time division multiplexed output data stream. Time-division switches are commonly also used as tandem switches where time slots from an input time division multiplexed trunk are selectively connected to time slots in an output time division multiplexed trunk.

time domain A term used to refer to a situation in which the amplitude of a *signal varies with time. *See also* space domain.

time-of-day clock A digital device that provides time-of-day information. It is typically used as a means of scheduling control applications or data collection activities.

timeout A condition that occurs when a process which is waiting for either an external event or the expiry of a preset time interval reaches the end of the time interval before the external event is detected. For example, if the process has sent a message and no acknowledgment has been detected at the end of the preset time period, then the process may take appropriate action, such as retransmitting the message. The word is also used as a verb.

time quantization (sampling) *See* quantization, discrete and continuous systems.

timer clock A timing device that can generate a *timeout signal after a fixed period of time. These devices are often made programmable, i.e. presetable, so that various timing durations can be obtained. In addition the timeout signal may be generated continuously, i.e. after every timing period, or on a one-shot basis.

time response of a linear channel. *See* convolution.

time series A set of observations ordered in time and usually equally spaced; each observation may be related in some way to its predecessors. Time-series problems arise in economics, commerce, industry, meteorology, demography, or any fields in which the same measurements are regularly recorded.
Time-series analysis is based on models of the variability of observations in a time series, by postulating trends, cyclic effects, and short-term relationships, with a view to understanding the causes of variation and to improving forecasting.

Autoregression is the use of *regression analysis to relate observations to their predecessors. *Moving-average methods* use the means of neighboring observations to reveal underlying trends. Autoregression and moving averages are combined in *ARMA* (or *Box-Jenkins*) forecasting techniques.

Cyclic influences may be of known period (months in a year or days in a week) and data may be seasonally adjusted on the basis of long-term means. Cyclic influences of unknown period may be studied by *spectral analysis*.

Analogous techniques may be used for data regularly ordered in space rather than time.

time sharing A technique, first advocated by Christopher Strachey, for sharing the time of a computer among several jobs, switching between them so rapidly that each job appears to have the computer to itself. *See also* multiaccess system.

time slicing Process scheduling in which a process is allowed to run for a predefined period of time, now called a *quantum, before rescheduling. *See also* scheduling algorithm.

timing diagram A graphical description of the operation of a *sequential circuit; the state(s) of all the relevant variables (inputs, internal memory, and outputs) are shown as functions along the time dimension.

TIP *Acronym for* terminal interface processor. *See* IMP.

tip node *Another name for* leaf node.

T²L *See* TTL.

TLU *Abbrev. for* table look-up.

TM *Abbrev. for* Turing machine.

toggling speed *Another name for* switching speed.

token ring A *ring network architecture configured on the basis that each station (node) on the ring awaits the arrival of a unique short sequence of bits – a *token* – from the adjacent upstream node, indicating that it is allowed to send information toward the downstream node. The network is configured in a manner that ensures that only a single token is present on the ring at one time. When a sending node intercepts the token, it first sends its message to the downstream node followed by the token, which is then passed to each succeeding node until it is again intercepted by a node with a message awaiting transmission.

top-down development An approach to program development in which progress is made by defining required elements in terms of more basic elements, beginning with the required program and ending when the implementation language is reached. At every stage during top-down development each of the undefined elements from the previous stage is defined. In order to do this, an appropriate collection of more basic elements is introduced, and the undefined elements are defined in terms of these more basic elements ("more basic" meaning that the element is closer to the level that can be directly expressed in the implementation language). These more basic elements will in turn be defined at the next stage in terms of still more basic elements, and so on until at some stage the elements can be defined directly in the implementation language.

In practice, "pure" top-down development is not possible; the choice of more basic elements at each stage must always be guided by an awareness of the facilities of the implementation language, and even then it will often be discovered at a later stage that some earlier choice was inappropriate, leading to a need for iteration. *Compare* bottom-up development.

top-down parsing A strategy for *parsing sentences of *context-free grammars that attempts to construct a *parse tree from the top down. The term includes techniques that may or may not involve backtracking.

Beginning with a parse tree consisting of just the start symbol of the *grammar, a top-down parser attempts to expand those leaf nodes labeled by nonterminals from left to right using the productions of the grammar. As leaves labeled by terminals are created they are matched against the input string. Should the match fail, new alternatives for the interior nodes are tried in a systematic way until the entire input string has been matched or no more alternatives are possible. A top-down parser without backtracking uses the information contained in the portion of the input string not yet matched to decide once and for all which alternatives to choose. The *LL parsing technique is the most powerful such technique.

Top-down parsing is often implemented as a set of recursive procedures, one for each nonterminal in the grammar, and is then called *recursive descent parsing*.

topology **1.** The study of those properties of *sets that are shared by all images (homeomorphic images) of the sets under certain mappings that might be described as deformations. Topology is sometimes described as geometry done on a rubber sheet; this sheet can be pulled or stretched into different shapes. Topological properties are unaltered by distortions of this kind. Topological properties can be attributed to *graphs, *grammars, and even *programs themselves.

2. (interconnection topology) *See* network architecture.

TOPS *Trademark, acronym for* terminal operating system. One of the multiprogramming systems available on Digital Equipment Corporation's larger machines, the DEC-10 and DEC-20 systems.

total correctness, proof of. *See* program correctness proof.

total function A *function

$$f: S \rightarrow T$$

whose value is defined for all elements x in the set S; thus for each x, $f(x)$ produces some value in T. *Compare* partial function.

totally ordered structure *Another name for* linear structure.

total ordering A *partial ordering with the added property that there is always order between any two elements. The usual "less than" ordering between integers is a total ordering. The relation "is a subset of" defined on the *algebra of sets is not.

trace program A program that monitors the execution of some software system and provides information on the dynamic behavior of that system in the form of a *trace*, i.e. a report of the sequence of actions carried out. Typically a trace program will offer several options as to the kind of trace produced. For example, there may be options to produce a statement-by-statement trace, or to trace just those statements that alter the flow of control, or to trace changes to the value of a specific variable.

track **1.** The portion of a magnetic storage medium that is accessible to the read/write heads. In magnetic disks the tracks are concentric and circular. In current magnetic tapes generated on tape transports there are usually 9 tracks that run parallel to the edges. *See also* optical disk.
2. The portion of a paper tape that may be punched with holes. On conventional data tapes there may be 5, 6, 7, or 8 tracks running parallel to the edges. Other numbers have been used for special purposes, as with carriage control tapes.

trade secrets Pieces of confidential information about a device, process, or product. The value of the information is that receiving it would enable the recipient to short-circuit an otherwise necessary course of development. Thus a source listing containing debugged code for one or more algorithms, if given in circumstances of confidence, may be protected by the law as a trade secret and the recipient barred from using the algorithms in programs of his own. Like *privacy, the law on trade secrets is not at all clear. *See also* copyright.

traffic A measure of the quantity of data or other messages taking place between points of a communication network.

traffic control A term sometimes used in reference to the control of input and output. It covers both the hardware (channels and interrupts) and software (resource allocation and process synchronization) necessary to achieve the orderly and correct movement of data in a multiprogramming system.

trailer label A *sentinel that occurs at the end of data organized in sequential form, e.g. on magnetic tape. Trailer labels typically include summary statistics of the data, e.g. the total number of records in the file.

trailer record A record that follows a group of related records and contains data relevant to those records. For example, a trailer record may appear at the end of a file and contain a total of monetary fields held on that file, which may be used as a security check.

train printer A type of *impact *line printer in which the type font is etched or engraved upon metal slugs that are pushed around a guide track. It was introduced by IBM in 1965 to supersede the *chain printer. The slugs of the train printer generally have three characters on the face and a gear form at the back. The track guides them around a loop, one section of which runs parallel to the line to be printed. The character set is repeated a number of times to ensure that the track is full. The use of slugs in a track enables greater accuracy of print to be achieved and also yields flexibility of character repertoire. Heavily used characters can be easily replaced and special symbols can be substituted for other characters. Speeds of up to 3000 lpm are achieved.

Train printers dominated the high-speed printer market up to 1982, when the *band printer offered superior performance at lower cost and nonimpact printers with superior print quality and versatility became financially viable.

transaction 1. A single coherent action on a *file or *database: different transactions (for different users working concurrently) can be carried out sequentially without interfering with one another. *See also* transaction processing.

2. The data generated by a transaction or a single record arising from any cause. In batch processing it is usual to accumulate the transactions on a storage medium such as tape. The data will usually cause some change to a related set of records held on a *master file.

transaction file (movement file) A file that contains relatively transient data. It is processed together with a *master file, the transaction file details being used to update the master file. Once the update has been accomplished successfully the transaction file need only be kept for backup purposes.

transaction processing A fairly general term associated with a system having a number of users submitting concurrent tasks requiring access to the same *files or *database. The tasks must be partitioned into *transactions, which are processed separately. The concept of a transaction is important in modern systems in connection with issues of integrity, backup, and restart.

transborder dataflow The most complex legal topic yet to be created by the use of computers in society. When a person in Germany contacts an Irish database, combines the information with information extracted from a Swiss reference manual stored in digital format on a computer in France, and sends the output to Australia,

Zambia, and Taiwan where it is recorded on disk with no eye-readable copies produced, he creates a literary work that falls outside any conventions that at present exist concerning *copyright. He also may have breached the *data protection legislation of several countries. With the growth in the use of satellites and broadband communication facilities, the importance of transborder dataflow will grow in the 1980s and hence new conventions will have to be drafted.

transceiver *Acronym for* transmitter and receiver. A device that can both transmit and receive signals on a communication medium. Many communication devices, including *modems, *codecs, and terminals, are transceivers.

transducer 1. Any device that converts energy in the form of sound, light, pressure, etc., into an equivalent electrical signal, or vice versa. For example, a photoconductor converts light and ultraviolet radiation into electrical energy, a piezoelectric device converts mechanical stress into electrical energy (and vice versa).
2. In formal language theory, any *automaton that produces output.

transfer instruction *Another name for* branch instruction.

transfer rate *See* data transfer rate.

transfinite *See* cardinality.

transformation 1. *Another name for* function, used especially in geometry.
2. of programs. *See* program transformation.

transformational semantics *See* program transformation.

transformation matrix An $m \times n$ matrix of numbers used to map vectors with n elements onto vectors with m elements.

transformation monoid *See* transformation semigroup.

transformation semigroup A *semigroup consisting of a collection C of transformations of a *set S into itself (*see* function), the *binary operation $\circ$ being the *composition of functions; it is essential that the set C should be *closed with respect to composition, i.e. if c_1 and c_2 are in C then so is $c_1 \circ c_2$.
If the identity transformation (*see* identity function) is included in the transformation semigroup, a *transformation monoid* results. Every monoid is isomorphic to a transformation monoid.

transform domain *See* filtering.

transient error of magnetic tape. *See* error rate.

transistor A semiconductor device having, in general, three terminals that are attached to electrode regions within the device. Current flowing between two of these electrodes is made to vary in response to voltage or current variations imposed on the third electrode. The device is capable of current or voltage amplification depending on the particular circuit implementation employed. It can also be used as a switch by driving it between its maximum and minimum of current flow.
The transistor was invented in 1948 by Shockley, Brattain, and Bardeen at Bell Telephone Labs. As performance and manufacturing techniques improved, there was a huge growth in computer technology.
See also bipolar transistor, field-effect transistor, MOSFET.

transistor-transistor logic *See* TTL.

transitive closure of a *transitive *binary relation R. A relation R^* defined as follows:

$$x\ R^*\ y$$

iff there exists a sequence

$$x = x_0, x_1, \ldots, x_n = y$$

such that $n > 0$ and

$$x_i\ R\ x_{i+1},\ i = 0,1,2, \ldots, n-1$$

It follows from the transitivity property that

if $x\ R\ y$ then $x\ R^*\ y$
and that R is a subset of R^*.
Reflexive closure is similar to transitive closure but includes the possibility that $n = 0$. Transitive and reflexive closures play important roles in parsing and compiling techniques and in finding paths in graphs.

transitive relation A *relation R defined on a set S and having the property that, for all x, y, and z in S,
whenever $x\ R\ y$ and $y\ R\ z$
then $x\ R\ z$
The relations "is less than" defined on integers, and "is subset of" defined on sets are transitive.

translation (protocol translation) *See* internetworking.

translation table A table of information stored within a processor or a peripheral that is used to convert encoded information into another form of code with the same meaning. There are a variety of codes used within the field of computing and sometimes more than one code may be used within a single system. For output devices such as printers the *ASCII code is widely used but the code used within the processor may be *EBCDIC. A translation table is used to make the required conversion.

translator A program that converts a program written in one language to the equivalent program in another language. A *compiler is a specific example of a translator: it takes a program written in a high-level language such as FORTRAN or Algol and converts it into machine code or assembly language.

translator writing system A set of *software tools that are designed to aid the production of new language translators. A *compiler-compiler is an example of one such tool.

transmission channel *See* channel.

transmission control unit *See* communication processor.

transmission rate The speed at which information may be transferred from a device or via a circuit. The unit used is usually related to the amount of information transferred per cycle, e.g. characters per second or bits per second. With data transmission circuits the *baud rate is sometimes used.

Transpac The French PTT's *public packet network. It started operation in 1978 after testbed development of the *RCP network. Transpac provides an X.25 interface.

transparent 1. Denoting a property or a component of a computer system that provides some facilities without restrictions or interference arising from the way it is implemented. For example, if a machine with 32-bit wide words has an 8-bit wide ALU yet performs correct 32-bit arithmetic, then the ALU size is transparent in such use.
2. Denoting or using a transmission path that passes a signal, or some particular feature of a signal, without restricting or changing it. Note that nontransparent systems would not allow particular signals to be transmitted as data, reserving them for special purposes. *See also* data transparency.

transport 1. A mechanism for transporting an information storage medium past an access station. The word is most frequently used to refer to either a tape transport (*see* magnetic tape) or a document transport.
2. A service provided by a (local or wide area) communication network, or the architectural layer or interface with this service.

transportable *See* portable.

transport layer of network protocol function. *See* seven-layer reference model.

transpose of an $m \times n$ matrix A. The $n \times m$ matrix, symbol A^T, given by interchanging rows and columns. Thus the i,jth element of A^T is equal to the j,ith element of A.

trap A system state similar to that caused by an *interrupt but synchronous to the system rather than asynchronous as in the case of an interrupt. There are a variety of conditions that can cause a trap to occur. Examples of such conditions include the attempted execution of an illegal instruction, or an attempt to access another user's resources in a system that supports multiuser protection. The attempted operation is detected by the hardware and control is transferred to a different part of the system, usually in the operating system, which can then decide on what action to take.

trap door *Another name for* Trojan horse.

trapezium rule *See* numerical integration.

trapezoidal rule *See* ordinary differential equations.

traversal A *path through a *graph in which every vertex is visited at least once. Traversals are usually discussed in connection with special kinds of graphs, namely *trees. Examples include *preorder traversal, *postorder traversal, and *symmetric order (or inorder) traversal. When parse trees for arithmetic expressions are traversed, these tree traversals lead to prefix (*Polish) notation, postfix (*reverse Polish) notation, and *infix notation respectively.

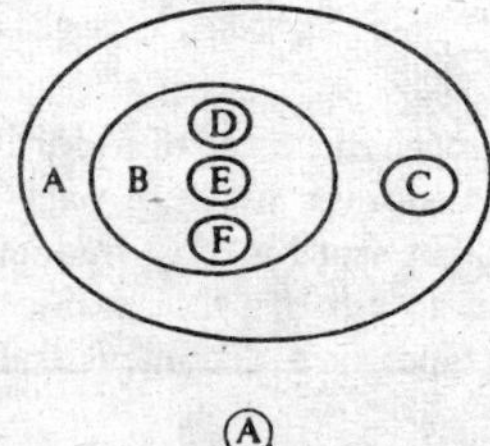

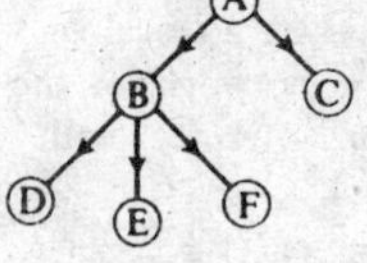

Sample tree represented as a Venn diagram (top) and as a directed graph

tree 1. Most commonly, short for *rooted tree*, i.e. a finite set of one or more *nodes such that firstly there is a single designated node called the *root* and secondly the remaining nodes are partitioned into $n \geq 0$ *disjoint sets, $T_1, T_2, \ldots, T_n$, where each of these sets is itself a tree. The sets $T_1, T_2, \ldots, T_n$ are called *subtrees* of the root. If the order of these subtrees is significant, the tree is called an *ordered tree*, otherwise it is sometimes called an *unordered tree*.
A tree can be represented as a *graph with the root node represented by a vertex connected by (directed) arcs to the vertices representing the root nodes of each of its subtrees. An alternative definition of a (*directed*) *tree* can thus be given in terms from graph theory: a tree is a directed *acyclic graph such that firstly there is a unique vertex, which no arcs enter, called the root, secondly every other vertex has exactly one arc entering it, and thirdly there is a unique path from the root to any vertex.
The diagram shows different representations of a tree.
2. Any *connected acyclic graph.
3. Any data structure representing a tree (def. 1 or 2). For example, a rooted tree can be represented as a pointer to the representation of the root node. A representation of a node would contain pointers to the subtrees of the node as well as the data associated with the node itself. Because the number of subtrees of a node may vary, it is common practice to use a *binary-tree representation.
The terminology associated with trees is either of a botanic nature, as with *forest, *leaf, root, or is genealogical, as with *ancestor, *descendant, *child, *parent, *sibling. *See also* binary tree.

tree automaton A generalization of the notion of a *finite-state automaton, applying to trees rather than strings (*see* tree language). There are two versions. A *top-down* machine begins at the root of the tree; having read the symbol at a node it changes state accordingly and splits into n machines to process separately the n descendants. A *bottom-up* machine begins with several separate activations of itself – one at each leaf node of the tree. When all the subtrees of a particular node have been processed, the machines that have processed the subtrees are replaced by a single one at that node. Its state is determined by the symbol at the node and the final states of the descendant machines. It is itself then available for coalescing further up.

trees: c etc.

frontiers: c acb aacbb etc.

Language generated by a tree grammar

tree grammar A generalization of the notion of *grammar, applying to trees (often called *terms* in this context) rather than strings (*see* tree language). A *regular tree grammar* is the corresponding generalization of the notion of *regular grammar. Productions have the form

$$A \rightarrow t,$$

where A is a nonterminal and t a term, e.g.

$$S \rightarrow h(a,g(S),b) \mid c$$

These productions generate the *regular tree language* shown in the diagram. Note that the *frontiers* of these trees are the strings shown below each tree in the diagram. A set of strings is *context-free if and only if it is the set of frontiers of the trees in a regular tree language.

The notion of *context-free grammar can be similarly generalized. This time nonterminals can themselves be function symbols having an arbitrary number of arguments, e.g.

$$F(x_1,x_2) \rightarrow$$
$$f(x_2,F(x_1,g(x_2))) \mid h(x_1,x_1,x_2)$$

This means, for example, that $F(a,b)$ could be rewritten to

$$f(b,F(a,g(b))),$$

and then to

$$f(b,f(g(b),F(a,g(g(b))))),$$

and then to

$$f(b,f(g(b),h(a,a,g(g(b)))))$$

tree language (term language) In *formal language theory, a generalization of the notion of language, applying to trees (often called *terms* in this context) rather than strings. Alphabets are extended to give each symbol an *arity*, the arity of each symbol dictating the number of subterms, or descendants in the tree, that it has.

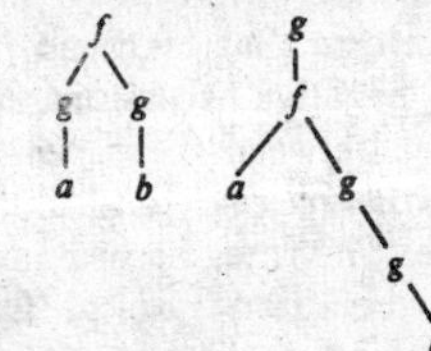

terms: $f(a,b)$ $f(g(a),g(b))$ $g(f(a,g(g(b))))$

Examples of Σ-trees and Σ-terms

For example, let Σ be the alphabet $\{f,g,a,b\}$ and give arities 2,1,0,0 to f,g,a,b respectively. Then examples of *Σ-trees* and their equivalent representations as *Σ-terms* (or *well-formed expressions over* Σ) are shown in the diagram. A Σ-language is now any set of Σ-terms. *See also* tree grammar, tree automaton.

tree search Any method of searching a body of data structured as a tree. *See* breadth-first search, depth-first search.

tree selection sort A refinement of *straight selection sort that makes use of the information gained in the first step to save on the subsequent number of comparisons required. It was proposed in 1956 by E. H. Friend and modified by K. E. Iverson in 1962. *See also* heapsort.

tree walking *Traversal of a tree.

trial function *See* finite-element method.

triangular matrix A square matrix in which every element lying to one side of the main diagonal is equal to zero. Thus for a *lower triangular matrix*, *L*,

$$l_{ij} = 0 \text{ if } i < j$$

and for an *upper triangular matrix*, *U*,

$$u_{ij} = 0 \text{ if } i > j$$

If, in addition,

$$l_{ii} = 0 \text{ or } u_{ii} = 0$$

then *L* or *U* is said to be *strictly lower* or *strictly upper triangular* respectively. The inverse of a lower (or an upper) triangular matrix, if it exists, is easy to calculate and is itself lower (or upper) triangular.

triangular waveform A periodic repetitive waveform that takes on its peak positive and negative excursions at fixed points in time. Between these peaks the waveform alternately rises and falls linearly with time. The rates of rise and fall determine the repetition rate or frequency of the waveform and in general are made equal. *Compare* sawtooth waveform.

tridiagonal matrix A band matrix *A* in which

$$a_{ij} = 0 \text{ if } |i - j| > 1$$

trie search A searching algorithm that examines data stored in a *trie* (name derived from information re*trie*val). A trie is essentially an *n*-ary tree with nodes that are *n*-place vectors, the components of which correspond to digits or characters.

trigger To initiate the operation of an electrical circuit or device. Thus a signal supplied to the trigger input of a circuit may cause the circuit's output signal to be synchronized to this input.

trim of an array. The array obtained by constraining the subscripts to lie in some specified subrange. For example, the trim of a vector

$$v = (v_1\ v_2\ \dots\ v_{10})$$

obtained by constraining the index i so that $3 \leqslant i \leqslant 7$ is the vector

$$(v_3\ v_4\ v_5\ v_6\ v_7)$$

See also slice.

trim erase *Another term for* tunnel erase.

triple precision The use of three times the usual number of bits to represent a number. It is seldom required. *See also* double precision.

tri-state output (three-state output) An electronic output stage consisting of a logic gate, commonly an inverter or buffer, that exhibits three possible *logic states, namely logic 1, logic 0, and an inactive (high-impedance or open-circuit) state. The inactive state allows the device outputs to be combined with other similar outputs in a busing structure such that only one device is active on the bus at any one time.

trivial graph A *graph with just one vertex.

Trojan horse 1. (trap door) An entry point that is placed in a computer system and is unknown to the system administrators and to the ordinary users. It may be permanent or temporary (self-erasing) in nature.
2. An unexpected or malicious side-effect of a program that otherwise operates correctly.

trouble shooting The resolution of a particular problem associated with a project or system. This activity is exceptional rather than part of the planned life of the project or system.

true complement *Another name for* radix complement.

truncation *See* roundoff error.

truncation error *Another name for* discretization error.

trunk *Another (US) name for* bus.

trunk circuit An interconnecting transmission channel between a switching machine in one location and a switching machine in an adjacent node.

truth table 1. A tabular description of a *combinational circuit (such as an *AND gate, *OR gate, *NAND gate), listing all possible states of the input variables together with a statement of the output variable(s) for each of those possible states.
2. A tabular description of a *logic operation (such as *AND, *OR, *NAND), listing all possible combinations of the truth values – i.e. *true* (T) or *false* (F) – of the operands together with the truth value of the outcome for each of the possible combinations.

TTL *Abbrev. for* transistor-transistor logic. A widely used family of logic circuits that is produced in integrated-circuit form and whose principal switching components are *bipolar transistors. It is available in low power and high switching speed versions (*see* Schottky TTL), in addition to the standard form.
The diagram shows the equivalent circuit of a TTL two-input *NAND gate. The basic circuit uses a multiemitter bipolar transistor, Q_1, which is easily fabricated in integrated-circuit form. Each base-emitter junction of Q_1 effectively acts as a *diode, in a similar manner to a *DTL input stage. Thus if all inputs are at a high voltage (logic 1), all input "diodes" are reverse biased; the collector voltage of Q_1 rises to V_{cc}, turning on Q_2 (which acts as a phase splitter). The emitter voltage of Q_2 rises while its collector voltage falls, turning Q_3 on and Q_4 off. The output thus falls to logic 0, i.e. zero volts.
If any one of the Q_1 inputs is returned to logic 0, 0 volts, then Q_1 is turned hard on, turning off Q_2 whose collector voltage rises; this turns on Q_4 whose emitter voltage falls, turning off Q_3. The output thus increases to +5 volts, i.e. logic 1. Diode D_1 is included to establish the correct bias conditions for Q_4. The output stage, consisting of Q_3, D_1, Q_4, and R, acts as a power amplifier and is often termed a *totem-pole output*.
TTL is the most commonly used technology for SSI and MSI devices due to its low cost, high speed, and ready availability.

T-type flip-flop *See* T flip-flop.

tunnel erase (trim erase) The use in floppy-disk drives (and occasionally in serial tape transports) of an auxiliary erase head that follows the write head and is designed to erase the edges of the written pattern of magnetization, thus defining it more accurately and reducing cross-talk between adjacent tracks.

Turing computable *See* Turing machine.

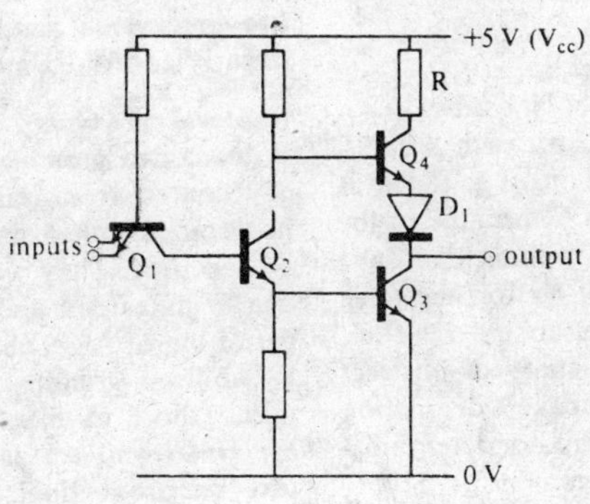

TTL NAND gate

Turing machine (TM) An imaginary computing machine used as a mathematical abstraction by Alan Turing to make precise the notion of an effective procedure (i.e. an algorithm). There are many equivalent ways of dealing with this problem; the first was Turing's version, published in 1936.

A Turing machine is an *automaton that includes a potentially infinite linear tape (in both directions) divided into boxes or cells and read by a read-head that scans one cell at a time. Symbols written on the tape are drawn from a finite alphabet:

$$s_0, \ldots, s_p$$

The control or processing unit of the machine can assume one of a finite number of distinct internal states:

$$q_0, \ldots, q_m$$

The "program" for a given machine is assumed to be made up from a finite set of instructions that are quintuples of the form

$$q_i s_j s_k X q_j$$

where X is R, L, or N

The first symbol indicates that the machine is in state q_i while the second indicates that the head is reading s_j on the tape. In this state the machine will replace s_j by s_k and if $X = R$ the head will move to the right; if $X = L$ it will move to the left and if $X = N$ it will remain where it is. To complete the sequence initiated by this triple the machine will go into state q_j.

A function f,

$$f: \mathbf{N}^k \rightarrow \mathbf{N}$$

where $\mathbf{N} = \{0,1,2, \ldots\}$,

$$\mathbf{N}^k = \mathbf{N} \times \ \ldots \ \times \mathbf{N} \ k \text{ times}$$

is *(Turing) computable* if for each x in $\mathbf{N}^k$, when some representation of x in $\mathbf{N}^k$ is placed on the tape (the N machine in the initial state of q_0 say), the machine halts with a representation of $f(x)$ on the tape. *See also* effective computability.

It is customary in the study of abstract computation models to make a distinction between deterministic and nondeterministic algorithms. In a *deterministic Turing machine* the overall course of the computation is completely determined by the Turing machine (program), the starting state, and the initial tape-inputs; in a *nondeterministic Turing machine* there are several possibilities at each stage of the computation: it can execute one out of possibly several basic modes. The class of problems solvable by deterministic Turing machines in *polynomial time is the class ***P***; the class of problems solvable by nondeterministic Turing machines in polynomial time is the class ***NP***. *See also* P=NP question.

turnaround document *See* document processing.

turnaround time (turnround time) 1. The time that elapses between the submission of a job to a computing facility and the return of results.

2. In data communications, the time taken to reverse the direction of transmission on a channel.

turnkey operation The delivery and installation of a complete computer system plus application programs so that the system can be placed into immediate operational use.

two-address instruction *See* instruction format. *See also* multiple-address machine.

two-dimensional array *Another name for* matrix. *See also* array.

two-dimensional memory *Another name for* linearly addressed memory.

two-level grammars (VW-grammars, van Wijngaarden grammars) A generalization of *context-free grammars that enables non-context-free aspects of a language to be specified. They were developed by A. van Wijngaarden and used in the formal definition of Algol 68. The productions of a two-level grammar are split into two parts: those in the first part are called *hyperrules* and act as templates for context-free productions; those in the second part are called *metaproductions*. The metaproductions are context-free productions and they define the set of nonterminals to be used in the hyperrules. The power of two-level grammars comes from the fact that the hyperrules can be templates for an infinite set of productions. It is in this way that they are used to define non-context-free aspects of a language.

two-level memory A memory system with two memories of different capacities and speeds. *See* multilevel memory, memory hierarchy.

two-norm (Euclidean norm) *See* approximation theory.

two-plus-one address *See* instruction format.

two's complement *See* radix complement.

two-way linked list *Another name for* doubly linked list.

two-way merge An algorithm that merges two ordered files into one single sorted file. It may be viewed as a generalization of sorting by insertion, and was proposed by John von Neumann in 1945.

Tymnet The US public packet-switching carrier that developed from Tymshare Inc.'s internal terminal network used by their public time-sharing service. Network switches are interconnected by voice-grade lines. A central supervisor creates a *virtual connection route for each call at call initialization. Flow control is performed on a link-by-link basis for each virtual connection. Messages between nodes contain data for up to 20 different calls, packed into 66-byte frames. Data is repackaged at each node into new blocks for the next hop.

type of a data object. A definition of the structure of the object, its legal values, and the operations that may be performed on it. For example, if an object is of type Boolean, it is probably very simple in structure, can only take the values TRUE and FALSE, and legal operations would only be logic operations such as AND and OR.

Types may be very complicated and defined in terms of other more primitive types. For example, Ada, Pascal, and Modula allow the programmer to define very complex types. The concept of types is not limited to variables. Some languages consider procedures to be an example of a type, and permit their use in the construction of more complex types such as arrays of procedures.

type 0 (1, 2, 3) language (or grammar) *See* Chomsky hierarchy.

typewriter terminal *Another name for* teleprinter.

U

UART *Acronym for* universal asynchronous receiver/transmitter. A *logic circuit, usually an integrated circuit, that will convert an asynchronous serial data stream into a byte-parallel form and vice versa. The normal application is in the interfaces for data transmission lines and peripherals.

ULA *Abbrev. for* uncommitted logic array.

unary operation (monadic operation) defined on a set *S*. A *function from the domain *S* into *S* itself. The *identity function is monadic. Other examples are the operations of *negation in arithmetic or logic and of taking *complements in set theory or in *Boolean algebra. Although basically functions, unary operations are frequently represented using a special notation, e.g. $\neg A$ or A'. When the set *S* is finite, a *truth table can be used to define the meaning of the operation.

unbundling The separation of system software charges from hardware charges in the marketing of computer systems. Historically, when system software was minimal and represented a small part of total system cost, it was included without additional charge. Unbundling was a natural result of system hardware becoming less expensive while software was becoming a much larger proportion of the cost.

uncertainty *See* entropy.

uncommitted logic array (ULA) A form of programmable logic array. *See* PLA.

unconditional branch instruction A *branch instruction that causes the program sequence to start at a new address; the instruction address becomes the contents of the *program counter.

undecidable *See* solvable.

undefined *See* partial function.

underflow The condition that arises when the result of an arithmetic operation is smaller than the allowable range of numbers that can be represented, or the result so obtained.

undetected error of magnetic tape. *See* error rate.

undirected graph *See* graph.

Unibus *Trademark* A minicomputer *bus structure devised by DEC and used in their PDP 11 series of computers. It is a single bus structure that has 56 bidirectional lines and is common to peripherals, memory, and the processor. The maximum transfer rate is one 16 bit word every 750 nanoseconds. All transfers are initiated by a master device and acknowledged by the receiving or storage device. The allocation of the role of master device is dynamic and the processor can grant control of the bus in response to a request from a peripheral.

unilaterally connected graph *See* reachability.

union 1. of two *sets. The set that results from combining the elements of two sets S and T, say, usually expressed as

$$S \cup T$$

$\cup$ is regarded as an *operation on sets, the *union operation*, which is *commutative and *associative. Symbolically

$$S \cup T = \{x \mid x \in S \text{ or } x \in T\}$$

The union of S and the *empty set is S. *See also* set algebra.

2. of two *graphs, G_1 and G_2. The graph that includes all the vertices and edges of G_1 and G_2, i.e. that contains the union of the two sets of vertices and of the two sets of edges as its vertices and edges.

unipolar signal A signal whose signaling elements are constrained to lie either between zero volts and some arbitrary positive voltage or less commonly between zero volts and some negative voltage. Unipolar signals are used in data-communication systems. *Compare* bipolar signal.

uniquely decodable (uniquely decipherable) A term usually applied to *variable-length codes: unique decodability ensures that codewords can be recognized unambiguously in the received signal so that the decoding process is the exact inverse of the encoding process.

unitary semiring *See* semiring.

unit matrix *Another name for* identity matrix.

unit-record device *See* record.

unit testing (module testing) *See* testing.

Univac The generic name of the products of *Sperry Univac. (It is an acronym for universal automatic computer.) The first Univac, UNIVAC I, was the product of the Eckert–Mauchly Corporation, formed in 1947. (Eckert–Mauchly was acquired by Remington–Rand, which later became Sperry Univac.) This machine was the second commercially available computer system (delivered slightly later than the Ferranti Mark I), and from 1951 through the mid-1950s was one of the leading computers.

universal flip-flop *See* flip-flop.

universal quantifier *See* quantifier.

universal set A *set that, in a particular application, includes every other set under discussion. Such sets give a more definite meaning to notions like *complement and *membership: in asking whether or not x is in S, where S is some set, it is assumed that x is a member of some universal set.

universal Turing machine A *Turing machine M that, given any two numbers n and m as input – one of them a suitable encoding of a Turing machine K – outputs the result of applying K to m. A universal Turing machine therefore serves as an executive program for the class of Turing machines.

UNIX *Trademark* An operating system that was introduced by Bell Laboratories in 1971 for DEC PDP 11 minicomputers. The aims of UNIX were to provide a simple uniform environment in which a relatively small number of users, with a considerable degree of cooperation, could collaborate on a single system. UNIX has proved extremely popular and is in many respects the de facto operating-system standard for 16-bit minicomputer systems. UNIX has also appeared in versions for much larger machines, and for single-user microprocessor-based systems.

unlock (unlock primitive) An indivisible operation by which a process indicates that it has completed its access to a particular resource. *See also* lock, semaphore.

unordered tree *See* tree.

unpack To convert from a packed format to a form in which individual items are directly accessible. *See* pack.

unsolvable *See* solvable.

UPC *Abbrev. for* Universal Product Code. *See* bar code.

updating Any process that changes the state of a system in an irreversible manner.

upline The direction from a remote node toward a central or controlling node in a hierarchical network. The word may also be used as a verb: to upline or to *upline load*, i.e. to send programs or data from a remote node to a more central or controlling node. Upline loading may be used for the storage of programs or data that were created or modified at the remote node, but cannot be stored there permanently. Upline loading may also be used to transmit data collected at a remote node to a more central node for further processing. *Compare* downline.

up operation *Another name for* V operation. *See* semaphore.

upper bound of a set S on which the *partial ordering $<$ is defined. An element u with the property that $s < u$ for all s in S. Also u is a *least upper bound* if, for any other upper bound v, $u < v$.
Since numerical computing demands the truncation of infinite arithmetic to finite arithmetic, the computation of least upper bounds of real numbers, indeed of any limit, can only be achieved to a machine tolerance, usually defined to be machine precision: the smallest epsilon eps, such that

$$1.0 + \text{eps} > 1.0$$

See also array, lower bound.

uptime The time or percentage of time during which a computer system is actually operating correctly.

upward compatibility *See* compatibility.

user area The part of the main memory of a computer that is available for use by the users' programs. A significant portion of the main memory may be dedicated to the operating system and the facilities that it requires, e.g. buffers.

user state *See* execution states.

utility programs The collection of programs that forms part of every computer system and provides a variety of generally useful functions, including file copying and deleting, text preparation, and program cross-referencing.

uvwxy lemma *Another name for* the *pumping lemma for context-free languages.

V

V.24 A standard electrical interface defined by the CCITT for interconnecting *DTE (data terminal equipment) to a *modem. The interface includes definition of control signals as well as clocking and data signaling standards. It is essentially equivalent to the *RS232C interface standard developed by the EIA in the US.

vacuum column *See* buffer.

validation *See* verification and validation.

validity check Any check that some entity respects the constraints applying to that entity. For example, when the value of a data item is input by a program, a validity check is normally performed to ensure that this value is within the acceptable range.

V and V *Short for* verification and validation.

van Wijngaarden grammar *Another name for* two-level grammar.

variable 1. A string of characters that is used to denote some value stored within the computer and may be changed during execution. Thus when a program reads the value of a data object, that object is said to be a variable or variable if the value read changes on subsequent reads or can be modified by the program. A variable may be internal to the program, in which case it is held in memory, or external if the program must perform an input operation in order to read its value. *See also* name. **2.** *See* parameter.

variable-length code A *code in which a fixed number of source symbols are encoded into a variable number of output symbols. This variable number (the *code length) may be made to depend on some property of the source symbols input to the encoder, often their relative frequency of occurrence. If a variable-length code is to be instantaneously decodable (i.e. a *prefix code), it must obey *Kraft's inequality. *See also* source coding theorem. *Compare* fixed-length code.

variable-length vector A *vector, i.e. a one-dimensional array, that usually has a fixed lower bound but its upper bound may vary according to values assigned to the array. *See also* string.

variable word length computer A computer that does not have a *fixed word length but operates on data of different word lengths; this may also apply to instruction sizes. The lengths of data words that can be handled are usually in units of *characters or *bytes, so that the computer handles strings of characters or bytes. It is then known as a *character machine* or *byte machine* respectively. A variable word length computer is particularly important where data is itself of varying lengths (e.g. strings of characters) as well as cases where natural data lengths do not fit word (hardware-restricted) boundaries.

variance *See* measures of variation.

variant field An optional part of a *record.

variation *See* measures of variation.

variational method A technique for the solution of certain classes of *ordinary and *partial differential equations that involves the use of a *variational principle*. That is, the solution of the differential equation is expressed as the solution of a minimization problem that involves an integral expression. The equation is then solved by carrying out an approximate minimization. Variational principles arise naturally in many branches of physics and engineering. As an example, the solution of

$$y'' + q(x)y = f(x), 0 \leqslant x \leqslant 1$$
$$y(0) = y(1) = 0$$

is also the solution of the problem

$$\underset{v \in V}{\text{minimize}} \int_0^1 \{v'(x)^2 - q(x)\, v(x)^2 - 2f(x)\, v(x)\}\, dx$$

where V is a class of sufficiently differentiable functions that are zero at $x = 0$ and $x = 1$. An approximate minimization can be carried out by minimizing over the subspace of functions

$$\sum_{j=1}^{n} c_j \phi_j(x)$$

When the trial functions $\phi_j(x)$ are *splines, the resulting method is an example of the *finite-element method.

VAX *See* DEC.

VAX/VMS *Trademark* The operating system offered by DEC as the standard system for their VAX range of processors. The system functions by producing a *virtual machine for each user of the VAX hardware.

VDU *Abbrev. for* visual display unit. An output device that can temporarily display information. The information can be both alphanumeric and graphical, and can be erased or changed under the control of a processor that may be remote or part of the unit. The display is generally achieved via a *cathode-ray tube but other technologies are in use (*see* display). In most cases the image is formed from a raster of horizontal lines similar to a television picture, but for displays that may be used for prolonged periods by a single operator the quality and stability of the image has to be significantly better than can be achieved on a domestic TV.

Most devices have a selection of display attributes that can be used to emphasize or differentiate items of information, e.g.
(a) blink or flash – in which the items are intermittently displayed at a rate that can be readily perceived;
(b) brilliance – in which a noticeable difference in illumination is applied in a steady state;
(c) reverse video – in which the character is displayed in the opposite contrast to the surrounding information; in a display that has bright characters on an apparently black screen the reverse video characters appear as black characters within a bright character-sized rectangle;
(d) underline – in which a line, usually displayed at the same brilliance or blink rate as the associated character, is drawn beneath the character;
(e) color – the color of the character and its background may be controlled individually.

vector A one-dimensional *array. In computing, vectors are widely used since the memory is essentially a vector of words. The notation for vectors is determined by the programming language. In mathematics (and in this dictionary), the conventional notation is to use a bold italic lower-case letter, e.g. $\boldsymbol{v}$, to denote a vector in its entirety, and the corresponding plain italic lower-case letter indexed by a subscript, e.g. v_i, to denote an element of the vector.
A vector may also be used to express a deficient *matrix, in which case it is necessary to distinguish between a row vector and a column vector.

vectored interrupts An efficient method implemented in hardware for dealing with many different devices, each of which is capable of interrupting and each different type of device requiring a unique *interrupt handler. The *interrupt vector* is an array of interrupt handler locations. When a device successfully interrupts the processor, it supplies the processor with a reference to its entry in the interrupt vector. The processor then uses this to transfer control to the appropriate interrupt handler.

vector-mode graphic display (vector graphics) A method of presenting graphical or pictorial images in which the pen of a plotter or the spot on a VDU moves along the path of the line to be drawn. *Compare* raster-mode graphic display.

vector norm *See* approximation theory.

vector processing Processing of sequences of data in a uniform manner, a common occurrence in manipulation of matrices (whose elements are vectors) or other arrays of data. This orderly progression of data can capitalize on the use of *pipeline processing. *See also* array processor.

Veitch diagram *Another name for* Karnaugh map.

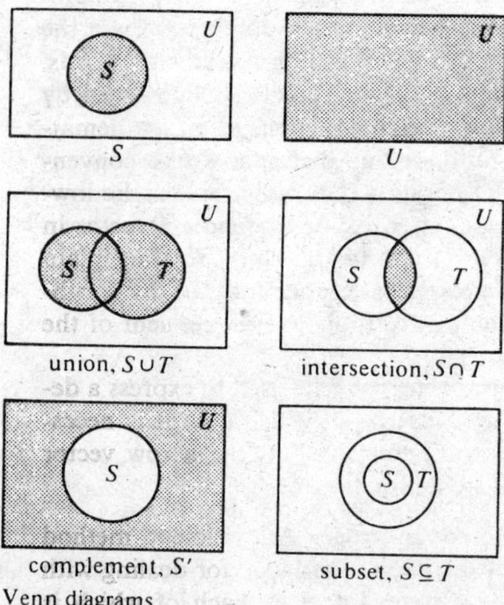

Venn diagrams

Venn diagram A schematic representation of a *set, first used in the 19th century by John Venn. A universal set U will typically be represented by a rectangle, and a subset S of U by the interior of a circle (or another simple closed curve) lying wholly within the rectangle. Some examples are shown in the diagram. Where appropriate, the shaded areas represent the sets indicated beneath each figure.

verification The process of checking the accuracy of transcription of information. It is generally applied to data that has been encoded via a data-preparation machine by an operator reading from a document. The documents are subsequently read by another operator and entered into a machine that compares the input with that prepared by the first operator. Any differences are signaled and a correction or confirmation action is made by the second operator.

The verification process may be performed on a machine dedicated to that process, and called a *verifier*, or it may be performed on a machine that can be switched to preparation or verification mode. When using media such as paper tape or cards, on which encoded data cannot be changed, separate machines are generally used. When the data is being recorded on magnetic media, the same device – which may be just a keyboard and display connected to a system – can be used for both processes.

verification and validation (V & V) A generic term for the complete range of checks that are performed on a system in order to increase confidence that the system is suitable for its intended purpose. This range might include a rigorous set of functional tests, performance testing, reliability testing, and so on. Although a precise distinction is not always drawn, the verification aspect normally refers to completely objective checking of conformity to some well-defined specification, while the validation aspect normally refers to a somewhat subjective assessment of likely suitability in the intended environment.

verification condition *See* program correctness proof.

verifier *See* verification.

version control Control of the creation and usage of the various versions of a given entity. For a recognizable entity, e.g. a software component, there may be various reasons for developing several distinct versions of the entity. A later version may represent an improvement over an earlier one, in that certain errors have been corrected or new capabilities added, or it may employ an alternative approach to meeting the same requirements.
Version control promotes correct usage of the various versions, perhaps by restricting access to existing versions and creation of new versions. For example, the "current release" version of some software component may be protected against modification or deletion, while access to (or even knowledge of) a version under development may be limited to the development team.

version number (generation number) *See* file updating.

vertex An element of the set of points that underlies the concept of a *graph. Edges are obtained by joining together pairs of vertices.

vertical check *See* cyclic redundancy check.

vertical format unit (VFU) The part of the control electronics of a printer that governs the vertical format of the document to be printed. Information about the desired format may be encoded into a loop of paper tape, sometimes called a *carriage control tape*, or it may be sent via the interface from the host system to which the printer is connected. The paper tape loop may be formed from standard 1″ paper tape or it may be a special tape with provision for 12 channels. The number of character positions in the tape loop is arranged to be the same as the number of lines on the form to be processed, or for short forms may be a multiple of the lines. The paper tape may be moved in synchronism with the document to be printed. Each channel of the tape represents a selectable tab stop, and the printer can be instructed to move paper continuously until a punching is detected in a designated channel.
In more recent designs of printer the reliability problems involved with the repeated cycling of the tape loop have been overcome by an *electronic VFU (EVFU)*. The information about the format may still be encoded on paper tape but prior to starting the print operation the printer cycles the tape twice: during the first cycle the information is read into a memory and during the second cycle the information is checked. During the printing operation the stored information is scanned in synchronism with the movement of the printing paper. This type of VFU usually has a facility to allow the host system to transmit the format data over the interface and directly into the printer memory.

vertical microinstruction *See* microprogramming.

vertical recording *See* magnetic encoding.

very large-scale integration *See* VLSI, integrated circuit.

VFU *Abbrev. for* vertical format unit.

video terminal A *VDU that displays information on a cathode-ray tube and generally has an associated keyboard. Normally the image is formed by a raster of horizontal lines similar to a television picture.

videotex A system that enables a keyboard to be used in conjunction with an ordinary television receiver and a telephone, forming a terminal that provides interactive dial-up access to one or more remote services providing information. The information-providing capacity of a videotex service is limited only (a) by the amount of on-line file store that the operator of the service can provide with reasonable response times, and (b) by the effectiveness of the indexing facilities provided

to enable users to find the information they want.
Although initially conceived as a domestic service, the take-up of videotex has been mainly by businesses; in some cases, companies use it as a straightforward means of providing a data communication network linking geographically dispersed locations.
Among countries in which videotex services are available are Australia, Canada (Telidon and Vista), France (Tictac and Titan), West Germany (Bildschirmtext), Japan (Captain), UK (Prestel), and US (Qube). *Viewdata* was an early generic name for videotex, and also an early name for the UK Prestel service, and it is still sometimes encountered.
Compare teletext.

viewdata *See* videotex.

virgin medium Material such as a magnetic tape or disk or paper tape that is suitable for the recording of data, but has not been used or preformatted for that purpose. *Compare* empty medium.

virtual call service In a *packet switching network, a technique of setting up a *virtual connection between terminals prior to the transmission of user data.

virtual connection A logical connection between two network terminating points that appears to the end equipment as a physical connection (generally with some transport delay). The use of virtual connections has found application in both voice and data transmission as a means of increasing utilization of trunking facilities where the physical facility is time-shared between a multiplicity of terminating equipments.

virtual machine A collection of resources that emulates the behavior of an actual machine. The virtual machine concept originated in Cambridge, Mass., in the late 1960s as an extension of the *virtual memory system of the Manchester Atlas computer.
A process is defined in its totality by the contents of the workspace to which it has access. Provided that the behavior of the workspace is consistent with the expected behavior, there is no means by which a process can determine whether a resource that it manipulates is realized by a physical resource of that type, or by the cooperative actions of other resources that jointly present the same changes in the contents of the process' workspace. As an example, a process cannot determine whether its output is passed directly to a printer or is sent via some form of *spooling system. Similarly it cannot determine whether it has sole use of a processor or is *multiprogramming with other processes. In a virtual machine environment no particular process has sole use of any system resource, and all system resources are regarded as being potentially sharable. In addition, use of virtual machines provides *isolation between multiple users of a single physical computer system, giving some level of computer security.
The virtual machine approach forms the basis of a number of commercially produced operating systems, especially of IBM's VM/CMS and of DEC's VAX/VM products.

virtual memory A system in which a process' workspace is held partly in high-speed memory and partly on some slower, and cheaper, backing-store device. When the process refers to a memory location the system hardware detects whether or not the required location is physically present in memory, and generates an interrupt if it is not; this allows the system supervisor to transfer the required data area from backing store into memory. For this purpose the address space is subdivided into *pages typically holding 4 kilobytes of data. Addresses within a page are defined by the 12 low-order bits in the address. The high-order bits can be thought of as the page number; they are used to search an *associative memory that shows either the physical location within memory of word zero of the page, or indicates that the page is not present in memory – at which point an interrupt is generated. The system supervisor then locates the page on backing store and transfers it into memory, updating the associative memory as it does so.

virtual storage access method (VSAM) An *access method suitable for files with sequential or relative organization on direct-access storage devices (*see* file organization). The whole file is mapped into *virtual memory so that records can be accessed at random using a calculated virtual address.

virtual terminal A nonphysical terminal that is defined as a superset of characteristics of a class of physical terminal types. The virtual terminal idea is analogous to defining a non-real-world language into which some set of real-world languages can be translated bilaterally.
In some *packet switching networks, attempts have been made to use the virtual terminal concept as a means of performing protocol translation between dissimilar terminals. At the input node the message is translated into the virtual terminal format, and at the output node it is retranslated into the receiving terminal's protocol. The generality of the concept is somewhat limited because of nontranslatable characteristics of certain types of terminals with respect to others.

visual display unit *See* VDU.

Viterbi decoding The decoding of a *convolutional code by Viterbi's algorithm.

VLSI *Abbrev. for* very large-scale integration, i.e. integrated-circuit fabrication technology that allows over 100 000 transistors to be integrated on a single chip. *See* integrated circuit.

VM/CMS *Trademark, acronym for* virtual machine, conversational monitor system. An operating system originally produced in Cambridge, Mass. (On its first introduction the C stood for Cambridge.) The original system ran on a specially modified IBM 360/44, and was the first to make formal use of the concept of a *virtual machine, as distinct from a *virtual memory. The basis of the system is a supervisory level that creates a number of virtual machines (VMs); in each of these VMs a user can run his own program, using his terminal to control the VM and also to provide the route by which he passes input to, or receives output from, his VM. Most users run a copy of CMS, the monitor system, which in turn actually controls the running of the jobs.

VME 29 *Trademark, acronym for* virtual machine environment for 2900 series. One of the operating systems offered by ICL for use with their 2900 range of computer systems.

voiceband *See* bandwidth.

voice coil *See* actuator.

void set *Another name for* empty set.

volatile memory A type of memory whose contents are destroyed on the removal of power to the memory. When volatile memories are used for crucial applications, they can be backed up with temporary battery-power supplies. *Compare* nonvolatile memory.

Volterra integral equation *See* integral equation.

volume of magnetic tape. *See* magnetic tape.

volume label *See* label.

von Neumann machine Any computer characterized by the following concepts:
(a) the main units are a *control unit, *arithmetic and logic unit, a *memory, and input and output facilities;
(b) programs and data share the same memory, thus the concept of a *stored program is fundamental;
(c) the control and arithmetic units, usually combined into a *central processor

(which may contain internal storage – accumulators and other registers), determine the actions to be carried out by reading instructions from the memory.
It follows that a program for a von Neumann machine consists of a set of instructions that are examined one after another; a "program counter" in the control unit indicates the next location in the memory from which an instruction is to be taken. It also follows that the data on which the program operates may include variables: storage locations can be named so that the stored value may be subsequently referenced or changed during execution of the program.
The vast majority of present-day computers are von Neumann machines. The name is taken from that of the American, John von Neumann. *Compare* non von Neumann architecture.

V operation (up operation) *See* semaphore.

VSAM *Abbrev. for* virtual storage access method.

VW-grammar *Short for* van Wijngaarden grammar, *another name for* two-level grammar.

W

wait list A list of the processes that are awaiting the completion of some activity before they can again run on a processor. Typically the activity is associated with input or output, but may in theory be associated with any activity that can cause a process to be suspended while awaiting the freeing of a *semaphore (or an equivalent mechanism that may be in use to control process synchronization).

wait operation *See* semaphore.

walk through A product review performed by a formal team. A number of such reviews may be held during the lifetime of a software project, covering, for example, requirements specification, program specifications, design, and implementation. The review is formally constituted; there is a clear statement of the contribution that each member of the review team is required to make, and a step-by-step procedure for carrying out the review. The person responsible for development of the product under review "walks through" the product for the benefit of the other reviewers, and the product is then openly debated with a view to uncovering problems or identifying desirable improvements.

Walsh analysis One of the many forms of orthogonal analysis (especially of *signals); it employs the *Walsh functions as its orthogonal basis (*see* orthonormal basis). Walsh analysis is especially suited to *digital signal processing since the Walsh functions themselves, and the operations based upon them, are easily represented and rapidly carried out by simple digital systems. The analysis of a signal in terms of Walsh functions is called its *Walsh transform*. *See also* discrete and continuous systems, filtering, sequency, bandwidth.

Walsh functions A complete set of functions that form an *orthonormal basis for *Walsh analysis: they take only the values +1 and −1, and are defined on a set of 2^n points for some n. For purposes of computer representation, and also for their use in coding, it is usual to represent "+1" by "0", and "−1" by "1". As an example, the 8-point Walsh functions are then as follows:

wal(8,0) = 00000000
wal(8,1) = 11110000
wal(8,2) = 00111100
wal(8,3) = 11001100
wal(8,4) = 10011001
wal(8,5) = 01101001
wal(8,6) = 01011010
wal(8,7) = 10101010

Note that the Walsh functions (usually denoted *wal*) consist alternatively of even

and odd functions (usually denoted *cal* and *sal* by analogy with *cos* and *sin*). Furthermore, within the set of 2^n functions there is one function of zero *sequency, one of (normalized) sequency 2^{n-1}, and one pair (odd and even) of each (normalized) sequency from 1 to $2^{n-1} - 1$.
A pair of Walsh functions corresponds, with some permutation of columns, to a *Reed–Muller code and, with a column deleted, to a *simplex code. *See also* Hadamard matrices.

Walsh transform *See* Walsh analysis.

WAN *Abbrev. for* wide area network.

WATFIV An improved version of *WATFOR.

WATFOR A fast load-and-go *FORTRAN compiler developed at the University of Waterloo in Canada (hence WATerloo FORtran) and used for the teaching of programming in the FORTRAN era.

weakest precondition For some given program statement S and some *postcondition R there is a (possibly empty) set of program states such that if execution of S is initiated from one of these states then S is guaranteed to terminate in a state for which R is true. The weakest precondition of S with respect to R, normally written

wp (S,R)

is a predicate that characterizes this set of states. Use of the adjective weakest explicitly indicates that the predicate must characterize all states that guarantee termination of S in a state for which R is true.
The term was introduced by Dijkstra in 1975 in conjunction with a calculus for the derivation of programs; this provides for development of a program to be guided by the simultaneous development of a total correctness proof for the program. *See* program correctness proof, predicate transformer.

weakly connected graph *See* connected graph.

weighted code A *block code in which a weight has been assigned to each of the symbol positions in a codeword. *See also* 8421 code, excess-3 code.

weighted graph A *graph that has weights associated with the edges of the graph. The weight can be regarded as a *function from the set of edges into some appropriate codomain. This function is sometimes called a *cost function*. For example, in graphs with geographical origins, weight might represent distance or cost of travel.

weighted least squares *See* least squares, method of.

weighted mean *See* measures of location.

well-formed formula (wff) *See* propositional calculus, predicate calculus.

well-ordered set A set S on which the relation $<$ is defined, satisfying the following properties:
(a) given x,y,z in S,
if $x < y$ and $y < z$, then $x < z$
(b) given x,y in S, then exactly one of the following three possibilities is true:
$x < y$, $x = y$, or $y < x$
(c) if T is any nonempty subset of S, then there exists an element x in T, such that
$x = y$ or $x < y$, i.e. $x \leqslant y$
for all y in T
This relation $<$ is said to be a *well ordering* of the set S.

wff *Short for* well-formed formula. *See* propositional calculus.

W grammar *Another name for* two-level grammar.

while loop *See* do-while loop.

Whirlwind The first real-time computer, built at the Massachusetts Institute of Technology and capable of calculating at high speed. The Whirlwind project had its origins in wartime defense and was officially launched in December 1944. The first version, operational in 1950, used electrostatic storage tubes but a ferrite core store was in use (its first appearance) by 1953.

white noise Noise occurring in a channel and regarded as continuous in time and continuous in amplitude, the noise being uniform in energy over equal intervals of *frequency. (Note that, by contrast, white light is uniform in energy over equal intervals of wavelength.) *Compare* impulse noise.

wide area network (WAN) A communication network distinguished from a *local area network (of which it may contain one or more) because of its longer-distance communications, which may or may not be provided by a *common carrier or *PTT. The term is sometimes used as another name for the *public packet network of a particular country or region.

wideband (broadband) *See* bandwidth.

width of a bus. The number of signal lines in the *bus.

Williams-tube store *See* electrostatic storage device.

Winchester technology The name given to the design approach used in the IBM 3340 disk drive, which was introduced in 1973. It was developed at their laboratories in Winchester, UK and demonstrated a significant advance in technology, allowing an increase in recording density to 300 tracks per inch and 5600 bits per inch. The technology has been adopted by many manufacturers.
The read/write heads and the carriage assembly that supports them are enclosed with the disks in a hermetically sealed enclosure called a *data module*. When the data module is mounted in the drive unit it is automatically coupled to a system that supplies it with filtered cooling air. An entirely new head design was introduced having a trimaran structure with two outriggers supporting a much narrower "hull" that carries the read/write head. The surface of the disk has an oxide coating of only 44 microinches (1.12 μm), compared to 185 microinches of previous designs, and a lubricant coating to prevent damage during head take-off and landings. When the disk is rotating the film of air drawn around with it provides an air bearing that causes the head to fly at a height of only 19 microinches (0.5 μm). In earlier drives, e.g. IBM 2311, the heads flew at 120 microinches.
The head used in the Winchester technology has a very low mass and is loaded toward the disk with a force of only 10 grams compared to the 350 grams used in earlier designs. To prevent damage to the data through repeated landing and take-off of the heads, an area of the disk is usually reserved for this purpose. The low mass and loading force are such that if as a result of malfunction – or by intention in some designs – the heads do land on a data area, the probability of the data being corrupted is very low.
Most recent designs using aspects of Winchester technology have the disk pack permanently fixed within the drive. The capacity of these disks ranges from a few megabytes in the case of microcomputer systems to hundreds of megabytes.

window 1. An allocation of messages, data units, or both, given by a receiver to a sender in a data communication protocol. It controls how much data the sender may transmit before it receives an *acknowledgment from the receiver. The window is used for *flow control by the receiver, to prevent the sender from transmitting more rapidly than the receiver can process. The window is also used for *error control, by establishing the range of data that is unacknowledged and thus may need to be retransmitted. The selection of a proper window size is dependent upon the properties of the path between the sender and receiver: bandwidth, delay, and network congestion are important factors.
2. A rectangular area on a display screen inside which part of an image or file is displayed. The window can be any size up to

that of the screen, and more than one window can be displayed at once. The process of obtaining the part of the image or file visible through the window is called *windowing.

windowing (scissoring) Processing the stored data of a large image so that part of it can be displayed. The visible *window formed by the process can be moved to allow examination of the entire stored image. Some graphics terminals have hardware windowing, but this is only effective when the complete image can be contained in the display file.

wired logic A form of digital logic in which some logic functions are implemented by directly connecting together the outputs of one or more logic gates. The success of this technique depends on the electronic characteristics of the gates involved. The technique is commonly used in bus communication systems with *tri-state output or with *open-collector devices.

wired-program computer A digital computer, usually a special-purpose one, in which the sequence of operations is fixed and cannot be self-altered. The sequence may take different paths in accordance with data-dependent conditions. Speed of operation is gained at a decrease in flexibility.

wire printer *See* dot matrix printer.

wire wrapping A technique for connecting components into *circuit boards by tightly wrapping wires around specialized terminals instead of soldering wires to them.

word 1. (machine word; computer word) A vector of bits that is treated as a unit by the computer hardware. The number of bits, referred to as the *word length* or *word size*, is now usually 16 or 32. The memory of a computer is divided into words (and possibly subdivided into *bytes). A word is usually long enough to contain an *instruction or an integer.

2. (string) In *formal language theory, a finite sequence of *symbols* drawn from some set of symbols Σ. We then speak of a *word over the alphabet* Σ or a *Σ-word*. The elements of Σ are also called *letters*. Common notation includes:

$|w|$ – the length of the word w,

w_i – the ith symbol in w,

Λ, the *empty word* – the unique word of length 0,

Σ^* – the set of all Σ-words.

Σ^* is infinite unless Σ is empty, in which case

$$\Sigma^* = \{\Lambda\}$$

See also concatenation.

word length (word size) *See* word.

word processing (text processing) An office automation facility that enables users to compose documents using a computer with facilities to edit, re-format, store, and print documents with maximum flexibility. A typical word processing system consists of a video terminal, probably specially designed or modified for word processing applications, some backing store such as a floppy-disk device for filing documents, and an associated printer capable of producing high-quality output at least comparable with that from a modern electric typewriter.

The systems available today fall into three main categories: stand-alone systems supporting one operator; clustered systems enabling several operators to share printers and files; hybrid systems attached to a central mainframe or minicomputer and able to perform additional functions. The following features are generally provided.

Document creation and editing, including the ability to (a) insert, delete, copy, and move text around in a document; (b) include text and/or graphics from other files; (c) search for and replace strings in the document.

Document formatting and printing using a choice of paper sizes and formats with multiple copies as required.

Text justification to specified margins with automatic hyphenation.
Ability to create a document from a standard template, e.g. one containing a company letter heading.
Use of alternative character sets such as bold, italic, underlined.
Layout of tables, figures, etc.
Substitution of variable information when printing the document for easy production of form letters, etc.

word size (word length) *See* word.

Wordstar *Trademark* A popular *word processing program for microcomputers with the *CP/M operating system. It is one of a family of compatible products from the MicroPro International Corporation.

work area *Another name for* workspace.

work file (scratch file) A file that is used to provide temporary storage space for data that is required only for the lifetime of one job, e.g. for data that is being sorted.

work function The *complexity function of an algorithm.

working set The set of *pages currently in use by a process. A process running in a *virtual memory environment can be regarded as having a subset of its total address space actually in use over any short period of time. The objective of the *memory management system is to ensure that for each process those pages, and only those pages, that are actually in use are retained in memory, thus maximizing the *hit rate for these pages.

workspace (work area) A block of locations within the main memory that are used for the temporary storage of data during processing.

workstation A position for an operator that is equipped with all of the facilities required to perform a particular type of task. In data processing and office systems the basic electronic equipment would normally be a visual display and keyboard; however there may also be ancillary electronic equipment such as magnetic storage devices, printer, OCR or bar code reader.

worst-case analysis *See* algorithm.

wrap around A facility of a VDU, allowing it to display lines of text that would otherwise be too long to be displayed completely: the line appears on the screen as two or more successive lines. This division into shorter lines that can fit within the available screen size is a function of the VDU electronics and there is no need for a format character to be included in the data stream.

write (often followed by *to*) To cause data to be recorded in some form of storage. The word is often used to qualify the meaning of a noun, as in write head.

writeable control store (WCS) *See* microprogramming.

write error *See* error rate. *See also* error management.

write head *See* head, magnetic tape.

write instruction A program instruction that causes an item of data to be recorded in some form of storage.

write ring A ring that is attached to the hub of a reel of magnetic tape to permit its content to be overwritten or erased. When the reel is mounted on a tape transport the ring actuates a switch that permits the writing process. An interrupt is normally sent to the system if writing is attempted without the write ring.

write time The elapsed time during which a given amount of data is being recorded in some storage device. It does not include any latency or check read time.

X

X.25 The CCITT standard interface protocol for *packet switching networks that defines the message structure required by data terminal equipment (*DTE) to interface to a *public packet network conforming to CCITT standards. The X.25 standard consists of three levels of protocol: the *physical layer*, the *link layer*, and the *network* (or *packet*) *layer*. These three levels conform to the lower three layers of the ISO *seven-layer reference model for open system interconnection.

X.75 The CCITT standard interface protocol for *packet switching networks that defines the message structure required for *gateway nodes of *public packet networks to intercommunicate.

X.121 An international standard for numbering networks and stations that will be interconnected using the *X.25 and related protocols.

XS3 code *Short for* excess-3 code.

xy plotter *See* plotter.

xy recorder *See* plotter.

Y

YACC *Acronym for* yet another compiler-compiler. A widely used *compiler-compiler provided as part of the *UNIX operating system environment.

Z

Z3 An electromechanical programmed calculator built in Berlin by Konrad Zuse and fully operational in 1941. Like the earlier (nonprogrammed) calculators, Z1 (mechanical) and Z2 (electromechanical), constructed by Zuse, it did not survive the war. An improved machine, the Z4, was completed by 1945.

zero function The *function whose value is zero for every element in its domain. The term is usually applied more specifically to the function

$$Z : N \rightarrow N$$

$$\text{for which } Z(n) = 0$$

for all n in N, the set of nonnegative integers. This function is basic to the theory of *recursive and *primitive recursive functions.

zero matrix *Another name for* null matrix.

zero suppression The elimination of nonsignificant zeros. While numerical data is being processed it may be expanded to a uniform number of digits by the addition of nonsignificant zeros to the left of the most significant digit. For printout or display these nonsignificant zeros are suppressed.

zero-trip loop *See* do-while loop.

zero word In coding theory, a word consisting entirely of zero digits. It lies at the origin of *Hamming space. *See also* Hamming weight.

ZX80 A small microcomputer made by Sinclair Research Ltd., UK, available both in kit and premade form. It was aimed at initial use by novice computer users. It has been superseded by the ZX81, which has more capability and greater capacity, and by the ZX Spectrum, which has color capability.